UNDERSTANDING ORGANIZATIONAL BEHAVIOR

A MULTIMEDIA APPROACH

Debra L. Nelson

Oklahoma State University

James Campbell Quick

The University of Texas at Arlington

SOUTH-WESTERN
★
THOMSON LEARNING

Australia · Canada · Mexico · Singapore · Spain · United Kingdom · United States

Understanding Organizational Behavior: A Multimedia Approach, 1e
by Debra L. Nelson & James Campbell Quick

Vice President/Publisher: Jack W. Calhoun
Executive Editor: John Szilagyi
Marketing Manager: Rob Bloom
Developmental Editor: Leslie Kauffman/Litten Editing and Production, Inc.
Production Editor: Elizabeth A. Shipp
Media Technology Editor: Vicky True
Media Developmental Editor: Kristen Meere
Media Production Editor: Mark Sears
Manufacturing Coordinator: Sandee Milewski
Internal Design: Joe Devine
Cover Design: Rick Moore
Cover Image: Barbara Friedman, Stock Illustration Source
Production House: Litten Editing and Production, Inc.
Printer: Westgroup

Printed in Canada
2 3 4 5 04 03 02 01

For more information contact South-Western, 5191 Natorp Blvd, Mason, Ohio 45040 or find us on the Internet at http://www.swcollege.com

For permission to use material from this text or product, contact us by

- telephone: 1-800-730-2214
- fax: 1-800-730-2215
- web: http://www.thomsonrights.com

Library of Congress Cataloging-in-Publication Data

Nelson, Debra L., 1956–
     Understanding organizational behavior : a multimedia approach / by Debra L. Nelson
and James Campbell Quick. — 1st ed.
        p. cm.
     Includes bibliographical references and index.
     ISBN 0-324-10077-9 (alk. paper)
     1. Organizational behavior.   I. Quick, James C.   II. Title.
HD58.7.N448 2001
658—dc21

                                                                              00-068746

To our students, who challenge us to be better than we are, who keep us in touch with reality, and who are the foundation of our careers.

Contents in Brief

PREFACE   xiv

PART 1 • INTRODUCTION

1. Organizational Behavior in Changing Times   2
2. Organizations 2001 and Managerial Challenges   29

PART 2 • INDIVIDUAL PROCESSES AND BEHAVIOR

3. Personality, Perception, and Attribution   70
4. Attitudes, Values, and Ethics   101
5. Motivation at Work   132
6. Learning and Performance Management   160
7. Stress and Well-Being at Work   189

PART 3 • INTERPERSONAL PROCESSES AND BEHAVIOR

8. Work Teams and Groups   220
9. Decision Making by Individuals and Groups   246
10. Power and Political Behavior   284
11. Leadership and Followership   314
12. Conflict at Work   349

PART 4 • ORGANIZATIONAL PROCESSES AND STRUCTURE

13. Jobs and the Design of Work   386
14. Organizational Design and Structure   416
15. Organizational Culture   447
16. Managing Change   476
References   511
Glossary   535
Company Index   I-1
Name Index   I-5
Subject Index   I-7

Contents

PART 1 • INTRODUCTION

1. Organizational Behavior in Changing Times 2
THINKING AHEAD Change, Challenge, and Gateway 2
Human Behavior in Organizations 3
Organizational Reality 1.1: Changing Work Environments—The Virtual Office 4
Understanding Human Behavior 4
Interdisciplinary Influences 5
The Organizational Context 7
Organizations as Systems 7
The Formal and Informal Organization 9
Six Focus Organizations 11
Ford Motor Company 12
Gateway, Inc. 12
Southwest Airlines 13
Starbucks Corporation 13
Harpo Entertainment Group 14
American Red Cross 14
The Challenge of Change 15
International Competition in Business 15
Challenge 1.1: Analyze Your Perceptions of a Change 16
Four Themes Related to Change 16
Customer Focused for High Quality 17
Behavior and Quality at Work 17
Managing Organizational Behavior in Changing Times 18
Learning About Organizational Behavior 19
Objective Knowledge 19
Challenge 1.2: Learning Style Inventory 20
Skill Development 21
Application of Knowledge and Skills 22
Plan for the Book 23
Managerial Implications: Foundations for the Future 24
LOOKING BACK Gateway . . . in the 21st Century 25
Chapter Summary 25

Key Terms 26
Review Questions 26
Discussion and Communication Questions 26
Ethics Questions 27
Experiential Exercises 27

2. Organizations 2001 and Managerial Challenges 29
THINKING AHEAD Ford Goes Global with an International Team of Executives 29
Competition: The Challenges Managers Face 30
Managing in a Global Environment 31
Changes in the Global Marketplace 32
Organizational Reality 2.1: Two CEOs, Two Strategies: Global Coke 34
Understanding Cultural Differences 34
Developing Cross-Cultural Sensitivity 37
Managing Workforce Diversity 40
Cultural Diversity 40
Gender Diversity 41
Age Diversity 42
Ability Diversity 44
Differences Are Assets 45
Diversity's Benefits and Problems 46
Managing Technological Innovation 48
Alternative Work Arrangements 49
The Changing Nature of Managerial Work 50
Helping Employees Adjust to Technological Change 51
Managing Ethical Issues at Work 52
Employee Rights 54
Sexual Harassment 55
Challenge 2.1: How Much Do You Know about AIDS? 56
Romantic Involvements 57
Organizational Reality 2.2: Sexual Harassment and the CEO 58
Organizational Justice 59

Whistle-blowing 59
Social Responsibility 60
Codes of Ethics 60
Managerial Implications: Facing the Challenges 61
LOOKING BACK Ford Cars and Trucks on Demand in the Future 63

Chapter Summary 63
Key Terms 64
Review Questions 64
Discussion and Communication Questions 64
Ethics Questions 65
Experiential Exercises 65

PART 2 • INDIVIDUAL PROCESSES AND BEHAVIOR

---

3. Personality, Perception, and Attribution 70
THINKING AHEAD The Woman (Oprah) behind the Company (Harpo) 70
Individual Differences and Organizational Behavior 71
Personality 72
Personality Theories 73
Personality Characteristics in Organizations 74
Organizational Reality 3.1: At Cisco Systems, Self-Esteem Produces Success 76
Challenge 3.1: Are You a High or Low Self-Monitor? 77
Measuring Personality 79
A Popular Application of Personality Theory in Organizations: The Myers-Briggs Type Indicator 79
The Preferences 80
The Sixteen Types 82
Social Perception 83
Characteristics of the Perceiver 86
Characteristics of the Target 87
Characteristics of the Situation 88
Barriers to Social Perception 88
Impression Management 91
Attribution in Organizations 92
Internal and External Attributions 92
Attributional Biases 93
Organizational Reality 3.2: "Chainsaw Al's" Self-Serving Bias 94
Managerial Implications: Using Personality, Perception, and Attribution at Work 95
LOOKING BACK Oprah's Reflections on Management 95
Chapter Summary 96
Key Terms 97
Review Questions 97

Discussion and Communication Questions 97
Ethics Questions 98
Experiential Exercises 98

4. Attitudes, Values, and Ethics 101
THINKING AHEAD Starbucks' Values Are Reflected in Its Mission Statement 101
Attitudes 102
The ABC Model 103
Organizational Reality 4.1: New Attitudes at Xionics Brought About by an Unusual Partnership 104
Attitude Formation 105
Attitudes and Behavior 106
Work Attitudes 108
Challenge 4.1: Assess Your Job Satisfaction 109
Persuasion and Attitude Change 113
Values 115
Instrumental and Terminal Values 116
Work Values 117
Challenge 4.2: What Do You Value at Work? 118
Cultural Differences in Values 119
Ethical Behavior 120
Value Systems 122
Locus of Control 123
Machiavellianism 124
Cognitive Moral Development 124
Managerial Implications: Attitudes, Values, and Ethics at Work 126
LOOKING BACK Environmental Responsibility Makes Good Business Sense at Starbucks 127
Chapter Summary 128
Key Terms 128
Review Questions 128
Discussion and Communication Questions 129
Ethics Questions 129
Experiential Exercises 129

5. Motivation at Work 132

THINKING AHEAD Motivation without Compensation—The Red Cross at Work 132

Motivation and Work Behavior 133
Internal Needs 134
Challenge 5.1: Protestant Ethic 134
External Incentives 135
Maslow's Need Hierarchy 136
The Hierarchy of Needs 136
Theory X and Theory Y 137
ERG Theory 139
McClelland's Need Theory 139
Herzberg's Two-Factor Theory 140
Motivation Factors 140
Hygiene Factors 142
Critique of the Two-Factor Theory 143
Challenge 5.2: What's Important to Employees? 143
Need for Achievement 144
Need for Power 144
Need for Affiliation 145
Social Exchange and Equity Theory 146
Demands and Contributions 146
Adams's Theory of Inequity 148
The Resolution of Inequity 149
New Perspectives on Equity Theory 149
Organizational Reality 5.1: The Equity-Sensitive Female Entrepreneur 150
Expectancy Theory of Motivation 151
Motivational Problems 153
Motivation and Moral Maturity 153
Cultural Differences in Motivation 154
Managerial Implications: Many Ways to Motivate People 154
LOOKING BACK The Intrinsic Motivation of Mission Commitment 155
Chapter Summary 156
Key Terms 156
Review Questions 156
Discussion and Communication Questions 156
Ethics Questions 157
Experiential Exercises 157

6. Learning and Performance Management 160

THINKING AHEAD Motivation, Goals, and the Consequences of Behavior 160

Learning in Organizations 161
Classical Conditioning 161
Operant Conditioning 162
The Strategies of Reinforcement, Punishment, and Extinction 162
Bandura's Social Learning Theory 165
Learning and Personality Differences 166
Goal Setting at Work 167
Organizational Reality 6.1: A Sense of Purpose at Medtronic 168
Characteristics of Effective Goals 168
Increasing Work Motivation and Task Performance 169
Reducing Role Stress of Conflicting and Confusing Expectations 170
Improving the Accuracy and Validity of Performance Evaluation 171
Performance: A Key Construct 172
Defining Performance 172
Measuring Performance 173
Performance Feedback: A Communication Challenge 175
Developing People and Enhancing Careers 176
Key Characteristics of an Effective Appraisal System 177
Rewarding Performance 177
A Key Organizational Decision Process 177
Individual versus Team Reward Systems 178
The Power of Earning 178
Organizational Reality 6.2: Individual Incentive versus Profit Sharing 179
Correcting Poor Performance 180
Challenge 6.1: Correcting Poor Performance 180
Attribution and Performance Management 181
Coaching, Counseling, and Mentoring 184
Managerial Implications: Performance Management Is a Key Task 184
LOOKING BACK Oprah's Rewards and Recognition for Successful Performance 185
Chapter Summary 186
Key Terms 186
Review Questions 186
Discussion and Communication Questions 186
Ethics Questions 187
Experiential Exercises 187

7. Stress and Well-Being at Work 189

THINKING AHEAD Deregulation Stress, Financial Risk, and Airline Safety 189

What Is Stress? 190

Challenge 7.1: The Frazzle Factor 191
    Four Approaches to Stress 191
    The Stress Response 193
Sources of Stress at Work 193
    Task Demands 194
Organizational Reality 7.1: Infotech-Stressor? Stress-
    Reliever? 195
    Role Demands 196
    Interpersonal Demands 196
    Physical Demands 197
    Nonwork Demands 197
The Consequences of Stress 198
    Performance and Health Benefits of Stress 198
    Individual Distress 199
    Organizational Distress 201
Individual Differences in the Stress–Strain Relationship
    202
    Gender Effects 202

    Type A Behavior Pattern 202
    Personality Hardiness 203
    Self-Reliance 204
Preventive Stress Management 205
    Organizational Stress Prevention 207
Challenge 7.2: Are You Self-Reliant? 206
    Individual Prevention 209
    Comprehensive Health Promotion 213
Managerial Implications: Stress without Distress 213
**LOOKING BACK Serious Fun at Southwest
    Airlines 214**
Chapter Summary 215
Key Terms 215
Review Questions 215
Discussion and Communication Questions 216
Ethics Questions 216
Experiential Exercises 217

Other Individual Influences on Decision Making 255
Challenge 9.1: Which Side of Your Brain Do You
    Favor? 256
  The Role of Intuition 258
  Creativity at Work 259
Challenge 9.2: Creative Problem Solving 261
Participation in Decision Making 263
  The Effects of Participation 263
  Foundations for Participation and Empowerment 264
  What Level of Participation? 265
The Group Decision-Making Process 265
  Advantages and Disadvantages of Group Decision
    Making 266
  Groupthink 266
  Group Polarization 269
Techniques for Group Decision Making 269
  Brainstorming 269
  Nominal Group Technique 270
  Delphi Technique 270
  Devil's Advocacy 270
  Dialectical Inquiry 271
  Quality Circles and Quality Teams 271
  Self-Managed Teams 272
Cultural Issues in Decision Making 273
Technological Aids to Decision Making 273
  Expert Systems 273
  Decision Support Systems 274
  Group Decision Support Systems 275
  Decision Making in the Virtual Workplace 276
Ethical Issues in Decision Making 277
Managerial Implications: Decision Making Is a Critical
  Activity 277
**LOOKING BACK Starbucks Makes the Chicago
  Decision Work 278**
Chapter Summary 278
Key Terms 279
Review Questions 279
Discussion and Communication Questions 279
Ethics Questions 280
Experiential Exercises 280

10. Power and Political Behavior 284
**THINKING AHEAD Texas Cattle Ranchers versus
  Harpo Productions: The Real Issue Is Power
  and Influence 284**
The Concept of Power 285
Forms and Sources of Power in Organizations 286
  Interpersonal Forms of Power 286

Using Power Ethically 288
  Two Faces of Power: One Positive, One Negative
    289
  Intergroup Sources of Power 290
Power Analysis: A Broader View 291
Symbols of Power 293
  Kanter's Symbols of Power 293
  Kanter's Symbols of Powerlessness 293
  Korda's Symbols of Power 294
Political Behavior in Organizations 295
  Influence Tactics 295
Organizational Reality 10.1: Etiquette Training for
    "Technogeeks" 297
  Managing Political Behavior in Organizations 299
Managing Up: Managing the Boss 300
Sharing Power: Empowerment 302
Challenge 10.1: Are You Self-Empowered? 303
Organizational Reality 10.2: "Empowerment Is Not for
    Everybody" 307
Managerial Implications: Using Power Effectively 308
LOOKING BACK Harpo, Oprah, and Power 309
Chapter Summary 309
Key Terms 310
Review Questions 310
Discussion and Communication Questions 310
Ethics Questions 311
Experiential Exercises 311

11. Leadership and Followership 314
**THINKING AHEAD Howard Schultz's Leadership
  Role in Changing Starbucks Coffee 314**
Leadership and Management 315
Organizational Reality 11.1: Kelleher's Inspiring
    Leadership at Southwest Airlines 316
Type I Universal Trait Theories 318
  Physical Attributes, Personality, and Abilities 318
  Transformational Leadership 319
  Leaders as Distinct Personalities 320
  Women Leaders 321
  Charismatic Leadership 321
Type II Universal Behavior Theories 322
  Leadership Style and Emotional Climate at Work
    322
  Leadership Behaviors 324
  Leadership Styles in Japan 324
  The Leadership Grid 325
Challenge 11.1: How Does Your Supervisor Lead? 326
Type III Situational Trait Theories 328

Fiedler's Contingency Theory 328
Leadership Effectiveness 330
Type IV Situational Behavior Theories 331
The Path–Goal Theory 331
Vroom-Yetton-Jago Normative Decision Model 333
The Situational Leadership Model 334
Guidelines for Leadership 336
Followership 336
Types of Followers 337
The Dynamic Follower 338
Challenge 11.2: Are You an Effective Follower? 339
Cultural Differences in Leadership 340
Managerial Implications: Leaders and Followers as
Partners 340
LOOKING BACK Focusing the Shooting Stars 341
Chapter Summary 342
Key Terms 342
Review Questions 342
Discussion and Communication Questions 343
Ethics Questions 343
Experiential Exercises 343

12. Conflict at Work 349
**THINKING AHEAD Conflict Management Pays
Off at Ford 349**
The Nature of Conflicts in Organizations 350
Importance of Conflict Management Skills for the
Manager 350
Functional versus Dysfunctional Conflict 350
Causes of Conflict in Organizations 352
Structural Factors 352
Personal Factors 354
Organizational Reality 12.1: "By the Way . . . Your Staff
Hates You!!!!!" 355

Globalization and Conflict 356
Forms of Conflict in Organizations 357
Interorganizational Conflict 357
Organizational Reality 12.2: Physicians Open New
Hospital and Old Wounds 358
Intergroup Conflict 359
Interpersonal Conflict 359
Intrapersonal Conflict 359
Intrapersonal Conflict 361
Interpersonal Conflict 361
Power Networks 361
Defense Mechanisms 363
Coping with Difficult Behavior 365
Conflict Management Strategies and Techniques 367
Ineffective Techniques 369
Effective Techniques 369
Conflict Management Styles 371
Avoiding 371
Accommodating 372
Competing 374
Compromising 374
Collaborating 374
Challenge 12.1: What Is Your Conflict-Handling Style?
375
Managerial Implications: Creating a Conflict-Positive
Organization 376
**LOOKING BACK The Secrets to Ford's Success in
Managing Relationships with the United Auto
Workers 377**
Chapter Summary 378
Key Terms 379
Review Questions 379
Discussion and Communication Questions 379
Ethics Questions 380
Experiential Exercises 380

PART 4 • ORGANIZATIONAL PROCESSES AND STRUCTURE

13. Jobs and the Design of Work 386
**THINKING AHEAD Jobs, Work Rules, and the
Airline Industry 386**
Work in Organizations 387
The Meaning of Work 388
Jobs in Organizations 389
Traditional Approaches to Job Design 390
Scientific Management 390
Job Enlargement/Job Rotation 391

Job Enrichment 392
Job Characteristics Theory 393
Challenge 13.1: Diagnosing Your Job 396
Alternative Approaches to Job Design 398
Social Information Processing 398
Interdisciplinary Approach 399
International Perspectives on the Design of Work
401
Work Design and Well-Being 403

Challenge 13.2: Is Your Work Environment a Healthy One? 404
Emerging Issues in the Design of Work 405
Organizational Reality 13.1: Telecommuting, Job Sharing, and Flexibility at Baxter Export 405
  Telecommuting 406
  Alternative Work Patterns 406
  Technology at Work 407
  Task Revision 408
  Skill Development 409
Managerial Implications: The Changing Nature of Work 409
LOOKING BACK Good Relations and Job Flexibility at Southwest Airlines 410
Chapter Summary 411
Key Terms 411
Review Questions 411
Discussion and Communication Questions 412
Ethics Questions 412
Experiential Exercises 412

14. Organizational Design and Structure 416
THINKING AHEAD Organizing for Emergencies, Crises, and Disaster Relief 416
Key Organizational Design Processes 417
Organizational Reality 14.1: Family Values at the SAS Institute 418
  Differentiation 419
  Integration 421
Basic Design Dimensions 423
Five Structural Configurations 424
  Simple Structure 424
Challenge 14.1: How Decentralized Is Your Company? 425
  Machine Bureaucracy 426
  Professional Bureaucracy 426
  Divisionalized Form 426
  Adhocracy 427
Contextual Variables 427
  Size 427
  Technology 429
  Environment 431
Organizational Reality 14.2: The Everglades—An Environmental Treasure Cleanup 432
  Strategy and Goals 434
Forces Reshaping Organizations 346
  Life Cycles in Organizations 436

Globalization 438
Changes in Information-Processing Technologies 438
Demands on Organizational Processes 439
Emerging Organizational Structures 440
Cautionary Notes about Structure 440
Managerial Implications: Fitting People and Structures Together 441
LOOKING BACK American Red Cross Disaster Response Field Organizations 442
Chapter Summary 442
Key Terms 443
Review Questions 443
Discussion and Communication Questions 443
Ethics Questions 444
Experiential Exercises 444

15. Organizational Culture 447
THINKING AHEAD A Culture of Family, Fun, and Luv 447
The Key Role of Organizational Culture 448
  Culture and Its Levels 448
  Artifacts 449
  Values 453
  Assumptions 453
Organizational Reality 15.1: A Culture of Climbers 454
Functions and Effects of Organizational Culture 455
  The Strong Culture Perspective 455
  The Fit Perspective 456
  The Adaptation Perspective 456
The Leader's Role in Shaping and Reinforcing Culture 458
  What Leaders Pay Attention To 458
  How Leaders React to Crises 458
  How Leaders Behave 458
  How Leaders Allocate Rewards 459
  How Leaders Hire and Fire Individuals 459
Organizational Socialization 460
  The Stages of the Socialization Process 460
  Outcomes of Socialization 462
  Socialization as Cultural Communication 463
Assessing Organizational Culture 463
  Organizational Culture Inventory 463
  Kilmann-Saxton Culture-Gap Survey 464
  Triangulation 464
Changing Organizational Culture 465
Organizational Reality 15.2: The Stalking Tiger Meets the Flying Horse 465

Developing a Global Organizational Culture 468
Developing an Ethical Organizational Culture 469
Challenge 15.1: Organizational Culture and Ethics 470
Developing a Culture of Empowerment and Quality 471
Managerial Implications: The Organizational Culture Challenge 472
LOOKING BACK Culture and Performance at Southwest Airlines 472
Chapter Summary 473
Key Terms 473
Review Questions 474
Discussion and Communication Questions 474
Ethics Questions 474
Experiential Exercises 474

16. Managing Change 476
THINKING AHEAD Transformation of the American Red Cross Biomedical Services 476
Forces for Change in Organizations 477
External Forces 478
Internal Forces 481
Organizational Reality 16.1: Continental's New Flight Plan 482
Change Is Inevitable 483
The Scope of Change 483
The Change Agent's Role 483
The Process of Change in Organizations 484
Resistance to Change 485

Challenge 16.1: Tolerance for Ambiguity 486
Managing Resistance to Change 487
Behavioral Reactions to Change 489
Lewin's Change Model 491
Challenge 16.2: Applying Force Field Analysis 492
Organization Development Interventions 494
Diagnosis and Needs Analysis 495
Organization- and Group-Focused Techniques 496
Individual-Focused Techniques 500
Ethical Considerations in Organization Development 503
Are Organization Development Efforts Effective? 504
Managerial Implications: Managing Change 504
LOOKING BACK Technology Keeps the American Red Cross Running Smoothly 505
Chapter Summary 505
Key Terms 506
Review Questions 506
Discussion and Communication Questions 507
Ethics Questions 507
Experiential Exercises 507
References 511

Glossary 535

Company Index I-1

Name Index I-6

Subject Index I-10

UNDERSTANDING ORGANIZATIONAL BEHAVIOR

A MULTIMEDIA APPROACH

ALL KINDS OF

RESOURCES FOR

ALL KINDS OF MINDS

Preface

ALL KINDS OF MINDS

Every learner approaches learning differently. Some learn best listening in a lecture environment, while others like to privately reflect on readings. Many learners struggle with concepts until they actually can see them in a model or graph, and there are those who need first-hand experience to gain understanding. Then, of course, there are those who learn best through a combination of any number of these. Fortunately, today's technology allows us to build learning environments tailored to all these unique learning styles.

Understanding Organizational Behavior takes advantage of those technologies to provide learners the most robust learning environment possible, providing tools for learners who study best through one particular style or a combination of styles. It combines the proven scholarship of an academic textbook with the most extensive multimedia learning package available. The textbook provides an exceptionally balanced presentation of modern organizational behavior theory and its application to today's global environment. Then to emphasize key concepts, the authors integrate "Experiencing Organizational Behavior," an award-winning collection of on-line modules that reinforce key concepts. In addition, the package includes a rich learning support package, including a Study Aid audio CD, a multimedia CD-ROM, InfoTrac College Edition, and more, to create the most comprehensive student learning package available.

While *Understanding Organizational Behavior: A Multimedia Approach* provides many options to accommodate different learning styles, it offers instructors the complete flexibility to assign all or parts of the package.

CORRELATION CHART OF TEXT CHAPTERS AND MULTIMEDIA RESOURCES

	Instructor's Manual on IRCD	Test Bank on IRCD: Multiple-Choice **MC** True/False **TF** Essay **ESS** Matching **MAT**	PowerPoint™ Slides on IRCD (# of slides)	Videos	Experiencing Organizational Behavior Online Concepts and Activities	Student CD-ROM	Audio CD-ROM	Web Site
Chapter 1	Chapter 1	MC: 48 ESS: 8 TF: 14 MAT: 4	25			The student CD-ROM offers a video case that explores the characteristics of learning organizations. It features Yahoo!, the company that leads the way for more traditional organizations on the Web, learning as it goes. Case questions are programmed to allow students to e-mail their solutions directly to their instructors. Also available on the CD-ROM are additional videos, interactive quiz questions for each chapter, plus complete business and organizational behavior glossaries.	The audio CD-ROM is a complete study guide on disc — providing students with comprehensive audio lectures of each chapter in the text. On-the-go students will find this a must-have portable study tool.	*Understanding Organizational Behavior: A Multimedia Approach* has its own Web site at **http:// nelson-quick. swcollege.com** The full PowerPoint presentation is available for you to download as lecture support for yourself as well as a study aid for your students. The "Features Archive" includes some of the more popular pedagogical features from *Organizational Behavior, third edition,* by Nelson and Quick. A multiple-choice and true/false tutorial and a glossary organized by chapter to help students study for exams are also featured.
Chapter 2	Chapter 2	MC: 73 ESS: 7 TF: 22 MAT: 5	25					
Chapter 3	Chapter 3	MC: 62 ESS: 5 TF: 13 MAT: 5	24		Personality & Attitudes; Perception & Attribution			
Chapter 4	Chapter 4	MC: 61 ESS: 5 TF: 15 MAT: 5	25		Personality & Attitudes			
Chapter 5	Chapter 5	MC: 48 ESS: 5 TF: 14 MAT: 5	25	Valassis Communications: A Case Study in Motivating for Performance	Motivation			
Chapter 6	Chapter 6	MC: 61 ESS: 5 TF: 11 MAT: 5	25	LaBelle Management: A Case Study in Performance Appraisals	Learning			
Chapter 7	Chapter 7	MC: 58 ESS: 5 TF: 20 MAT: 4	25		Stress			
Chapter 8	Chapter 8	MC: 54 ESS: 5 TF: 25 MAT: 5	25		Teams			
Chapter 9	Chapter 9	MC: 70 ESS: 5 TF: 19 MAT: 5	25	Next Door Food Stores: A Case Study of Self-Directed Work Teams	Decision Making			
Chapter 10	Chapter 10	MC: 65 ESS: 5 TF: 17 MAT: 5	25		Power & Politics			
Chapter 11	Chapter 11	MC: 68 ESS: 5 TF: 23 MAT: 4	25		Leadership			
Chapter 12	Chapter 12	MC: 62 ESS: 5 TF: 19 MAT: 5	25	JIAN Corporation: A Case Study in Conflict Management	Conflict & Negotiation			
Chapter 13	Chapter 13	MC: 66 ESS: 5 TF: 21 MAT: 5	25					
Chapter 14	Chapter 14	MC: 79 ESS: 5 TF: 21 MAT: 5	25		Organizational Design			
Chapter 15	Chapter 15	MC: 56 ESS: 5 TF: 15 MAT: 5	25	W.B. Doner and Company: A Case Study of Culture in the Organization				
Chapter 16	Chapter 16	MC: 68 ESS: 5 TF: 22 MAT: 5	25		Innovation & Change			

UNDERSTANDING ORGANIZATIONAL BEHAVIOR

. . . represents the solid scholarly foundations on which the science of organizational behavior was built, the realities of contemporary life in organizations, and the challenges that constantly present themselves. Our book is steeped in research tradition and contains not only classic research, but also leading-edge contributions to the field. This research and theory form the foundations of our knowledge base. This text reflects what is happening in the real world, in all types of organizations: public and private, large and small, product- and service-oriented. Some of the examples show successes and failures of managers applying organizational behavior knowledge. Individual and group activities offer proactive learning and reflect the opportunities we have to grow and develop both as individuals and organizations.

Our overarching theme of change is accompanied by four supporting subthemes: globalization, diversity, technology, and ethics. Each theme presents its own challenges and presents demands on individuals to learn, grow, and adjust. The global marketplace has brought with it a boundaryless world, with no constraints on time and distance. Diversity can be a tremendous asset, with its wealth of skills and knowledge, if managers can build an organizational culture that views differences as assets. While new technologies have vastly improved the efficiency of work, managers must balance high-tech with high-touch. Managing ethical behavior means doing the right thing in an age of increased white-collar crime and public scrutiny of organizations.

One of the new organizational realities is that employment in today's organizations is not forever. Organizations expect employees to learn continually. Our book rests on the assumption that learning involves not only acquiring knowledge but also developing skills. The rich theory and research in organizational behavior must be translated into application. Thus, the text presents the opportunity to know concepts, ideas, and theories, and practice skills, abilities, and behaviors to enhance the management of human behavior at work. Both knowledge and skills are essential for future managers. We hope the knowledge and skills presented here empower them to succeed in the changing world of work.

FEATURES

Thinking Ahead opening vignettes help preview upcoming chapter topics by presenting one of six different companies: Gateway, Starbucks, Southwest Airlines, Ford, Harpo Productions, or American Red Cross. ***Looking Back*** at the end of the chapter completes the example.

Organizational Reality boxes spotlighting contemporary organizational life reflect the themes of globalization, diversity, technology, and ethics.

Self-assessment ***Challenge Exercises*** in each chapter provide students with feedback on one aspect of the topic. Students can use the results of the Challenge for self-discovery or behavorial change.

Discussion and Communication Questions assist students in developing written and oral communication skills.

Ethics Questions provoke critical thinking and encourage students to think about ways to resolve ethical conflicts in organizations.

Experiential Exercises at the end of each chapter provide opportunity for group learning and development of interpersonal working skills in a team environment.

Thinking Ahead

Ford Goes Global with an International Team of Executives

Ford is a company with a global strategy for the twenty-first century. Ford's CEO, Jacques Nasser, heads an internationally trained team of executives whose g...

Looking Back

Ford Cars and Trucks on Demand in the Future

Ford's in-house Web site and intranet may save billions of dollars for the company during the next few years and could even change the way Ford does business. The company is trying to move from a "make and sell" strategy to a more flexible, cars-on-demand approach. Ford's intranet connects 120,000 workstations around the world to thousands of Ford Web sites. The information on the Web sites is proprietary—things like market research, analysis of competitors' models, and rankings of suppliers. Ford's product development system documents thousands of steps in manufacturing, assembling, and testing vehicles, and it's on the intranet. Engineers, designers, and suppliers can access and work from the same data, which are updated hourly. Each vehicle team has its own Web site, where questions are posted and quality issues are resolved. This system has helped Ford reduce the time it takes to get new models into production from thirty-six months to twenty-four months.

In an effort to integrate the Internet into all parts of Ford's business, the company has signed e-commerce agreements with Oracle, Cisco Systems, Yahoo!, and Carpoint. Ford and Oracle created the world's first automotive online supply chain network and the world's largest

---

ORGANIZATIONAL REALITY 3.1

At Cisco Systems, Self-Esteem Produces Success

Once every four months, Cisco Systems' chief executive puts on a red apron, picks up a canvas bag full of ice cream treats, and walks through corporate headquarters handing out ice cream to his staff. He greets employees with "Hi, my name is John Chambers. Corporate overhead here at Cisco." You might think this behavior unusual for a CEO, but Chambers's belief in himself and his employees lends itself to good humor, and to success.

Cisco dominates the business for data networking equipment that makes up the plumbing of the Internet and corporate computer networks. Between January 1995 when Chambers became CEO and 1998, Cisco's share price increased by 600 percent, giving the company a market value of over $100 billion in a mere 8.5 years—the fastest to do so in history. (Even Microsoft took 11 years to accomplish this!)

Chambers is preparing Cisco to compete in a much bigger league, the $250 billion per year market for telecommunication equipment. He'll have to do battle with Nortel, twice as big as Cisco, Lucent, three times as big, and Siemens, seven times as big as Cisco. "I want Cisco to be a dynasty," he says. "I think it can be a company that changes the world." His own self-esteem and self-efficacy (his "can do" attitude), along with a

to read. His childhood reading coach recalls about Chambers: "He knew that he had a problem, and he had no doubt in his mind that he was going to do something about it. He made no excuses for not being able to read, and that's very rare." His hard work paid off. He graduated second in his class from high school.

At Cisco, Chambers built a culture where it's not a sign of weakness, but a sign of strength, to say, "I can't do everything myself. I will find a partner and trust myself to be able to manage the process." Teamwork is essential; managers who are not team players are flushed out of the company. He constantly polls his staff on problems. How is the Scottish factory coming? Is the softball team on track? Do we have the right people in the right jobs? Having a day care center on site, combined with success, fuels self-esteem.

Despite the formidable competition Cisco Systems faces in the telecommunication industry, Wall Street is bullish on the company. Most analysts attribute the success in large measure to Chambers and the way he encourages his managers to stay focused on their

Discussion Question

Challenge 4.1

Assess Your Job Satisfaction

Think of the job you have now or a job you've had in the past. Indicate how satisfied you are with each aspect of your job below, using the following scale:

```
1 = Extremely dissatisfied
2 = Dissatisfied
3 = Slightly dissatisfied
4 = Neutral
5 = Slightly satisfied
6 = Satisfied
7 = Extremely satisfied
```

1. The amount of job security I have.
2. The amount of pay and fringe benefits I receive.
3. The amount of personal growth and development I get in doing my job.
4. The people I talk to and work with on my job.
5. The degree of respect and fair treatment I receive from my boss.
6. The feeling of worthwhile accomplishment I get from doing my job.
7. The chance to get to know other people while on the job.
8. The amount of support and guidance I receive from my supervisor.
9. The degree to which I am fairly paid for what I contribute to this organization.
10. The amount of independent thought and action I can exercise in my job.
11. How secure things look for me in the future in this organization.
12. The chance to help other people while at work.
13. The amount of challenge in my job.
14. The overall quality of the supervision I receive on my work.

Now, compute your scores for the facets of job satisfaction.

Pay satisfaction:
Q2 ___ + Q9 ___ Divided by 2: ___

Security satisfaction:
Q1 ___ + Q11 ___ Divided by 2: ___

Social satisfaction:
Q4 ___ + Q7 ___ + Q12 ___ Divided by 3: ___

Supervisory satisfaction:
Q5 ___ + Q8 ___ + Q14 ___ Divided by 3: ___

Growth satisfaction:
Q3 ___ + Q6 ___ + Q10 ___ + Q13 ___ Divided by 4: ___

Scores on the facets range from 1 to 7. (Scores lower than 4 suggest there is room for change.)

This questionnaire is an abbreviated version of the Job Diagnostic Survey, a widely used tool for assessing individuals' attitudes about their jobs. Compare your scores on each facet to the following norms for a large sample of managers.

Pay satisfaction:	4.6
Security satisfaction:	5.2
Social satisfaction:	5.6
Supervisory satisfaction:	5.2
Growth satisfaction:	5.3

How do your scores compare? Are there actions you can take to improve your job satisfaction?

SOURCE: R. Hackman/G. Oldham, *Work Redesign* (pp. 284 & 317). Copyright © 1980 by Addison-Wesley Publishing Company, Inc. Reprinted by permission of Addison-Wesley Longman.

Chapter 4 • Attitudes, Values, and Ethics / 129

DISCUSSION AND COMMUNICATION QUESTIONS

1. What jobs do you consider to be most satisfying? Why?
2. How can managers increase their employees' job satisfaction?
3. Suppose you have an employee whose lack of commitment is affecting others in the work group. How would you go about persuading the person to change this attitude?
4. In Rokeach's studies on values, the most recent data are from 1981. Do you think values have changed since then? If so, how?
5. What are the most important influences on an individual's perceptions of ethical behavior? Can organizations change these perceptions? If so, how?
6. How can managers encourage organizational citizenship?
7. (*communication question*) Suppose you are a manager in a customer service organization. Your group includes seven supervisors who report directly to you. Each supervisor manages a team of seven cus- tomer service representatives. One of your supervisors, Linda, has complained that Joe, one of her employees, has "an attitude problem." She has requested that Joe be transferred to another team. Write a memo to Linda explaining your position on this problem and what should be done.
8. (*communication question*) Select a company that you admire for its values. Use the resources of your university library to answer two questions. First, what are the company's values? Second, how do employees enact these values? Prepare an oral presentation to present in class.
9. (*communication question*) Think of a time when you have experienced cognitive dissonance. Analyze your experience in terms of the attitude and behavior involved. What did you do to resolve the cognitive dissonance? What other actions could you have taken? Write a brief description of your experience and your responses to the questions.

ETHICS QUESTIONS

1. Is it ethical for an organization to influence an individual's ethical behavior? In other words, is ethics a personal issue that organizations should stay away from? Is it an invasion of privacy to enforce codes of conduct?
2. Suppose a coworker is engaging in behavior that you find personally unethical, but the behavior is not prohibited by the company's ethical standards. How would you handle the issue?
3. Some people have argued that the biggest deficiency of business school graduates is that they have no sense of ethics. What do you think?
4. Is it possible to operate in a completely ethical manner and be successful in business when your competitors engage in unethical tactics?
5. How do Machiavellianism and locus of control affect an individual's cognitive moral development?

Experiential Exercises

4.1 Chinese, Indian, and American Values

Purpose
To learn some differences between Chinese, Indian, and American value systems.

Group size
Any number of groups of five to eight people.
Time required
50+ minutes

EXPERIENCING ORGANIZATIONAL BEHAVIOR

Experiencing Organizational Behavior, by R. Dennis Middlemist, is the on-line teaching assistant that helps students understand and reinforce OB concepts – 24 hours a day.

This award-winning, Web-based teaching tool is a fully integrated, on-line instructional system that engagingly and dynamically presents organizational behavior content and scenarios. Four areas of information (Overview, important Terms, relevant Exercises, and illustrated Scenario) are presented for a variety of key topics.

Experiencing Organizational Behavior's content was developed through extensive reviews of organizational behavior textbooks and publications, as well as the author's teaching experience.

Below is a walk-through of the *Experiencing Organizational Behavior* Motivation module. Since all the modules follow the same organization and include the same exercises, you may use this model to walk through any of the other modules. The address of the site is:

http://www.experiencingob.com

As you can see, the first page of *Experiencing Organizational Behavior* contains detailed directions on how to use the modules.
To get started, select a topic from the drop-down box in the top right corner. This box is found throughout the product so you may move to another module at any time. To follow this example, select **MOTIVATION**.

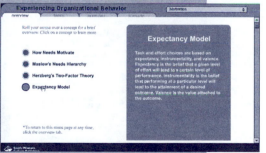

This is the first screen of the Motivation module. Note the key concepts are on the left-hand side. If you pass the mouse over each key term, you will see a definition appear in the green box to the right. This provides the learner with a brief introduction to the concept. Click on the key term **EXPECTANCY MODEL** to learn more.

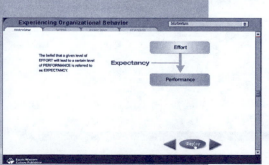

A short paragraph introduces you to the model or graph you are going to view. Select **BEGIN** and then move through the sequence by pressing the green arrow to the right. At any point you may move back a step or replay the entire model. It is important to note that these models and animations will move at the same speed, *no matter what your Internet connection rate*. When completed, you may select the Overview to return to the main menu and more motivation topics. When ready, select the **TERMS** tab.

Each module contains two crossword puzzles on two of the major concepts. For this example, we have selected **Herzberg's Two-Factor Theory**. To complete the crossword, type the letter in the correct box to complete the answer. Correct letters remain in the puzzle while incorrect letters disappear. By clicking **HINT**, a letter will be added to help the learner along. After viewing the crossword, select the **EXERCISES** tab.

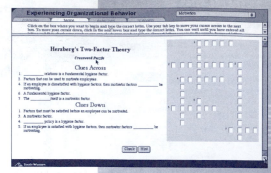

The exercises in each module present students with either a matching or "drag and drop" exercise and an integrated activity. We have selected the **Maslow's Needs Hierarchy** exercise, which is a "drag and drop" exercise. After matching key terms with their statements, click the **CHECK** box to check your scores. When completed, click the **EXERCISES** tab to move on to the Integrated Application.

The Integrated Application presents the learner with a short scenario and photos that represent real business situations. Students are asked to respond through the questions on the left. Responses to their answers appear in **red** at the top of the screen. After exploring the Integrated Application, select the **SCENARIO** tab.

Each module contains an animated scenario that presents a situation relating to the most difficult or important concepts. This scenario is on **Expectancy Model**.

It is important to note again that these animations run at the same rate, regardless of Internet connection speed.

Each scenario is divided into three parts, and learners are asked to respond to what they see happening at the end of each section. If the question is answered incorrectly, the rationale is provided as to why the answer was wrong and the learner is given an opportunity to answer again. The learner cannot move on in the animation until they answer correctly.

AUDIO CD

The Audio CD is a comprehensive study guide on disc. Detailed outlines are provided for each chapter of the text. This portable study tool can be conveniently used most anywhere – in the dorm room, walking to class, driving in the car – to give reinforcement of key organizational concepts.

STUDENT CD-ROM

The Student CD-ROM offers a video case that explores the characteristics of learning organizations. It features Yahoo!, the hi-tech company that leads the way for more traditional organizations on the Web, learning as it goes. Case questions are programmed to allow students to e-mail their solutions directly to their instructors. Also available on the CD-ROM are additional videos, interactive quiz questions for each chapter, plus complete business and organizational behavior glossaries.

 WIZEUP DIGITAL EDITION

The WizeUp Digital Edition of *Understanding Organizational Behavior: A Multimedia Approach* contains the complete South-Western text, powered by WizeUp software. It features powerful study tools to help students study faster and easier (available at **http://www.wizeup.com**).

With the digital version students can...

- instantly find exactly what they need by using powerful search tools;
- add notes anywhere in their textbooks;
- search, sort, and print their notes to make a custom study guide;
- trade notes digitally with their classmates and professors;
- create custom hyperlinks from their books to the Web or any other digital resource;
- highlight any text and erase highlights if they make a mistake.

WEB SITE

http://nelson-quick.swcollege.com

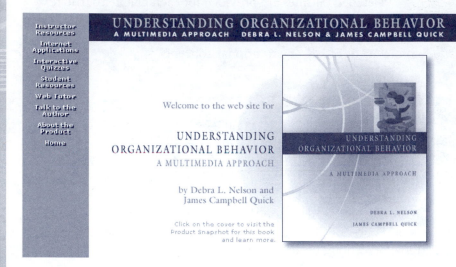

This dynamic, comprehensive Web site features the following teaching and learning support:

- *Experiencing Organizational Behavior* margin notes
- How to use *Experiencing Organizational Behavior* effectively
- Quizzes
- Glossary organized by chapter
- Instructor resources, including Instructor's Manual and PowerPoint™ presentation slides
- Additional boxed features not included in the text
- Two appendices (*A Brief Historical Perspective* and *How Do We Know What We Know About Organizational Behavior?*)
- Internet exercises

INSTRUCTOR RESOURCES

 INSTRUCTOR'S RESOURCE CD-ROM Key instructor ancillaries (Instructor's Manual, Test Bank, and PowerPoint™ slides) are provided on CD-ROM, giving instructors the ultimate tool for customizing lectures and presentations.

Exam*View*® **EXAMVIEW** This supplement contains all of the questions in the test bank. This program is an easy-to-use test creation software compatible with Microsoft Windows. Instructors can add or edit questions, instructions, and answers, and select questions (randomly or numerically) by previewing them on the screen. Instructors can also create and administer quizzes on line, whether over the Internet, a local area network (LAN), or a wide area network (WAN).

 **VIDEO** Video segments have been selected to support the themes of the book and to deepen students' understanding of the organizational behavior concepts presented throughout the text. Information on using the videos can be found in the Instructor's Manual on the Instructor's Resource CD-ROM. Companies profiled in the video series include Valassis Communications, LaBelle Management, Next Door Food Stores, JIAN Corporation, and W.B. Doner and Company.

PART 1

Introduction

1. Organizational Behavior in Changing Times   2

2. Organizations 2001 and Managerial
Challenges   29

Learning Objectives

After reading this chapter, you should be able to do the following:

1. Define *organizational behavior.* p. 3

2. Identify six interdisciplinary contributions to the study of organizational behavior. *p. 5*

3. Identify the important system components of an organization. *p. 7*

4. Describe the formal and informal elements of an organization. *p. 9*

5. Understand the diversity of organizations in the economy, as exemplified by the six focus organizations. *p. 11*

6. Recognize the challenge of change for organizational behavior. *p. 15*

7. Demonstrate the value of objective knowledge and skill development in the study of organizational behavior. *p. 19*

1

Organizational Behavior in Changing Times

Thinking Ahead

Change, Challenge, and Gateway

The challenge of managing constant change is nowhere more present than in the information systems, communication, and computer industries. The past twenty-five years have seen a series of hardware and software revolutions through which information systems, communications, and computers are converging into a single industry. Information technology is even becoming a passé term as an information industry emerges. The amount of computer work and support accomplished today by one expert on a desktop computer system required fifteen people using mainframe punch card–based systems supported by card sorters, punch card collators, and aisles of files less than thirty years ago.

This information revolution has dramatically changed the nature of managerial work, eased the workload of many, and challenged people to learn new skills and to modify their behavior at work.[1] For example, American Airlines' department of Weight and Balance Planning at System Operation Control in Fort Worth, Texas, does all load planning for all of American Airlines' aircraft worldwide. The department achieves this with an artificial intelligence system that enables one load planner to work forty-five flights in a normal eight-hour shift, compared to eight to ten flights locally in the precomputer days. The beat goes on! Continuing change and innovation are resulting in a computer hardware and software half-life of less than a year, and in many cases only six months. How can people keep pace with this rate of change and avoid technological obsolescence? What can computer manufacturers do to help individuals gain access to the information age, travel on the electronic highway of the Internet, and transform the way they interact with other people at work and play? Gateway introduced one revolutionary way to respond to this challenge.

HUMAN BEHAVIOR IN ORGANIZATIONS

Organizational behavior is individual behavior and group dynamics in organizations. The study of organizational behavior is primarily concerned with the psychosocial, interpersonal, and behavioral dynamics in organizations. However, organizational variables that affect human behavior at work are also relevant to the study of organizational behavior. These organizational variables include jobs, the design of work, communication, performance appraisal, organizational design, and organizational structure. Therefore, although individual behavior and group dynamics are the primary concerns in the study of organizational behavior, organizational variables are also important.

1. Define *organizational behavior.*

organizational behavior
The study of individual behavior and group dynamics in organizational settings.

This chapter presents an introduction to organizational behavior. The first section provides an overview of human behavior in organizations and its interdisciplinary origins. The second section presents an organizational context within which behavior occurs and briefly introduces the six focus companies used in the book. The third section highlights the importance of *change* and *challenge* for organizational behavior in these changing times. The fourth section addresses the ways people learn about organizational behavior and explains how the text's pedagogical features relate to the various ways of learning. The final section of the chapter presents the plan for the book.

change
The transformation or modification of an organization and/or its stakeholders.

challenge
The call to competition, contest, or battle.

Human behavior in organizations is complex and often difficult to understand. Organizations have been described as clockworks in which human behavior is logical and rational, but they often seem like snake pits to those who work in them.[2] The clockwork metaphor reflects an orderly, idealized view of organizational behavior devoid of conflict or dilemma because all the working parts (the people) mesh smoothly. The snake pit metaphor conveys the daily conflict, distress, and struggle in organizations. Each metaphor reflects reality from a different perspective—the organization's versus the individual's point of view. These metaphors still apply in the virtual work environments that are emerging. Organizational Reality 1.1 briefly describes virtual offices. These new environments have important and as yet unspecified implications for what human behavior in organizations means.

ORGANIZATIONAL REALITY 1.1

Changing Work Environments—The Virtual Office

Home-based entrepreneurs, those on the go who want to avoid high overhead in one location, and multinationals with needs for short-term projects are all learning to take advantage of virtual offices. High-tech communications through videoconferencing, electronic mail, and telecommuting have provided the technological platform with which people have transformed the ways and places in which they work. Home-based entrepreneurs can couple a comfortable home office with panoramic views of rolling hills, seashores, countrysides, or cityscapes, depending on individual preferences. Virtual office and private club locations enable the entrepreneur to avoid the expensive overhead costs of dedicated office space. Private clubs afford the opportunity for luncheons, receptions, meeting spaces, or high-tech communication support for the conduct of business. Hence, the entrepreneur has financial and operational flexibility.

Virtual office companies provide central-city space, with high-tech features yet without the high costs, for many entrepreneurs and businesspeople in Europe and the United States. Virtual Office is a U.K. company offering a prestigious London address, central London telephone number, and secretarial services for a monthly fee with the option of adding other required services on a chargeable basis. Virtual offices—made possible by the revolutions in information and communication systems—enable entrepreneurs and businesspeople to have an established, secure base of operation from which they can access any point in the world.

Lifestyle balance is a driving force for some who seek virtual offices in proximity to their residence to support a home-based entrepreneurial business. The very high quality of contemporary communication and information technology often makes it impossible for clients, customers, or suppliers to know whether you are in the office next door, your home office, your virtual office, the Montreux jazz festival in Switzerland, or between contract negotiation meetings in Beijing, China.

Discussion Questions

1. What are some advantages and some disadvantages of a virtual office arrangement?

2. What are some of the implications of virtual office arrangements for employees and their supervisors?

SOURCES: P. Baldwin, "Using Your Club as a Virtual Office," *Private Clubs*, August 1998, 36–39; K. A. Strassel, "'Virtual Office' Space Gives Executives High-Tech Features without High Costs," *The Wall Street Journal*, December 23, 1996, A5A.

This section briefly contrasts two perspectives for understanding human behavior, the external and the internal perspectives. It then discusses the six scientific disciplines from which the study of organizational behavior has emerged. Each discipline has made a unique contribution to organizational behavior.

Understanding Human Behavior

The vast majority of theories and models of human behavior fall into one of two basic categories. One category has an internal perspective, and the other has an external perspective. The internal perspective considers factors inside the person to understand behavior. This view is psychodynamically oriented. People who subscribe to this view understand human behavior in terms of the thoughts, feelings, past experiences, and needs of the individual. The internal perspective explains people's actions and behavior in terms of their history and personal value systems. The internal processes of thinking, feeling, perceiving, and judging lead people to act in specific ways. The internal perspective has given rise to a wide range of motivational and leadership theories. This perspective implies that people are best understood from the inside and that people's behavior is best interpreted after understanding their thoughts and feelings.

The other category of theories and models of human behavior takes an external perspective. This perspective focuses on factors outside the person to understand behavior. People who subscribe to this view understand human behavior in terms of external events, consequences of behavior, and the environmental forces to which a person is subject. From the external perspective, a person's history, feelings, thoughts, and personal value systems are not very important in interpreting actions and behavior. This perspective has given rise to an alternative set of motivational and leadership theories. The external perspective implies that a person's behavior is best understood by examining the surrounding external events and environmental forces.

The internal and external perspectives offer alternative explanations for human behavior. For example, the internal perspective might say Mary is an outstanding employee because she has a high need for achievement, whereas the external perspective might say Mary is an outstanding employee because she is paid extremely well for her work. Kurt Lewin captured both perspectives in saying that behavior is a function of both the person and the environment.[3]

Interdisciplinary Influences

Organizational behavior is a blended discipline that has grown out of contributions from numerous earlier fields of study, only one of which is the psychological discipline from which Kurt Lewin came. These interdisciplinary influences are the roots for what is increasingly recognized as the independent discipline of organizational behavior. The sciences of psychology, sociology, engineering, anthropology, management, and medicine are the disciplines from which organizational behavior has emerged or by which it has been influenced. Each of these sciences has had its own important and unique influence on the discipline of organizational behavior.

Psychology is the science of human behavior and dates back to the closing decades of the nineteenth century. Psychology traces its own origins to philosophy and the science of physiology. One of the most prominent early psychologists, William James, actually held a degree in medicine (M.D.). Since its origin, psychology has itself become differentiated into a number of specialized fields, such as clinical, experimental, military, organizational, and social psychology. The topics in organizational psychology, which include work teams, work motivation, training and development, power and leadership, human resource planning, and workplace wellness, are very

2. Identify six interdisciplinary contributions to the study of organizational behavior.

psychology
The science of human behavior.

similar to the topics covered by organizational behavior.[4] An early leader in the field of psychology was Robert Yerkes, whose research efforts for the American military during World War I had later implications for sophisticated personnel selection methods used by corporations such as Johnson & Johnson, Valero Energy, and Chaparral Steel.[5]

sociology
The science of society.

Sociology, the science of society, has made important contributions to knowledge about group and intergroup dynamics in the study of organizational behavior. Because sociology takes the society rather than the individual as its point of departure, the sociologist is concerned with the variety of roles within a society or culture, the norms and standards of behavior that emerge within societies and groups, and the consequences of compliant and deviant behavior within social groups. For example, the concept of *role set* was a key contribution to role theory by Robert Merton.[6] The role set consisted of a person in a social role and all others who had expectations of that person. A team of Harvard educators used the concept to study the school superintendent role in Massachusetts.[7] These sociological contributions were the basis for subsequent studies of role conflict and ambiguity in companies such as Tenneco, Purex, and The Western Company of North America.

engineering
The applied science of energy and matter.

Engineering is the applied science of energy and matter. Engineering has made important contributions to our understanding of the design of work. By taking basic engineering ideas and applying them to human behavior in work organizations, Frederick Taylor had a profound influence on the early years of the study of organizational behavior.[8] Taylor's engineering background led him to place special emphasis on human productivity and efficiency in work behavior. His notions of performance standards and differential piece-rate systems contributed to a congressional investigation into scientific management at the behest of organized labor. Taylor was ahead of his times in many ways, and his ideas were often controversial during his lifetime. Nevertheless, applications of his original ideas are embedded in organizational goal-setting programs, such as those at Black & Decker, IBM, and Weyerhauser.[9] Even the notions of *stress* and *strain* have their origins in the lexicon of engineering.

anthropology
The science of the learned behavior of human beings.

Anthropology is the science of human learned behavior and is especially important to understanding organizational culture. Cultural anthropology focuses on the origins of culture and the patterns of behavior as culture is communicated symbolically. Current research in this tradition has examined the effects of efficient cultures on organization performance[10] and how pathological personalities may lead to dysfunctional organizational cultures.[11] Schwartz used a psychodynamic, anthropological mode of inquiry in exploring corporate decay at General Motors and NASA during the 1980s.[12]

management
The study of overseeing activities and supervising people in organizations.

Management, originally called administrative science, is a discipline concerned with the study of overseeing activities and supervising people in organizations. It emphasizes the design, implementation, and management of various administrative and organizational systems. March and Simon take the human organization as their point of departure and concern themselves with the administrative practices that will enhance the effectiveness of the system.[13] Management is the first discipline to take the modern corporation as the unit of analysis, and this viewpoint distinguishes the discipline's contribution to the study of organizational behavior.

Medicine is the applied science of healing or treatment of diseases to enhance an individual's health and well-being. Medicine embraces concern for both physical and psychological health, with the concern for industrial mental health dating back at least sixty years.[14] More recently, as the war against acute diseases is being won, medical attention has shifted from the acute diseases, such as influenza, to the more chronic, such as hypertension. Attention has also been directed to occupational health and well-being.[15] Individual behavior and lifestyle patterns play a more important role in treating chronic diseases than in treating acute diseases.[16] These trends have contributed to the growth of corporate wellness programs, such as Johnson & Johnson's "Live for Life Program" and Control Data Corporation's STAY-WELL program. Such programs have led to increasing attention to medicine in organizational behavior. The surge in health care costs over the past two decades has also contributed to increased organizational concern with medicine and health care in the workplace.[17]

medicine
The applied science of healing or treatment of diseases to enhance an individual's health and well-being.

THE ORGANIZATIONAL CONTEXT

A complete understanding of organizational behavior requires both an understanding of human behavior and an understanding of the organizational context within which human behavior is acted out. The organizational context is the specific setting within which organizational behavior is enacted. This section discusses several aspects of this organizational context and includes specific organizational examples. First, organizations are presented as systems. Second, the formal and informal organizations are discussed. Finally, six focus companies are presented as contemporary examples, which are drawn on throughout the text.

3. Identify the important system components of an organization.

Organizations as Systems

Just as two different perspectives offer complementary explanations for human behavior, two other perspectives offer complementary explanations of organizations. Organizations are systems of interacting components, which are people, tasks, technology, and structure. These internal components also interact with components in the organization's task environment. Organizations as open systems have people, technology, structure, and purpose, which interact with elements in the organization's environment.

What, exactly, is an organization? Today, the corporation is the dominant organizational form for much of the Western world, but other organizational forms have dominated other times and societies. Some societies have been dominated by religious organizations, such as the temple corporations of ancient Mesopotamia and the churches in colonial America.[18]

Other societies have been dominated by military organizations, such as the clans of the Scottish Highlands and the regional armies of the People's Republic of China.[19, 20] All these societies are woven together by family organizations, which themselves may vary from nuclear and extended families to small, collective communities.[21, 22] The purpose and structure of the religious, military, and family organizational forms may vary, but people's behavior in these organizations may be very similar. In fact, early discoveries about power and leadership in work organizations were remarkably similar to findings about power and leadership within families.[23]

Organizations may manufacture products, such as aircraft components or steel, or deliver services, such as managing money or providing insurance protection. To understand how organizations do these things requires an understanding of the open system components of the organization and the components of its task environment.

Leavitt sets out a basic framework for understanding organizations, a framework that emphasizes four major internal components: task, people, technology, and structure.[24] These four components, along with the organization's inputs, outputs, and key elements in the task environment, are depicted in Figure 1.1. The *task* of the organization is its mission, purpose, or goal for existing. The *people* are the human resources of the organization. The technology is the wide range of tools, knowledge, and/or tech-

task
An organization's mission, purpose, or goal for existing.

people
The human resources of the organization.

Figure 1.1
A Systems View of Organization

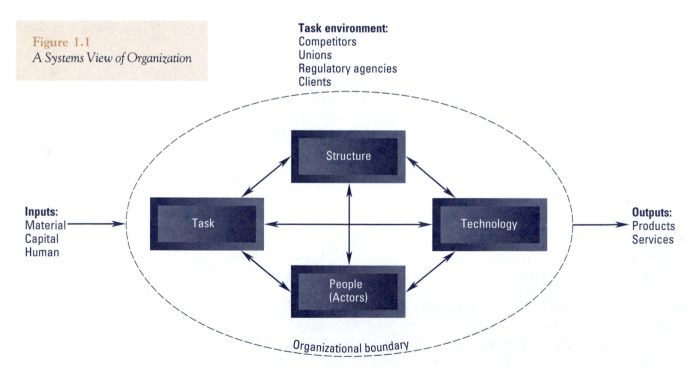

Task environment:
Competitors
Unions
Regulatory agencies
Clients

Inputs:
Material
Capital
Human

Outputs:
Products
Services

Structure

Task

Technology

People
(Actors)

Organizational boundary

SOURCE: Based on Harold Leavitt, "Applied Organizational Change in Industry: Structural, Technological, and Humanistic Approaches," in J. G. March, ed., *Handbook of Organizations* (Chicago: Rand McNally, 1965), p. 1145. Reprinted by permission of James G. March.

niques used to transform the inputs into outputs. The *structure* is how work is designed at the micro level, as well as how departments, divisions, and the overall organization are designed at the macro level.

In addition to these major internal components, the organization as a system also has an external task environment. The task environment is composed of different constituents, such as suppliers, customers, and federal regulators. Thompson describes the task environment as that element of the environment related to the organization's degree of goal attainment; that is, the task environment is composed of those elements of the environment related to the organization's basic task.[25] For example, when steel was a major component in the production of cars, U.S. Steel was a major supplier for General Motors and Ford Motor Company—U.S. Steel was a major component of their task environments. As less steel and more aluminum was used to make cars, U.S. Steel became a less important supplier for General Motors and Ford—it was no longer a major component in their task environments.

The organization system works by taking inputs, converting them into throughputs, and delivering outputs to its task environment. Inputs consist of the human, informational, material, and financial resources used by the organization. Throughputs are the materials and resources as they are transformed by the organization's technology component. Once the transformation is complete, they become outputs for customers, consumers, and clients. The actions of suppliers, customers, regulators, and other elements of the task environment affect the organization and the behavior of people at work. For example, Onsite Engineering and Management of Norcross, Georgia, experienced a threat to its survival in the mid-1980s by being totally dependent on one large utility for its outputs. By broadening its client base and improving the quality of its services (that is, its outputs) over the next several years, Onsite became a healthier, more successful small company. Transforming inputs into high-quality outputs is critical to an organization's success.

The Formal and Informal Organization

The systems view of organization may lead one to view the design of an organization as a clockwork with a neat, precise, interrelated functioning. The *formal organization* is the part of the system that has legitimacy and official recognition. The snake pit organizational metaphor mentioned earlier has its roots in the study and examination of the *informal organization*, which is the unofficial part of the system. The informal organization was first fully appreciated as a result of the *Hawthorne studies*, conducted during the 1920s and 1930s. It was during the interview study, the third of the four Hawthorne studies, that the researchers began to develop a fuller appreciation for the informal elements of the Hawthorne Works as an organization.[26] The formal and informal elements of the organization are depicted in Figure 1.2.[27]

structure
The manner in which an organization's work is designed at the micro level, as well as how departments, divisions, and the overall organization are designed at the macro level.

4. Describe the formal and informal elements of an organization.

formal organization
The part of the organization that has legitimacy and official recognition.

informal organization
The unofficial part of the organization.

Hawthorne studies
Studies conducted during the 1920s and 1930s that discovered the existence of the informal organization.

Figure 1.2
*Formal and Informal Elements
of Organizations*

Formal organization (overt)
Goals and objectives
Policies and procedures
Job descriptions
Financial resources

Social surface

Informal organization
(covert)
Beliefs and assumptions
about:
    people
    work
    the organization
Perceptions and attitudes
Values
Feelings, such as fear,
    rage, despair, and hope
Group norms

Potential conflict between the formal and informal elements of the organization makes an understanding of both important. Conflicts between these two elements erupted in many organizations during the early years of the twentieth century and were embodied in the union–management strife of that era. The conflicts escalated into violence in a number of cases. For example, during the 1920s every supervisor at the Homestead Works of U.S. Steel was issued a pistol and a box of ammunition "just in case" it became necessary to shoot an unruly, dangerous steelworker. Not all organizations are characterized by such potential formal–informal, management–labor conflict. During the same era, Eastman Kodak was very progressive. The company helped with financial backing for employees' neighborhood communities, such as Meadowbrook in Rochester, New York. Kodak's concern for employees and attention to informal issues made unions unnecessary within the company.

The informal organization is a frequent point of diagnostic and intervention activities in organization development.[28] The informal organization is important because people's feelings, thoughts, and attitudes about their work do make a difference in their behavior and performance. Individual behavior plays out in the context of the formal and informal elements of the system, becoming organizational behavior. The existence of the informal organization was one of the major discoveries of the Hawthorne studies.

Six Focus Organizations

Organizational behavior always occurs in the context of a specific organizational setting. Most attempts at explaining or predicting organizational behavior rely heavily on factors within the organization and give less weight to external environmental considerations.[29] Students can benefit from being sensitive to the industrial context of organizations and from developing an appreciation for each organization as a whole. In this vein, six organizations are featured in the Thinking Ahead and Looking Back sections of three chapters. Gateway, Inc. and the computer industry are illustrated in this chapter.

The U.S. economy is the largest in the world, with a gross domestic product of more than $9.3 trillion in 1999. Figure 1.3 shows the major sectors of the economy. The largest sectors are service (40 percent) and product manufacture of nondurable goods (19 percent) and durable goods (8 percent). Taken together, the production of products and the delivery of services account for 67 percent of the U.S. economy. Government and fixed investments account for the remaining 33 percent. Large and small organizations operate in each sector of the economy shown in Figure 1.3.

The private sectors are an important part of the economy. The manufacturing sector includes the production of basic materials, such as steel, and the production of finished products, such as automobiles and electronic

5. Understand the diversity of organizations in the economy, as exemplified by the six focus organizations.

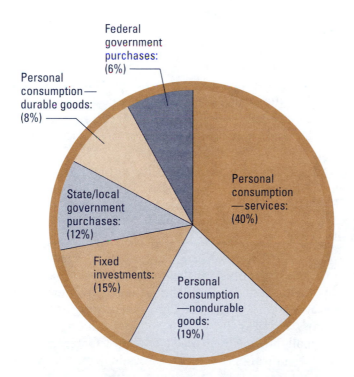

Figure 1.3
U.S. Gross Domestic Product

(Total $9.3 trillion for 1999)

Federal government purchases: (6%)

Personal consumption— durable goods: (8%)

State/local government purchases: (12%)

Fixed investments: (15%)

Personal consumption —services: (40%)

Personal consumption —nondurable goods: (19%)

equipment. The service sector includes transportation, financial services, insurance, and retail sales. The government sectors, which provide essential infrastructure, and nonprofit organizations are also important to our collective well-being because they meet needs not addressed in these economic sectors. We have chosen two manufacturing, two service, one privately owned, and one nonprofit organization to highlight throughout the text. The manufacturing organizations are Ford Motor Company and Gateway, Inc. The two service organizations are Southwest Airlines and Starbucks. The privately owned company is Harpo Entertainment and the nonprofit organization is the American Red Cross.

Each of these six organizations makes an important and unique contribution to the manufacturing or service sectors of the national economy and/or to our national well-being. These organizations are not alone, however. Hundreds of other small, medium, and large organizations are making valuable and significant contributions to the economic health and human welfare of the United States. Brief examples from many organizations are used throughout the book. We hope that by better understanding these organizations, you will have a greater appreciation for your own organization and others within the diverse world of private business enterprises and nonprofit organizations.

Ford Motor Company

Ford Motor Company is the world's second largest industrial corporation, and one of a handful of companies that contributed significantly to the growth of the United States.[30] Ford's two principal business segments are automotive and financial services. Ford is best known for the cars and trucks it manufactures.

At the end of the 1970s, Ford committed to "make quality Job One" in the production of its cars and trucks. The 1980s saw an internal revolution within Ford Motor Company resulting in a dramatic improvement in its financial health and the quality of its cars and trucks.

Ford faces continuing quality pressure from the Japanese and domestic pressure for safer and more fuel-efficient cars. A successful business of 365,000 people and $168 billion in sales estimated for 2000, one of Ford's major challenges is the overcapacity in the automotive industry. A more immediate crisis for Ford in 2000 was the Firestone tire recall, which fully engaged CEO Jacques Nasser and other top Ford officers.

Gateway, Inc.

Gateway, whose name came from the view that its computers were the gateway to the twenty-first century, is the leading American seller of personal computers by mail.[31] Founded in 1985, the company grew dramatically in its first five years and moved to diversify its marketing strategy in the early 1990s. Gateway's early expansion in corporate standing came through its business with small- and medium-sized companies. Gateway topped the *Inc. 500* list of fastest growing private companies in 1991 and went public in

1993, raising $150 million through the sale of 10.9 million shares, or 15 percent of the company.

With over $10 billion in sales and 21,000 employees in 2000, Gateway has manufacturing plants in Ireland, Malaysia, and the United States as well as other facilities in Australia, Austria, Belgium, France, Germany, Hong Kong, Japan, Luxembourg, the Netherlands, Sweden, and Switzerland. The company added software and peripherals to its catalog of computers in 1994, along with showrooms in France and Germany. In 1995, Gateway expanded its business in the Pacific Rim by selling its products in Japan and Australia. Dell and Compaq are Gateway's two primary competitors, and founder Ted Waitt rejected a $7 billion takeover bid by Compaq's management team in 1997. Gateway's new Country Store concept blends the order-by-telephone model with the hands-on approach.

Southwest Airlines

Southwest Airlines is an air transportation service company that became a major airline in the 1990s by providing single-class, high-frequency service to fifty-two cities in twenty-six states across the United States.[32] Founded in 1966 by a group of Texas investors, Southwest is a medium-sized service organization based on number of employees, yet it is the seventh largest airline based on number of passengers carried in 1997. The company benefited from its competitors' 1991 misfortunes, expanding its fleet and services. Southwest, which is headquartered in Dallas, has been recognized with numerous awards based on service quality; in 1997, it was named the Best Company to Work for in America. In 2000, Southwest had 29,000 employees and estimated over $5 billion in revenues, with expansion efforts to continue on the East Coast.

Southwest has an informal organizational culture. In 1998, the company celebrated its twenty-seventh anniversary of incorporation. Southwest emphasizes high aircraft utilization and high employee productivity. It has created a unique niche in the air transportation industry by offering low fares that enable it to compete against ground and rail transportation as well as other major airlines.

Starbucks Corporation

Starbucks Corporation is the leading roaster, retailer, and brand of specialty coffee in North American.[33] This company began as a single small store entrepreneurial venture in 1971 by three coffee aficionados who, legend goes, named the company for the coffee-loving first mate in *Moby Dick*. The company went public in 1992, and expanded to over 2,300 stores in North America by the year 2000. It went international in 1996 with operations in Japan and Singapore and a total of nearly 150 stores overseas by 2000, but still maintains its headquarters in Seattle, Washington. This over 3 billion-dollar-a-year business serves more than two million customers each week, primarily through retail outlets. In addition, 14 percent of Starbucks' business is through specialty sales and direct mail. Starbucks says it sells its coffee "one cup at a time." It was not always so. The founders aimed to buy the finest coffee and sell it by the pound. After employee Howard Schultz bought the name Starbucks and the assets of the Starbucks Coffee Company in 1987, he expanded the company by opening coffee shops and office building kiosks that sold coffee by the cup. In the early 1990s, Starbucks made the transformation from an entrepreneurship to a professionally managed company while working to retain an entrepreneurial spirit and *esprit de corps* among its 25,000 employees. The company's challenge is to continue its global expansion; to that end, Starbucks International works with business partners in global markets, including Japan, Singapore, Philippines, Korea, and Taiwan. Overseas expansion is still robust.

Harpo Entertainment Group

Harpo Entertainment Group, a privately held entrepreneurial business in television and film production, is the creation of Oprah Winfrey who serves as chairwoman and CEO. Although led by a female entrepreneur, the company has two presidents, both men. Harpo is "Oprah" spelled backward. Harpo, which produces the highest rated talk show in television history, qualifies as a small business with 175 employees and as a medium-sized business with $150 million in annual revenues. The business is built on a foundation of talk. Harpo produces *The Oprah Winfrey Show*, which is seen by forty million viewers daily in 200 U.S. and 130 foreign markets. In addition, the company produces feature films and made-for-TV movies, maintains the Oprah Online feature for America Online, and rents studio space.[34]

Oprah Winfrey believes that knowledge is power. With knowledge, a person can soar and reach as high as his or her dreams will take the person. Oprah was born in 1954 and lived in Mississippi, Wisconsin, and Tennessee before moving to Chicago. She was challenged in 1997–1998 by a group of Texas cattle ranchers who sued unsuccessfully under the "veggie libel" laws over a 1996 show on mad cow disease. As the owner of Harpo Entertainment Group, Oprah Winfrey topped the *Forbes* list of Top 40 earning entertainers for 1993 with two-year earnings of $98 million.

American Red Cross

The American Red Cross is a not-for-profit organization chartered by the U.S. Congress to provide relief services to those in need and is a member of the International Red Cross and Red Crescent Movement.[35] As a humanitarian organization led by volunteers, the Red Cross provides relief to victims of more than 60,000 natural and human-made U.S. disasters each year; teaches CPR, first aid, and water safety; helps people prevent, prepare for, and respond to emergencies; provides counseling and emergency message transmission for U.S. military personnel; and is guardian of the nation's largest blood bank. The Red Cross is guided by seven fundamental principles of the International Red Cross and Red Crescent Movement: humanity, impartiality, neutrality, independence, voluntary service, unity, and universality.

Founded in 1881 by Clara Barton as a result of her war relief experiences, the Red Cross quickly expanded to aid victims of natural disasters. The president of the Red Cross oversees a paid staff of 29,850 and a budget of nearly $2 million annually, but the major work of the American Red Cross is accomplished through nearly 1.4 million volunteers. The majority of volunteers are adults (63 percent), but a sizable minority are youths aged eighteen or under (31 percent). The Red Cross, which distributes nearly one-half the nation's blood supply, recently faced the challenge of rising costs and quasi competition from low-cost blood banks. Then-president Elizabeth Dole announced a plan to improve blood bank organization and operation, which has already substantially reduced the health risks from blood transfusions.

THE CHALLENGE OF CHANGE

Changing times always pose a challenge for people and organizations. Global competition is a leading force driving change at work. Competition in the United States and world economies has increased significantly during the past couple of decades, especially in industries such as banking, finance, and air transportation. Corporate competition creates performance and cost pressures, which have a ripple effect on people and their behavior at work. The competition may lead to downsizing and restructuring, yet it provides the opportunity for revitalization as well.[36] Further, small companies are not necessarily the losers in this competitive environment. Scientech, a small power and energy company headquartered in Idaho Falls, Idaho, found it had to enhance its managerial talent and service quality to meet the challenges of growth and big-company competitors. Product and service quality is one tool that can help companies become winners in a competitive environment. Problem-solving skills are another tool used by IBM, CDC, Northwest Airlines, and Northwestern National Life to help achieve high-quality products and services.

Too much change leads to chaos; too little change leads to stagnation. Terrence Murray is chairman of FleetBoston Financial, a New England financial organization that has grown dramatically in recent years. As Mr. Murray says, "When there is change, morale is never going to be perfect." What are your perceptions of change? Complete Challenge 1.1 and see how you perceive change.

International Competition in Business

Organizations in the United States are changing radically in response to increased international competition. According to noted economist Lester Thurow, the next several decades in business will be characterized by intense competition among the United States, Japan, and Europe in core industries.[37] Economic competition places pressure on all categories of employees to be productive and to add value to the firm. The uncertainty of unemployment resulting from corporate warfare and competition is an

6. Recognize the challenge of change for organizational behavior.

Challenge 1.1

Analyze Your Perceptions of a Change

Everyone perceives change differently. Think of a change situation you are currently experiencing. It can be any business, school-related, or personal experience that requires a significant change in your attitude or behavior. Rate your feelings about this change using the following scales. For instance, if you feel the change is more of a threat than an opportunity, you would circle 0, 2, or 4 on the first scale.

1. Threat	0	2	4	6	8	10	Opportunity
2. Holding on to the past	0	2	4	6	8	10	Reaching for the future
3. Immobilized	0	2	4	6	8	10	Activated
4. Rigid	0	2	4	6	8	10	Versatile
5. A loss	0	2	4	6	8	10	A gain
6. Victim of change	0	2	4	6	8	10	Agent of change
7. Reactive	0	2	4	6	8	10	Proactive
8. Focused on the past	0	2	4	6	8	10	Focused on the future
9. Separate from change	0	2	4	6	8	10	Involved with change
10. Confused	0	2	4	6	8	10	Clear

How positive are your perceptions of this change?

SOURCE: H. Woodward and S. Buchholz, *Aftershock: Helping People through Corporate Change*, p. 15. Copyright © 1987 John Wiley & Sons, Inc. Reprinted by permission of John Wiley & Sons, Inc.

ongoing feature of organizational life for people in companies or industries that pursue cost-cutting strategies to achieve economic success. The international competition in the automotive industry among the Japanese, U.S., and European car companies embodies the intensity that can be expected in other industries in the future.

Some people feel that the future must be the focus in coming to grips with this international competition, whereas others believe we can deal with the future only by studying the past.[38] Global, economic, and organizational changes have dramatic effects on the study and management of organizational behavior. How positive were your perceptions of the change you analyzed in Challenge 1.1? Are you an optimist who sees opportunity, or a pessimist who sees threat?

Four Themes Related to Change

Chapter 2 develops four themes related to change in contemporary organizations: globalization, technology, diversity, and ethics. These are four driving forces creating and shaping changes at work. Further, success in global competition requires organizations to be more responsive to ethnic, religious, and gender diversity in the workforce, in addition to responding positively to the competition in the international marketplace. Workforce demographic change and diversity are critical challenges in themselves for the study and management of organizational behavior.[39, 40] The theories of motivation, leadership, and group behavior based on research in a workforce of one composition may not be applicable in a workforce of a very different composition. This may be especially problematic if ethnic, gender, and/or religious differences lead to conflict between leaders and followers in organizations. For example, the former Soviet Union's military establishment found ethnic and religious conflicts between the officers and enlisted corps a real impediment to unit cohesion and performance during the 1980s.

Customer Focused for High Quality

Organizations are becoming more customer focused to meet changing product and service demands as well as customers' expectations of high quality. Quality has the potential for giving organizations in viable industries a competitive edge in meeting international competition.

Quality has become a rubric for products and services that are of high status. Total quality has been defined in many ways.[41] We define ***total quality management*** as the total dedication to continuous improvement and to customers so that the customers' needs are met and their expectations exceeded. Quality is a customer-oriented philosophy of management with important implications for virtually all aspects of organizational behavior. Quality cannot be optimized, because customer needs and expectations are always changing. Quality is a cultural value embedded in highly successful organizations. Ford Motor Company's dramatic metamorphosis as an automotive leader is attributable to the decision to "make quality Job One" in all aspects of the design and manufacture of cars.

The pursuit of total quality improves the probability of organizational success in increasingly competitive industries. Quality is more than a fad; it is an enduring feature of an organization's culture and of the economic competition we face today. Quality is not an end in itself. It leads to competitive advantage through customer responsiveness, results acceleration, and resource effectiveness.[42] The three key questions in evaluating quality-improvement ideas for people at work are these: (1) Does the idea improve customer response? (2) Does the idea accelerate results? (3) Does the idea increase the effectiveness of resources? A "yes" answer means the idea should be implemented to improve total quality. Total quality is also dependent on how people behave at work.

Behavior and Quality at Work

Whereas total quality may draw on reliability engineering or just-in-time management, total quality improvement can be successful only when employees have the skills and authority to respond to customer needs.[43] Total quality has direct and important effects on the behavior of employees at all levels in the organization, not just on employees working directly with

total quality management
The total dedication to continuous improvement and to customers so that the customers' needs are met and their expectations exceeded.

customers. Chief executives can advance total quality by engaging in participative management, being willing to change everything, focusing quality efforts on customer service (not cost cutting), including quality as a criterion in reward systems, improving the flow of information regarding quality-improvement successes or failures, and being actively and personally involved in quality efforts. George Fisher, chairman and CEO of Eastman Kodak, considers behavioral attributes such as leadership, cooperation, communication, and participation important elements in a total quality system.

Quality has become so important to our future competitiveness that the U.S. Department of Commerce now sponsors an annual award in the name of Malcolm Baldrige, former secretary of commerce in the Reagan administration, to recognize companies excelling in total quality management. The Malcolm Baldrige National Quality Award examination evaluates an organization in seven categories: leadership, information and analysis, strategic quality planning, human resource utilization, quality assurance of products and services, quality results, and customer satisfaction.

According to former president George Bush, "Quality management is not just a strategy. It must be a new style of working, even a new style of thinking. A dedication to quality and excellence is more than good business. It is a way of life, giving something back to society, offering your best to others."

Quality is one watchword for competitive success. Organizations that do not respond to customer needs find their customers choosing alternative product and service suppliers who are willing to exceed customer expectations. With this said, you should not conclude that total quality is a panacea for all organizations or that total quality guarantees unqualified success.

Managing Organizational Behavior in Changing Times

Over and above the challenge of enhancing quality to meet international competition, managing organizational behavior during changing times is challenging for at least four reasons: (1) the increasing globalization of organizations' operating territory, (2) the increasing diversity of organizational workforces, (3) continuing technological innovation with its companion need for skill enhancement, and (4) the continuing demand for higher levels of moral and ethical behavior at work. These are the issues managers need to address in managing people at work.

Each of these four issues is explored in detail in Chapter 2 and highlighted throughout the text because they are intertwined in the contemporary practice of organizational behavior. For example, the issue of women in the workplace concerns workforce diversity and at the same time overlaps the globalization issue. Gender roles are often defined differently in various cultures and societies. In addition, sexual harassment is a frequent ethical problem for organizations in the United States, Europe, Israel, and South Africa as more women enter these workforces. The student of organizational behavior must appreciate and understand the importance of these issues.

LEARNING ABOUT ORGANIZATIONAL BEHAVIOR

Organizational behavior is neither a purely scientific area of inquiry nor a strictly intellectual endeavor. It involves the study of abstract ideas, such as valence and expectancy in motivation, as well as the study of concrete matters, such as observable behaviors and physiological symptoms of distress at work. Therefore, learning about organizational behavior is a multidimensional activity, as shown in Figure 1.4. First, it requires the mastery of a certain body of *objective knowledge*. Objective knowledge results from research and scholarly activities. Second, the study of organizational behavior requires *skill development* and the mastery of abilities essential to successful functioning in organizations. Third, it requires the integration of objective knowledge and skill development in order to apply both appropriately in specific organizational settings.

Researchers have found that increasing student diversity is best addressed through more diverse learning options for students and greater responsibility on the part of students as coproducers in the work of learning.[44] To gain a better understanding of yourself as a learner, so as to maximize your potential and develop strategies in specific learning environments, you need to evaluate the way you prefer to learn and process information. Challenge 1.2 offers you a short, quick way of assessing your learning style. If you are a visual learner, then use charts, maps, filmstrips, notes, or flash cards, and write things out for visual review. If you are an auditory learner, listen and take notes during lectures, but also consider taping them so you can fill in gaps later; review your notes frequently; and recite key concepts out loud. If you are a tactile learner, trace words as you are saying them, write down facts several times, and make study sheets.

Objective Knowledge

Objective knowledge, in any field of study, is developed through basic and applied research. Research in organizational behavior has continued since early research on scientific management. Acquiring objective knowledge requires the cognitive mastery of theories, conceptual models, and research findings. In this book, the objective knowledge in each chapter is reflected in the notes that support the text material. Mastering the concepts and ideas that come from these notes enables you to intelligently discuss topics such as motivation, performance, leadership,[45] and executive stress.[46]

We encourage instructors and students of organizational behavior to think critically about the objective knowledge in organizational behavior. Only by engaging in critical thinking can one question or challenge the

7. Demonstrate the value of objective knowledge and skill development in the study of organizational behavior.

objective knowledge
Knowledge that results from research and scholarly activities.

skill development
The mastery of abilities essential to successful functioning in organizations.

Figure 1.4
Learning about Organizational Behavior

Challenge 1.2

Learning Style Inventory

Directions: This twenty-four-item survey is not timed. Answer each question as honestly as you can. Place a check on the appropriate line after each statement.

	OFTEN	SOMETIMES	SELDOM
1. Can remember more about a subject through the lecture method with information, explanations, and discussion.	_____	_____	_____
2. Prefer information to be written on the chalkboard, with the use of visual aids and assigned readings.	_____	_____	_____
3. Like to write things down or to take notes for visual review.	_____	_____	_____
4. Prefer to use posters, models, or actual practice and some activities in class.	_____	_____	_____
5. Require explanations of diagrams, graphs, or visual directions.	_____	_____	_____
6. Enjoy working with my hands or making things.	_____	_____	_____
7. Am skillful with and enjoy developing and making graphs and charts.	_____	_____	_____
8. Can tell if sounds match when presented with pairs of sounds.	_____	_____	_____
9. Remember best by writing things down several times.	_____	_____	_____
10. Can understand and follow directions on maps.	_____	_____	_____
11. Do better at academic subjects by listening to lectures and tapes.	_____	_____	_____
12. Play with coins or keys in pockets.	_____	_____	_____
13. Learn to spell better by repeating the words out loud than by writing the word on paper.	_____	_____	_____
14. Can better understand a news development by reading about it in the paper than by listening to the radio.	_____	_____	_____
15. Chew gum, smoke, or snack during studies.	_____	_____	_____
16. Feel the best way to remember is to picture it in your head.	_____	_____	_____
17. Learn spelling by "finger spelling" words.	_____	_____	_____
18. Would rather listen to a good lecture or speech than read about the same material in a textbook.	_____	_____	_____
19. Am good at working and solving jigsaw puzzles and mazes.	_____	_____	_____
20. Grip objects in hands during learning period.	_____	_____	_____
21. Prefer listening to the news on the radio rather than reading about it in the newspaper.	_____	_____	_____
22. Obtain information on an interesting subject by reading relevant materials.	_____	_____	_____
23. Feel very comfortable touching others, hugging, handshaking, etc.	_____	_____	_____
24. Follow oral directions better than written ones.	_____	_____	_____

Scoring Procedures

Score 5 points for each OFTEN, 3 points for each SOMETIMES, and 1 point for each SELDOM.

Visual Preference Score = Points for questions 2 + 3 + 7 + 10 + 14 + 16 + 19 + 22   = _____
Auditory Preference Score = Points for questions 1 + 5 + 8 + 11 + 13 + 18 + 21 + 24   = _____
Tactile Preference Score = Points for questions 4 + 6 + 9 + 12 + 15 + 17 + 20 + 23   = _____

SOURCE: Adapted from J. N. Gardner and A. J. Jewler, *Your College Experience: Strategies for Success, Third Concise Edition* (Belmont, Calif.: Wadsworth/ITP, 1998), pp. 62–63; and E. Jensen, *Student Success Secrets,* 4th ed. (Hauppauge, N.Y.: Barron's, 1996), pp. 33–36.

results of specific research and responsibly consider how to apply research results in a particular work setting. Rote memorization does not enable the student to appreciate the complexity of specific theories or the interrelationships among concepts, ideas, and topics. Good critical thinking, in contrast, enables the student to identify inconsistencies and limitations in the current body of objective knowledge.

Critical thinking, based on knowledge and understanding of basic ideas, leads to inquisitive exploration and is a key to accepting the responsibility of coproducer in the learning process. A questioning, probing attitude is at the core of critical thinking. The student of organizational behavior should evolve into a critical consumer of knowledge related to organizational behavior—one who is able to intelligently question the latest research results and distinguish plausible, sound new approaches from fads that lack substance or adequate foundation. Ideally, the student of organizational behavior develops into a scientific professional manager who is knowledgeable in the art and science of organizational behavior.

Skill Development

Learning about organizational behavior requires doing as well as knowing. The development of skills and abilities requires that students be challenged, by the instructor or by themselves. Skill development is a very active component of the learning process.

The U.S. Department of Labor is concerned that people achieve the necessary skills to be successful in the workplace.[47] The essential skills identified by the Department of Labor are (1) resource management skills, such as time management; (2) information management skills, such as data interpretation; (3) personal interaction skills, such as teamwork; (4) systems behavior and performance skills, such as cause–effect relationships; and (5) technology utilization skills, such as troubleshooting. Many of these skills, such as decision making and information management, are directly related to the study of organizational behavior.[48]

Developing skills is different from acquiring objective knowledge in that it requires structured practice and feedback. A key function of experiential learning is to engage the student in individual or group activities that are systematically reviewed, leading to new skills and understandings. Objective knowledge acquisition and skill development are interrelated. The process for learning from structured or experiential activities is depicted in Figure 1.5. The student engages in an individual or group structured activity and systematically reviews that activity, which leads to new or modified knowledge and skills.

If skill development and structured learning occur in this way, there should be an inherently self-correcting element to learning because of the modification of the student's knowledge and skills over time.[49] To ensure that skill development does occur and that the learning is self-correcting as it occurs, three basic assumptions that underlie the previous model must be followed.

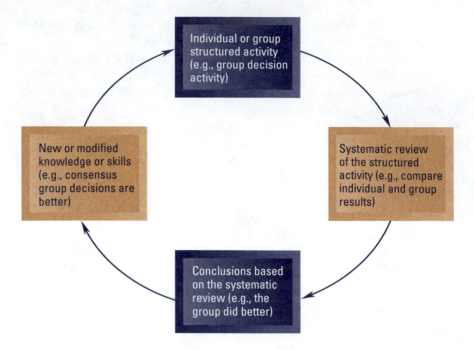

Figure 1.5
Learning from Structured Activity

First, each student must accept responsibility for his or her own behavior, actions, and learning. This is a key to the coproducer role in the learning process. A group cannot learn for its members. Each member must accept responsibility for what he or she does and learns. Denial of responsibility helps no one, least of all the learner.

Second, each student must actively participate in the individual or group structured learning activity. Structured learning is not passive; it is active. In group activities, everyone suffers if just one person adopts a passive attitude. Hence, all must actively participate.

Third, each student must be open to new information, new skills, new ideas, and experimentation. This does not mean that students should be indiscriminately open. It does mean that students should have a nondefensive, open attitude so that change is possible through the learning process.

Application of Knowledge and Skills

One of the advantages of structured, experiential learning is that a person can explore new behaviors and skills in a comparatively safe environment. Losing your temper in a classroom activity and learning about the potential adverse impact on other people will probably have dramatically different consequences from losing your temper with an important customer in a tense work situation. The ultimate objective of skill development and experiential learning is that one transfers the process employed in learning from structured activities in the classroom to learning from unstructured opportunities in the workplace.

Although organizational behavior is an applied discipline, a student is not "trained" in organizational behavior. Rather, one is "educated" in organizational behavior and is a coproducer in learning. The distinction between these two modes of learning is found in the degree of direct and immediate applicability of either knowledge or skills. As an activity, training more nearly ties direct objective knowledge or skill development to specific applications. By contrast, education enhances a person's residual pool of objective knowledge and skills that may then be selectively applied later—sometimes significantly later—when the opportunity presents itself. Hence, education is highly consistent with the concept of lifelong learning. Especially in a growing area of knowledge such as organizational behavior, the student can think of the first course as the outset of lifelong learning about the topics and subject.

PLAN FOR THE BOOK

Change and challenge are watchwords in organizations during these changing times. Managers and employees alike are challenged to meet change in the workplace: change in how work gets done, change in psychological and legal contracts between individuals and organizations, change in who is working in the organization, and change in the basis for organization. The four major challenges facing managers are the global environment, workplace diversity, technological innovation, and ethical issues at work. These four challenges, which are discussed in detail in Chapter 2, are shaping the changes occurring in organizations throughout the world. For example, the increasing globalization of business has led to intense international competition in core industries, and the changing demographics of the workplace have led to gender, age, racial, and ethnic diversity among working populations.

The first two chapters compose Part I of the book, the introduction. It is against the backdrop of the challenges discussed here that the specific content subjects in organizational behavior must be understood. In addition to the introduction, the text has three major parts. Part II addresses individual processes and behavior. Part III addresses interpersonal processes and behavior. Part IV addresses organizational processes and behavior.

The five chapters in Part II are designed to help the reader understand specific aspects of human behavior. Chapter 3 discusses personality, perception, and attribution. Chapter 4 examines attitudes, values, and ethics (see, for example, your attitude toward change in Challenge 1.1). Chapters 5 and 6 address the broad range of motivational theories, learning, and performance management in organizations. Finally, Chapter 7 considers stress and well-being at work.

Part III is composed of five chapters designed to help the reader better understand interpersonal and group dynamics in organizations. Chapter 8 focuses on an increasingly prominent feature of the workplace, teamwork and groups. Chapter 9 examines how individuals and groups make decisions. Chapter 10 is about power and politics, the bases of which shift as the organization shifts. Chapter 11 addresses the companion topics of leadership and followership. Finally, Chapter 12 examines conflict at work.

Part IV's four chapters are designed to help the reader better understand organizational processes and the organizational context of behavior at work. Chapter 13 examines traditional and contemporary approaches to job design.[50] Chapter 14 develops the topics of organizational design and structure, giving special attention to contemporary forces reshaping organizations and to emerging forms of organization. Chapter 15 addresses the culture of the organization. Finally, Chapter 16 brings closure to the text and the main theme of change by addressing the topic of managing change.

Managerial Implications: Foundations for the Future

Managers must consider personal and environmental factors to understand fully how people behave in organizations and to help them grow to be all they can be. Human behavior is complex and at times confusing. Characteristics of the organizational system and formal–informal dynamics at work are important environmental factors that influence people's behavior. Managers should look for similarities and differences in manufacturing, service-oriented, nonprofit, and governmental organizations.

Change is a primary concern for contemporary managers. Changing customer demands for high-quality outputs challenge companies to meet the global competition. Globalization, workforce diversity, technology, and ethics are four themes related to change that are developed in Chapter 2. Another aspect of meeting the competition is learning. Managers must continually upgrade their knowledge about all aspects of their businesses, to include especially the human side of the enterprise. They must hone both their technical and their interpersonal skills, engaging in a lifelong educational process.

Several business trends and ongoing changes are affecting managers across the globe. These include continuing industrial restructuring, a dramatic increase in the amount and availability of information, a need to attract and retain the best employees, a need to understand a wide range of human and cultural differences, and a rapid shortening of response times in all aspects of business activities. Further, the old company towns are largely relics of the past, and managers are being called on to reintegrate their businesses with communities, cultures, and societies at a much broader level than has ever been required before. Trust, predictability, and a sense of security become important issues in this context. Reweaving the fabric of human relationships within, across, and outside the organization is a challenge for managers today.

Knowledge becomes power in tracking these trends and addressing these issues. Facts and information are two elements of knowledge in this context. Theories are a third element of a manager's knowledge base. Good theories are tools that help managers understand human and organizational behavior, help them make good business decisions, and inform them about actions to take or to refrain from taking. Managers always use theories, if not those generated from systematic research, then those evolved from the manager's implicit observation. Theories tell us how organizations, business, and people work—or do not work. Therefore, the student is challenged to master the theories in each topic area, then apply and test the theory in the real world of organizational life. The challenge for the student and the manager is to see what works and what does not work in their specific work context.

Looking Back

Gateway...in the 21st Century

The two biggest barriers for individuals who want to purchase a PC to enter the information age and ride the electronic highway are (1) the up-front cost and (2) fear of technology obsolescence. Gateway designed a breakthrough purchase program to clear away these two barriers.[51] The revolutionary program is called "Your:)Ware," the first and only computer purchase plan that lowers the cost of buying a PC, provides unlimited Internet access, and simultaneously protects against technology obsolescence. Is Gateway's Your:)Ware the computer industry's answer to Ford's Model T in the automotive industry? There are parallels. Your:)Ware, like the Model T, is aimed at enabling everyone to have an affordable, simple, usable product, in this case a PC. Gateway consultants make a complex purchase process simpler by knowing the right questions to ask to help people create a customized solution for their individual computing needs. A unique feature of Your:)Ware is the trade-in option, which enables individuals to purchase or finance their own PC and then between the start of the last month of the second year of ownership and the end of the fourth year, trade it in for the average wholesale price. (Thus, Your:)Ware combines a customized PC, software, unlimited Internet access, and obsolescence protection into one monthly payment that is much smaller than most people's monthly car payment.) As computers, communication technology, and the Internet transform people's behavior at work and at home, Gateway is changing how it does business so that more people can enter the information age.

CHAPTER SUMMARY

1. Organizational behavior is individual behavior and group dynamics in organizations.

2. The disciplines of psychology, sociology, engineering, anthropology, management, and medicine have contributed to the discipline of organizational behavior.

3. Organizations are systems composed of people, structure, and technology committed to a task.

4. Organizations have formal and informal elements within them.

5. Manufacturing organizations, service organizations, privately owned companies, and nonprofit organizations all contribute to our national well-being.

6. The changes and challenges facing managers are driven by international competition and customer demands.

7. Learning about organizational behavior requires a mastery of objective knowledge and specific skill development.

KEY TERMS

organizational behavior 3	**anthropology** 6	**formal organization** 9
change 3	**management** 6	**informal organization** 9
challenge 3	**medicine** 7	**Hawthorne studies** 9
psychology 5	**task** 8	**total quality management** 17
sociology 6	**people** 8	**objective knowledge** 19
engineering 6	**structure** 9	**skill development** 19

REVIEW QUESTIONS

1. Define *organizational behavior*. What is the focus of organizational behavior?
2. Identify six disciplines relevant to the development of organizational behavior. How does each contribute?
3. What is an organization? What are its four system components? Give an example of each.
4. Briefly describe the elements of the formal and the informal organization. Give examples of each.
5. Discuss the six focus organizations used in the book.
6. Describe how competition and total quality are affecting organizational behavior. Why is managing organizational behavior in changing times challenging?

DISCUSSION AND COMMUNICATION QUESTIONS

1. How do the formal aspects of your work environment affect you? What informal aspects of your work environment are important?
2. What is the biggest competitive challenge or change facing the businesses in your industry today? Will that change in the next five years?
3. What will the next chief executive of your company be like?
4. Discuss two ways people learn about organizational behavior.
5. Which of the focus companies is your own company most like? Do you work for one of these focus companies? Which company would you most like to work for?
6. (*communication question*) Prepare a memo about an organizational change occurring where you work or in your college or university. Write a 100-word description of the change and, using Figure 1.1, identify how it is affecting the people, structure, task, and/or technology of the organization.
7. (*communication question*) Develop an oral presentation about the changes and challenges facing your college or university based on an interview with a faculty member or administrator. Be prepared to describe the changes and challenges, as well as whether they are good or bad.
8. (*communication question*) Prepare a brief description of a service or manufacturing company, entrepreneurial venture, or nonprofit organization of your choice. Go to the library and read about the organization from several sources, then use these multiple sources to write your description.

ETHICS QUESTIONS

1. Suppose two people at work have a personal, informal relationship unrelated to the formal organization. Further assume their relationship could affect people in the formal organization. As an aware employee, should you tell the people who are unaware of it and may be affected by the relationship?

2. Which disciplines are important in understanding moral and ethical issues for organizations and management?

3. Suppose you would be able to beat the competition if you presented a prospective customer with negative information about the competition's quality program. Should you provide the information? Further assume that the information relates to safety. Would that make a difference in whether you told the customer?

4. What are the most sensitive ethical issues in your business or organization today?

Experiential Exercises

1.1 What's Changing at Work?

This exercise provides an opportunity to discuss changes occurring in your workplace and university. These changes may be for the better or the worse. However, rather than evaluating whether they are good or bad changes, begin by simply identifying the changes that are occurring. Later you can evaluate whether they are good or bad.

Step 1. The class forms into groups of approximately six members each. Each group elects a spokesperson and answers the following questions. The group should spend at least five minutes on each question. Make sure that each member of the group makes a contribution to each question. The spokesperson for each group should be ready to share the group's collective responses to these questions.

   a. *What are the changes occurring in your workplace and university?* Members should focus both on internal changes, such as reorganizations, and on external changes, such as new customers or competitors. Develop a list of the changes discussed in your group.

   b. *What are the forces that are driving the changes?* To answer this question, look for the causes of the changes members of the group are observing. For example, a reorganization may be caused by new business opportunities, by new technologies, or by a combination of factors.

   c. *What signs of resistance to change do you see occurring?* Change is not always easy for people or organizations. Do you see signs of resistance, such as frustration, anger, increased absences, or other forms of discomfort with the changes you observe?

Step 2. Once you have answered the three questions in Step 1, your group needs to spend some time evaluating whether these changes are good or bad. Decide whether each change on the list developed in Step 1a is a good or bad change. In addition, answer the question "Why?" That is, why is this change good? Why is that change bad?

Step 3. Each group shares the results of its answers to the questions in Step 1 and its evaluation of the changes completed in Step 2. Cross-team questions and discussion follow.

Step 4. Your instructor may allow a few minutes at the end of the class period to comment on his or her perceptions of changes occurring within the university, or businesses with which he or she is familiar.

1.2 My Absolute Worst Job

Purpose: To become acquainted with fellow class-mates.
Group size: Any number of groups of two.
Exercise schedule:

1. Write answers to the following questions:
   a. What was the worst job you ever had? Describe the following:
      (1) The type of work you did
      (2) Your boss
      (3) Your coworkers
      (4) The organization and its policies
      (5) What made the job so bad
   b. What is your dream job?

2. Find someone you do not know, and share your responses.

3. Get together with another dyad, preferably new people. Partner a of one dyad introduces partner b to the other dyad, then b introduces a. The same process is followed by the other dyad. The introduction should follow this format: "This is Mary Cullen. Her very worst job was putting appliqués on bibs at a clothing factory, and she disliked it for the following reason. What she would rather do is be a financial analyst for a big corporation."

4. Each group of four meets with another quartet and is introduced, as before.

5. Your instructor asks for a show of hands on the number of people whose worst jobs fit into the following categories:

   a. Factory
   b. Restaurant
   c. Manual labor
   d. Driving or delivery
   e. Professional
   f. Health care
   g. Phone sales or communication
   h. Other

6. Your instructor gathers data on worst jobs from each group and asks the groups to answer these questions:
   a. What are the common characteristics of the worst jobs in your group?
   b. How did your coworkers feel about their jobs?
   c. What happens to morale and productivity when a worker hates the job?
   d. What was the difference between your own morale and productivity in your worst job and in a job you really enjoyed?
   e. Why do organizations continue to allow unpleasant working conditions to exist?

7. Your instructor leads a group discussion on Parts a through e of Question 6.

SOURCE: D. Marcic, "My Absolute Worst Job: An Icebreaker," *Organizational Behavior: Experiences and Cases* (St. Paul, Minn.: West, 1989), 5–6. Copyright 1988 Dorothy Marcic. All rights reserved. Reprinted by permission.

For more practice exercises, consult the fifth edition of *Organizational Behavior: Experiences and Cases* by Dorothy Marcic and Joseph Seltzer (South-Western, 1998).

Learning Objectives

After reading this chapter, you should be able to do the following:

1. Describe the dimensions of cultural differences in societies that affect work-related attitudes. *p. 34*

2. Explain the social and demographic changes that are producing diversity in organizations. *p. 40*

3. Describe actions managers can take to help their employees value diversity. *p. 46*

4. Understand the alternative work arrangements produced by technological advances. *p. 49*

5. Explain the ways managers can help employees adjust to technological change. *p. 52*

6. Discuss the assumptions of consequential, rule-based, and cultural ethical theories. *p. 53*

7. Explain six issues that pose ethical dilemmas for managers. *p. 54*

2

Organizations 2001 and Managerial Challenges

Thinking Ahead

Ford Goes Global with an International Team of Executives

Ford is a company with a global strategy for the twenty-first century. Ford's CEO, Jacques Nasser, heads an internationally trained team of executives whose goal is to grow Ford's global operations while developing new vehicles for about half of what the company used to spend, and in less time. This is an ambitious undertaking and incredibly complex to execute.

Nasser was born in Lebanon and grew up in Australia. He has been with Ford for more than thirty years but has spent only seven years at Ford headquarters in Detroit. His other assignments at Ford have taken him to Thailand, the Philippines, Mexico, Venezuela, Argentina, Brazil, Australia, and Europe. Nasser combines a degree in international business with global experience and an obsession with cars. One of his pet projects is the Ka, a sporty three-door model that emerged from a laboratory in Europe. It proved too costly to reengineer for U.S. safety standards, but in Europe it was a hit and proved to Nasser that Ford could put out a new vehicle in a mere twenty-four months.

Going global at Ford has not been problem free. At one point, the company's North American, European, and Asian operations were all making Ford Escorts—but they were not using common parts. Now uniform parts are used in all markets, resulting in a tremendous savings of money. In Brazil, Ford lost more than $600 million because of inadequate preparation for the demise of its joint venture with Volkswagen and poor financial control. After careful attention, that market seems to be on the mend. With support from the North American and European operations, volume in Brazil is up 70 percent.

Ford's global future looks bright. A new worldwide production system is working in 170 factories, and productivity is improving. A huge amount of growth is occurring in Asia Pacific and South America. Factories are going up in Bombay, Madras, Thailand, and Vietnam. Five joint-venture component factories are up and running in China. Although most of Ford's profits now come from Europe, the United States, Canada, and Mexico, the long-term outlook is that the Asian Pacific markets will be bigger than Western Europe and North America. Ford has made great strides in the global market and is committed to major expansion around the world.[1]

COMPETITION: THE CHALLENGES MANAGERS FACE

Ford is not alone in its attempt to meet the competitive challenges of today's environment. The vast majority of U.S. executives believe U.S. firms are encountering unprecedented global competition.[2] Although it has had its longest economic expansion period since World War II, the U.S. faces competition from other robust economies. Singapore, Finland, the Netherlands, and Switzerland are all growing in competitiveness while Japan is losing ground.[3] With competition increasing both at home and abroad, managers must find creative ways to deal with the competitive challenges they face.

What are the major challenges that managers must deal with in order to remain competitive? Chief executive officers of U.S. corporations cite four issues that are paramount: (1) globalizing the firm's operations to compete in global markets, (2) managing a diverse workforce, (3) keeping up with technological change and implementing technology in the workplace, and (4) managing ethical behavior.[4, 5]

Successful organizations manage all four challenges well. Our focus companies, Ford, Southwest Airlines, Harpo, Starbucks, the Red Cross, and Gateway, owe their success to their ability to meet these challenges. You'll be reading about how they do this throughout the book and how other organizations tackle these challenges as well. In this chapter, we introduce you to these four challenges and the complexities of trying to manage them.

Globalization is a challenge that Ford has handled well, as you saw in the opening vignette. Ford saw early on that the European and Asian markets were ripe with opportunity and quickly became a force in those markets. Rapid political and social changes have broken down old national barriers to competition, and the market has become a boundaryless one in which all firms, large and small, must compete.

Managing a diverse workforce is something organizations like Levi Strauss and Coors Brewing Company do extremely well, and they reap success from it. The workforce of today is more diverse than ever before, and managers have the task of bringing together employees of different backgrounds in work teams. Often, this means having to deal with communication barriers, insensitivity, stereotypes, and ignorance of others' motivations and cultures.[6]

Technological change is one of the keys to strategic competitiveness. Imagine yourself as a small business owner of a package delivery firm. You'll be competing with FedEx, the proud owner of the most technologically advanced package tracking and delivery system in the world. Would you be able to compete? When organizations try to keep pace with technological change, they find that these changes aren't simple. Changing technology often means changes in individual jobs, information flows, social interactions, and the structure of the organization.

Managing ethical behavior is a challenge that organizations like Johnson & Johnson are known for. The company's credo guides employee behavior and has helped employees do the right thing in some tough situations. Ethical behavior in business has been at the forefront of public consciousness for some time now. Insider trading scandals, influence peddling, and contract frauds are in the news daily, and the companies that are involved pay the price in terms of lost profits and loss of reputation.

Organizations must manage these four challenges well in order to remain competitive, or even to survive in today's turbulent environment. Throughout the book, we'll show you how organizational behavior can contribute to managing the challenges.

MANAGING IN A GLOBAL ENVIRONMENT

Only a few years ago, business conducted across national borders was referred to as "international" activity. The word *international* carries with it a connotation that the individual's or the organization's nationality is held strongly in consciousness.[7] *Globalization*, in contrast, implies that the world is free from national boundaries and that it is really a borderless world.[8] U.S. workers are now competing with workers in other countries. Organizations from other countries are locating subsidiaries in the United States, such as the U.S. manufacturing locations of Honda, Mazda, and Mercedes.

Similarly, what were once referred to as multinational organizations (organizations that did business in several countries) are now referred to as transnational companies. In **transnational organizations**, the global viewpoint supersedes national issues.[9] Transnational organizations operate over large global distances and are multicultural in terms of the people they employ. 3M, Dow Chemical, Coca-Cola, and other transnational organizations operate worldwide with diverse populations of employees.

transnational organization
An organization in which the global viewpoint supersedes national issues.

Changes in the Global Marketplace

Social and political upheavals have led organizations to change the way they conduct business and to encourage their members to think globally. The collapse of Eastern Europe was followed quickly by the demise of the Berlin Wall. East and West Germany were united into a single country. In the Soviet Union, perestroika led to the liberation of the satellite countries and the breaking away of the Soviet Union's member nations. Perestroika also brought about many opportunities for U.S. businesses, as witnessed by the press releases showing extremely long waiting lines at Moscow's first McDonald's restaurant.

Business ventures in China have become increasingly attractive to U.S. businesses. Coca-Cola has led the way, as shown in Organizational Reality 2.1. One challenge U.S. managers have tackled is attempting to understand the Chinese way of doing business. Chinese managers' business practices have been shaped by the Communist Party, socialism, feudalistic values, and *guanxi* (building networks for social exchange). Once *guanxi* is established, individuals can ask favors of each other with the expectation that the favor will be returned. For example, it is common in China to use *guanxi*, or personal connections, to conduct business or to obtain jobs. The term *guanxi* is sometimes a sensitive word, because Communist Party policies oppose the use of such practices to gain influence. In China, the family is regarded as being responsible for a worker's productivity, and in turn, the company is responsible for the worker's family. Because of socialism, Chinese managers have very little experience with rewards and punishments and are reluctant to use them in the workplace. The concept of *guanxi* is not unique to China. There are similar concepts in many other countries, including Russia and Haiti. It is a broad term that can mean anything from strongly loyal relationships to ceremonial gift-giving, sometimes seen as bribery. *Guanxi* is more common in societies with underdeveloped legal support for private businesses.[10]

To work with Chinese managers, Americans can learn to build their own *guanxi*; understand the Chinese chain of command; and negotiate slow, general agreements in order to interact effectively. Using the foreign government as the local franchisee may be effective in China. For example, Kentucky Fried Chicken's operation in China is a joint venture between KFC (60 percent) and two Chinese government bodies (40 percent).[11]

In 1993, the European Union integrated fifteen nations into a single market by removing trade barriers. The member nations of the European Union are Belgium, Denmark, France, Germany, Greece, Ireland, Italy, Luxembourg, the Netherlands, Portugal, Spain, Austria, Finland, Sweden, and the United Kingdom. The integration of Europe provides many opportunities for U.S. organizations, including 350 million potential customers. Companies like Ford Motor Company and IBM, which entered the market early with wholly owned subsidiaries, will have a head start on these opportunities.[12] Competition within the European Union will increase, however, as will competition from Japan and the former Soviet nations.

guanxi
The Chinese practice of building networks for social exchange.

ORGANIZATIONAL REALITY 2.1

Two CEOs, Two Strategies: Global Coke

China is Coke's eighth largest market, and former CEO Doug Ivester visited China to deliver the message that Coke wants to be a good global citizen—to be a good guest in China, to help its schools, to help its economy. Each Coke job creates ten more jobs to support it. "Did you understand the relevance of the egg?" he asked his troops after the nighttime tour of Nanjing Road. "We are competing against that egg." He was talking about a woman running a kiosk who was selling tons of tea eggs (eggs marinated in tea and soy sauce that sell in Shanghai like hot dogs in New York) but very few Cokes. "We have to . . . show that lady that she will make more money selling Coke than selling eggs."

Ivester said his goal was on the cover of Coke's annual report. The cover reflected a milestone that Coke reached in 1998: selling one billion drinks a day, or 2 percent of the world's daily beverage consumption. The cover showed forty-eight Coke bottles on it, representing the 48 billion beverages consumed in the world per day. One bottle is red, representing Coke's share. Ivester's goal is for two bottles to be red; that is, to double worldwide consumption of Coke. That goal, among others, was not met, and Ivester was ousted.

Enter Douglas Daft, the new chief executive, who was eager to turn around Coke's two-year streak of disappointing profits. His strategy is one of localism—adapting to local markets. Daft broke Europe into ten different geographic units, with non-Americans running nine of the ten. While Ivester wanted managers to push only Coke, Fanta, Sprite, and Diet Coke, Daft has turned teams loose to develop flavors with European appeal. The Turkish division has designed a pear-flavored drink, and the German group has developed a berry-flavored Fanta.

Daft's rationale is that Coke must recognize the local nature of its business in its global operations. As the former head of Coke's operations in Asia, he knows that Coke will always be the core of the company, but locally made beverages are now the name of the game. Decisions about advertising are now also made locally. In the past, Coke's commercials for China were made in Atlanta. Given Daft's emphasis on localism, this will soon be a thing of the past.

Discussion Question

1. What challenges might Coke face in expanding its global markets?

SOURCES: W. Echikson & D. Foust, "For Coke, Local Is It," *Business Week* (July 3, 2000): 122; "Coke's New Formula," *Far Eastern Economic Review* (April 20, 2000): 64.

The United States, Canada, and Mexico have dramatically reduced trade barriers in accordance with the North American Free Trade Agreement (NAFTA), which took effect in 1994. Organizations have found promising new markets for their products, and many companies have located plants in Mexico to take advantage of low labor costs. Daimler-Chrysler, for example, has a massive assembly plant in Saltillo. Prior to NAFTA, Mexico placed heavy tariffs on U.S. exports. The agreement immediately eliminated many of these tariffs and provided that the remaining tariffs be phased out over time.

All of these changes have brought about the need to think globally. To benefit from global thinking, managers will also need to take a long-term view. Entry into global markets is a long-term proposition, and it requires long-term strategies.

Understanding Cultural Differences

1. Describe the dimensions of cultural differences in societies that affect work-related attitudes.

One of the keys for any company competing in the global marketplace is to understand the diverse cultures of the individuals involved. Whether managing culturally diverse individuals within a single location or managing individuals at remote locations around the globe, an appreciation of the differences among cultures is crucial. Knowing cultural differences in symbols may even be important. Computer icons may not translate well in other cultures. The thumbs up sign, for example, means approval in the United States. In Australia, however, it is an obscene gesture. And manila file folders, like the icons used in Windows applications, aren't used in many European countries and therefore aren't recognized.[13]

Do cultural differences translate into differences in work-related attitudes? The pioneering work of Dutch researcher Geert Hofstede has focused on this question.[14] He and his colleagues surveyed 160,000 managers and employees of IBM who were working in sixty different countries.[15] In this way, the researchers were able to study individuals from the same company in the same jobs, but working in different countries. Hofstede's work is important, because his studies showed that national culture explains more differences in work-related attitudes than do age, gender, profession, or position within the organization. Thus, cultural differences do affect individuals' work-related attitudes. Hofstede found five dimensions of cultural differences that formed the basis for work-related attitudes. These dimensions are shown in Figure 2.1.

individualism
A cultural orientation in which people belong to loose social frameworks, and their primary concern is for themselves and their families.

collectivism
A cultural orientation in which individuals belong to tightly knit social frameworks, and they depend strongly on large extended families or clans.

Individualism Versus Collectivism In cultures where *individualism* predominates, people belong to loose social frameworks, but their primary concern is for themselves and their families. People are responsible for taking care of their own interests. They believe that individuals should make decisions. Cultures characterized by *collectivism* are tightly knit social frameworks in which individual members depend strongly on extended families or clans. Group decisions are valued and accepted.

Figure 2.1
Hofstede's Dimensions of Cultural Differences

SOURCE: Reprinted with permission of Academy of Management, PO Box 3020, Briar Cliff, NY 10510-8020. *Cultural Constraints in Management Theories* (Figure). G. Hofstede, *Academy of Management Executive 7* (1993). Reproduced by permission of the publisher via Copyright Clearance Center, Inc.

The North American culture is individualistic in orientation. It is a "can-do" culture that values individual freedom and responsibility. In contrast, collectivist cultures emphasize group welfare and harmony. Israeli kibbutzim and the Japanese culture are examples of societies in which group loyalty and unity are paramount. Organization charts show these orientations. In Canada and the United States, which are individualistic cultures, organization charts show individual positions. In Malaysia, which is a collectivist culture, organization charts show only sections or departments.

This dimension of cultural differences has other workplace implications. Individualistic managers, as found in Great Britain and the Netherlands, emphasize and encourage individual achievement. In contrast, collectivistic managers, such as in Japan and Colombia, seek to fit harmoniously within the group. They also encourage these behaviors among their employees. There are also cultural differences within regions of the world. Arabs are more collectivist than Americans. Within the Arab culture, however, Egyptians are more individualistic than Arabs from the Gulf States (Saudi Arabia, Oman, Bahrain, Kuwait, Quatar, United Arab Emirates). This may be due to the fact that Egyptian businesspeople tend to have longer and more intense exposures to Western culture.[16]

Power Distance The second dimension of cultural differences examines the acceptance of unequal distribution of power. In countries with a high *power distance*, bosses are afforded more power simply because they are the bosses. Titles are used, formality is the rule, and authority is seldom bypassed. Power holders are entitled to their privileges, and managers and employees see one another as fundamentally different kinds of people. India is a country with a high power distance, as are Venezuela and Mexico.

In countries with a low power distance, people believe that inequality in society should be minimized. People at various power levels are less threatened by, and more willing to trust, one another. Managers and employees see one another as similar. Managers are given power only if they have expertise. Employees frequently bypass the boss in order to get work done in countries with a low power distance, such as Denmark and Australia.

Uncertainty Avoidance Some cultures are quite comfortable with ambiguity and uncertainty, whereas others do not tolerate these conditions as well. Cultures with high *uncertainty avoidance* are concerned with security and tend to avoid conflict. People have a need for consensus. The inherent uncertainty in life is a threat against which people in such cultures constantly struggle.

Cultures with low uncertainty avoidance are more tolerant of ambiguity. People are more willing to take risks and more tolerant of individual differences. Conflict is seen as constructive, and people accept dissenting viewpoints. Norway and Australia are characterized by low uncertainty avoidance, and this trait is seen in the value placed on job mobility. Japan and Italy are characterized by high uncertainty avoidance, so career stability is emphasized.

power distance
The degree to which a culture accepts unequal distribution of power.

uncertainty avoidance
The degree to which a culture tolerates ambiguity and uncertainty.

masculinity
The cultural orientation in which assertiveness and materialism are valued.

femininity
The cultural orientation in which relationships and concern for others are valued.

Masculinity Versus Femininity In cultures that are characterized by *masculinity*, assertiveness and materialism are valued. Men should be assertive, tough, and decisive, whereas women should be nurturing, modest, and tender.[17] Money and possessions are important, and performance is what counts. Achievement is admired. Cultures that are characterized by *femininity* emphasize relationships and concern for others. Men and women are expected to assume both assertive and nurturing roles. Quality of life is important, and people and the environment are emphasized.

Masculine societies, such as in Austria and Venezuela, define gender roles strictly. Feminine societies, in contrast, tend to blur gender roles. Women may be the providers, and men may stay home with the children. The Scandinavian countries of Norway, Sweden, and Denmark exemplify the feminine orientation.

time orientation
Whether a culture's values are oriented toward the future (long-term orientation) or toward the past and present (short-term orientation).

Time Orientation Cultures also differ in *time orientation*; that is, whether the culture's values are oriented toward the future (long-term orientation) or toward the past and present (short-term orientation).[18] In China, a culture with a long-term orientation, values such as thrift and persistence, which focus on the future, are emphasized. In Russia, the orientation is short term. Values such as respect for tradition (past) and meeting social obligations (present) are emphasized.

U.S. Culture The position of the United States on these five dimensions is interesting. Hofstede found the United States to be the most individualistic country of any studied. On the power distance dimension, the United States ranked among the countries with weak power distance. Its rank on uncertainty avoidance indicated a tolerance of uncertainty. The United States also ranked as a masculine culture with a short-term orientation. These values have shaped U.S. management theory, so Hofstede's work casts doubt on the universal applicability of U.S. management theories. Because cultures differ so widely on these dimensions, management practices should be adjusted to account for cultural differences. Managers in transnational organizations must learn as much as they can about other cultures in order to lead their culturally diverse organizations effectively.

Careers in management have taken on a global dimension. Working in transnational organizations will likely give managers the opportunity to work in other countries. *Expatriate managers*, those who work in a country other than their home country, should know as much as possible about cultural differences. Because many future managers will have global work experience, it is never too early to begin planning for this aspect of your career.

expatriate manager
A manager who works in a country other than his or her home country.

International executives are executives whose jobs have international scope, whether in an expatriate assignment or in a job dealing with international issues. What kind of competencies should an individual develop in order to prepare for an international career? There seem to be several attributes, all of them centering around core competencies and the ability to learn from experience. Some of the key competencies are integrity, insightfulness, risk taking, courage to take a stand, and ability to bring out the best in people. Learning-oriented attributes of international executives include cultural adventurousness, flexibility, openness to criticism, desire to seek learning opportunities, and sensitivity to cultural differences.[19]

Understanding cultural differences becomes especially important for companies that are considering opening foreign offices, because workplace customs can vary widely from one country to another. Carefully searching out this information in advance can help companies successfully manage foreign operations. Consulate offices and companies operating within the foreign country are excellent sources of information about national customs and legal requirements. Table 2.1 presents a series of differences among five countries to highlight what a company might encounter in opening a foreign office in any one of them.

Another reality that can affect global business practices is the cost of layoffs in other countries. The practice of downsizing is not unique to the United States. Dismissing a forty-five-year-old middle manager with twenty years of service and a $50,000 annual salary can vary in cost from a low of $13,000 in Ireland to a high of $130,000 in Italy.[20] The cost of laying off this manager in the United States would be approximately $19,000. The wide variability in costs stems from the various legal protections that certain countries give workers. In Italy, laid-off employees must receive a "notice period" payment (one year's pay if they have nine years or more of service) plus a severance payment (based on pay and years of service). U.S. companies operating overseas often adopt the European tradition of training and retraining workers to avoid overstaffing and potential layoffs. An appreciation of the customs and rules for doing business in another country is essential if a company wants to go global.

Developing Cross-Cultural Sensitivity

As organizations compete in the global marketplace, employees must learn to deal with individuals from diverse cultural backgrounds. Stereotypes may pervade employees' perceptions of other cultures. In addition, employees may be unaware of others' perceptions of the employees' national culture. A potentially valuable exercise is to ask members of various cultures to describe one another's cultures. This provides a lesson on the misinterpretation of culture.

Intel wants interns and employees to understand the company's culture, but more importantly, it wants to understand the employees' cultures. In an effort to increase diversity, Intel's proportion of ethnic minorities in managerial positions increased from 13 percent in 1993 to 17 percent in 1997, and is still climbing. Many individuals feel their cultural heritage is important and may walk into uncomfortable situations at work. To prevent this, Intel's new workers are paired carefully with mentors, and mentors and protégés learn about each others' cultures.

Cultural sensitivity training is a popular method for helping employees recognize and appreciate cultural differences. Another way of developing sensitivity is to use cross-cultural task forces or teams. The Milwaukee-based

Some of the knottiest problems a company faces when it opens a foreign office are right inside that office. Few U.S. companies are prepared for how different the workplace "rules" abroad can be from U.S. norms—and how these norms differ from one country to another. Knowing some of these customs in advance can make a huge difference in the ability to manage a foreign operation successfully, as well as in the profitability of the operation.

Few prerequisites and compensation levels are mandated. The benefits offered by companies are typically a blend of what is legally required and what is voluntary. The following are workforce highlights from five countries, gathered from consulate offices and owners of U.S. companies.

BELGIUM   **Perks:** As elsewhere in Europe, a car and a cellular phone for managers and salespeople. Discretionary use of an expense account. **Benefits:** Health care and social security are required by law; these amount to 33% of gross salary. Even a secretary signs a contract when hired, and cannot be fired just like that. Severance provisions are much higher than in the United States. After ten years, a middle manager could expect severance pay of one to two years' salary. **Compensation:** Almost every employee participates in a bonus plan. Employees also get a separate bonus, equal to three weeks' salary, when they take their vacation. Cost of a good electronic engineer: $35,000. **Vacation:** Four weeks, by law. **Holidays:** Twelve days. **Language:** English is all that's necessary. **U.S. workers:** Relatively easy to bring in. **Other:** Dated attitudes toward women employees and minorities prevail here and throughout Europe, but upcoming legislation should force attitudes to change.

GREAT BRITAIN   **Perks:** Managers and salespeople expect company cars, often with cellular phones. High tax rates have made objects, rather than cash, preferred by employees. **Benefits:** Private medical insurance to complement national health care. Pension plans are not as common as in the United States. **Compensation:** It's difficult to find people to work for straight commission. A Christmas bonus is expected by all. Cost of a good electronic engineer: $25,000. **Vacation:** Three to five weeks typically, but not mandated by law. **Holidays:** Eight legal holidays; most companies offer twelve. **Language:** English. **U.S. workers:** It's not easy, but the Brits are cooperative if you want to bring in U.S. citizens to seed a company. **Other:** The buying cycle is much longer. What takes two visits to sell here might take five there.

HUNGARY   **Perks:** Company car for managers and salespeople. Pay in hard currency. Travel abroad is prized. **Benefits:** Health care coverage is legally required and costs plenty—some 40% of wages. But wage rates are low. Many companies also make home-construction loans and provide lunch, commuting, and day-care allowances. There's a heavy penalty for trying to reduce benefits to employees. **Compensation:** High tax rate makes bonuses not very rewarding, so they aren't expected. Cost of a good electronic engineer: $10,000. **Vacation:** Fifteen days required by law. Companies typically add one to nine days for every three years of service. **Holidays:** Eight days. **Language:** Most Hungarians speak German or Russian as a second language. **U.S. workers:** Laws recently became more restrictive, but there's little problem for managers or technical employees. **Other:** Buying a Hungarian property is complicated because of the privatization process, but overhead is easily lowered. Office space is scarce and expensive. Never toast a contract with beer mugs—it recalls the conquest of Hungary. Use slivovitz instead.

(continued)

Table 2.1
Opening a Foreign Office: A Five-Country Comparison

GE Medical Systems Group (GEMS) has 7,000 of its 15,000 employees working outside the United States. GEMS has developed a vehicle for bringing managers from each of its three regions (the Americas, Europe, and Asia) together to work on a variety of business projects. Under the Global Leadership Program, several work groups made up of managers from various regions of the world are formed. The teams work on important projects, such as worldwide employee integration to increase the employees' sense of belonging throughout the GEMS international organization.[22]

JAPAN **Perks:** Company car for executives. Add a chauffeur for the president, vice-presidents, and perhaps managing director of a U.S. company's office. **Benefits:** National health care and social-security costs are split 50–50 by employer and employee. Companies also pay for workers' compensation insurance, unemployment insurance, and pension costs. Transportation allowance (four-hour daily train commutes aren't unusual), lunch allowance. Expense budgets can run very high; a middle manager might entertain clients five nights a week. **Compensation:** Bonuses for individual performance are unpopular. Employees prefer straight salary. All receive New Year's bonus based on company's performance: 1.2 times a month's salary in a good year, half a month's salary in a bad year. Cost of a good electronic engineer: $30,000. **Vacation:** Two weeks, by law, usually taken a day or two at a time. **Holidays:** Twenty legally mandated days, including New Year's and August holidays, during which the whole country shuts down. **Language:** English fluency is very rare. Many Japanese understand English, but they are taught to write, rather than speak it. Outside the cities, no English. **U.S. workers:** Not difficult; U.S. limitations pose more difficulty than Japanese rules do. **Other:** There's a tremendous shortage of people for management positions, and head-hunting is not accepted. Communication problems can be awesome. There is no effective, acceptable way to say no in Japanese, so you often don't know where you stand.

SOUTH KOREA **Perks:** Pick-up by a car pool, graduating to a company car and driver. For a vice-president, a golf-club membership and lessons, for any salesperson, a generous lump-sum expense account, which employee may keep if he or she does not spend it all. **Benefits:** Law requires companies with more than ten employees to pay for one medical examination each year and set aside one month's salary per year, per employee, as severance. Many companies offer low- or no-interest car and housing loans; some build their own apartment buildings and offer cheap leases to key employees. **Compensation:** Employees respond well to commission only. Spring, fall, and New Year's bonuses are expected; size of bonus reflects company performance. Cost of a good electronic engineer: $19,000. **Vacation:** Law requires three vacation days. **Holidays:** Nineteen days. **U.S. workers:** Company must prove no Korean could do the job, but criteria for this are not rigorous. **Language:** It's easy to find people who speak English, though not as easy among production people. **Other:** South Koreans hold the United States in high esteem.

SOURCE: Reprinted with permission of *Inc. Magazine*, Goldhirsh Group, Inc., 38 Commercial Wharf, Boston, MA 02110 (http://www.inc.com). Opening a Foreign Office: A Five-Country Comparison (Table), Inc. Magazine, April 1992. Reproduced by permission of the publisher via Copyright Clearance Center, Inc.

The globalization of business affects all parts of the organization, and human resource management is affected in particular. Companies have employees around the world, and human resource managers face the daunting task of effectively supporting a culturally diverse workforce. Human resource managers must adopt a global view of all functions, including human resource planning, recruitment and selection, compensation, and training and development. They must have a working knowledge of the legal systems in various countries, as well as of global economics, culture, and customs. Human resource managers must not only prepare U.S. workers to live outside their native country, but also help foreign employees interact with U.S. culture. Global human resource management is a complex endeavor, but it is critical to the success of organizations in the global marketplace.

Globalization is one challenge managers must meet in order to remain competitive in the changing world. Related to globalization is the challenge of managing an increasingly diverse workforce. Cultural differences contribute a great deal to the diversity of the workforce, but there are other forms of diversity as well.

MANAGING WORKFORCE DIVERSITY

Workforce diversity has always been an important issue for organizations. The United States, as a melting pot nation, has always had a mix of individuals in its workforce. We once sought to be all alike, as in the melting pot, but we now recognize and try to appreciate individual differences. *Diversity* encompasses all forms of differences among individuals, including culture, gender, age, ability, religious affiliation, personality, economic class, social status, military attachment, and sexual orientation.

Attention to diversity has increased in recent years, particularly because of the changing demographics of the working population. Managers feel that dealing with diversity successfully is a paramount concern for two reasons. First, managers may lack the knowledge of how to motivate diverse work groups. Second, managers are unsure of how to communicate effectively with employees who have different values and language skills.[23]

Several demographic trends are affecting organizations. By the year 2020, the workforce will be more culturally diverse, more female, and older than ever. In addition, legislation and new technologies have brought more workers with disabilities into the workforce.

Cultural Diversity

Cultural diversity in the workplace is growing because of the globalization of business, as we discussed earlier. People of diverse national origins—Koreans, Bolivians, Pakistanis, Vietnamese, Swedes, Australians, and others—will find themselves cooperating in teams to perform the work of the organization. In addition, changing demographics within the United States will significantly affect the cultural diversity in organizations. By 2020, minorities will constitute more than one-half of the new entrants to the U.S. workforce. The participation rates of African Americans and Hispanic Americans in the labor force have increased dramatically in recent years. By 2020, white non-Hispanics will constitute 68 percent of the labor force (down from 76 percent in 1997); 14 percent of the workforce will be Hispanic (up from 9 percent); African Americans' share will remain at 11 percent, and 6 percent will be Asian.[24]

These trends have important implications for organizations. African Americans and Hispanic Americans are overrepresented in declining occupations, thus limiting their opportunities. Further, African Americans and Hispanic Americans tend to live in a small number of large cities that are facing severe economic difficulties and high crime rates. Because of these factors, minority workers are likely to be at a disadvantage within organizations.

The jobs available in the future will require more skill than has been the case in the past. Often, minority workers have not had opportunities to

---

diversity
All forms of individual differences, including culture, gender, age, ability, religious affiliation, personality, economic class, social status, military attachment, and sexual orientation.

2. Explain the social and demographic changes that are producing diversity in organizations.

develop their skills. Minority skills deficits are large, and the proportions of African Americans and Hispanic Americans who are qualified for higher-level jobs are often much lower than the proportions of qualified whites and Asian Americans.[25] Minority workers are less likely to be prepared because they are less likely to have had satisfactory schooling and on-the-job training. Educational systems within the workplace are needed to supply minority workers with the skills necessary for success. Companies such as Motorola are already recognizing and meeting this need by focusing on basic skills training.

The globalization of business and changing demographic trends will present organizations with a tremendously culturally diverse workforce. This represents both a challenge and a risk. The challenge is to harness the wealth of differences that cultural diversity provides. The risk is that prejudices and stereotypes will prevent managers and employees from developing synergies that can benefit the organization.

Gender Diversity

The feminization of the workforce has increased substantially. The number of women in the labor force increased from 31.5 million in 1970 to 63 million in 1998. This increase accounts for almost 60 percent of the overall expansion of the entire labor force in the United States for this time period. In 1998, women made up almost 46 percent of the labor force, and by the year 2020, the labor force is predicted to be balanced with respect to gender. Women are also better prepared to contribute in organizations than ever before. Women now earn 40 percent of all doctorates, 56 percent of master's degrees, and 55 percent of all undergraduate degrees. Thus, women are better educated, and more are electing to work. In 1998, 70 percent of U.S. women were employed.[26]

Women's participation in the workforce is increasing, but their share of the rewards of participation is not increasing commensurately. Women hold only 11.9 percent of corporate officer positions in the *Fortune 500* companies.[27] Only 2.4 percent of the chairpersons and CEOs of *Fortune 500* firms are women.[28] Salaries for women persist at a level of 76 percent of their male counterparts' earnings.[29] Furthermore, because benefits are tied to compensation, women also receive lower levels of benefits.

In addition to lower earnings, women face other obstacles at work. The *glass ceiling* is a transparent barrier that keeps women from rising above a certain level in organizations. In the United States, it is rare to find women in positions above middle management in corporations.[30] The glass ceiling is not based on women's lack of ability to handle upper-level management positions. Instead, the barrier keeps women from advancing higher in an organization because they are women.

There is reason to believe that, on a global basis, the leadership picture for women is improving and will continue to improve. For example, the number of female political leaders around the world increased dramatically in recent decades. In the 1970s there were only five such leaders. In the

glass ceiling
A transparent barrier that keeps women from rising above a certain level in organizations.

1990s, twenty-one female leaders came into power. Countries such as Ireland, Sri Lanka, Iceland, and Norway all had female political leaders in the 1990s. Women around the world are leading major global companies, albeit not in the United States. These global female business leaders do not come predominantly from the West. In addition, a large number of women have founded entrepreneurial businesses. Women now own one-third of all American businesses, and these women-owned businesses employ more people than the entire *Fortune 500* combined.[31]

Removing the glass ceiling and other obstacles to women's success represents a major challenge to organizations. Policies that promote equity in pay and benefits, encourage benefit programs of special interest to women, and provide equal starting salaries for jobs of equal value are needed in organizations. Corporations that shatter the glass ceiling have several practices in common. Upper managers clearly demonstrate support for the advancement of women, often with a statement of commitment issued by the CEO. Women are represented on standing committees that address strategic business issues of importance to the company. Women are targeted for participation in executive education programs, and systems are in place for identifying women with high potential for advancement.[32] Three of the best companies in terms of their advancement and development of women are Motorola, Deloitte and Touche, and the Bank of Montreal.[33]

Although women in our society have adopted the provider role, men have not been as quick to share domestic responsibilities. Managing the home and arranging for child care are still seen as the woman's domain. In addition, working women often find themselves having to care for their elderly parents. Because of their multiple roles, women are more likely than men to experience conflicts between work and home. Organizations can offer incentives such as flexible work schedules, child care, elder care, and work site health promotion programs to assist working women in managing the stress of their lives.[34]

More women in the workforce means that organizations must help them achieve their potential. To do less would be to underutilize the talents of half of the U.S. workforce.

The glass ceiling is not the only gender barrier in organizations. Males may suffer from discrimination when they are employed in traditionally female jobs such as nursing, elementary school teaching, and social work. Males may be overlooked as candidates for managerial positions in traditionally female occupations.[35]

Age Diversity

The graying of the U.S. workforce is another source of diversity in organizations. Aging baby boomers (those individuals born from 1946 through 1964) contributed to the rise of the median age in the United States to thirty-six in the year 2000—six years older than at any earlier time in history. This also means that the number of middle-aged Americans will rise dramatically. In the workforce, the number of younger workers will decline, as will the number of older workers (over age sixty-five). The net result will be a gain in workers aged thirty-five to fifty-four. By 2030, there will be seventy million older persons, more than twice their number in 1996. People over age sixty-five will comprise 13 percent of the population in 2010, and 20 percent of the population by 2030.[36]

This change in worker profile has profound implications for organizations. The job crunch among middle-aged workers will become more intense as companies seek flatter organizations and the elimination of middle-management jobs. Older workers are often higher paid, and companies that employ large numbers of aging baby boomers may find these pay scales a handicap to competitiveness.[37] However, a more experienced, stable, reliable, and healthy workforce can pay dividends to companies. The baby boomers are well trained and educated, and their knowledge can be a definite asset to organizations.

Another effect of the aging workforce is greater intergenerational contact in the workplace.[38] As organizations grow flatter, workers who were traditionally segregated by old corporate hierarchies (with older workers at the top and younger workers at the bottom) will be working together. Four generations will be cooperating: the silent generation (people born from 1930 through 1945), a small group that includes most organizations' top managers; the baby boomers, whose substantial numbers give them a strong influence; the baby bust generation, popularly known as Generation X (those born from 1965 through 1976); and the subsequent generation, tentatively called Generation Y or the baby boomlet.[39] Although there is certainly diversity within each generation, each generation differs in general ways from other generations.

The differences in attitudes and values among these four generations can be substantial, and managers face the challenge of integrating these individuals into a cohesive group. Currently, as already noted, most positions of leadership are held by members of the silent generation. Baby boomers regard the silent generation as complacent and as having done little to reduce social inequities. Baby boomers strive for moral rights in the workplace and take a more activist position regarding employee rights. The baby busters, newer to the workplace, are impatient, want short-term gratification, and believe that family should come before work. They scorn the achievement orientation and materialism of the baby boomers. Managing such diverse perspectives is a challenge that must be addressed.

One company that is succeeding in accommodating the baby busters is Patagonia, a manufacturer of products for outdoor enthusiasts. Although the company does not actively recruit twenty-year-olds, approximately 20 percent of Patagonia's workers are in this age group because they are attracted to its products. To retain baby busters, the company offers several options, one of which is flextime. Employees can arrive at work as early as 6 A.M., and work as late as 6 P.M., as long as they work the core hours between 9 A.M. and 3 P.M. Workers also have the option of working at the office for five hours a day and at home for three hours.

Personal leaves of absence are also offered, generally unpaid, for as much as four months per year. This allows employees to take an extended summer break and prevents job burnout. Patagonia has taken into consideration the baby busters' desires for more time for personal concerns and has incorporated these desires into the company.[40]

Younger workers may have false impressions of older workers, viewing them as resistant to change, unable to learn new work methods, less physically capable, and less creative than younger employees. Research indicates, however, that older employees are more satisfied with their jobs, are more committed to the organization, and possess more internal work motivation than their younger cohorts.[41] Research also indicates that direct experience with older workers reduces younger workers' negative beliefs.[42] Motivating aging workers and helping them maintain high levels of contribution to the organization will be a key task for managers.

Ability Diversity

The workforce is full of individuals with different abilities, presenting another form of diversity. Individuals with disabilities are an underutilized human resource. An estimated 54 million individuals with disabilities live in the United States, and their unemployment rate is estimated to exceed 50 percent.[43] Nevertheless, the representation of individuals with disabilities in the workforce has increased because of the Americans with Disabilities Act, which went into effect in the summer of 1992. Under this law, employers are required to make reasonable accommodations to permit workers with disabilities to perform jobs. The act defines a person with a disability as "anyone possessing a physical or mental impairment that substantially limits one or more major life activities."[44] It protects individuals with temporary, as well as permanent, disabilities. The act's protection encompasses a broad range of illnesses that produce disabilities. Among these are acquired immune deficiency syndrome (AIDS), cancer, hypertension, anxiety disorders, dyslexia, blindness, and cerebral palsy, to name only a few.

Some companies recognized the value of employing workers with disabilities long before the legislation. Pizza Hut employs 3,000 workers with disabilities and plans to hire more. The turnover rate for Pizza Hut workers with disabilities is only one-fifth of the normal turnover rate.[45]

McDonald's created McJobs, a program that has trained and hired more than 9,000 mentally and physically challenged individuals since 1981.[46] McJobs is a corporate plan to recruit, train, and retain individuals with disabilities. Its participants include workers with visual, hearing, or orthopedic impairments; learning disabilities; and mental retardation. Through classroom and on-site training, the McJobs program prepares individuals with disabilities for the work environment. Before McJobs workers go on-site, sensitivity training sessions are held with store managers and crew members. These sessions help workers without disabilities understand what it means to be a worker with a disabling condition. Most McJobs workers start part-time and advance according to their own abilities and the opportunities available. Some McJobs workers with visual impairments prefer to work on the back line, whereas others who use wheelchairs can work the drive-through window.

Companies like Pizza Hut and McDonald's have led the way in hiring individuals with disabilities. One key to the success of these firms is helping able-bodied employees understand how workers with disabilities can contribute to the organization. In this way, ability diversity becomes an asset and helps organizations meet the challenge of unleashing the talents of workers with disabilities.

Differences Are Assets

Diversity involves much more than culture, gender, age, ability, or personality. It also encompasses religious affiliation, economic class, social status, military attachment, and sexual orientation. The scope of diversity is broad and inclusive. All these types of diversity lend heterogeneity to the work-force.

The issue of sexual orientation as a form of diversity has received increasing attention from organizations. Approximately 1.5 million households in the United States are identified as homosexual domestic partnerships.[47] Sexual orientation is an emotionally charged issue. Often, heterosexual resistance to accepting gay, lesbian, or bisexual workers is caused by moral beliefs. Although organizations must respect these beliefs, they must also send a message that all people are valued. The threat of job discrimination leads many gay men and lesbians to keep their sexual orientation secret at work. This secrecy has a cost, however. Closeted gay workers report lower job satisfaction and organizational commitment, and more role conflict and conflict between work and home life issues than do openly gay workers or heterosexual workers.[48] People who work in organizations full of fear, distrust, stigmatization, and harassment are not likely to be able to perform well. A tolerant atmosphere can improve the productivity of heterosexual and homosexual workers alike. Training must explain how homophobia hinders everyone's productivity. Education and training can be supplemented by everyday practices like using inclusive language—for example, using the term "partner" instead of "spouse" in verbal and written communication. Some companies offer benefits to same-sex partners. Coors Brewing Company, the Walt Disney Company, and Lotus Development Corporation were among the first to extend these benefits.

Part of the challenge in managing diversity lies in attempting to combat prejudices and discrimination. Whereas prejudice is an attitude, discrimination is behavior. Both are detrimental to organizations that depend on productivity from every single worker. Often, in studies of ratings of promotion potential, minorities are rated lower than whites, and females are rated lower than males.[49] The disparity between the pay of women and minority-group members relative to white men increases with age.[50] It is to organizations' benefit to make sure that good workers are promoted and compensated fairly, but as the workforce becomes increasingly diverse, the potential for unfair treatment also increases.

Diversity is advantageous to the organization in a multitude of ways. Some organizations have recognized the potential benefits of aggressively working to increase the diversity of their workforces. TRICON Global Restaurants' Kentucky Fried Chicken (KFC) has a goal of attracting and retaining female and minority-group executives. A president of KFC's U.S. operations said, "We want to bring in the best people. If there are two equally qualified people, we'd clearly like to have diversity."[51]

Digital Equipment Corporation (DEC—now part of Compaq Computer) faced a challenge in managing diversity in its Springfield, Massachusetts, plant, which employed predominantly African American workers. The task was to overcome the perception that the plant was separate from, different from, and not as good as DEC's predominantly white plants. DEC's Springfield employees tackled the issue by stressing empowerment (sharing power throughout the organization) and pushing for high-technology products that would give it a solid identity. The model used by the plant, called Valuing Differences, was based on two key ideas. First, people work best when they are valued and when diversity is taken into account. Second, when people feel valued, they build relationships and work together as a team.[52]

Managing diversity is one way a company can become more competitive. It is more than simply being a good corporate citizen or complying with affirmative action.[53] It is also more than assimilating women and minorities into a dominant male culture. Managing diversity includes a painful examination of hidden assumptions that employees hold. Biases and prejudices about people's differences must be uncovered and dealt with so that differences can be celebrated and exploited to their full advantage.

Diversity's Benefits and Problems

Diversity can enhance organizational performance. Organizations can reap five main benefits from diversity. First, diversity management can help firms attract and retain the best available human talent. The companies that appear at the top of "Best Places to Work" lists are usually excellent at managing diversity. Second, diversity can enhance marketing efforts. Just as workforces are becoming more diverse, so are markets. Having a diverse workforce can help the company improve its marketing plans by drawing on insights of employees from various cultural backgrounds. Third, diversity promotes creativity and innovation. The most innovative companies deliberately put together diverse teams to foster creativity. Fourth, diversity results in better problem solving. Diverse groups bring more expertise and experience to bear on problems and decisions. They also encourage higher levels of critical thinking. Fifth, diversity enhances organizational flexibility. Inflexible organizations are characterized by narrow thinking, rigidity, and standard definitions of "good" work styles. In contrast, diversity makes an organization challenge old assumptions and become more adaptable.

3. Describe actions managers can take to help their employees value diversity.

These five benefits can add up to competitive advantage for a company that manages diversity well.

Lest we paint an overly rosy picture of diversity, we must recognize its potential problems. Five problems are particularly important: resistance to change, cohesiveness, communication problems, conflicts, and decision making. People are more highly attracted to, and feel more comfortable with, others like themselves. It stands to reason that diversity efforts may be met with considerable resistance when individuals are forced to interact with others unlike themselves. Managers should be prepared for this resistance rather than naively assuming that everybody supports diversity. (Managing resistance to change is presented at length in Chapter 16.) Another potential problem with diversity is the issue of cohesiveness, that invisible "glue" that holds a group together. Cohesive, or tightly knit, groups are preferred by most people. It takes longer for a diverse group of individuals to become cohesive. In addition, cohesive groups have higher morale and better communication. We can reason that it may take longer for diverse groups to develop high morale.

Another obstacle to performance in diverse groups is communication. Culturally diverse groups may encounter special challenges in terms of communication barriers. Misunderstandings can occur that can lower work group effectiveness. Conflicts can also arise, and decision making may take more time.[54]

In summary, diversity has several advantages that can lead to improved productivity and competitive advantage. In diverse groups, however, certain aspects of group functioning can become problematic. The key is to maximize the benefits of diversity and prevent or resolve the potential problems.

Pillsbury is one company that lays out the performance case for managing and valuing differences. Pillsbury's managers argue that the same business rationale for cross-functional teams is relevant to all kinds of diversity. Managing differences includes bringing race and gender, as well as marketing expertise, into a team. To open up a very profitable baked-goods market in a tough-to-crack niche, Pillsbury hired some Spanish-speaking Hispanics. The company lacked the language expertise and cultural access to the Hispanic community. Pillsbury's vice-president of human resources conducted his own study of the food industry, asking an independent group to rate the diversity performance of ten companies and correlating it with financial performance over a ten-year period. Along with many other studies, the Pillsbury research suggests that diversity is a strong contributor to financial performance.[55]

Whereas the struggle for equal employment opportunity is a battle against racism and prejudice, managing diversity is a battle to value the differences that individuals bring to the workplace. Organizations that manage diversity effectively can reap the rewards of increased productivity and improved organizational health.

MANAGING TECHNOLOGICAL INNOVATION

Another challenge that managers face is effectively managing technological innovation. *Technology* consists of the intellectual and mechanical processes used by an organization to transform inputs into products or services that meet organizational goals. Managers face the challenge of rapidly changing technology and of putting the technology to optimum use in organizations. The inability of managers to incorporate new technologies successfully into their organizations is a major factor that has limited economic growth in the United States.[56] Although the United States still leads the way in developing new technologies, it lags behind in making productive use of these new technologies in workplace settings.[57]

The Internet has radically changed the way organizations communicate and perform work. By integrating computer, cable, and telecommunications technologies, businesses have learned new ways to compete. In networked organizations, time, distance, and space become irrelevant. A networked organization can do business anytime and anywhere, which is essential in the global marketplace. And networking is essential for companies that want to provide quality service to customers. Del Monte Foods gets daily inventory reports electronically from grocers. When inventory falls to a certain level, the Del Monte network processes a restocking order. This allows retailers to drastically cut their investments in inventories. The World Wide Web has created a virtual commercial district. Customers can book air travel, buy compact disks, and "surf the Net" to conduct business around the globe.[58]

One fascinating technological change is the development of *expert systems*, computer-based applications that use a representation of human expertise in a specialized field of knowledge to solve problems. Expert systems can be used in many ways, including providing advice to nonexperts, providing assistance to experts, replacing experts, and serving as a training and development tool in organizations.[59] MYCIN, a medically oriented expert system, diagnoses diseases and recommends treatment.[60] One organization currently using an expert system is Anheuser Busch.[61] The company uses an expert system to assist managers in ensuring that personnel decisions comply with antidiscrimination laws.

Robots, another technological innovation, were invented in the United States, and advanced research on *robotics* is still conducted here. However, Japan leads the world in the use of robotics in organizations. Organizations in the United States have fewer total robots than were added in 1989 alone in Japan.[62] Robots in Japan are treated like part of the family. They are even named after favorite celebrities, singers, and movie stars. Whereas Japanese workers are happy to let robots take over repetitive or dangerous work, Americans are more suspicious of labor-saving robots because employers often use them to cut jobs.[63] The main reason for the reluctance of U.S. organizations to use robots is their slow payout. Robotics represents a big investment that does not pay off in the short term. Japanese managers are more willing to use a long-term horizon to evaluate the effectiveness of ro-

technology
The intellectual and mechanical processes used by an organization to transform inputs into products or services that meet organizational goals.

expert system
A computer-based application that uses a representation of human expertise in a specialized field of knowledge to solve problems.

robotics
The use of robots in organizations.

botics technology. Labor unions may also resist robotics because of the fear that robots will replace employees.

Some U.S. companies that experimented with robotics had bad experiences. John Deere and Company originally used robots to paint its tractors, but the company scrapped them because programming the robots for the multitude of types of paint used took too long. Now Deere uses robots to torque cap screws on tractors, a repetitive job that once had a high degree of human error.

It is tempting to view technology from only the positive side; however, a little realism is in order. Some firms that have been disappointed with costly technologies are electing to *de-*engineer. And computer innovations often fail; 42 percent of information technology projects are abandoned before completion, and half of all technology projects fail to meet managers' expectations. Pacific Gas and Electric (part of PG&E Corporation) spent tens of millions of dollars on a new IBM-based system. Deregulation then hit the utility industry, and customers were permitted to choose among utility companies. Keeping up with multiple suppliers and fast-changing prices was too much, and the massive new system couldn't handle the additional burden quickly enough. It was scrapped in favor of a new project using the old first-generation computer system, which is being updated and gradually replaced. So, some innovations fail to live up to expectations, and some simply fail.[64]

Alternative Work Arrangements

Technological advances have been responsible, to a large degree, for the advent of alternative work arrangements, the nontraditional work practices, settings, and locations that are now supplementing traditional workplaces. One alternative work arrangement is *telecommuting*, transmitting work from a home computer to the office using a modem. IBM, for example, was one of the first companies to experiment with the notion of installing computer terminals at employees' homes and having employees work at home. By telecommuting, employees gain flexibility, save the commute to work, and enjoy the comforts of being at home. Telecommuting also has disadvantages, however, including distractions, lack of opportunities to socialize with other workers, lack of interaction with supervisors, and decreased identification with the organization. Despite these disadvantages, telecommuters still feel "plugged in" to the communication system at the office. Studies show that telecommuters often report higher satisfaction with office communication than do workers in traditional office environments.[65]

Estimates are that 30 to 40 million Americans are telecommuting. Why do companies encourage telecommuting? Cost reductions are an obvious motivator. Since 1991, AT&T has gained $550 million in cash flow from eliminating office space and reducing overhead costs. Another reason is to increase productivity. At IBM, a survey of telecommuters indicated that 87 percent believed they were more productive in the alternative work arrangement. Telecommuting also allows companies access to workers with key

4. Understand the alternative work arrangements produced by technological advances.

telecommuting
Transmitting work from a home computer to the office using a modem.

skills regardless of their locations. Alternative workplaces also give companies an advantage in hiring and keeping talented employees, who find the flexibility of working at home very attractive.

There is a spectrum of other alternative work arrangements. *Hoteling* is a shared-office arrangement wherein employees have mobile file cabinets and lockers for personal storage, and "hotel" work spaces are furnished for them. These spaces must be reserved instead of being permanently assigned. The computer system routes phone calls and e-mail as necessary. Individuals' personal photos and memorabilia are stored electronically and "placed" on occupants' computer desktops upon arrival.

Satellite offices comprise another alternative work arrangement. In such offices, large facilities are broken into a network of smaller workplaces that are located close to employees' homes. Satellites are often located in comparatively inexpensive cities and suburban areas. They usually have simpler and less costly furnishings and fixtures than the more centrally located offices. Satellites can save a company as much as 50 percent in real estate costs and can be quite attractive to employees who don't want to work in a large urban area. This can broaden the pool of potential employees, who can communicate with the home office via various technologies.[66]

All of these alternative work arrangements signal a trend toward *virtual offices*, in which people work anytime, anywhere, and with anyone. The concept involves work being where people are, rather than people moving to where the work is. Information technologies make connectivity, collaboration, and communication easy. Critical voice-mails and messages can be delivered to and from the central office, a client's office, the airport, the car, or home.

The Changing Nature of Managerial Work

Technological innovation affects the very nature of the management job. Managers who once had to coax workers back to their desks from coffee breaks now find that they need to encourage workers mesmerized by new technology to take more frequent breaks.[67] Working with a computer can be stressful, both physically and psychologically. Eye strain, neck and back strain, and headaches can result from sitting at a computer terminal too long. In addition, workers can become accustomed to the fast response time of the computer and expect the same from their coworkers. When coworkers do not respond with the speed and accuracy of the computer, they may receive a harsh retort.

Computerized monitoring provides managers with a wealth of information about employee performance, but it also holds great potential for misuse. The telecommunications, airline, and mail-order merchandise industries make wide use of systems that secretly monitor employees' interactions with customers. Employers praise such systems, saying that they improve customer service. Workers, however, are not so positive; they react with higher levels of depression, anxiety, and exhaustion from working under such secret scrutiny. At Bell Canada, operators were evaluated on a system that tabulated average working time with customers. Operators found the practice highly stressful, and they sabotaged the system by giving callers wrong directory assistance numbers rather than taking the time to look up the correct ones. As a result, Bell Canada now uses average working time scores for entire offices rather than for individuals.[68]

New technologies and rapid innovation place a premium on a manager's technical skills. Early management theories rated technical skills as less important than human and conceptual skills, but this has become wisdom of the past. Managers today must develop technical competence in order to gain workers' respect, which does not come automatically. Computer-integrated manufacturing systems, for example, have been shown to require managers to use participative management styles, open communication, and greater technical expertise in order to be effective.[69]

In a world of rapid technological innovation, managers must focus more carefully on helping workers manage the stress of their work. They must also take advantage of the wealth of information at their disposal to motivate, coach, and counsel workers rather than try to control them more stringently or police them. In addition, managers will need to develop their technical competence in order to gain workers' respect.

Technological change occurs so rapidly that turbulence characterizes most organizations. Workers must constantly learn and adapt to changing technology so that organizations can remain competitive. Managers must grapple with the challenge of helping workers adapt and make effective use of new technologies.

Helping Employees Adjust to Technological Change

Most workers are well aware of the benefits of modern technologies. The availability of skilled jobs and improved working conditions have been by-products of innovation in many organizations. Technology is also bringing disadvantaged individuals into the workforce. Microchips have dramatically increased opportunities for workers with visual impairments. Information can be decoded into speech using a speech synthesizer, into braille using a hard-copy printer, or into enlarged print visible on a computer monitor. Workers with visual impairments are no longer dependent on sighted persons to translate printed information for them, and this has opened new doors of opportunity.[70] Engineers at Carnegie-Mellon University have developed PizzaBot, a robot that individuals with disabilities can operate using a voice-recognition system. Despite these and other benefits of new technology in the workplace, however, employees may still resist change.

Technological innovations bring about changes in employees' work environments, and change has been described as the ultimate stressor. Many workers react negatively to change that they perceive will threaten their work situation. Many of their fears center around loss—of freedom, of control, of the things they like about their jobs.[71] Employees may fear that their quality of work life will deteriorate and that pressure at work will increase.

5. Explain the ways managers can help employees adjust to technological change.

Further, employees may fear being replaced by technology or being displaced into jobs of lower skill levels.

Managers can take several actions to help employees adjust to changing technology. The workers' participation in early phases of the decision-making process regarding technological changes is important. Individuals who participate in planning for the implementation of new technology gain important information about the potential changes in their jobs; therefore, they are less resistant to the change. Workers are the users of the new technology. Their input in early stages can lead to a smoother transition into the new ways of performing work.

Managers should also keep in mind the effects that new technology will have on the skill requirements of workers. Many employees support changes that increase the skill requirements of their jobs. Increased skill requirements often lead to increases in job autonomy, more responsibility, and potential pay increases, all of which are received positively by employees. Whenever possible, managers should select technology that increases workers' skill requirements.

Providing effective training about ways to use the new technology also is essential. Training helps employees perceive that they control the technology rather than being controlled by it. The training should be designed to match workers' needs, and it should increase the workers' sense of mastery of the new technology.

Support groups within the organization are another way of helping employees adjust to technological change. Technological change is stressful, and support groups are important emotional outlets for workers. Support groups can also function as information exchanges so that workers can share advice on using the technology. Workers feel less alone with the problem when they know that other workers share their frustration.

reinvention
The creative application of new technology.

A related challenge is to encourage workers to invent new uses for technology already in place. *Reinvention* is the term for creatively applying new technology.[72] Innovators should be rewarded for their efforts. Individuals who explore the boundaries of a new technology can personalize the technology and adapt it to their own job needs, as well as share this information with others in the work group. In one large public utility, service representatives (without their supervisor's knowledge) developed a personal note-passing system that later became the basis of a formal communication system that improved the efficiency of their work group.

Managers face a substantial challenge in leading organizations to adopt new technologies more humanely and effectively. Technological changes are essential for earnings growth and for expanded employment opportunities. The adoption of new technologies is a critical determinant of U.S. competitiveness in the global marketplace.

MANAGING ETHICAL ISSUES AT WORK

In addition to the challenges of globalization, workforce diversity, and technology, managers must confront the ethical challenges that are encountered in organizations. Some organizations manage ethical issues well. Johnson & Johnson employees operate under an organizational credo, which we will present later in this section. Another organization that manages ethical issues well is Merck and Company. This pharmaceutical company's emphasis on ethical behavior has earned it recognition as one of America's most admired companies in *Fortune*'s polls of CEOs.

Despite the positive way some organizations handle ethical issues, however, unethical conduct does occur in some organizations. A few of the ethical problems that managers report as toughest to resolve include employee theft, environmental issues, comparable worth of employees, conflicts of interest, and sexual harassment.[73]

How can people in organizations rationally think through ethical decisions so that they make the "right" choices? Ethical theories give us a basis for understanding, evaluating, and classifying moral arguments and then defending conclusions about what is right and wrong. Ethical theories can be classified as consequential, rule based, or cultural.

Consequential theories of ethics emphasize the consequences or results of behavior. John Stuart Mill's utilitarianism, a well-known consequential theory, suggests that right and wrong are determined by the consequences of the action.[74] "Good" is the ultimate moral value, and we should maximize the most good for the greatest number of people. But do good ethics make for good business?[75] Right actions do not always produce good consequences, and good consequences do not always follow from right actions. And how do we determine the greatest good—in short-term or long-term consequences? Using the "greatest number" criterion can imply that minorities (less than 50 percent) might be excluded in evaluating the morality of actions. An issue that may be important for a minority but unimportant for the majority might be ignored. These are but a few of the dilemmas raised by utilitarianism.

In contrast, *rule-based theories* of ethics emphasize the character of the act itself, not its effects, in arriving at universal moral rights and wrongs.[76] Moral rights, the basis for legal rights, are associated with such theories. In a theological context, the Bible, the Talmud, and the Koran are rule-based guides to ethical behavior. Immanuel Kant worked toward the ultimate moral principle in formulating his categorical imperative, a universal standard of behavior.[77] Kant argued that individuals should be treated with respect and dignity and that they should not be used as a means to an end. He argued that we should put ourselves in the other person's position and ask if we would make the same decision if we were in the other person's situation.

Corporations and business enterprises are more prone to subscribe to consequential ethics than rule-based ethics, in part due to the persuasive arguments of the Scottish political economist and moral philosopher Adam Smith.[78] He believed that the self-interest of human beings is God's providence, not the government's. Smith set forth a doctrine of natural liberty, presenting the classical argument for open market competition and free trade. Within this framework, people should be allowed to pursue what is

6. Discuss the assumptions of consequential, rule-based, and cultural ethical theories.

consequential theory
An ethical theory that emphasizes the consequences or results of behavior.

rule-based theory
An ethical theory that emphasizes the character of the act itself rather than its effects.

in their economic self-interest, and the natural efficiency of the marketplace would serve the well-being of society.

cultural theory
An ethical theory that emphasizes respect for different cultural values.

Cultural theories are a third type of ethical theory.[79] Cultural relativism contends that there are no universal ethical principles and that people should not impose their own ethical standards on others. Local standards should be the guides for ethical behavior. Cultural theories encourage individuals to operate under the old adage "When in Rome, do as the Romans do." Strict adherence to cultural relativism can lead individuals to deny their accountability for their own decisions and to avoid difficult ethical dilemmas.

Levi Strauss Company made a costly decision when its leadership decided not to do business in mainland China. That market alone could have doubled its revenues from international operations. But concerns about human rights violations, child labor, and the Chinese government's role in plant operations made the venture inconsistent with the company's basic values, ethics, and social responsibility. The company elected to forgo the opportunity rather than to follow cultural relativism.[80]

People need ethical theories to help them think through confusing, complex, difficult moral choices and ethical decisions. In contemporary organizations, people face ethical and moral dilemmas in many diverse areas. The key areas we will address are employee rights, sexual harassment, romantic involvements, organizational justice, whistle-blowing, and social responsibility. We conclude with a discussion of professionalism and codes of ethics.

Employee Rights

7. Explain six issues that pose ethical dilemmas for managers.

Managing the rights of employees at work creates many ethical dilemmas in organizations. Some of these dilemmas are privacy issues related to technology. Computerized monitoring, as we discussed earlier in the chapter, constitutes an invasion of privacy in the minds of some individuals. The use of employee data from computerized information systems presents many ethical concerns. Safeguarding the employee's right to privacy and at the same time preserving access to the data for those who need it requires that the manager balance competing interests.

Drug testing, free speech, downsizing and layoffs, and due process are but a few of the issues involving employee rights that managers face. Perhaps no issue generates as much need for managers to balance the interests of employees and the interests of the organization as the reality of AIDS in the workplace. New drugs have shown the promise of extended lives for people with human immunodeficiency virus (HIV), and this means that HIV-infected individuals can remain in the workforce and stay productive. Managers may be caught in the middle of a conflict between the rights of HIV-infected workers and the rights of their coworkers who feel threatened.

Employers are not required to make concessions to coworkers, but employers do have obligations to educate, reassure, and provide emotional support to coworkers. Confidentiality may also be a difficult issue. Some employees with HIV or AIDS will not wish to waive confidentiality and will not want to reveal their condition to their coworkers because of fears of stigmatization or even reprisals. In any case, management should discuss with the affected employee the ramifications of trying to maintain confidentiality and should assure the employee that every effort will be made to prevent negative consequences for him or her in the workplace.[81]

Laws exist that protect HIV-infected workers. As mentioned earlier, the Americans with Disabilities Act requires employees to treat HIV-infected workers as disabled individuals and to make reasonable accommodations for them. The ethical dilemmas involved with this situation, however, go far beyond the legal issues. How does a manager protect the dignity of the person with AIDS and preserve the morale and productivity of the work group when so much prejudice and ignorance surround this disease? Many organizations, such as Wells Fargo, believe the answer is education.[82] Wells Fargo has a written AIDS policy because of the special issues associated with the disease—such as confidentiality, employee socialization, coworker education, and counseling—that must be addressed. The Body Shop's employee education program consists of factual seminars combined with interactive theater workshops. The workshops depict a scenario in which an HIV-positive worker must make decisions, and the audience decides what the worker should do. This helps participants explore the emotional and social issues surrounding HIV.[83] Many of us do not know as much about AIDS as we should, and many of our fears arise because of a lack of knowledge. Assessment tools like the one in Challenge 2.1 are used by employers to help employees express their concerns about AIDS and pinpoint specific content needed in education programs.

Sexual Harassment

According to the Equal Employment Opportunity Commission, sexual harassment is unwelcome sexual attention, whether verbal or physical, that affects an employee's job conditions or creates a hostile working environment.[84] Court rulings, too, have broadened the definition of sexual harassment beyond job-related abuse to include acts that create a hostile work environment. In addition, Supreme Court rulings presume companies are to blame when managers create a sexually hostile working environment. Some organizations are more tolerant of sexual harassment. Complaints are not taken seriously, it is risky to complain, and perpetrators are unlikely to be punished. In these organizations, sexual harassment is more likely to occur. Sexual harassment is also more likely to occur in male-dominated workplaces.[85] Managers can defend themselves by demonstrating that they took action to eliminate workplace harassment and that the complaining employee did not take advantage of company procedures to deal with harassment. Even the best sexual harassment policy, however, won't absolve a company when harassment leads to firing, demotions, or undesirable working assignments.[86]

Challenge 2.1

How Much Do You Know about AIDS?

Rate the following statements on a scale of 1 to 5 to indicate the extent to which you agree or disagree with each statement (1 = strongly disagree, 5 = strongly agree).

____ **1.** It may be dangerous for me to work around someone with AIDS.
____ **2.** Working with employees who have AIDS places coworkers in a life-threatening situation.
____ **3.** There is a reason to fear employees who have AIDS.
____ **4.** Employees who have AIDS pose a threat to their coworkers.
____ **5.** There is a reason to single out employees who have AIDS.

Indicate whether you believe each statement below is true (T) or false (F).

____ **6.** AIDS is a highly contagious disease.
____ **7.** Most people who contract AIDS die from the disease.
____ **8.** AIDS can be contracted when an employee with AIDS sneezes or coughs on others.
____ **9.** AIDS can be contracted through nonsexual touching, such as shaking hands.
____ **10.** Persons who share tools or equipment with employees who have AIDS are likely to contract the disease.
____ **11.** AIDS cannot be contracted through face-to-face conversation with an AIDS-infected coworker.
____ **12.** AIDS can be transmitted when people eat or drink after one another.
____ **13.** AIDS cannot be transmitted through blood.
____ **14.** There is a vaccine to prevent AIDS.
____ **15.** AIDS can be contracted from toilet seats.

Now add your score for items 1 through 5. Your total reflects your fear of AIDS. Scores range from 5 (low fear) to 25 (high fear). Score greater than 15 indicate a high-level, work-related fear of AIDS.

Finally, look at items 6 through 15. All of these items are false except 7 and 11. Give yourself 1 point for each correct answer. This scale reflects knowledge of AIDS. Scores can range from 0 (poorly informed about AIDS) to 10 (well informed about AIDS). If your score was less than 5, you need to learn more about AIDS.

SOURCE: J. M. Vest, F. P. O'Brien, and M. J. Vest, "AIDS Training in the Workplace," *Training and Development Journal* 45 (1991): 59–64. Reprinted by permission of Michael J. Vest.

There are three types of sexual harassment. *Gender harassment* includes crude comments or sexual jokes and behaviors that disparage someone's gender or convey hostility toward a particular gender. *Unwanted sexual attention* involves unwanted touching or repeated unwanted pressures for dates. *Sexual coercion* consists of implicit or explicit demands for sexual favors by threatening negative job-related consequences or promising job-related rewards.[87]

Sexual harassment costs the typical *Fortune 500* company $6.7 million per year in absenteeism, turnover, and loss of productivity. Plaintiffs may now sue not only for back pay, but also for compensatory and punitive damages. And these costs do not take into account the negative publicity that firms may encounter from sexual harassment cases, which can cost untold millions. Sexual harassment can have strong negative effects on victims. Victims are less satisfied with their work, supervisors, and coworkers and may psychologically withdraw at work. They may suffer poorer mental health and even exhibit symptoms of post-traumatic stress disorder in conjunction with the harassment experience. Some victims report alcohol abuse, depression, headaches, and nausea.[88, 89]

One company that has had to settle four sexual harassment complaints is ICN Pharmaceuticals. Organizational Reality 2.2 describes ICN's dilemmas, which were especially problematic because the accused harasser was the chief executive officer.

Several companies have created comprehensive sexual harassment programs that seem to work. Atlantic Richfield (ARCO), a player in the male-dominated energy industry, has a handbook on preventing sexual harassment that includes phone numbers of state agencies where employees can file complaints. In essence, it gives employees a road map to the courthouse, and the openness seems to work. Lawsuits rarely happen at ARCO. When sexual harassment complaints come in, the company assumes the allegations are true and investigates thoroughly. The process has resulted in the firing of highly placed managers—the captain of an oil tanker was fired for sexually harassing coworkers. Other companies believe in the power of training programs. Some of the best training programs use role-playing, videotapes, and group discussions of real cases to help supervisors recognize unlawful sexual harassment and investigate complaints properly.

Romantic Involvements

Hugging, sexual innuendos, and repeated requests for dates may constitute sexual harassment for some, but they are a prelude to romance for others. This situation carries with it a different set of ethical dilemmas for organizations.

A recent fax poll indicated that three-fourths of the respondents felt it was okay to date a coworker, while three-fourths disapproved of dating a superior or subordinate. In *Meritor vs. Vinson*, the Supreme Court ruled that the agency principle applies to supervisor–subordinate relationships. Employers are liable for acts of their agents (supervisors) and can thus be held liable for sexual harassment. Other employees might claim that the subordinate who is romantically involved with the supervisor gets preferential treatment. Dating between coworkers poses less liability for the company because the agency principle doesn't apply. Policing coworker dating can also backfire: Wal-Mart lost a lawsuit when it tried to forbid coworkers from dating.

Workplace romances may result, for the participants, in experiences that can be positive or negative, temporary or permanent, exploitative to non-

ORGANIZATIONAL REALITY 2.2

Sexual Harassment and the CEO

Individuals in the top spots of today's corporations are sometimes targets for complaints. When allegations of sexual misconduct were made against President Clinton, many contended that if he had been in corporate America, he would have been fired. That may not really be the case.

Consider the experience of ICN Pharmaceuticals, a multinational that once had the best performing stock in the industry and a market value of over $3 billion. ICN's chief executive officer, Milan Panic, is considered the architect of that success, with his connections to powerful people in Eastern Europe, where ICN does a lot of business. Panic is also accused of numerous sexual harassment incidents, and he and ICN have paid out millions in four separate cases, with many other accusations being leveled. At least six women have come forward to say that Panic repeatedly propositioned them, groped them, and rewarded or punished female employees based on whether they complied or complained.

Is Panic an innocent victim of extortion? Do women target him because of his power and wealth? If so, why does the company continue to settle the claims out of court for millions of dollars? ICN, focusing on its rapid global expansion, contends that the settlements are the only way to avoid bad publicity, distraction from company goals, and even more costly and time-consuming litigation.

In the wake of the first few complaints, ICN appeased the women who claimed harassment and secured their silence with money. Yet it did not make any fundamental changes in company policy. Down the road, however, ICN formed a special committee of board members to deal with harassment allegations. ICN's lawyers would investigate and make a report to the committee, which would recommend a response. Whereas many companies bring in impartial investigators, ICN chose to use its own lawyers. The sexual harassment suits were settled, and Panic remained CEO.

Panic may be losing his grip on ICN, however, because of falling stock prices. ICN shares have fallen behind the pharmaceuticals' index and market averages. Panic devised a restructuring plan to split ICN into three companies, and he would retain control of all three. The announcement caused ICN stock to fall even lower.

Discussion Question

1. What effects do allegations of sexual harassment have within a company? How will the way ICN handles this matter affect its reputation?

SOURCES: M. Horn, "Sex and the CEO," *U.S. News and World Report* (July 6, 1998): 32–40; C. Palmeri & D. Polek, "Will Investors Pull the Plug on Milan Panic?" *Business Week* (Sept. 4, 2000): 108–109.

exploitative. The effects of office romances can similarly be positive or negative, or they can simply be mild diversions. Romances can be damaging to organizational effectiveness, or they can occasionally enhance effectiveness through their positive effects on participants. Two particular kinds of romances are hazardous in the workplace. Hierarchical romances, in which one person directly reports to another, can create tremendous conflicts of interest. Utilitarian romances, in which one person satisfies the needs of another in exchange for task-related or career-related favors, are potentially damaging in the workplace. Though most managers realize that workplace romance cannot be eliminated through rules and policies, they believe that intervention is a must when romance constitutes a serious threat to productivity or workplace morale.[90]

Organizational Justice

Another area in which moral and ethical dilemmas may arise for people at work concerns organizational justice, both distributive and procedural. ***Distributive justice*** concerns the fairness of outcomes individuals receive. For example, the salaries and bonuses of U.S. corporate executives became a central issue with Japanese executives when President George Bush and American CEOs in key industries visited Japan in 1992. The Japanese CEOs questioned the distributive justice in keeping the American CEOs' salaries at high levels at a time when so many companies were in difficulty and laying off workers.

Procedural justice concerns the fairness of the process by which outcomes are allocated.[91] The ethical questions here do not concern the just or unjust distribution of organizational resources. Rather, the ethical questions in procedural justice concern the process. Has the organization used the correct procedures in allocating resources? Have the right considerations, such as competence and skill, been brought to bear in the decision process? And have the wrong considerations, such as race and gender, been excluded from the decision process?

distributive justice
The fairness of the outcomes that individuals receive in an organization.

procedural justice
The fairness of the process by which outcomes are allocated in an organization.

Whistle-blowing

Whistle-blowers are employees who inform authorities of wrongdoings by their companies or coworkers. Whistle-blowers can be perceived as either heroes or "vile wretches" depending on the circumstances of the situation. For a whistle-blower to be considered a public hero, the gravity of the situation that the whistle-blower reports to authorities must be of such magnitude and quality as to be perceived as abhorrent by others.[92] In contrast, the whistle-blower is considered a vile wretch if others see the act of whistle-blowing as more offensive than the situation the whistle-blower reports to authorities.

whistle-blower
An employee who informs authorities of the wrongdoings of his or her company or coworkers.

Whistle-blowing is important in the United States because committed organizational members sometimes engage in unethical behavior in an intense desire to succeed. Many examples of whistle-blowing can be found in corporate America. In a suit that may top the current record for a whistle-blower award, a $171.6 million award was leveled against FMC Corporation, a government defense contractor. A testing supervisor, Henry Boisvert, was fired for refusing to sign his name to a report he thought was inaccurate. The issue in the suit was the Bradley fighting vehicle, a tanklike troop carrier purchased by the Army that is supposed to be able to "swim" across rivers and lakes. Boisvert tested the Bradley and found that its viability in water was not good; in fact, it "swam" like a rock. He wrote a report, and his supervisor told him the report was not to leave the company. When he refused to sign a falsified report, he was fired. Former FMC welders testified at the trial that they weren't given enough time to do their work and filled gaps with putty. Quality control measures were a sham. Through Boisvert's whistle-blowing, the government will recover damages from FMC.[93] Laws are now in place to provide remedies for workers who suffer employment discrimination in retaliation for whistle-blowing.

Organizations can manage whistle-blowing by communicating the conditions that are appropriate for the disclosure of wrongdoing. Clearly delineating wrongful behavior and the appropriate ways to respond are important organizational actions.

Social Responsibility

social responsibility
The obligation of an organization to behave in ethical ways.

Corporate *social responsibility* is the obligation of an organization to behave in ethical ways in the social environment in which it operates. Ethical conduct at the individual level can translate into social responsibility at the organizational level. When Malden Mills, the maker of Polartec, burned down in 1995, the company's president, Aaron Feuerstein, paid workers during the months it took to rebuild the company. Although doing so cost the company a lot of money and wasn't required by law, Feuerstein said his own values caused him to do the socially responsible thing. Malden Mills recovered financially and continues its success with Polartec.

Socially responsible actions are expected of organizations. Current concerns include protecting the environment, promoting worker safety, supporting social issues, and investing in the community, among others. Some organizations, like IBM, loan executives to inner-city schools to teach science and math. Other organizations like Patagonia demonstrate social responsibility through environmentalism. Firms that are seen as socially responsible have a competitive advantage in attracting applicants.[94]

Codes of Ethics

One of the characteristics of mature professions is the existence of a code of ethics to which the practitioners adhere in their actions and behavior. An example is the Hippocratic oath in medicine. Although some of the individual differences we will address in Chapter 4 produce ethical or unethical orientations in specific people, a profession's code of ethics becomes a standard against which members can measure themselves in the absence of internalized standards.

No universal code of ethics or oath exists for business as it does for medicine. However, Paul Harris and four business colleagues, who founded Rotary International in 1904, made an effort to address ethical and moral behavior right from the beginning. They developed the four-way test, shown in Figure 2.2, which is now used in more than 180 nations throughout the world by the nearly two million Rotarians in 25,000 Rotary clubs. Figure 2.2 focuses the questioner on key ethical and moral questions.

Beyond the individual and profession level, corporate culture is another excellent starting point for addressing ethics and morality. In Chapter 15 we will examine how corporate culture and leader behavior trickles down the company, setting a standard for all below. In some cases, the corporate ethics may be captured in a regulation. For example, the Joint Ethics Reg-

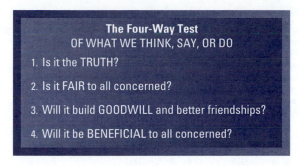

Figure 2.2
The Four-Way Test

ulation (DOD 5500.7-R, August 1993) specifies the ethical standards to which all U.S. military personnel are to adhere. In other cases, the corporate ethics may be in the form of a credo. Johnson & Johnson's credo, shown in Figure 2.3, helped hundreds of employees ethically address the criminal tampering with Tylenol products. In its 1986 centennial annual report, J & J attributed its success in this crisis, as well as its long-term business growth (a compound sales rate of 11.6 percent for 100 years), to "our unique form of decentralized management, our adherence to the ethical principles embodied in our credo, and our emphasis on managing the business for the long term."

Individual codes of ethics, professional oaths, and organizational credos all must be anchored in a moral, ethical framework. They are always open to question and continuous improvement using ethical theories as a tool for reexamining the soundness of the current standard. Although a universal right and wrong may exist, it would be hard to argue that there is only one code of ethics to which all individuals, professions, and organizations can subscribe.

MANAGERIAL IMPLICATIONS: FACING THE CHALLENGES

The success of organizations in the new millennium will depend on managers' ability to address the challenges of globalization, diversity, technology, and ethics. Failure to address the challenges can be costly. Think about Pepsi's losses to Coke in the global cola wars. As you saw in Organizational Reality 2.1, Coke is winning the battle and capitalizing on the huge opportunities and profits from global markets. A racial discrimination lawsuit against Texaco not only cost the company millions in a settlement, but also damaged the company's reputation. Mitsubishi suffered a similar fate in a sexual harassment scandal. Failure to address these challenges can mean costly losses, damage to reputations, and ultimately an organization's demise.

These four challenges are also important because the way managers handle them shapes employee behavior. Developing global mind-sets among

Figure 2.3
The Johnson & Johnson Credo

We believe our first responsibility is to the doctors, nurses and patients,
to mothers and all others who use our products and services.
In meeting their needs everything we do must be of high quality.
We must constantly strive to reduce our costs
in order to maintain reasonable prices.
Customers' orders must be serviced promptly and accurately.
Our suppliers and distributors must have an opportunity
to make a fair profit.

We are responsible to our employees,
the men and women who work with us throughout the world.
Everyone must be considered as an individual.
We must respect their dignity and recognize their merit.
They must have a sense of security in their jobs.
Compensation must be fair and adequate,
and working conditions clean, orderly and safe.
Employees must feel free to make suggestions and complaints.
There must be equal opportunity for employment, development
and advancement for those qualified.
We must provide competent management,
and their actions must be just and ethical.

We are responsible to the communities in which we live and work
and to the world community as well.
We must be good citizens—support good works and charities
and bear our fair share of taxes.
We must encourage civic improvements and better health and education.
We must maintain in good order
the property we are privileged to use,
protecting the environment and natural resources.

Our final responsibility is to our stockholders.
Business must make a sound profit.
We must experiment with new ideas.
Research must be carried on, innovative programs developed
and mistakes paid for.
New equipment must be purchased, new facilities provided
and new products launched.
Reserves must be created to provide for adverse times.
When we operate according to these principles,
the stockholders should realize a fair return.

employees expands their worldview and puts competition on a larger scale. Knowing that diversity is valued and differences are assets causes employees to think twice about engaging in behaviors that are discriminatory. Valuing technological change leads employees to experiment with new technologies and develop innovative ways to perform their jobs. Sending a message that unethical behavior is not tolerated lets employees know that doing the right thing pays off.

These four challenges are recurring themes that you'll see throughout this book. We'll show you how companies are tackling these challenges and how organizational behavior can be used to do this effectively. It's a must, if organizations are to remain competitive.

Looking Back

Ford Cars and Trucks on Demand in the Future

Ford's in-house Web site and intranet may save billions of dollars for the company during the next few years and could even change the way Ford does business. The company is trying to move from a "make and sell" strategy to a more flexible, cars-on-demand approach. Ford's intranet connects 120,000 workstations around the world to thousands of Ford Web sites. The information on the Web sites is proprietary—things like market research, analysis of competitors' models, and rankings of suppliers. Ford's product development system documents thousands of steps in manufacturing, assembling, and testing vehicles, and it's on the intranet. Engineers, designers, and suppliers can access and work from the same data, which are updated hourly. Each vehicle team has its own Web site, where questions are posted and quality issues are resolved. This system has helped Ford reduce the time it takes to get new models into production from thirty-six months to twenty-four months.

In an effort to integrate the Internet into all parts of Ford's business, the company has signed e-commerce agreements with Oracle, Cisco Systems, Yahoo!, and Carpoint. Ford and Oracle created the world's first automotive online supply chain network and the world's largest business-to-business electronic network. The network, called Auto-xchange, added Cisco Systems as a partner and is now a $300 billion supply chain linking suppliers, dealers, and consumers. The goal of Auto-xchange is to extend Ford's core business into virtual e-business, connecting the supply chain to the consumer, which will reduce Ford's time to market.

CHAPTER SUMMARY

1. To ensure that their organizations meet the competition, managers must tackle four important challenges: globalization, workforce diversity, technological change, and ethical behavior at work.

2. The five cultural differences that affect work-related attitudes are individualism versus collectivism, power distance, uncertainty avoidance, masculinity versus femininity, and time orientation.

3. Diversity encompasses gender, culture, personality, sexual orientation, religion, military affiliation, ability, economic class, social status, and a host of other differences.

4. Managers must take a proactive approach to managing diversity so that differences are valued and capitalized upon.

5. Alternative work arrangements, facilitated by technology, are changing the way work is performed.

6. Through supportive relationships and training, managers can help employees adjust to technological change.

7. Three types of ethical theories include consequential theories, rule-based theories, and cultural theories.

8. Ethical dilemmas emerge for people at work in the areas of employee rights, sexual harassment, romantic involvements, organizational justice, whistle-blowing, and social responsibility.

KEY TERMS

transnational organization 31

guanxi 32

individualism 34

collectivism 34

power distance 35

uncertainty avoidance 35

masculinity 36

femininity 36

time orientation 36

expatriate manager 36

diversity 40

glass ceiling 41

technology 48

expert system 48

robotics 48

telecommuting 49

reinvention 52

consequential theory 53

rule-based theory 53

cultural theory 54

distributive justice 59

procedural justice 59

whistle-blower 59

social responsibility 60

REVIEW QUESTIONS

1. What are Hofstede's five dimensions of cultural differences that affect work attitudes? Using these dimensions, describe the United States.
2. What are the primary sources of diversity in the U.S. workforce?
3. What are the potential benefits and problems of diversity?
4. What is the reality of the glass ceiling? What would it take to change this reality?
5. Why do employees fear technological innovations, and how can managers help employees adjust?
6. What are some of the ethical challenges encountered in organizations?
7. Describe the difference between distributive and procedural justice.

DISCUSSION AND COMMUNICATION QUESTIONS

1. How can managers be encouraged to develop global thinking? How can managers dispel stereotypes about other cultures?
2. Some people have argued that in designing expert systems, human judgment is made obsolete. What do you think?
3. Why do some companies encourage alternative work arrangements?
4. What effects will the globalization of business have on a company's culture? How can an organization with a strong "made in America" identity compete in the global marketplace?
5. Why is diversity such an important issue? Is the workforce more diverse today than in the past?
6. How does a manager strike a balance between encouraging employees to celebrate their own cultures and forming a single unified culture within the organization?
7. Do you agree with Hofstede's findings about U.S. culture? On what do you base your agreement or disagreement?
8. (*communication question*) Select one of the four challenges (globalization, diversity, technology, ethics) and write a brief position paper arguing for its importance to managers.
9. (*communication question*) Find someone whose home country is not your own. This might be a classmate or an international student at your university. Interview the person about his or her culture, using Hofstede's dimensions. Also ask what you might need to know about doing business in the person's country (e.g., customs, etiquette). Be prepared to share this information in class.

ETHICS QUESTIONS

1. Suppose your company has the opportunity to install a marvelous new technology, but it will mean that 20 percent of the jobs in the company will be lost. As a manager, would you adopt the new technology? How would you make the decision?

2. What is the most difficult ethical dilemma you have ever faced at work or school? Why? How was it resolved?

3. Some companies have a policy that employees should not become romantically involved with each other. Is this ethical?

4. What are some of the concerns that a person with AIDS would have about his or her job? What are some of the fears that coworkers would have? How can a manager balance these two sets of concerns?

5. Suppose you are visiting Taiwan and attempting to do business there. You are given a gift by your Taiwanese host, who is your prospective client. Your interpreter explains that it is customary to exchange gifts before transacting business. You have no gift to offer. How would you handle the situation?

Experiential Exercises

2.1 International Orientations

1 Preparation (pre-class)
Read the background on the International Orientation Scale and the case study "Office Supplies International—Marketing Associate," complete the ratings and questions, and fill out the self-assessment inventory.

2 Group Discussions
Groups of four to six people discuss their answers to the case study questions and their own responses to the self-assessment.

3 Class Discussion
Instructor leads a discussion on the International Orientation Scale and the difficulties and challenges of adjusting to a new culture. Why do some people adjust more easily than others? What can you do to adjust to a new culture? What can you regularly do that will help you adjust in the future to almost any new culture?

Office Supplies International—Marketing Associate*
Jonathan Fraser is a marketing associate for a large multinational corporation, Office Supplies International (OSI), in Buffalo, New York. He is being considered for a transfer to the international division of OSI. This position will require that he spend between one and three years working abroad in one of OSI's three foreign subsidiaries: OSI-France, OSI-Japan, or OSI-Australia. This transfer is considered a fast track career move at OSI, and Jonathan feels honored to be in the running for the position.

Jonathan has been working at OSI since he graduated with his bachelor's degree in marketing ten years ago. He is married and has lived and worked in Buffalo all his life. Jonathan's parents are first-generation German Americans. His grandparents, although deceased, spoke only German at home and upheld many of their ethnic traditions. His parents, although quite "Americanized," have retained some of their German traditions. To communicate better with his grandparents, Jonathan took German in high school, but never used it because his grandparents had passed away.

In college, Jonathan joined the German Club and was a club officer for two years. His other collegiate extracurricular activity was playing for the varsity baseball team. Jonathan still enjoys playing in a summer softball league with his college friends. Given his athletic interests, he volunteered to be the athletic programming coordinator at OSI, where he organizes the company's softball and volleyball teams. Jonathan has been making steady progress at OSI. Last year, he was named marketing associate of the year.

His wife, Sue, is also a Buffalo native. She teaches English literature at the high school in one of the middle-class suburbs of Buffalo. Sue took five years off from teaching after she had a baby, but returned to teaching this year when Janine, their five-year-old daughter, started kindergarten. She is happy to be resuming her career. One or two nights a week, Sue volunteers at the city mission where she works as a career counselor and a basic skills trainer. For fun, she takes both pottery and ethnic cooking classes.

Both Sue and Jonathan are excited about the potential transfer and accompanying pay raise. They are, however, also feeling apprehensive and cautious. Neither Sue nor Jonathan has ever lived away from their families in Buffalo, and Sue is concerned about giving up her newly reestablished career. Their daughter Janine has just started school, and Jonathan and Sue are uncertain whether living abroad is the best thing for her at her age.

Using the three-point scale below, try to rate Jonathan and Sue as potential expatriates. Write a sentence or two on why you gave the ratings you did.

Rating Scale

1. Based on this dimension, this person would adjust well to living abroad.

2. Based on this dimension, this person may or may not adjust well to living abroad.

3. Based on this dimension, this person would not adjust well to living abroad.

Jonathan's International Orientation

rating dimension	rating and reason for rating
International attitudes	
Foreign experiences	
Comfort with differences	
Participation in cultural events	

Sue's International Orientation

rating dimension	rating and reason for rating
International attitudes	
Foreign experiences	
Comfort with differences	
Participation in cultural events	

Discussion Questions: Office Supplies International

1. Imagine that you are the international human resource manager for OSI. Your job is to interview both Jonathan and Sue to determine whether they should be sent abroad. What are some of the questions you would ask? What critical information do you feel is missing? It might be helpful to role-play the three parts and evaluate your classmates' responses as Jonathan and Sue.

2. Suppose France is the country where they would be sent. To what extent woud your ratings change? What else would you change about the way you are assessing the couple?

3. Now answer the same questions, except this time they are being sent to Japan. Repeat the exercise for Australia.

4. For those dimensions that you rated Sue and Jonathan either 2 or 3 (indicating that they might have a potential adjustment problem), what would you suggest for training and development? What might be included in a training program?

5. Reflect on your own life for a moment and give yourself a rating on each of the following dimensions. Try to justify why you rated yourself as you did. Do you feel that you would adjust well to living abroad? What might be difficult for you?

rating dimension	rating and reason for rating France, Japan, Australia (or other)
International attitudes	
Foreign experiences	
Comfort with differences	
Participation in cultural events	

6. Generally, what are some of the potential problems a dual-career couple might face? What are some of the solutions to those problems?

7. How would the ages of children affect the expatriate's assignment? At what age should the children's international orientations be assessed along with their parents?

International Orientation Scale

The following sample items are taken from the International Orientation Scale. Answer each question and give yourself a score for each dimension. The highest possible score for any dimension is 20 points.

Dimension 1: International Attitudes

Use the following scale to answer questions Q1 through Q4.

1	*Strongly agree*
2	*Agree somewhat*
3	*Maybe or unsure*
4	*Disagree somewhat*
5	*Strongly disagree*

Q1. Foreign language skills should be taught as early as elementary school. _____

Q2. Traveling the world is a priority in my life. _____

Q3. A year-long overseas assignment (from my company) would be a fantastic opportunity for my family and me. _____

Q4. Other countries fascinate me. _____

Total Dimension 1 _____

Dimension 2: Foreign Experiences

Q1. I have studied a foreign language.

1	Never
2	For less than a year
3	For a year
4	For a few years
5	For several years

Q2. I am fluent in another language.

1	I don't know another language.
2	I am limited to very short and simple phrases.
3	I know basic grammatical structure and speak with a limited vocabulary.
4	I understand conversation on most topics.
5	I am very fluent in another language.

Q3. I have spent time overseas (traveling, studying abroad, etc.).

1	Never
2	About a week
3	A few weeks
4	A few months
5	Several months or years

Q4. I was overseas before the age of 18.

1	Never
2	About a week
3	A few weeks
4	A few months
5	Several months or years

Total Dimension 2 _____

Dimension 3: Comfort with Differences

Use the following scale for questions Q1 through Q4.

1	*Quite similar*
2	*Mostly similar*
3	*Somewhat different*
4	*Quite different*
5	*Extremely different*

Q1. My friends' career goals, interests, and education are . . . _____

Q2. My friends' ethnic backgrounds are . . . _____

Q3. My friends' religious affiliations are . . . _____

Q4. My friends' first languages are . . . _____

Total Dimension 3 _____

Dimension 4: Participation in Cultural Events

Use the following scale to answer questions Q1 through Q4.

1	*Never*
2	*Seldom*
3	*Sometimes*
4	*Frequently*
5	*As often as possible*

Q1. I eat at a variety of ethnic restaurants (e.g., Greek, Polynesian, Thai, German). _____

Q2. I watch the major networks' world news programs. _____

Q3. I attend ethnic festivals. _____

Q4. I visit art galleries and museums. _____

Total Dimension 4 _____

Self-Assessment Discussion Questions:

Do any of these scores suprise you?

Would you like to improve your international orientation?

If so, what could you do to change various aspects of your life?

2.2 Ethical Dilemmas

Divide the class into five groups. Each group should choose one of the following scenarios and agree on a course of action.

1. Sam works for you. He is technically capable and a good worker, but he does not get along well with others in the work group. When Sam has an opportunity to transfer, you encourage him to take it. What would you say to Sam's potential supervisor when he asks about Sam?

2. Your boss has told you that you must reduce your work group by 30 percent. Which of the following criteria would you use to lay off workers?
   a. Lay off older, higher paid employees.
   b. Lay off younger, lower paid employees.
   c. Lay off workers based on seniority only.
   d. Lay off workers based on performance only.

3. You are an engineer, but you are not working on your company's Department of Transportation (DOT) project. One day you overhear a conversation in the cafeteria between the program manager and the project engineer that makes you reasonably sure a large contract will soon be given to the ABC Company to develop and manufacture a key DOT subsystem. ABC is a small firm, and its stock is traded over the counter. You feel sure that the stock will rise from its present $2.25 per share as soon as news of the DOT contract gets out. Would you go out and buy ABC's stock?

4. You are the project engineer working on the development of a small liquid rocket engine. You know that if you could achieve a throttling ratio greater than 8 to 1, your system would be considered a success and continue to receive funding support. To date, the best you have achieved is a 4 to 1 ratio. You have an un-

proven idea that you feel has a 50 percent chance of being successful. Your project is currently being reviewed to determine if it should be continued. You would like to continue it. How optimistically should you present the test results?

5. Imagine that you are the president of a company in a highly competitive industry. You learn that a competitor has made an important scientific discovery that is not patentable and will give that company an advantage that will substantially reduce the profits of your company for about a year. There is some hope of hiring one of the competitor's employees who knows the details of the discovery. Would you try to hire this person?

Each group should present its scenario and chosen course of action to the class. The class should then evaluate the ethics of the course of action, using the following questions to guide discussion:

1. Are you following rules that are understood and accepted?

2. Are you comfortable discussing and defending your action?

3. Would you want someone to do this to you?

4. What if everyone acted this way?

5. Are there alternatives that rest on firmer ethical ground?

For more practice exercises, consult the fifth edition of Organizational Behavior: Experiences and Cases by Dorothy Marcic and Joseph Seltzer (South-Western, 1998).

PART 2

Individual Processes and Behavior

3. Personality, Perception, and Attribution   70

4. Attitudes, Values, and Ethics   101

5. Motivation at Work   132

6. Learning and Performance Management   160

7. Stress and Well-Being at Work   189

Learning Objectives

After reading this chapter, you should be able to do the following:

1. Describe individual differences and their importance in understanding behavior. *p. 71*

2. Define *personality*. *p. 72*

3. Explain four theories of personality. *p. 73*

4. Identify several personality characteristics and their influences on behavior in organizations. *p. 74*

5. Explain how personality is measured. *p. 79*

6. Discuss Carl Jung's contribution to our understanding of individual differences, and explain how his theory is used in the Myers-Briggs Type Indicator. *p. 79*

7. Define *social perception* and explain how characteristics of the perceiver, the target, and the situation affect it. *p. 83*

8. Identify five common barriers to social perception. *p. 89*

9. Explain the attribution process and how attributions affect managerial behavior. *p. 92*

3

Personality, Perception, and Attribution

Thinking Ahead

The Woman (Oprah) behind the Company (Harpo)

Most companies reflect the personality of the leader—Southwest Airlines' culture reflects Herb Kelleher's love of fun, Microsoft reflects Bill Gates's intensity and love of technology. Another company, perhaps less visible, undoubtedly reflects the personality of the woman at the helm. Harpo Productions (Oprah spelled backward) is led by one of the most visible, and most admired, women in the world.

Harpo employs around 175 employees and has revenues of approximately $140 million per year. Although the public may perceive Oprah as larger than life, her company, Harpo, is small in terms of number of employees. One of Harpo's products, *The Oprah Winfrey Show*, has tremendous visibility. The show is seen in 206 U.S. markets and 136 foreign markets. More than 33 million people per day tune in to the show, which has been the number one talk show for fourteen years in a row. Oprah's Web site, **http://www.oprah.com**, has 115 million visitors per month.

Such exposure leads to tremendous speculation about Oprah's personality. But is the Oprah we see on television the "real" Oprah or just our perception of who she is? From all accounts, she seems to practice what she preaches. "I've tried to have the show be an extension of what I am and what I stand for," she has said. Oprah created the "Angel Network" to encourage people to be charitable; she gives millions each year to charity herself. She encourages free dialogue on her show, and her own revelations about child abuse galvanized support for America's first national database of child abusers. Oprah encourages viewers to write down things they are thankful for—and does so herself each morning, listing five things she is grateful for. Her Oprah's Book Club was started to enrich people's lives through reading—Oprah herself is a voracious reader. And Harpo Productions receives no financial benefit from book selections or sales.

Harpo Productions, its *Oprah Winfrey Show*, and its other projects, such as films, appear to represent Oprah's own personality. Oprah herself has said, "You really have to work hard to let what you are come through." A more accurate case might be built for this supposition when Oprah's autobiography is published—if it ever is. She wrote it, and then canceled its publication because she felt the book didn't reflect her true spirit. In the Looking Back feature, you can learn more about the management philosophy on which Harpo was built.[1]

INDIVIDUAL DIFFERENCES AND ORGANIZATIONAL BEHAVIOR

In this chapter and continuing in Chapter 4, we explore the concept of *individual differences*. Individuals are unique in terms of their skills, abilities, personalities, perceptions, attitudes, values, and ethics. These are just a few of the ways individuals may be similar to or different from one another. Individual differences represent the essence of the challenge of management, because no two individuals are completely alike. Managers face the challenge of working with people who possess a multitude of individual characteristics, so the more managers understand individual differences, the better they can work with others. Figure 3.1 illustrates how individual differences affect human behavior.

The basis for understanding individual differences stems from Lewin's early contention that behavior is a function of the person and the environment.[2] Lewin expressed this idea in an equation: $B = f(P, E)$, where B = behavior, P = person, and E = environment. This idea has been developed by the *interactional psychology* approach.[3] Basically, this approach says that in order to understand human behavior, we must know something about the person and something about the situation. There are four basic propositions of interactional psychology:

1. Behavior is a function of a continuous, multidirectional interaction between the person and the situation.

2. The person is active in this process and is both changed by situations and changes situations.

1. Describe individual differences and their importance in understanding behavior.

individual differences
The way in which factors such as skills, abilities, personalities, perceptions, attitudes, values, and ethics differ from one individual to another.

interactional psychology
The psychological approach that emphasizes that in order to understand human behavior, we must know something about the person and about the situation.

Figure 3.1
Variables Influencing Individual Behavior

2. Define *personality*.

personality
A relatively stable set of characteristics that influence an individual's behavior.

3. People vary in many characteristics, including cognitive, affective, motivational, and ability factors.

4. Two interpretations of situations are important: the objective situation and the person's subjective view of the situation.[4]

The interactional psychology approach points out the need to study both persons and situations. We will focus on personal and situational factors throughout the text. The person consists of individual differences such as those we emphasize in this chapter and Chapter 4: personality, perception, attribution, attitudes, values, and ethics. The situation consists of the environment the person operates in, and it can include things like the organization, work group, personal life situation, job characteristics, and many other environmental influences. One important and fascinating individual difference is personality.

PERSONALITY

What makes an individual behave in consistent ways in a variety of situations? Personality is an individual difference that lends consistency to a person's behavior. *Personality* is defined as a relatively stable set of characteristics that influence an individual's behavior. Although there is debate about the determinants of personality, we conclude that there are several origins. One determinant is heredity, and some interesting studies have supported this position. Identical twins who are separated at birth and raised apart in very different situations have been found to share personality traits and job preferences. For example, about half of the variation in traits like extraversion, impulsiveness, and flexibility was found to be genetically determined; that is, identical twins who grew up in different environments shared these traits.[5] In addition, the twins held similar jobs.[6] Thus, there does appear to be a genetic influence on personality.

Another determinant of personality is the environment a person is exposed to. Family influences, cultural influences, educational influences, and other environmental forces shape personality. Personality is therefore shaped by both heredity and environment.

Personality Theories

Four major theories of personality are the trait theory, psychodynamic theory, humanistic theory, and the integrative approach. Each theory has influenced the study of personality in organizations.

Trait Theory Some early personality researchers believed that to understand individuals, we must break down behavior patterns into a series of observable traits. According to *trait theory*, combining these traits into a group forms an individual's personality. Gordon Allport, a leading trait theorist, saw traits as broad, general guides that lend consistency to behavior.[7] Thousands of traits have been identified over the years. Raymond Cattell, another prominent trait theorist, identified sixteen traits that formed the basis for differences in individual behavior. He described traits in bipolar adjective combinations such as self-assured/apprehensive, reserved/outgoing, and submissive/dominant.[8]

More recently, researchers have argued that all traits can be reduced to five basic factors. The "Big Five" traits include extraversion, agreeableness, conscientiousness, emotional stability, and openness to experience.[9] Descriptions of the "Big Five" are shown in Table 3.1. The "Big Five" are broad, global traits. Although there is evidence to support the existence of the Big Five traits, research is needed to see whether these five traits actually predict behavior at work.

From preliminary research, we know that introverted and conscientious employees are less likely to be absent from work.[10] The traits most associated with high-performing employees are conscientiousness and emotional stability.[11]

The trait approach has been the subject of considerable criticism. Some theorists argue that simply identifying traits is not enough; instead, personality is dynamic and not completely stable. Further, trait theorists tended to ignore the influence of situations.[12]

Psychodynamic Theory Based on the work of Sigmund Freud, *psychodynamic theory* emphasizes the unconscious determinants of behavior.[13] Freud saw personality as the interaction among three elements of personality: the id, ego, and superego. The id is the most primitive element, the source of drives and impulses that operate in an uncensored manner. The superego, similar to what we know as conscience, contains values and the "shoulds and should nots" of the personality. There is an ongoing conflict between

3. Explain four theories of personality.

trait theory
The personality theory that states that in order to understand individuals, we must break down behavior patterns into a series of observable traits.

Experiencing OB

Psychologists have identified dozens of traits that influence a person's behavior. Five of these traits are called the "Big Five" because of their global effects on behavior. To learn about these, visit our animated concept and activity site. Choose Personality&Attitudes from the "select a topic" pull-down menu, then Big Five Personality Factors from the "overview tab."

http://www.experiencingob.com

psychodynamic theory
The personality theory that emphasizes the unconscious determinants of behavior.

Table 3.1
The "Big Five" Personality Traits

Extraversion	The person is gregarious, assertive, and sociable (as opposed to reserved, timid, and quiet).
Agreeableness	The person is cooperative, warm, and agreeable (rather than cold, disagreeable, and antagonistic).
Conscientiousness	The person is hardworking, organized, and dependable (as opposed to lazy, disorganized, and unreliable).
Emotional stability	The person is calm, self-confident, and cool (as opposed to insecure, anxious, and depressed).
Openness to experience	The person is creative, curious, and cultured (rather than practical with narrow interests).

SOURCES: P. T. Costa and R. R. McCrae, *The NEO-PI Personality Inventory* (Odessa, Fla.: Psychological Assessment Resources, 1992); J. F. Salgado, "The Five Factor Model of Personality and Job Performance in the European Community," *Journal of Applied Psychology* 82 (1997): 30–43.

the id and the superego. The ego serves to manage the conflict between the id and the superego. In this role, the ego compromises, and the result is the individual's use of defense mechanisms such as denial of reality. The contribution of psychodynamic theory to our understanding of personality is its focus on unconscious influences on behavior.

Humanistic Theory Carl Rogers believed that all people have a basic drive toward self-actualization, which is the quest to be all you can be.[14] The *humanistic theory* focuses on individual growth and improvement. It is distinctly people centered and also emphasizes the individual's view of the world. The humanistic approach contributes an understanding of the self to personality theory and contends that the self-concept is the most important part of an individual's personality.

humanistic theory
The personality theory that emphasizes individual growth and improvement.

Integrative Approach Recently, researchers have taken a broader, more *integrative approach* to the study of personality.[15] To capture its influence on behavior, personality is described as a composite of the individual's psychological processes. Personality dispositions include emotions, cognitions, attitudes, expectancies, and fantasies.[16] *Dispositions*, in this approach, simply mean the tendencies of individuals to respond to situations in consistent ways. Influenced by both genetics and experiences, dispositions can be modified. The integrative approach focuses on both person (dispositions) and situational variables as combined predictors of behavior.

integrative approach
The broad theory that describes personality as a composite of an individual's psychological processes.

Personality Characteristics in Organizations

4. Identify several personality characteristics and their influences on behavior in organizations.

Managers should learn as much as possible about personality in order to understand their employees. Hundreds of personality characteristics have been identified. We have selected four characteristics because of their particular influences on individual behavior in organizations: locus of control, self-esteem, self-monitoring, and positive/negative affect. Because these characteristics affect performance at work, managers need to have a working knowledge of them.

Locus of Control An individual's generalized belief about internal (self) versus external (situation or others) control is called *locus of control*. People who believe they control what happens to them are said to have an internal locus of control, whereas people who believe that circumstances or other people control their fate have an external locus of control.[17] Research on locus of control has strong implications for organizations. Internals (those with an internal locus of control) have been found to have higher job satisfaction, to be more likely to assume managerial positions, and to prefer participative management styles.[18] In addition, internals have been shown to display higher work motivation, hold stronger beliefs that effort leads to performance, receive higher salaries, and display less anxiety than externals (those with an external locus of control).[19]

Knowing about locus of control can prove valuable to managers. Because internals believe they control what happens to them, they will want to exercise control in their work environment. Allowing internals considerable voice in how work is performed is important. Internals will not react well to being closely supervised. Externals, in contrast, may prefer a more structured work setting, and they may be more reluctant to participate in decision making.

Self-Esteem *Self-esteem* is an individual's general feeling of self-worth. Individuals with high self-esteem have positive feelings about themselves, perceive themselves to have strengths as well as weaknesses, and believe their strengths are more important than their weaknesses.[20] Individuals with low self-esteem view themselves negatively. They are more strongly affected by what other people think of them, and they compliment individuals who give them positive feedback while cutting down people who give them negative feedback.[21]

A person's self-esteem affects a host of other attitudes and has important implications for behavior in organizations. People with high self-esteem perform better and are more satisfied with their jobs.[22] When they are involved in a job search, they seek out higher status jobs.[23] A work team made up of individuals with high self-esteem is more likely to be successful than a team with lower average self-esteem.[24]

Very high self-esteem may be too much of a good thing. When people with high self-esteem find themselves in stressful situations, they may brag inappropriately.[25] This may be viewed negatively by others, who see spontaneous boasting as egotistical.

Self-esteem may be strongly affected by situations. Success tends to raise self-esteem, whereas failure tends to lower it. Given that high self-esteem is generally a positive characteristic, managers should encourage employees to raise their self-esteem by giving them appropriate challenges and opportunities for success. Cisco Systems is a company that believes in self-esteem. See how John Chambers, Cisco's CEO, creates a culture that enhances self-esteem in Organizational Reality 3.1.

locus of control
An individual's generalized belief about internal control (self-control) versus external control (control by the situation or by others).

self-esteem
An individual's general feeling of self-worth.

ORGANIZATIONAL REALITY 3.1

At Cisco Systems, Self-Esteem Produces Success

Once every four months, Cisco Systems's chief executive puts on a red apron, picks up a canvas bag full of ice cream treats, and walks through corporate headquarters handing out ice cream to his staff. He greets employees with "Hi, my name is John Chambers. Corporate overhead here at Cisco." You might think this behavior unusual for a CEO, but Chambers's belief in himself and his employees lends itself to good humor, and to success.

Cisco dominates the business for data networking equipment that makes up the plumbing of the Internet and corporate computer networks. Between January 1995 when Chambers became CEO and 1998, Cisco's share price increased by 800 percent, giving the company a market value of over $100 billion in a mere 8.5 years—the fastest to do so in history. (Even Microsoft took 11 years to accomplish this!)

Chambers is preparing Cisco to compete in a much bigger league, the $250 billion per year market for telecommunication equipment. He'll have to do battle with Nortel, twice as big as Cisco, Lucent, three times as big, and Siemens, seven times as big as Cisco. "I want Cisco to be a dynasty," he says. "I think it can be a company that changes the world." His own self-esteem and self-efficacy (his "can do" attitude), along with a culture that enhances employees' self-esteem, will help the company do this.

A belief in himself was essential in Chambers's childhood. He grew up in an era where learning disabilities were undiagnosed, and because he was severely dyslexic, he couldn't learn to read. His childhood reading coach recalls about Chambers: "He knew that he had a problem, and he had no doubt in his mind that he was going to do something about it. He made no excuses for not being able to read, and that's very rare." His hard work paid off. He graduated second in his class from high school.

At Cisco, Chambers built a culture where it's not a sign of weakness, but a sign of strength, to say, "I can't do everything myself. I will find a partner and trust myself to be able to manage the process." Teamwork is essential; managers who are not team players are flushed out of the company. He constantly polls his staff on problems. How is the Scottish factory coming along? Is our softball team on track? Do we need to consider having a day care center on site? Such teamwork, combined with success, fuels employee self-esteem.

Despite the formidable competition Cisco Systems faces in the telecommunications industry, Wall Street is bullish on the company. Many analysts attribute the success and promising future to Chambers and the way he has motivated his managers to stay focused on the customer.

Discussion Question

1. What can managers do to encourage the development of self-esteem among employees? Why is this an important thing to do?

SOURCE: A. Kupfer, "The Real King of the Internet," *Fortune* (September 7, 1998): 84–92.

---

self-monitoring

The extent to which people base their behavior on cues from other people and situations.

Self-Monitoring A characteristic with great potential for affecting behavior in organizations is *self-monitoring*—the extent to which people base their behavior on cues from other people and situations.[26] High self-monitors pay attention to what is appropriate in particular situations and to the behavior of other people, and they behave accordingly. Low self-monitors, in contrast, are not as vigilant to situational cues and act from internal states rather than paying attention to the situation. As a result, the behavior of low self-monitors is consistent across situations. High self-monitors, because their behavior varies with the situation, appear to be more unpredictable and less consistent. You can use Challenge 3.1 to assess your own self-monitoring tendencies.

Research is currently focusing on the effects of self-monitoring in organizations. In one study, the authors tracked the careers of 139 MBAs for five years to see whether high self-monitors were more likely to be promoted, change employers, or make a job-related geographic move. The results were "yes" to each question. High self-monitors get promoted because

Challenge 3.1

Are You a High or Low Self-Monitor?

For the following items, circle T (true) if the statement is characteristic of your behavior. Circle F (false) if the statement does not reflect your behavior.

1. I find it hard to imitate the behavior of other people.	T	F
2. At parties and social gatherings, I do not attempt to do or say things that others will like.	T	F
3. I can only argue for ideas that I already believe.	T	F
4. I can make impromptu speeches even on topics about which I have almost no information.	T	F
5. I guess I put on a show to impress or entertain others.	T	F
6. I would probably make a good actor.	T	F
7. In a group of people, I am rarely the center of attention.	T	F
8. In different situations and with different people, I often act like very different persons.	T	F
9. I am not particularly good at making other people like me.	T	F
10. I am not always the person I appear to be.	T	F
11. I would not change my opinions (or the way I do things) in order to please others or win their favor.	T	F
12. I have considered being an entertainer.	T	F
13. I have never been good at games like charades or at improvisational acting.	T	F
14. I have trouble changing my behavior to suit different people and different situations.	T	F
15. At a party, I let others keep the jokes and stories going.	T	F
16. I feel a bit awkward in company and do not show up quite as well as I should.	T	F
17. I can look anyone in the eye and tell a lie with a straight face (if it is for a good cause).	T	F
18. I may deceive people by being friendly when I really dislike them.	T	F

To score this questionnaire, give yourself 1 point for each of the following items that you answered T (true): 4, 5, 6, 8, 10, 12, 17, and 18. Now give yourself 1 point for each of the following items that you answered F (false): 1, 2, 3, 7, 9, 11, 13, 14, 15, and 16. Add both subtotals to find your overall score. If you scored 11 or above, you are probably a *high self-monitor*. If you scored 10 or under, you are probably a *low self-monitor*.

they accomplish tasks through meeting the expectations of others. However, the high self-monitor's flexibility may not be suited for every job, and the tendency to move may not fit every organization.[27] Because high self-monitors base their behavior on cues from others and from the situation, they demonstrate higher levels of managerial self-awareness. This means that, as managers, they assess their own workplace behavior accurately.[28]

Although research on self-monitoring in organizations is in its early stages, we can speculate that high self-monitors respond more readily to work group norms, organizational culture, and supervisory feedback than do low self-monitors, who adhere more to internal guidelines for behavior ("I am who I am"). In addition, high self-monitors may be enthusiastic participants in the trend toward work teams because of their ability to assume flexible roles.

positive affect
An individual's tendency to accentuate the positive aspects of himself or herself, other people, and the world in general.

negative affect
An individual's tendency to accentuate the negative aspects of himself or herself, other people, and the world in general.

Positive/Negative Affect Recently, researchers have explored the effects of persistent mood dispositions at work. Individuals who focus on the positive aspects of themselves, other people, and the world in general are said to have *positive affect*.[29] In contrast, those who accentuate the negative in themselves, others, and the world are said to possess *negative affect* (also referred to as negative affectivity).[30] Interviewers who exhibit positive affect evaluate job candidates more favorably than do interviewers whose affect is neutral.[31] Employees with positive affect are absent from work less often.[32] Individuals with negative affect report more work stress.[33] Individual affect also influences the work group. Negative individual affect produces negative group affect, and this leads to less cooperative behavior in the work group.[34]

Positive affect is a definite asset in work settings. Managers can do several things to promote positive affect, including allowing participative decision making and providing pleasant working conditions. We need to know more about inducing positive affect in the workplace.

The characteristics previously described are but a few of the personality characteristics that affect behavior and performance in organizations. Can managers predict the behavior of their employees by knowing their personalities? Not completely. You may recall that the interactional psychology model (Figure 3.1) requires both person and situation variables to predict behavior. Another idea to remember in predicting behavior is the strength of situational influences. Some situations are *strong situations* in that they overwhelm the effects of individual personalities. These situations are interpreted in the same way by different individuals, evoke agreement on the appropriate behavior in the situation, and provide cues to appropriate behavior. A performance appraisal session is an example of a strong situation. Employees know to listen to their boss and to contribute when asked to do so.

strong situation
A situation that overwhelms the effects of individual personalities by providing strong cues for appropriate behavior.

A weak situation, in contrast, is one that is open to many interpretations. It provides few cues to appropriate behavior and no obvious rewards for one behavior over another. Thus, individual personalities have a stronger influence in weak situations than in strong situations. An informal meeting without an agenda can be seen as a weak situation.

Organizations present combinations of strong and weak situations; therefore, personality has a stronger effect on behavior in some situations than in others.[35]

Measuring Personality

Several methods can be used to assess personality. These include projective tests, behavioral measures, and self-report questionnaires.

The *projective test* is one method used to measure personality. In these tests, individuals are shown a picture, abstract image, or photo and are asked to describe what they see or to tell a story about what they see. The rationale behind projective tests is that each individual responds to the stimulus in a way that reflects his or her unique personality. The Rorschach ink blot test is a projective test commonly used to assess personality.[36] Like other projective tests, however, it has low reliability.

There are *behavioral measures* of personality as well. Measuring behavior involves observing an individual's behavior in a controlled situation. We might assess a person's sociability, for example, by counting the number of times he or she approaches strangers at a party. The behavior is scored in some manner to produce an index of personality.

The most common method of assessing personality is the *self-report questionnaire*. Individuals respond to a series of questions, usually in an agree/disagree or true/false format. One of the more widely recognized questionnaires is the Minnesota Multiphasic Personality Inventory (MMPI). The MMPI is comprehensive and assesses a variety of traits, as well as various neurotic or psychotic disorders. Used extensively in psychological counseling to identify disorders, the MMPI is a long questionnaire. The Big Five traits we discussed earlier are measured by another self-report questionnaire, the NEO Personality Inventory.

Another popular self-report questionnaire is the Myers-Briggs Type Indicator (MBTI). In the next section, we will introduce the Jungian theory of personality. The Myers-Briggs Type Indicator is an instrument that has been developed to measure Jung's ideas about individual differences. Many organizations use the MBTI, and we will focus on it as an example of how some organizations use personality concepts to help employees appreciate diversity.

A POPULAR APPLICATION OF PERSONALITY THEORY IN ORGANIZATIONS: THE MYERS-BRIGGS TYPE INDICATOR

One approach to applying personality theory in organizations is the Jungian approach and its measurement tool, the MBTI.

Swiss psychiatrist Carl Jung built his work on the notion that people are fundamentally different, but also fundamentally alike. His classic treatise

---

5. Explain how personality is measured.

projective test
A personality test that elicits an individual's response to abstract stimuli.

behavioral measures
Personality assessments that involve observing an individual's behavior in a controlled situation.

self-report questionnaire
A common personality assessment that involves an individual's responses to a series of questions.

6. Discuss Carl Jung's contribution to our understanding of individual differences, and explain how his theory is used in the Myers-Briggs Type Indicator.

Psychological Types proposed that the population was made up of two basic types—extraverted and introverted.[37] He went on to identify two types of perception (sensing and intuiting) and two types of judgment (thinking and feeling). Perception (how we gather information) and judgment (how we make decisions) represent the basic mental functions that everyone uses.

Jung suggested that human similarities and differences could be understood by combining preferences. We prefer and choose one way of doing things over another. We are not exclusively one way or another; rather, we have a preference for extraversion or introversion, just as we have a preference for right-handedness or left-handedness. We may use each hand equally well, but when a ball is thrown at us by surprise, we will reach to catch it with our preferred hand. Jung's type theory argues that no preferences are better than others. Differences are to be understood, celebrated, and appreciated.

During the 1940s, a mother–daughter team became fascinated with individual differences among people and with the work of Carl Jung. Katharine Briggs and her daughter, Isabel Briggs Myers, developed the **Myers-Briggs Type Indicator** to put Jung's type theory into practical use. The MBTI is used extensively in organizations as a basis for understanding individual differences. More than 3 million people complete the instrument per year in the United States.[38] The MBTI has been used in career counseling, team building, conflict management, and understanding management styles.[39]

The Preferences

There are four basic preferences in type theory and two possible choices for each of the four preferences. Table 3.2 shows these preferences. The combination of these preferences makes up an individual's psychological type.

Extraversion/Introversion The *extraversion/introversion* preference represents where you get your energy. The extravert (E) is energized by interaction with other people. The introvert (I) is energized by time alone. Extraverts typically have a wide social network, whereas introverts have a more narrow range of relationships. As articulated by Jung, this preference has nothing to do with social skills. Many introverts have excellent social skills but prefer the internal world of ideas, thoughts, and concepts. Extraverts represent approximately 70 percent of the U.S. population.[40] Our culture rewards extraversion and nurtures it. Jung contended that the extraversion/introversion preference reflects the most important distinction between individuals.

In work settings, extraverts prefer variety, and they do not mind the interruptions of the phone or visits from coworkers. They communicate freely but may say things that they regret later. Introverts prefer quiet for concentration, and they like to think things through in private. They do not mind working on a project for a long time and are careful with details. Introverts dislike telephone interruptions, and they may have trouble recalling names and faces.

Myers-Briggs Type Indicator (MBTI)
An instrument developed to measure Carl Jung's theory of individual differences.

extraversion
A preference indicating that an individual is energized by interaction with other people.

introversion
A preference indicating that an individual is energized by time alone.

EXTRAVERSION	**INTROVERSION**	Table 3.2 *Type Theory Preferences and Descriptions*
Outgoing	Quiet	
Publicly expressive	Reserved	
Interacting	Concentrating	
Speaks, then thinks	Thinks, then speaks	
Gregarious	Reflective	
SENSING	**INTUITING**	
Practical	General	
Specific	Abstract	
Feet on the ground	Head in the clouds	
Details	Possibilities	
Concrete	Theoretical	
THINKING	**FEELING**	
Analytical	Subjective	
Clarity	Harmony	
Head	Heart	
Justice	Mercy	
Rules	Circumstances	
JUDGING	**PERCEIVING**	
Structured	Flexible	
Time oriented	Open ended	
Decisive	Exploring	
Makes lists/uses them	Makes lists/loses them	
Organized	Spontaneous	

Sensing/Intuiting The *sensing/intuiting* preference represents perception or how we prefer to gather information. In essence this preference reflects what we pay attention to. The sensor (S) pays attention to information gathered through the five senses and to what actually exists. The intuitor (N) pays attention to a "sixth sense" and to what could be rather than to what actually exists.[41] Approximately 70 percent of people in the United States are sensors.[42]

At work, sensors prefer specific answers to questions and can become frustrated with vague instructions. They like jobs that yield tangible results, and they enjoy using established skills more than learning new ones. Intuitors like solving new problems and are impatient with routine details. They enjoy learning new skills more than actually using them. Intuitors tend to think about several things at once, and they may be seen by others as absentminded. They like figuring out how things work just for the fun of it.

Thinking/Feeling The *thinking/feeling* preference represents the way we prefer to make decisions. The thinker (T) makes decisions in a logical, objective fashion, whereas the feeler (F) makes decisions in a personal, value-

sensing
Gathering information through the five senses.

intuiting
Gathering information through "sixth sense" and focusing on what could be rather than what actually exists.

thinking
Making decisions in a logical, objective fashion.

feeling
Making decisions in a personal, value-oriented way.

oriented way. The general U.S. population is divided 50/50 on the thinking/feeling preference, but it is interesting that two-thirds of all males are thinkers, whereas two-thirds of all females are feelers. It is the one preference in type theory that has a strong gender difference. Thinkers tend to analyze decisions, whereas feelers sympathize. Thinkers try to be impersonal, whereas feelers base their decisions on how the outcome will affect the people involved.

In work settings, thinkers do not show much emotion, and they may become uncomfortable with people who do. They respond more readily to other people's thoughts. They are firm minded and like putting things into a logical framework. Feelers, in contrast, are more comfortable with emotion in the workplace. They enjoy pleasing people and need a lot of praise and encouragement.

judging
Preferring closure and completion in making decisions.

perceiving
Preferring to explore many alternatives and flexibility.

Judging/Perceiving   The *judging/perceiving* preference reflects one's orientation to the outer world. The judger (J) loves closure. Judgers prefer to lead a planned, organized life and like making decisions. The perceiver (P), in contrast, prefers a more flexible and spontaneous life and wants to keep options open. Imagine a J and a P going out for dinner. The J asks the P to choose a restaurant, and the P suggests ten alternatives. The J just wants to decide and get on with it, whereas the P wants to explore all the options.

For judgers in all arenas of life, and especially at work, there is a right and a wrong way to do everything. They love getting things accomplished and delight in marking off the completed items on their calendars. Perceivers tend to adopt a wait-and-see attitude and to collect new information rather than draw conclusions. Perceivers are curious and welcome new information. They may start too many projects and not finish them.

The Sixteen Types

The preferences combine to form sixteen distinct types, as shown in Table 3.3. For example, let's examine ESTJ. This type is extraverted, sensing, thinking, and judging. ESTJs see the world as it is (S); make decisions objectively (T); and like structure, schedules, and order (J). Combining these qualities with their preference for interacting with others makes them natural managers. ESTJs are seen by others as dependable, practical, and able to get any job done. They are conscious of the chain of command and see work as a series of goals to be reached by following rules and regulations. They may have little tolerance for disorganization and have a high need for control. Research results from the *MBTI Atlas* show that most of the 7,463 managers studied were ESTJs.[43]

There are no good and bad types, and each type has its own strengths and weaknesses. There is a growing volume of research on type theory. The MBTI has been found to have good reliability and validity as a measurement instrument for identifying type.[44, 45] Type has been found to be related to learning style, teaching style, choice of occupation, decision-making style, and management style.

Recent studies have begun to focus on the relationship between type and specific managerial behaviors. The introvert (I) and the feeler (F), for example, have been shown to be more effective at participative management than their counterparts, the extravert and the thinker.[46] Companies like AT&T, ExxonMobil, and Honeywell use the MBTI in their management development programs to help employees understand the different viewpoints of others in the organization. The MBTI can also be used for team building. Hewlett-Packard and Armstrong World Industries use the MBTI to help teams realize that diversity and differences lead to successful performance.

Type theory is valued by managers for its simplicity and accuracy in depicting personalities. It is a useful tool for helping managers develop interpersonal skills. Managers also use type theory to build teams that capitalize on individuals' strengths and to help individual team members appreciate differences.

It should be recognized that there is the potential for individuals to misuse the information from the MBTI in organizational settings. Some inappropriate uses include labeling one another, providing a convenient excuse that they simply can't work with someone else, and avoiding responsibility for their own personal development with respect to working with others and becoming more flexible. One's type is not an excuse for inappropriate behavior.

We turn now to another psychological process that forms the basis for individual differences. Perception shapes the way we view the world, and it varies greatly among individuals.

SOCIAL PERCEPTION

Perception involves the way we view the world around us. It adds meaning to information gathered via the five senses of touch, smell, hearing, vision, and taste. Perception is the primary vehicle through which we come to understand ourselves and our surroundings. **Social perception** is the process of interpreting information about another person. Virtually all management activities rely on perception. In appraising performance, managers use their perceptions of an employee's behavior as a basis for the evaluation.

One work situation that highlights the importance of perception is the selection interview. The consequences of a bad match between an individual and the organization are devastating for both parties, so it is essential that the data gathered be accurate. Typical first interviews are brief, and the candidate is usually one of many seen by an interviewer during a day. How long does it take for the interviewer to reach a decision about a candidate? In the first four to five minutes, the interviewer often makes an accept or reject decision based on his or her perception of the candidate.[47]

Perception is also culturally determined. Based on our cultural backgrounds, we tend to perceive things in certain ways. Read the following sentence:

Finished files are the result of years of scientific study combined with the experience of years.

social perception
The process of interpreting information about another person.

7. Define *social perception* and explain how characteristics of the perceiver, the target, and the situation affect it.

Experiencing OB

The social perception process involves the perceiver, the target, and the situation. To interact with a model of this process, visit our animated concept and activity site. Choose Perception&Attribution from the "select a topic" pull-down menu, then Social (Person) Perception from the "overview tab."

http://www.experiencingob.com

	Sensing Types		Intuitive Types	

Introverts

ISTJ

Quiet, serious, earn success by thoroughness and dependability. Practical, matter-of-fact, realistic, and responsible. Decide logically what should be done and work toward it steadily, regardless of distractions. Take pleasure in making everything orderly and organized— their work, their home, their life. Value traditions and loyalty.

ISFJ

Quiet, friendly, responsible, and conscientious. Committed and steady in meeting their obligations. Thorough, painstaking and accurate. Loyal, considerate, notice and remember specifics about people who are important to them, concerned with how others feel. Strive to create an orderly and harmonious environment at work and at home.

INFJ

Seek meaning and connection in ideas, relationships, and material possessions. Want to understand what motivates people and are insightful about others. Conscientious and committed to their firm values. Develop a clear vision about how best to serve the common good. Organized and decisive in implementing their vision.

INTJ

Have original minds and great drive for implementing their ideas and achieving their goals. Quickly see patterns in external events and develop long-range explanatory perspectives. When committed, organize a job and carry it through. Skeptical and independent, have high standards of competence and performance for themselves and others.

ISTP

Tolerant and flexible, quiet observers until a problem appears, then act quickly to find workable solutions. Analyze what makes things work and readily get through large amounts of data to isolate the core of practical problems. Interested in cause and effect, organize facts using logical principles, value efficiency.

ISFP

Quiet, friendly, sensitive, and kind. Enjoy the present moment, what's going on around them. Like to have their own space and to work within their own time frame. Loyal and committed to their values and to people who are important to them. Dislike disagreements and conflicts, do not force their opinions or values on others.

INFP

Idealistic, loyal to their values and to people who are important to them. Want an external life that is congruent with their values. Curious, quick to see possibilities, can be catalysts for implementing ideas. Seek to understand people and to help them fulfill their potential. Adaptable, flexible, and accepting unless a value is threatened.

INTP

Seek to develop logical explanations for everything that interests them. Theoretical and abstract, interested more in ideas than in social interaction. Quiet, contained, flexible, and adaptable. Have unusual ability to focus in depth to solve problems in their area of interest. Skeptical, sometimes critical, always analytical.

(continued)

Table 3.3
Characteristics Frequently Associated with Each Type

Now quickly count the number of *F*s in the sentence. Individuals for whom English is their second language see all six *F*s. Most native English speakers report that there are three *F*s. Because of cultural conditioning, *of* is not an important word and is ignored.[48] Culture affects our interpretation of the data we gather, as well as the way we add meaning to it.

Valuing diversity, including cultural diversity, has been recognized as the key to international competitiveness.[49] This challenge and others make social perception skills essential to managerial success.

Sensing Types		Intuitive Types	

Extraverts

ESTP
Flexible and tolerant, they take a pragmatic approach focused on immediate results. Theories and conceptual explanations bore them—they want to act energetically to solve the problem. Focus on the here-and-now, spontaneous, enjoy each moment that they can be active with others. Enjoy material comforts and style. Learn best through doing.

ESFP
Outgoing, friendly, and accepting. Exuberant lovers of life, people, and material comforts. Enjoy working with others to make things happen. Bring common sense and a realistic approach to their work and make work fun. Flexible and spontaneous, adapt readily to new people and environments. Learn best by trying a new skill with other people.

ENFP
Warmly enthusiastic and imaginative. See life as full of possibilities. Make connections between events and information very quickly, and confidently proceed based on the patterns they see. Want a lot of affirmation from others, and readily give appreciation and support. Spontaneous and flexible, often rely on their ability to improvise and their verbal fluency.

ENTP
Quick, ingenious, stimulating alert, and outspoken. Resourceful in solving new and challenging problems. Adept at generating conceptual possibilities and then analyzing them strategically. Good at reading other people. Bored by routine, will seldom do the same thing the same way, apt to turn to one new interest after another.

ESTJ
Practical, realistic, matter-of-fact. Decisive, quickly move to implement decisions. Organize projects and people to get things done, focus on getting results in the most efficient way possible. Take care of routine details. Have a clear set of logical standards, systematically follow them and want others to also. Forceful in implementing their plans.

ESFJ
Warmhearted, conscientious, and cooperative. Want harmony in their environment, work with determination to establish it. Like to work with others to complete tasks accurately and on time. Loyal, follow through even in small matters. Notice what others need in their day-by-day lives and try to provide it. Want to be appreciated for who they are and for what they contribute.

ENFJ
Warm, empathetic, responsive, and responsible. Highly attuned to the emotions, needs, and motivations of others. Find potential in everyone, want to help others fulfill their potential. May act as catalysts for individual and group growth. Loyal, responsive to praise and criticism. Sociable, facilitate others in a group, and provide inspiring leadership.

ENTJ
Frank, decisive, assume leadership readily. Quickly see logical and inefficient procedures and policies, develop and implement comprehensive systems to solve organizational problems. Enjoy long-term planning and goal setting. Usually well informed, well read, enjoy expanding their knowledge and passing it on to others. Forceful in presenting their ideas.

NOTE: I = introvert; E = extravert; S = sensor; N = intuitor; T = thinker; F = feeler; J = judger; and P = perceiver.

Three major categories of factors influence our perception of another person: characteristics of ourselves, as perceivers; characteristics of the target person we are perceiving; and characteristics of the situation in which the interaction takes place. Figure 3.2 shows a model of social perception.

Characteristics of the Perceiver

Several characteristics of the perceiver can affect social perception. One such characteristic is *familiarity* with the target (the person being perceived). When we are familiar with a person, we have multiple observations on which to base our impression of him or her. If the information we have gathered during these observations is accurate, we may have an accurate perception of the other person. Familiarity does not always mean accuracy, however. Sometimes, when we know a person well, we tend to screen out information that is inconsistent with what we believe the person is like. This is a particular danger in performance appraisals where the rater is familiar with the person being rated.

The perceiver's *attitudes* also affect social perception. Suppose you are interviewing candidates for a very important position in your organization— a position that requires negotiating contracts with suppliers, most of whom

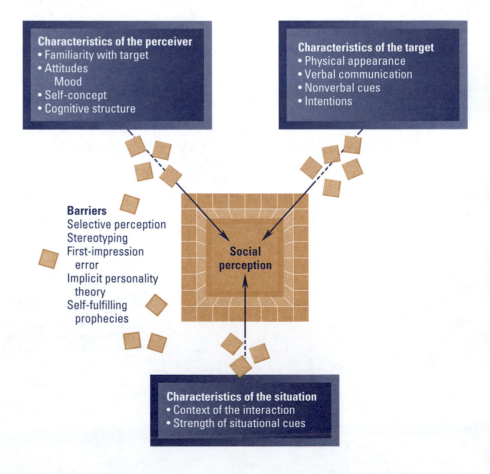

Figure 3.2
A Model for Social Perception

Characteristics of the perceiver
• Familiarity with target
• Attitudes
   Mood
• Self-concept
• Cognitive structure

Characteristics of the target
• Physical appearance
• Verbal communication
• Nonverbal cues
• Intentions

Barriers
Selective perception
Stereotyping
First-impression
   error
Implicit personality
   theory
Self-fulfilling
   prophecies

Social perception

Characteristics of the situation
• Context of the interaction
• Strength of situational cues

are male. You may feel that women are not capable of holding their own in tough negotiations. This attitude will doubtless affect your perceptions of the female candidates you interview.

Mood can have a strong influence on the way we perceive someone.[50] We think differently when we are happy than we do when we are depressed. In addition, we remember information that is consistent with our mood state better than information that is inconsistent with our mood state. When in a positive mood, we form more positive impressions of others. When in a negative mood, we tend to evaluate others unfavorably.

Another factor that can affect social perception is the perceiver's *self-concept*. An individual with a positive self-concept tends to notice positive attributes in another person. In contrast, a negative self-concept can lead a perceiver to pick out negative traits in another person. Greater understanding of self allows us to have more accurate perceptions of others.

Cognitive structure, an individual's pattern of thinking, also affects social perception. Some people have a tendency to perceive physical traits, such as height, weight, and appearance, more readily. Others tend to focus more on central traits, or personality dispositions. Cognitive complexity allows a person to perceive multiple characteristics of another person rather than attending to just a few traits.

Characteristics of the Target

Characteristics of the target, who is the person being perceived, influence social perception. *Physical appearance* plays a big role in our perception of others. The perceiver will notice the target's physical features like height, weight, estimated age, race, and gender. Clothing says a great deal about a person. Blue pin-striped suits, for example, are decoded to mean banking or Wall Street. Perceivers tend to notice physical appearance characteristics that contrast with the norm, that are intense, or that are new or unusual.[51] A loud person, one who dresses outlandishly, a very tall person, or a hyperactive child will be noticed because he or she provides a contrast to what is commonly encountered. In addition, people who are novel can attract attention. Newcomers or minorities in the organization are examples of novel individuals.

Physical attractiveness often colors our entire impression of another person. Interviewers rate attractive candidates more favorably, and attractive candidates are awarded higher starting salaries.[52, 53] People who are perceived as physically attractive face stereotypes as well. We will discuss these and other stereotypes later in this chapter.

Verbal communication from targets also affects our perception of them. We listen to the topics they speak about, their voice tone, and their accent and make judgments based on this input.

Nonverbal communication conveys a great deal of information about the target. Eye contact, facial expressions, body movements, and posture all are deciphered by the perceiver in an attempt to form an impression of the target. It is interesting that some nonverbal signals mean very different things in different cultures. The "okay" sign in the United States (forming a circle with the thumb and forefinger) is an insult in South America. Facial expressions, however, seem to have universal meanings. Individuals from different cultures are able to recognize and decipher expressions the same way.[54]

The *intentions* of the target are inferred by the perceiver, who observes the target's behavior. We may see our boss appear in our office doorway and think, "Oh no! She's going to give me more work to do." Or we may perceive that her intention is to congratulate us on a recent success. In any case, the perceiver's interpretation of the target's intentions affects the way the perceiver views the target.

Characteristics of the Situation

The situation in which the interaction between the perceiver and the target takes place also influences the perceiver's impression of the target. The *social context* of the interaction is a major influence. Meeting a professor in his or her office affects your impression in a certain way that may contrast with the impression you would form had you met the professor in a local restaurant. In Japan, social context is very important. Business conversations after working hours or at lunch are taboo. If you try to talk business during these times, you may be perceived as rude.[55]

The *strength of situational cues* also affects social perception. As we discussed earlier in the chapter, some situations provide strong cues as to appropriate behavior. In these situations, we assume that the individual's behavior can be accounted for by the situation, and that it may not reflect the individual's disposition. This is the **discounting principle** in social perception.[56] For example, you may encounter an automobile salesperson who has a warm and personable manner, asks about your work and hobbies, and seems genuinely interested in your taste in cars. Can you assume that this behavior reflects the salesperson's personality? You probably cannot, because of the influence of the situation. This person is trying to sell you a car, and in this particular situation he or she probably treats all customers in this manner.

You can see that characteristics of the perceiver, the target, and the situation all affect social perception. It would be wonderful if all of us had accurate social perception skills. Unfortunately, barriers often prevent us from perceiving another person accurately.

Barriers to Social Perception

Several factors lead us to form inaccurate impressions of others. Five of these barriers to social perception are selective perception, stereotyping, first-impression error, implicit personality theories, and self-fulfilling prophecies.

We receive a vast amount of information. **Selective perception** is our tendency to choose information that supports our viewpoints. Individuals often ignore information that makes them feel uncomfortable or threatens their viewpoints. Suppose, for example, that a sales manager is evaluating

discounting principle
The assumption that an individual's behavior is accounted for by the situation.

selective perception
The process of selecting information that supports our individual viewpoints while discounting information that threatens our viewpoints.

the performance of his employees. One employee does not get along well with colleagues and rarely completes sales reports on time. This employee, however, generates the most new sales contracts in the office. The sales manager may ignore the negative information, choosing to evaluate the salesperson only on contracts generated. The manager is exercising selective perception.

A *stereotype* is a generalization about a group of people. Stereotypes reduce information about other people to a workable level, and they are efficient for compiling and using information. Stereotypes can be accurate, and when they are accurate, they can be useful perceptual guidelines. Most of the time, however, stereotypes are inaccurate. They harm individuals when inaccurate impressions of them are inferred and are never tested or changed.[57] Thus, stereotypes may not be effective if they are too rigid or based on false information.

Suppose that a white male manager passes the coffee area and notices two African American men talking there. He becomes irritated at them for wasting time. Later in the day, he sees two women talking in the coffee area. He thinks they should do their gossiping on their own time. The next morning, the same manager sees two white men talking in the coffee area. He thinks nothing of it; he is sure they are discussing business. The manager may hold a stereotype that women and minorities do not work hard unless closely supervised.

In multicultural work teams, members often stereotype foreign coworkers rather than getting to know them before forming an impression. Team members from less developed countries are often assumed to have less knowledge simply because their homeland is economically or technologically less developed.[58] Stereotypes like these can deflate the productivity of the work team, as well as create low morale.

Attractiveness is a powerful stereotype. We assume that attractive individuals are also warm, kind, sensitive, poised, sociable, outgoing, independent, and strong. Are attractive people really like this? Certainly, all of them are not. A study of romantic relationships showed that most attractive individuals do not fit the stereotype, except for possessing good social skills and being popular.[59]

Some individuals may seem to us to fit the stereotype of attractiveness because our behavior elicits from them behavior that confirms the stereotype. Consider, for example, a situation in which you meet an attractive fellow student. Chances are that you respond positively to this person, because you assume he or she is warm, sociable, and so on. Even though the person may not possess these traits, your positive response may bring out these behaviors in the person. The interaction between the two of you may be channeled such that the stereotype confirms itself.[60]

First impressions are lasting impressions, so the saying goes. Individuals place a good deal of importance on first impressions, and for good reason. We tend to remember what we perceive first about a person, and sometimes we are quite reluctant to change our initial impressions.[61] *First-impression*

Experiencing OB

Inaccurate perceptions lead to many problems between people. Five common barriers to accurate perception are presented at our animated concept and activity site. Choose Perception&Attribution from the "select a topic" pull-down menu, then Perceptual Barriers (Errors) from the "overview tab."

http://www.experiencingob.com

stereotype
A generalization about a group of people.

8. Identify five common barriers to social perception.

first-impression error
The tendency to form lasting opinions about an individual based on initial perceptions.

implicit personality theory
Opinions formed about other people that are based on our own mini-theories about how people behave.

error occurs when we observe a very brief bit of a person's behavior in our first encounter and infer that this behavior reflects what the person is really like. Primacy effects can be particularly dangerous in interviews, given that we form first impressions quickly and that these impressions may be the basis for long-term employment relationships.

Implicit personality theories can also lead to inaccurate perceptions.[62] We tend to have our own mini-theories about how people look and behave. These theories help us organize our perceptions and take shortcuts instead of integrating new information all the time. We are *cognitive misers*. Because the world is complex and ambiguous and we have a limited mental capacity, we try to expend the least amount of effort possible in attempting to make sense of the world.[63] We group traits and appearances into clusters that seem to go together. For example, you may believe that introverted people are also worriers and intellectuals, or that fashionable dressers are also up on current events and like modern music. These implicit personality theories are barriers, because they limit our ability to take in new information when it is available.

self-fulfilling prophecy
The situation in which our expectations about people affect our interaction with them in such a way that our expectations are fulfilled.

Self-fulfilling prophecies are also barriers to social perception. Sometimes our expectations affect the way we interact with others such that we get what we wish for. Self-fulfilling prophecy is also known as the Pygmalion effect, named for the sculptor in Greek mythology who prayed that a statue of a woman he had carved would come to life, a wish that was granted by the gods.

Early studies of self-fulfilling prophecy were conducted in elementary school classrooms. Teachers were given bogus information that some of their pupils had high intellectual potential. These pupils were chosen randomly; there were really no differences among the students. Eight months later, the "gifted" pupils scored significantly higher on an IQ test. The teachers' expectations had elicited growth from these students, and the teachers had given them tougher assignments and more feedback on their performance.[64] Self-fulfilling prophecy has been studied in many settings, including at sea. The Israeli Defense Forces told one group of naval cadets that they probably wouldn't experience seasickness, and even if they did, it wouldn't affect their performance. The self-fulfilling prophecy worked! These cadets were rated better performers than other groups, and they also had less seasickness. The information improved the cadets' self-efficacy—they believed they could perform well even if they became seasick.[65]

The Pygmalion effect has been observed in work organizations as well. A manager's expectations of an individual affect both the manager's behavior toward the individual and the individual's response.[66] For example, suppose your initial impression is that an employee has the potential to move up within the organization. Chances are you will spend a great deal of time coaching and counseling the employee, providing challenging assignments, and grooming the individual for success.

Managers can harness the power of the Pygmalion effect to improve productivity in the organization. It appears that high expectations of individuals come true. Can a manager extend these high expectations to an entire group and have similar positive results? The answer is yes. When a manager expects positive things from a group, the group delivers.[67]

Impression Management

Most people want to make favorable impressions on others. This is particularly true in organizations, where individuals compete for jobs, favorable performance evaluations, and salary increases. The process by which individuals try to control the impressions others have of them is called *impression management*. Individuals use several techniques to control others' impressions of them.[68]

Some impression management techniques are self-enhancing. These techniques focus on enhancing others' impressions of the person using the technique. Name-dropping, which involves mentioning an association with important people in the hopes of improving one's image, is often used. Managing one's appearance is another technique for impression management. Individuals dress carefully for interviews because they want to "look the part" in order to get the job. Self-descriptions, or statements about one's characteristics, are used to manage impressions as well.

Another group of impression management techniques are *other-enhancing*. The aim of these techniques is to focus on the individual whose impression is to be managed. Flattery is a common other-enhancing technique whereby compliments are given to an individual in order to win his or her approval. Favors are also used to gain the approval of others. Agreement with someone's opinion is a technique often used to gain a positive impression.

Some employees may engage in impression management to intentionally look bad at work. Methods for creating a poor impression include decreasing performance, not working to one's potential, skipping work, displaying a bad attitude, or broadcasting one's limitations. Why would someone try to look bad to others? Sometimes employees want to avoid additional work or a particular task. They may try to look bad in hopes of being laid off, or they may create poor impressions in order to get attention.[69]

Are impression management techniques effective? Most of the research has focused on employment interviews, and the results indicate that candidates who engage in impression management by self-promoting performed better in interviews, were more likely to obtain site visits with potential employers, and were more likely to get hired.[70,71] In addition, employees who engage in impression management are rated more favorably in performance appraisals than those who do not.[72]

Impression management seems to have an impact on others' impressions. As long as the impressions conveyed are accurate, this process can be a beneficial one in organizations. If the impressions are found to be false, however, a strongly negative overall impression may result. Furthermore, excessive impression management can lead to the perception that the user is manipulative or insincere.[73] We have discussed the influences on social

impression management
The process by which individuals try to control the impressions others have of them.

perception, the potential barriers to perceiving another person, and impression management. Another psychological process that managers should understand is attribution.

ATTRIBUTION IN ORGANIZATIONS

As human beings, we are innately curious. We are not content merely to observe the behavior of others; rather, we want to know *why* they behave the way they do. We also seek to understand and explain our own behavior. **Attribution theory** explains how we pinpoint the causes of our own behavior and that of other people.[74]

The attributions, or inferred causes, we provide for behavior have important implications in organizations. In explaining the causes of our performance, good or bad, we are asked to explain the behavior that was the basis for the performance.

Internal and External Attributions

Attributions can be made to an internal source of responsibility (something within the individual's control) or an external source (something outside the individual's control). Suppose you perform well on an exam in this course. You might say you aced the test because you are smart or because you studied hard. If you attribute your success to ability or effort, you are making an internal attribution.

Alternatively, you might make an external attribution for your performance. You might say it was an easy test (you would attribute your success to degree of task difficulty) or that you had good luck. In this case, you are attributing your performance to sources beyond your control, or external sources. You can see that internal attributions include such causes as ability and effort, whereas external attributions include causes like task difficulty or luck.

Attribution patterns differ among individuals.[75] Achievement-oriented individuals attribute their success to ability and their failures to lack of effort, both internal causes. Failure-oriented individuals attribute their failures to lack of ability, and they may develop feelings of incompetence as a result of their attributional pattern. Evidence indicates that this attributional pattern also leads to depression.[76]

Attribution theory has many applications in the workplace. The way you explain your own behavior affects your motivation. For example, suppose you must give an important presentation to your executive management group. You believe you have performed well, and your boss tells you that you've done a good job. To what do you attribute your success? If you believe careful preparation and rehearsal led to your success, you're likely to take credit for the performance and to have a sense of self-efficacy about future presentations. If, however, you believe that you were just lucky, you may not be motivated to repeat the performance because you believe you had little influence on the outcome.

---

attribution theory
A theory that explains how individuals pinpoint the causes of their own behavior and that of others.

9. Explain the attribution process and how attributions affect managerial behavior.

Experiencing OB

Success- and failure-oriented persons differ in their attributions of their successes and failures. A table highlighting these differences is presented at our animated concept and activity site. Choose Perception&Attribution from the "select a topic" pull-down menu, then Internal/External Attributions from the "overview tab."

http://www.experiencingob.com

One situation in which a lot of attributions are made is the employment interview. Candidates are often asked to explain the causes of previous performance (Why did you perform poorly in math classes?) to interviewers. In addition, candidates often feel they should justify why they should be hired (I work well with people, so I'm looking for a managerial job). Research shows that successful and unsuccessful candidates differ in the way they make attributions for negative outcomes. Successful candidates are less defensive and make internal attributions for negative events. Unsuccessful candidates attribute negative outcomes to things beyond their control (external attributions), which gives interviewers the impression that the candidate failed to learn from the event. In addition, interviewers fear that the individuals would be likely to blame others when something goes wrong in the workplace.[77]

Attributional Biases

The attribution process may be affected by two very common errors: the fundamental attribution error and the self-serving bias. The tendency to make attributions to internal causes when focusing on someone else's behavior is known as the ***fundamental attribution error***.[78] The other error, ***self-serving bias***, occurs when focusing on one's own behavior. Individuals tend to make internal attributions for their own successes and external attributions for their own failures.[79] In other words, when we succeed, we take credit for it; when we fail, we blame the situation on other people. Organizational Reality 3.2 illustrates how "Chainsaw Al" Dunlap fell prey to self-serving bias. Even CEOs are not immune to these biases.

Both of these biases were illustrated in a study of health care managers who were asked to cite the causes of their employees' poor performance.[80] The managers claimed that internal causes (their employees' lack of effort or lack of ability) were the basis for their employees' poor performance. This is an example of the fundamental attribution error. When the employees were asked to pinpoint the cause of their own performance problems, they blamed a lack of support from the managers (an external cause), which illustrates self-serving bias.

There are cultural differences in these two attribution errors. As described above, these biases apply to people from the United States. In more fatalistic cultures, such as India's, people tend to believe that fate is responsible for much that happens. People in such cultures tend to emphasize external causes of behavior.[81]

In China, people are taught that hard work is the route to accomplishment. When faced with either a success or a failure, Chinese individuals first introspect about whether they tried hard enough or whether their attitude was correct. In a study of attributions for performance in sports, Chinese athletes attributed both their successes and failures to internal causes. Even when the cause of poor athletic performance was clearly external, such as bad weather, the Chinese participants made internal attributions. In terms of the Chinese culture, this attributional pattern is a reflection of moral

fundamental attribution error
The tendency to make attributions to internal causes when focusing on someone else's behavior.

self-serving bias
The tendency to attribute one's own successes to internal causes and one's failures to external causes.

Experiencing OB

We often attribute causes to our own behavior very differently than we attribute causes to others' behaviors. To interact with this idea, visit our animated concept and activity site. Choose Perception&Attribution from the "select a topic" pull-down menu, then Attribution Biases from the "overview tab."

http://www.experiencingob.com

ORGANIZATIONAL REALITY 3.2

"Chainsaw Al's" Self-Serving Bias

Al Dunlap is possibly one of the most notorious men in business, known both for his successes and for his failures. In his case, these successes and failures have been very public, and he has taken credit for the successes and blamed others, or circumstances, for the failures. Is this a case of self-serving bias?

Al Dunlap acquired a reputation as the king of downsizing. At Scott Paper, he fired thousands of employees and sold the company to Kimberly-Clark for huge profits, earning him the nickname "Chainsaw Al." The Scott Paper deal netted him around $100 million. Dunlap wrote a best seller, *Mean Business*, in which he sang his own praises (the subtitle of the book tells it all—*How I Save Bad Companies and Make Good Companies Great*). In the book, he claims he's worth every penny: "I'm a superstar in my field, much like Michael Jordan in basketball and Bruce Springsteen in rock 'n roll" (p. 21).

He was hired in 1996 by Sunbeam, a maker of blenders, electric blankets, and gas grills, and Sunbeam's stock doubled in six weeks. Over the course of a year at Sunbeam, he cut half of Sunbeam's 12,000 employees, cut back its product line, and took massive writeoffs. Dunlap declared victory and put the company up for sale after just a year, but no buyers emerged. Instead, Dunlap bought three consumer products companies. With tricky accounting, the acquisitions looked good. When his accounting tricks were uncovered, however, Sunbeam had over $2 billion in debt and a negative cash flow. It was in worse shape than when "Chainsaw Al" took over.

Dunlap blamed the results on an executive he fired, on underlings who were allowed to make "stupid, low-margin deals," and even on El Niño—"People don't think about buying grills during a storm." He claimed he was blindsided by the bad results. Facing the board of directors, he claimed that a billionaire financier was conspiring to buy the company at a bargain by orchestrating a torrent of negative media coverage.

The board didn't buy his story. Chainsaw Al got the ax. Would the situation have been different if he had owned up to the failures? We will never know.

Discussion Question

1. How did "Chainsaw Al" exhibit self-serving bias? Do you think things would have turned out differently if he had made more accurate attributions?

SOURCES: P. Sellers, "Exit for Chainsaw?" *Fortune* (June 8, 1998): 300–331; M. Schifrin, "The Unkindest Cut," *Forbes* (May 4, 1998): 44–45; A. Dunlap and B. Andelman, *Mean Business* (New York: Random House, 1996).

values that are used to evaluate behavior. The socialistic value of selfless morality dictates that individual striving must serve collective interests. Mao Ze-dong stressed that external causes function only through internal causes; therefore, the main cause of results lies within oneself. Chinese are taught this from childhood and form a corresponding attributional tendency. In analyzing a cause, they first look to their own effort.[82]

The way individuals interpret the events around them has a strong influence on their behavior. People try to understand the causes of behavior in order to gain predictability and control over future behavior. Managers use attributions in all aspects of their jobs. In evaluating performance and rewarding employees, managers must determine the causes of behavior and a perceived source of responsibility. One tough call managers often make is whether allegations of sexual harassment actually resulted from sexual conduct and, if harassment did occur, what should be done about it. To make such tough calls, managers use attributions.

Attribution theory can explain how performance evaluation judgments can lead to differential rewards. A supervisor attributing an employee's good performance to internal causes, such as effort or ability, may give a larger raise than a supervisor attributing the good performance to external causes, such as help from others or good training. Managers are often called on to explain their own actions as well, and in doing so they make attributions about the causes of their own behavior. We continue our discussion of attributions in Chapter 6 in terms of how attributions are used in managing employee performance.

MANAGERIAL IMPLICATIONS: USING PERSONALITY, PERCEPTION, AND ATTRIBUTION AT WORK

Managers need to know as much as possible about individual differences in order to understand themselves and those with whom they work. An understanding of personality characteristics can help a manager appreciate differences in employees. With the increased diversity of the workforce, tools like the MBTI can be used to help employees see someone else's point of view. These tools can also help make communication among diverse employees more effective.

Managers use social perception constantly on the job. Knowledge of the forces that affect perception and the barriers to accuracy can help the manager form more accurate impressions of others.

Determining the causes of job performance is a major task for the manager, and attribution theory can be used to explain how managers go about determining causality. In addition, knowledge of the fundamental attribution error and self-serving bias can help a manager guard against these biases in the processes of looking for causes of behavior on the job.

In this chapter, we have explored the psychological processes of personality, perception, and attribution as individual differences. In the following chapter, we will continue our discussion of individual differences in terms of attitudes, values, and ethics.

Looking Back

Oprah's Reflections on Management

Many of us see Oprah, the television celebrity, rather than Oprah, head of Harpo Productions. Let's take a look at her role as manager, and her view of it, in her own words. Here are a few of her thoughts on management.

On management style:

> To me one of the most important things about being a good manager is to rule with a heart. You have to know the business, but you also have to know what's at the heart of the business, and that's the people. People matter.
>
> You have to surround yourself with people you trust, and people that are good. But they also have to be people who will tell the emperor you have no clothes.

She inspires loyalty by treating people "like I would want to be treated, and I allow them to make mistakes."

On the 1994 personnel shakeup at Harpo Productions:

> I made mistakes. My goal is to be fair.

On decision making at Harpo:

> I don't do anything unless it feels good. I don't move on logic. I move on my gut. And I have a good gut.

On her personal mission:

> My fortune gives me choices. If a child is in need, I help. My money enables me to make an important difference in people's lives.

On Harpo's mission:

> The mission of Harpo Productions is "to inform, enlighten, uplift and entertain; to use our lives and voices as a means of service to the viewing public."[83]

CHAPTER SUMMARY

1. Individual differences are factors that make individuals unique. They include personalities, perceptions, skills and abilities, attitudes, values, and ethics.

2. The trait theory, psychodynamic theory, humanistic theory, and integrative approach are all personality theories.

3. Managers should understand personality because of its effect on behavior. Several characteristics affect behavior in organizations, including locus of control, self-esteem, self-monitoring, and positive/negative affect.

4. Personality has a stronger influence in weak situations, where there are few cues to guide behavior.

5. One useful framework for understanding individual differences is type theory, developed by Carl Jung and measured by the Myers-Briggs Type Indicator (MBTI).

6. Social perception is the process of interpreting information about another person. It is influenced by characteristics of the perceiver, the target, and the situation.

7. Barriers to social perception include selective perception, stereotyping, first-impression error, implicit personality theories, and self-fulfilling prophecies.

8. Impression management techniques such as name-dropping, managing one's appearance, self-

descriptions, flattery, favors, and agreement are used by individuals to control others' impressions of them.

9. Attribution is the process of determining the cause of behavior. It is used extensively by managers, especially in evaluating performance.

KEY TERMS

individual differences   71

interactional psychology   71

personality   72

trait theory   73

psychodynamic theory   73

humanistic theory   74

integrative approach   74

locus of control   75

self-esteem   75

self-monitoring   76

positive affect   78

negative affect   78

strong situation   78

projective test   79

behavioral measures   79

self-report questionnaire   79

Myers-Briggs Type Indicator (MBTI)   80

extraversion   80

introversion   80

sensing   81

intuiting   81

thinking   81

feeling   81

judging   82

perceiving   82

social perception   83

discounting principle   88

selective perception   88

stereotype   89

first-impression error   89

implicit personality theory   90

self-fulfilling prophecy   90

impression management   91

attribution theory   92

fundamental attribution error   93

self-serving bias   93

REVIEW QUESTIONS

1. What are individual differences, and why should managers understand them?
2. Define *personality*, and describe its origins.
3. Describe four theories of personality and explain what each contributes to our knowledge of personality.
4. Describe the eight preferences of the Myers-Briggs

Type Indicator. How does this instrument measure Carl Jung's ideas?
5. What factors influence social perception? What are the barriers to social perception?
6. Describe the errors that affect the attribution process.

DISCUSSION AND COMMUNICATION QUESTIONS

1. What contributions can high self-monitors make in organizations? Low self-monitors?
2. How can managers improve their perceptual skills?
3. Which has the stronger impact on personality: heredity or environment?
4. How can managers make more accurate attributions?
5. How can managers encourage self-efficacy in employees?
6. How can self-serving bias and the fundamental attribution error be avoided?
7. (*communication question*) You have been asked to develop a training program for interviewers. An

integral part of this training program focuses on helping interviewers develop better social perception skills. Write an outline for this section of the training program. Be sure to address barriers to social perception and ways to avoid these barriers.
8. (*communication question*) Form groups of four to six, then split each group in half. Debate the origins of personality, with one half taking the position that personality is inherited, and the other half taking the position that personality is formed by the environment. Each half should also discuss the implications of its position for managers.

ETHICS QUESTIONS

1. What are the ethical uses of personality tests? What are the unethical uses?

2. Suppose a manager makes an incorrect attribution for an employee's poor performance (for instance, the manager cites equipment failure), and peers know the employee is at fault. Should they blow the whistle on their colleague?

3. Suppose one of your colleagues wants to eliminate all biases and stereotypes from the hiring process.

He suggests that only résumés be used, with no names or other identifying data—only experience and education. What are the ethical consequences of this approach? Would any group be unfairly disadvantaged by this approach?

4. Suppose a manager makes a misattribution of an employee's poor performance. What are the ethical consequences of this?

Experiential Exercises

3.1 MBTI Types and Management Styles

Part I. This questionnaire will help you determine your preferences. For each item, circle either a or b. If you feel both a and b are true, decide which one is more like you, even if it is only slightly more true.

1. I would rather
   a. Solve a new and complicated problem.
   b. Work on something I have done before.

2. I like to
   a. Work alone in a quiet place.
   b. Be where the action is.

3. I want a boss who
   a. Establishes and applies criteria in decisions.
   b. Considers individual needs and makes exceptions.

4. When I work on a project, I
   a. Like to finish it and get some closure.
   b. Often leave it open for possible changes.

5. When making a decision, the most important considerations are
   a. Rational thoughts, ideas, and data.
   b. People's feelings and values.

6. On a project, I tend to
   a. Think it over and over before deciding how to proceed.
   b. Start working on it right away, thinking about it as I go along.

7. When working on a project, I prefer to
   a. Maintain as much control as possible.
   b. Explore various options.

8. In my work, I prefer to
   a. Work on several projects at a time, and learn as much as possible about each one.
   b. Have one project that is challenging and keeps me busy.

9. I often
   a. Make lists and plans whenever I start something and may hate to seriously alter my plans.
   b. Avoid plans and just let things progress as I work on them.

10. When discussing a problem with colleagues, it is easy for me to
    a. See "the big picture."
    b. Grasp the specifics of the situation.

11. When the phone rings in my office or at home, I usually
    a. Consider it an interruption.
    b. Do not mind answering it.

12. Which word describes you better?
    a. Analytical.
    b. Empathetic.

13. When I am working on an assignment, I tend to
    a. Work steadily and consistently.
    b. Work in bursts of energy with "down time" in between.

14. When I listen to someone talk on a subject, I usually try to
    a. Relate it to my own experience and see if it fits.
    b. Assess and analyze the message.

15. When I come up with new ideas, I generally
    a. "Go for it."
    b. Like to contemplate the ideas some more.

16. When working on a project, I prefer to
    a. Narrow the scope so it is clearly defined.
    b. Broaden the scope to include related aspects.

17. When I read something, I usually
    a. Confine my thoughts to what is written there.
    b. Read between the lines and relate the words to other ideas.

18. When I have to make a decision in a hurry, I often
    a. Feel uncomfortable and wish I had more information.
    b. Am able to do so with available data.

19. In a meeting, I tend to
    a. Continue formulating my ideas as I talk about them.
    b. Only speak out after I have carefully thought the issue through.

20. In work, I prefer spending a great deal of time on issues of
    a. Ideas.
    b. People.

21. In meetings, I am most often annoyed with people who

a. Come up with many sketchy ideas.
b. Lengthen meetings with many practical details.

22. I am a
    a. Morning person.
    b. Night owl.

23. What is your style in preparing for a meeting?
    a. I am willing to go in and be responsive.
    b. I like to be fully prepared and usually sketch an outline of the meeting.

24. In a meeting, I would prefer for people to
    a. Display a fuller range of emotions.
    b. Be more task oriented.

25. I would rather work for an organization where
    a. My job was intellectually stimulating.
    b. I was committed to its goals and mission.

26. On weekends, I tend to
    a. Plan what I will do.
    b. Just see what happens and decide as I go along.

27. I am more
    a. Outgoing.
    b. Contemplative.

28. I would rather work for a boss who is
    a. Full of new ideas.
    b. Practical.

In the following, choose the word in each pair that appeals to you more:

29. a. Social.
    b. Theoretical.

30. a. Ingenuity.
    b. Practicality.

31. a. Organized.
    b. Adaptable.

32. a. Active.
    b. Concentration.

SCORING KEY

Count one point for each item listed below that you have circled in the inventory.

Score for I	Score for E	Score for S	Score for N
2a	2b	1b	1a
6a	6b	10b	10a
11a	11b	13a	13b
15b	15a	16a	16b
19b	19a	17a	17b
22a	22b	21a	21b
27b	27a	28b	28a
32b	32a	30b	30a

Total ___

Circle the one with more points—I or E.

Circle the one with more points—S or N.

Score for T	Score for F	Score for J	Score for P
3a	3b	4a	4b
5a	5b	7a	7b
12a	12b	8b	8a
14b	14a	9a	9b
20a	20b	18b	18a
24b	24a	23b	23a
25a	25b	26a	26b
29b	29a	31a	31b

Total ___

Circle the one with more points—T or F.

Circle the one with more points—J or P.

Your score is

I or E ____   T or F ____

S or N ____   J or P ____

Part II. The purpose of this part of the exercise is to give you experience in understanding some of the individual differences that were proposed by Carl Jung and are measured by the MBTI.

Step 1. Your instructor will assign you to a group.

Step 2. Your group is a team of individuals who want to start a business. You are to develop a mission statement and a name for your business.

Step 3. After you have completed Step 2, analyze the decision process that occurred within the group. How did you decide on your company's name and mission?

Step 4. Your instructor will have each group report to the class the name and mission of the company, and then the decision process used. Your instructor will also give you some additional information about the exercise and provide some interesting insights about your management style.

SOURCE: "MBTI Types and Management Styles" from D. Marcic and P. Nutt, "Personality Inventory," in D. Marcic, ed., *Organizational Behavior: Experiences and Cases* (St. Paul: West, 1989), 9–16. Reprinted by permission.

3.2 Stereotypes in Employment Interviews

Step 1. Your instructor will give you a transcript that records an applicant's interview for a job as a laborer. Your task is to memorize as much of the interview as possible.

Step 2. Write down everything you can remember about the job candidate.

Step 3. Your instructor will lead you in a discussion.

SOURCE: Adapted from D. A. Sachau and M. Hussang, "How Interviewers' Stereotypes Influence Memory: An Exercise," *Journal of Management Education* 16 (1992): 391–396. Copyright © 1992 by Sage Publications. Reprinted with permission of Sage Publications, Inc.

For more practice exercises, consult the fifth edition of *Organizational Behavior: Experiences and Cases* by Dorothy Marcic and Joseph Seltzer (South-Western, 1998).

Learning Objectives

After reading this chapter, you should be able to do the following:

1. Explain the ABC model of an attitude. *p. 103*

2. Describe how attitudes are formed. *p. 105*

3. Define *job satisfaction* and *organizational commitment* and discuss the importance of these two work attitudes. *p. 108*

4. Identify the characteristics of the source, target, and message that affect persuasion. *p. 114*

5. Distinguish between instrumental and terminal values. *p. 116*

6. Explain how managers can deal with the diverse value systems that characterize the global environment. *p. 120*

7. Describe a model of individual and organizational influences on ethical behavior. *p. 123*

8. Discuss how value systems, locus of control, Machiavellianism, and cognitive moral development affect ethical behavior. *p. 124*

4

Attitudes, Values, and Ethics

Thinking Ahead

Starbucks' Values Are Reflected in Its Mission Statement

Starbucks' first chairman and CEO, Howard Schultz, wanted the company to have a mission statement that represented its values: people first, profits last. The mission statement is an organic body of beliefs and founding principles that all Starbucks' partners (Starbucks' term for employees) hold in common. It is more than a decoration for the walls—instead, it reflects the basic values that guide behavior in the company.

Starbucks Mission Statement

Establish Starbucks as the premier purveyor of the finest coffee in the world while maintaining our uncompromising principles as we grow. The following six guiding principles will help us measure the appropriateness of our decisions.

*Provide a great work environment and treat
each other with respect and dignity.*

*Embrace diversity as an essential component
in the way we do business.*

*Apply the highest standards of excellence
to the purchasing, roasting, and fresh
delivery of our coffee.*

*Develop enthusiastically satisfied
customers all of the time.*

*Contribute positively to our communities
and our environment.*

*Recognize that profitability is essential
to our future success.*

Starbucks' partners helped craft the mission statement, and it is a vital link to the values of the large and scattered workforce. A "mission review" team was created to examine behaviors that are not in accordance with the values. Partners can make a suggestion or report actions that seem contradictory to the values, and managers reply within two weeks. Hundreds of suggestions are submitted each year, and actions are taken to align behavior with the values expressed in the mission statement. In this way, partners monitor both themselves and management and hold managers to their own high standards.[1]

You'll note that one important company value is contributing positively to the environment. In the Looking Back segment, we'll examine the ways that Starbucks implements this value.

In this chapter, we continue the discussion of individual differences we began in Chapter 3 with personality, perception, and attribution. Persons and situations jointly influence behavior, and individual differences help us to better understand the influence of the person. Our focus now is on three other individual difference factors: attitudes, values, and ethics.

ATTITUDES

attitude
A psychological tendency expressed by evaluating an entity with some degree of favor or disfavor.

An *attitude* is a psychological tendency that is expressed by evaluating a particular entity with some degree of favor or disfavor.[2] We respond favorably or unfavorably toward many things: animals, coworkers, our own appearance, politics.

Attitudes are important because of their links to behavior. Attitudes are also an integral part of the world of work. Managers speak of workers who have "bad attitudes" and conduct "attitude adjustment" talks with employees. Often, poor performance attributed to bad attitudes really stems from lack of motivation, minimal feedback, lack of trust in management, or other problems. These are areas that managers must explore.

Organizational Reality 4.1 presents the story of an unusual pair in business: a staid, white, British CEO and a young, black, upstart engineer. They refused to let attitudes get in their way, and the result has been a change in their company's culture.

You can see that it is important for managers to understand the antecedents to attitudes as well as their consequences. Managers also need to understand the different components of attitudes, how attitudes are formed, the major attitudes that affect work behavior, and how to use persuasion to change attitudes.

The ABC Model

Attitudes develop on the basis of evaluative responding. An individual does not have an attitude until he or she responds to an entity (person, object, situation, issue) on an affective, cognitive, or behavioral basis. To understand the complexity of an attitude, we can break it down into three components, as depicted in Table 4.1.

These components—affect, behavioral intentions, and cognition—compose what we call the ABC model of an attitude.[3] *Affect* is the emotional component of an attitude. It refers to an individual's feeling about something or someone. Statements such as "I like this" or "I prefer that" reflect the affective component of an attitude. Affect is measured by physiological indicators such as galvanic skin response (changes in electrical resistance of skin that indicate emotional arousal) and blood pressure. These indicators show changes in emotions by measuring physiological arousal. An individual's attempt to hide his or her feelings might be shown by a change in arousal.

The second component is the intention to behave in a certain way toward an object or person. Our attitudes toward women in management, for

1. Explain the ABC model of an attitude.

affect
The emotional component of an attitude.

Table 4.1
The ABC Model of an Attitude

	Component	Measured By	Example
A	Affect	Physiological indicators Verbal statements about feelings	I don't like my boss.
B	Behavioral intentions	Observed behavior Verbal statements about intentions	I want to transfer to another department.
C	Cognition	Attitude scales Verbal statements about beliefs	I believe my boss plays favorites at work.

SOURCE: Adapted from M. J. Rosenberg and C. I. Hovland, "Cognitive, Affective, and Behavioral Components of Attitude," in M. J. Rosenberg, C. I. Hovland, W. J. McGuire, R. P. Abelson, and J. H. Brehm, *Attitude Organization and Change* (New Haven: Yale University Press, 1960). Copyright 1960 Yale University Press. Used with permission.

ORGANIZATIONAL REALITY 4.1

New Attitudes at Xionics Brought About by an Unusual Partnership

Xionics Document Technologies was not your typical high-tech firm. It had a conservative dress code, and even supposedly "fun" activities didn't materialize. An opening-day baseball party fell through when managers objected to employees watching the game on television. Young engineers ignored the company in favor of the flashier and more liberal Silicon Valley firms.

Attitudes changed at the company, however, due to an unusual partnership. Robert Gilkes, Xionics's former chairman, was fifty-eight, white, and British. His background included three years as a magistrate in an African colony, and his bearing and aloofness led most employees to address him as "sir." Omar Green was twenty-seven, black, and a graduate of MIT. His usual fashion at work was three earrings, lots of hair gel, baggy pants, and oversized T-shirts. Mr. Gilkes invited Mr. Green to his customary open-door session and said, "So, Omar, tell me what's wrong with Xionics."

Green took advantage of the moment, telling Gilkes that the company lacked vision and innovation, and spent the next hour describing new markets, the Internet, and ways to make Xionics's culture more entrepreneurial. Gilkes was energized by Green's honesty. Green was ". . . prepared to talk to me as an equal, saying what he thought was right, not what he thought I wanted to hear." Since that meeting, Green became a key player in the company's journey to change. He was the junior member of a group that meets twice a month to discuss strategy. His days often ended in Gilkes's office, with discussions of new personnel, products, and the competition. The bond between Gilkes and Green can be described as a partnership, a friendship, and a mentor–protégé relationship. It is unique, however, in that in most similar relationships, CEOs seek out employees just like themselves. Attitudes didn't prevent the two from forging a dynamic partnership.

In their first discussion during the open-door policy, Green thought Gilkes would grill him on the race issue—that didn't happen. "The fact that he was a funky-style dresser suggested that he would have ideas that were younger," said Gilkes. "I wanted to see if we could connect." That connection was a crucial one in the drive to turn Xionics around.

Xionics changed its culture. Dress codes were relaxed. Managers were told to stop hiring in their own images. And attitudes changed, thanks to a duo who did not let their own attitudes get in the way. Xionics was acquired by Oak Technologies in 1999 and became the Oak Imaging Group.

Discussion Question

1. What stereotypes did Mr. Gilkes and Mr. Green have to overcome in order to work together? Are stereotypes ever a good thing?

SOURCE: J. Kaufman, "The Funky-Style Dresser," *The Wall Street Journal*, July 22, 1997, A1. Permission conveyed through Copyright Clearance Center, Inc.

example, may be inferred from observing the way we behave toward a female supervisor. We may be supportive, passive, or hostile, depending on our attitude. The behavioral component of an attitude is measured by observing behavior or by asking a person about behavior or intentions. The statement "If I were asked to speak at commencement, I'd be willing to try to do so, even though I'd be nervous" reflects a behavioral intention.

The third component of an attitude, cognition (thought), reflects a person's perceptions or beliefs. Cognitive elements are evaluative beliefs and are measured by attitude scales or by asking about thoughts. The statement

"I believe Japanese workers are industrious" reflects the cognitive component of an attitude.

The ABC model shows that to thoroughly understand an attitude, we must assess all three components. Suppose, for example, you want to evaluate your employees' attitudes toward flextime (flexible work scheduling). You would want to determine how they feel about flextime (affect), whether they would use flextime (behavioral intention), and what they think about the policy (cognition). The most common method of attitude measurement, the attitude scale, measures only the cognitive component.

As rational beings, individuals try to be consistent in everything they believe in and do. They prefer consistency (consonance) between their attitudes and behavior. Anything that disrupts this consistency causes tension (dissonance), which motivates individuals to change either their attitudes or their behavior to return to a state of consistency. The tension produced when there is a conflict between attitudes and behavior is *cognitive dissonance*.[4]

Suppose, for example, a salesperson is required to sell damaged televisions for the full retail price, without revealing the damage to customers. She believes, however, that doing so constitutes unethical behavior. This creates a conflict between her attitude (concealing information from customers is unethical) and her behavior (selling defective TVs without informing customers about the damage).

The salesperson, experiencing the discomfort from dissonance, will try to resolve the conflict. She might change her behavior by refusing to sell the defective TV sets. Alternatively, she might rationalize that the defects are minor and that the customers will not be harmed by not knowing about them. These are attempts by the salesperson to restore equilibrium between her attitudes and behavior, thereby eliminating the tension from cognitive dissonance.

Managers need to understand cognitive dissonance because employees often find themselves in situations in which their attitudes conflict with their behavior. They manage the tension by changing their attitudes or behavior. Employees who display sudden shifts in behavior may be attempting to reduce dissonance. Some employees find the conflicts between strongly held attitudes and required work behavior so uncomfortable that they leave the organization to escape the dissonance.

Attitude Formation

Attitudes are learned. Our responses to people and issues evolve over time. Two major influences on attitudes are direct experience and social learning.

Direct experience with an object or person is a powerful influence on attitudes. How do you know that you like biology or dislike math? You have probably formed these attitudes from experience in studying the subjects. Research has shown that attitudes that are derived from direct experience are stronger, held more confidently, and more resistant to change than attitudes formed through indirect experience.[5] One reason attitudes derived

cognitive dissonance
A state of tension that is produced when an individual experiences conflict between attitudes and behavior.

2. ■ Describe how attitudes are formed.

social learning
The process of deriving attitudes from family, peer groups, religious organizations, and culture.

from direct experience are so powerful is their availability. This means that the attitudes are easily accessed and are active in our cognitive processes.[6] When attitudes are available, we can call them quickly into consciousness. Attitudes that are not learned from direct experience are not as available, so we do not recall them as easily.

In *social learning*, the family, peer groups, religious organizations, and culture shape an individual's attitudes in an indirect manner.[7] Children learn to adopt certain attitudes by the reinforcement they are given by their parents when they display behaviors that reflect an appropriate attitude. This is evident when very young children express political preferences similar to their parents'. Peer pressure molds attitudes through group acceptance of individuals who express popular attitudes and through sanctions, such as exclusion from the group, placed on individuals who espouse unpopular attitudes.

Substantial social learning occurs through *modeling*, in which individuals acquire attitudes by merely observing others. After overhearing other individuals expressing an opinion or watching them engaging in a behavior that reflects an attitude, the observer adopts the attitude.

For an individual to learn from observing a model, four processes must take place:

1. The learner must focus attention on the model.
2. The learner must retain what was observed from the model. Retention is accomplished in two basic ways. In one, the learner "stamps in" what was observed by forming a verbal code for it. The other way is through symbolic rehearsal, by which the learner forms a mental image of himself or herself behaving like the model.
3. Behavioral reproduction must occur; that is, the learner must practice the behavior.
4. The learner must be motivated to learn from the model.

Culture also plays a definitive role in attitude development. Consider, for example, the contrast in the North American and European attitudes toward vacation and leisure. The typical vacation in the United States is two weeks, and some workers do not use all of their vacation time. In Europe, the norm is longer vacations; and in some countries, *holiday* means everyone taking a month off. The European attitude is that an investment in longer vacations is important to health and performance.

Attitudes and Behavior

If you have a favorable attitude toward participative management, will your management style be participative? As managers, if we know an employee's attitude, to what extent can we predict the person's behavior? These questions illustrate the fundamental issue of attitude–behavior correspondence, that is, the degree to which an attitude predicts behavior.

This correspondence has concerned organizational behaviorists and social psychologists for quite some time. Can attitudes predict behaviors like being absent from work or quitting your job? Some studies suggested that attitudes and behavior are closely linked, while others found no relationship at all or a weak relationship at best. Attention then became focused on when attitudes predict behavior and when they do not. Attitude–behavior correspondence depends on five things: attitude specificity, attitude relevance, timing of measurement, personality factors, and social constraints.

Individuals possess both general and specific attitudes. You may favor women's right to reproductive freedom (a general attitude) and prefer prochoice political candidates (a specific attitude), but not attend pro-choice rallies or send money to Planned Parenthood. That you don't perform these behaviors may make the link between your attitude and behavior on this issue seem rather weak. However, given a choice between a pro-choice and an anti-abortion political candidate you will probably vote for the pro-choice candidate. In this case, your attitude seems quite predictive of your behavior. The point is that the greater the attitude specificity, the stronger its link to behavior.[8]

Another factor that affects the attitude–behavior link is relevance.[9] Attitudes that address an issue in which we have some self-interest are more relevant for us, and our subsequent behavior is consistent with our expressed attitude. Suppose there is a proposal to raise income taxes on those who earn $150,000 or more. If you are a student, you may not find the issue of great personal relevance. Individuals in that income bracket, however, might find it highly relevant; their attitude toward the issue would be strongly predictive of whether they would vote for the tax increase.

The timing of the measurement also affects attitude–behavior correspondence. The shorter the time between the attitude measurement and the observed behavior, the stronger the relationship. For example, voter preference polls taken close to an election are more accurate than earlier polls are.

Personality factors also influence the attitude–behavior link. One personality disposition that affects the consistency between attitudes and behavior is self-monitoring. Recall from Chapter 3 that low self-monitors rely on their internal states when making decisions about behavior, while high self-monitors are more responsive to situational cues. Low self-monitors therefore display greater correspondence between their attitudes and behaviors.[10] High self-monitors may display little correspondence between their attitudes and behavior because they behave according to signals from others and from the environment.

Finally, social constraints affect the relationship between attitudes and behavior.[11] The social context provides information about acceptable attitudes and behaviors.[12, 13] New employees in an organization, for example, are exposed to the attitudes of their work group. Suppose a newcomer from Afghanistan holds a negative attitude toward women in management because in his country the prevailing attitude is that women should not be in positions of power. He sees, however, that his work group members respond positively to their female supervisor. His own behavior may therefore be

job satisfaction
A pleasurable or positive emotional state resulting from the appraisal of one's job or job experiences.

3. Define *job satisfaction* and *organizational commitment* and discuss the importance of these two work attitudes.

compliant because of social constraints. This behavior is inconsistent with his attitude and cultural belief system.

Work Attitudes

Attitudes at work are important because, directly or indirectly, they affect work behavior. This was dramatically illustrated in a comparison of the product quality of air conditioners manufactured in the United States versus those made in Japan.[14] In general, there is a perception that Japanese products are of higher quality. When air conditioners from nine U.S. plants and seven Japanese plants were compared, the results were bad news for the U.S. plants. The Japanese products had significantly fewer defects than the U.S. products.

The researchers continued their study by asking managers in both countries' plants about their attitudes toward various goals. Japanese supervisors reported that their companies had strong attitudes favoring high-quality products, while U.S. supervisors reported quality goals to be less important. U.S. supervisors reported strong attitudes favoring the achievement of production scheduling goals, while Japanese supervisors indicated that schedules were less important. The researchers concluded that the attitudes of U.S. managers toward quality were at least partly responsible for lower quality products.

Although many work attitudes are important, two attitudes in particular have been emphasized. Job satisfaction and organizational commitment are key attitudes of interest to managers and researchers.

Job Satisfaction   Most of us believe that work should be a positive experience. *Job satisfaction* is a pleasurable or positive emotional state resulting from the appraisal of one's job or job experiences.[15] It has been treated both as a general attitude and as satisfaction with five specific dimensions of the job: pay, the work itself, promotion opportunities, supervision, and coworkers.[16] You can assess your own job satisfaction by completing Challenge 4.1.

An individual may hold different attitudes toward various aspects of the job. For example, an employee may like her job responsibilities but be dissatisfied with the opportunities for promotion. Characteristics of individuals also affect job satisfaction. Those with high negative affectivity are more likely to be dissatisfied with their jobs. Challenging work, valued rewards, opportunities for advancement, competent supervision, and supportive coworkers are dimensions of the job that can lead to satisfaction.

There are several measures of job satisfaction. One of the most widely used measures comes from the Job Descriptive Index (JDI). This index measures the specific facets of satisfaction by asking employees to respond yes, no, or cannot decide to a series of statements describing their jobs. Another popular measure is the Minnesota Satisfaction Questionnaire (MSQ).[17] This survey also asks employees to respond to statements about their jobs, using a five-point scale that ranges from very dissatisfied to very satisfied. Figure 4.1 presents some sample items from each questionnaire.

Challenge 4.1

Assess Your Job Satisfaction

Think of the job you have now or a job you've had in the past. Indicate how satisfied you are with each aspect of your job below, using the following scale:

1 = Extremely dissatisfied
2 = Dissatisfied
3 = Slightly dissatisfied
4 = Neutral
5 = Slightly satisfied
6 = Satisfied
7 = Extremely satisfied

1. The amount of job security I have.
2. The amount of pay and fringe benefits I receive.
3. The amount of personal growth and development I get in doing my job.
4. The people I talk to and work with on my job.
5. The degree of respect and fair treatment I receive from my boss.
6. The feeling of worthwhile accomplishment I get from doing my job.
7. The chance to get to know other people while on the job.
8. The amount of support and guidance I receive from my supervisor.
9. The degree to which I am fairly paid for what I contribute to this organization.
10. The amount of independent thought and action I can exercise in my job.
11. How secure things look for me in the future in this organization.
12. The chance to help other people while at work.
13. The amount of challenge in my job.
14. The overall quality of the supervision I receive on my work.

Now, compute your scores for the facets of job satisfaction.

Pay satisfaction:

Q2 ___ + Q9 ___ = ___ Divided by 2: ___

Security satisfaction:

Q1 ___ + Q11 ___ = ___ Divided by 2: ___

Social satisfaction:

Q4 ___ + Q7 ___ + Q12 ___ = ___ Divided by 3: ___

Supervisory satisfaction:

Q5 ___ + Q8 ___ + Q14 ___ = ___ Divided by 3: ___

Growth satisfaction:

Q3 ___ + Q6 ___ + Q10 ___ + Q13 ___ = ___ Divided by 4: ___

Scores on the facets range from 1 to 7. (Scores lower than 4 suggest there is room for change.)

This questionnaire is an abbreviated version of the Job Diagnostic Survey, a widely used tool for assessing individual's attitudes about their jobs. Compare your scores on each facet to the following norms for a large sample of managers.

Pay satisfaction:	4.6
Security satisfaction:	5.2
Social satisfaction:	5.6
Supervisory satisfaction:	5.2
Growth satisfaction:	5.3

How do your scores compare? Are there actions you can take to improve your job satisfaction?

SOURCE: R. Hackman/G. Oldham, *Work Redesign* (pp. 284 & 317). Copyright © 1980 by Addison-Wesley Publishing Company, Inc. Reprinted by permission of Addison-Wesley Longman.

Figure 4.1
Sample Items from Satisfaction Questionnaires

Job Descriptive Index

Think of the work you do at present. How well does each of the following words or phrases describe your work? In the blank beside each word given below, write

__Y__	for "Yes" if it describes your work
__N__	for "No" if it does NOT describe it
__?__	if you cannot decide

WORK ON YOUR PRESENT JOB:

_____	Routine
_____	Satisfying
_____	Good

Think of the majority of the people that you work with now or the people you meet in connection with your work. How well does each of the following words or phrases describe these people? In the blank beside each word, write

__Y__	for "Yes" if it describes the people you work with
__N__	for "No" if it does NOT describe them
__?__	if you cannot decide

CO-WORKERS (PEOPLE):

_____	Boring
_____	Responsible
_____	Intelligent

Minnesota Satisfaction Questionnaire

1 = Very dissatisfied
2 = Dissatisfied
3 = I can't decide whether I am satisfied or not
4 = Satisfied
5 = Very satisfied

On my present job, this is how I feel about:

_____	The chance to work alone on the job (Independence)
_____	My chances for advancement on this job (Advancement)
_____	The chance to tell people what to do (Authority)
_____	The praise I get for a good job (Recognition)
_____	My pay and the amount of work I do (Compensation)

SOURCES: The Job Descriptive Index is copyrighted by Bowling Green State University. The complete forms, scoring key, instructions, and norms can be obtained from Dr. Patricia C. Smith, Department of Psychology, Bowling Green State University, Bowling Green, OH 43403. Minnesota Satisfaction Questionnaire from D. J. Weiss, R. V. Davis, G. W. England, and L. H. Lofquist, *Manual for the Minnesota Satisfaction Questionnaire* (University of Minnesota Vocational Psychology Research, 1967).

Are satisfied workers more productive? Or, are more productive workers more satisfied? The link between satisfaction and performance has been widely explored. One view holds that satisfaction causes good performance. If this were true, then the manager's job would simply be to keep workers happy. Although this may be the case for certain individuals, job satisfaction for most people is one of several causes of good performance.

Another view holds that good performance causes satisfaction. If this were true, managers would need to help employees perform well, and satisfaction would follow. However, some employees who are high performers are not satisfied with their jobs.

The research shows modest support for both views, but no simple, direct relationship between satisfaction and performance has been found.[18] One reason for these results may be the difficulty of demonstrating the attitude–behavior links we described earlier in this chapter. Future studies using specific, relevant attitudes and measuring personality variables and behavioral intentions may be able to demonstrate a link between job satisfaction and performance.

Another reason for the lack of a clear relationship between satisfaction and performance is the intervening role of rewards. Employees who receive valued rewards are more satisfied. In addition, employees who receive rewards that are contingent on performance (the higher the performance, the larger the reward) tend to perform better. Rewards thus influence both satisfaction and performance. The key to influencing both satisfaction and performance through rewards is that the rewards are valued by employees and are tied directly to performance.

Job satisfaction has been shown to be related to many other important personal and organizational outcomes. Job satisfaction is related to ***organizational citizenship behavior***—behavior that is above and beyond the call of duty.[19] Satisfied employees are more likely to help their coworkers, make positive comments about the company, and refrain from complaining when things at work do not go well. Going beyond the call of duty is especially important to organizations using teams to get work done. Employees depend on extra help from each other to get things accomplished.

organizational citizenship behavior
Behavior that is above and beyond the call of duty.

Satisfied workers are more likely to want to give something back to the organization because they want to reciprocate their positive experiences.[20] Often, employees may feel that citizenship behaviors are not recognized because they occur outside the confines of normal job responsibilities. Organizational citizenship behaviors do, however, influence performance evaluations. Employees who exhibit behaviors such as helping others, making suggestions for innovations, and developing their skills receive higher performance ratings.[21]

Organizational citizenship behaviors vary from everyday individual acts to group efforts. Albany Ladder, a New York–based construction equipment sales firm, can attest to the value of such behaviors. Top managers at the company believe that they owe their company's ability to make it through cyclical declines in the construction industry to employees who go the extra mile without being asked. For example, Albany Ladder desperately needed to put a concrete pad for equipment in the corner of its parking lot. A crew of employee volunteers, doing a job that didn't remotely resemble their regular ones, pitched in and built the pad on a Saturday, with no pay. Organizational citizenship behaviors like this can be essential to a firm's survival; thus, they are an important part of performance.

Although researchers have had a tough time demonstrating the link between job satisfaction and individual performance, this has not been the case for the link between job satisfaction and organizational performance. Companies with satisfied workers have better performance than companies with dissatisfied workers.[22] This may be due to the more intangible elements of performance, like organizational citizenship behavior, that contribute to organizational effectiveness but aren't necessarily captured by just measuring individual job performance.

Job satisfaction is related to some other important outcomes. People who are dissatisfied with their jobs are absent more frequently. The type of dissatisfaction that most often leads employees to miss work is dissatisfaction with the work itself. In addition, dissatisfied workers are more likely to quit their jobs, and turnover at work can be very costly to organizations. Dissatisfied workers also report more psychological and medical problems than do satisfied employees.[23]

Like all attitudes, job satisfaction is influenced by culture. One study found that Japanese workers reported significantly lower job satisfaction than did U.S. workers.[24] Interestingly, the study showed that job satisfaction in both Japan and the United States could be improved by participative techniques such as quality circles and social activities sponsored by the company. Research also has shown that executives in less industrialized countries have lower levels of job satisfaction.[25]

Culture may also affect the factors that lead to job satisfaction. In a comparison of employees in the United States and India, the factors differed substantially. Leadership style, pay, and security influenced job satisfaction for the Americans. For the employees in India, however, recognition, innovation, and the absence of conflict led to job satisfaction.[26]

Because organizations face the challenge of operating in the global environment, managers must understand that job satisfaction is significantly affected by culture. Employees from different cultures may have differing expectations of their jobs; thus, there may be no single prescription for increasing the job satisfaction of a multicultural workforce.

organizational commitment
The strength of an individual's identification with an organization.

affective commitment
The type of organizational commitment that is based on an individual's desire to remain in an organization.

continuance commitment
The type of organizational commitment that is based on the fact that an individual cannot afford to leave.

Organizational Commitment The strength of an individual's identification with an organization is known as *organizational commitment*. There are three kinds of organizational commitment: affective, continuance, and normative. *Affective commitment* is an employee's intention to remain in an organization because of a strong desire to do so. It consists of three factors:

- A belief in the goals and values of the organization
- A willingness to put forth effort on behalf of the organization
- A desire to remain a member of the organization.[27]

Affective commitment encompasses loyalty, but it is also a deep concern for the organization's welfare.

Continuance commitment is an employee's tendency to remain in an organization because the person cannot afford to leave.[28] Sometimes, employees believe that if they leave, they will lose a great deal of their investments in time, effort, and benefits and that they cannot replace these investments.

Normative commitment is a perceived obligation to remain with the organization. Individuals who experience normative commitment stay with the organization because they feel that they should.[29]

Certain organizational conditions encourage commitment. Participation in decision making and job security are two such conditions. Certain job characteristics also positively affect commitment. These include autonomy, responsibility, and interesting work.[30]

Affective and normative commitments are related to lower rates of absenteeism, higher quality of work, increased productivity, and several different types of performance.[31] Managers should encourage affective commitment because committed individuals expend more task-related effort and are less likely than others to leave the organization.[32]

Several researchers have examined organizational commitment in different countries. One study of workers in Saudi Arabia found that Asians working there were more committed to the organization than were Westerners and Arab workers.[33] Another study revealed that American workers displayed higher affective commitment than did Korean and Japanese workers.[34] The reasons for these differences need to be explored.

Job satisfaction and organizational commitment are two important work attitudes that managers can strive to improve among their employees. And these two attitudes are strongly related. Both affective and normative commitment are related to job satisfaction. Increasing job satisfaction is likely to increase commitment as well. To begin with, managers can use attitude surveys to reveal employees' satisfaction or dissatisfaction with specific facets of their jobs. Then they can take action to make the deficient aspects of the job more satisfying. Participative management has been shown to increase both satisfaction and commitment. Managers can give employees opportunities to participate in decision making to help improve these attitudes.

> **normative commitment**
> The type of organizational commitment that is based on an individual's perceived obligation to remain with an organization.

Persuasion and Attitude Change

To understand how attitudes can change, it is necessary to understand the process of persuasion. Through persuasion, one individual (the source) tries to change the attitude of another person (the target). Certain characteristics of the source, the target, and the message affect the persuasion process. There are also two cognitive routes to persuasion.

Source Characteristics Three major characteristics of the source affect persuasion: expertise, trustworthiness, and attractiveness.[35] A source who is perceived as an expert is particularly persuasive. Ken Cooper, founder of Cooper Aerobics Center, is a persuasive force for changing attitudes toward aerobic fitness. His expertise persuaded many sedentary people to get moving and led to the boom in aerobics classes, running, swimming, and other aerobic activities. Trustworthiness is also important. Richard Simmons, also a persuasive force in the fitness movement, has a style that certainly contrasts with that of Dr. Cooper. His energetic, sometimes zany approach has motivated many overweight people to exercise. Simmons's ability to persuade comes from the trust he has earned by being forthright about his own weight problems. Because he combated obesity himself and won, many people trust him to help them succeed in the battle to become fit. Finally, attractiveness and likability play a role in persuasion. Attractive communicators have long been used in advertising to persuade consumers to buy certain products. As a source of persuasion, managers who are perceived as being experts, who are trustworthy, or who are attractive or likable will have an edge in changing employee attitudes.

Target Characteristics   Some people are more easily persuaded than others. Individuals with low self-esteem are more likely to change their attitudes in response to persuasion than are individuals with high self-esteem. Individuals who hold very extreme attitudes are more resistant to persuasion, and people who are in a good mood are easier to persuade.[36] Undoubtedly, individuals differ widely in their susceptibility to persuasion. Managers must recognize these differences and realize that their attempts to change attitudes may not receive universal acceptance.

4.▪ Identify the characteristics of the source, target, and message that affect persuasion.

Message Characteristics   Suppose you must implement an unpopular policy at work. You want to persuade your employees that the policy is a positive change. Should you present one side of the issue or both sides? Given that your employees are already negatively inclined toward the policy, you will have more success in changing their attitudes if you present both sides. This shows support for one side of the issue while acknowledging that another side does exist. Moreover, refuting the other side makes it more difficult for the targets to hang on to their negative attitudes.

Messages that are obviously designed to change the target's attitude may be met with considerable negative reaction. In fact, undisguised deliberate attempts at changing attitudes may cause attitude change in the opposite direction! This is most likely to occur when the target of the persuasive communication feels her or his freedom is threatened.[37] Less threatening approaches are less likely to elicit negative reactions.

Cognitive Routes to Persuasion   When are message characteristics more important, and when are other characteristics more important in persuasion? The elaboration likelihood model of persuasion, presented in Figure 4.2, proposes that persuasion occurs over two routes: the central route and the peripheral route.[38] The routes are differentiated by the amount of elaboration, or scrutiny, the target is motivated to give the message.

The *central route* to persuasion involves direct cognitive processing of the message's content. When an issue is personally relevant, the individual is motivated to think carefully about it. In the central route, the content of the message is very important. If the arguments presented are logical and convincing, attitude change will follow.

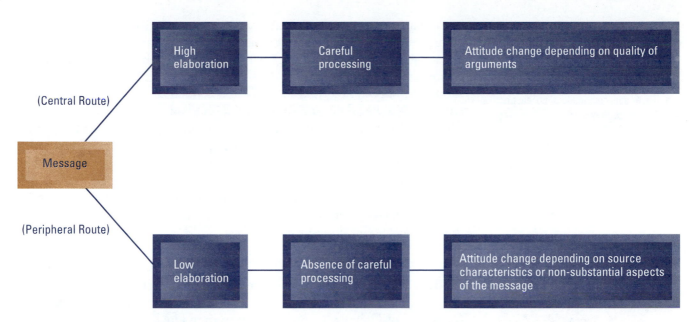

SOURCE: Adapted from R. E. Petty and J. T. Cacioppo, "The Elaboration Likelihood Model of Persuasion," in L. Berkowitz, ed., *Advances in Experimental Social Psychology*, vol. 19 (New York: Academic Press, 1986), 123–205.

Figure 4.2
The Elaboration Likelihood Model of Persuasion

In the *peripheral route* to persuasion, the individual is not motivated to pay much attention to the message's content. This is because the message may not be perceived as personally relevant, or the individual may be distracted. Instead, the individual is persuaded by characteristics of the persuader—for example, expertise, trustworthiness, and attractiveness. In addition, the individual may be persuaded by statistics, the number of arguments presented, or the method of presentation—all of which are non-substantial aspects of the message.

The elaboration likelihood model shows that the target's level of involvement with the issue is important. That involvement also determines which route to persuasion will be more effective. In some cases, attitude change comes about through both the central and the peripheral routes. To cover all of the bases, managers should structure the content of their messages carefully, develop their own attributes that will help them be more persuasive, and choose a method of presentation that will be attractive to the audience.[39]

We have seen that the process of persuading individuals to change their attitudes is affected by the source, the target, the message, and the route. When all is said and done, however, managers are important catalysts for encouraging attitude change.

VALUES

Another source of individual differences is values. Values exist at a deeper level than attitudes and are more general and basic in nature. We use them

values

Enduring beliefs that a specific mode of conduct or end state of existence is personally or socially preferable to an opposite or converse mode of conduct or end state of existence.

to evaluate our own behavior and that of others. As such, they vary widely among individuals. *Values* are enduring beliefs that a specific mode of conduct or end state of existence is personally or socially preferable to an opposite or converse mode of conduct or end state of existence.[40] This definition was proposed by Rokeach, an early scholar of human values. Values give us a sense of right and wrong, good and bad.

As individuals grow and mature, they learn values, which may change over the life span as an individual develops a sense of self. Cultures, societies, and organizations shape values. Parents and others who are respected by the individual play crucial roles in value development by providing guidance about what is right and wrong. Values come to the forefront of an individual's development during adolescence, and many individuals stabilize their value systems during this life stage.

Businesses have shown increasing interest in values over recent years. This interest goes along with the emphasis on ethics in organizations that we described in Chapter 2. Because values are general beliefs about right and wrong, they form the basis for ethical behavior. Tandem Computers (now part of Compaq Computer) hired individuals who shared the company's values of personal growth and freedom. Six-week sabbaticals every four years allowed Tandem employees to pursue personal growth in areas as diverse as climbing the mountains of Nepal and studying at a world-renowned cooking school.[41] We will focus on the importance of shared values in the organization in Chapter 15. Our emphasis in this chapter is on values as sources of variation among individuals.

Instrumental and Terminal Values

5. Distinguish between instrumental and terminal values.

instrumental values

Values that represent the acceptable behaviors to be used in achieving some end state.

terminal values

Values that represent the goals to be achieved or the end states of existence.

Rokeach distinguished between two types of values: instrumental and terminal. *Instrumental values* reflect the means to achieving goals; that is, they represent the acceptable behaviors to be used in achieving some end state. Instrumental values identified by Rokeach include ambition, honesty, self-sufficiency, and courage. *Terminal values*, in contrast, represent the goals to be achieved or the end states of existence. Rokeach identified happiness, love, pleasure, self-respect, and freedom among the terminal values. A complete list of instrumental and terminal values is presented in Table 4.2. Terminal and instrumental values work in concert to provide individuals with goals to strive for and acceptable ways to achieve the goals.

Americans' rankings of instrumental and terminal values have shown remarkable stability over time.[42] Rokeach studied their rankings in four national samples from 1968, 1971, 1974, and 1981. There was considerable stability in the rankings across the studies, which spanned a thirteen-year period. Most of the values shifted only one position in the rankings over this time span. The highest ranked instrumental values were honesty, ambition, responsibility, forgiving nature, open-mindedness, and courage. The highest ranked terminal values were world peace, family security, freedom, happiness, self-respect, and wisdom.

INSTRUMENTAL VALUES		
Honesty	Ambition	Responsibility
Forgiving nature	Open-mindedness	Courage
Helpfulness	Cleanliness	Competence
Self-control	Affection/love	Cheerfulness
Independence	Politeness	Intelligence
Obedience	Rationality	Imagination
TERMINAL VALUES		
World peace	Family security	Freedom
Happiness	Self-respect	Wisdom
Equality	Salvation	Prosperity
Achievement	Friendship	National security
Inner peace	Mature love	Social respect
Beauty in art and nature	Pleasure	Exciting, active life

Table 4.2
Instrumental and Terminal Values

SOURCE: Table adapted with the permission of The Free Press, a Division of Simon & Schuster, Inc. from *The Nature of Human Values* by Milton Rokeach. Copyright © 1973 by The Free Press.

Although the values of Americans as a group have been stable, individuals vary widely in their value systems. For example, social respect is one terminal value that people differ on. Some people desire respect from others and work diligently to achieve it, and other people place little importance on what others think of them. Individuals may agree that achievement is an important terminal value but may disagree on how to attain that goal.

Age also affects values. Baby boomers' values contrast with those of the baby busters, who are beginning to enter the workforce. The baby busters value family life and time off from work and prefer a balance between work and home life. This contrasts with the more driven, work-oriented value system of the boomers. The United States is not the only nation affected by age differences in values. Many European nations have found that values of young workers differ from those of older generations. Younger generations place more emphasis on personal development at work and on good pay as compared with previous generations.

Work Values

Work values are important because they affect how individuals behave on their jobs in terms of what is right and wrong.[43] Four work values relevant to individuals are achievement, concern for others, honesty, and fairness.[44] Achievement is a concern for the advancement of one's career. This is shown in such behaviors as working hard and seeking opportunities to develop new skills. Concern for others is shown in caring, compassionate behaviors such as encouraging other employees or helping others work on difficult tasks. These behaviors constitute organizational citizenship, as we discussed earlier. Honesty is providing accurate information and refusing to mislead others for personal gain. Fairness emphasizes impartiality and recognizes different points of view. Individuals can rank-order these values in terms of their importance in their work lives.[45] Challenge 4.2 gives you a chance to see what your work values are and whether they match those of an organization.

Although individuals' value systems differ, when they share similar values at work, the results are positive. Employees who share their supervisor's values are more satisfied with their jobs and more committed to the orga-

Challenge 4.2

What Do You Value at Work?

The fifty-four items listed below cover the full range of personal and institutional values you'd be likely to encounter at any company. Divide it into two groups: the twenty-seven that would be the most evident in your ideal workplace and the twenty-seven that would be the least. Keep halving the groups until you have a rank-ordering, then fill in the numbers of your top and bottom ten choices. Test your fit at a firm by seeing whether the company's values match your top and bottom ten.

TOP TEN CHOICES

BOTTOM TEN CHOICES

THE CHOICE MENU
YOU ARE: 1. Flexible. **2.** Adaptable. **3.** Innovative. **4.** Able to seize opportunities. **5.** Willing to experiment. **6.** Risk-taking. **7.** Careful. **8.** Autonomy-seeking. **9.** Comfortable with rules. **10.** Analytical. **11.** Attentive to detail. **12.** Precise. **13.** Team-oriented. **14.** Ready to share information. **15.** People-oriented. **16.** Easygoing. **17.** Calm. **18.** Supportive. **19.** Aggressive. **20.** Decisive. **21.** Action-oriented. **22.** Eager to take initiative. **23.** Reflective. **24.** Achievement-oriented. **25.** Demanding. **26.** Comfortable with individual responsibility. **27.** Comfortable with conflict. **28.** Competitive. **29.** Highly organized. **30.** Results-oriented. **31.** Interested in making friends at work. **32.** Collaborative. **33.** Eager to fit with colleagues. **34.** Enthusiastic about the job. **YOUR COMPANY OFFERS: 35.** Stability. **36.** Predictability. **37.** High expectations of performance. **38.** Opportunities for professional growth. **39.** High pay for good performance. **40.** Job security. **41.** Praise for good performance. **42.** A clear guiding philosophy. **43.** A low level of conflict. **44.** An emphasis on quality. **45.** A good reputation. **46.** Respect for the individual's rights. **47.** Tolerance. **48.** Informality. **49.** Fairness. **50.** A unitary culture throughout the organization. **51.** A sense of social responsibility. **52.** Long hours. **53.** Relative freedom from rules. **54.** The opportunity to be distinctive, or different from others.

SOURCE: M. Siegel, "The Perils of Culture Conflict." Reprinted from the November 9, 1998 issue of *Fortune* by special permission; copyright © 1998, Time Inc.

nization.[46] Values also have profound effects on the choice of jobs. Traditionally, pay and advancement potential have been the strongest influences on job choice decisions. One study, however, found that three other work values—achievement, concern for others, and fairness—exerted more influence on job choice decisions than did pay and promotion opportunities.[47]

This means that organizations recruiting job candidates should pay careful attention to individuals' values and to the messages that organizations send about company values. At Prudential Insurance, the key value is integrity; it is Prudential's "rock" in guiding relationships among employees, customers, and regulatory agencies.[48]

Cultural Differences in Values

As organizations face the challenges of an increasingly diverse workforce and a global marketplace, it becomes more important than ever for them to understand the influence of culture on values. Doing business in a global marketplace often means that managers encounter a clash of values between different cultures. Take the value of loyalty, for example. In Japan, loyalty means "compassionate overtime." Even though you have no work to do, you should stay late to give moral support to your peers who are working late.[49] In contrast, Koreans value loyalty to the person for whom one works.[50] In the United States, family and other personal loyalties are more highly valued than is loyalty to the company or one's supervisor.

Doing business in Russia has its challenges in terms of value differences. When Cargill, a Minnesota company, established a food-processing plant in Russia in the early 1990s, it had to deal not only with Russia's nonconvertible currency, but also with value differences. Jules Carson, who headed the project, said "The main obstacle is getting the people to adopt a business attitude and business ethics. I don't know any short way to solve that. It will take persistence and coaching."[51]

Values also affect individuals' views of what constitutes authority. French managers value authority as a right of office and rank. Their behavior reflects this value, as they tend to use power based on their position in the organization. In contrast, managers from the Netherlands and Scandinavia value group inputs to decisions and expect their decisions to be challenged and discussed by employees.[52]

Conducting business on a global scale often presents managers with dilemmas that call their own value systems into question. The solicitation or exchange of gifts among businesspeople in the United States is frowned on. In Asia and in some parts of Mexico, however, it is traditional to exchange gifts in business relationships. These gifts begin a cycle of future favors to be exchanged between the parties. What American managers may consider payoffs and bribes may be considered legitimate ways of doing business in other countries.

Value differences between cultures must be acknowledged in today's global economy. We may be prone to judging the value systems of others, but we should resist the temptation to do so. Tolerating diversity in values can help us understand other cultures. Value systems of other nations are not necessarily right or wrong—they are merely different. The following suggestions can help managers understand and work with the diverse values that characterize the global environment:[53]

6. Explain how managers can deal with the diverse value systems that characterize the global environment.

1. Learn more about and recognize the values of other peoples. They view their values and customs as moral, traditional, and practical.
2. Avoid prejudging the business customs of others as immoral or corrupt. Assume they are legitimate unless proved otherwise.
3. Find legitimate ways to operate within others' ethical points of view—do not demand that they operate within your value system.
4. Avoid rationalizing "borderline" actions with excuses such as the following:
   - "This isn't really illegal or immoral."
   - "This is in the organization's best interest."
   - "No one will find out about this."
   - "The organization will back me up on this."
5. Refuse to do business when stakeholder actions violate or compromise laws or fundamental organizational values.
6. Conduct relationships as openly and as aboveboard as possible.

Values are important because they provide guidance for behavior. They are intertwined with the concept of ethics, the next dimension of individual differences to be examined.

ETHICAL BEHAVIOR

ethical behavior
Acting in ways consistent with one's personal values and the commonly held values of the organization and society.

Ethics is the study of moral values and moral behavior. ***Ethical behavior*** is acting in ways consistent with one's personal values and the commonly held values of the organization and society.[54] As we saw in Chapter 2, ethical issues are a major concern in organizations. There is evidence that paying attention to ethical issues pays off for companies. In the early 1990s, James Burke, then the CEO of Johnson & Johnson, put together a list of companies that devoted a great deal of attention to ethics. The group included Johnson & Johnson, Coca-Cola, Gerber, Kodak, 3M, and Pitney Bowes. Over a forty-year period, the market value of these organizations grew at an annual rate of 11.3 percent, as compared to 6.2 percent for the Dow Jones industrials as a whole.[55] Doing the right thing can have a positive effect on an organization's performance.

Unethical behavior by employees can affect individuals, work teams, and even the organization. Organizations thus depend on individuals to act ethically. One company recognized for its comprehensive efforts to encourage ethical behavior is General Dynamics. Several years ago, the company launched a program to integrate its ethical standards into everyday business conduct.[56] It developed a booklet of ethical standards, distributed it to all employees, and undertook a massive training effort to express to all employees the importance of ethical behavior. The company also appointed employees throughout the corporation to serve as ethics directors. The directors answer employees' questions about ethical problems and screen allegations about potential violations of General Dynamics' code of conduct. Many of the directors maintain hotlines for employees to use.

In the first two years after the hotlines were established, General Dynamics employees contacted ethics directors more than 30,000 times. Although most employee calls were requests for information or advice, some calls were more serious. Ethics contacts resulted in 1,400 sanctions, the most common being warnings. Time-reporting violations, in which employees overstated the number of hours they worked, were the most frequent reasons for warnings.

Today's high-intensity business environment makes it more important than ever to have a strong ethics program in place. In a survey of more than 4,000 employees conducted by the Washington, D.C.–based Ethics Resource Center, one-third of the employees said that they had witnessed ethical misconduct in the past year. If that many employees actually saw unethical acts, imagine how many unethical behaviors occurred behind closed doors! The most common unethical deeds witnessed were lying to supervisors (56 percent), lying on reports or falsifying records (41 percent,) stealing or theft (35 percent), sexual harassment (35 percent), drug or alcohol abuse (31 percent), and conflicts of interest (31 percent).[57]

One of the toughest challenges managers face is aligning the ideal of ethical behavior with the reality of everyday business practices. Violations of the public's trust are costly. Since Jack in the Box restaurants' *E. coli* crisis, the company has faced image and financial problems. Studies show that firms experience lower accounting returns and slow sales growth for as long as five years after being convicted of a corporate illegality.[58]

The ethical issues that individuals face at work are complex. A review of articles appearing in *The Wall Street Journal* during just one week revealed more than sixty articles dealing with ethical issues in business.[59] As Table 4.3 shows, the themes appearing throughout the articles were distilled into twelve major ethical issues. You can see that few of these issues are clearcut. All of them depend on the specifics of the situation, and their interpretation depends on the characteristics of the individuals examining them. For example, look at issue 2: lying. We all know that "white lies" are told in business. Is this acceptable? The answer to this question varies from person to person. Thus, the perception of what constitutes ethical versus unethical behavior in organizations varies among individuals.

Ethical behavior is influenced by two major categories of factors: individual characteristics and organizational factors.[60] Our purpose in this section is to look at the individual influences on ethical behavior. We examine organizational influences throughout the remainder of the book—particularly in Chapter 15, where we focus on creating an organizational culture that reinforces ethical behavior.

Table 4.3
Ethical Issues from One Week in The Wall Street Journal

1. **Stealing:** Taking things that don't belong to you.
2. **Lying:** Saying things you know aren't true.
3. **Fraud and deceit:** Creating or perpetuating false impressions.
4. **Conflict of interest and influence buying:** Bribes, payoffs, and kickbacks.
5. **Hiding versus divulging information:** Concealing information that another party has a right to know, or failing to protect personal or proprietary information.
6. **Cheating:** Taking unfair advantage of a situation.
7. **Personal decadence:** Aiming below excellence in terms of work performance (e.g., careless or sloppy work).
8. **Interpersonal abuse:** Behaviors that are abusive of others (e.g., sexism, racism, emotional abuse).
9. **Organizational abuse:** Organizational practices that abuse members (e.g., inequitable compensation, misuses of power).
10. **Rule violations:** Breaking organizational rules.
11. **Accessory to unethical acts:** Knowing about unethical behavior and failing to report it.
12. **Ethical dilemmas:** Choosing between two equally desirable or undesirable options.

SOURCE: Adapted from J. O. Cherrington and D. J. Cherrington, "A Menu of Moral Issues: One Week in the Life of *The Wall Street Journal*," *Journal of Business Ethics* 11 (1992): 255–265. Reprinted by permission of Kluwer Academic Publishers.

The model that guides our discussion of individual influences on ethical behavior is presented in Figure 4.3. It shows both individual and organizational influences.

Making ethical decisions is part of each manager's job. It has been suggested that ethical decision making requires three qualities of individuals:[61]

1. The competence to identify ethical issues and evaluate the consequences of alternative courses of action

2. The self-confidence to seek out different opinions about the issue and decide what is right in terms of a particular situation

3. Toughmindedness—the willingness to make decisions when all that needs to be known cannot be known and when the ethical issue has no established, unambiguous solution.

What are the individual characteristics that lead to these qualities? Our model presents four major individual differences that affect ethical behavior: value systems, locus of control, Machiavellianism, and cognitive moral development.

Value Systems

Values are systems of beliefs that affect what the individual defines as right, good, and fair. Ethics reflects the way the values are acted out. Ethical be-

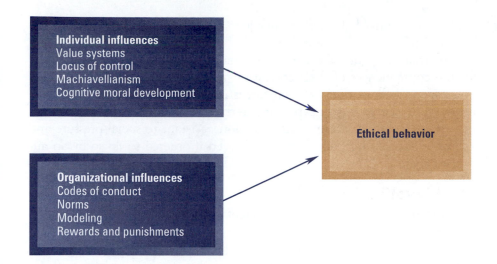

Figure 4.3
*Individual/Organizational
Model of Ethical Behavior*

havior, as noted earlier, is acting in ways consistent with one's personal values and the commonly held values of the organization and society.

Employees are exposed to multiple value systems: their own, their supervisor's, the company's, the customers', and others'. In most cases, the individual's greatest allegiance will be to personal values. When the value system conflicts with the behavior the person feels must be exhibited, the person experiences a value conflict. Suppose, for example, that an individual believes honesty is important in all endeavors. Yet this individual sees that those who get ahead in business fudge their numbers and deceive other people. Why should the individual be honest if honesty doesn't pay? It is the individual's values, a basic sense of what is right and wrong, that override the temptation to be dishonest.[62]

One person who believes that good values make good business is Kim Dawson, founder of the internationally known Kim Dawson Agency. Values have shaped her approach to the modeling and talent industries. One important value is the long-term development of people. The product that the Dawson Agency sells is the freshness of a youthful face. The modeling career ends for some at a very early age, so the agency counsels young models to pursue their education at college and plan for the future. When Dawson models work in Europe or Japan, they study by correspondence. By emphasizing honesty and long-term development, Kim Dawson demonstrates concern for her models' futures.

7. Describe a model of individual and organizational influences on ethical behavior.

Locus of Control

Another individual influence on ethical behavior is locus of control. In Chapter 3, we introduced locus of control as a personality variable that affects individual behavior. Recall that individuals with an internal locus of control believe that they control events in their lives and that they are responsible for what happens to them. In contrast, individuals with an external locus of control believe that outside forces such as fate, chance, or other people control what happens to them.[63]

Internals are more likely than externals to take personal responsibility for the consequences of their ethical or unethical behavior. Externals are more apt to believe that external forces caused their ethical or unethical behavior. Research has shown that internals make more ethical decisions than do externals.[64] Internals also are more resistant to social pressure and are less willing to hurt another person, even if ordered to do so by an authority figure.[65]

Machiavellianism

Another individual difference that affects ethical behavior is Machiavellianism. Niccolò Machiavelli was a sixteenth-century Italian statesman. He wrote *The Prince*, a guide for acquiring and using power.[66] The primary method for achieving power that he suggested was manipulation of others. *Machiavellianism*, then, is a personality characteristic indicating one's willingness to do whatever it takes to get one's own way.

A high-Mach individual behaves in accordance with Machiavelli's ideas, which include the notion that it is better to be feared than loved. High-Machs tend to use deceit in relationships, have a cynical view of human nature, and have little concern for conventional notions of right and wrong.[67] They are skilled manipulators of other people, relying on their persuasive abilities. Low-Machs, in contrast, value loyalty and relationships. They are less willing to manipulate others for personal gain and are concerned with others' opinions.

High-Machs believe that the desired ends justify any means. They believe that manipulation of others is fine if it helps achieve a goal. Thus, high-Machs are likely to justify their manipulative behavior as ethical.[68] They are emotionally detached from other people and are oriented toward objective aspects of situations. And high-Machs are likelier than low-Machs to engage in behavior that is ethically questionable.[69] Employees can counter Machiavellian individuals by focusing on teamwork instead of on one-on-one relationships, where high-Machs have the upper hand. It is also beneficial to make interpersonal agreements public and thus less susceptible to manipulation by high-Machs.

Cognitive Moral Development

An individual's level of *cognitive moral development* also affects ethical behavior. Psychologist Lawrence Kohlberg proposed that as individuals mature, they move through a series of six stages of moral development.[70] With each successive stage, they become less dependent on other people's opinions of right and wrong and less self-centered (acting in one's own interest). At higher levels of moral development, individuals are concerned with broad principles of justice and with their self-chosen ethical principles. Kohlberg's model focuses on the decision-making process and on how individuals justify ethical decisions. His model is a cognitive developmental theory about

Machiavellianism
A personality characteristic indicating one's willingness to do whatever it takes to get one's own way.

8. Discuss how value systems, locus of control, Machiavellianism, and cognitive moral development affect ethical behavior.

cognitive moral development
The process of moving through stages of maturity in terms of making ethical decisions.

how people think about what is right and wrong and how the decision-making process changes through interaction with peers and the environment.

Cognitive moral development occurs at three levels, and each level consists of two stages. In Level I, called the premoral level, the person's ethical decisions are based on rewards, punishments, and self-interest. In Stage 1, the individual obeys rules to avoid punishment. In Stage 2, the individual follows the rules only if it is in his or her immediate interest to do so.

In Level II, the conventional level, the focus is on the expectations of others (parents, peers) or society. In Stage 3, individuals try to live up to the expectations of people close to them. In Stage 4, they broaden their perspective to include the laws of the larger society. They fulfill duties and obligations and want to contribute to society.

In Level III, the principled level, what is "right" is determined by universal values. The individual sees beyond laws, rules, and the expectations of other people. In Stage 5, individuals are aware that people have diverse value systems. They uphold their own values despite what others think. For a person to be classified as being in Stage 5, decisions must be based on principles of justice and rights. For example, a person who decides to picket an abortion clinic just because his religion says abortion is wrong is not a Stage 5 individual. A person who arrives at the same decision through a complex decision process based on justice and rights may be a Stage 5 individual. The key is the process rather than the decision itself. In Stage 6, the individual follows self-selected ethical principles. If there is a conflict between a law and a self-selected ethical principle, the individual acts according to the principle.

As individuals mature, their moral development passes through these stages in an irreversible sequence. Research suggests that most adults are in Stage 3 or 4. Most adults thus never reach the principled level of development (Stages 5 and 6).

Since it was proposed, more than thirty years ago, Kohlberg's model of cognitive moral development has received a great deal of research support. Individuals at higher stages of development are less likely to cheat,[71] more likely to engage in whistle-blowing,[72] and more likely to make ethical business decisions.[73, 74]

Kohlberg's model has also been criticized. Gilligan, for example, has argued that the model does not take gender differences into account. Kohlberg's model was developed from a twenty-year study of eighty-four boys.[75] Gilligan contends that women's moral development follows a different pattern—one that is based not on individual rights and rules but on responsibility and relationships. Women and men face the same moral dilemmas but approach them from different perspectives—men from the perspective of equal respect and women from the perspective of compassion and care. More research is needed on gender differences in cognitive moral development.

There is evidence to support the idea that men and women view ethics differently. A large-scale review of sixty-six studies found that women were more likely than men to perceive certain business practices as unethical.

Young women were more likely to see breaking the rules and acting on insider information as unethical. Both sexes agreed that collusion, conflicts of interest, and stealing are unethical. It takes about twenty-one years for the gender gap to disappear. Men seem to become more ethical with more work experience; the longer they are in the workforce, the more their attitudes become similar to those held by women. There is an age/experience effect for both sexes: experienced workers are more likely to think lying, bribing, stealing, and colluding are unethical.[76]

Individual differences in values, locus of control, Machiavellianism, and cognitive moral development are important influences on ethical behavior in organizations. Given that these influences vary widely from person to person, how can organizations use this knowledge to increase ethical behavior? One action would be to hire individuals who share the organization's values. Another would be to hire only internals, low-Machs, and individuals at higher stages of cognitive moral development. This strategy obviously presents practical and legal problems.

There is evidence that cognitive moral development can be increased through training.[77] Organizations could help individuals move to higher stages of moral development by providing educational seminars. However, values, locus of control, Machiavellianism, and cognitive moral development are fairly stable in adults.

The best way to use the knowledge of individual differences may be to recognize that they help explain why ethical behavior differs among individuals and to focus managerial efforts on creating a work situation that supports ethical behavior.

Most adults are susceptible to external influences; they do not act as independent ethical agents. Instead, they look to others and to the organization for guidance. Managers can offer such guidance by encouraging ethical behavior through codes of conduct, norms, modeling, and rewards and punishments, as shown in Figure 4.3. We discuss these areas further in Chapter 15.

MANAGERIAL IMPLICATIONS: ATTITUDES, VALUES, AND ETHICS AT WORK

Managers must understand attitudes because of their effects on work behavior. By understanding how attitudes are formed and how they can be changed, managers can shape employee attitudes. Attitudes are learned through observation of other employees and by the way they are reinforced. Job satisfaction and organizational commitment are important attitudes to encourage among employees, and participative management is an excellent tool for doing so.

Values affect work behavior because they affect employees' views of what constitutes right and wrong. The diversity of the workforce makes it imperative that managers understand differences in value systems. Shared values within an organization can provide the foundation for cooperative efforts toward achieving organizational goals.

Ethical behavior at work is affected by individual and organizational influences. A knowledge of individual differences in value systems, locus of control, Machiavellianism, and cognitive moral development helps managers understand why individuals have diverse views about what constitutes ethical behavior.

This chapter concludes our discussion of individual differences that affect behavior in organizations. Attitudes, values, and ethics combine with personality, perception, and attribution to make individuals unique. Individual uniqueness is a major managerial challenge, and it is one reason there is no single best way to manage people.

Looking Back

Environmental Responsibility Makes Good Business Sense at Starbucks

Starbucks is concerned about the environmental impact of its operations. It created a "Green Team" of regional coordinators and asked them to devise ways to reduce, reuse, and recycle and to rethink the company's environmental practices. As a result, Starbucks now uses unbleached napkins, environmentally friendly cleaning supplies, and recycling bins in its stores. The company also rewards customers who bring their own coffee mugs. Starbucks' retail stores recycle coffee grounds and give customers the grounds to use in backyard compost piles.

More than five million customers a week visit Starbucks for hot drink "to-go" orders that use disposable paper cups. Starbucks joined the Alliance for Environmental Innovation to develop environmentally sound disposable cups and to test alternatives to disposable cups. More than forty cup ideas have been evaluated in the complex investigation. Coffee drinkers like their coffee hot, but they don't want cups that transfer the heat to their fingers. Things customers may not be as concerned about, such as best retention, use of virgin or recycled fibers, and minimal use of materials, all must be considered. It's a complex issue, and Starbucks continually seeks solutions to minimize the environmental impact and improve the performance of its cups. This effort is balanced, of course, with the determination to enhance the quality of the customers' experience. In addition, Starbucks and the Alliance are working on ways to encourage consumers to use reusable cups. Ceramic cups can be used an average of 3,000 times, providing considerable environmental benefits. Starbucks is also encouraging customers to use commuter mugs for "to-go" orders.

These environmentally sound practices reflect Starbucks' values, as you saw in the Thinking Ahead segment. In addition, they have decreased costs, improved Starbucks' market position, and gained competitive advantage for the company.[78]

CHAPTER SUMMARY

1. The ABC model of an attitude contends that an attitude has three components: affect, behavioral intentions, and cognition. Cognitive dissonance is the tension produced by a conflict between attitudes and behavior.
2. Attitudes are formed through direct experience and social learning. Direct experience creates strong attitudes because the attitudes are easily accessed and active in cognitive processes.
3. Attitude–behavior correspondence depends on attitude specificity, attitude relevance, timing of measurement, personality factors, and social constraints.
4. Two important work attitudes are job satisfaction and organizational commitment. There are cultural differences in these attitudes, and both attitudes can be improved by providing employees with opportunities for participation in decision making.
5. A manager's ability to persuade employees to change their attitudes depends on characteristics of the manager (expertise, trustworthiness, and attractiveness), the employees (self-esteem, original attitude, and mood), the message (one-sided versus two-sided), and the route (central versus peripheral).
6. Values are enduring beliefs and are strongly influenced by cultures, societies, and organizations.
7. Instrumental values reflect the means to achieving goals; terminal values represent the goals to be achieved.
8. Ethical behavior is influenced by the individual's value system, locus of control, Machiavellianism, and cognitive moral development.

KEY TERMS

attitude   102

affect   103

cognitive dissonance   105

social learning   106

job satisfaction   108

organizational citizenship behavior   111

organizational commitment   112

affective commitment   112

continuance commitment   112

normative commitment   113

values   116

instrumental values   116

terminal values   116

ethical behavior   120

Machiavellianism   124

cognitive moral development   124

REVIEW QUESTIONS

1. Describe the ABC model of an attitude. How should each component be measured?
2. How are attitudes formed? Which source is stronger?
3. Discuss cultural differences in job satisfaction and organizational commitment.
4. What are the major influences on attitude–behavior correspondence? Why do some individuals seem to exhibit behavior that is inconsistent with their attitudes?
5. What should managers know about the persuasion process?
6. Define *values*. Distinguish between instrumental values and terminal values. Are these values generally stable, or do they change over time?
7. What is the relationship between values and ethics?
8. How does locus of control affect ethical behavior?
9. What is Machiavellianism, and how does it relate to ethical behavior?
10. Describe the stages of cognitive moral development. How does this concept affect ethical behavior in organizations?

DISCUSSION AND COMMUNICATION QUESTIONS

1. What jobs do you consider to be most satisfying? Why?

2. How can managers increase their employees' job satisfaction?

3. Suppose you have an employee whose lack of commitment is affecting others in the work group. How would you go about persuading the person to change this attitude?

4. In Rokeach's studies on values, the most recent data are from 1981. Do you think values have changed since then? If so, how?

5. What are the most important influences on an individual's perceptions of ethical behavior? Can organizations change these perceptions? If so, how?

6. How can managers encourage organizational citizenship?

7. (communication question) Suppose you are a manager in a customer service organization. Your group includes seven supervisors who report directly to you. Each supervisor manages a team of seven customer service representatives. One of your supervisors, Linda, has complained that Joe, one of her employees, has "an attitude problem." She has requested that Joe be transferred to another team. Write a memo to Linda explaining your position on this problem and what should be done.

8. (communication question) Select a company that you admire for its values. Use the resources of your university library to answer two questions. First, what are the company's values? Second, how do employees enact these values? Prepare an oral presentation to present in class.

9. (communication question) Think of a time when you have experienced cognitive dissonance. Analyze your experience in terms of the attitude and behavior involved. What did you do to resolve the cognitive dissonance? What other actions could you have taken? Write a brief description of your experience and your responses to the questions.

ETHICS QUESTIONS

1. Is it ethical for an organization to influence an individual's ethical behavior? In other words, is ethics a personal issue that organizations should stay away from? Is it an invasion of privacy to enforce codes of conduct?

2. Suppose a coworker is engaging in behavior that you find personally unethical, but the behavior is not prohibited by the company's ethical standards. How would you handle the issue?

3. Some people have argued that the biggest deficiency of business school graduates is that they have no sense of ethics. What do you think?

4. Is it possible to operate in a completely ethical manner and be successful in business when your competitors engage in unethical tactics?

5. How do Machiavellianism and locus of control affect an individual's cognitive moral development?

Experiential Exercises

4.1 Chinese, Indian, and American Values

Purpose
To learn some differences between Chinese, Indian, and American value systems.

Group size
Any number of groups of five to eight people.

Time required
50+ minutes

Exercise Schedule

1. Complete rankings (preclass)

Students rank the fifteen values for either Chinese and American orientations or for Indian and American systems. If time permits, all three can be done.

	Unit time	Total time
2. Small groups (optional)	15 min.	15 min.

Groups of five to eight members try to achieve consensus on the ranking values for both Chinese and American cultures.

3. Group presentations (optional)	15 min.	30 min.

Each group presents its rankings and discusses reasons for making those decisions.

4. Discussion	20+ min.	50 min.

Instructor leads a discussion on the differences between Chinese and American value systems and presents the correct rankings.

Value Rankings

Rank each of the fifteen values below according to what you think they are in the Chinese, Indian (from India), and American cultures. Use "1" as the most important value for the culture and "15" as the least important value for that culture.

Value	American	Chinese	Indian
Achievement			
Deference			
Order			
Exhibition			
Autonomy			
Affiliation			
Intraception			
Succorance			
Dominance			
Abasement			
Nurturance			
Change			
Endurance			
Heterosexuality			
Aggression			

Some Definitions

Intraception: The tendency to be governed by subjective factors, such as feelings, fantasies, speculations, and aspirations. The other side of extraception, where one is governed by concrete, clearly observable physical conditions.

Succorance: Willingness to help another or to offer relief.

Abasement: To lower oneself in rank, prestige, or esteem.

Internal/External Locus of Control

Consider American and Chinese groups. Which would tend to have more internal locus of control (tend to feel in control of one's destiny, that rewards come as a result of hard work, perseverance, and responsibility)? Which would be more external (fate, luck or other outside forces control destiny)?

Machiavellianism

This concept was defined by Christie and Geis as the belief that one can manipulate and deceive people for personal gain. Do you think Americans or Chinese would score higher on the Machiavellian scale?

Discussion Questions

1. What are some main differences among the cultures? Did any pattern emerge?

2. Were you surprised by the results?

3. What behaviors could you expect in business dealings with Chinese (or Indians) based on their value system?

4. How do American values dictate Americans' behaviors in business situations?

SOURCE: "Chinese, Indian, and American Values" by Dorothy Marcic, copyright 1993. Adapted from Michael Harris Bond, ed., *The Psychology of the Chinese People*, Hong Kong: Oxford University Press, 200 Madison Ave., NY 10016, 1986. The selection used here is a portion of "Chinese Personality and Its Change," by Kuo-Shu Yang, pp. 106–170. Reprinted by permission.

4.2 Is This Behavior Ethical?

The purpose of this exercise is to explore your opinions about ethical issues faced in organizations. The class should be divided into twelve groups. Each group will randomly be assigned one of the following issues, which reflect the twelve ethical themes found in *The Wall Street Journal* study shown in Table 4.3.

1. Is it ethical to take office supplies from work for home use? Make personal long-distance calls from the office? Use company time for personal business? Or do these behaviors constitute stealing?

2. If you exaggerate your credentials in an interview, is it lying? Is lying in order to protect a coworker acceptable?

3. If you pretend to be more successful than you are in order to impress your boss, are you being deceitful?

4. How do you differentiate between a bribe and a gift?

5. If there are slight defects in a product you are selling, are you obligated to tell the buyer? If an advertised "sale" price is really the everyday price, should you divulge the information to the customer?

6. Suppose you have a friend who works at the ticket office for the convention center where Garth Brooks will be appearing. Is it cheating if you ask the friend to get you tickets so that you won't have to fight the crowd to get them? Is buying merchandise for your family at your company's cost cheating?

7. Is it immoral to do less than your best in terms of work performance? Is it immoral to accept workers' compensation when you are fully capable of working?

8. What behaviors constitute emotional abuse at work? What would you consider an abuse of one's position power?

9. Are high-stress jobs a breach of ethics? What about transfers that break up families?

10. Are all rule violations equally important? Do employees have an ethical obligation to follow company rules?

11. To what extent are you responsible for the ethical behavior of your coworkers? If you witness unethical behavior and don't report it, are you an accessory?

12. Is it ethical to help one work group at the expense of another group? For instance, suppose one group has excellent performance and you want to reward its members with an afternoon off. The other work group will have to pick up the slack and work harder if you do this. Is this ethical?

Once your group has been assigned its issue, you have two tasks:

1. First, formulate your group's answer to the ethical dilemmas.

2. After you have formulated your group's position, discuss the individual differences that may have contributed to your position. You will want to discuss the individual differences presented in this chapter as well as any others that you feel affected your position on the ethical dilemma.

Your instructor will lead the class in a discussion of how individual differences may have influenced your positions on these ethical dilemmas.

SOURCE: Issues adapted from J. O. Cherrington and D. J. Cherrington, "A Menu of Moral Issues: One Week in the Life of *The Wall Street Journal*," *Journal of Business Ethics* 11 (1992): 255–265. Reprinted by permission of Kluwer Academic Publishers.

For more practice exercises, consult the fifth edition of *Organizational Behavior: Experiences and Cases* by Dorothy Marcic and Joseph Seltzer (South-Western, 1998).

Learning Objectives

After reading this chapter, you should be able to do the following:

1. Define *motivation.* *p. 133*

2. Explain how Theory X and Theory Y relate to Maslow's hierarchy of needs. *p. 137*

3. Discuss the needs for achievement, power, and affiliation. *p. 139*

4. Describe the two-factor theory of motivation. *p. 140*

5. Describe how inequity influences individual motivation and behavior. *p. 146*

6. Explain seven different strategies for resolving inequity. *p. 149*

7. Describe the expectancy theory of motivation. *p. 151*

8. Describe the cultural differences in motivation. *p. 154*

5

Motivation at Work

Thinking Ahead

Motivation without Compensation—The Red Cross at Work

Most companies and organizations pay people for the work they do, a conventional feature of the American free enterprise system. Money provides for most of the necessities of life, and the majority of workers in the world expect to be paid for their work. However, this is not universally true. Each year, throughout the United States and the world, a significant amount of valuable, important work is done on a voluntary basis for the common good. Various religious and civic organizations rely heavily on unpaid volunteers to accomplish their work and achieve their missions. This is especially true for the American Red Cross, the largest volunteer organization in the United States. The American Red Cross is a humanitarian organization under the leadership of volunteers. The Red Cross's nearly 1.4 million volunteers outnumber the paid staff 45 to 1; the volunteers are a force to be reckoned with in times of disaster and need.[1] When floods, forest fires, bombings, or hostile military actions create human suffering and the need for relief and a human touch, American

Red Cross volunteers are there. When the Oklahoma City bombing devastated the community, Red Cross volunteers were there. They provide first aid, perform cardiopulmonary resuscitation, oversee the collection of blood, provide service on military installations in the United States and around the world, and help communities prepare for disasters. The diverse, intergenerational workforce of volunteers is made up of young adults (6 percent), adults over the age of twenty-five (63 percent), and a significant minority of youths aged eighteen or under (31 percent). Whereas employees in business enterprises are often motivated by external or economic incentives, Red Cross volunteers are intrinsically motivated by the need to care for and nurture others and by a commitment to the common good. At the end of this chapter, we see how American Red Cross volunteers receive recognition and rewards for their contributions to the well-being of their communities, the nation, and the world.

This is the first of two chapters about motivation, behavior, and performance at work. A comprehensive approach to understanding motivation, behavior, and performance must consider three elements of the work situation—the individual, the job, and the work environment—and how these elements interact.[2] This chapter emphasizes internal and process theories of motivation. It begins with individual need theories of motivation; turns to the two-factor theory of motivation, which foreshadows theories of job design discussed in Chapter 13; and finishes by examining two individual–environment interaction or process theories of motivation. The next chapter (Chapter 6) emphasizes external theories of motivation and focuses on factors in the environment to help understand good or bad performance.

MOTIVATION AND WORK BEHAVIOR

Motivation is the process of arousing and sustaining goal-directed behavior. Motivation is one of the more complex topics in organizational behavior. *Motivation* comes from the Latin root word *movere*, which means "to move."

Motivation theories attempt to explain and predict observable behavior. The wide range and variety of motivation theories result from the great diversity of people and complexity of their behavior in organizations. Early attempts were made to develop universal theories of motivation, but more recent research recognizes the limitations as well as the power of the various theories and classes of theories. Motivation theories may be broadly classified into internal, process, and external theories of motivation. Internal theories of motivation give primary consideration to variables within the individual that give rise to motivation and behavior. The hierarchy of needs theory exemplifies the internal theories. Process theories of motivation emphasize the nature of the interaction between the individual and the environment. Expectancy theory exemplifies the process theories. External theories of motivation focus on the elements in the environment, including

1. Define *motivation*.

motivation
The process of arousing and sustaining goal-directed behavior.

the consequences of behavior, as the basis for understanding and explaining people's behavior at work. Any single motivation theory explains only a small portion of the variance in human behavior. Therefore, alternative theories have developed over time in an effort to account for the unexplained portions of the variance in behavior.

Internal Needs

Philosophers and scholars have theorized for centuries about human needs and motives. Over the past century, attention narrowed to understanding motivation in businesses and other organizations.[3] Max Weber, an early German organizational scholar, argued that the meaning of work lay not in the work itself but in its deeper potential for contributing to a person's ultimate salvation.[4] From this Calvinistic perspective, the Protestant ethic was the fuel for human industriousness. The Protestant ethic said people should work hard because those who prospered at work were more likely to find a place in heaven. Challenge 5.1 gives you an opportunity to evaluate

Challenge 5.1

Protestant Ethic

Rate the following statements from 1 (for *disagree completely*) to 6 (for *agree completely*).

____ **1.** When the workday is finished, people should forget their jobs and enjoy themselves.
____ **2.** Hard work makes us better people.
____ **3.** The principal purpose of people's jobs is to provide them with the means for enjoying their free time.
____ **4.** Wasting time is as bad as wasting money.
____ **5.** Whenever possible, a person should relax and accept life as it is rather than always striving for unreachable goals.
____ **6.** A good indication of a person's worth is how well he or she does his or her job.
____ **7.** If all other things are equal, it is better to have a job with a lot of responsibility than one with little responsibility.
____ **8.** People who "do things the easy way" are the smart ones.

____ Total your score for the pro-Protestant ethic items (2, 4, 6, and 7).
____ Total your score for the non-Protestant ethic items (1, 3, 5, and 8).

A pro-Protestant ethic score of 20 or over indicates you have a strong work ethic; 15–19 indicates a moderately strong work ethic; 9–14 indicates a moderately weak work ethic; 8 or less indicates a weak work ethic.

A non-Protestant ethic score of 20 or over indicates you have a strong non-work ethic; 15–19 indicates a moderately strong non-work ethic; 9–14 indicates a moderately weak non-work ethic; 8 or less indicates a weak non-work ethic.

SOURCE: M. R. Blood, "Work Values and Job Satisfaction," *Journal of Applied Psychology* 53 (1969): 456–459. Copyright © 1969 by the American Psychological Association. Reprinted with permission.

how strongly you have a pro-Protestant versus a non-Protestant ethic. Although Weber, and later Blood, both used the term *Protestant ethic*, many see the value elements of this work ethic in the broader Judeo-Christian tradition. We concur.

A more complex motivation theory was proposed by Sigmund Freud. For him, a person's organizational life was founded on the compulsion to work and the power of love.[5] He saw much of human motivation as unconscious by nature. ***Psychoanalysis*** was Freud's method for delving into the unconscious mind to better understand a person's motives and needs. Freud's psychodynamic theory offers explanations for irrational and self-destructive behavior, such as the behavior manifested by the postal worker in Oklahoma who gunned down several coworkers in the late 1980s.[6] The motives underlying such traumatic work events may be understood by analyzing a person's unconscious needs and motives. Freud's theorizing is important as the basis for subsequent need theories of motivation.

Internal needs and external incentives both play an important role in motivation. Although extrinsic motivation is important, so too is intrinsic motivation, which varies by the individual.[7] Therefore, it is important for managers to consider both internal needs and external incentives when attempting to motivate their employees. Further, managers who are more supportive and less controlling appear to elicit more intrinsic motivation from their employees.

External Incentives

Early organizational scholars made economic assumptions about human motivation and developed corresponding differential piece rate systems of pay that emphasized external incentives. These organizational scholars assumed that people were motivated by self-interest and economic gain. The Hawthorne studies confirmed the beneficial effects of pay incentives on productivity but also found that social and interpersonal motives in behavior were important.[8]

Those who made economic assumptions about human motivation emphasized financial incentives for behavior. The Scottish political economist and moral philosopher Adam Smith argued that a person's ***self-interest*** was God's providence, not the government's.[9] Gordon E. Forward, a member of the board of Texas Industries (TXI), believes people are motivated by "enlightened" self-interest. Self-interest is what is in the best interest and benefit to the individual; enlightened self-interest additionally recognizes the self-interest of other people. Adam Smith laid the cornerstone for the free enterprise system of economics when he formulated the "invisible hand" and the free market to explain the motivation for individual behavior. The "invisible hand" refers to the unseen forces of a free market system that shape the most efficient use of people, money, and resources for productive ends. His theory of political economy subsequently explained collective economic behavior. Smith's basic assumption was that people are motivated by self-interest for economic gain to provide the necessities and conveniences

psychoanalysis
Sigmund Freud's method for delving into the unconscious mind to better understand a person's motives and needs.

self-interest
What is in the best interest and benefit to an individual.

of life. This implies that financial and economic incentives to work are the most important considerations in understanding human behavior. Further, employees are most productive when motivated by self-interest.

Technology is an important concept in Smith's view, because he believed that a nation's wealth is determined by two circumstances: (1) the skill, dexterity, and judgment with which labor is applied and (2) the proportion of the nation's population employed in useful labor versus the proportion not so employed. He considered the first circumstance to be more important. The more efficient and effective labor is, the greater the abundance of the nation. Technology is important as a force multiplier for the productivity of labor in creating products or delivering services.

Frederick Taylor, the founder of scientific management, was also concerned with labor efficiency and effectiveness.[10] His central concern was to change the relationship between management and labor from one of conflict to one of cooperation.[11] Taylor believed the basis of their conflict was the division of the profits within the company. Instead of continuing this conflict over how to divide the profits, labor and management should form a cooperative relationship aimed at enlarging the total profits.

MASLOW'S NEED HIERARCHY

Abraham Maslow, a psychologist, proposed a need theory of motivation emphasizing psychological and interpersonal needs in addition to physical needs and economic necessity. His theory was based on a need hierarchy later applied through Theory X and Theory Y, two sets of assumptions about people at work. In addition, his need hierarchy was reformulated in an ERG theory of motivation using a revised classification scheme for basic human needs.

The Hierarchy of Needs

The core of Maslow's theory of human motivation is a hierarchy of five need categories.[12] Although he recognized that there were factors other than one's needs (for example, culture) that were determinants of behavior, he focused his theoretical attention on specifying people's internal needs. Maslow labeled the five hierarchical categories as physiological needs, safety and security needs, love (social) needs, esteem needs, and the need for self-actualization. Maslow's *need hierarchy* is depicted in Figure 5.1, which also shows how the needs relate to Douglas McGregor's assumptions about people, which will be discussed next.

Maslow conceptually derived the five need categories from the early thoughts of William James[13] and John Dewey,[14] coupled with the psychodynamic thinking of Sigmund Freud and Alfred Adler.[15] Maslow's need theory was later tested in research with working populations. For example, one study reported that middle managers and lower level managers had different perceptions of their need deficiencies and the importance of their needs.[16] More recently, Motorola adapted motivational techniques aimed

Experiencing OB

Need-based theories of motivation are based on drive theory of behavior. To examine drive theory before you read about Maslow's need hierarchy, visit our animated concept and activity site. Choose Motivation from the "select a topic" pull-down menu, then How Needs Motivate from the "overview tab."

http://www.experiencingob.com

need hierarchy
The theory that behavior is determined by a progression of physical, social, and psychological needs by higher order needs.

Figure 5.1
Human Needs, Theory X, and Theory Y

at social and interpersonal needs for its teamwork from its Penang operations in Malaysia to its 2,300-worker factory in Plantation, Florida. One distinguishing feature of Maslow's need hierarchy is the following progression hypothesis. Although some research has challenged the assumption, the theory says that only ungratified needs motivate behavior.[17] Further, it is the lowest level of ungratified needs in the hierarchy that motivates behavior. As one level of need is met, a person progresses to the next higher level of need as a source of motivation. Hence, people progress up the hierarchy as they successively gratify each level of need. For example, an employee may satisfy security needs by obtaining two big promotions and then be motivated by developing good working relationships with coworkers. The problem with the progression hypothesis is that it leaves no way to move down the hierarchy, which could occur, for example, if a person at the esteem level lost a job and was now worried about security.

Theory X and Theory Y

One important organizational implication of the need hierarchy concerns how to manage people at work (see Figure 5.1). Douglas McGregor understood people's motivation using Maslow's need theory. He grouped the physiological and safety needs as "lower order" needs and the social, esteem, and self-actualization needs as "upper order" needs. McGregor proposed two alternative sets of assumptions about people at work based upon which set of needs were the motivators.[18] He labeled these sets of assumptions *Theory X* and *Theory Y*. They are included in Table 5.1. Regardless of people's motivation to work, McGregor saw the responsibility of management as being the same. Specifically, "management is responsible

Experiencing OB

Maslow proposed that an unsatisfied need on a lower level must be satisfied before a need on the next higher level would become active on behavior. To interact with this idea, visit our animated concept and activity site. Choose Motivation from the "select a topic" pull-down menu, then Maslow's Need Hierarchy from the "overview tab."

http://www.experiencingob.com

2. Explain how Theory X and Theory Y relate to Maslow's hierarchy of needs.

Theory X
A set of assumptions of how to manage individuals who are motivated by lower order needs.

THEORY X	THEORY Y
■ People are by nature indolent. That is, they work as little as possible.	■ People are not by nature passive or resistant to organizational needs. They have become so as a result of experience in organizations.
■ People lack ambition, dislike responsibility, and prefer to be led.	■ The motivation, the potential for development, the capacity for assuming responsibility, and the readiness to direct behavior toward organizational goals are all present in people. Management does not put them there. It is a responsibility of management to make it possible for people to recognize and develop these human characteristics for themselves.
■ People are inherently self-centered and indifferent to organizational needs.	
■ People are by nature resistant to change.	
■ People are gullible and not very bright, the ready dupes of the charlatan and the demagogue.	■ The essential task of management is to arrange conditions and methods of operation so that people can achieve their own goals best by directing their own efforts toward organizational objectives.

Table 5.1
McGregor's Assumptions about People

Theory Y
A set of assumptions of how to manage individuals who are motivated by higher order needs.

for organizing the elements of productive enterprise—money, materials, equipment, people—in the interest of economic ends."[19]

According to McGregor, people should be treated differently depending on whether they are motivated by lower order or higher order needs. Specifically, McGregor believed that Theory X assumptions are appropriate for employees motivated by lower order needs. Theory Y assumptions, in contrast, are appropriate for employees motivated by higher order needs, and Theory X assumptions are then inappropriate. In addition, McGregor believed that in the 1950s, when he was writing, the majority of American workers had satisfied their lower order needs and were therefore motivated by higher order needs.

Employee participation programs are one consequence of McGregor's Theory Y assumptions. Ford Motor Company's first step in revitalizing its workforce through an employee involvement (EI) program was based on Theory Y assumptions about human nature.[20] However, some companies, such as Lincoln Electric, use money as the chief source of employee motivation.

Gordon E. Forward, a member of the board of Texas Industries (TXI), considers the assumptions made about people central to motivation and management.[21] He views employees as resources to be developed, not labor costs to be charged off. A future-thinking, enlightened executive, Forward has fun at work and at play. Using Maslow's need hierarchy and Theory Y assumptions about people, he cultivated and developed a productive, loyal workforce in TXI's Chaparral Steel unit.

ERG Theory

Clayton Alderfer, while recognizing the value of Maslow's contribution to understanding motivation, believed that the original need hierarchy was not quite accurate in identifying and categorizing human needs.[22] As an evolutionary development of the need hierarchy, Alderfer proposed the ERG theory of motivation, which grouped human needs into only three basic categories: existence, relatedness, and growth.[23] Alderfer classified Maslow's physiological and physical safety needs in an existence need category; Maslow's interpersonal safety, love, and interpersonal esteem needs in a relatedness need category; and Maslow's self-actualization and self-esteem needs in a growth need category.

In addition to the differences in categorizing human needs, ERG theory added a regression hypothesis to go along with the progression hypothesis originally proposed by Maslow. Alderfer's regression hypothesis helped explain people's behavior when frustrated at meeting needs at the next higher level in the hierarchy. Specifically, the regression hypothesis states that people regress to the next lower category of needs and intensify their desire to gratify these needs. Hence, ERG theory explains both progressive need and gratification up the hierarchy and regression when people are faced with frustration. Figure 5.2 shows the relationship between Maslow's hierarchy of needs and Alderfer's ERG theory.

MCCLELLAND'S NEED THEORY

A second major need theory of motivation focuses on personality and learned needs. Henry Murray developed a long list of motives and manifest needs in his early studies of personality.[24] David McClelland, a psycholo-

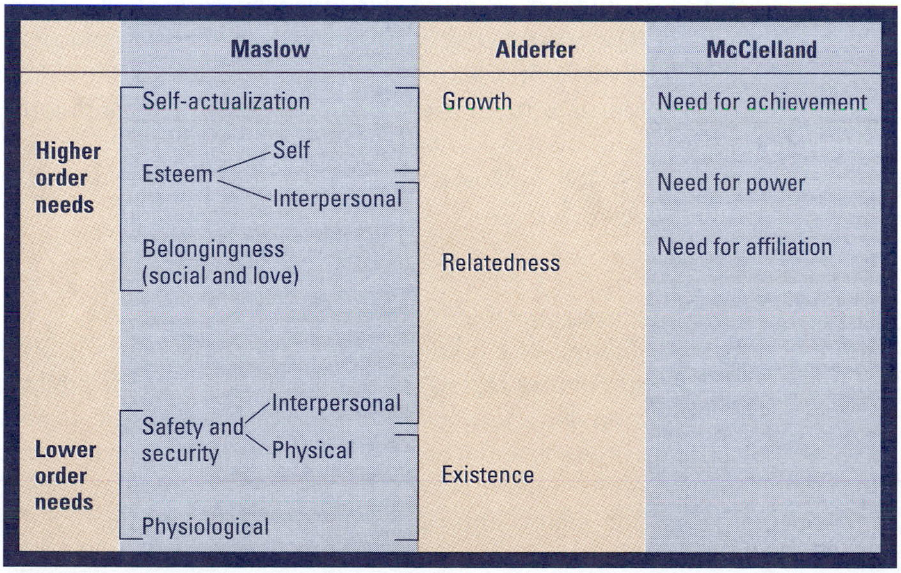

3. Discuss the needs for achievement, power, and affiliation.

	Maslow		Alderfer	McClelland
Higher order needs	Self-actualization		Growth	Need for achievement
	Esteem — Self			
	— Interpersonal			Need for power
	Belongingness (social and love)		Relatedness	Need for affiliation
Lower order needs	Safety and security — Interpersonal — Physical		Existence	
	Physiological			

Figure 5.2
Three Need Theories of Motivation

gist, was inspired by Murray's early work.[25] McClelland identified three learned or acquired needs he called manifest needs. These manifest needs were the needs for achievement, for power, and for affiliation. Individuals and national cultures differ in their levels of these needs. Some individuals have a high need for achievement, whereas others have a moderate or low need for achievement. The same is true for the other two needs. Hence, it is important to emphasize that different needs are dominant in different people. For example, a manager may have a strong need for power, a moderate need for achievement, and a weak need for affiliation. Each need has quite different implications for people's behavior. The Murray Thematic Apperception Test (TAT) was used as an early measure of the achievement motive and was further developed, both qualitatively and quantitatively, by McClelland and his associates.[26] The TAT is a projective test, and projective tests were discussed in Chapter 3.

HERZBERG'S TWO-FACTOR THEORY

4. Describe the two-factor theory of motivation.

Frederick Herzberg departed from the need theories of motivation and examined the experiences that satisfied or dissatisfied people at work. This motivation theory became known as the two-factor theory.[27] Herzberg's original study included 200 engineers and accountants in western Pennsylvania during the 1950s. Herzberg asked these people to describe two important incidents at their jobs: one that was very satisfying and made them feel exceptionally good at work, and another that was very dissatisfying and made them feel exceptionally bad at work.

Herzberg and his colleagues believed that people had two sets of needs—one related to the animalistic avoidance of pain and one related to the humanistic desire for psychological growth. Conditions in the work environment would affect one or the other of these needs. Work conditions related to satisfaction of the need for psychological growth were labeled *motivation factors*. Work conditions related to dissatisfaction caused by discomfort or pain were labeled *hygiene factors*. Each set of factors related to one aspect of what Herzberg identified as the human being's dual nature regarding the work environment. Thus, motivation factors relate to job satisfaction, and hygiene factors relate to job dissatisfaction.[28] These two independent factors are depicted in Figure 5.3.

motivation factor
A work condition related to satisfaction of the need for psychological growth.

hygiene factor
A work condition related to dissatisfaction caused by discomfort or pain.

Motivation Factors

Job satisfaction is produced by building motivation factors into a job, according to Herzberg. This process is known as job enrichment. In the original research, the motivation factors were identified as responsibility, achievement, recognition, advancement, and the work itself. These factors relate to the content of the job and what the employee actually does on the job. When these factors are present, they lead to superior performance and effort on the part of job incumbents. These factors directly influence the way people feel about their work. Figure 5.3 also shows that salary is a motivational factor in some studies. Many organizational reward systems now

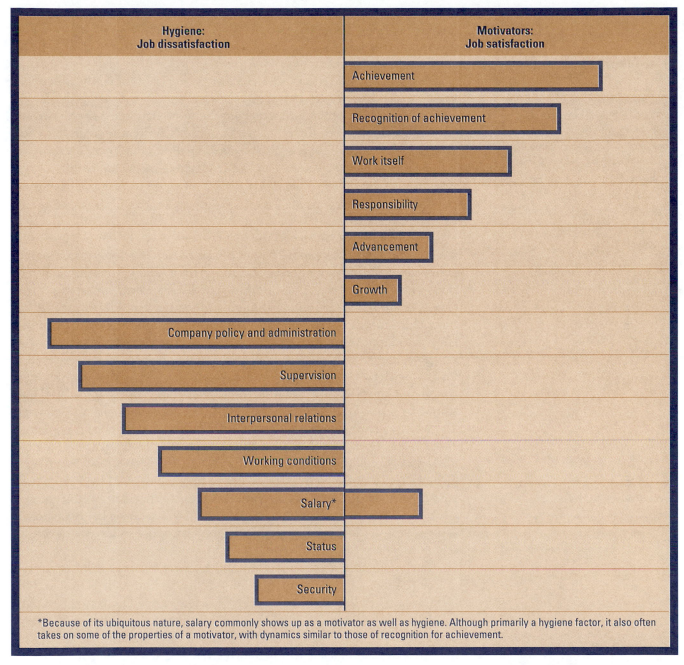

Hygiene: Job dissatisfaction	Motivators: Job satisfaction
	Achievement
	Recognition of achievement
	Work itself
	Responsibility
	Advancement
	Growth
Company policy and administration	
Supervision	
Interpersonal relations	
Working conditions	
Salary*	
Status	
Security	

*Because of its ubiquitous nature, salary commonly shows up as a motivator as well as hygiene. Although primarily a hygiene factor, it also often takes on some of the properties of a motivator, with dynamics similar to those of recognition for achievement.

SOURCE: Reprinted from Frederick Herzberg, *The Managerial Choice: To Be Efficient or to Be Human* (Salt Lake City: Olympus, 1982). Reprinted by permission.

Figure 5.3
The Motivation–Hygiene Theory of Motivation

include other financial benefits, such as stock options, as part of an employee's compensation package.

Motivation factors lead to positive mental health and challenge people to grow, contribute to the work environment, and invest themselves in the organization. During the 1980s, recognition was used as an important mo-

Experiencing OB

Herzberg believed that hygiene factors and motivation factors have quite different effects on employee behavior. An interactive presentation of his ideas is found at our animated concept and activity site. Choose Motivation from the "select a topic" pull-down menu, then Herzberg's Two-Factor Theory from the "overview tab."

http://www.experiencingob.com

tivation factor at the former Perpetual Financial Corporation, which hosted a companywide "Salute to Associates" to thank employees. However, programs like this one require constant supervision and do not eliminate the need for other rewards.

According to the theory and Herzberg's original results, the absence of these factors does not lead to dissatisfaction. Rather, it leads to the lack of satisfaction. The motivation factors are the more important of the two sets of factors, because they directly affect a person's motivational drive to do a good job. When they are absent, the person will be demotivated to perform well and achieve excellence. The hygiene factors are a completely distinct set of factors unrelated to the motivation to achieve and do excellent work.

Hygiene Factors

Job dissatisfaction occurs when the hygiene factors are either not present or not sufficient. In the original research, the hygiene factors were company policy and administration, technical supervision, salary, interpersonal relations with one's supervisor, and working conditions, salary, and status. These factors relate to the context of the job and may be considered support factors. They do not directly affect a person's motivation to work but influence the extent of the person's discontent. These factors cannot stimulate psychological growth or human development. They may be thought of as maintenance factors, because they contribute to an individual's basic needs. Excellent hygiene factors result in employees' being *not dissatisfied* and contribute to the absence of complaints about these contextual considerations.

When these hygiene factors are poor or absent, the person complains about "poor supervision," "poor medical benefits," or whatever hygiene factor is poor. Employees experience a deficit and are dissatisfied when the hygiene factors are not present. Even in the absence of good hygiene factors, employees may still be very motivated to perform their jobs well if the motivation factors are present. Although this may appear to be a paradox, it is not, because the motivation and hygiene factors are independent of each other.

The combination of motivation and hygiene factors can result in one of four possible job conditions. First, a job high in both motivation and hygiene factors leads to high motivation and few complaints among employees. In this job condition, employees are motivated to perform well and are contented with the conditions of their work environment. Second, a job low in both factors leads to low motivation and many complaints among employees. Under such conditions, employees are not only demotivated to perform well but are also discontented with the conditions of their work environment. Third, a job high in motivation factors and low in hygiene factors leads to high employee motivation to perform coupled with complaints about aspects of the work environment. Discontented employees may still be able to do an excellent job if they take pride in the product or service. Fourth, a job low in motivation factors and high in hygiene factors leads to low employee motivation to excel but few complaints about the work environment. These complacent employees have little motivation to do an outstanding job.

Two conclusions may be drawn at this point. First, hygiene factors are of some importance up to a threshold level, but beyond the threshold there is little value in improving the hygiene factors. Second, the presence of motivation factors is essential to enhancing employee motivation to excel at work. Challenge 5.2 asks you to rank a set of ten job reward factors in terms of their importance to the average employee, to supervisors, and to you.

Critique of the Two-Factor Theory

Herzberg's two-factor theory has been criticized. One criticism concerns the classification of motivation and hygiene factors. Data have not shown a clear dichotomization of incidents into hygiene and motivator factors. For example, employees almost equally classify pay as a hygiene factor and as a motivation factor. A second criticism is the absence of individual differences in the theory. Specifically, individual differences such as age, sex,

Challenge 5.2

What's Important to Employees?

There are many possible job rewards that employees may receive. Listed below are ten possible job reward factors. Rank these factors three times. First, rank them as you think the average employee would rank them. Second, rank them as you think the average employee's supervisor would rank them for the employee. Finally, rank them according to what you consider important.

Employee   Supervisor   You

1. job security
2. full appreciation of work done
3. promotion and growth in the organization
4. good wages
5. interesting work
6. good working conditions
7. tactful discipline
8. sympathetic help with personal problems
9. personal loyalty to employees
10. a feeling of being in on things

Your instructor has normative data for 1,000 employees and their supervisors that will help you interpret your results and place the results in the context of Maslow's need hierarchy and Herzberg's two-factor theory of motivation.

SOURCE: "Crossed Wires on Employee Motivation," *Training and Development* 49 (1995): 59–60. American Society for Training and Development. Reprinted with permission. All rights reserved.

social status, education, or occupational level may influence the classification of factors as motivation or hygiene. A third criticism is that intrinsic job factors, such as the work flow process, may be more important in determining satisfaction or dissatisfaction on the job.[29] Finally, almost all of the supporting data for the theory come from Herzberg and his students using his peculiar type of critical-incident storytelling technique. These criticisms challenge and qualify, yet do not invalidate, the theory. Herzberg's two-factor theory has important implications for job enrichment and the design of work, as discussed in Chapter 13.

Need for Achievement

need for achievement
A manifest (easily perceived) need that concerns individuals' issues of excellence, competition, challenging goals, persistence, and overcoming difficulties.

The *need for achievement* concerns issues of excellence, competition, challenging goals, persistence, and overcoming difficulties.[30] A person with a high need for achievement seeks excellence in performance, enjoys difficult and challenging goals, and is persevering and competitive in work activities. Questions that address the need for achievement are ones like these: Do you enjoy difficult, challenging work activities? Do you strive to exceed your performance objectives? Do you seek out new ways to overcome difficulties?

McClelland found that people with a high need for achievement perform better than those with a moderate or low need for achievement, and he has noted national differences in achievement motivation. Individuals with a high need for achievement have three unique characteristics. First, they set goals that are moderately difficult yet achievable, because they want both challenge and a good chance for success. Second, they like to receive feedback on their progress toward these goals. Because success is important to them, they like to know how they are doing. Third, they do not like having external events or other people interfere with their progress toward the goals. They are most comfortable working on individual tasks and activities that they control.

High achievers often hope and plan for success. They may be quite content to work alone or with other people—whichever is more appropriate to their task. High achievers like being very good at what they do, and they develop expertise and competence in their chosen endeavors. An example of a person with a high need for achievement is an information systems engineer who declines supervisory or managerial responsibility and devotes her energy to being the very best information systems engineer she can be.

Recent research shows that need for achievement generalizes well across countries with adults who are employed full-time.[31] In addition, international differences in the tendency for achievement have been found in global research on achievement. Specifically, achievement tendencies are highest for the United States, an individualistic culture, and lowest for Japan and Hungary, collectivistic societies.[32]

Need for Power

need for power
A manifest (easily perceived) need that concerns an individual's need to make an impact on others, influence others, change people or events, and make a difference in life.

The *need for power* is concerned with making an impact on others, the desire to influence others, the urge to change people or events, and the desire to make a difference in life. The need for power is interpersonal, because it involves influence attempts directed at other people. People with a high need for power like to be in control of people and events. McClelland makes an important distinction between socialized power, which is used for the social benefit of many, and personalized power, which is used for the personal gain of the individual. The former is a constructive force in organizations, whereas the latter may be a very disruptive, destructive force in organizations.

A high need for power was one distinguishing characteristic of managers rated the "best" in McClelland's research. Specifically, the best managers had a very high need for socialized power, used for the collective well-being of the group, as opposed to personalized power.[33] These managers are concerned for others; have an interest in the organization's larger goals; and have a desire to be useful to the larger group, organization, and society.

Social and hierarchical status are important considerations for people with a high need for power. The more they are able to rise to the top of their organizations, the greater is their ability to exercise power, influence, and control so as to make an impact. Successful managers have the greatest upward velocity in an organization; they rise to higher managerial levels more quickly than their contemporaries.[34] These successful managers benefit their organizations most if they have a high socialized power need. The need for power is discussed further in Chapter 10, on power and politics.

Need for Affiliation

The *need for affiliation* is concerned with establishing and maintaining warm, close, intimate relationships with other people.[35] People with a high need for affiliation are motivated to express their emotions and feelings to others while expecting other people to do the same in return. They find conflicts and complications in their relationships disturbing and are strongly motivated to work through any such barriers to closeness. The relationships they have with others are therefore close and personal, emphasizing friendship and companionship.

People who have moderate to low needs for affiliation are more likely to feel comfortable working alone for extended periods of time. Modest or low levels of interaction with others are likely to satisfy these people's affiliation needs, allowing them to focus their attention on other needs and activities. People with a high need for affiliation, in contrast, always hope to be included in a range of interpersonal activities, in or away from work. They may play important integrative roles in group or intergroup activities because they work to achieve harmony and closeness in all relationships.

Over and above these three needs, Murray's manifest needs theory included the need for autonomy. This is the desire for independence and freedom from any constraints. People with a high need for autonomy like to work alone and to control the pace of their work. They dislike bureaucratic rules, regulations, and procedures. Figure 5.2 is a summary chart of the three

need for affiliation
A manifest (easily perceived) need that concerns an individual's need to establish and maintain warm, close, intimate relationships with other people.

need theories of motivation just discussed; it shows the parallel relationships between the needs in each of the theories. While Maslow and Alderfer would refer to higher and lower order needs, McClelland does not make a similar distinction.

SOCIAL EXCHANGE AND EQUITY THEORY

5. Describe how inequity influences individual motivation and behavior.

Equity theory is a social exchange process theory of motivation that focuses on the individual–environment interaction. In contrast to internal needs theories of motivation, equity theory is concerned with the social processes that influence motivation and behavior. Peter Blau suggests that power and exchange are important considerations in understanding human behavior.[36] In the same vein, Amitai Etzioni developed three categories of exchange relationships or involvements people have with organizations: committed, calculated, and alienated involvements.[37] The implications of these involvements for power are discussed in detail in Chapter 10. Etzioni characterized committed involvements as moral relationships of high positive intensity, calculated involvements as ones of low positive or low negative intensity, and alienated involvements as ones of high negative intensity. Committed involvements may characterize a person's relationship with a religious group, and alienated involvements may characterize a person's relationship with a prison system. Calculated involvements and Blau's ideas about power in social exchange are the best frameworks for understanding (the equity or inequity of) a person's relationship with a work organization.

Demands and Contributions

Calculated involvements are based on the notion of social exchange in which each party in the relationship demands certain things of the other and contributes accordingly to the exchange. Business partnerships and commercial deals are excellent examples of calculated involvements. When they work well and both parties to the exchange benefit, the relationship has a positive orientation. When losses occur or conflicts arise, the relationship has a negative orientation. A model for examining these calculated exchange relationships is set out in Figure 5.4. We use this model to examine the nature of the relationship between a person and his or her employing organization.[38] The same basic model can be used to examine the relationship between two individuals or two organizations.

Demands   Each party to the exchange makes demands upon the other. These demands express the expectations that each party has of the other in the relationship. The organization expresses its demands on the individual in the form of goal or mission statements, job expectations, performance objectives, and performance feedback. These are among the primary and formal mechanisms through which people learn about the organization's demands and expectations of them.

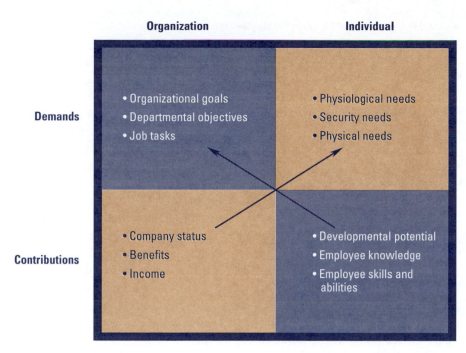

Figure 5.4
The Individual–Organizational Exchange Relationship

SOURCE: Reproduced with permission from McGraw-Hill, Inc.

The organization is not alone in making demands of the relationship. The individual has needs to be satisfied as well, as we have previously discussed. These needs form the basis for the expectations or demands placed on the organization by the individual. These needs may be conceptualized from the perspective of Maslow, Alderfer, Herzberg, or McClelland. Different individuals have different needs.

Contributions Just as each party to the exchange makes demands upon the other, each also has contributions to make to the relationship. These contributions are the basis for satisfying the demands expressed by the other party in the relationship. Employees are able to satisfy organizational demands through a range of contributions, including their skills, abilities, knowledge, energy, professional contacts, and native talents. As people grow and develop over time, they are able to increasingly satisfy the range of demands and expectations placed upon them by the organization.

In a similar fashion, organizations have a range of contributions available to the exchange relationship to meet individual needs. These contributions include salary, benefits, advancement opportunities, security, status, and social affiliation. Some organizations are richer in resources and better able to meet employee needs than other organizations. Thus, one of the concerns that individuals and organizations alike have is whether the relationship is a fair deal or an equitable arrangement for both members of the relationship.

inequity
The situation in which a person perceives he or she is receiving less than he or she is giving, or is giving less than he or she is receiving.

Adams's Theory of Inequity

Blau's and Etzioni's ideas about social process and exchange provide a context for understanding fairness, equity, and inequity in work relationships. Stacy Adams explicitly developed the idea that *inequity* in the social exchange process is an important motivator.[39] Adams's theory of inequity suggests that people are motivated when they find themselves in situations of inequity or unfairness.[40] Inequity occurs when a person receives more, or less, than the person believes is deserved based on effort and/or contribution. Inequity leads to the experience of tension, and tension motivates a person to act in a manner to resolve the inequity.

When does a person know that the situation is inequitable or unfair? Adams suggests that people examine the contribution portion of the exchange relationship just discussed. Specifically, people consider their inputs (their own contributions to the relationship) and their outcomes (the organization's contributions to the relationship). People then calculate an input/outcome ratio, which they compare with that of a generalized or comparison other. Figure 5.5 shows one equity situation and two inequity situations, one negative and one positive. For example, inequity in (b) could occur if the comparison other earned a higher salary, and inequity in (c) could occur if the person had more vacation time, in both cases all else being equal. Although not illustrated in the example, nontangible inputs, like emotional investment, and nontangible outcomes, like job satisfaction, may well enter into a person's equity equation.

Pay inequity has been a particularly thorny issue for women in some professions and companies. Eastman Kodak and other companies have made real progress in addressing this inequity through pay equity.[41] As organizations become increasingly international, it may be difficult to determine pay and benefit equity/inequity across national borders.

Adams would consider the inequity in Figure 5.5(b) to be a first level of inequity. A more severe, second level of inequity would occur if the comparison other's inputs were lower than the person's. Inequalities in one (inputs or outcomes) coupled with equality in the other (inputs or outcomes)

Figure 5.5
Equity and Inequity at Work

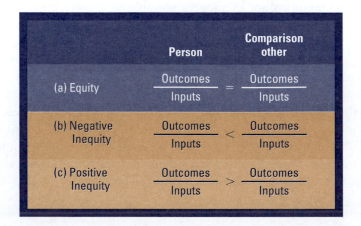

are experienced as a less severe inequity than inequalities in both inputs and outcomes. Adams's theory, however, does not provide a way of determining if some inputs (such as effort or experience) or some outcomes are more important or weighted more than others, such as a degree or certification.

The Resolution of Inequity

Once a person establishes the existence of an inequity, a number of strategies can be used to restore equity to the situation. Adams's theory provides seven basic strategies to restore equity for the person: (1) alter the person's outcomes, (2) alter the person's inputs, (3) alter the comparison other's outcomes, (4) alter the comparison other's inputs, (5) change who is used as a comparison other, (6) rationalize the inequity, and (7) leave the organizational situation.

6. Explain seven different strategies for resolving inequity.

Within each of the first four strategies, a wide variety of tactics can be employed. For example, if an employee has a strategy to increase his or her income by $11,000 per year to restore equity, the tactic might be a meeting between the employee and his or her manager concerning the issue of salary equity. The person would present relevant data on the issue. Another tactic would be for the person to work with the company's compensation specialists. A third tactic would be for the person to bring the matter before an equity committee in the company. A fourth tactic would be for the person to seek advice from the legal department.

The selection of a strategy and a set of tactics is a sensitive issue with possible long-term consequences. In this example, a strategy aimed at reducing the comparison other's outcomes may have the desired short-term effect of restoring equity while having adverse long-term consequences in terms of morale and productivity. Similarly, the choice of legal tactics may result in equity but have the long-term consequence of damaged relationships in the workplace. Therefore, as a person formulates the strategy and tactics to restore equity, the range of consequences of alternative actions must be taken into account. Hence, not all strategies or tactics are equally preferred. The equity theory does not include a hierarchy predicting which inequity reduction strategy a person will or should choose.

Field studies on equity theory suggest that it may help explain important organizational behaviors. For example, one study found that workers who perceived compensation decisions as equitable displayed greater job satisfaction and organizational commitment.[42] In addition, equity theory may play an important role in labor–management relationships with regard to union-negotiated benefits.

New Perspectives on Equity Theory

Since the original formulation of the theory of inequity, now usually referred to as equity theory, a number of revisions have been made in light of new theories and research. One important theoretical revision proposes three types of individuals based on preferences for equity.[43] **Equity sensitives** are

equity sensitive
An individual who prefers an equity ratio equal to that of his or her comparison other.

benevolent
An individual who is comfortable with an equity ratio less than that of his or her comparison other.

entitled
An individual who is comfortable with an equity ratio greater than that of his or her comparison other.

those people who prefer equity based on the originally formed theory. Equity sensitivity contributes significantly to variation in free time spent working.[44] *Benevolents* are people who are comfortable with an equity ratio less than that of their comparison other, as exhibited in the Calvinistic heritage of the Dutch.[45] These people may be thought of as givers. *Entitleds* are people who are comfortable with an equity ratio greater than that of their comparison other, as exhibited by some offspring of the affluent who want and expect more.[46] These people may be thought of as takers. Females and minorities have not always been equitably treated in business and commerce. Organizational Reality 5.1 shows how one female entrepreneur has built a healthy manufacturing business while being sensitive to equity and fairness for women and minorities.

Research suggests that a person's organizational position influences self-imposed performance expectations.[47] Specifically, a two-level move up in an organization with no additional pay creates a higher self-imposed performance expectation than a one-level move up with modest additional pay. Similarly, a two-level move down in an organization with no reduction in

---

ORGANIZATIONAL REALITY 5.1

The Equity-Sensitive Female Entrepreneur

Kim Peacock is a female entrepreneur who has built an award-winning $6 million manufacturing business. GNS Foods, Inc., manufactures, packages, and distributes nuts, snack mixes, and candy to 250 customers (distributors, repackers, and retailers) throughout the United States. In addition to building the business through growth, GNS Foods has expanded through the acquisition of the assets of a candy manufacturer in 1994. The manufacturing operations and warehouse are located in a 25,000-square-foot company-owned building.

As a certified Disadvantaged Business enterprise with twenty-five employees, GNS Foods is sensitive and committed to motivating, training, and promoting women and minorities from within the company. Women hold four of the six management positions in the company, one of which is held by Kim who serves as president and CEO. Another woman holds the plant manager's job, a typically male role in manufacturing organizations. All six lead worker positions are held by minorities. Kim Peacock has learned to speak Spanish fluently as a second language and has encouraged a bilingual culture (English and Spanish) in the business. The one full-time Vietnamese employee, who was GNS's 1995 Employee of the Year, takes private one-on-one, company-paid English lessons. Company-wide memos and announcements are issued in English and Spanish.

Kim Peacock is an equity entrepreneur who encourages an organizational culture in which women and minorities feel equitably treated and are motivated to work hard, perform well, and be rewarded for their effort and success.

Discussion Questions

1. What are the pros and cons of an actively bilingual work environment?

2. What elements of Kim Peacock's approach are or could be applied where you work?

SOURCE: Mid-Cities Entrepreneurship Council, Mid-Cities Entrepreneurship Achievement Award and videotape (Arlington, Tex.: The University of Texas at Arlington, 1997).

pay creates a lower self-imposed performance expectation than a one-level move down with a modest decrease in pay. This suggests that organizational position may be more important than pay in determining the level of a person's performance expectations. Some limitations of equity theory are its heavy emphasis on pay as an outcome, the difficulty in controlling the choices of a comparison other, and the difficulty the theory has had in explaining the overpayment condition.

Although most studies of equity theory take a short-term perspective, equity comparisons over the long term should be considered as well. Increasing, decreasing, or constant experiences of inequity over time may have very different consequences for people.[48] For example, do increasing experiences of inequity have a debilitating effect on people? In addition, equity theory may help companies implement two-tiered wage structures, such as the one used by American Airlines in the early 1990s. In a two-tiered system, one group of employees receives different pay and benefits than another group of employees. A study of 1,935 rank-and-file members in one retail chain using a two-tiered wage structure confirmed the predictions of equity theory.[49] The researchers suggest that unions and management may want to consider work location and employment status (part-time versus full-time) prior to the implementation of a two-tiered system.

EXPECTANCY THEORY OF MOTIVATION

Whereas equity theory focuses on a social exchange process, Vroom's expectancy theory of motivation focuses on personal perceptions of the performance process. His theory is founded on the basic notions that people desire certain outcomes of behavior and performance, which may be thought of as rewards or consequences of behavior, and that they believe there are relationships between the effort they put forth, the performance they achieve, and the outcomes they receive. Expectancy theory is a cognitive process theory of motivation.

The key constructs in the expectancy theory of motivation are the *valence* of an outcome, *expectancy*, and *instrumentality*.[50] Valence is the value or importance one places on a particular reward. Expectancy is the belief that effort leads to performance (for example, "If I try harder, I can do better"). Instrumentality is the belief that performance is related to rewards (for example, "If I perform better, I will get more pay"). A model for the expectancy theory notions of effort, performance, and rewards is depicted in Figure 5.6.

Valence, expectancy, and instrumentality are all important to a person's motivation. Expectancy and instrumentality concern a person's beliefs about how effort, performance, and rewards are related. For example, a person may firmly believe that an increase in effort has a direct, positive effect on performance and that a reduced amount of effort results in a commensurate reduction in performance. Another person may have a very different set of beliefs about the effort–performance link. The person might believe that

7. Describe the expectancy theory of motivation.

valence
The value or importance one places on a particular reward.

expectancy
The belief that effort leads to performance.

instrumentality
The belief that performance is related to rewards.

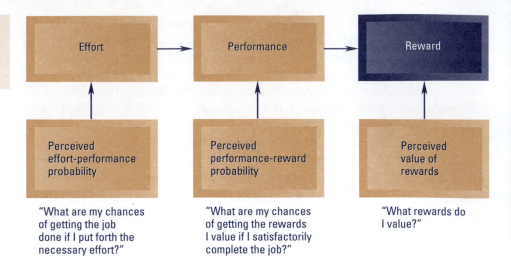

Figure 5.6
An Expectancy Model for Motivation

Experiencing OB

To learn how effort, expectancy, performance, instrumentality, rewards, and valence affect motivation, interact with the Expectancy concept at our animated concept and activity site. Choose Motivation from the "select a topic" pull-down menu, then Expectancy Model from the "overview tab."

http://www.experiencingob.com

regardless of the amount of additional effort put forth, no improvement in performance is possible. Therefore, the perceived relationship between effort and performance varies from person to person and from activity to activity.

In a similar fashion, people's beliefs about the performance–reward link vary. One person may believe that an improvement in performance has a direct, positive effect on the rewards received, whereas another person may believe that an improvement in performance has no effect on the rewards received. Again, the perceived relationship between performance and rewards varies from person to person and from situation to situation. From a motivation perspective, it is the person's belief about the relationships between these constructs that is important, not the actual nature of the relationship.

Expectancy theory has been used by managers and companies to design motivation programs,[51] such as Tenneco's PP&E (Performance Planning and Evaluation) system in the 1970s.[52] In Tenneco's case, the PP&E system was designed to enhance a person's belief that effort would lead to better performance and that better performance would lead to merit pay increases and other rewards. Valence and expectancy are particularly important in establishing priorities for people pursuing multiple goals.[53]

A person's motivation increases along with his or her belief that effort leads to performance and that performance leads to rewards, assuming the person wants the rewards. This is the third key idea within the expectancy theory of motivation. It is the idea that the valence, or value, that people place on various rewards varies. One person prefers salary to benefits, whereas another person prefers just the reverse. All people do not place the same value on each reward.

Motivational Problems

Within the expectancy theory framework, motivational problems stem from three basic causes. These causes are a disbelief in a relationship between effort and performance, a disbelief in a relationship between performance and rewards, and lack of desire for the rewards offered.

If the motivational problem is related to the person's belief that effort will not result in performance, the solution lies in altering this belief. The person can be shown how an increase in effort or an alteration in the kind of effort put forth can be converted into improved performance. For example, the textbook salesperson who does not believe more calls (effort) will result in greater sales (performance) might be shown how to distinguish departments with high-probability sales opportunities from those with low-probability sales opportunities. Hence, more calls (effort) can be converted into greater sales (performance).

If the motivational problem is related to the person's belief that performance will not result in rewards, the solution lies in altering this belief. The person can be shown how an increase in performance or a somewhat altered form of performance will be converted into rewards. For example, the textbook salesperson who does not believe greater sales (performance) will result in overall higher commissions (rewards) might be shown computationally or graphically that a direct relationship does exist. Hence, greater sales (performance) are directly converted into higher commissions (rewards).

If the motivational problem is related to the value the person places on, or the preference the person has for, certain rewards, the solution lies in influencing the value placed on the rewards or altering the rewards themselves. For example, the textbook salesperson may not particularly want higher commissions, given the small incremental gain he would receive at his tax level. In this case, the company might establish a mechanism for sheltering commissions from being taxed or alternative mechanisms for deferred compensation.

Research results on expectancy theory have been mixed.[54] The theory has been shown to predict job satisfaction accurately.[55] However, the theory's complexity makes it difficult to test the full model, and the measures of instrumentality, valence, and expectancy have only weak validity.[56] In addition, measuring the expectancy constructs is time-consuming, and the values for each construct change over time for an individual. Finally, a theory assumes the individual is totally rational and acts as a minicomputer, calculating probabilities and values. In reality, the theory may be more complex than people as they typically function.

Motivation and Moral Maturity

Expectancy theory would predict that people work to maximize their personal outcomes. This is consistent with Adam Smith's ideas of working in one's own self-interest. Ultimately, Adam Smith and expectancy theories

moral maturity
The measure of a person's cognitive moral development.

believe that people work to benefit themselves alone. Expectancy theory would not explain altruistic behavior for the benefit of others. Therefore, it may be necessary to consider an individual's *moral maturity* in order to better understand altruistic, fair, and equitable behavior. Moral maturity is the measure of a person's cognitive moral development, which was discussed in Chapter 4. Morally mature people act and behave based on universal ethical principles, whereas morally immature people act and behave based on egocentric motivations.[57]

Cultural Differences in Motivation

Most motivation theories in use today have been developed by Americans in the United States and are about Americans.[58] When researchers have examined the universality of these theories, they have found cultural differences, at least with regard to Maslow's, McClelland's, Herzberg's, and Vroom's theories. For example, while self-actualization may be the pinnacle need for Americans in Maslow's need hierarchy, security may be the most important need for people in cultures such as Greece and Japan who have a high need to avoid uncertainty.[59] Although achievement is an important need for Americans, research noted earlier in the chapter suggested that other cultures do not value achievement as much as Americans do.

The two-factor theory has been tested in other countries as well. Results in New Zealand did not replicate the results found in the United States; supervision and interpersonal relationships were important motivators in New Zealand rather than hygienic factors as in America.[60] Finally, expectancy theory may hold up very nicely in cultures that value individualism but break down in more collectivist cultures that value cooperative efforts. In collectivist cultures, rewards are more closely tied to group and team efforts, thus obviating the utility of expectancy theory.

MANAGERIAL IMPLICATIONS: MANY WAYS TO MOTIVATE PEOPLE

8. Describe the cultural differences in motivation.

Managers must realize that all motivation theories are not equally good or equally useful. The later motivation theories, such as the equity and expectancy theories, may be more scientifically sound than earlier theories, such as the two-factor theory. Nevertheless, the older theories of motivation have conceptual value, show us the importance of human needs, and provide a basis for the later theories. The individual, internal theories of motivation and the individual–environment interaction process theories uniquely contribute to our overall understanding of human behavior and motivation at work.

Managers cannot assume they understand employees' needs. They should recognize the variety of needs that motivate employee behavior and ask employees to better understand their needs. Individual employees differ in their needs, and managers should be sensitive to ethnic, national, gender, and age differences in this regard. Employees with high needs for power must be given opportunities to exercise influence, and employees with high needs for achievement must be allowed to excel at work.

Managers can increase employee motivation by training (increased perceptions of success because of increased ability), coaching (increased confidence), and task assignments (increased perceptions of success because of more experience). Managers should ensure that rewards are contingent on good performance and that valued rewards, such as time off or flexible work schedules, are available. Managers must understand what their employees want.

Finally, managers should be aware that morally mature employees are more likely to be sensitive to inequities at work. At the same time, these employees are less likely to be selfish or self-centered and more likely to be concerned about equity issues for all employees. Morally mature employees will act ethically for the common good of all employees and the organization.

Looking Back

The Intrinsic Motivation of Mission Commitment

Although primarily motivated intrinsically for the common good, American Red Cross volunteers also receive recognition for the valuable, important work they do in ceremonies and community recognition programs. These ceremonies and recognition programs may not be flashy events, but they are a small token of the community's gratitude for the volunteers' contributions to the community and to the national and international welfare.

These volunteers are intrinsically motivated by the mission and purpose of the Red Cross as an organization. Turnover among volunteers is surprisingly low, and many stay committed through the years, sometimes taking breaks in service. Rather than calculating their rewards and being primarily motivated by self-interest and economic gain, American Red Cross volunteers exhibit the kind of intrinsic motivation identified by Etzioni in committed relationships, as discussed earlier in the chapter. Unconcerned with economic incentives and social equity, volunteers deliver a variety of services for the common good because it is the right thing to do and because they feel the personal satisfaction of helping others who are in need or suffering. For the volunteers, the acts of caring, serving, giving, and lifting up others are their own rewards. These acts enhance the well-being of the local, national, and international communities within which we all live and work. The volunteers' work does not get counted in the economic activity of the country or the world, yet it certainly enriches the fabric of human relationships that weaves the world into a global village.

CHAPTER SUMMARY

1. Early economic theories of motivation emphasized extrinsic incentives as the basis for motivation and technology as a force multiplier.
2. Early psychological theories of motivation emphasized internal needs but did not take into account individual diversity in these needs.
3. Maslow's hierarchy of needs theory of motivation was the basis for McGregor's Theory X and Theory Y assumptions about people at work.
4. According to McClelland, the needs for achievement, power, and affiliation are learned needs that differ among cultures.
5. The two-factor theory found that the presence of motivation factors led to job satisfaction, and the presence of hygiene factors prevented job dissatisfaction.
6. Social exchange theory holds that people form calculated working relationships and expect fair, equitable, ethical treatment.
7. Expectancy theory says that effort is the basis for motivation and that people want their effort to lead to performance and rewards.
8. Theories of motivation are culturally bound and differences occur between nations.

KEY TERMS

motivation   133
psychoanalysis   135
self-interest   135
need hierarchy   136
Theory X   137
Theory Y   137
motivation factor   140

hygiene factor   140
need for achievement   144
need for power   144
need for affiliation   145
inequity   148
equity sensitive   149

benevolent   150
entitled   150
valence   151
expectancy   151
instrumentality   151
moral maturity   154

REVIEW QUESTIONS

1. Define the terms *motivation*, *needs*, and *equity*.
2. How can knowledge of motivation theories help managers?
3. What are the five categories of motivational needs described by Maslow? Give an example of how each can be satisfied.
4. What are the Theory X and Theory Y assumptions about people at work? How do they relate to the hierarchy of needs?
5. What three manifest needs does McClelland identify?
6. How do hygiene and motivational factors differ? What are the implications of the two-factor theory for managers?
7. How is inequity determined by a person in an organization? How can inequity be resolved if it exists?
8. What are the key concepts in the expectancy theory of motivation?

DISCUSSION AND COMMUNICATION QUESTIONS

1. What do you think are the most important motivational needs for the majority of people? Do you think your needs differ from those of most people?
2. At what level in Maslow's hierarchy of needs are you living? Are you basically satisfied at this level?

3. Assume you are leaving your current job to look for employment elsewhere. What will you look for that you do not have now? If you do not have a job, assume you will be looking for one soon. What are the most important factors that you will seek?

4. If you were being inequitably paid in your job, which strategy do you think would be the most helpful to you in resolving the inequity? What tactics would you consider using?

5. Do you believe you can do a better job of working or do a better job of studying than you are currently doing? Do you think you would get more pay and benefits or better grades if you did a better job? Do you care about the rewards (or grades) in your organization (or university)?

6. What important experiences have contributed to your moral and ethical development? Are you working to further your own moral maturity at this time?

7. *(communication question)* Prepare a memo describing the two employees you work with who most closely operate according to Theory X and Theory Y assumptions about human nature. Be as specific and detailed in your description as you can, using quotes and/or observational examples.

8. *(communication question)* Develop an oral presentation about the most current management practices in employee motivation. Find out what at least four different companies are doing in this area. Be prepared to compare these practices with the theory and research in the chapter.

9. *(communication question)* Interview a manager and prepare a memo summarizing the relative importance that manager places on the needs for achievement, power, and affiliation. Include (1) whether these needs have changed over time and (2) what job aspects satisfy these needs.

ETHICS QUESTIONS

1. Is it ethical for you to pursue your own needs first at work? Are your needs in conflict with what is fair and equitable for others at work? Do you consider the thoughts and feelings of other people at work?

2. Suppose your company knew what employees wanted at work and was unwilling to spend the money to meet their needs. Do you think this would be unethical?

3. Assume you know an employee who is being underpaid because the company believes it can save money and the employee will not complain. Is this unethical? Should you tell the employee about the underpayment condition?

4. Suppose your company has an employee who has been with the company for a long time and now has health problems that will prevent him or her from being fully productive for at least a year. Should the company attempt to carry this person for that period of time, even though the person will not be able to perform? Should the person's pay and benefits be reduced according to performance?

Experiential Exercises

5.1 What Do You Need from Work?

This exercise provides an opportunity to discuss your basic needs and those of other students in your class. Refer back to Challenge 5.2: What's Important to Employees? on page 143 and look over your ranking of the ten possible job reward factors. Think about basic needs you may have that are possibly work related and yet would not be satisfied by one or another of these ten job reward factors.

Step 1. The class will form into groups of approximately six members each. Each group elects a spokesperson and answers the following questions. The group should spend at least five minutes on the first question and make sure each member of the group makes a contribution. The second question will probably take longer for your group to answer, up to fifteen minutes. The spokesperson should be ready to share the group's answers.

    a. *What important basic needs do you have that are not addressed by one or another of these ten job reward factors?* Members should focus on the whole range of needs discussed in the different need theories of motivation covered in Chapter 5. Develop a list of the basic needs overlooked by these ten factors.

    b. *What is important to members of your group?* Rank-order all job reward factors (the original ten and any new ones your group came up with in Step 1) in terms of their importance for your group. If group members disagree about the rankings, take time to discuss the differences among group members. Work for consensus and also note points of disagreement.

Step 2. Each group will share the results of its answers to the questions in Step 1. Cross-team questions and discussion follow.

Step 3. If your instructor has not already shared the normative data for 1,000 employees and their supervisors mentioned in Challenge 5.2, the instructor may do that at this time.

Step 4 (Optional). Your instructor may ask you to discuss the similarities and differences in your group's rankings with the employee and supervisory normative rankings. If he or she does, spend some time addressing two questions.

    a. *What underlying reasons do you think may account for the differences that exist?*

    b. *How have the needs of employees and supervisors changed over the past twenty years? Are they likely to change in the future?*

5.2 What to Do?

According to Stacy Adams, the experience of inequity or social injustice is a motivating force for human behavior. This exercise provides you and your group with a brief scenario of an inequity at work. Your task is to consider feasible actions for redress of this inequity.

    John and Mary are full professors in the same medical school department of a large private university. As a private institution, neither the school nor the university makes the salaries and benefits of its faculty a matter of public record. Mary has pursued a long-term (fourteen years) career in the medical school, rising through the academic ranks while married to a successful businessman with whom she has raised three children. Her research and teaching contributions have been broad ranging and award winning. John joined the medical school within the last three years and was recruited for his leading-edge contribution to a novel line of research on a new procedure. Mary thought he was probably attracted with a comprehensive compensation package, yet she had no details until an administrative assistant gave her some information about salary and benefits a month ago. Mary learned that John's base contract salary is 16 percent higher than hers ($250,000 versus $215,000), that he was awarded an incentive pay component for the commercialization of his new procedure, and that he was given an annual discretionary travel budget of $35,000 and a membership in an exclusive private club. Mary is in a quandary about what to do. Given pressures from the board of trustees to hold down costs associated with public and private pressure to keep tuition increases low, Mary wonders how to begin to close this $70,000+ inequity gap.

Step 1. Working in groups of six, discuss the equity issues in this medical school department situation using the text material on social exchange and equity theory. Do the outcome differences here appear to be gender based, age based, performance based, or marital status based? Do you need more information? If so, what additional information do you need?

Step 2. Consider each of the seven strategies for the resolution of inequity as portrayed in this situation. Which ones are feasible to pursue based on what you know? Which ones are not feasible? Why? What are the likely consequences of each strategy or course of action? What would you advise Mary to do?

Step 3. Once your group has identified feasible resolution strategies, choose the best strategy. Next, develop a specific plan of action for Mary to follow in attempting to resolve the inequity so that she can achieve the experience and the reality of fair treatment at work.

Step 4 (Optional). Your group may be asked to share its preferred strategy for this situation and your rationale for the strategy.

Learning Objectives

After reading this chapter, you should be able to do the following:

1. Define *learning*, *reinforcement*, *punishment*, *extinction*, and *goal setting*. *p. 161*

2. Distinguish between classical and operant conditioning. *p. 161*

3. Explain the use of positive and negative consequences of behavior in strategies of reinforcement and punishment. *p. 162*

4. Identify the purposes of goal setting and five characteristics of effective goals. *p. 167*

5. Describe effective strategies for giving and receiving performance feedback. *p. 175*

6. Compare individual and team-oriented reward systems. *p. 178*

7. Describe strategies for correcting poor performance. *p. 180*

6

Learning and Performance Management

Thinking Ahead

Motivation, Goals, and the Consequences of Behavior

Oprah Winfrey is a talk show host, actress, producer, philanthropist, businesswoman, and chair of Harpo Entertainment Group in Chicago.[1] She was not always a success. Oprah's childhood years were difficult at times, but her life began changing positively when she went at age thirteen to live with the man she believes is her father. A strict disciplinarian, Vernon Winfrey challenged Oprah to read and expand her vocabulary. Oprah found constructive behavior had positive consequences, and she learned to be self-disciplined. Keys to her adulthood success include setting challenging goals and the discipline of daily assessment.

She began her career in broadcasting at the age of nineteen as the youngest and the first African American woman ever to anchor the news at Nashville's WTVF-TV. Oprah moved from Nashville to Baltimore where she co-anchored the six o'clock news until she was recruited to co-host Baltimore's WJZ-TV's local talk show *People Are Talking*. Seven years later, she relocated to Chicago to host

WLS-TV's morning talk show, *AM Chicago*, which became the number one talk show one month after Oprah became its host. In less than a year, the show expanded to an hour and was renamed *The Oprah Winfrey Show*.

Maintaining self-discipline and achieving her goals are still difficult in some areas of her life. Oprah was challenged by her weight and engaged personal trainer Bob Greene to help her achieve her weight goals through exercise, physical fitness, and healthy diet. The creation and success of Harpo Entertainment Group are a result of her business goals. Oprah is also motivated to help others and makes significant charitable contributions to aid women and children. Her philanthropic efforts have established scholarships for hundreds of students in schools and universities throughout the country. As discussed in the Looking Back feature, Oprah Winfrey's learned self-discipline, goal setting, and motivation have led to wide recognition and rewards, many of which she shares with others.

This is the second of two chapters addressing motivation and behavior. Chapter 5 emphasized internal and process theories of motivation. This chapter focuses on external theories of motivation and factors in the work environment that influence good and bad performance. The first section addresses learning theory and the use of reinforcement, punishment, and extinction at work. It also touches on Bandura's social learning theory and Jung's personality approach to learning. The second section presents theory, research, and practice related to goal setting in organizations. The third section addresses the definition and measurement of performance. The fourth section is concerned with rewarding performance. The fifth and concluding section addresses how to correct poor performance.

LEARNING IN ORGANIZATIONS

Learning is a change in behavior acquired through experience. Learning may begin with the cognitive activity of developing knowledge about a subject, which then leads to a change in behavior. Alternatively, the behaviorist approach to learning assumes that observable behavior is a function of its consequences. According to the behaviorists, learning has its basis in classical and operant conditioning. Learning helps guide and direct motivated behavior.

1. Define *learning, reinforcement, punishment, extinction,* and *goal setting*.

learning
A change in behavior acquired through experience.

Classical Conditioning

Classical conditioning is the process of modifying behavior so that a conditioned stimulus is paired with an unconditioned stimulus and elicits an unconditioned response. It is largely the result of the research on animals (primarily dogs) by the Russian physiologist Ivan Pavlov.[2] Pavlov's professional exchanges with Walter B. Cannon and other American researchers during the early 1900s led to the application of his ideas in the United States.[3] Classical conditioning builds on the natural consequence of an

2. Distinguish between classical and operant conditioning.

classical conditioning
Modifying behavior so that a conditioned stimulus is paired with an unconditioned stimulus and elicits an unconditioned response.

unconditioned response to an unconditioned stimulus. In dogs, this might be the natural production of saliva (unconditioned response) in response to the presentation of meat (unconditioned stimulus). By presenting a conditioned stimulus (for example, a bell) simultaneously with the unconditioned stimulus (the meat), the researcher caused the dog to develop a conditioned response (salivation in response to the bell).

Classical conditioning may occur in a similar fashion in humans.[4] For example, a person working at a computer terminal may get lower back tension (unconditioned response) as a result of poor posture (unconditioned stimulus). If the person becomes aware of that tension only when the manager enters the work area (conditioned stimulus), then the person may develop a conditioned response (lower back tension) to the appearance of the manager.

Although this example is logical, classical conditioning has real limitations in its applicability to human behavior in organizations—for at least three reasons. First, humans are more complex than dogs and less amenable to simple cause-and-effect conditioning. Second, the behavioral environments in organizations are complex and not very amenable to single stimulus–response manipulations. Third, complex human decision making makes it possible to override simple conditioning.

Operant Conditioning

Operant conditioning is the process of modifying behavior through the use of positive or negative consequences following specific behaviors. It is based on the notion that behavior is a function of its consequences,[5] which may be either positive or negative. The consequences of behavior are used to influence, or shape, behavior through three strategies: reinforcement, punishment, and extinction. Organizational behavior modification is a form of operant conditioning used successfully in a variety of organizations to shape behavior.[6]

The Strategies of Reinforcement, Punishment, and Extinction

Reinforcement is used to enhance desirable behavior, and punishment and extinction are used to diminish undesirable behavior. The application of reinforcement theory is central to the design and administration of organizational reward systems. Well-designed reward systems help attract and retain the very best employees. Strategic rewards help motivate behavior, actions, and accomplishments, which advance the organization toward specific business goals.[7] Strategic rewards go beyond cash to include training and educational opportunities, stock options, and recognition awards such as travel. Strategic rewards are important positive consequences of people's work behavior.

Reinforcement and punishment are administered through the management of positive and negative consequences of behavior. *Positive consequences* are the results of a person's behavior that the person finds

Experiencing OB

Learn more about the operant conditioning process by interacting with the concept at our animated concept and activity site. Choose Learning from the "select a topic" pull-down menu, then Operant Conditioning Process from the "overview tab."

http://www.experiencingob.com

operant conditioning
Modifying behavior through the use of positive or negative consequences following specific behaviors.

3. Explain the use of positive and negative consequences of behavior in strategies of reinforcement and punishment.

positive consequences
Results of a behavior that a person finds attractive or pleasurable.

attractive or pleasurable. They might include a pay increase, a bonus, a promotion, a transfer to a more desirable geographic location, or praise from a supervisor. ***Negative consequences*** are the results of a person's behavior that the person finds unattractive or aversive. They might include disciplinary action, an undesirable transfer, a demotion, or harsh criticism from a supervisor. Positive and negative consequences must be defined for the person receiving them. Therefore, individual, gender, and cultural differences may be important in their classification.

The use of positive and negative consequences following a specific behavior either reinforces or punishes that behavior.[8] Thorndike's law of effect states that behaviors followed by positive consequences are more likely to recur and behaviors followed by negative consequences are less likely to recur.[9] Figure 6.1 shows how positive and negative consequences may be applied or withheld in the strategies of reinforcement and punishment.

Reinforcement *Reinforcement* is the attempt to develop or strengthen desirable behavior by either bestowing positive consequences or withholding negative consequences. Positive reinforcement results from the application of a positive consequence following a desirable behavior. Bonuses paid at the end of successful business years are an example of positive reinforcement. Marriott International provides positive reinforcement by honoring fifteen to twenty employees each year with its J. Willard Marriott Award of Excellence. Each awardee receives a medallion engraved with the words that express the basic values of the company: dedication, achievement, character, ideals, effort, and perseverance.

Negative reinforcement results from withholding a negative consequence when a desirable behavior occurs. For example, a manager who reduces an employee's pay (negative consequence) if the employee comes to work late (undesirable behavior) and refrains from doing so when the employee is on time (desirable behavior) has negatively reinforced the employee's on-time behavior. The employee avoids the negative consequence

negative consequences
Results of a behavior that a person finds unattractive or aversive.

Experiencing OB

Some reinforcement strategies are used to increase desired behavior, while other strategies are used to decrease undesired behavior. To test your understanding of reinforcement strategies, visit our animated concept and activity site. Choose Learning from the "select a topic" pull-down menu, then Strategies of Reinforcement from the "overview tab."

http://www.experiencingob.com

reinforcement
The attempt to develop or strengthen desirable behavior by either bestowing positive consequences or withholding negative consequences.

	Reinforcement (desirable behavior)	Punishment (undesirable behavior)
Positive consequences	Apply	Withhold
Negative consequences	Withhold	Apply

Figure 6.1
Reinforcement and Punishment Strategies

punishment
The attempt to eliminate or weaken undesirable behavior by either bestowing negative consequences or withholding positive consequences.

(a reduction in pay) by exhibiting the desirable behavior (being on time to work).

Either continuous or intermittent schedules of reinforcement may be used. These reinforcement schedules are described in Table 6.1. When managers design organizational reward systems, they consider not only the type of reinforcement but also how often the reinforcement should be provided.

Punishment *Punishment* is the attempt to eliminate or weaken undesirable behavior. It is used in two ways. One way to punish a person is to ap-

Table 6.1
Schedules of Reinforcement

Schedule	Description	Effects on Responding
Continuous		
	Reinforcer follows every response	1. Steady high rate of performance as long as reinforcement follows every response 2. High frequency of reinforcement may lead to early satiation 3. Behavior weakens rapidly (undergoes extinction) when reinforcers are withheld 4. Appropriate for newly emitted, unstable, low-frequency responses
Intermittent		
	Reinforcer does not follow every response	1. Capable of producing high frequencies of responding 2. Low frequency of reinforcement precludes early satiation 3. Appropriate for stable or high-frequency responses
Fixed Ratio	A fixed number of responses must be emitted before reinforcement occurs	1. A fixed ratio of 1:1 (reinforcement occurs after every response) is the same as a continuous schedule 2. Tends to produce a high rate of response that is vigorous and steady
Variable Ratio	A varying or random number of responses must be emitted before reinforcement occurs	Capable of producing a high rate of response that is vigorous, steady, and resistant to extinction
Fixed Interval	The first response after a specific period of time has elasped is reinforced	Produces an uneven response pattern varying from a very slow, unenergetic response immediately following reinforcement to a very fast, vigorous response immediately preceding reinforcement
Variable Interval	The first response after varying or random periods of time have elapsed is reinforced	Tends to produce a high rate of response that is vigorous, steady, and resistant to extinction

SOURCE: Table from *Organizational Behavior Modification* by Fred Luthans and Robert Kreitner. Copyright © 1985, p. 58 by Scott Foresman and Company and the authors. Reprinted by permission of the authors.

ply a negative consequence following an undesirable behavior. For example, a professional athlete who is excessively offensive to an official (undesirable behavior) may be ejected from a game (negative consequence). The other way to punish a person is to withhold a positive consequence following an undesirable behavior. For example, a salesperson who makes few visits to companies (undesirable behavior) and whose sales are well below the quota (undesirable behavior) is likely to receive a very small commission check (positive consequence) at the end of the month.

One problem with punishment is that it may have unintended results. Because punishment is discomforting to the individual being punished, the experience of punishment may result in negative psychological, emotional, performance, or behavioral consequences. For example, the person being punished may become angry, hostile, depressed, or despondent. From an organizational standpoint, this result becomes important when the punished person translates negative emotional and psychological responses into negative actions. A General Motors employee who had been disciplined pulled an emergency cord and shut down an entire assembly line. A hardware store owner was killed by a man he had fired for poor performance. Work slowdowns, sabotage, and subversive behavior are all unintended negative consequences of punishment.

Extinction An alternative to punishing undesirable behavior is *extinction*—the attempt to weaken a behavior by attaching no consequences (either positive or negative) to it. It is equivalent to ignoring the behavior. The rationale for using extinction is that a behavior not followed by any consequence is weakened. Some patience and time may be needed for extinction to be effective, however.

Extinction may be practiced, for example, by not responding (no consequence) to the sarcasm (behavior) of a colleague. Extinction may be most effective when used in conjunction with the positive reinforcement of desirable behaviors. Therefore, in the example, the best approach might be to compliment the sarcastic colleague for constructive comments (reinforcing desirable behavior) while ignoring sarcastic comments (extinguishing undesirable behavior).

Extinction is not always the best strategy, however. In cases of dangerous behavior, punishment might be preferable to deliver a swift, clear lesson. It might also be preferable in cases of seriously undesirable behavior, such as employee embezzlement and other illegal or unethical behavior.

Bandura's Social Learning Theory

A social learning theory proposed by Albert Bandura is an alternative to the strictly behavioristic approaches of Pavlov and Skinner.[10] Bandura believes learning occurs through the observation of other people and the modeling of their behavior. Executives might teach their subordinates a wide range of behaviors, such as leader–follower interactions and stress

Experiencing OB

Reinforcement schedules may affect the effectiveness of reinforcement strategies. Learn more about reinforcement schedules by visiting our animated concept and activity site. Choose Learning from the "select a topic" pull-down menu, then Reinforcement Schedules from the "overview tab."

http://www.experiencingob.com

extinction
The attempt to weaken a behavior by attaching no consequences to it.

self-efficacy
An individual's beliefs and expectancies about his or her ability to perform a specific task effectively.

management, by exhibiting these behaviors. Since employees look to their supervisors for acceptable norms of behavior, they are likely to pattern their own responses on the supervisor's.

Central to Bandura's social learning theory is the notion of *self-efficacy*, an individual's beliefs and expectancies about his or her ability to perform a specific task effectively. Individuals with high self-efficacy believe that they have the ability to get things done, that they are capable of putting forth the effort to accomplish the task, and that they can overcome any obstacles to their success. Employees with low self-efficacy quit trying prematurely and may even fail at a task. There are four sources of self-efficacy: prior experiences, behavior models (witnessing the success of others), persuasion from other people, and assessment of current physical and emotional capabilities.[11] Believing in one's own capability to get something done is an important facilitator of success. There is strong evidence that self-efficacy leads to high performance on a wide variety of physical and mental tasks.[12] High self-efficacy has also led to success in breaking addictions, increasing pain tolerance, and recovering from illnesses.

Managers can help employees develop self-efficacy. The strongest way for an employee to develop self-efficacy is to succeed at a challenging task.[13] Managers can help by providing job challenges, coaching and counseling for improved performance, and rewarding employees' achievements. Empowerment, or sharing power with employees, can be accomplished by interventions that help employees increase their self-esteem and self-efficacy. Given the increasing diversity of the workforce, managers may want to target their efforts toward women and minorities in particular. Research has indicated that women and minorities tend to have lower than average self-efficacy.[14]

Experiencing OB

Individuals often learn which behaviors will be rewarded and which will be punished by observing what happens to others. You may learn more about this concept at our animated concept and activity site. Choose Learning from the "select a topic" pull-down menu, then Bandura's Social Learning Theory from the "overview tab."

http://www.experiencingob.com

Learning and Personality Differences

The cognitive approach to learning mentioned at the beginning of the chapter is based on the *Gestalt* school of thought and draws on Jung's theory of personality differences (discussed in Chapter 3). Two elements of Jung's theory have important implications for learning and subsequent behavior.

The first element is the distinction between introverted and extraverted people. Introverts need quiet time to study, concentrate, and reflect on what they are learning. They think best when they are alone. Extraverts need to interact with other people, learning through the process of expressing and exchanging ideas with others. They think best in groups and while they are talking.

The second element is the personality functions of intuition, sensing, thinking, and feeling. These functions are listed in Table 6.2, along with their implications for learning by individuals. The functions of intuition and sensing determine the individual's preference for information gathering. The functions of thinking and feeling determine how the individual evaluates and makes decisions about newly acquired information.[15] Each person has a preferred mode of gathering information and a preferred mode of evalu-

Personality Preference	Implications for Learning by Individuals
Information Gathering	
Intuitors	Prefer theoretical frameworks. Look for the meaning in material. Attempt to understand the grand scheme. Look for possibilities and interrelations.
Sensors	Prefer specific, empirical data. Look for practical applications. Attempt to master details of a subject. Look for what is realistic and doable.
Decision Making	
Thinkers	Prefer analysis of data and information. Work to be fairminded and evenhanded. Seek logical, just conclusions. Do not like to be too personally involved.
Feelers	Prefer interpersonal involvement. Work to be tenderhearted and harmonious. Seek subjective, merciful results. Do not like objective, factual analysis.

Table 6.2
Personality Functions and Learning

SOURCE: O. Kroeger and J. M. Thuesen, *Type Talk: The 16 Personality Types That Determine How We Live, Love, and Work* (New York: Dell Publishing Co., 1989).

ating and making decisions about that information. For example, an intuitive thinker may want to skim research reports about implementing total quality programs and then, based on hunches, decide how to apply the research findings to the organization. A sensing feeler may prefer viewing videotaped interviews with people in companies that implemented total quality programs and then identify people in the organization most likely to be receptive to the approaches presented.

GOAL SETTING AT WORK

Goal setting is the process of establishing desired results that guide and direct behavior. Goal-setting theory is based on laboratory studies, field research experiments, and comparative investigations by Edwin Locke, Gary Latham, John M. Ivancevich, and others.[16] Goals help crystallize the sense of purpose and mission that is essential to success at work. Organizational Reality 6.1 discusses the sense of purpose at Medtronic, the Minneapolis-based medical products company. Purpose, mission, and goals are important sources of motivation for people at work, often leading to collective achievement, as at Medtronic.

4. Identify the purposes of goal setting and five characteristics of effective goals.

goal setting
The process of establishing desired results that guide and direct behavior.

ORGANIZATIONAL REALITY 6.1

A Sense of Purpose at Medtronic

Medtronic is a fifty-year-old, Minneapolis-based high-technology, global medical products company with a sense of purpose and direction. CEO Bill George says, "Shareholder value is a hollow notion as a sole source of employee motivation." Employees need a sense of purpose, mission, and direction. Medtronic's mission is to contribute to human welfare by applying biomedical engineering in the research, design, manufacture, and sale of instruments or appliances that alleviate pain, restore health, and extend life. Founded as a partnership in April 1949, Medtronic has grown into a world-class organization of 19,000 employees conducting business in 120 countries. Medtronic is the world's leading medical technology company specializing in implants and interventional therapies.

Rather than focusing on shareholder value as a source of employee motivation, Medtronic employees concentrate on the people and patients who will have the company's products implanted inside them. Hence, their purpose is to help sick people get well, and they do not have to be physicians or surgeons to do that. Medtronic made a major advance in 1960 when it acquired the rights to the first transistorized, self-contained, implantable pacemaker for the long-term correction of complete heart block. After this technological innovation, significant advances in all areas of pacing occurred rapidly, from transvenous leads to screw-in myocardial leads and dual-chamber pacing. Hence, Medtronic is a high-tech organization responding to high-touch needs within people. Employees turn out so many new gizmos that 50 percent of the company's revenue come from products introduced in the past twelve months.

Medtronic employees project their sense of purpose and mission around the globe. The company has had an international distribution network for forty years and its own international sales force for thirty years; it expanded internationally during the 1980s through the acquisition of Vitatron, an international pacemaker company located in the Netherlands. Medtronic's global activity is anchored in its sense of purpose or mission, which is a motivating force for employees and for the business.

Discussion Questions

1. What are some of the best ways to reinforce a sense of purpose among employees in high-technology companies?

2. Is there a possible conflict between high-tech innovation and concern for patients and customers?

SOURCE: R. B. Lieber, "100 Best Companies to Work for in America," *Fortune* (January 12, 1998): 72+.

Characteristics of Effective Goals

Various organizations define the characteristics of effective goals differently. For the former Sanger-Harris, a retail organization, the acronym SMART communicated the approach to effective goals. SMART stands for Specific, Measurable, Attainable, Realistic, and Time-bound. Five commonly accepted characteristics of effective goals are specific, challenging, measurable, time-bound, and prioritized.

Specific and challenging goals serve to cue or focus the person's attention on exactly what is to be accomplished and to arouse the person to peak performance. In a wide range of occupations, people who set specific, challenging goals consistently outperform people who have easy or unspecified goals, as Figure 6.2 shows.

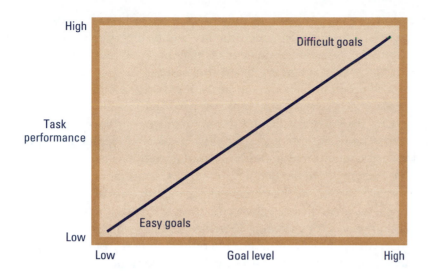

Figure 6.2
Goal Level and Task Performance

Measureable, quantitative goals are useful as a basis for feedback about goal progress. Qualitative goals are also valuable. The Western Company of North America (now part of BJ Services Corporation) allowed about 15 percent of a manager's goals to be of a qualitative nature.[17] A qualitative goal might be to improve relationships with customers. Further work might convert the qualitative goal into quantitative measures such as number of complaints or frequency of complimentary letters. In this case, however, the qualitative goal may well be sufficient and most meaningful.

Time-bound goals enhance measurability. The time limit may be implicit in the goal, or it may need to be made explicit. For example, without the six-month time limit, an insurance salesperson might think the sales goal is for the whole year rather than for six months. Many organizations work on standardized cycles, such as quarters or years, where very explicit time limits are assumed. If there is any uncertainty about the time period of the goal effort, the time limit should be explicitly stated.

The priority ordering of goals allows for effective decision making about the allocation of resources.[18] As time, energy, or other resources become available, a person can move down the list of goals in descending order. The key concern is with achieving the top-priority goals. Priority helps direct a person's efforts and behavior. Although these characteristics help increase motivation and performance, that is not the only function of goal setting in organizations, however.

Goal setting serves one or more of three functions. First, it can increase work motivation and task performance.[19] Second, it can reduce the role stress that is associated with conflicting or confusing expectations.[20] Third, it can improve the accuracy and validity of performance evaluation.[21]

Increasing Work Motivation and Task Performance

Goals are often used to increase employee effort and motivation, which in turn improve task performance. The higher the goal, the better the performance; that is, people work harder to reach difficult goals. The positive relationship between goal difficulty and task performance is depicted in Figure 6.2. Even unreasonable goals may improve motivation, although there is not universal agreement on this point.[22]

Three important behavioral aspects of enhancing performance motivation through goal setting are employee participation, supervisory commitment, and useful performance feedback. Employee participation in goal setting leads to goal acceptance by employees. Goal acceptance is thought to lead to goal commitment and then to goal accomplishment. Special attention has been given to factors that influence commitment to difficult goals, such as participation in the process of setting the difficult goals.[23] Even in the case of assigned goals, goal acceptance and commitment are considered essential prerequisites to goal accomplishment.

Supervisory goal commitment is a reflection of the organization's commitment to goal setting. Organizational commitment is a prerequisite for successful goal-setting programs, such as management by objectives (MBO) programs.[24] The organization must be committed to the program, and the employee and supervisors must be committed to specific work goals as well as to the program. (MBO will be discussed in more detail later in the chapter.)

The supervisor plays a second important role by providing employees with interim performance feedback on progress toward goals. Performance feedback is most useful when the goals are specific, and specific goals improve performance most when interim feedback is given.[25] For example, assume an insurance salesperson has a goal of selling $500,000 worth of insurance in six months but has sold only $200,000 after three months. During an interim performance feedback session, the supervisor may help the salesperson identify his problem—that he is not focusing his calls on the likeliest prospects. This useful feedback coupled with the specific goal helps the salesperson better focus his efforts to achieve the goal. Feedback is most helpful when it is useful (helping the salesperson identify high-probability prospects) and timely (halfway through the performance period).

Reducing Role Stress of Conflicting and Confusing Expectations

A second function of goal setting is to reduce the role stress associated with conflicting and confusing expectations. This is done by clarifying the task–role expectations communicated to employees. Supervisors, coworkers, and employees are all important sources of task-related information. A fourteen-month evaluation of goal setting in reducing role stress found that conflict, confusion, and absenteeism were all reduced through the use of goal setting.[26]

The improved role clarity resulting from goal setting may be attributable to improved communication between managers and employees. An early study of the MBO goal-setting program at Ford Motor Company found an initial 25 percent lack of agreement between managers and their bosses concerning the definition of the managers' jobs. Through effective goal-setting activities, this lack of agreement was reduced to about 5 percent.[27] At FedEx, managers are encouraged to include communication-related targets in their annual MBO goal-setting process.[28]

Improving the Accuracy and Validity of Performance Evaluation

The third major function of goal setting is improving the accuracy and validity of performance evaluation. One of the best methods of doing so is to use *management by objectives (MBO)*—a goal-setting program based on interaction and negotiation between employees and managers. MBO programs have been pervasive in organizations for nearly thirty years.[29]

According to Peter Drucker, who originated the concept, the objectives-setting process begins with the employee writing an "employee's letter" to the manager. The letter explains the employee's general understanding of the scope of the manager's job, as well as the scope of the employee's own job, and lays out a set of specific objectives to be pursued over the next six months or year. After some discussion and negotiation, the manager and the employee finalize these items into a performance plan.

Drucker considers MBO a participative and interactive process. This does not mean that goal setting begins at the bottom of the organization. It means that goal setting is applicable to all employees, with lower level organizational members and professional staff having a clear influence over the goal-setting process.[30] (The performance aspect of goal setting is discussed in the next section of the chapter.)

Goal-setting programs have operated under a variety of names, including goals and controls at Purex (now part of Dial Corporation), work planning and review at Black & Decker and General Electric, and performance planning and evaluation at the former Tenneco, Inc., and IBM. Most of these programs are designed to enhance performance,[31] especially when incentives are associated with goal achievement.

The two central ingredients in goal-setting programs are planning and evaluation. The planning component consists of organizational and individual goal setting. Organizational goal setting is an essential prerequisite to individual goal setting; the two must be closely linked for the success of both.[32] At FedEx, all individual objectives must be tied to the overall corporate objectives of people, service, and profit.

In planning, discretionary control is usually given to individuals and departments to develop operational and tactical plans to support the corporate objectives. The emphasis is on formulating a clear, consistent, measurable, and ordered set of goals to articulate *what* to do. It is also assumed that operational support planning helps determine *how* to do it. The concept of intention is used to encompass both the goal (*what*) and the set of pathways that lead to goal attainment (*how*), thus recognizing the importance of both what and how.[33]

management by objectives (MBO)
A goal-setting program based on interaction and negotiation between employees and managers.

The evaluation component consists of interim reviews of goal progress, conducted by managers and employees, and formal performance evaluation. The reviews are mid-term assessments designed to help employees take self-corrective action. They are not designed as final or formal performance evaluations. The formal performance evaluation occurs at the close of a reporting period, usually once a year. Tenneco's program in the 1970s was an example of a goal-setting program that systematically incorporated planning and evaluation components.[34]

Because goal-setting programs are somewhat mechanical by nature, they are most easily implemented in stable, predictable industrial settings. Although most programs allow for some flexibility and change, they are less useful in organizations where high levels of unpredictability exist, as in basic research and development, or where the organization requires substantial adaptation or adjustment. Finally, individual, gender, and cultural differences do not appear to threaten the success of goal-setting programs.[35, 36] Thus, goal-setting programs may be widely applied and effective in a diverse workforce.

PERFORMANCE: A KEY CONSTRUCT

Goal setting is designed to improve work performance, an important organizational behavior directly related to the production of goods or the delivery of services. Performance is most often thought of as task accomplishment, the term *task* coming from Taylor's early notion of a worker's required activity.[37] Some early management research found performance standards and differential piece-rate pay to be key ingredients in achieving high levels of performance, while other early research found stress helpful in improving performance up to an optimum point.[38] Hence, outcomes and effort are both important for good performance. This section focuses on task-oriented performance.

One company that elicits high levels of performance from its people is FedEx. Chairman, president, and CEO Frederick W. Smith emphasizes People-Service-Profit (P-S-P) and the importance of performance feedback and performance-based rewards in ensuring sustained high levels of performance.

Defining Performance

Performance must be clearly defined and understood by the employees who are expected to perform well at work. Performance in most lines of work is multidimensional. For example, a sales executive's performance may require administrative and financial skills along with the interpersonal skills needed to motivate a sales force. Or a medical doctor's performance may demand the positive interpersonal skills of a bedside manner to complement the necessary technical diagnostic and treatment skills for enhancing the healing process. Each specific job in an organization requires the definition of skills and behaviors essential to excellent performance. Defining performance is a prerequisite to measuring and evaluating performance on the job.

Although different jobs require different skills and behaviors, organizational citizenship behavior (OCB) is one dimension of individual performance that spans many jobs. It was defined in Chapter 4 as behavior that is above and beyond the call of duty. OCB involves individual discretionary behavior that promotes the organization and is not explicitly rewarded; it includes helping behavior, sportsmanship, and civic virtue. According to supervisors, OCB is enhanced most through employee involvement programs aimed at engaging employees in the work organization rather than through employee involvement in employment decisions in nonunion operations.[39] OCB emphasizes collective performance in contrast to individual performance or achievement. OCB is just one of a number of performance dimensions to consider when defining performance for a specific job within an organization.

Performance appraisal is the evaluation of a person's performance once it is well defined. Accurate appraisals help supervisors fulfill their dual roles as evaluators and coaches. As a coach, a supervisor is responsible for encouraging employee growth and development. As an evaluator, a supervisor is responsible for making judgments that influence employees' roles in the organization.

The major purposes of performance appraisals are to give employees feedback on performance, to identify the employees' developmental needs, to make promotion and reward decisions, to make demotion and termination decisions, and to develop information about the organization's selection and placement decisions. For example, a review of 57,775 performance appraisals found higher ratings on appraisals done for administrative reasons and lower ratings on appraisals done for research or for employee development.[40]

performance appraisal
The evaluation of a person's performance.

Measuring Performance

Ideally, actual performance and measured performance are the same. Practically, this is seldom the case. Measuring operational performance is easier than measuring managerial performance because of the availability of quantifiable data. Measuring production performance is easier than measuring research and development performance because of the reliability of the measures.

Performance appraisal systems are intended to improve the accuracy of measured performance and increase its agreement with actual performance. The extent of agreement is called the true assessment, as Figure 6.3 shows. The figure also identifies the performance measurement problems that contribute to inaccuracy. These include deficiency, unreliability, and invalidity. Deficiency results from overlooking important aspects of a person's actual performance. Unreliability results from poor-quality performance measures. Invalidity results from inaccurate definition of the expected job performance.

Early performance appraisal systems were often quite biased. See, for example, Table 6.3, which is a sample of officer effectiveness reports from an

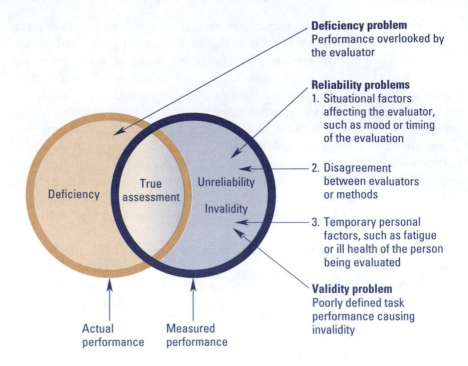

Figure 6.3
Actual and Measured Performance

Deficiency problem
Performance overlooked by the evaluator

Reliability problems
1. Situational factors affecting the evaluator, such as mood or timing of the evaluation

2. Disagreement between evaluators or methods

3. Temporary personal factors, such as fatigue or ill health of the person being evaluated

Validity problem
Poorly defined task performance causing invalidity

Deficiency

True assessment

Unreliability

Invalidity

Actual performance

Measured performance

infantry company in the early 1800s. Even contemporary executive appraisals have a dark side. One study of eighty-two executives in manufacturing and service companies concluded that senior executives had extraordinary latitude in evaluating the performance of subordinate executives, often using appraisals as political tools to control people and resources.[41]

Performance-monitoring systems using modern electronic technology are sometimes used to measure the performance of vehicle operators, computer technicians, and customer service representatives. For example, such systems might record the rate of keystrokes or the total number of keystrokes for a computer technician. The people subject to this type of monitoring are in some cases unaware that their performance is being measured. What is appropriate performance monitoring? What constitutes inappropriate electronic spying on the employee? Are people entitled to know when their performance is being measured? The ethics of monitoring performance may differ by culture. The United States and Sweden, for example, respect individual freedom more than Japan and China do. The overriding issue, however, is how far organizations should go in using modern technology to measure human performance.

Goal setting and MBO are results-oriented methods of performance appraisal that do not necessarily rely on modern technology. Like performance-monitoring systems, they shift the emphasis from subjective, judgmental performance dimensions to observable, verifiable results. Goals established in the planning phase of goal setting become the standard against which to measure subsequent performance. However, rigid adherence to a results-oriented approach may risk overlooking performance opportunities.

Alexander Brown—Lt. Col., Comdg.—A good natured man.
Clark Crowell—first Major—A good man, but no officer.
Jess B. Wordsworth—2nd Major—An excellent officer.
Captain Shaw—A man of whom all unite in speaking ill. A knave despised
      by all.
Captain Thomas Lord—Indifferent, but promises well.
Captain Rockwell—An officer of capacity, but imprudent and a man of
      violent passions.
1st Lt. Jas. Kearns—Merely good, nothing promising.
1st Lt. Robert Cross—Willing enough—has much to learn—with small
      capacity.
2nd Lt. Stewart Berry—An ignorant unoffending fellow.
Ensign North—A good young man who does well.

Table 6.3
Officer Effectiveness Reports, circa 1813

SOURCE: Table from *The Air Officer's Guide*, 6th ed., Copyright © 1952 Stackpole Books. Used with permission.

Another method for improving the accuracy of performance appraisal is to have multiple evaluators contribute to the final appraisal. Superiors, peers, employees, and clients all contribute something unique because each group has a different vantage point. Most traditional evaluations are completed by superiors. Peer and employee evaluations may add a new dimension by covering such areas as cooperation and supervisory style. For example, one mid-level executive behaved very differently in dealing with superiors, peers, and employees. With superiors, he was positive, compliant, and deferential. With peers, he was largely indifferent, often ignoring them. With employees, he was tough and demanding, bordering on cruel and abusive. Without each of these perspectives, the executive's performance would not have been accurately assessed.

FedEx has incorporated a novel and challenging approach to evaluation in its blueprint for service quality. All managers at FedEx are evaluated by their employees through a survey-feedback-action system. Employees evaluate their managers using a five-point scale on twenty-nine standard statements and ten local option ones. Low ratings suggest problem areas requiring management attention. For example, the following statement received low ratings from employees in 1990: Upper management pays attention to ideas and suggestions from people at my level. CEO Fred Smith became directly involved in addressing this problem area. One of the actions he took to correct the problem was the development of a biweekly employee newsletter.

Performance Feedback: A Communication Challenge

Once clearly defined and accurate performance measures are developed, there is still the challenge of performance feedback. Feedback sessions are

5. Describe effective strategies for giving and receiving performance feedback.

among the more stressful events for supervisors and employees. Early research at General Electric found employees responded constructively to positive feedback and were defensive over half the time in response to critical or negative feedback. Typical responses to negative feedback included shifting responsibility for the shortcoming or behavior, denying it outright, or providing a wide range of excuses for it.[42]

Both parties to a performance feedback session should try to make it a constructive learning experience, since positive and negative performance feedback has long-term implications for the employee's performance and for the working relationship. American Airlines follows three guidelines in providing evaluative feedback so that the experience is constructive for supervisor and employee alike.[43] First, refer to specific, verbatim statements and specific, observable behaviors displayed by the person receiving the feedback. This enhances the acceptance of the feedback while reducing the chances of denial. Second, focus on changeable behaviors, as opposed to intrinsic or personality-based attributes. People are often more defensive about who they are than about what they do. Third, plan and organize for the session ahead of time. Be sure to notify the person who will receive the feedback. Both the leader and the follower should be ready.

In addition to these ideas, many companies recommend beginning coaching and counseling sessions with something positive. The intent is to reduce defensiveness and enhance useful communication. There is almost always at least one positive element to emphasize. Once the session is under way and rapport is established, then the evaluator can introduce more difficult and negative material. Because people are not perfect, there is always an opportunity for them to learn and to grow through performance feedback sessions. Critical feedback is the basis for improvement and is essential to a performance feedback session.

Self-evaluations are increasingly used for performance feedback, and there is evidence they lead to more satisfying, constructive evaluation interviews and less defensiveness concerning the evaluation process.[44] In addition, self-evaluations may improve job performance through greater commitment to organizational goals. On the other hand, a key criticism of self-evaluations is their low level of agreement with supervisory evaluations.[45] High levels of agreement may not necessarily be desirable, however, if the intent of the overall evaluation process is to provide a full picture of the person's performance.

Developing People and Enhancing Careers

A key function of a good performance appraisal system is to develop people and enhance careers.[46] Developmentally, performance appraisals should emphasize individual growth needs and future performance. If the supervisor is to coach and develop employees effectively, there must be mutual trust. The supervisor must be vulnerable and open to challenge from the subordinate while maintaining a position of responsibility for what is in the subordinate's best interests.[47] The supervisor must also be a skilled, empathetic listener who encourages the employee to talk about hopes and aspirations.[48]

The employee must be able to take active responsibility for future development and growth. This might mean challenging the supervisor's ideas about future development as well as expressing individual preferences and goals. Passive, compliant employees are unable to accept responsibility for themselves or to achieve full emotional development. Individual responsibility is a key characteristic of the culture of the Chaparral Steel Company (part of Texas Industries). The company joke is that the company manages by "adultry" (pun intended). Chaparral Steel treats people like adults and expects adult behavior from them.

Key Characteristics of an Effective Appraisal System

An effective performance appraisal system has five key characteristics: validity, reliability, responsiveness, flexibility, and equitability. Its validity comes from capturing multiple dimensions of a person's job performance. Its reliability comes from capturing evaluations from multiple sources and at different times over the course of the evaluation period. Its responsiveness allows the person being evaluated some input into the final outcome. Its flexibility leaves it open to modification based on new information, such as federal requirements. Its equitability results in fair evaluations against established performance criteria, regardless of individual differences.

REWARDING PERFORMANCE

One function of a performance appraisal system is to provide input for reward decisions. If an organization wants good performance, then it must reward good performance. If it does not want bad performance, then it must not reward bad performance. If companies talk "teamwork," "values," and "customer focus," then they need to reward behaviors related to these ideas. Although this idea is conceptually simple, it can become very complicated in practice. Reward decisions are among the most difficult and complicated decisions made in organizations, and among the most important decisions. When leaders confront decisions about pay every day, they should know that it is a myth that people work for money.[49] While pay and rewards for performance have value, so too do trust, fun, and meaningful work.

A Key Organizational Decision Process

Reward and punishment decisions in organizations affect many people throughout the system, not just the persons being rewarded or punished. Reward allocation involves sequential decisions about which people to reward, how to reward them, and when to reward them. Taken together, these decisions shape the behavior of everyone in the organization, because of the vicarious learning that occurs as people watch what happens to others, especially when new programs or initiatives are implemented. People carefully watch what happens to peers who make mistakes or have problems with the new system; then they gauge their own behavior accordingly.

Individual versus Team Reward Systems

6. Compare individual and team-oriented reward systems.

One of the distinguishing characteristics of Americans is the value they place on individualism. Systems that reward individuals are common in organizations in the United States. One of the strengths of these systems is that they foster autonomous and independent behavior that may lead to creativity, to novel solutions to old problems, and to distinctive contributions to the organization. Individual reward systems directly affect individual behavior and may encourage competitive striving within a work team. Although motivation and reward techniques in the United States are individually focused, they are often group focused outside the United States.[50]

Too much competition within a work environment, however, may be dysfunctional. At the Western Company of North America (now part of BJ Services Corporation), individual success in the MBO program was tied too tightly to rewards, and individual managers became divisively competitive. For example, some managers took last-minute interdepartmental financial actions in a quarter to meet their objectives, but by doing so, they caused other managers to miss their objectives. These actions raise ethical questions about how far individual managers should go in serving their own self-interest at the expense of their peers.

Team reward systems solve the problems caused by individual competitive behavior. These systems emphasize cooperation, joint efforts, and the sharing of information, knowledge, and expertise. The Japanese and Chinese cultures, with their collectivist orientations, place greater emphasis than Americans on the individual as an element of the team, not a member apart from the team. Digital Equipment Corporation (now part of Compaq Computer) used a partnership approach to performance appraisals. Self-managed work group members participated in their own appraisal process. Such an approach emphasizes teamwork and responsibility.

Some organizations have experimented with individual and group alternative reward systems.[51] At the individual level, these include skill-based and pay-for-knowledge systems. Each emphasizes skills or knowledge possessed by an employee over and above the requirements for the basic job. At the group level, gain-sharing plans emphasize collective cost reduction and allow workers to share in the gains achieved by reducing production or other operating costs. In such plans, everyone shares equally in the collective gain. Organizational Reality 6.2 describes a shift from an individual incentive program for salespeople at Marshall Industries to a collective profit-sharing program. The results were very positive, suggesting collective profit sharing can improve performance.

The Power of Earning

The purpose behind both individual and team reward systems is to shape productive behavior. Effective performance management can be the lever

ORGANIZATIONAL REALITY 6.2

Individual Incentive versus Profit Sharing

About ten years ago, Rob Rodin, CEO of Marshall Industries (now part of Avnet, Inc.), did something radical with rewards—he did away with all individual incentives for his sales force. At that time, Marshall Industries was a big ($1+ billion in annual sales) distributor of electronic components based in El Monte, California. Until Rodin's changes, Marshall had rewarded the performance of its salespeople through individual incentives and compensation, with relatively small base salaries as a core of the reward system. Hence, Rodin's plan to do away with all commissions, all bonuses, all Alaskan cruises or Acapulco vacations or Hawaiian pig roasts, and all televisions or plaques was truly a radical concept. How did Rodin reward Marshall's salespeople and best performers?

Rob Rodin was standing smack in the middle of one of the nastiest battle zones in modern management, which concerns how people should be rewarded for performance. He raised the question "Does money motivate?" and answered it with a "Yes, but . . . ." Rodin put into place a base salary system with the opportunity for profit sharing. Profit sharing was the same percentage of salary for everyone based on the whole company's performance.

His heretical move worked very well at Marshall Industries. Productivity per person almost tripled. Profit sharing got rid of distortions that had masked real results, such as people shipping early to meet quotas and pushing costs from one quarter into the next to make budget, as well as cost allocation fights over computer systems. In addition, the profit-sharing system built trust within the company.

Discussion Questions

1. Could Rob Rodin's profit-sharing plan at Marshall Industries work in most companies?

2. How do you think profit sharing built trust within Marshall Industries?

SOURCE: G. Colvin, "Value Driven: What Money Makes You Do," *Fortune* (August 17, 1998): 213+.

of change that boosts individual and team achievements in an organization. So, if one wants the rewards available in the organization, then one should work to earn them. Performance management and reward systems assume a demonstrable connection between performance and rewards. Organizations get the performance they reward, not the performance they say they want.[52] Further, when there is no apparent link between performance and rewards, people may begin to believe they are entitled to rewards regardless of how they perform. The concept of entitlement is very different from the concept of earning, which assumes a performance–reward link.

The notion of entitlement at work is counterproductive when taken to the extreme because it counteracts the power of earning.[53] People who believe they are entitled to rewards regardless of their behavior or performance are not motivated to behave constructively. Merit raises in some organizations, for example, have come to be viewed as entitlements, thus reducing their positive value in the organizational reward system. People believe they have a right to be taken care of by someone, whether that is the organization or a specific person. Entitlement engenders passive, irresponsible behavior, whereas earning engenders active, responsible, adult behavior. If rewards depend on performance, then people must perform responsibly to receive them. The power of earning rests on a direct link between performance and rewards.

CORRECTING POOR PERFORMANCE

7. Describe strategies for correcting poor performance.

Often a complicated, difficult challenge for supervisors, correcting poor performance is a three-step process. First, the cause or primary responsibility for the poor performance must be identified. Second, if the primary responsibility is a person's, then the source of the personal problem must be determined. Third, a plan of action to correct the poor performance must be developed. Challenge 6.1 gives you an opportunity to examine a poor performance you have experienced.

Poor performance may result from a variety of causes, the more important being poorly designed work systems, poor selection processes, inadequate training and skills development, lack of personal motivation, and personal problems intruding on the work environment. Not all poor performance is self-motivated; some is induced by the work system. Therefore, a good diagnosis should precede corrective action. For example, it may be that an employee is subject to a work design or selection system that

Challenge 6.1

Correcting Poor Performance

At one time or another, each of us has had a poor performance of some kind. It may have been a poor test result in school, a poor presentation at work, or a poor performance in an athletic event. Think of a poor performance event that you have experienced and work through the following three steps.

1. _____
2. _____
3. _____
4. _____
5. _____
6. _____
7. _____

Step 1. Briefly describe the specific event in some detail. Include why you label it a poor performance (bad score? someone else's evaluation?).

Step 2. Analyze the Poor Performance

a. List all the possible contributing causes to the poor performance. Be specific, such as the room was too hot, you did not get enough sleep, you were not told how to perform the task, etc. You might ask other people for possible ideas, too.

b. Is there a primary cause for the poor performance? What is it?

Step 3. Plan to Correct the Poor Performance

Develop a step-by-step plan of action that specifies what you can change or do differently to improve your performance the next time you have an opportunity. Include seeking help if it is needed. Once your plan is developed, look for an opportunity to execute it.

does not allow the person to exhibit good performance. Identifying the cause of the poor performance comes first and should be done in communication with the employee. If the problem is with the system and the supervisor can fix it, then everyone wins as a result.

If the poor performance is not attributable to work design or organizational process problems, then attention should be focused on the employee. At least three possible causes of poor performance can be attributed to the employee. The problem may lie in (1) some aspect of the person's relationship to the organization or supervisor, (2) some area of the employee's personal life, or (3) a training or developmental deficiency. In the latter two cases, poor performance may be treated as a symptom as opposed to a motivated consequence. In such cases, identifying financial problems, family difficulties, or health disorders may enable the supervisor to help the employee solve problems before they become too extensive. Employee assistance programs (EAPs) can be helpful to employees managing personal problems and are discussed in Chapter 7 in relation to managing stress.

Poor performance may also be motivated by an employee's displaced anger or conflict with the organization or supervisor. In such cases, the employee may or may not be aware of the internal reactions causing the problem. In either event, sabotage, work slowdowns, work stoppages, and similar forms of poor performance may result from such motivated behavior. The supervisor may attribute the cause of the problem to the employee, and the employee may attribute it to the supervisor or organization. To solve motivated performance problems requires treating the poor performance as a symptom with a deeper cause. Resolving the underlying anger or conflict results in the disappearance of the symptom (poor performance).

Attribution and Performance Management

According to attribution theory, managers make attributions (inferences) concerning employees' behavior and performance.[54] The attributions may not always be accurate. For example, an executive with Capital Cities Corporation (now part of the Disney Company) who had a very positive relationship with his boss was not held responsible for profit problems in his district. The boss attributed the problem to the economy instead. Supervisors and employees who share perceptions and attitudes, as in the Capital Cities situation, tend to evaluate each other highly.[55] Supervisors and employees who do not share perceptions and attitudes are more likely to blame each other for performance problems.

Harold Kelley's attribution theory aims to help us explain the behavior of other people. He also extended attribution theory by trying to identify the antecedents of internal and external attributions. Kelley proposed that individuals make attributions based on information gathered in the form of three informational cues: consensus, distinctiveness, and consistency.[56, 57] We observe an individual's behavior and then seek out information in the form of these three cues. *Consensus* is the extent to which peers in the same situation behave the same way. *Distinctiveness* is the degree to which the

consensus
An informational cue indicating the extent to which peers in the same situation behave in a similar fashion.

distinctiveness
An informational cue indicating the degree to which an individual behaves the same way in other situations.

consistency
An informational cue indicating the frequency of behavior over time.

person behaves the same way in other situations. *Consistency* refers to the frequency of a particular behavior over time.

We form attributions based on whether these cues are low or high. Figure 6.4 shows how the combination of these cues helps us form internal or external attributions. Suppose you have received several complaints from customers regarding one of your customer service representatives, John. You have not received complaints about your other service representatives (low consensus). Upon reviewing John's records, you note that he also received customer complaints during his previous job as a sales clerk (low distinctiveness). The complaints have been coming in steadily for about three months (high consistency). In this case, you would most likely make an internal attribution and conclude that the complaints must stem from John's behavior. The combination of low consensus, low distinctiveness, and high consistency leads to internal attributions.

Figure 6.4
Informational Cues and Attributions

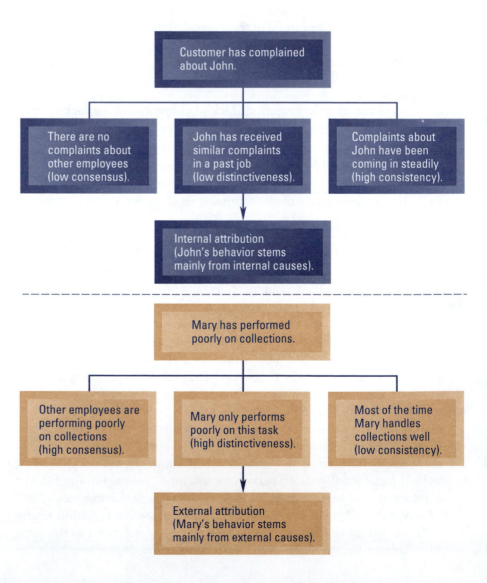

Other combinations of these cues, however, produce external attributions. High consensus, high distinctiveness, and low consistency, for example, produce external attributions. Suppose one of your employees, Mary, is performing poorly on collecting overdue accounts. You find that the behavior is widespread within your work team (high consensus) and that Mary is performing poorly only on this aspect of the job (high distinctiveness), and that most of the time she handles this aspect of the job well (low consistency). You will probably decide that something about the work situation caused the poor performance—perhaps work overload or an unfair deadline.

Consensus, distinctiveness, and consistency are the cues used to determine whether the cause of behavior is internal or external. The process of determining the cause of a behavior may not be simple and clear-cut, however, because of some biases that occur in forming attributions.

Figure 6.5 presents an attribution model that specifically addresses how supervisors respond to poor performance. A supervisor who observes poor performance seeks cues about the employee's behavior in the three forms discussed above: consensus, consistency, and distinctiveness.

On the basis of this information, the supervisor makes either an internal (personal) attribution or an external (situational) attribution. Internal attributions might include low effort, lack of commitment, or lack of ability. External attributions are outside the employee's control and might include equipment failure or unrealistic goals. The supervisor then determines the source of responsibility for the performance problem and tries to correct the problem.

Supervisors may choose from a wide range of responses. They can, for example, express personal concern, reprimand the employee, or provide training. Supervisors who attribute the cause of poor performance to a person (an internal cause) will respond more harshly than supervisors who attribute the cause to the work situation (an external cause). Supervisors should try not to make either of the two common attribution errors discussed in Chapter 3: the fundamental attribution error and the self-serving bias.

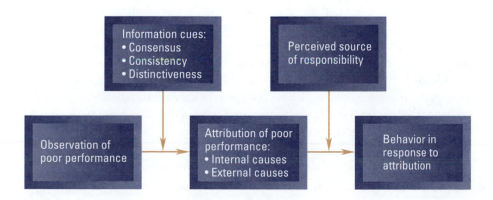

Figure 6.5
Attribution Model

Coaching, Counseling, and Mentoring

Supervisors have important coaching, counseling, and mentoring responsibilities to their subordinates. They should maintain a helping relationship with employees.[58] This relationship may be one where performance-based deficiencies are addressed or one where personal problems that diminish employee performance, such as depression, are addressed.[59] In either case, the supervisors can play a helpful role in employee problem-solving activities without accepting responsibility for the employees' problems. One important form of help is to refer the employee to trained professionals.

Coaching and counseling are among the career and psychosocial functions of a mentoring relationship.[60] *Mentoring* is a work relationship that encourages development and career enhancement for people moving through the career cycle. Mentor relationships typically go through four phases: initiation, cultivation, separation, and redefinition. The relationship can significantly enhance the early development of a newcomer and the mid-career development of an experienced employee. One study found that good performance by newcomers resulted in leaders giving more delegation.[61] Career development can be enhanced through peer relationships as an alternative to traditional mentoring relationships.[62] Informational, collegial, and special peers aid the individual's development through information sharing, career strategizing, job-related feedback, emotional support, and friendship. Hence, mentors and peers may both play constructive roles in correcting an employee's poor performance and in enhancing overall career development.

mentoring
A work relationship that encourages development and career enhancement for people moving through the career cycle.

MANAGERIAL IMPLICATIONS: PERFORMANCE MANAGEMENT IS A KEY TASK

People in organizations learn from the consequences of their actions. Therefore, managers must exercise care in applying positive and negative consequences to ensure that they are connected to the behaviors the managers intend to reward or punish. Managers should also be judicious in the use of punishment and should consider extinction coupled with positive reinforcement as an alternative to punishment for shaping employee behavior. The strategic use of training and educational opportunities, stock options, and recognition awards is instrumental to successful organizational reward systems. Managers can serve as positive role models for employees' vicarious learning about ethical behavior and high-quality performance.

Goal-setting activities may be valuable to managers in bringing out the best performance from employees. Managers can use challenging, specific goals for this purpose and must be prepared to provide employees with timely, useful feedback on goal progress so that employees will know how they are doing. Goal-setting activities that are misused may create dysfunctional competition in an organization and lead to lower performance.

Good performance evaluation systems are a valuable tool for providing employees with clear feedback on their actions. Managers who rely on valid and reliable performance measures may use them in employee development and to correct poor performance. Managers who use high-technology performance monitoring systems must remember that employees are humans, not machines. Managers are responsible for creating a positive learning atmosphere in performance feedback sessions, and employees are responsible for learning from these sessions.

Finally, managers can use rewards as one of the most powerful positive consequences for shaping employee behavior. If rewards are to improve performance, managers must make a clear connection between specific performance and the rewards. Employees should be expected to earn the rewards they receive; they should expect rewards to be related to performance quality and skill development.

Looking Back

Oprah's Rewards and Recognition for Successful Performance

Self-discipline, goal setting, and daily assessements of her progress have led to a variety of rewards and recognitions for Oprah Winfrey, many of which she shares with others. Since entering syndication in 1986, *The Oprah Winfrey Show* has received thirty-two Emmys, seven of which went to Oprah as host. In 2000, Harpo films won an Emmy for *Tuesdays with Morrie*. In 1997, Oprah was named *Newsweek's* "Most Important Person" in books and media and *TV Guide's* "Television Performer of the Year." She was also awarded a People's Choice Award for "Favorite Television Performer." At the end of the 1995–1996 television season, Oprah was honored with the most prestigious award in broadcasting, the George Foster Peabody Individual Achievement Award. Oprah also received the IRTS Gold Medal Award and was recognized by *Time* magazine as one of "America's 25 Most Influential People of 1996."

Since receiving both Golden Globe and Academy Award nominations for her role in Steven Spielberg's *The Color Purple*, Oprah has been critically acclaimed for her performances in *There Are No Children Here* and *The Women of Brewster Place*, stories portraying strong and determined women and representing triumphs of the human spirit. Oprah's fitness book, *Make the Connection*, which she co-authored with Bob Greene, became a bestseller. These various awards and recognitions are the long-term, positive consequences of the daily habits of self-discipline, goal setting, and assessment of progress toward her goals.

CHAPTER SUMMARY

1. Learning is a change in behavior acquired through experience.
2. The operant conditioning approach to learning states that behavior is a function of positive and negative consequences.
3. Reinforcement is used to develop desirable behavior; punishment and extinction are used to decrease undesirable behavior.
4. Bandura's social learning theory suggests that self-efficacy is important to effective learning.
5. Goal setting improves work motivation and task performance, reduces role stress, and improves the accuracy and validity of performance appraisal.
6. Performance appraisals help organizations develop employees and make decisions about them.
7. Making accurate attributions about the behavior of others is an essential prerequisite to correcting poor performance.
8. High-quality performance should be rewarded and poor performance should be corrected.
9. Mentoring is a relationship for encouraging development and career enhancement for people moving through the career cycle.

KEY TERMS

learning   161

classical conditioning   161

operant conditioning   162

positive consequences   162

negative consequences   163

reinforcement   163

punishment   164

extinction   165

self-efficacy   166

goal setting   167

management by objectives (MBO)   171

performance appraisal   173

consensus   181

distinctiveness   181

consistency   182

mentoring   184

REVIEW QUESTIONS

1. Define the terms *learning, reinforcement, punishment,* and *extinction*.
2. What are positive and negative consequences in shaping behavior, and how should they be managed? Explain the value of extinction as a strategy.
3. How can self-efficacy be enhanced? What are the differences in the way introverted and extroverted and intuitive and sensing people learn?
4. What are the five characteristics of well-developed goals? Why is feedback on goal progress important?
5. What are the purposes of conducting performance appraisals? Who should appraise performance? Why?
6. What are the two possible attributions of poor performance? What are the implications of each?
7. How can supervisors best provide useful performance feedback?
8. How do mentors and peers help people develop and enhance their careers?

DISCUSSION AND COMMUNICATION QUESTIONS

1. Which learning approach—the behavioral approach or Bandura's social learning theory—do you find more appropriate for people?
2. Given your personality type, how do you learn best? Do you miss learning some things because of how they are taught?
3. What goals do you set for yourself in your work and personal life? Will you know if you achieve them?
4. If a conflict occurred between your self-evaluation and the evaluation given to you by your supervisor or instructor, how would you respond? What,

specifically, would you do? What have you learned from your supervisor or instructor during the last reporting period?

5. What rewards are most important to you? How hard are you willing to work to receive them?

6. *(communication question)* Prepare a memo detailing the consequences of behavior in your work or university environment (e.g., grades, awards, suspensions, and scholarships). Include in your memo your classification of these consequences as positive or negative. Should your organization or university change the way it applies these consequences?

7. *(communication question)* Develop an oral presentation about the most current management practices in employee rewards and performance management. Find out what at least four different companies are doing in this area. Be prepared to discuss their fit with the text materials.

8. *(communication question)* Interview a manager or supervisor who is responsible for completing performance appraisals on people at work. Ask the manager which aspects of performance appraisal and the performance appraisal interview process are most difficult and how he or she manages these difficulties. Include the aspects of his or her job that enable the manager to meet these three different needs.

ETHICS QUESTIONS

1. Suppose a team of behavioral experts was asked to enhance the motivation of military personnel to kill their enemy: Is this request ethical? Is it socially desirable? Should the team have accepted the assignment? Explain.

2. Suppose the organization you work for simply assigns employees their task goals without consulting them. Is there an ethical problem with this approach? Does the organization have to consult its employees?

3. Assume you are an experienced technical employee with a better understanding of your work than your supervisor has. Further assume that your supervisor sets such high performance standards for an inexperienced coworker that the person cannot ever meet them and therefore is fired. What should you do? Is your supervisor's action ethical? Explain.

4. Suppose your company announced that it would pay bonuses to employees who met a certain performance standard. The company did not realize, however, that many employees would be able to reach the standard with hard work and that the bonuses would cost the company much more than expected. Is it fair to lower the bonus rate? Is it fair to increase the performance standard for bonuses after the fact? Explain.

Experiential Exercises

6.1 Positive and Negative Reinforcement

Purpose: To examine the effects of positive and negative reinforcement on behavior change.

1. Two or three volunteers are selected to receive reinforcement from the class while performing a particular task. The volunteers leave the room.

2. The instructor identifies an object for the student volunteers to locate when they return to the room.

(The object should be unobtrusive but clearly visible to the class. Some that have worked well are a small triangular piece of paper that was left behind when a notice was torn off a classroom bulletin board, a smudge on the chalkboard, and a chip in the plaster of a classroom wall.)

3. The instructor specifies the reinforcement contingencies that will be in effect when the volunteers

return to the room. For negative reinforcement, students should hiss, boo, and throw things (although you should not throw anything harmful) when the first volunteer is moving away from the object; cheer and applaud when the second volunteer is getting closer to the object; and, if a third volunteer is used, use both negative and positive reinforcement.

4. The instructor should assign a student to keep a record of the time it takes each of the volunteers to locate the object.

5. Volunteer number 1 is brought back into the room and is instructed: "Your task is to locate and touch a particular object in the room, and the class has agreed to help you. You may begin."

6. Volunteer number 1 continues to look for the object until it is found while the class assists by giving negative reinforcement.

7. Volunteer number 2 is brought back into the room and is instructed: "Your task is to locate and touch a particular object in the room, and the class has agreed to help you. You may begin."

8. Volunteer number 2 continues to look for the object until it is found while the class assists by giving positive reinforcement.

9. Volunteer number 3 is brought back into the room and is instructed: "Your task is to locate and touch a particular object in the room, and the class has agreed to help you. You may begin."

10. Volunteer number 3 continues to look for the object until it is found while the class assists by giving both positive and negative reinforcement.

11. In a class discussion, answer the following questions:
   a. How did the behavior of the volunteers differ when different kinds of reinforcement (positive, negative, or both) were used?
   b. What were the emotional reactions of the volunteers to the different kinds of reinforcement?
   c. Which type of reinforcement—positive or negative—is most common in organizations? What effect do you think this has on motivation and productivity?

6.2 Correcting Poor Performance

This exercise provides an opportunity for you to engage in a performance diagnosis role-play as either the assistant director of the Academic Computing Service Center or as a member of a university committee appointed by the president of the university at the request of the center director. The instructor will form the class into groups of five or six students and either ask the group to select who is to be the assistant director or assign one group member to be the assistant director.

Performance diagnosis, especially where some poor performance exists, requires making attributions and determining causal factors as well as formulating a plan of action to correct any poor performance.

Step 1. (5 minutes) Once the class is formed into groups, the instructor provides the assistant director with a copy of the role description and each university committee member with a copy of the role context information. Group members are to read through the materials provided.

Step 2. (15 minutes) The university committee is to call in the assistant director of the Academic Computing Service Center for a performance diagnostic interview. This is an information-gathering interview, not an appraisal session. The purpose is to gather information for the center director.

Step 3. (15 minutes) The university committee is to agree on a statement that reflects their understanding of the assistant director's poor performance, to include a specification of the causes. Based on this problem statement, the committee is to formulate a plan of action to correct the poor performance. The assistant director is to do the same, again ending with a plan of action.

Step 4. (10–15 minutes, optional) The instructor may ask the groups to share the results of their work in Step 3 of the role-play exercise.

Learning Objectives

After reading this chapter, you should be able to do the following:

1. Define *stress, distress, strain*, and *eustress*. *p. 190*

2. Compare four different approaches to stress. *p. 191*

3. Explain the psycho-physiology of the stress response. *p. 193*

4. Identify work and non-work causes of stress. *p. 193*

5. Describe the benefits of eustress and the costs of distress. *p. 198*

6. Discuss four moderators of the stress–strain relationship. *p. 202*

7. Distinguish the primary, secondary, and tertiary stages of preventive stress management. *p. 205*

8. Discuss organizational and individual methods of preventive stress management. *p. 207*

7

Stress and Well-Being at Work

Thinking Ahead

Deregulation Stress, Financial Risk, and Airline Safety

The deregulation of the U.S. airline industry more than twenty years ago introduced competitive pressures to this previously regulated industry, increasing stress for employees and companies alike. What were the effects of deregulation stress on employees, airlines, and the traveling public? Did deregulation increase stress and risk for air travelers as it did for airlines and their employees? Significantly, deregulation seems to have had no effect on the safety of airline travel.[1] The effects on the airlines, however, appear to have been mixed. Although the airlines' operating profits did not decline under deregulation, their financial risk increased as did the job insecurity of their employees. This increased financial risk in the business appears not to have increased risk for the traveling public, however, for two reasons. First, deregulation was never intended to deregulate safety, but to restore competitive market forces to this sector of the economy. Second, many studies have shown that deregulation and the increased competition that resulted from it have reduced airfares. Lower airfares increase the number of passenger revenue miles flown by airlines. Increased miles flown are bound to increase crew experience and lead to new innovations in all aspects of the industry, including safety. Because of the continued supervision of the Federal Aviation Administration, direct investment effects, and the competitive structure of the industry, the airline industry has maintained an adequate level of safety in air traffic. While air travelers may be secure, how have the men and women of Southwest Airlines successfully managed the stress, pressure, insecurity, and increased financial risk in this competitive, deregulated environment? In the Looking Back feature, CEO Herb Kelleher talks about putting humor to work at Southwest Airlines.

During the past decade, stress has become a significant topic in organizational behavior, in part due to the increase in competitive pressures in many industries, as in the case of the airline industry just discussed. This chapter has five major sections, each addressing one aspect of stress. The first section examines the question "What is stress?" The discussion includes four approaches to the stress response. The second section reviews the demands and stressors that trigger the stress response at work. The third section examines the performance and health benefits of stress and the individual and organizational forms of distress. The fourth section considers individual difference factors, such as gender and personality hardiness, that help moderate the stress–distress relationship. The fifth section presents a framework for preventive stress management and reviews a wide range of individual and organizational stress management methods.

1. Define *stress, distress, strain,* and *eustress.*

stress
The unconscious preparation to fight or flee that a person experiences when faced with any demand.

stressor
The person or event that triggers the stress response.

distress
The adverse psychological, physical, behavioral, and organizational consequences that may arise as a result of stressful events.

strain
Distress.

WHAT IS STRESS?

Stress is one of the most creatively ambiguous words in the English language, with as many interpretations as there are people who use the word. In other languages, the term *stress* has a variety of meanings, and Spanish does not even have a direct translation of the word. Even the stress experts do not agree on its definition. Stress carries a negative connotation for some people, as though it were something to be avoided. This is unfortunate, because stress is a great asset in managing legitimate emergencies and achieving peak performance. **Stress**, or the stress response, is the unconscious preparation to fight or flee that a person experiences when faced with any demand.[2] A **stressor**, or demand, is the person or event that triggers the stress response. **Distress** or **strain** refers to the adverse psychological, physical, behavioral, and organizational consequences that *may* occur as a result of stressful events. Challenge 7.1 gives you an opportunity to examine how overstressed and angry you may be.

Challenge 7.1

The Frazzle Factor

Read each of the following statements and rate yourself on a scale of 0 to 3, giving the answer that best describes how you generally feel (3 points for *always*, 2 points for *often*, 1 point for *sometimes*, and 0 points for *never*). Answer as honestly as you can, and do not spend too much time on any one statement.

Am I Overstressed?

____ 1. I have to make important snap judgments and decisions.

____ 2. I am not consulted about what happens on my job or in my classes.

____ 3. I feel I am underpaid.

____ 4. I feel that no matter how hard I work, the system will mess it up.

____ 5. I do not get along with some of my coworkers or fellow students.

____ 6. I do not trust my superiors at work or my professors at school.

____ 7. The paperwork burden on my job or at school is getting to me.

____ 8. I feel people outside the job or the university do not respect what I do.

Am I Angry?

____ 1. I feel that people around me make too many irritating mistakes.

____ 2. I feel annoyed because I do good work or perform well in school, but no one appreciates it.

____ 3. When people make me angry, I tell them off.

____ 4. When I am angry, I say things I know will hurt people.

____ 5. I lose my temper easily.

____ 6. I feel like striking out at someone who angers me.

____ 7. When a coworker or fellow student makes a mistake, I tell him or her about it.

____ 8. I cannot stand being criticized in public.

SCORING

To find your level of anger and potential for aggressive behavior, add your scores from both quiz parts.

40–48: The red flag is waving, and you had better pay attention. You are in the danger zone. You need guidance from a counselor or mental health professional, and you should be getting it now.

30–39: The yellow flag is up. Your stress and anger levels are too high, and you are feeling increasingly hostile. You are still in control, but it would not take much to trigger a violent flare of temper.

10–29: Relax, you are in the broad normal range. Like most people, you get angry occasionally, but usually with some justification. Sometimes you take overt action, but you are not likely to be unreasonably or excessively aggressive.

0–9: Congratulations! You are in great shape. Your stress and anger are well under control, giving you a laid-back personality not prone to violence.

SOURCE: Questionnaire developed by C. D. Spielberger. Appeared in W. Barnhill, "Early Warning." *The Washington Post*, August 11, 1992, B5.

Four Approaches to Stress

The stress response was discovered by Walter B. Cannon, a medical physiologist, early in the twentieth century.[3] Later researchers defined stress differently than Cannon. We will review four different approaches to defin-

2. Compare four different approaches to stress.

Experiencing OB

The fight-or-flight choice is a common dilemma for people facing a stressful situation. Learn more about the fight-or-flight response at our animated concept and activity site. Choose Stress from the "select a topic" pull-down menu, then The Stress Response from the "overview tab."

http://www.experiencingob.com

homeostasis
A steady state of bodily functioning and equilibrium.

ego-ideal
The embodiment of a person's perfect self.

self-image
How a person sees himself or herself, both positively and negatively.

ing stress: the homeostatic/medical, cognitive appraisal, person–environment fit, and psychoanalytic approaches. These four approaches to stress will give you a more complete understanding of what stress really is.

The Homeostatic/Medical Approach When Walter B. Cannon originally discovered stress, he called it "the emergency response" or "the militaristic response," arguing that it was rooted in "the fighting emotions." His early writings provide the basis for calling the stress response the *fight-or-flight* response. According to Cannon, stress resulted when an external, environmental demand upset the person's natural steady-state balance.[4] He referred to this steady-state balance, or equilibrium, as **homeostasis**. Cannon believed the body was designed with natural defense mechanisms to keep it in homeostasis. He was especially interested in the role of the sympathetic nervous system in activating a person under stressful conditions.[5]

The Cognitive Appraisal Approach Richard Lazarus was more concerned with the psychology of stress. He de-emphasized the medical and physiological aspects, emphasizing instead the psychological and cognitive aspects of the response.[6] Like Cannon, Lazarus saw stress as a result of a person–environment interaction, and he emphasized the person's cognitive appraisal in classifying persons or events as stressful or not. Individuals differ in their appraisal of events and people. What is stressful for one person may not be stressful for another. Perception and cognitive appraisal are important processes in determining what is stressful, and a person's organizational position can shape such perception. For example, an employee would more likely be stressed by an upset supervisor than another supervisor would be. Lazarus also introduced problem-focused and emotion-focused coping. Problem-focused coping emphasizes managing the stressor, and emotion-focused coping emphasizes managing your response.

The Person–Environment Fit Approach Robert Kahn was concerned with the social psychology of stress. His approach emphasized how confusing and conflicting expectations of a person in a social role create stress for the person.[7] He extended the approach to examine a person's fit in the environment. A good person–environment fit occurs when a person's skills and abilities match a clearly defined, consistent set of role expectations. This results in a lack of stress for the person. Stress occurs when the role expectations are confusing and/or conflicting, or when a person's skills and abilities are not able to meet the demands of the social role. After a period of this stress, the person can expect to experience strain, such as strain in the form of depression.

The Psychoanalytic Approach Harry Levinson defined stress based on Freudian psychoanalytic theory.[8] Levinson believes that two elements of the personality interact to cause stress. The first element is the **ego-ideal**, the embodiment of a person's perfect self. The second element is the **self-image**—how the person really sees himself or herself, both positively and negatively. Although not sharply defined, the ego-ideal encompasses admirable attributes of parental personalities, wished-for and/or imaginable qualities a person would like to possess, and the absence of any negative or distasteful qualities. Stress results from the discrepancy between the idealized self (ego-ideal) and the real self-image; the greater the discrepancy, the more stress a person experiences. More generally, psychoanalytic theory helps us understand the role of unconscious personality factors as causes of stress within a person.

The Stress Response

Whether activated by an ego-ideal/self-image discrepancy, a poorly defined social role, cognitive appraisal suggesting threat, or a lack of balance, the resulting stress response is characterized by a predictable sequence of mind and body events. The stress response begins with the release of chemical messengers, primarily adrenaline, into the bloodstream. These messengers activate the sympathetic nervous system and the endocrine (hormone) system. These two systems work together and trigger four mind–body changes to prepare the person for fight or flight:

3. ■ Explain the psychophysiology of the stress response.

1. The redirection of the blood to the brain and large-muscle groups and away from the skin, internal organs, and extremities.
2. Increased alertness by way of improved vision, hearing, and other sensory processes through the activation of the brainstem (ancient brain).
3. The release of glucose (blood sugar) and fatty acids into the bloodstream to sustain the body during the stressful event.
4. Depression of the immune system, as well as restorative and emergent processes (such as digestion).

This set of four changes shifts the person from a neutral, or naturally defensive, posture to an offensive posture. The stress response can be very functional in preparing a person to deal with legitimate emergencies and to achieve peak performance. It is neither inherently bad nor necessarily destructive.

SOURCES OF STRESS AT WORK

The four approaches to defining stress emphasize demands, or sources of stress, for people at work. We can organize these demands into the general categories of task demands, role demands, interpersonal demands, and physical demands. In addition, the organization needs to be sensitive to non-work stressors, such as demands from the person's family or nonwork activities. For example, child-care considerations are an increasing concern for organizations as more women have gone to work and more men are the primary caregivers. Finally, global factors, such as general economic conditions within a society and the international economy, create widespread stress for individuals. Table 7.1 summarizes the specific demands that we discuss.

4. ■ Identify work and nonwork causes of stress.

Table 7.1
Work and Nonwork Demands

Work Demands	
Task Demands	**Role Demands**
Change	Role conflict:
Lack of control	Interrole
Career progress	Intrarole
New technologies	Person–role
Work overload	Role ambiguity
Interpersonal Demands	**Physical Demands**
Abrasive personalities	Extreme environments
Sexual harassment	Strenuous activities
Leadership styles	Hazardous substances
Nonwork Demands	
Family Demands	**Personal Demands**
Marital expectations	Religious activities
Child-rearing/day-care arrangements	Self-improvement tasks
Parental care	Traumatic events

Experiencing OB

Test your understanding of sources of stress at our animated concept and activity site. Choose Stress from the "select a topic" pull-down menu, then Sources of Stress from the "overview tab."

http://www.experiencingob.com

Task Demands

Change and lack of control are two of the most stressful demands people face at work.[9] Change leads to uncertainty, a lack of predictability in a person's daily tasks and activities, and may be caused by job insecurity related to difficult economic times. During the 1980s, U.S. Steel had to lay off tens of thousands of workers because of the economic difficulties in the industry resulting from intense international competition. Corporate warfare led to extensive mergers, acquisitions, and downsizing during the 1980s; these changes resulted in significant uncertainty for thousands of employees. Technology and technological innovation also create change and uncertainty for many employees, requiring adjustments in training, education, and skill development. Organizational Reality 7.1 discusses modern electronic information and communication technology. Intended to make life and work easier and more convenient, information technology may have a paradoxical effect and be a source of stress rather than a stress-reliever.

Lack of control is a second major source of stress, especially in work environments that are difficult and psychologically demanding. The lack of control may be caused by inability to influence the timing of tasks and activities, to select tools or methods for accomplishing the work, to make decisions that influence work outcomes, or to exercise direct action to affect the work outcomes. One study found that male workers in occupations with low job autonomy (lack of control) and high job demands (heavy workloads) experienced more heart attacks than other male workers.[10]

ORGANIZATIONAL REALITY 7.1

Infotech-Stressor? Stress-Reliever?

Being "wired" is a euphemism for being stressed-up and a double entendre for being plugged in to electronic information or communication technology. In 2000, executives can be wired and unplugged at the same time. Mark Kvamme, chairman of USWeb/CKS, an Internet marketing firm, has a satellite dish atop his house that provides Internet access seven times faster than a 56K modem, and his laptop contains global positioning software that can pinpoint his location anywhere in the world if he gets lost.

Information, communication, and electronic technology are intended to make life easier for managers and executives, but do they? Is being wired and plugged in a stress-reliever? Infotech may just as easily display the other edge of its sword, becoming a stressor for the manager or executive who is wired in a hyperfrenetic, pass-the-Valium kind of way. For example, a corporate lobbyist who checked into an upstate New York spa for a stress management weekend, including mud baths and massages, brought along her pager just to stay connected. The lobbyist was beeped so often during the weekend that she was asked to leave before it was finished. A Pitney Bowes study conducted by Gallup found the average executive received 190 "communications" a day, including 30 e-mails, 22 voice messages, 4 pager beeps, and 3 express mailings. Although infotech is intended to be a world-expanding, labor-saving, stress-reliever, it is all too often a stressor playing to a manager's vulnerability: belief in total accessibility, total awareness, and absolute control. Technology is neither a manager's salvation nor the enemy, despite the power infotech may have in a manager's work and life. The manager's challenge is to use infotech as a tool, mastering its utility and power rather than allowing the tool to become the master.

Discussion Questions

1. Why is information technology a stressor for managers?

2. What are good ways to manage information technology so that it is *not* a stressor?

SOURCE: J. Martin, "Smart Managing/Best Practices, Careers, and Ideas: Ultra-Wired," *Fortune* (August 3, 1998): 241+.

Concerns over career progress, new technologies, and work overload (or work underload) are three additional task demands triggering stress for the person at work. Career stress is related to the career gridlock that has occurred in many organizations as the middle-manager ranks have been thinned due to mergers, acquisitions, and downsizing during the past two decades.[11] Thinning the organizational ranks also often leaves an abundance of work for those who are still employed. Work overload is seen as the leading stressor for people at work. In some cases, the reverse, work underload, can be an equally stressful problem. New technologies also create both career stress and "technostress" for people at work who wonder if they will be replaced by "smart" machines.[12] Although they enhance the organization's productive capacity, new technologies may be viewed as the enemy by workers who must ultimately learn to use them. This creates a real dilemma for management.

Role Demands

The social–psychological demands of the work environment may be every bit as stressful as task demands at work. People encounter two major categories of role stress at work: role conflict and role ambiguity.[13] Role conflict results from inconsistent or incompatible expectations communicated to a person. The conflict may be an interrole, intrarole, or person–role conflict.

Interrole conflict is caused by conflicting expectations related to two separate roles, such as employee and parent. For example, the employee with a major sales presentation on Monday and a sick child at home Sunday night is likely to experience interrole conflict.

Intrarole conflict is caused by conflicting expectations related to a single role, such as employee. For example, the manager who presses employees for both very fast work *and* high-quality work may be viewed at some point as creating a conflict for employees.

Ethics violations are likely to cause person–role conflicts. Employees expected to behave in ways that violate personal values, beliefs, or principles experience conflict. The unethical acts of committed employees exemplify this problem. Organizations with high ethical standards, such as Johnson & Johnson, are less likely to create ethical conflicts for employees. Person–role conflicts and ethics violations create a sense of divided loyalty for an employee.

The second major cause of role stress is role ambiguity. Role ambiguity is the confusion a person experiences related to the expectations of others. Role ambiguity may be caused by not understanding what is expected, not knowing how to do it, or not knowing the result of failure to do it. For example, a new magazine employee asked to copyedit a manuscript for the next issue may experience confusion because of lack of familiarity with copyediting procedures and conventions for the specific magazine.

A twenty-one-nation study of middle managers examined their experiences of role conflict, role ambiguity, and role overload. The results indicated that role stress varies more by country than it does by demographic and organizational factors. For example, non-Western managers experience less role ambiguity and more role overload than do their Western counterparts.[14] Another study found that simultaneous increases in both role conflict and role ambiguity were associated with lower levels of job performance.[15]

Interpersonal Demands

Abrasive personalities, sexual harassment, and the leadership style in the organization are interpersonal demands for people at work. The abrasive person may be an able and talented employee, but one who creates emotional waves that others at work must accommodate. Abrasive personalities stand out at work, and some organizational cultures tolerate them. Organizations are increasingly less tolerant of sexual harassment, a gender-related interpersonal demand that creates a stressful working environment both for the person being harassed and for others. The vast majority of sexual harassment is directed at women in the workplace. Leadership styles in organizations, whether authoritarian or participative, create stress for different personality types. Employees who feel secure with firm, directive leadership may be anxious with an open, participative style. Those comfortable with participative leadership may feel restrained by a directive style. Trust is an important characteristic of the leader–follower interpersonal relationship, and a threat to a worker's reputation with her or his supervisor may be especially stressful.[16]

Physical Demands

Extreme environments, strenuous activities, hazardous substances, and global travel create physical demands for people at work. Work environments that are very hot or very cold place differing physical demands on people and create unique risks. One cross-cultural study that examined the effects of national culture and ambient temperature on role stress concluded that ambient temperature does affect human well-being, leading to the term *sweat shop* for inhumane working conditions.[17] Dehydration is one problem of extremely hot climates, whereas frostbite is one problem of extremely cold climates. The strenuous job of a steelworker and the hazards associated with bomb disposal work are physically demanding in different ways. The unique physical demands of work are often occupation specific, such as the risk of gravitationally induced loss of consciousness for military pilots flying high-performance fighters[18] or jet lag and loss of sleep for globe-trotting CEOs like IBM's Louis Gerstner and General Electric's Jack Welch.

Office work has its physical hazards as well. Noisy, crowded offices, such as those of some stock brokerages, can prove stressful to work in. Working with a computer terminal can also be stressful, especially if the ergonomic fit between the person and machine is not correct. Eyestrain, neck stiffness, and arm and wrist problems can occur. Office designs that use partitions (cubicles) rather than full walls can create stress. These systems offer little privacy for the occupant (for example, to conduct employee counseling or performance appraisal sessions) and little protection from interruptions.

Nonwork Demands

Nonwork demands create stress for people, which may carry over into the work environment, or vice versa.[19] Not all workers are subject to family demands related to marriage, child rearing, and parental care. For those who are, these demands may create role conflicts or overloads that are difficult to manage. For example, the loss of good day care for children may be especially stressful for dual-career and single-parent families.[20] The tension between work and family may lead to a real struggle to achieve balance in life. This struggle led Rocky Rhodes, cofounder of Silicon Graphics, to establish four priorities for his life: God, family, exercise, and work.[21] These priorities helped him reallocate his time to achieve better balance in his life. As a result of the maturing of the American population, an increasing number of people face the added demand of parental care. Even when a person works to achieve an integrative social identity, integrating many social roles into a "whole" identity for a more stress-free balance in work and nonwork identities, the process of integration is not an easy one.[22]

In addition to family demands, people have personal demands related to nonwork organizational commitments, such as in churches, synagogues, and public service organizations. These demands become more or less stressful depending on their compatibility with the person's work and family life and their capacity to provide alternative satisfactions for the person. Finally, traumatic events and their aftermath are stressful for people who experience them.[23] Traumatic events need not be catastrophic in nature, although catastrophic events related to war or death of a loved one are traumatic. Job loss, examination failures, and termination of romantic attachments are all traumatic and may lead to distress if not addressed and resolved.

THE CONSEQUENCES OF STRESS

5. Describe the benefits of eustress and the costs of distress.

eustress
Healthy, normal stress.

Contrary to one report, Americans are not failing the stress test, and not all the consequences of stress are bad or destructive.[24] Interestingly, BellSouth won the Best of Show television sweepstakes at the 34th International Broadcasting Awards with its commercial entitled "Stress Test." The consequences of healthy, normal stress (called *eustress*, for "euphoria + stress") include a number of performance and health benefits to be balanced against the more commonly known costs of individual and organizational distress.[25] The benefits of eustress and the costs of distress are listed in Table 7.2. An organization striving for high-quality products and services needs a healthy workforce to support the effort. Eustress is a characteristic of healthy people; distress is not.

Performance and Health Benefits of Stress

Experiencing OB

You may learn more about the relationship between stress level and performance by visiting our animated concept and activity site. Choose Stress from the "select a topic" pull-down menu, then Consequences of Stress from the "overview tab."

http://www.experiencingob.com

The Yerkes-Dodson law, shown in Figure 7.1, indicates that stress leads to improved performance up to an optimum point.[26] Beyond the optimum point, further stress and arousal have a detrimental effect on performance. Therefore, healthy amounts of eustress are desirable to improve performance by arousing a person to action. It is in the midrange of the curve that the greatest performance benefits from stress are achieved. Joseph McGrath has suggested that performance declines beyond the midpoint in the Yerkes-Dodson curve because of the increasing difficulty of the task to be performed.[27] The stress response does provide momentary strength and physical force for brief periods of exertion, thus providing a basis for peak performance in athletic competition or other events.

Specific stressful activities, including aerobic exercise, weight training, and flexibility training, improve health and enhance a person's ability to manage stressful demands or situations. Cannon argued that the stress response better prepares soldiers for combat.[28] In survival or combat situa-

Benefits of Eustress	
Performance	**Health**
Increased arousal	Cardiovascular efficiency
Bursts of physical strength	Enhanced focus in an emergency
Costs of Distress	
Individual	**Organizational**
Psychological disorders	Participation problems
Medical illnesses	Performance decrements
Behavioral problems	Compensation awards

Table 7.2
Benefits of Eustress and Costs of Distress

tions, stress provides one with the necessary energy boost to manage the situation successfully.

The stress response is not inherently bad or destructive. The various individual and organizational forms of distress often associated with the word *stress* are the result of prolonged activation of the stress response, mismanagement of the energy induced by the response, or unique vulnerabilities in a person. We next examine the forms of individual distress and then the forms of organizational distress.

Individual Distress

An extreme preoccupation with work may result in acute individual distress, such as the unique Japanese phenomenon of *karoshi*, or death by over-

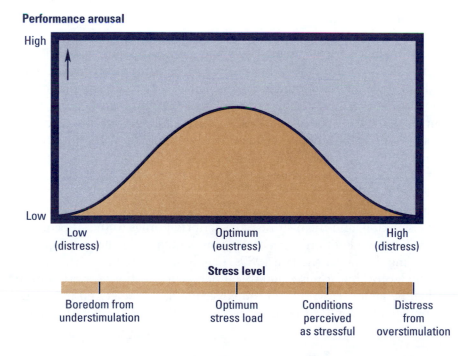

Figure 7.1
Yerkes-Dodson Law

Performance arousal

High

Low

Low
(distress)

Optimum
(eustress)

High
(distress)

Stress level

Boredom from
understimulation

Optimum
stress load

Conditions
perceived
as stressful

Distress
from
overstimulation

work.[29] In general, individual distress usually takes one of the three basic forms shown in Table 7.2. Work-related psychological disorders are among the ten leading health disorders and diseases in the United States, according to the National Institute for Occupational Safety and Health.[30] The most common types of psychological distress are depression, burnout, and psychosomatic disorders. In the early stages, depression and burnout result in a decline in efficiency; diminished interest in work; fatigue; and an exhausted, run-down feeling. Psychosomatic disorders are physical disorders with a psychological origin. For example, the intense stress of public speaking may result in a speech disorder; that is, the person is under so much stress that the mind literally will not allow speech to occur.

A number of medical illnesses have a stress-related component.[31] The most significant medical illnesses of this form are heart disease and strokes, backaches, peptic ulcers, and headaches. Ford Motor Company found that cardiovascular diseases, the leading cause of death in the United States since 1910, constituted only 1.5 percent of the medical incidents among 800 salaried employees at its headquarters but accounted for 29 percent of the reported medical costs.[32] On the positive side, premature death and disability rates have dropped 24 to 36 percent since the mid-1970s. Backaches are a nonfatal medical problem to which stress contributes through the strong muscular contractions related to preparation for fight or flight. Headaches may be related to eyestrain or have a migraine component, but tension headaches are caused by the contraction of the head and neck muscles under stressful conditions. Finally, stress is a contributing factor to peptic ulcers. A popular comedian commented, "I don't get angry; I just grow a tumor!" There is no clear evidence that stress is a direct causal agent in the onset of cancer. However, stress may play an indirect role in the progression of the disease.[33]

Behavioral problems are the third form of individual distress. These problems include violence, substance abuse of various kinds, and accidents. Violence need not necessarily be physical to be destructive. Interpersonal conflicts can be a form of nonphysical violence. One study found that conflicts with workmates, neighbors, and other "nonintimates" account for about 80 percent of our bad moods.[34] Ethnic and cultural differences are too often a basis for interpersonal conflicts and may escalate into physical violence in the workplace. For example, some U.S. employees of Arab descent experienced ethnic slurs at work during the Gulf War with Iraq, a largely Arab nation.

Substance abuse ranges from legal behaviors such as alcohol abuse, excessive smoking, and the overuse of prescription drugs to illegal behaviors such as heroin addiction. Former surgeon general C. Everett Koop's war on smoking, begun in the late 1980s, may be warranted from the health-risk standpoint, but it raises an ethical debate about the restriction of individual behavior. How far can the government or society go in restricting individual behavior that has adverse health consequences for many?

This is even more problematic in light of recent research results showing the adverse health effects of passive smoking (that is, nonsmokers breathing smoky air).

Accidents, both on and off the job, are another behavioral form of distress that can sometimes be traced to work-related stressors. For example, an unresolved problem at work may continue to preoccupy or distract an employee driving home and result in the employee having an automobile accident.

These three forms of individual distress—psychological disorders, medical illnesses, and behavioral problems—cause a burden of personal suffering. They also cause a collective burden of suffering reflected in organizational distress.

Organizational Distress

The University of Michigan studies on organizational stress identified a variety of indirect costs of mismanaged stress for the organization, such as low morale, dissatisfaction, breakdowns in communication, and disruption of working relationships. Subsequent research at the Survey Research Center at Michigan established behavioral costing guidelines, which specify the direct costs of organizational distress.[35]

Participation problems are the costs associated with absenteeism, tardiness, strikes and work stoppages, and turnover. In the case of absenteeism, the organization may compensate by hiring temporary personnel who take the place of the absentee, thus elevating personnel costs. When considering turnover, a distinction should be made between dysfunctional and functional turnover. Dysfunctional turnover occurs when an organization loses a valuable employee. It is costly for the organization. Replacement costs, including recruiting and retraining, for the valued employee range from five to seven months of the person's monthly salary. Functional turnover, in contrast, benefits the organization by creating opportunities for new members, new ideas, and fresh approaches. Functional turnover occurs when an organization loses an employee who has little or no value, or is a problem. Functional turnover is good for the organization. The "up or out" promotion policy for members of some organizations is designed to create functional turnover.

Performance decrements are the costs resulting from poor quality or low quantity of production, grievances, and unscheduled machine downtime and repair. As in the case of medical illnesses, stress is not the only causal agent in these performance decrements. Stress does play a role, however, whether the poor quality or low quantity of production is motivated by distressed employees or by an unconscious response to stress on the job. In California, some employees have the option of taking a "stress leave" rather than filing a grievance against the boss.

Compensation awards are the organizational costs resulting from court awards for job distress.[36] Given the case law framework of most of the na-

participation problem
A cost associated with absenteeism, tardiness, strikes and work stoppages, and turnover.

performance decrement
A cost resulting from poor quality or low quantity of production, grievances, and unscheduled machine downtime and repair.

compensation award
An organizational cost resulting from court awards for job distress.

tion's legal system, it takes a history of judgments to determine how far the courts will go in honoring stress-related claims. One former insurance employee in Louisiana filed a federal suit against the company, alleging it created a high-strain job for him that resulted in an incapacitating depression.[37] A jury awarded him a $1.5 million judgment that was later overturned by the judge. Job-stress-related claims have skyrocketed and threaten to bankrupt the workers' compensation system in some states, although claims and costs are down in other states.[38]

INDIVIDUAL DIFFERENCES IN THE STRESS–STRAIN RELATIONSHIP

6. Discuss four moderators of the stress–strain relationship.

The same stressful events may lead to distress and strain for one person and to excitement and healthy results for another. Individual differences play a central role in the stress–strain relationship. The weak organ hypothesis in medicine, also known as the Achilles' heel phenomenon, suggests that a person breaks down at his or her weakest point. Some individual differences, such as gender and Type A behavior pattern, enhance vulnerability to strain under stressful conditions. Other individual differences, such as personality hardiness and self-reliance, reduce vulnerability to strain under stressful conditions.

Gender Effects

According to Estelle Ramey, women are designed for long, miserable lives, whereas men are designed for short, violent ones.[39] The truth of this is that the life expectancy for American women is approximately seven years longer than for American men. Ramey attributes part of the increased life span to hormonal differences between the sexes.

Some literature suggests that there are differences in the stressors to which the two sexes are subject.[40] For example, sexual harassment is a gender-related source of stress for many working women. There is also substantive evidence that the important differences in the sexes are in vulnerabilities.[41] For example, males are more vulnerable at an earlier age to fatal health problems, such as cardiovascular disorders, whereas women report more nonfatal, but long-term and disabling, health problems. Although we can conclude that gender indeed creates a differential vulnerability between the two sexes, it may actually be more important to examine the differences *among* women or *among* men.

Type A Behavior Pattern

Type A behavior pattern
A complex of personality and behavioral characteristics, including competitiveness, time urgency, social status insecurity, aggression, hostility, and a quest for achievements.

Type A behavior pattern is also labeled *coronary-prone behavior*.[42] *Type A behavior pattern* is a complex of personality and behavioral characteristics, including competitiveness, time urgency, social status insecurity, aggression, hostility, and a quest for achievements. Table 7.3 lists four primary components of the Type A behavior pattern.

1. Sense of time urgency (a kind of "hurry sickness").
2. The quest for numbers (success is measured by the number of achievements).
3. Status insecurity (feeling unsure of oneself deep down inside).
4. Aggression and hostility expressed in response to frustration and conflict.

Table 7.3
Type A Behavior Pattern Components

There are two primary hypotheses concerning the lethal part of the Type A behavior pattern. One hypothesis suggests that the problem is time urgency, whereas the other hypothesis suggests that it is the hostility and aggression. The weight of evidence suggests that hostility and aggression, not time urgency, are the lethal agents.[43] Look back at your result in Challenge 7.1. Are you too angry and overstressed?

The alternative to the Type A behavior pattern is the Type B behavior pattern. People with Type B personalities are relatively free of the Type A behaviors and characteristics identified in Table 7.3. Type B people are less coronary prone, but if they do have a heart attack, they do not appear to recover as well as those with Type A personalities. Organizations can also be characterized as Type A or Type B organizations.[44] Type A individuals in Type B organizations and Type B individuals in Type A organizations experience stress related to a misfit between their personality type and the predominant type of the organization. However, preliminary evidence suggests that Type A individuals in Type A organizations are most at risk of health disorders.

Type A behavior can be modified. The first step is recognizing that an individual is prone to the Type A pattern. Another possible step in modifying Type A behavior is to spend time with Type B individuals. Type B people often recognize Type A behavior and can help Type A individuals take hassles less seriously and see the humor in situations. Type A individuals can also pace themselves, manage their time well, and try not to do multiple things at once. Focusing only on the task at hand and its completion, rather than worrying about other tasks, can help Type A individuals cope more effectively.

Personality Hardiness

People who have personality hardiness resist strain reactions when subjected to stressful events more effectively than do people who are not hardy.[45] The components of *personality hardiness* are commitment (versus alienation), control (versus powerlessness), and challenge (versus threat). Commitment is a curiosity and engagement with one's environment that leads to the experience of activities as interesting and enjoyable. Control is an ability to influence the process and outcomes of events that leads to the experience of activities as personal choices. Challenge is the viewing of change as a stimulus to personal development, which leads to the experience of activities with openness.

personality hardiness
A personality resistant to distress and characterized by commitment, control, and challenge.

transformational coping
A way of managing stressful events by changing them into less subjectively stressful events.

The hardy personality appears to use these three components actively to engage in transformational coping when faced with stressful events.[46] *Transformational coping* is the act of actively changing an event into something less subjectively stressful by viewing it in a broader life perspective, by altering the course and outcome of the event through action, and/or by achieving greater understanding of the process. The alternative to transformational coping is regressive coping, a much less healthy form of coping with stressful events characterized by a passive avoidance of events by decreasing interaction with the environment. Regressive coping may lead to short-term stress reduction at the cost of long-term healthy life adjustment.

Self-Reliance

self-reliance
A healthy, secure, *interdependent* pattern of behavior related to how people form and maintain supportive attachments with others.

There is increasing evidence that social relationships have an important impact on health and life expectancy.[47] *Self-reliance* is a personality attribute related to how people form and maintain supportive attachments with others. Self-reliance was originally based in attachment theory, a theory about normal human development.[48] The theory identifies three distinct patterns of attachment, and research suggests that these patterns extend into behavioral strategies during adulthood, in professional as well as personal relationships.[49] Self-reliance results in a secure pattern of attachment and interdependent behavior. Interpersonal attachment is emotional and psychological connectedness to another person. The two insecure patterns of attachment are counterdependence and overdependence.

Self-reliance is a healthy, secure, *interdependent* pattern of behavior. It may appear paradoxical, because a person appears independent while maintaining a host of supportive attachments.[50] Self-reliant people respond to stressful, threatening situations by reaching out to others appropriately. Self-reliance is a flexible, responsive strategy of forming and maintaining multiple, diverse relationships. Self-reliant people are confident, enthusiastic, and persistent in facing challenges.

counterdependence
An unhealthy, insecure pattern of behavior that leads to separation in relationships with other people.

Counterdependence is an unhealthy, insecure pattern of behavior that leads to separation in relationships with other people. When faced with stressful and threatening situations, counterdependent people draw into themselves, attempting to exhibit strength and power. Counterdependence may be characterized as a rigid, dismissing denial of the need for other people in difficult and stressful times. Counterdependent people exhibit a fearless, aggressive, and actively powerful response to challenges.

overdependence
An unhealthy, insecure pattern of behavior that leads to preoccupied attempts to achieve security through relationships.

Overdependence is also an unhealthy, insecure pattern of behavior. Overdependent people respond to stressful and threatening situations by clinging to other people in any way possible. Overdependence may be characterized as a desperate, preoccupied attempt to achieve a sense of security through relationships. Overdependent people exhibit an active, but disorganized and anxious response to challenges. Overdependence prevents a person from being able to organize and maintain healthy relationships and thus creates much distress. It is interesting to note that both counterdependence and overdependence are exhibited by some military personnel who are experiencing adjustment difficulties during the first thirty days of basic training.[51] In particular, basic military trainees who have the most difficulty have overdependence problems and find it difficult to function on their own during the rigors of training.

Challenge 7.2 gives you an opportunity to examine how self-reliant (interdependent), counterdependent, and/or overdependent you are.

PREVENTIVE STRESS MANAGEMENT

Stress is an inevitable feature of work and personal life. It is neither inherently bad nor destructive. Stress can be managed. The following is the central principle of *preventive stress management*: Individual and organizational distress are not inevitable. Preventive stress management is an organizational philosophy about people and organizations taking joint responsibility for promoting health and preventing distress and strain. Preventive stress management is rooted in the public health notions of prevention, which were first used in preventive medicine. The three stages of prevention are primary, secondary, and tertiary prevention. A framework for understanding preventive stress management is presented in Figure 7.2,

7. Distinguish the primary, secondary, and tertiary stages of preventive stress management.

preventive stress management
An organizational philosophy that holds that people and organizations should take joint responsibility for promoting health and preventing distress and strain.

Figure 7.2
A Framework for Preventive Stress Management

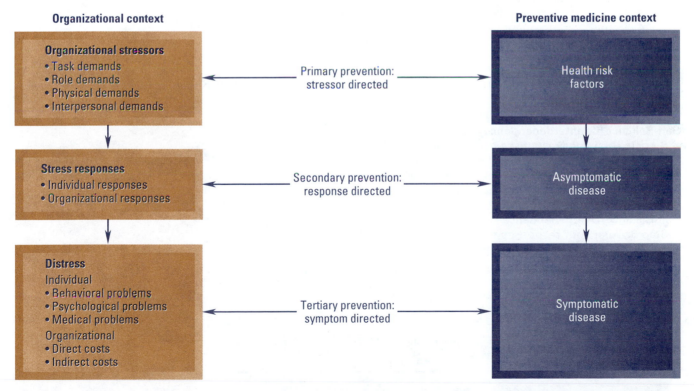

SOURCE: J. D. Quick, R. S. Horn, and J. C. Quick, "Health Consequences of Stress," *Journal of Organizational Behavior Management* 8, No. 2, figure 1 (Fall 1986): 21. Reprinted with permission of Haworth Press, Inc., 10 Alice Street, Binghamton, NY 13904. Copyright 1986.

Challenge 7.2

Are You Self-Reliant?

Each of the following questions relates to how you form relationships with people at work, at home, and in other areas of your life. Read each statement carefully and rate each on a scale from 0 (strongly disagree) to 5 (strongly agree) to describe your degree of disagreement or agreement with the statement. *Answer all 15 questions.*

____ **1.** It is difficult for me to delegate work to others.
____ **2.** Developing close relationships at work will backfire on you.
____ **3.** I avoid depending on other people because I feel crowded by close relationships.
____ **4.** I am frequently suspicious of other people's motives and intentions.
____ **5.** Asking for help makes me feel needy, and I do not like that.
____ **6.** It is difficult for me to leave home or work to go to the other.
____ **7.** People will always be there when I need them.
____ **8.** I regularly and easily spend time with other people during the workday.
____ **9.** I trust at least two other people to have my best interests at heart.
____ **10.** I have a healthy, happy home life.
____ **11.** I need to have colleagues or subordinates close in order to feel secure about my work.
____ **12.** I become very concerned when I have conflict with family members at home.
____ **13.** I get very upset and disturbed if I have conflicts in relationship(s) at work.
____ **14.** I prefer very frequent feedback from my boss to know I am performing well.
____ **15.** I always consult others when I make decisions.

Scoring:

Follow the instructions to determine your score for each subscale of the Self-Reliance Inventory. *Note: Question 6 is used twice in scoring.*

Self-Reliance/Counterdependence
   Step 1: Total your responses to Questions 1–6   ____
   Step 2: Total your responses to Questions 7–10   ____
   Step 3: Subtract your Step 2 total from 20 (20 − ____) =   ____
   Step 4: Add your results in Steps 1 and 3   ____

Self-Reliance/Overdependence
   Step 5: Total your responses to Questions 6 and 11–15   ____

A score lower than 16 in Step 4 or Step 5 indicates self-reliance on that particular subscale.

A score higher than 20 in Step 4 suggests possible counterdependence and a score higher than 20 in Step 5 suggests possible overdependence.

SOURCE: Adapted from J. C. Quick, D. L. Nelson, and J. D. Quick, "The Self-Reliance Inventory," in J. W. Pfeiffer, ed., *The 1991 Annual: Developing Human Resources* (San Diego: Pfeiffer & Co., 1991), pp. 149–161.

which includes the three stages of prevention in a preventive medicine context, as well as an organizational context.

Primary prevention is intended to reduce, modify, or eliminate the demand or stressor causing stress. The idea behind primary prevention is to eliminate or ameliorate the source of a problem. True organizational stress prevention is largely primary in nature, because it changes and shapes the demands the organization places on people at work. *Secondary prevention* is intended to alter or modify the individual's or the organization's response to a demand or stressor. People must learn to manage the inevitable, inalterable work stressors and demands so as to avert distress and strain while promoting health and well-being. *Tertiary prevention* is intended to heal individual or organizational symptoms of distress and strain. The symptoms may range from early warning signs (such as headaches or absenteeism) to more severe forms of distress (such as hypertension, work stoppages, and strikes). Tertiary prevention is therapeutic, aimed at arresting distress and healing the individual, the organization, or both. We will discuss these stages of prevention in the context of organizational prevention, individual prevention, and comprehensive health promotion.

Organizational Stress Prevention

Some organizations are low-stress, healthy environments, whereas others are high-stress environments that may place their employees' health at risk. Organizational stress prevention focuses on people's work demands and on ways to reduce distress at work. One comprehensive approach to organizational health and preventive stress management was pioneered in the U.S. Air Force by Lieutenant Colonel Joyce Adkins, who developed an Organizational Health Center (OHC) at the Sacramento Air Logistics Center.[52] The OHC's goal is to keep people happy, healthy, and on the job, while increasing efficiency and productivity to their highest levels by focusing on workplace stressors, organizational and individual forms of distress, and managerial and individual strategies for preventive stress management. This comprehensive, organizational health approach addresses primary, secondary, and tertiary prevention. Most organizational prevention, however, is primary prevention, including job redesign, goal setting, role negotiation, and career management. Two organizational stress prevention methods, team building and social support at work, are secondary prevention. Because team building is discussed extensively in Chapter 8, we do not discuss it separately here. Finally, companies such as Kraft Foods (a subsidiary of Philip Morris Companies), and Hardee's Food Systems (part of CKE Restaurants, Inc.) have developed specific violence prevention programs to combat the rise in workplace violence. Violence in organizations is a category of dysfunctional behaviors that are often motivated by stressful events and whose negative consequences organizations want to prevent.[53]

Job Redesign The job strain model presented in Figure 7.3 suggests that the combination of high job demands and restricted job decision latitude

primary prevention
The stage in preventive stress management designed to reduce, modify, or eliminate the demand or stressor causing stress.

secondary prevention
The stage in preventive stress management designed to alter or modify the individual's or the organization's response to a demand or stressor.

tertiary prevention
The stage in preventive stress management designed to heal individual or organizational symptoms of distress and strain.

8. Discuss organizational and individual methods of preventive stress management.

Experiencing OB

Interact with various individual and organizational methods of stress management at our animated concept and activity site. Choose Stress from the "select a topic" pull-down menu, then Managing Stress from the "overview tab."

http://www.experiencingob.com

Figure 7.3
Job Strain Model

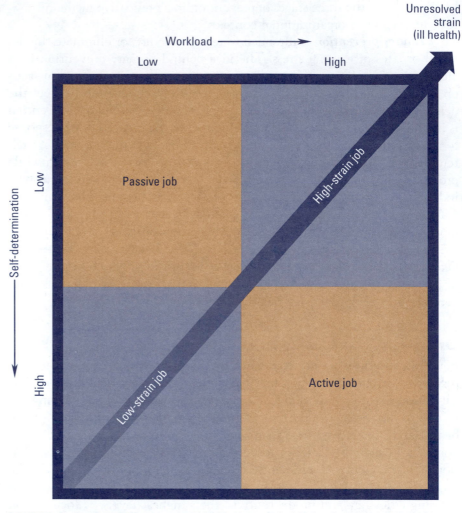

SOURCE: B. Gardell, "Efficiency and Health Hazards in Mechanized Work," in J. C. Quick, R. S. Bhagat, J. E. Dalton, and J. D. Quick, eds., *Work Stress: Health Care Systems in the Workplace.* Copyright © 1987. Reproduced with permission of Greenwood Publishing Group, Inc., Westport, CT.

or worker control leads to a high-strain job. A major concern in job redesign should be to enhance worker control. Increasing worker control reduces distress and strain without necessarily reducing productivity in many cases.

Job redesign to increase worker control is one strategy of preventive stress management. It can be accomplished in a number of ways, the most common being to increase job decision latitude. Increased job decision latitude might include greater decision authority over the sequencing of work activities, the timing of work schedules, the selection and sequencing of work tools, or the selection of work teams. A second objective of job redesign should be to reduce uncertainty and increase predictability in the workplace. Uncertainty is a major stressor.

Goal Setting Organizational preventive stress management can also be achieved through goal-setting activities. These activities are designed to increase task motivation, as discussed in Chapter 6, while reducing the degree of role conflict and ambiguity to which people at work are subject. Goal setting focuses a person's attention while directing energy in a productive channel. Implicit in much of the goal-setting literature is the assumption that people participate in, and accept, their work goals. Chapter 6 addressed goal setting in depth.

Role Negotiation The organizational development technique of role negotiation has value as a stress management method, because it allows people to modify their work roles.[54] Role negotiation begins with the definition of a specific role, called the focal role, within its organizational context. The person in the focal role then identifies the expectations understood for that role, and key organizational members specify their expectations of the person in the focal role. The actual negotiation follows from the comparison of the role incumbent's expectations and key members' expectations. The points of confusion and conflict are opportunities for clarification and resolution. The final result of the role negotiation process should be a clear, well-defined focal role with which the incumbent and organizational members are both comfortable.

Social Support Systems Team building, discussed in Chapter 8, is one way to develop supportive social relationships in the workplace. However, team building is primarily task oriented, not socioemotional, in nature. Although employees may receive much of their socioemotional support from personal relationships outside the workplace, some socioemotional support within the workplace is also necessary for psychological well-being.

Social support systems can be enhanced through the work environment in a number of ways. For example, some research has shown that psychologically intimate, cross-sex relationships in the workplace are possible and enhance social identity integration.[55] Figure 7.4 identifies key elements in a person's work and nonwork social support system. These relations provide emotional caring, information, evaluative feedback, modeling, and instrumental support.

Individual Prevention

Individual prevention focuses on how the person can manage stress before it becomes a problem. Individual prevention can be of a primary, secondary, or tertiary nature. The primary prevention activities we discuss are learned optimism, time management, and leisure time activities. The secondary prevention activities we discuss are physical exercise, relaxation, and diet. The tertiary prevention activities we discuss are opening up and professional help. These eight methods and their benefits are summarized in Table 7.4.

Learned Optimism Optimism and pessimism are two different thinking styles people use to explain the good and bad events in their lives to themselves.[56] These explanatory styles are habits of thinking learned over time,

Figure 7.4
Social Support at Work and Home

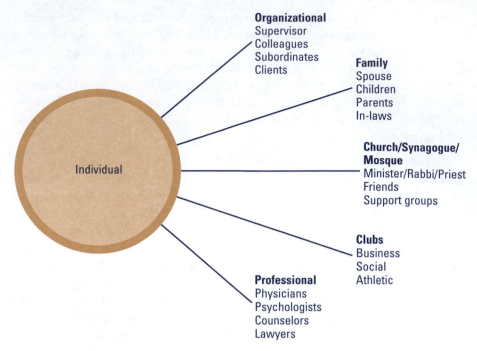

SOURCE: From J. C. Quick, J. D. Quick, D. L. Nelson, and J. J. Hurrell, Jr., in *Preventive Stress Management in Organizations*, 1997, p. 198. Copyright © 1997 by The American Psychological Association. Reprinted with permission.

not inborn attributes. Pessimism is an explanatory style leading to depression, physical health problems, and low levels of achievement. Optimism is an alternative explanatory style that enhances physical health and achievement and averts susceptibility to depression.

Optimistic people avoid distress by viewing the bad events and difficult times in their lives as temporary, limited, and caused by something other than themselves. Optimistic people face difficult times and adversity with hope. Optimistic people take more credit for the good events in their lives; they see these good events as more pervasive and generalized. Learned optimism begins with identifying pessimistic thoughts and then distracting oneself from these thoughts or disputing them with evidence and alternative thoughts. Learned optimism is nonnegative thinking.

Time Management Work overload, the major job stressor, can lead to time pressure and overtime work. Time management skills can help employees make the most effective, efficient use of the time they spend at work and can help students who are not working make more productive use of their time. The good time manager is not necessarily the person who gets the most done. Rather, the good time manager is a "macro time manager" who knows the activities that contribute most to his or her long-term life development.[57] Time management enables a person to minimize the stress of work overload and to prioritize work and leisure time activities. Organizing

Primary Prevention		Table 7.4 *Individual Preventive Stress Management*
Learned optimism:	Alters the person's internal self-talk and reduces depression.	
Time management:	Improves planning and prioritizes activities.	
Leisure time activity:	Balances work and nonwork activities.	
Secondary Prevention		
Physical exercise:	Improves cardiovascular function and muscular flexibility.	
Relaxation training:	Lowers all indicators of the stress response.	
Diet:	Lowers the risk of cardiovascular disease and improves overall physical health.	
Tertiary Prevention		
Opening up:	Releases internalized traumas and emotional tensions.	
Professional help:	Provides information, emotional support, and therapeutic guidance.	

and prioritizing may be the two most important time management skills for successful people managing very busy activity schedules.

Leisure Time Activities Unremitted striving characterizes many people with a high need for achievement. Leisure time activities provide employees an opportunity for rest and recovery from strenuous activities either at home or at work. Many individuals, when asked what they do with their leisure time, say that they clean the house or mow the lawn. These activities are fine, as long as the individual gets the stress-reducing benefit of pleasure from them. Some say our work ethic is a cultural barrier to pleasure. We work longer hours, and two-income families are the norm. Leisure is increasingly a luxury among working people. The key to the effective use of leisure time is enjoyment. Leisure time can be used for spontaneity, joy, and connection with others in our lives. While vacations can be a relief from job burnout, there can be fade-out effects.[58] Hence, leisure time and vacations must be periodic, recurring activities.

Physical Exercise Two different types of physical exercise are important secondary stress prevention activities for individuals. First, aerobic exercise improves a person's responsiveness to stressful activities. Kenneth Cooper has long advocated aerobic exercise.[59] Research at the Aerobics Center in Dallas has found that aerobically fit people (1) have lower levels of adrenaline in their blood at rest; (2) have a slower, stronger heart functioning; and (3) recover from stressful events more quickly.

Second, flexibility training is important because of the muscular contractions associated with the stress response. One component of the stress response is the contraction of the flexor muscles, which prepares a person to fight or flee. Flexibility training enables a person to stretch and relax these muscles to prevent the accumulation of unnecessary muscular tension.[60] Flexibility exercises help maintain joint mobility, increase strength, and play an important role in the prevention of injury.

Relaxation Training Herbert Benson was one of the first people to identify the relaxation response as the natural counterresponse to the stress response.[61] In studying Western and Eastern peoples, Benson found that Judeo-Christian people have elicited this response through their time-honored tradition of prayer, whereas Eastern people have elicited it through meditation. The relaxation response does not require a theological or religious component. If you have a practice of regular prayer or meditation, you may already elicit the relaxation response regularly. Keep in mind that digestion may interfere with the elicitation of the response, so avoid practicing relaxation shortly after eating.

Diet Diet may play an indirect role in stress and stress management. High sugar content in the diet can stimulate the stress response, and foods high in cholesterol can adversely affect blood chemistry. Good dietary practices contribute to a person's overall health, making the person less vulnerable to distress. In his nonsurgical, nonpharmacological approach to reversing heart disease, Dean Ornish proposes a very stringent "reversal diet" for people with identifiable blockage of the arteries.[62] Ornish recommends a somewhat less stringent "prevention diet" as one of four elements for opening up the arteries. Another element in his program is being open in relationships with other people.

Opening Up Everyone experiences a traumatic, stressful, or painful event in life at one time or another. One of the most therapeutic, curative responses to such an event is to confide in another person.[63] Discussing difficult experiences with another person is not always easy, yet health benefits, immune system improvement, and healing accrue through self-disclosure. In one study comparing those who wrote once a week about traumatic events with those who wrote about nontraumatic events, significant health benefits and reduced absenteeism were found in the first group.[64] Confession need not be through a personal relationship with friends. It may occur through a private diary. For example, a lawyer might write each evening about all of his or her most troubling thoughts, feelings, and emotions during the course of the day. The process of opening up and confessing appears to counter the detrimental effects of stress.

Professional Help Confession and opening up may occur through professional helping relationships. People who need healing have psychological counseling, career counseling, physical therapy, medical treatment, surgical intervention, and other therapeutic techniques available. Employee assistance programs (EAPs) may be very helpful in referring employees to the appropriate caregivers. Even combat soldiers who experience battle stress reactions severe enough to take them out of action can heal and be ready for subsequent combat duty.[65] The early detection of distress and strain reactions, coupled with prompt professional treatment, can be instrumental in averting permanent physical and psychological damage.

Comprehensive Health Promotion

Whereas organizational stress prevention is aimed at eliminating health risks at work, comprehensive health promotion programs are aimed at establishing a "strong and resistent host" by building on individual prevention and lifestyle change.[66] Physical fitness and exercise programs characterize corporate health promotion programs in the United States and Canada.[67] A health promotion and wellness survey of the 143 accredited medical schools in the United States, Canada, and Puerto Rico found that these programs place the most emphasis on physical well-being and the least emphasis on spiritual well-being.[68] A review of the most intensively researched programs, such as Johnson & Johnson's "Live for Life," AT&T's "TLC," the former Control Data's "STAY-WELL," and the Coors wellness program, shows a strong emphasis on lifestyle change.[69] Unfortunately, programs such as these may be among those most at risk in corporate cost-cutting and downsizing programs.

Johnson & Johnson's Health and Wellness program is a comprehensive health promotion program with a significant number of educational modules for individuals and groups. Each module addresses a specific topic, such as Type A behavior, exercise, diet (through cooperative activities with the American Heart Association), stress, and risk assessment (through regular risk assessments and health profiles for participants). Johnson & Johnson Health Care Systems Inc., has found that the health status of employees who are not participating in health promotion programs in the workplace improves if the worksite does have a health promotion program.

MANAGERIAL IMPLICATIONS: STRESS WITHOUT DISTRESS

Stress is an inevitable result of work and personal life. Distress is not an inevitable consequence of stressful events, however; in fact, well-managed stress can improve health and performance. Managers must learn how to create healthy stress for employees to facilitate performance and well-being without distress. Managers can help employees by adjusting workloads, avoiding ethical dilemmas, being sensitive to diversity among individuals concerning what is stressful, and being sensitive to employees' personal life demands.

New technologies create demands and stress for employees. Managers can help employees adjust to new technologies by ensuring that their design and implementation are sensitive to employees and that employee involvement is strong.

Managers can be sensitive to early signs of distress at work, such as employee fatigue or changes in work habits, in order to avoid serious forms of distress. The serious forms of distress include violent behavior, psychological depression, and cardiovascular problems. Distress is important to the organization because of the costs associated with turnover and absenteeism, as well as poor-quality production.

Managers should be aware of gender, personality, and behavioral differences when analyzing stress in the workplace. Men and women have different vulnerabilities when it comes to distress. Men are at greater risk of fatal disorders, for example, and women are more vulnerable to nonfatal disorders, such as depression. Personality hardiness and self-reliance are helpful in managing stressful events.

Managers can use the principles and methods of preventive stress management to create healthier work environments. They can practice several forms of individual stress prevention to create healthier lifestyles for themselves, and they can encourage employees to do the same. Large organizations can create healthier workforces through the implementation of comprehensive health promotion programs. Setting an example is one of the best things a manager can do for employees when it comes to preventive stress management.

Looking Back

Serious Fun at Southwest Airlines

Serious fun is not an oxymoron. CEO Herb Kelleher is serious about having fun at work.[70] Having fun and a sense of humor make good business sense because they facilitate people working together and coping with the inevitable stress and work demands. At the same time, because fun and humor rely on individual spontaneity and lightheartedness, they can lose their effectiveness as corporate programs. Kelleher and Southwest Airlines encourage employees to feel free to be humorous and spontaneous at work, without going to extremes. Humor that demeans people, especially customers, is mean spirited, or puts people down is an out-of-bounds extreme at Southwest. If a humorous antic happens to make someone uncomfortable, Kelleher does not put in a rule that says the person cannot do that anymore. Rather, Southwest people talk to the individual personally and explain why they think the antic was carried too far.

At Southwest, fun and humor are seen as lubricants that grease and smooth human interaction at work, increase cooperative get-along behavior, and reduce the stress and tension of the workday. Southwest makes lots of room for employees and managers who may not have a sense of humor or a funny bone, but manage stress and work demands in alternatively healthy ways. Kelleher does see ways in which managers can foster humor among employees. Specifically, he encourages spontaneity, communication with all employees, and informal gatherings, such as picnics or family get-togethers. Although deregulation in the airline industry has increased the financial business risk for companies and employees, Kelleher has fostered an organizational culture at Southwest Airlines in which fun and humor help lift the stress load and inevitable pressure of work demands in a competitive environment.

CHAPTER SUMMARY

1. Stress is the unconscious preparation to fight or flee when faced with any demand. Distress is the adverse consequence of stress.
2. Four approaches to understanding stress are the homeostatic/medical approach, the cognitive appraisal approach, the person–environment fit approach, and the psychoanalytic approach.
3. The stress response is a natural mind–body response characterized by four basic mind–body changes.
4. Employees face task, role, interpersonal, and physical demands at work, along with nonwork (extraorganizational) demands. Global competition and advanced technologies create new stresses at work.
5. Nonwork stressors, such as family problems and work–home conflicts, can affect an individual's work life and home life.

6. Stress has health benefits, including enhanced performance.
7. Distress is costly to both individuals and organizations.
8. Individual diversity requires attention to gender, Type A behavior, personality hardiness, and self-reliance in determining the links between stress and strain.
9. Preventive stress management aims to enhance health and reduce distress or strain. Primary prevention focuses on the stressor, secondary prevention focuses on the response to the stressor, and tertiary prevention focuses on symptoms of distress.

KEY TERMS

stress   190
stressor   190
distress   190
strain   190
homeostasis   192
ego-ideal   192
self-image   192

eustress   198
participation problem   201
performance decrement   201
compensation award   201
Type A behavior pattern   202
personality hardiness   203
transformational coping   204

self-reliance   204
counterdependence   204
overdependence   204
preventive stress management   205
primary prevention   207
secondary prevention   207
tertiary prevention   207

REVIEW QUESTIONS

1. Define *stress*, *distress*, *strain*, and *eustress*.
2. Describe four approaches to understanding stress. How does each add something new to our understanding of stress?

3. What are the four changes associated with the stress response?
4. List three demands of each type: task, role, interpersonal, and physical.

5. What is a nonwork demand? How does it affect an individual?
6. Describe the relationship between stress and performance.
7. What are the major medical consequences of distress? The behavioral consequences? The psychological consequences?
8. Why should organizations be concerned about stress at work? What are the costs of distress to organizations?
9. How do gender, the Type A behavior pattern, personality hardiness, and self-reliance moderate the relationship between stress and strain?
10. What is primary prevention? Secondary prevention? Tertiary prevention? Describe major organizational stress prevention methods.
11. Describe eight individual preventive stress management methods.
12. What is involved in comprehensive health promotion programs?

DISCUSSION AND COMMUNICATION QUESTIONS

1. Why should organizations help individuals manage stress? Isn't stress basically the individual's responsibility?
2. Is there more stress today than in past generations? What evidence is available concerning this question?
3. Discuss the following statement: Employers should be expected to provide stress-free work environments.
4. If an individual claims to have job-related depression, should the company be liable?
5. Do you use any stress prevention methods that are not discussed in the chapter?
6. (*communication question*) Write a memo describing the most challenging demands and/or stressors at your workplace (or university). Be specific in describing the details of these demands and/or stressors. How might you go about changing these demands and/or stressors?
7. (*communication question*) Interview a medical doctor, a psychologist, or another health care professional about the most common forms of health problems and distress seen in their work. Summarize your interview and compare the results to the categories of distress discussed in the chapter.
8. (*communication question*) Do research on social support and diaries as ways to manage stressful and/or traumatic events. Develop an oral presentation for class that explains the benefits of each of these approaches for preventive stress management. Include guidelines on how to practice each.

ETHICS QUESTIONS

1. Suppose a company knows that health risks are associated with the very high stress levels in one operation and decides it is willing to pay for employee health problems rather than lower the stress levels. Is this ethical on the company's part? Should employees be informed of the risks?
2. Suppose a company prescribes certain healthy behaviors, such as regular exercise and the practice of relaxation, for all employees. Is it ethical for a company to influence these employee behaviors, or does this infringe on their individual rights?
3. Assume that personality hardiness, Type B behavior, and self-reliance are positive personal attributes, and assume further that individuals with these attributes will cope better with stress. Is it appropriate for organizations to use these attributes as hiring criteria? That is, can organizations hire only hardy, self-reliant, Type B people?
4. Assume that a company finds that many employees have lower back problems associated with bending over work benches. In looking into the problem, the company finds that it can either raise the benches so that employees bend less or send all the employees to a lower back care class. Should the company choose the more cost-efficient approach? What else should the company consider?

Experiential Exercises

7.1 Gender Role Stressors

The major sources of stress are not necessarily the same for men and women. This exercise will help you identify the similarities and differences in the stressors and perceptions of men and women.

Step 1. Individually, list the major sources of stress for you because of your gender. Be as specific as possible, and within your list, prioritize your stressors.

Step 2. Individually, list what you think are the major sources of stress for those of the opposite gender. Again, be as specific as possible, and prioritize your list.

Step 3. In teams of five or six members of the same sex, share your two lists of stressors. Discuss these stressors, and identify the top five sources of stress for your group because of your gender and the top five sources of stress for those of the opposite gender. Again, be as specific as possible, and prioritize your list.

Step 4. The class will then engage in a cross-team exchange of lists. Look for similarities and differences among the teams in your class as follows. Select one gender to be addressed first. If the females are first, for example, the male groups will post their predictions. This will be followed by the actual stressor lists from the female groups. Then do the same for the other gender.

7.2 Workplace Stress Diagnosis

The following exercise gives you an opportunity to work within a group to compare the work demands and job stressors found in different work settings. Intervention for preventive stress management should always be based on a good diagnosis. This exercise gives you a start in this direction.

Step 1. Rate the degree to which each of the following work demands is a source of stress for you and your coworkers at work. Use a 7-point rating scale for assigning the stressfulness of the work demand, with 7 = very high source of stress, 4 = moderate source of stress, and 1 = very little source of stress.

____ Uncertainty about various aspects of the work environment

____ Lack of control over people, events, or other aspects of work

____ Lack of career opportunities and progress

____ The implementation of new technologies

____ Work overload; that is, too much to do and not enough time

____ Conflicting expectations from one or more people at work

____ Confusing expectations from one or more people at work

____ Dangerous working conditions and/or hazardous substances

____ Sexual harassment by supervisors, coworkers, or others

____ Abrasive personalities and/or political conflicts

____ Rigid, insensitive, unresponsive supervisors or managers

Step 2. Write a brief description of the most stressful event that has occurred in your work environment during the past twelve-month period.

Step 3. The class will form into groups of approximately six members each. Each group elects a spokesperson and then compares the information developed by each person in Steps 1 and 2 above. In the process of this comparison, answer the following questions:

a. What are the similarities between work environments in terms of their most stressful work demands?

b. What are the differences between work environments in terms of their most stressful work demands?

c. Are there similarities in the descriptions of the most stressful events? If so, what are they?

Step 4. Each group will share the results of its answers to the questions in Step 3. Cross-team questions and discussion follow.

Step 5 (Optional). Your instructor may ask you to choose one or another of the work environments in which to develop some preventive stress management strategies. Complete parts a and b below in your group.

a. Identify one to three preventive stress management strategies that you think are the best to use in the work environment. Why have you chosen them?

b. How should the effectiveness of these strategies be evaluated?

PART 3

Interpersonal Processes and Behavior

8.	Work Teams and Groups	220
9.	Decision Making by Individuals and Groups	246
10.	Power and Political Behavior	284
11.	Leadership and Followership	314
12.	Conflict at Work	349

Learning Objectives

After reading this chapter, you should be able to do the following:

1. Define *group* and *team*. *p. 221*

2. Explain four important aspects of group behavior. *p. 222*

3. Describe group formation, the four stages of a group's development, and the characteristics of a mature group. *p. 223*

4. Discuss quality circles and quality teams. *p. 232*

5. Identify the social benefits of group and team membership. *p. 232*

6. Explain the task and maintenance functions in teams. *p. 233*

7. Discuss empowerment, teamwork, and self-managed teams. *p. 234*

8. Explain the importance of upper echelons and top management teams. *p. 238*

8

Work Teams and Groups

Thinking Ahead

Competition in the Subcompact Car Market

The use of teams can enhance product quality in a competitive market. The subcompact car market in America is rife with extremely strong competitors, both domestic (e.g., General Motors' Saturn) and foreign (any Japanese car company has a serious competitor in the lineup).[1] Although subcompacts are the least expensive class of vehicles in the automobile industry, consumers demand the same quality from them as from mid-size and luxury cars. Companies that have attempted to scrimp on quality in the subcompact car market have either left the market, as in the case of the Yugo, or have a serious consumer-confidence rebuilding program under way, as in the case of the Hyundai.

The Ford Escort has been the leading subcompact car in America for the past eighteen years—an outstanding accomplishment in light of the strong competition. Key factors in this sustained outstanding level of performance are the best-in-class quality of the Ford Escort and Ford's efforts to benchmark Escort quality against the best-quality car possibly built. Only two plants in North America produce the Ford Escort: the Wayne Stamping & Assembly Plant in Wayne, Michigan, and the Hermosillo Stamping & Assembly Plant in Hermosillo, Mexico. In the 3.2-million-square-foot Wayne plant, 3,700 people produce approximately 200,000 vehicles annually. That's 74 jobs per hour (net) and 1,184 units during two eight-hour shifts. How has Ford Motor's Wayne assembly plant been able to sustain this best-in-class quality for eighteen years? Ford has done it through teams and teamwork at the Wayne assembly plant. More specifically, Ford has done it through variable reduction teams (VRTs). Ford's Wayne VRTs are discussed in the Looking Back feature at the end of the chapter.

Teamwork, as discussed in the Thinking Ahead and Looking Back features, has been a long-standing feature of the Ford work culture. For example, Lee Iacocca relied on a traditional group and teamwork in the design and production of the first Ford Mustang in 1965.[2] In today's information age, advanced computer and telecommunications technologies enable organizations to be more flexible through the use of virtual teams.[3] Virtual teams also address new workforce demographics, enabling companies to access expertise and the best employees who may be located anywhere in the world. Whether a traditional group or a virtual team, groups and teams continue to play a vital role in organizational behavior and performance at work.

A *group* is two or more people having common interests or objectives. Table 8.1 summarizes the characteristics of a well-functioning, effective group.[4] A *team* is a small number of people with complementary skills who are committed to a common mission, performance goals, and approach for which they hold themselves mutually accountable.[5] Groups emphasize individual leadership, individual accountability, and individual work products.

1. Define *group* and *team*.

group
Two or more people with common interests or objectives.

team
A small number of people with complementary skills who are committed to a common mission, performance goals, and approach for which they hold themselves mutually accountable.

- The atmosphere tends to be relaxed, comfortable, and informal.
- The group's task is well understood and accepted by the members.
- The members listen well to one another; most members participate in a good deal of task-relevant discussion.
- People express both their feelings and their ideas.
- Conflict and disagreement are present and centered around ideas or methods, not personalities or people.
- The group is aware and conscious of its own operation and function.
- Decisions are usually based on consensus, not majority vote.
- When actions are decided, clear assignments are made and accepted by members of the group.

Table 8.1
Characteristics of a Well-Functioning, Effective Group

Teams emphasize shared leadership, mutual accountability, and collective work products.

The chapter begins with a traditional discussion of group behavior and group development in the first two sections. The third section discusses teams. The final two sections explore the contemporary team issues of empowerment, self-managed teams, and upper echelon teams.

GROUP BEHAVIOR

2. Explain four important aspects of group behavior.

Group behavior has been a subject of interest in social psychology for a long time, and many different aspects of group behavior have been studied over the years. We now look at four topics relevant to groups functioning in organizations: norms of behavior, group cohesion, social loafing, and loss of individuality. Group behavior topics related to decision making, such as polarization and groupthink, are addressed in Chapter 9.

Norms of Behavior

norms of behavior
The standards that a work group uses to evaluate the behavior of its members.

The standards that a work group uses to evaluate the behavior of its members are its **norms of behavior**. These norms may be written or unwritten, verbalized or not verbalized, implicit or explicit. So long as individual members of the group understand the norms, the norms can be effective in influencing behavior. Norms may specify what members of a group should do (such a specified dress code for men and for women), or they may specify what members of a group should not do (such as executives not behaving arrogantly with employees).

Norms may exist in any aspect of work group life. They may evolve informally or unconsciously within a group, or they may arise in response to challenges, such as the norm of disciplined behavior by firefighters in responding to a three-alarm fire to protect the group.[6] Performance norms are among the most important group norms from the organization's perspective, as we discuss in a later section of this chapter. Organizational culture and corporate codes of ethics, such as Johnson & Johnson's credo (see Chapter 2), reflect behavioral norms expected within work groups.

Group Cohesion

group cohesion
The "interpersonal glue" that makes members of a group stick together.

The "interpersonal glue" that makes the members of a group stick together is **group cohesion**. Group cohesion can enhance job satisfaction for members and improve organizational productivity.[7] Highly cohesive groups at work may not have many interpersonal exchanges away from the workplace. Nevertheless, they are able to control and manage their membership better than work groups low in cohesion. This is due to the strong motivation in highly cohesive groups to maintain good, close relationships among the members. We examine group cohesion in further detail, along with factors leading to high levels of group cohesion, when discussing the common characteristics of well-developed groups.

Social Loafing

Social loafing occurs when one or more group members rely on the efforts of other group members and fail to contribute their own time, effort, thoughts, or other resources to a group.[8] This may create a real drag on the group's efforts and achievements. Although some scholars argue that, from the individual's standpoint, social loafing, or free riding, is rational behavior in response to an experience of inequity or when individual efforts are hard to observe, it nevertheless shortchanges the group, which loses potentially valuable resources possessed by individual members.[9]

A number of methods for countering social loafing exist, such as having identifiable individual contributions to the group product and member self-evaluation systems. For example, if each group member is responsible for a specific input to the group, a member's failure to contribute will be noticed by everyone. If members must formally evaluate their contributions to the group, they are less likely to loaf.

social loafing
The failure of a group member to contribute personal time, effort, thoughts, or other resources to the group.

Experiencing OB

Cement your understanding of the social loafing concept by interacting with the concept and related materials at our animated concept and activity site. Choose Teams from the "select a topic" pull-down menu, then Social Loafing from the "overview tab."

http://www.experiencingob.com

Loss of Individuality

Social loafing may be detrimental to group achievement, but it does not have the potentially explosive effects of **loss of individuality**. Loss of individuality, or deindividuation, is a social process in which individual group members lose self-awareness and its accompanying sense of accountability, inhibition, and responsibility for individual behavior.[10]

When individuality is lost, people may engage in morally reprehensible acts and even violent behavior as committed members of their group or organization. For example, loss of individuality was one of several contributing factors in the violent and aggressive acts that led to the riot that destroyed sections of Los Angeles following the Rodney King verdict in the early 1990s. Loss of individuality is not always negative or destructive, however. The loosening of normal ego control mechanisms in the individual may lead to prosocial behavior and heroic acts in dangerous situations.[11] A group that successfully develops into a mature group may not encounter problems with loss of individuality.

loss of individuality
A social process in which individual group members lose self-awareness and its accompanying sense of accountability, inhibition, and responsibility for individual behavior.

GROUP FORMATION AND DEVELOPMENT

After its formation, a group goes through predictable stages of development. If successful, it emerges as a mature group. One logical group development model proposes four stages following the group's formation.[12] These stages are mutual acceptance, decision making, motivation and commitment, and control and sanctions. To become a mature group, each of the stages in development must be successfully negotiated.

According to this group development model, a group addresses three issues: interpersonal issues, task issues, and authority issues.[13] The interpersonal issues include matters of trust, personal comfort, and security. The task issues include the mission or purpose of the group, the methods the

3. Describe group formation, the four stages of a group's development, and the characteristics of a mature group.

group employs, and the outcomes expected of the group. The authority issues include decisions about who is in charge, how power and influence are managed, and who has the right to tell whom to do what. This section addresses group formation, each stage of group development, and the characteristics of a mature group.

Group Formation

Formal and informal groups form in organizations for different reasons. Formal groups are sometimes called official or assigned groups, and informal groups may be called unofficial or emergent groups. Formal groups gather to perform various tasks and include an executive and staff, standing committees of the board of directors, project task forces, and temporary committees. An example of a formal group is the task force assembled by the Hospital Corporation of America (now part of HCA—The Healthcare Company) during the mid-1980s to examine the mission of the corporation. Headed by a divisional vice-president, the task force was composed of fifteen members with wide professional and geographic diversity. The task force met approximately once a month for about nine months to complete its task.

Diversity is an important consideration in the formation of groups. For example, Monsanto Agricultural Company (MAC—later Monsanto Company and now part of Pharmacia Corporation) created a task force titled Valuing Diversity to address subtle discrimination resulting from workforce diversity.[14] The original task force was titled Eliminating Subtle Discrimination (ESD) and was composed of fifteen women, minorities, and white males. Subtle discrimination might include the use of gender- or culture-specific language. MAC's and the task force's intent was to build on individual differences—whether in terms of gender, race, or culture—in developing a dominant heterogeneous culture. Diversity can enhance group performance. One study of gender diversity among U.S. workers found that men and women in gender-balanced groups had higher job satisfaction than those in homogeneous groups.[15]

Ethnic diversity has characterized many industrial work groups in the United States since the 1800s. This was especially true during the early years of the 1900s, when waves of immigrant workers arrived from Germany, Yugoslavia, Italy, Poland, Scotland, the Scandinavian countries, and many other nations. Organizations were challenged to blend these culturally and linguistically diverse peoples into effective work groups.

In addition to ethnic, gender, and cultural diversity, there is interpersonal diversity. Chaparral Steel Company (part of Texas Industries) has a team of officers who achieved compatibility through interpersonal diversity. Successful interpersonal relationships are the basis of group effort, a key foundation for business success. In the case of the Chaparral Steel officers, they differed in their needs for inclusion in activities, control of people and events, and interpersonal affection from others. Though diverse in their interpersonal needs, the officers as a group found strength through balance and complementarity.

Experiencing OB

Learn about a second model of team development at our animated concept and activity site. Choose Teams from the "select a topic" pull-down menu, then Stages of Development from the "overview tab."

http://www.experiencingob.com

Informal groups evolve in the work setting to gratify a variety of member needs not met by formal groups. For example, organizational members' inclusion and affection needs might be satisfied through informal athletic or interest groups. Athletic teams representing a department, unit, or company may achieve semiofficial status, such as the American Airlines long-distance running teams that use the corporate logo on their race shirts.

Stages of Group Development

All groups, formal and informal, go through four stages of development: mutual acceptance, decision making, motivation and commitment, and control and sanctions. Demographic diversity and group fault lines (i.e., potential breaking points in a group) are two potential predictors of the sense-making process, subgroup formation patterns, and the nature of group conflict at various stages of group development.[16] Hence, group development through these four stages may not always be smooth.

Mutual Acceptance Mutual acceptance is the first stage in a group's development. In this stage, the focus is on the interpersonal relations among the members. Members assess one another with regard to trustworthiness, emotional comfort, and evaluative acceptance. For the Valuing Diversity task force at MAC, trust was one of the early issues to be worked through. The power, influence, and authority issues may also emerge at this point if strong personalities immediately attempt to dominate other group members or dictate the group's agenda. This authority issue is also an interpersonal issue related to trust and acceptance. Once team members establish a comfortable level of mutual trust and acceptance, they can focus their attention on the work of the group.

Decision Making Planning and decision making occur during the second stage of a group's development. The focus turns from interpersonal relations to decision-making activities related to the group's task accomplishment. Specifically, the group must make decisions about what its task is and how to accomplish that task. Wallace Supply Company, an industrial distributor of pipes, valves, and fittings, has found employee teams particularly valuable in this aspect of work life.[17] This second stage may be thought of as the planning stage in a group's development. In addition, the issue of authority often begins to surface during this stage of development, if it did not surface during the first stage. The group addresses authority questions like these: Who is responsible for what aspects of the group's work? Does the group need one primary leader and spokesperson?

Motivation and Commitment In the third stage of development, the group has largely resolved the interpersonal and task issues. Member attention is directed to self-motivation and the motivation of other group members for task accomplishment. Some members focus on the task function of initiating activity and ensure that the work of the group really gets moving. Other members contribute to motivation and commitment within the group through maintenance functions such as supporting, encouraging, and recognizing the contributions of their teammates or through establishing the standards that the team may use in evaluating its performance and members.

The latter contribution is illustrated by a twenty-five-member leadership group that monitors "the flow," Eastman Kodak's unique black-and-white film production process named for its layout design. The people who work the flow are called Zebras. With motivation, commitment, and evaluative feedback from the twenty-five-person leadership team, the Zebras substantially enhanced productivity, profitability, and morale.

The emphasis during the motivation and commitment stage of team development is on execution and achievement, whether through a process of questioning and prodding or through facilitation and workload sharing. If key decisions or plans established in the second stage of development need to be revisited, they are, but only in the context of getting work done.

Control and Sanctions In its final stage of development, a group has become a mature, effective, efficient, and productive unit. The group has successfully worked through necessary interpersonal, task, and authority issues. A mature group is characterized by a clear purpose or mission; a well-understood set of norms of behavior; a high level of cohesion; and a clear, but flexible, status structure of leader–follower relationships. A mature group is able to control its members through the judicious application of specific positive and negative sanctions used in response to specific member behaviors. If the group's membership changes, either through a loss of an established member or the inclusion of a newcomer, it may well engage in some activities common in earlier stages of development as it accommodates the newcomer or adjusts to the loss.

Characteristics of a Mature Group

The description of a well-functioning, effective group in Table 8.1 characterizes a mature group. Such a group has four distinguishing characteristics: a clear purpose and mission, well-understood norms and standards of conduct, a high level of group cohesion, and a flexible status structure.

Purpose and Mission The purpose and mission may be assigned to a group (as in the case of Hospital Corporation of America task force's charter to examine the corporate mission) or emerge from within the group (as in the case of the American Airlines long-distance running team). Even in the case of an assigned mission, the group may reexamine, modify, revise, or question the mission. It may also embrace the mission as stated. The importance of mission is exemplified in IBM's Process Quality Management, which requires that a process team of not more than twelve people develop a clear understanding of mission as the first step in the process.[18] The IBM approach demands that all members agree to go in the same direction. The mission statement is converted into a specific agenda, clear goals, and a set of critical success factors. Stating the purpose and mission in the form of specific goals enhances productivity over and above any performance benefits achieved through individual goal setting.[19]

Behavioral Norms Behavioral norms, which evolve over a period of time, are well-understood standards of behavior within a group.[20] They are benchmarks against which team members are evaluated and judged by other team members. Some behavioral norms become written rules, such as an attendance policy or an ethical code for a team. Other norms remain informal, although they are no less well understood by team members. Dress codes and norms about after-hours socializing may fall into this category. Behavioral norms also evolve around performance and productivity.[21] The group's productivity norm may or may not be consistent with, and supportive of, the organization's productivity standards. A high-performance team sets productivity standards above organizational expectations with the intent to excel. Average teams set productivity standards based on, and consistent with, organizational expectations. Noncompliant or counterproductive teams may set productivity standards below organizational expectations with the intent of damaging the organization or creating change.

Group Cohesion Group cohesion was earlier described as the interpersonal attraction binding group members together. It enables a group to exercise effective control over its members in relation to its behavioral norms and standards. Goal conflict in a group, unpleasant experiences, and domination of a subgroup are among the threats to a group's cohesion. Groups with low levels of cohesion have greater difficulty exercising control over their members and enforcing their standards of behavior. A classic study of cohesiveness in 238 industrial work groups found cohesion to be an important factor influencing anxiety, tension, and productivity within the groups.[22] Specifically, work-related tension and anxiety were lower in teams high in cohesion, and they were higher in teams low in cohesion, as depicted in Figure 8.1. This suggests that cohesion has a calming effect on team members, at least concerning work-related tension and anxiety. In addition, actual productivity was found to vary significantly less in highly cohesive teams, making these teams much more predictable with regard to their productivity. The actual productivity levels were primarily determined by the productivity norms within each work group. That is, highly cohesive groups with high production standards are very productive. Similarly, highly cohesive groups with low productivity standards are unproductive. Member satisfaction, commitment, and communication are better in highly cohesive groups. Groupthink may be a problem in highly cohesive groups and is discussed in Chapter 9. Challenge 8.1 includes the three group cohesion questions from this research project. Complete Challenge 8.1 to determine the level of cohesion in a group of which you are a member.

Group cohesion is influenced by a number of factors, most notably time, size, the prestige of the team, external pressure, and internal competition. Group cohesion evolves gradually over time through a group's normal development. Smaller groups—those of five or seven members, for example— are more cohesive than those of over twenty-five, although cohesion does not decline much with size after forty or more members. Prestige or social

Experiencing OB

Learn more about factors affecting team cohesiveness and how cohesiveness affects the team's performance by visiting our animated concept and activity site. Choose Teams from the "select a topic" pull-down menu, then Team Cohesiveness from the "overview tab."

http://www.experiencingob.com

Figure 8.1
Cohesiveness and Work-Related Tension[a]

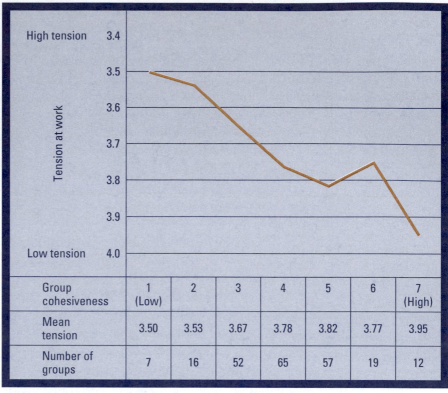

Group cohesiveness	1 (Low)	2	3	4	5	6	7 (High)
Mean tension	3.50	3.53	3.67	3.78	3.82	3.77	3.95
Number of groups	7	16	52	65	57	19	12

Note: Product-moment correlation is .28, and critical ratio is 4.20; p is less than .001.

[a]The measure of tension at work is based on group mean response to the question "Does your work ever make you feel 'jumpy' or nervous?" A low numerical score represents relatively high tension.

SOURCE: From S. E. Seashore, *Group Cohesiveness in the Industrial Work Group*, 1954. Research conducted by Stanley E. Seashore at the Institute for Social Research, University of Michigan. Reprinted by permission.

status also influences a group's cohesion, with more prestigious groups, such as the U.S. Air Force Thunderbirds or the U.S. Navy Blue Angels, being highly cohesive. However, even groups of very low prestige may be highly cohesive in how they stick together. Finally, external pressure and internal competition influence group cohesion. Although the mechanics' union, pilots, and other internal constituencies at Eastern Airlines had various differences of opinion, they all pulled together in a cohesive fashion in resisting Frank Lorenzo when he came in to reshape the airline before its demise. Whereas external pressures tend to enhance cohesion, internal competition usually decreases cohesion within a team. However, one study found that company-imposed work pressure disrupted group cohesion by increasing internal competition and reducing cooperative interpersonal activity.[23]

Status Structure *Status structure* is the set of authority and task relations among a group's members. The status structure may be hierarchical or egalitarian (i.e., democratic), depending on the group. Successful resolution of the authority issue within a team results in a well-understood status struc-

status structure
The set of authority and task relations among a group's members.

Challenge 8.1

How Cohesive Is Your Group?

Think about a group of which you are a member. Answer each of the following questions in relation to this group by circling the number next to the alternative that most reflects your feelings.

1. Do you feel that you are really a part of your group?

   5—Really a part of the group.
   4—Included in most ways.
   3—Included in some ways, but not in others.
   2—Do not feel I really belong.
   1—Do not work with any one group of people.

2. If you had a chance to do the same activities in another group, for the same pay if it is a work group, how would you feel about moving?

   1—Would want very much to move.
   2—Would rather move than stay where I am.
   3—Would make no difference to me.
   4—Would rather stay where I am than move.
   5—Would want very much to stay where I am.

3. How does your group compare with other groups that you are familiar with on each of the following points?

- The way people get along together.

   5—Better than most.
   3—About the same as most.
   1—Not as good as most.

- The way people stick together.

   5—Better than most.
   3—About the same as most.
   1—Not as good as most.

- The way people help one another on the job.

   5—Better than most.
   3—About the same as most.
   1—Not as good as most.

Add up your circled responses. If you have a number of 20 or above, you view your group as highly cohesive. If you have a number between 10 and 19, you view your group's cohesion as average. If you have a number of 7 or less, you view your group as very low in cohesion.

SOURCE: From S. E. Seashore, *Group Cohesiveness in the Industrial Work Group,* University of Michigan, 1954. Reprinted by permission.

ture of leader–follower relationships. Where leadership problems arise, it is important to find solutions and build team leader effectiveness.[24] Whereas groups tend to have one leader, teams tend to share leadership. For example, one person may be the team's task master, who sets the agenda, initiates much of the work activity, and ensures that the team meets its deadlines. Another team member may take a leadership role in maintaining effective interpersonal relationships in the group. Hence, shared leadership is very feasible in teams. An effective status structure results in role interrelatedness among group members.

Diversity in a group is healthy, and members may contribute to the collective effort through one of four basic styles.[25] These are the contributor, the collaborator, the communicator, and the challenger. The contributor is data driven, supplies necessary information, and adheres to high performance standards. The collaborator sees the big picture and is able to keep a constant focus on the mission and urge other members to join efforts for mission accomplishment. The communicator listens well, facilitates the group's process, and humanizes the collective effort. The challenger is the devil's advocate who questions everything from the group's mission, purpose, and methods to its ethics. Members may exhibit one or more of these four basic styles over a period of time. In addition, an effective group must have an integrator.[26] This can be especially important in cross-functional teams, where different perspectives carry the seeds of conflict. However, cross-functional teams are not necessarily a problem. Effectively managing cross-functional teams of artists, designers, printers, and financial experts enabled Hallmark Cards to cut its new-product development time in half.[27]

Emergent leadership in groups was studied among sixty-two men and sixty women.[28] Groups performed tasks not classified as either masculine or feminine, that is, "sex-neutral" tasks. Men and women both emerged as leaders, and neither gender had significantly more emergent leaders. However, group members who described themselves in masculine terms were significantly more likely to emerge as leaders than group members who described themselves in feminine, androgynous (both masculine and feminine), or undifferentiated (neither masculine nor feminine) terms. Hence, gender stereotypes may play a role in emergent leadership.

TEAMS AT WORK

Teams are task-oriented work groups; they can be formally designated or informally evolved. Both formal and informal teams make important and valuable contributions to the organization and are important to the member need satisfaction. For example, an informal Xerox team from accounting, sales, administration, and distribution saved the company $200 million in inventory costs during 1991 through innovative production and inventory planning.[29]

Several kinds of teams exist. One classification scheme uses a sports analogy. Some teams work like baseball teams with set responsibilities, other teams work like football teams through coordinated action, and still other teams work like doubles tennis teams with primary yet flexible responsibilities. Although each type of team may have a useful role in the organization, the individual expert should not be overlooked.[30]

Why Teams?

Teams are very useful in performing work that is complicated, complex, interrelated, and/or more voluminous than one person can handle. Harold Geneen, while chairman of ITT, said, "If I had enough arms and legs and time, I'd do it all myself." Obviously, people working in organizations cannot do everything because of the limitations of arms, legs, time, expertise, knowledge, and other resources. Individual limitations are overcome through teamwork and collaboration. For example, General Motors' NDH

Bearings plant in Sandusky, Ohio, has become a world-class supplier of automotive components in terms of quality, cost, and delivery by emphasizing teamwork, open communication, and advanced technology.[31] In particular, union–management teams, such as the "bid teams," enabled NDH to make impressive gains from 1985 through 1991.

Teams make important contributions to organizations in work areas that lend themselves to teamwork. Teamwork is a core value at Hewlett-Packard, according to former CEO Lew Platt. Complex, interdependent work tasks and activities that require collaboration particularly lend themselves to teamwork. Teams are appropriate where knowledge, talent, skills, and abilities are dispersed across organizational members and require integrated effort for task accomplishment. The recent emphasis on team-oriented work environments is based on empowerment with collaboration, not on power and competition. Larry Hirschhorn labels this "the new team environment" founded on a significantly more empowered workforce in the industrial sectors of the American economy. This new team environment is compared with the old work environment in Table 8.2.

That teams are necessary is a driving principle of total quality efforts in organizations. Total quality efforts often require the formation of teams—especially cross-functional teams composed of people from different functions, such as manufacturing and design, who are responsible for specific organizational processes. Eastman Kodak CEO George Fisher believes in the importance of participation and cooperation as foundations for teamwork and a total quality program. In a study of forty machine crews in a northeastern U.S. paper mill, organizational citizenship behaviors, specifically helping behavior and sportsmanship, contributed significantly to the quantity and quality of work group performance.[32]

Experiencing OB

You may learn more about types of teams and their relationship to the organization by interacting with team concepts at our animated concept and activity site. Choose Teams from the "select a topic" pull-down menu, then Types of Teams from the "overview tab."

http://www.experiencingob.com

New Team Environment	Old Work Environment
Person comes up with initiatives.	Person follows orders.
Team has considerable authority to chart its own steps.	Team depends on the manager to chart its course.
Members form a team because people learn to collaborate in the face of their emerging right to think for themselves. People both rock the boat and work together.	Members were a team because people conformed to direction set by the manager. No one rocked the boat.
People cooperate by using their thoughts and feelings. They link up through direct talk.	People cooperated by suppressing their thoughts and feelings. They wanted to get along.

Table 8.2
A Comparison of the New Team Environment versus the Old Work Environment

SOURCE: *Managing in the New Team Environment*, by Hirschhorn, © 1991. Reprinted by permission of Prentice-Hall, Inc., Upper Saddle River, N.J.

Quality Circles and Teams

4. Discuss quality circles and quality teams.

quality circle (QC)
A small group of employees who work voluntarily on company time, typically one hour per week, to address work-related problems such as quality control, cost reduction, production planning and techniques, and even product design.

Quality circles are one form of team in a total quality program. **Quality circles (QCs)** are small groups of employees who work voluntarily on company time—typically one hour per week—to address work-related problems such as quality control, cost reduction, production planning and techniques, and even product design. Membership in a QC is typically voluntary and is fixed once a circle is formed, although some changes may occur as appropriate. QCs are trained in various problem-solving techniques and use them to address the work-related problems.

QCs were popularized as a Japanese management method when an American, W. Edward Deming, exported his thinking about QCs to Japan following World War II.[33] QCs became popular in the United States in the 1980s, when companies such as Ford, Hewlett-Packard, and Eastman Kodak implemented them. KL Spring and Stamping Corporation is an automotive industry supplier that has used quality circles and employee involvement for successful productivity improvements.

QCs must deal with substantive issues if they are to be effective; otherwise, employees begin to believe the QC effort is simply a management ploy. QCs do not necessarily require final decision authority to be effective if their recommendations are always considered seriously and implemented when appropriate. One study found that QCs are effective for a period of time, and then their contributions begin to diminish.[34] This may suggest that QCs must be reinforced and periodically reenergized to maintain their effectiveness over long periods of time. Decision making in quality circles and **quality teams** is discussed in Chapter 9.

quality team
A team that is part of an organization's structure and is empowered to act on its decisions regarding product and service quality.

Quality teams are different from QCs in that they are more formal and are designed and assigned by upper-level management. Quality teams are not voluntary and have more formal power than QCs. Although QCs and quality teams are not intended to provide members with social benefits, all teams in an organization have the potential to afford team members a number of social benefits.

Social Benefits

5. Identify the social benefits of group and team membership.

psychological intimacy
Emotional and psychological closeness to other team or group members.

Two sets of social benefits are available to team or group members. One set of social benefits accrues from achieving psychological intimacy. The other comes from achieving integrated involvement.[35]

Psychological intimacy is emotional and psychological closeness to other team or group members. It results in feelings of affection and warmth, unconditional positive regard, opportunity for emotional expression, openness, security and emotional support, and giving and receiving nurturance. Failure to achieve psychological intimacy results in feelings of emotional isolation and loneliness. This may be especially problematic for chief executives who experience loneliness at the top. Although psychological intimacy is valuable for emotional health and well-being, it need not necessarily be achieved in the work setting.

Integrated involvement is closeness achieved through tasks and activities. It results in enjoyable and involving activities, social identity and self-definition, being valued for one's skills and abilities, opportunity for power and influence, conditional positive regard, and support for one's beliefs and values. Failure to achieve integrated involvement results in social isolation. Whereas psychological intimacy is more emotion based, integrated involvement is more behavior and activity based. Integrated involvement contributes to social psychological health and well-being.

Psychological intimacy and integrated involvement each contribute to overall health. It is not necessary to achieve both in the same team or group. For example, while chief executive at Xerox Corporation, David Kearns was also a marathon runner; he found integrated involvement with his executive team and psychological intimacy with his athletic companions on long-distance runs.

Teams and groups have two sets of functions that operate to enable members to achieve psychological intimacy and integrated involvement. These are task and maintenance functions.

integrated involvement
Closeness achieved through tasks and activities.

Task and Maintenance Functions

An effective team carries out various task functions to perform its work successfully and various maintenance functions to ensure member satisfaction and a sense of team spirit.[36] Teams that successfully fulfill these functions afford their members the potential for psychological intimacy and integrated involvement. Table 8.3 presents nine task and nine maintenance functions in teams or groups.

Task functions are those activities directly related to the effective completion of the team's work. For example, the task of initiating activity involves suggesting ideas, defining problems, and proposing approaches and/or solutions to problems. The task of seeking information involves asking for ideas, suggestions, information, or facts. Effective teams have members who fulfill various task functions as they are required.

Some task functions are more important at one time in the life of a group, and other functions are more important at other times. For example,

6. Explain the task and maintenance functions in teams.

task function
An activity directly related to the effective completion of a team's work.

Task Functions	Maintenance Functions
Initiating activities	Supporting others
Seeking information	Following others' leads
Giving information	Gatekeeping communication
Elaborating concepts	Setting standards
Coordinating activities	Expressing member feelings
Summarizing ideas	Testing group decisions
Testing ideas	Consensus testing
Evaluating effectiveness	Harmonizing conflict
Diagnosing problems	Reducing tension

Table 8.3
Task and Maintenance Functions in Teams or Groups

during the engineering test periods for new technologies, the engineering team needs members who focus on testing the practical applications of suggestions and those who diagnose problems and suggest solutions.

The effective use of task functions leads to the success of the team, and the failure to use them may lead to disaster. For example, the successful initiation and coordination of an emergency room (ER) team's activities by the senior resident saved the life of a knife wound victim.[37] The victim was stabbed one-quarter inch below the heart, and the ER team acted quickly to stem the bleeding, begin intravenous fluids, and monitor the victim's vital signs.

maintenance function
An activity essential to effective, satisfying interpersonal relationships within a team or group.

Maintenance functions are those activities essential to the effective, satisfying interpersonal relationships within a team or group. For example, following another group member's lead may be as important as leading others. Communication gatekeepers within a group ensure balanced contributions from all members. Because task activities build tension into teams and groups working together, tension-reduction activities are important to drain off negative or destructive feelings. For example, in a study of twenty-five work groups over a five-year period, humor and joking behavior were found to enhance the social relationships in the groups.[38] The researchers concluded that performance improvements in the twenty-five groups indirectly resulted from improved relationships attributable to the humor and joking behaviors. Maintenance functions enhance togetherness, cooperation, and teamwork, enabling members to achieve psychological intimacy while furthering the success of the team. Jody Grant's supportive attitude and comfortable demeanor as chairman and CEO of Texas Capital Bancshares enabled him to build a vibrant bank in the aftermath of the great Texas banking crash. Grant was respected for his expertise *and* his ability to build relationships. Both task and maintenance functions are important for successful teams.

EMPOWERMENT AND SELF-MANAGED TEAMS

7. Discuss empowerment, teamwork, and self-managed teams.

Quality circles and quality teams, as we discussed earlier, are one way to implement teamwork in organizations. Self-managed teams are broad-based work teams that deal with issues beyond quality. Decision making in self-managed teams is also discussed in Chapter 9. General Motors' NDH Bearings plant, for example, fostered teamwork by empowering employees to make important decisions at work. The company's approach was to push decision making down throughout the plant.

Empowerment may be thought of as an attribute of a person or of an organization's culture.[39] As an organizational culture attribute, empowerment encourages participation, an essential ingredient for teamwork.[40] Quality action teams (QATs) at FedEx are the primary quality improvement process (QIP) technique used by the company to engage management and hourly employees in four- to ten-member problem-solving teams.[41] The teams are empowered to act and solve problems as specific as charting the best route from the Phoenix airport to the local distribution center or as global as making major software enhancements to the online package-tracking system.

Empowerment may give employees the power of a lightning strike, but empowered employees must be properly focused through careful planning and preparation before they strike.[42]

Challenge 8.2 includes several items from FedEx's survey-feedback-action (SFA) survey related to employee empowerment. Complete Challenge 8.2 to see if you are empowered.

Challenge 8.2

Are You an Empowered Employee?*

Read each of the following statements carefully. Then, to the right, indicate which answer best expresses your level of agreement (5 = strongly agree, 4 = agree, 3 = sometimes agree/sometimes disagree, 2 = disagree, 1 = strongly disagree, and 0 = undecided/do not know). Mark only one answer for each item, and respond to all items.

____ 1. I feel free to tell my manager what I think.	5	4	3	2	1	0
____ 2. My manager is willing to listen to my concerns.	5	4	3	2	1	0
____ 3. My manager asks for my ideas about things affecting our work.	5	4	3	2	1	0
____ 4. My manager treats me with respect and dignity.	5	4	3	2	1	0
____ 5. My manager keeps me informed about things I need to know.	5	4	3	2	1	0
____ 6. My manager lets me do my job without interfering.	5	4	3	2	1	0
____ 7. My manager's boss gives us the support we need.	5	4	3	2	1	0
____ 8. Upper management (directors and above) pays attention to ideas and suggestions from people at my level.	5	4	3	2	1	0

Scoring

To determine if you are an empowered employee, add your scores.

32–40: You are empowered! Managers listen when you speak, respect your ideas, and allow you to do your work.

24–31: You have *some* power! Your ideas are considered sometimes, and you have some freedom of action.

16–23: You must exercise caution. You cannot speak or act too boldly, and your managers appear to exercise close supervision.

8–15: Your wings are clipped! You work in a powerless, restrictive work environment.

*If you are not employed, discuss these questions with a friend who is employed. Is your friend an empowered employee?

SOURCE: *Survey-Feedback-Action (SFA)*, FedEx Corporation, Memphis, TN.

Empowerment Skills

Empowerment through employee self-management is an alternative to empowerment through teamwork.[43] Whether through self-management or teamwork, empowerment requires the development of certain skills if it is to be enacted effectively. Competence skills are the first set of skills required for empowerment. Mastery and experience in one's chosen discipline and profession provide an essential foundation for empowerment. This means that new employees and trainees should experience only limited empowerment until they demonstrate the capacity to accept more responsibility, a key aspect of empowerment.

Empowerment also requires certain process skills. The most critical process skills for empowerment include negotiating skills, especially with allies, opponents, and adversaries.[44] Allies are the easiest people to negotiate with because they agree with you about the team's mission, and you can trust their actions and behavior. Opponents require a different negotiating strategy; although you can predict their actions and behavior, they do not agree with your concept of the team's mission. Adversaries are dangerous, difficult people to negotiate with because you cannot predict their actions or behaviors, and they do not agree with your concept of the team's mission.

A third set of empowerment skills involves the development of cooperative and helping behaviors.[45] Cooperative people are motivated to maximize the gains for everyone on the team; they engage in encouraging, helpful behavior to bring about that end. The alternatives to cooperation are competitive, individualistic, and egalitarian orientations. Competitive people are motivated to maximize their personal gains regardless of the expense to other people. This can be very counterproductive from the standpoint of the team. Individualistic people are motivated to act autonomously, though not necessarily to maximize their personal gains. They are less prone to contribute to the efforts of the team. Egalitarian people are motivated to equalize the outcomes for each team member, which may or may not be beneficial to the team's well-being.

Communication skills are a final set of essential empowerment skills.[46] These skills include self-expression skills and skills in reflective listening. Empowerment cannot occur in a team unless members are able to express themselves effectively, as well as listen carefully to one another.

Self-Managed Teams

self-managed team
A team that makes decisions that were once reserved for managers.

Self-managed teams are teams that make decisions that were once reserved for managers. They are also called *self-directed teams* or *autonomous work groups*. Self-managed teams are one way to implement empowerment in organizations. A one-year study of self-managed teams suggests they have a positive impact on employee attitudes but not on absenteeism or turnover.[47] Evaluative research is helpful in achieving a better understanding of this relatively new way of approaching teamwork and the design of work. Research can help in establishing expectations for self-managed teams. For example, it is probably unreasonable to expect these teams to be fully functional and self-directed in short periods of time. Further, there are risks, such as groupthink, in self-managing teams that must be prevented or managed if the team is to achieve full development and function.[48] Organizational Reality 8.1 describes the problems Levi Strauss encountered when it implemented self-managed teams in 1992. Morale dropped and conflict rose at Levi.

Other evaluations of self-managed teams are more positive. Southwest Industries, a high-technology aerospace manufacturing firm, embarked on a major internal reorganization in the early 1990s that included the creation of self-managed teams to fit its high-technology production process. Southwest's team approach resulted in a 30 percent increase in shipments, a 30 percent decrease in lead time, a 40 percent decrease in total inventory, a decrease in machinery downtime, and almost a one-third decrease in production costs.[49] Self-managed teams were also the foundation for the mirac-

---

ORGANIZATIONAL REALITY 8.1

Morale Takes a Hit in Levi's Factory Teams

During 1992, Levi Strauss implemented a teamwork system in its U.S. plants to replace the old piecework system. The teamwork system did not work well, however. Originally, the company felt that teamwork would be more humane, safe, and profitable. Levi's operations vice-president said, "This change will lead to a self-managed work environment that will reduce stress and help employees become more productive." Under the old piecework system, a worker repeatedly performed a single, specialized task, such as sewing zippers or attaching belt loops, and was paid according to the amount of work he or she completed. The teamwork system was intended to reduce monotony, offer stitchers task variety, and reduce repetitive-stress injuries. Levi prided itself on generous pay and charity support in factory towns within an industry notorious for low wages and poor working conditions. Levi kept its large U.S. manufacturing base long after other apparel firms moved offshore, but competitive industry pressures forced the 1992 change.

Unfortunately, the teamwork and self-managed work environment did not pan out as planned. Instead, the change led to skilled workers being pitted against slower colleagues who could not keep the pace, triggering infighting and damaging morale at several Levi plants. Longtime friendships became strained or broken when faster workers were assigned to interdependent work teams with slower workers. Threats and insults often followed. Although teams staffed with skilled equals did fairly well under the new system, on unbalanced teams lower skilled workers saw their pay increase while top performers saw their pay drop. Labor and overhead costs surged. Even though employees were prepared with team-building and problem-solving seminars, and in some cases a book on corporate change, the teamwork system caused a lot of anxiety, pain, and suffering for Levi employees. For Levi Strauss, teamwork did not work well.

Discussion Questions

1. How did Levi Strauss's factory teams cause morale problems?

2. What could Levi Strauss have done differently to achieve better teamwork?

SOURCE: R. T. King Jr., "Levi's Factory Workers Are Assigned to Teams, and Morale Takes a Hit," *The Wall Street Journal*, May 20, 1998, A1+. Permission conveyed through Copyright Clearance Center, Inc.

ulous resurrection of the former Chrysler (now DaimlerChrysler) Corporation's oldest plant in New Castle, Indiana, as the United Auto Workers' union and company management forged a partnership for success.[50]

A game (Learning Teams) is available to help people create self-directed teams, learn cooperatively, and master factual information.[51] With no outside help, an engineering team in the Defense Systems and Electronics Group (DSEG) now part of Raytheon, developed themselves into a highly effective, productive, self-managed team. They then helped DSEG in its successful effort to win a Malcolm Baldrige National Quality Award.

UPPER ECHELONS: TEAMS AT THE TOP

8. Explain the importance of upper echelons and top management teams.

upper echelon
A top-level executive team in an organization.

Self-managed teams at the top of the organization—top-level executive teams—are referred to as *upper echelons*. Organizations are often a reflection of these upper echelons.[52] Upper echelon theory argues that the background characteristics of the top management team can predict organizational characteristics. Furthermore, upper echelons are one key to the strategic success of the organization.[53] Thus, the teams at the top are instrumental in defining the organization over time such that the values, competence, ethics, and unique characteristics of the top management team are eventually reflected throughout the organization. This ability to exert power and influence throughout the entire organization makes the top management team a key to the organization's success.

For example, when Lee Iacocca became CEO at the former Chrysler Corporation, his top management team was assembled to bring about strategic realignment within the corporation by building on Chrysler's historical engineering strength. The dramatic success of Chrysler during the early 1980s was followed by struggle and accommodation during the late 1980s. This raises the question of how long a CEO and the top management team can sustain organizational success.

Hambrick and Fukutomi address this question by examining the dynamic relationship between a CEO's tenure and the success of the organization.[54] They found five seasons in a CEO's tenure: (1) response to a mandate, (2) experimentation, (3) selection of an enduring theme, (4) convergence, and (5) dysfunction. All else being equal, this seasons model has significant implications for organizational performance. Specifically, organizational performance increases during a CEO's tenure to a peak, after which performance declines. This relationship is depicted in Figure 8.2. The peak has been found to come at about seven years—somewhere in the middle of the executive's seasons. As indicated by the dotted lines in the figure, the peak may be extended, depending on several factors, such as diversity in the executive's support team.

From an organizational health standpoint, diversity and depth in the top management team enhance the CEO's well-being.[55] From a performance standpoint, the CEO's top management team can influence the timing of the performance peak, the degree of dysfunction during the closing season of the CEO's tenure, and the rate of decline in organizational performance. Diversity and heterogeneity in the top management team help sustain high levels of organizational performance at the peak and help maintain the CEO's vitality. The presence of a "wild turkey" in the top management team can be a particularly positive force. The wild turkey is a devil's advocate who challenges the thinking of the CEO and other top executives and provides a counterpoint during debates. If not shouted down or inhibited, the wild turkey helps the CEO and the team sustain peak performance and retard the CEO's dysfunction and decline. After General Motors acquired EDS (later spun off as Electronic Data Systems) in 1984, GM and Roger Smith, then its CEO, lost a possible opportunity to change and improve the corporation's performance when they silenced Ross Perot, EDS's founder and a wild turkey. Because Perot's ideas were never implemented at GM, we will never know if they would have been beneficial. Perot was inhibited, and GM's decline continued.

We can conclude that the leadership, composition, and dynamics of the top management team have an important influence on the organization's performance. In some cases, corporations have eliminated the single CEO. For example, in early 1992, Xerox and Microsoft announced plans for a team of executives to function in lieu of a president.[56] Walter Wriston created such a three-member team when he was chairman at Citicorp (now part of Citigroup).

Multicultural Teams

The backgrounds of group members may be quite different in the global workplace. Homogeneous groups in which all members share similar back-

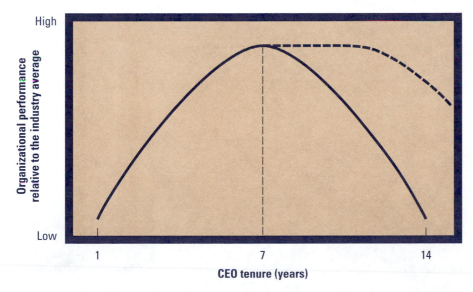

Figure 8.2
Executive Tenure and
Organizational Performance

SOURCE: D. Hambrick, The Seasons of an Executive's Tenure, keynote address, the Sixth Annual Texas Conference on Organizations, Lago Vista, Texas, April 1991.

grounds are giving way to token groups in which all but one member come from the same background, bicultural groups in which two or more members represent each of two distinct cultures, and multicultural groups in which members represent three or more ethnic backgrounds.[57] Diversity within a group may increase the uncertainty, complexity, and inherent confusion in group processes, making it more difficult for the group to achieve its full, potential productivity.[58] On the positive side, Ford was highly successful with Detroit's most diverse, international management team assembled by former chairman and CEO Alex Trotman.[59] Ford president and CEO Jacques Nasser has continued this international initiative while putting his own stamp on Ford's top-level management team. The advantages of culturally diverse groups include the generation of more and better ideas while limiting the risk of groupthink, to be discussed in Chapter 9.

MANAGERIAL IMPLICATIONS: TEAMWORK FOR PRODUCTIVITY AND QUALITY

Work groups and teams are important vehicles through which organizations achieve high-quality performance. The current emphasis on the new team environment, shown in Table 8.2, places unique demands on managers, teams and individuals in leading, working, and managing. Managing these demands requires an understanding of individual diversity and the interrelationships of individuals, teams, and managers, as depicted in the triangle in Figure 8.3. Expectations associated with these three key organizational roles for people at work are different. The first role is as an individual, empowered employee. The second is as an active member of one or more teams. The third is the role of manager or formal supervisor. Earlier in the chap-

Figure 8.3
The Triangle for Managing in the New Team Environment

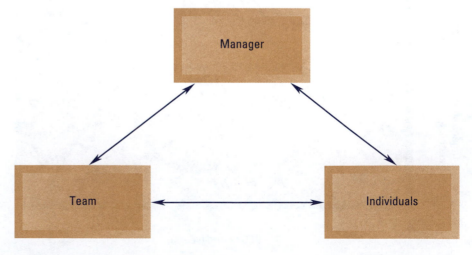

SOURCE: *Managing in the New Team Environment*, by Hirschhorn, © 1991. Reprinted by permission of Prentice-Hall, Inc., Upper Saddle River, N.J.

ter, we discussed the foundations for teamwork, empowerment, and skills for working in the new team environment. Individual empowerment must be balanced with collaborative teamwork.

The manager in the triangle is responsible for creating a receptive organizational environment for work groups and teams. This requires that the manager achieve a balance between setting limits (so that individuals and teams do not go too far afield) and removing barriers (so that empowered individuals and self-managed teams can accomplish their work). In addition, the manager should establish a flexible charter for each team. Once the charter is established, the manager continues to be available to the team as a coaching resource, as necessary. The manager establishes criteria for evaluating the performance effectiveness of the team, as well as the individuals, being supervised. In an optimum environment, this involves useful and timely performance feedback to teams that carries a sense of equity and fairness with it. The manager's responsibilities are different from the team leader's.

Effective team leaders may guide a work group or share leadership responsibility with their teams, especially self-managed teams. Team leaders are active team members with responsibility for nurturing the development and performance of the team.[60] They require skills different from those of the manager. Whereas the manager establishes the environment in which teams flourish, the team leader teaches, listens, solves problems, manages conflict, and enhances the dynamics of team functioning to ensure the team's success. It is the team leader's task to bring the team to maturity; help the team work through interpersonal, task, and authority issues; and be skilled in nurturing a cohesive, effective team. A team leader requires the hands-on skills of direct involvement and full membership in the team. Flexibility, delegation, and collaboration are characteristics of healthy teams and team leaders. Increasing globalization requires team leaders to be skilled at forging teamwork among diverse individuals, whereas managers must be skilled at forging collaboration among diverse groups.

Looking Back

People and Processes Produce Quality at Ford Wayne

Variable reduction teams (VRTs) at Ford's Wayne Stamping & Assembly Plant are a key method for ensuring the Ford Escort's outstanding quality.[61] The plant was retooled in 1996 for the March 1996 launch of a new model Escort and its sister design, the Mercury Tracer. During the retooling, the plant focused on ways to maintain its outstanding quality. In all, there are twelve VRTs at the Ford Wayne plant; each team represents a different subsystem in the Escort, such as Interior Trim, Sheet Metal, Powertrain, Chassis, and Paint. The purpose of the VRTs is to reduce variations in the production and assembly process that may detract from the outstanding quality of each job that comes off the assembly line. At 8:30 A.M. each working day, in a large, well-lighted room just off the factory floor, in a section where end-of-line tests are occurring, there is a meeting of the plant manager, quality control manager, manufacturing and area managers, hourly employees, engineering personnel, purchasing support, and sometimes supplier representatives. Using graphs, charts, drawings, matrices, and other visual displays, two VRTs go through the process in their subsystems for the assembled audience. Each VRT presents problems it has identified and discusses actions the team members are taking to resolve these issues. Using a solid sampling of data from within the plant and from the outside world developed by the VRTs, everyone looks for variations that may reduce Ford Escort quality below best in class, or even below the best quality achievable for any car.

CHAPTER SUMMARY

1. Groups are often composed of diverse people at work. Teams in organizations are a key to enhance quality and achieve success.

2. Important aspects of group behavior include norms of behavior, group cohesion, social loafing, and loss of individuality.

3. Once a group forms, it goes through four stages of development. If successful, the group emerges as a mature group with a purpose, clear behavioral norms, high cohesion, and a flexible status structure.

4. Quality circles, originally popularized in Japan, and quality teams contribute to solving technological and quality problems in the organization.

5. Teams provide social benefits for team members, as well as enhancing organizational performance.

6. Empowerment and teamwork require specific organizational design elements and individual psychological characteristics and skills.

7. Upper echelons and top management teams are key to the strategy and performance of an organization. Diversity and a devil's advocate in the top team enhance performance.

8. Managing in the new team environment places new demands on managers, teams, and individuals. Managers must create a supportive and flexible environment for collaborative teams and empowered individuals. Team leaders must nurture the team's development.

KEY TERMS

group 221
team 221
norms of behavior 222
group cohesion 222
social loafing 223

loss of individuality 223
status structure 228
quality circle (QC) 232
quality team 232
psychological intimacy 232

integrated involvement 233
task function 233
maintenance function 234
self-managed team 236
upper echelon 238

REVIEW QUESTIONS

1. What is a group? A team?
2. Explain four aspects of group behavior. How can each aspect help or hinder the group's functioning?
3. Explain what happens in each of the four stages of a group's development. When does the group address interpersonal issues? Task issues? Authority issues?
4. Describe the four characteristics of mature groups.
5. Why are teams important to organizations today? How and why are teams formed?
6. Describe at least five task and five maintenance functions that effective teams must perform.
7. Describe the necessary skills for empowerment and teamwork.
8. What are the benefits and potential drawbacks of self-managed teams?
9. What is the role of the manager in the new team environment? What is the role of the team leader?

DISCUSSION AND COMMUNICATION QUESTIONS

1. Which was the most effective group (or team) of which you have been a member? What made that group (or team) so effective?
2. Have you ever experienced peer pressure to act more in accordance with the behavioral norms of a group? Have you ever engaged in a little social loafing? Have you ever lost your head and been caught up in a group's destructive actions?
3. Name a company that successfully uses teamwork and empowerment. What has that company done that makes it so successful at teamwork and empowerment? Has its team approach made a difference in its performance? How?
4. Name a person you think is a particularly good team member. What makes this person a good team member? Name a person who is a problem as a team member. What makes this person a problem?
5. Think about your current work environment. Does your work environment use quality circles or self-managed teams? What are the barriers to teamwork and empowerment in that environment? What elements of the environment enhance or encourage teamwork and empowerment?
(If you do not work, discuss this question with a friend who does.)
6. (*communication question*) Prepare a memo describing your observations about teams and groups in your workplace or your university. Where have you observed teams or groups to be most effective? Why? What changes might be made at work or in the university to make teams more effective?
7. (*communication question*) Develop an oral presentation about what the most important norms of behavior should be in an academic community and workplace. Be specific. Discuss how these norms should be established and reinforced.
8. (*communication question*) Interview an employee or manager about what he or she believes contributes to cohesiveness in work groups and teams. Ask the person what the conclusions are based on. Be prepared to discuss what you have learned in class.
9. Do you admire the upper echelons in your organization or university? Why or why not? Do they communicate effectively with groups and individuals throughout the organization?

ETHICS QUESTIONS

1. Assume that someone is engaged in social loafing in a group of which you are a member. What should you do? Is this person acting in an unethical manner?
2. Does a moral dilemma arise when an individual is expected to subordinate his or her individuality and autonomy to the will of the work group or team? Suppose you are a member of a work group

or team that is getting ready to act in a way you believe is unethical or immoral. What should you do? Will you be responsible for the actions of the entire team?

3. Assume that a very mature group decides that it is necessary to resort to threats to one of the members to keep the person in line with the group's norms. Further assume that the behavior of the person in question is not endangering anyone inside or outside the group. Is the proposed group action unethical? What should your position be on the issue?

4. Suppose an empowered employee makes a mistake at your place of work that damages some property but does not hurt anyone. Assuming the employee was empowered to act, should the employee be punished for the unfortunate consequences of the action? Would your answer differ depending on whether the employee had been properly trained and supervised before being empowered?

Experiential Exercises

8.1 Tower Building: A Group Dynamics Activity

This exercise gives you an opportunity to study group dynamics in a task-oriented situation. Each group must bring materials to class for building a tower. All materials must fit in a box no greater than eight cubic feet (i.e., 2 ft. × 2 ft. × 2 ft. or 1 ft. × 2 ft. × 4 ft.).

Step 1. Each group is assigned a meeting place and a workplace. One or two observers should be assigned in each group. The instructor may assign a manager to each group.

Step 2. Each group plans for the building of the paper tower (no physical construction is allowed during this planning period). Towers will be judged on the basis of height, stability, beauty, and meaning. (Another option is to have the groups do the planning outside of class and come prepared to build the tower.)

Step 3. Each group constructs its tower.

Step 4. Groups inspect other towers, and all individuals rate towers other than their own. See the evaluation sheet at the right. Each group turns in its point totals (i.e., someone in the group adds up each person's total for all groups rated) to the instructor, and the instructor announces the winner.

Step 5. Group Dynamics Analysis. Observers report observations to their own groups, and each group analyzes the group dynamics that occurred during the planning and building of the tower.

Step 6. Groups report on major issues in group dynamics that arose during the tower planning and building. Complete the Tower Building Aftermath questionnaire as homework if requested by your instructor.

CRITERIA	GROUPS							
	1	2	3	4	5	6	7	8
Height								
Stability/ Strength								
Beauty								
Meaning/ Significance								
TOTALS								

Rate each criterion on a scale of 1–10, with 1 being lowest or poorest, and 10 being highest or best.

SOURCE: From *Organizational Behavior and Performance,* 5/e by Szilagyi/Wallace, © 1997. Reprinted by permission of Prentice-Hall, Inc., Upper Saddle River, N.J.

8.2 Design a Team

The following exercise gives you an opportunity to design a team. Working in a six-person group, address the individual characteristics, team composition, and norms for an effective group whose task is to make recommendations on improving customer relations. The president of a small clothing manufacturer is concerned that his customers are not satisfied with the company's responsiveness, product quality, and returned-orders process. He has asked your group to put together a team to address these problems.

Step 1. The class will form into groups of approximately six members each. Each group elects a spokesperson and answers the following questions. The group should spend an equal amount of time on each question.

a. *What characteristics should the individual members of the task team possess?* Members may consider professional competence, skills, department, and/or personality and behavioral characteristics in the group's discussion.

b. *What should the composition of the task team be?* Once your group has addressed individual characteristics, consider the overall composition of the task team. Have special and/or unique competencies, knowledge, skills, and abilities been considered in your deliberations?

c. *What norms of behavior do you think the task team should adopt?* A team's norms of behavior may evolve, or they may be consciously discussed and agreed upon. Take the latter approach.

Step 2. Each group will share the results of its answers to the questions in Step 1. Cross-team questions and discussion follows.

Decision Making by Individuals and Groups

Learning Objectives

After reading this chapter, you should be able to do the following:

1. Explain the assumptions of bounded rationality. *p. 249*

2. Describe Jung's cognitive styles and how they affect managerial decision making. *p. 253*

3. Understand the role of creativity in decision making, and practice ways to increase your own creativity. *p. 262*

4. Identify the advantages and disadvantages of group decision making. *p. 266*

5. Discuss the symptoms of groupthink and ways to prevent it. *p. 267*

6. Evaluate the strengths and weaknesses of several group decision-making techniques. *p. 269*

7. Describe the effects that expert systems and group decision support systems have on decision-making organizations. *p. 273*

8. Utilize an "ethics check" for examining managerial decisions. *p. 277*

Thinking Ahead

Starbucks in Chicago: Was It a Bad Decision?

In the early days, Howard Schultz had only three coffee bars, two in Seattle and one in Vancouver, British Columbia. He wanted Starbucks to be a national company, and a crucial step would be to see if people in other cities would like Starbucks coffee, with its stronger, robust taste. Chicago was the city on Schultz's mind. A number of business experts advised against Starbucks moving into Chicago. It was 2,000 miles away, and it was logistically hard to supply with such a perishable product as coffee. Chicagoans, Schultz was told, would never drink dark-roasted coffee; they lived in the heartland of Folger's and Maxwell House. They preferred the coffee from local convenience stores.

Schultz persisted, thinking that Chicago's cold climate and big downtown area were great for coffee. He leased a prime downtown location and opened the first Starbucks in Chicago in October 1987—the day of the stock market crash. Three more locations were opened during the next six months. But, by the time winter was over,

Chicagoans were not buying the coffee. Costs of goods were higher in Chicago. Employees were not buying into the coffee or the dream.

During the next two years, Starbucks lost tens of thousands of dollars in Chicago. The company's directors started asking tough questions. Venture capitalists balked at its expansion plans because of the problems in Chicago. Until Starbucks succeeded in Chicago, Schultz could not show that the Starbucks idea would work across North America. Was it a bad decision? Find out in the Looking Back feature as the Starbucks saga continues.[1]

THE DECISION-MAKING PROCESS

Decision making is a critical activity in the lives of managers. The decisions a manager faces can range from very simple, routine matters for which the manager has an established decision rule (*programmed decisions*) to new and complex decisions that require creative solutions (*nonprogrammed decisions*).[2] Scheduling lunch hours for one's work group is a programmed decision. The manager performs the decision activity on a daily basis, using an established procedure with the same clear goal in mind. In contrast, decisions like buying out another company are nonprogrammed. The decision to acquire a company is unique and unstructured, and requires considerable judgment. Regardless of the type of decision made, it is helpful to understand as much as possible about how individuals and groups make decisions.

Decision making is a process involving a series of steps, as shown in Figure 9.1. The first step is recognition of the problem; that is, the manager realizes that a decision must be made. Identification of the real problem is important; otherwise, the manager may be reacting to symptoms and firefighting rather than dealing with the root cause of the problem. Next, a manager must identify the objective of the decision. In other words, the manager must determine what is to be accomplished by the decision.

The third step in the decision-making process is gathering information relevant to the problem. The manager must pull together sufficient information about why the problem occurred. This involves conducting a thorough diagnosis of the situation and going on a fact-finding mission.

The fourth step is listing and evaluating alternative courses of action. During this step, a thorough "what if" analysis should also be conducted to determine the various factors that could influence the outcome. It is important to generate a wide range of options and creative solutions in order to be able to move on to the fourth step.

Next, the manager selects the alternative that best meets the decision objective. If the problem has been diagnosed correctly and sufficient alternatives have been identified, this step is much easier.

Finally, the solution is implemented. The situation must then be monitored to see whether the decision met its objective. Consistent monitoring and periodic feedback are essential parts of the follow-up process.

programmed decision
A simple, routine matter for which a manager has an established decision rule.

nonprogrammed decision
A new, complex decision that requires a creative solution.

Figure 9.1
The Decision-Making Process

Recognize the problem and the need for a decision.

Identify the objective of the decision.

Gather and evaluate data and diagnose the situation.

List and evaluate alternatives.

Select the best course of action.

Implement the decision.

Gather feedback.

Follow up.

Decision making can be stressful. Managers must make decisions with significant risk and uncertainty, and often without full information. They must trust and rely on others in arriving at their decisions, but they are ultimately responsible. Sometimes the decisions are painful and involve exiting businesses, firing people, and admitting wrong. Former AT&T CEO Bob Allen announced a layoff of 30,000 people in the wake of the company's losses from its purchase of NCR, which was a bad decision. The courage to make big, unpleasant, and often painful decisions is a quality that managers will need in the coming decade.[3]

effective decision
A timely decision that meets a desired objective and is acceptable to those individuals affected by it.

MODELS OF DECISION MAKING

The success of any organization depends on managers' abilities to make *effective decisions*. An effective decision is timely, is acceptable to the individuals affected by it, and meets the desired objective.[4] This section describes three models of decision making: the rational model, the bounded rationality model, and the garbage can model.

Rational Model

Rationality refers to a logical, step-by-step approach to decision making, with a thorough analysis of alternatives and their consequences. The rational model of decision making comes from classic economic theory and contends that the decision maker is completely rational in his or her approach. The rational model has the following important assumptions:

1. The outcome will be completely rational.
2. The decision maker has a consistent system of preferences, which is used to choose the best alternative.
3. The decision maker is aware of all the possible alternatives.
4. The decision maker can calculate the probability of success for each alternative.[5]

In the rational model, the decision maker strives to optimize, that is, to select the best possible alternative.

Given the assumptions of the rational model, it is unrealistic. There are time constraints and limits to human knowledge and information-processing capabilities. In addition, a manager's preferences and needs change often. The rational model is thus an ideal that managers strive for in making decisions. It captures the way a decision should be made but does not reflect the reality of managerial decision making.[6]

Bounded Rationality Model

Recognizing the deficiencies of the rational model, Herbert Simon suggested that there are limits on how rational a decision maker can actually be. His decision theory, the bounded rationality model, earned a Nobel Prize in 1978.

Simon's model, also referred to as the "administrative man" theory, rests on the idea that there are constraints that force a decision maker to be less than completely rational. The bounded rationality model has four assumptions:

1. Managers select the first alternative that is satisfactory.
2. Managers recognize that their conception of the world is simple.
3. Managers are comfortable making decisions without determining all the alternatives.
4. Managers make decisions by rules of thumb or heuristics.

Bounded rationality assumes that managers *satisfice*; that is, they select the first alternative that is "good enough," because the costs of optimizing in terms of time and effort are too great.[7] Further, the theory assumes that managers develop shortcuts, called *heuristics*, to make decisions in

rationality
A logical, step-by-step approach to decision making, with a thorough analysis of alternatives and their consequences.

Experiencing OB

There are many different models of rational decision making, but most of them contain common steps. To view an alternative decision-making model, visit our animated concept and activity site. Choose Decision_Making from the "select a topic" pull-down menu, then Decision-Making Process from the "overview tab."

http://www.experiencingob.com

1. Explain the assumptions of bounded rationality.

bounded rationality
A theory that suggests that there are limits to how rational a decision maker can actually be.

satisfice
To select the first alternative that is "good enough," because the costs in time and effort are too great to optimize.

heuristics
Shortcuts in decision making that save mental activity.

order to save mental activity. Heuristics are rules of thumb that allow managers to make decisions based on what has worked in past experiences.

Does the bounded rationality model more realistically portray the managerial decision process? Research indicates that it does.[8] One of the reasons managers face limits to their rationality is that they must make decisions under risk and time pressure. The situation they find themselves in is highly uncertain, and the probability of success is not known.

Garbage Can Model

garbage can model
A theory that contends that decisions in organizations are random and unsystematic.

Sometimes the decision-making process in organizations appears to be haphazard and unpredictable. In the *garbage can model*, decisions are random and unsystematic.[9] Figure 9.2 depicts the garbage can model. In this model, the organization is a garbage can in which problems, solutions, participants, and choice opportunities are floating around randomly. If the four factors happen to connect, a decision is made.[10] The quality of the decision depends on timing. The right participants must find the right solution to the right problem at the right time.

The garbage can model illustrates the idea that not all organizational decisions are made in a step-by-step, systematic fashion. Especially under conditions of high uncertainty, the decision process may be chaotic. Some decisions appear to happen out of sheer luck.

On the high-speed playing field of today's businesses, managers must make critical decisions quickly, with incomplete information, and must also involve employees in the process. Maybe they can learn from the military. Before you dismiss this idea, let's agree that the military might seem the last place to look for a fast-reacting, adaptable organization. The Marines, however, are different. You can see what they're up to in Organizational Reality 9.1. The tough competition and need for quick decisions reflect not only the heat of battle, but also the business environment today.

Figure 9.2
The Garbage Can Model

Problems — Solutions

Participants — Choice opportunities

SOURCE: From M. D. Cohen, J. G. March, and J. P. Olsen in *Administrative Science Quarterly* 17 (March 1972) 1–25. Reprinted by permission of the Administrative Science Quarterly.

ORGANIZATIONAL REALITY 9.1

The Few . . . The Proud . . . The Decision Makers

The Marines are making decisions a little differently, and they're proud of it. The heart of their approach to decision making can be found in two of their most basic beliefs: (1) War is chaos, confusion, and uncertainty. (2) The only way to succeed is to push the ability and authority for decision making down to the Marines who are on the spot.

One way the Marines get this done is by using the "rule of three," which means that a person should focus only on three tasks or goals. A decision can be boiled down to three alternative courses of action. When the Marines put together a plan to provide humanitarian aid, they have three hours to plan it and three hours to prepare for it. A sergeant has a squadron of three fire teams; a lieutenant has a platoon of three squads, and so on. While this creates a tall, narrow hierarchy, that hierarchy can collapse at a moment's notice when there is a decision to be made. The chain of command is not consulted. Even privates know that they can do whatever is necessary to complete a mission. Group decision making is also used. The group first comes up with the desired end state, and then it proposes three alternative missions for getting there (the "rule of three" again). Disagreement is not only allowed; it is demanded.

Another key to success is selection and training. Officer candidate school (OCS), which has a 25 percent washout rate, is essentially a ten-week, twenty-four-hour-a-day job interview that screens out those who lack the right stuff. OCS includes "brainteasers"—intense hands-on exercises in decision making and problem solving. In one brainteaser, candidates are told to move a wounded soldier across a mined stream using a rope and boards. If they make it past OCS, candidates enter Basic School, a six-month course in generic, high-speed chaos-proof leadership. Cross-training is emphasized, and so is exposure to as many decision-making scenarios as possible.

Indecisiveness is a fatal flaw in the Marines. The "70 percent" solution, which means an imperfect solution whose saving grace is that it can be made right now, is key. A mediocre decision is better than no decision. If swiftly made and executed, it stands a chance in an environment where the enemy can take the advantage in a heartbeat.

Technology is helping the Marines deal with high-speed, high-risk assaults that don't fare well in bureaucratic or autocratic environments. At the Marine Warfighting Laboratory in Quantico, Virginia, eighteen squads of Marines fan out over 1,500 miles of desert. Normally, squads stay within sight of each other to avoid calling in artillery fire on another squad. These squads, however, have handheld computers that can record enemy positions and send in signals of their own locations. Back at the command post, officers can construct a picture of the entire battle scene. The goal is to get information back to the squads so that they can make better decisions about where to call in fire.

Discussion Question

1. Can the Marines' method of decision making be used in other organizations? If so, what kind of organizations? Would it fail in certain organizations? Which ones?

SOURCE: D. H. Freedman, "Core Values," *Inc.* (April 1998): 54–66. Reprinted by permission of the publisher via Copyright Clearance Center, Inc.

DECISION MAKING AND RISK

Many decisions involve some element of risk. For the Marines, certain decisions are life or death issues, carrying with them extreme levels of risk. For managers, hiring decisions, promotions, delegation, acquisitions and mergers, overseas expansions, new product development, and other decisions make risk a part of the job.

risk aversion
The tendency to choose options that entail fewer risks and less uncertainty.

Experiencing OB

Decision-making conditions affect the predictability of possible decision outcomes, which then affects one's perception of the decision risk. You can interact with this idea at our animated concept and activity site. Choose Decision_Making from the "select a topic" pull-down menu, then Decision-Making Conditions from the "overview tab."

http://www.experiencingob.com

Risk and the Manager

Individuals differ in terms of their willingness to take risks. Some people experience *risk aversion*. They choose options that entail fewer risks, preferring familiarity and certainty. Other individuals are risk takers; that is, they accept greater potential for loss in decisions, tolerate greater uncertainty, and in general are more likely to make risky decisions.

Research indicates that women are more averse to risk taking than men and that older, more experienced managers are more risk averse than younger managers. There is also some evidence that successful managers take more risks than unsuccessful managers.[11] However, the tendency to take risks or avoid them is only part of behavior toward risk. Risk taking is influenced not only by an individual's tendency but also by organizational factors. In commercial banks, loan decisions that require the assessment of risk are made every day.

The way managers behave in response to uncertainty and risk has important implications for organizations. Many individuals find uncertainty stressful, and one of the negative consequences of distress in organizations is faulty decision making by managers. One way to manage the decision-making behavior of employees is to model effective decision making under uncertainty by displaying the desired behavior. This communicates to employees the acceptable level of risk-taking behavior in the organization.

Upper-level managers face a tough task in managing risk-taking behavior. By discouraging lower-level managers from taking risks, they may stifle creativty and innovation. If upper-level managers are going to encourage risk taking, however, they must allow employees to fail without fear of punishment. One way to accomplish this is to consider failure "enlightened trial and error."[12] The key is establishing a consistent attitude toward risk within the organization.

When individuals take risks, losses may occur. Suppose an oil producer thinks there is an opportunity to uncover oil by reentering an old drilling site. She gathers a group of investors and shows them the logs, and they chip in to finance the venture. The reentry is drilled to a certain depth, and nothing is found. Convinced they did not drill deep enough, the producer goes back to the investors and requests additional financial backing to continue drilling. The investors consent, and she drills deeper, only to find nothing. She approaches the investors, and after lengthy discussion, they agree to provide more money to drill deeper. Why do decision makers sometimes throw good money after bad? Why do they continue to provide resources to what looks like a losing venture?

Escalation of Commitment

escalation of commitment
The tendency to continue to commit resources to a losing course of action.

Continuing to commit resources to a losing course of action is known as *escalation of commitment*.[13] A situation often cited as an example is former President Lyndon Johnson's continued commitment of troops and money to the Vietnam War, even though many advisers had warned that U.S. involvement was a losing effort.

In situations characterized by escalation of commitment, individuals who make decisions that turn out to be poor choices tend to hold fast to those choices, even when substantial costs are incurred.[14] Why does escalation of commitment occur? One explanation is offered by cognitive dissonance theory, as we discussed in Chapter 4. This theory assumes that humans dislike inconsistency, and that when there is inconsistency among their attitudes or inconsistency between their attitudes and behavior, they strive to reduce the dissonance.[15]

Two other reasons why people may hang on to a losing course of action are optimism and control. Some people are overly optimistic and overestimate the likelihood that positive things will happen to them. Other people operate under an illusion of control—that they have special skills to control the future that other people don't have.[16]

Hanging on to a poor decision can be costly to organizations. Organizations can deal with escalation of commitment in several ways. One is to split the responsibility for decisions about projects. One individual can make the initial decision, and another individual can make subsequent decisions on the project. Another suggestion is to provide individuals with a graceful exit from poor decisions so that their images are not threatened. One way of accomplishing this is to reward people who admit to poor decisions before escalating their commitment to them. A study also suggested that having groups, rather than individuals, make an initial investment decision would reduce escalation. Support has been found for this idea. Participants in group decision making may experience a diffusion of responsibility for the failed decision rather than feeling personally responsible; thus, they can pull out of a bad decision without threatening their image.[17]

We have seen that there are limits to how rational a manager can be in making decisions. Most managerial decisions involve considerable risk, and individuals react differently to risk situations.

JUNG'S COGNITIVE STYLES

In Chapter 3 we introduced Jungian theory as a way of understanding and appreciating differences among individuals. This theory is especially useful in pointing out that individuals have different styles of making decisions. Carl Jung's original theory identified two styles of information gathering (sensing and intuiting) and two styles of making judgments (thinking and feeling). You already know what each individual preference means. Jung contended that individuals prefer one style of perceiving and one style of judging.[18] The combination of a perceiving style and a judging style is called a *cognitive style*. There are four cognitive styles: sensing/thinking (ST), sensing/feeling (SF), intuiting/thinking (NT), and intuiting/feeling (NF). Each of the cognitive styles affects managerial decision making.[19]

STs rely on facts. They conduct an impersonal analysis of the situation and then make an analytical, objective decision. The ST cognitive style is valuable in organizations because it produces a clear, simple solution. STs

2. Describe Jung's cognitive styles and how they affect managerial decision making.

cognitive style

An individual's preference for gathering information and evaluating alternatives.

remember details and seldom make factual errors. Their weakness is that they may alienate others because of their tendency to ignore interpersonal aspects of decisions. In addition, they tend to avoid risks.

SFs also gather factual information, but they make judgments in terms of how they affect people. They place great importance on interpersonal relationships but also take a practical approach to gathering information for problem solving. The SFs' strength in decision making lies in their ability to handle interpersonal problems well and their ability to take calculated risks. SFs may have trouble accepting new ideas that break the rules in the organization.

NTs focus on the alternative possibilities in a situation and then evaluate the possibilities objectively and impersonally. NTs love to initiate ideas, and they like to focus on the long term. They are innovative and will take risks. Weaknesses of NTs include their tendencies to ignore arguments based on facts and to ignore the feelings of others.

NFs also search out alternative possibilities, but they evaluate the possibilities in terms of how they will affect the people involved. They enjoy participative decision making and are committed to developing their employees. However, NFs may be prone to making decisions based on personal preferences rather than on more objective data. They may also become too responsive to the needs of others.

Research tends to support the existence of these four cognitive styles. One study asked managers to describe their ideal organization, and the researchers found strong similarities in the descriptions of managers with the same cognitive style.[20] STs wanted an organization that relied on facts and details and that exercised impersonal methods of control. SFs focused on facts, too, but they did so in terms of the relationships within the organization. NTs emphasized broad issues and described impersonal, idealistic organizations. NFs described an organization that would serve humankind well and focused on general, humanistic values. Other studies have found that MBA students with different cognitive styles exhibited these different styles in making strategic planning decisions and in making production decisions in a computer-simulated manufacturing environment.[21]

All four cognitive styles have much to contribute to organizational decision making.[22] Isabel Briggs Myers, creator of the MBTI, also developed the Z problem-solving model, which capitalizes on the strengths of the four separate preferences (sensing, intuiting, thinking, and feeling). By using the Z problem-solving model, managers can use both their preferences and non-preferences to make decisions more effectively. The Z model is presented in Figure 9.3.

According to this model, good problem solving has four steps:

1. *Examine the facts and details*. Use sensing to gather information about the problem.

2. *Generate alternatives*. Use intuiting to develop possibilities.

3. *Analyze the alternatives objectively*. Use thinking to logically determine the effects of each alternative.

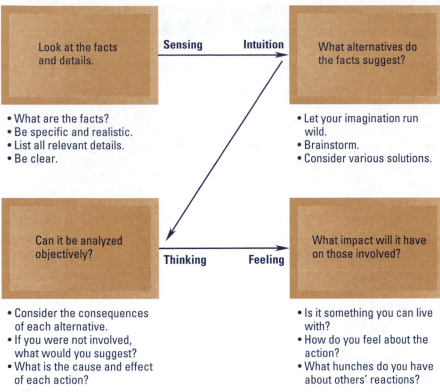

Figure 9.3
The Z Problem-Solving Model

Look at the facts and details.

Sensing **Intuition**

What alternatives do the facts suggest?

- What are the facts?
- Be specific and realistic.
- List all relevant details.
- Be clear.

- Let your imagination run wild.
- Brainstorm.
- Consider various solutions.

Can it be analyzed objectively?

Thinking **Feeling**

What impact will it have on those involved?

- Consider the consequences of each alternative.
- If you were not involved, what would you suggest?
- What is the cause and effect of each action?

- Is it something you can live with?
- How do you feel about the action?
- What hunches do you have about others' reactions?

SOURCE: Excerpted from *Type Talk at Work* by Otto Kroeger and Janet M. Thuesen, 1992, Delacorte Press. Reprinted by permission of Otto Kroeger Associates.

4. *Weigh the impact.* Use feeling to determine how the people involved will be affected.

Using the Z model can help an individual develop his or her nonpreferences. Another way to use the Z model is to rely on others to perform the nonpreferred activities. For example, an individual who is an NF might want to turn to a trusted NT for help in analyzing alternatives objectively.

OTHER INDIVIDUAL INFLUENCES ON DECISION MAKING

In addition to the cognitive styles just examined, many other individual differences affect a manager's decision making. Other personality characteristics, attitudes, and values, along with all of the individual differences variables that were discussed in Chapters 3 and 4, have implications for managerial decision making. Managers must use both their logic and their creativity to make effective decisions. Most of us are more comfortable using either logic or creativity, and we show that preference in everyday decision making. Challenge 9.1 is an activity that will tell you which process, logic or creativity, is your preferred one. Take Challenge 9.1 now, and then read on to interpret your score.

Challenge 9.1

Which Side of Your Brain Do You Favor?

There are no "right" or "wrong" answers to this questionnaire. It is more of a self-assessment than a test. Do not read the questions more than once. Don't over-analyze. Merely circle "A" or "B" to indicate which answer is more typical of you.

1. Typically, when I have a problem to solve,
   A I make a list of possible solutions, prioritize them, and then select the best answer.
   B I "let it sit" for a while or talk it over with someone before I attempt to reach a solution.

2. When I sit with my hands clasped in my lap (FOLD YOUR HANDS THAT WAY RIGHT NOW BEFORE GOING ON, THEN LOOK AT YOUR HANDS), the thumb that is on top is
   A my right thumb.
   B my left thumb.

3. I have hunches
   A sometimes, but do not place much faith in them.
   B frequently and I usually follow them.

4. If I am at a meeting or lecture, I tend to take extensive notes.
   A True
   B False

5. I am well-organized, have a system for doing things, have a place for everything and everything in its place, and can assimilate information quickly and logically.
   A True
   B False

6. I am good with numbers.
   A True
   B False

7. Finding words in a dictionary or looking up names in a telephone book is something I can do easily and quickly.
   A True
   B False

8. If I want to remember directions or other information,
   A I make notes.
   B I visualize the information.

9. I express myself well verbally.
   A True
   B False

10. To learn dance steps or athletic moves,
    A I try to understand the sequence of the steps and repeat them mentally.
    B I don't think about it; I just try to get the feel of the game or the music.

Interpretation:

• Four, five, or six "A" answers indicate lateralization—an ability to use either hemisphere easily and to solve problems according to their nature rather than according to a favored manner.

• One, two, or three "A" answers indicate right-hemisphere dominance; corresponding traits include inventiveness, creativity, innovation, risk taking, whimsy, and an ability to see the "big picture."

• Seven, eight, or nine "A" answers indicate a left-hemisphere dominance—a tendency toward attention to detail, the use of logic, and traits of thoroughness and accuracy.

SOURCE: "Which Side of the Brain Do You Favor?" from *Quality Driven Designs*. Copyright 1992 Pfeiffer/Jossey-Bass. Reprinted by permission of Jossey-Bass, Inc., a subsidiary of John Wiley & Sons, Inc.

Our brains have two lateral halves (Figure 9.4). The right side is the center for creative functions, while the left side is the center for logic, detail, and planning. There are advantages to both kinds of thinking, so the ideal situation is to be "brain-lateralized" or to be able to use either logic or creativity or both, depending on the situation. There are ways to develop the side of the brain you are not accustomed to using. To develop your right side, or creative side, you can ask "what if" questions, engage in play, and

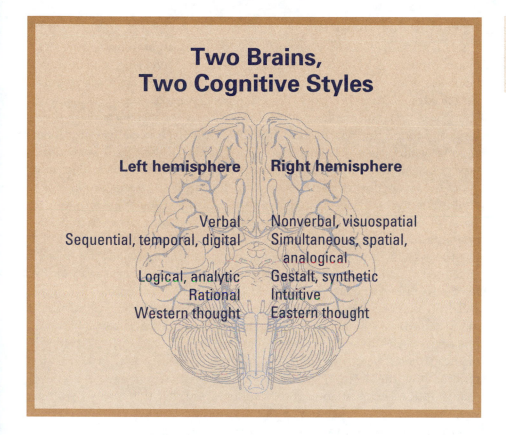

Figure 9.4
Functions of the Left and Right Brain Hemispheres

SOURCE: Based on an idea from *Left Brain, Right Brain* by Springer and Deutsch, p. 272. © 1993 by Sally P. Springer and Georg Deutsch (New York: W. H. Freeman and Company, 1993). DILBERT © UFS. Reprinted by permission.

follow your intuition. To develop the left side, you can set goals for completing tasks and work to attain these goals. For managers, it is important to see the big picture, craft a vision, and plan strategically—all of which require right-brain skills. It is equally important to be able to understand day-to-day operations and flow chart work processes, which are left-hemisphere brain skills.

Two particular individual influences that can enhance decision-making effectiveness will be highlighted next: intuition and creativity.

The Role of Intuition

intuition

A fast, positive force in decision making that is utilized at a level below consciousness and involves learned patterns of information.

There is some evidence that managers use their ***intuition*** to make decisions. Henry Mintzberg, in his work on managerial roles, found that in many cases managers do not appear to use a systematic, step-by-step approach to decision making. Rather, Mintzberg argued, managers make judgments based on "hunches."[23] Daniel Isenberg studied the way senior managers make decisions and found that intuition was used extensively, especially as a mechanism to evaluate decisions made more rationally.[24] Robert Beck studied the way managers at BankAmerica (now Bank of America) made decisions about the future direction of the company following the deregulation of the banking industry. Beck described their use of intuition as an antidote to "analysis paralysis," or the tendency to analyze decisions rather than developing innovative solutions.[25]

Just what is intuition? In Jungian theory, intuiting (N) is one preference used to gather data. This is only one way that the concept of intuition has been applied to managerial decision making, and it is perhaps the most widely researched form of the concept of intuition. There are, however, many definitions of *intuition* in the managerial literature. Chester Barnard, one of the early influential management researchers, argued that intuition's main attributes were speed and the inability of the decision maker to determine how the decision was made.[26] Other researchers have contended that intuition occurs at an unconscious level and that this is why the decision maker cannot verbalize how the decision was made.[27]

Intuition has been variously described as follows:

- The ability to know or recognize quickly and readily the possibilities of a situation.[28]
- Smooth automatic performance of learned behavior sequences.[29]
- Simply analyses frozen into habit and into the capacity for rapid response through recognition.[30]

These definitions share some common assumptions. First, there seems to be a notion that intuition is fast. Second, intuition is utilized at a level below consciousness. Third, there seems to be agreement that intuition involves learned patterns of information. Fourth, intuition appears to be a positive force in decision making.

The use of intuition may lead to more ethical decisions. Intuition allows an individual to take on another's role with ease, and role taking is a fundamental part of developing moral reasoning. You may recall from Chapter 4 the role of cognitive moral development in ethical decision making. One study found a strong link between cognitive moral development and intuition. The development of new perspectives through intuition leads to higher moral growth, and thus to more ethical decisions.[31]

One question that arises is whether managers can be taught to use their intuition. Weston Agor, who has conducted workshops on developing intuitive skills in managers, has attained positive results in organizations such as the former Tenneco and the city of Phoenix. Agor suggests relaxation techniques, using images to guide the mind, and taking creative pauses before making a decision.[32] A review of the research on intuition suggests that although intuition itself cannot be taught, managers can be trained to rely more fully on the promptings of their intuition.[33]

Intuition is an elusive concept, and one with many definitions. There is an interesting paradox regarding intuition. Some researchers view "rational" methods as preferable to intuition, yet satisfaction with a rational decision is usually determined by how the decision feels intuitively.[34] Intuition appears to have a positive effect on managerial decision making, but researchers need to agree on a common definition and conduct further research to increase our knowledge of the role of intuition at work and the influence of experience on our intuitive capabilities.

Creativity at Work

Creativity is a process influenced by individual and organizational factors that results in the production of novel and useful ideas, products, or both.[35] The social and technological changes that organizations face require creative decisions.[36] Managers of the future need to develop special competencies to deal with the turbulence of change, and one of these important competencies is the ability to promote creativity in organizations.[37]

Creativity is a process that is at least in part unconscious. The four stages of the creative process are preparation, incubation, illumination, and verification.[38] Preparation means seeking out new experiences and opportunities to learn, because creativity grows from a base of knowledge. Travel and educational opportunities of all kinds open the individual's mind. Incubation is a process of reflective thought and is often conducted subconsciously. During incubation, the individual engages in other pursuits while the mind considers the problem and works on it. Illumination occurs when the individual senses an insight for solving the problem. Finally, verification is conducted to determine if the solution or idea is valid. This is accomplished by thinking through the implications of the decision, presenting the idea to another person, or trying out the decision. Both individual and organizational influences affect the creative process.

Individual Influences Several individual variables are related to creativity. One group of factors involves the cognitive processes that creative individuals tend to use. One cognitive process is divergent thinking, meaning the individual's ability to generate several potential solutions to a

creativity
A process influenced by individual and organizational factors that results in the production of novel and useful ideas, products, or both.

Experiencing OB

Managers often emphasize creativity as an additional means of improving decision making. To learn about techniques that foster creativity in decision making, visit our animated concept and activity site. Choose Decision_Making from the "select a topic" pull-down menu, then Creativity in Decision Making from the "overview tab."

http://www.experiencingob.com

problem.[39] In addition, associational abilities and the use of imagery are associated with creativity.[40] Unconscious processes such as dreams are also essential cognitive processes related to creative thinking.[41]

Personality factors have also been related to creativity in studies of individuals from several different occupations. These characteristics include intellectual and artistic values, breadth of interests, high energy, concern with achievement, independence of judgment, intuition, self-confidence, and a creative self-image.[42] Tolerance of ambiguity, intrinsic motivation, risk taking, and a desire for recognition are also associated with creativity.[43]

There is also evidence that people who are in a good mood are more creative. One study found that individuals who were in a good mood were more successful at creative problem solving than people whose mood was neutral.[44]

Organizational Influences The organizational environment in which people work can either support creativity or impede creative efforts. Creativity killers include focusing on how work is going to be evaluated, being watched while you are working, competing with other people in win–lose situations, and having limits imposed on how you can do your work. In contrast, creativity facilitators include feelings of autonomy, being part of a team with diverse skills, and having supervisors who are creative role models.[45] High-quality, supportive relationships with supervisors are related to creativity.[46] Flexible organizational structures and participative decision making have also been associated with creativity. An organization can also present impediments to creativity. These barriers include internal political problems, harsh criticism of new ideas, destructive internal competition, and avoidance of risk.[47]

Studies of the role of organizational rewards in encouraging creativity have mixed results. Some studies have shown that monetary incentives improve creative performance, whereas others have found that material rewards do not influence innovative activity.[48] Still other studies have indicated that explicitly contracting to obtain a reward led to lower levels of creativity when compared with contracting for no reward, being presented with just the task, or being presented with the task and receiving the reward later.[49] Organizations can therefore enhance individuals' creative decision making by providing a supportive environment, participative decision making, and a flexible structure.

Individual/Organization Fit Research has indicated that creative performance is highest when there is a match, or fit, between the individual and organizational influences on creativity. For example, when individuals who desire to be creative are matched with an organization that values creative ideas, the result is more creative performance.[50]

A common mistaken assumption regarding creativity is that either you have it or you do not. Research refutes this myth and has shown that individuals can be trained to be more creative.[51] One company that has found success in this way is Frito-Lay (part of PepsiCo). Frito-Lay offers three

Challenge 9.2

Creative Problem Solving

Each of the following problems is an equation that can be solved by substituting the appropriate words for the letters. Have fun with them!

Examples: 3F = 1Y (3 feet = 1 yard.)
4LC = GL (4 leaf clover = Good luck.)

1. M + M + NH + V + C + RI = NE.
2. "1B in the H = 2 in the B."
3. 8D − 24H = 1W.
4. 3P = 6.
5. HH & MH at 12 = N or M.
6. 4J + 4Q + 4K = All the FC.
7. S & M & T & W & T & F & S are D of W.
8. A + N + AF + MC + CG = AF.
9. T = LS State.
10. 23Y − 3Y = 2D.
11. E − 8 = Z.
12. Y + 2D = T.
13. C + 6D = NYE.
14. Y − S − S − A = W.
15. A & E were in the G of E.
16. My FL and South P are both MC.
17. "NN = GN."
18. N + P + SM = S of C.
19. 1 + 6Z = 1M.
20. "R = R = R."
21. AL & JG & WM & JK were all A.
22. N + V + P + A + A + C + P + I = P of S.
23. S + H of R = USC.

(Your instructor can provide the solution to this Challenge.)

SOURCE: From *A Whack on the Side of the Head* by Roger Von Oech. Copyright © 1983, 1990, 1998 by Roger Von Oech. By permission of Warner Books.

courses in creative problem solving and trains its own trainers to hold creativity workshops within each plant. The company saved $500 million during the first six years of its creativity training effort and believes this is directly related to the employees' creative problem-solving skills.[52] Challenge 9.2 allows you to practice your own creative problem-solving skills.

Part of creativity training involves learning to open up mental locks that keep us from generating creative alternatives to a decision or problem. The following are some mental locks that diminish creativity:

- Searching for the "right" answer.
- Trying to be logical.
- Following the rules.
- Avoiding ambiguity.
- Striving for practicality.
- Being afraid to look foolish.
- Avoiding problems outside our own expertise.
- Fearing failure.
- Believing we are not really creative.
- Not making play a part of work.[53]

3. Understand the role of creativity in decision making, and practice ways to increase your own creativity.

Note that many of these mental locks stem from values within organizations. Organizations can facilitate creative decision making in many ways. Rewarding creativity, allowing employees to fail, making work more fun, and providing creativity training are a few suggestions. Also, companies can encourage creativity by exposing employees to new ideas. This can be done in several ways, including job rotation, which moves employees through different jobs and gives them exposure to different information, projects, and teams. Employees can also be assigned to work with groups outside the company, such as suppliers or consultants. Finally, managers can encourage employees to surround themselves with stimuli that they have found to enhance their creative processes. These may be music, artwork, books, or anything else that encourages creative thinking.[54]

3M consistently ranks among the top ten in *Fortune*'s annual list of most admired corporations. It earned this reputation through innovation: more than one-quarter of 3M's sales are from products less than four years old. Post-It Notes, for example, were created by a worker who wanted little adhesive papers to mark hymns for church service. He thought of another worker who had perfected a light adhesive, and the two spent their "free time" developing Post-It Notes. 3M now sells more than $100 million of them annually.

Leaders can play key roles in modeling creative behavior. Richard Branson, founder and chairman of U.K.-based Virgin Atlantic, believes that if you do not use your employees' creative potential, you are doomed to failure. At Virgin Atlantic, the culture encourages risk taking and rewards innovation. Rules and regulations are not its thing, nor is analyzing ideas to death. Branson says an employee can have an idea in the morning and implement it in the afternoon.[55]

Creativity is a global concern. Poland, for example, is undergoing a major shift from a centrally planned economy and monoparty rule to a market economy and Western-style democracy. One of the major concerns for Polish mangers is creativity. Finding ingenious solutions and having the ability to think creatively can be a question of life or death for Polish organizations, which are making the transition to a faster pace of learning and change.[56]

Japanese companies manage creativity in a much different way than do North American firms. Min Basadur visited several major Japanese companies, including Matsushita, Hitachi, and Toyota, to conduct comparative research on organizational creativity in Japan and North America. He found several differences between the two cultures. First, Japanese companies place a strong emphasis on problem finding. Companies in North America, in contrast, are more reluctant to identify problems, because rewards often go to individuals who appear not to have many problems. Furthermore, Japanese companies have a structured mechanism for encouraging problem finding. Workers are given cards on which to write down problems or areas of discontent, and these are posted on a wall. When others notice a problem that interests them, they join forces to solve it.

Another difference that Basadur found involves rewards. In North America, the motivating factor for suggestions is money. A few employees submit ideas that save a company large sums of money and reap large cash rewards. In Japan, all employees participate, and monetary rewards are small. Every suggestion gets a reward. For the Japanese, the most motivating rewards are intrinsic: accomplishment, recognition, and personal growth.[57]

Both intuition and creativity are important influences on managerial decision making. Both concepts require additional research so that managers can better understand how to use intuition and creativity, as well as how to encourage their employees to use them to make more effective decisions.

PARTICIPATION IN DECISION MAKING

Effective management of people can improve a company's economic performance. Firms that capitalize on this fact share several common practices. Chief among them is participation of employees in decision making.[58] Many companies do this through highly empowered self-managed teams like the ones we discussed in Chapter 8. Even in situations where formal teams are not feasible, decision authority can be handed down to front-line employees who have the knowledge and skills to make a difference. At Hampton Inn Hotels, for example, guest services personnel are empowered to do whatever is necessary to make guests happy—without consulting their superiors.

The Effects of Participation

Participative decision making occurs when individuals who are affected by decisions influence the making of those decisions.[59] Participation is associated with greater feelings of autonomy and meaningfulness of work.[60] In addition, participative management has been found to increase employee creativity and job satisfaction.[61] Some studies have reported a positive link between participation and productivity.[62]

Some individuals do not respond well to participative decision making. They prefer to have managers make the decisions.[63] Ralph Stayer at Johnsonville Foods learned this when he attempted to move his company toward participative management. He announced to his management team that they would be responsible for making their own decisions; yet two years after the announcement, his plan was not working. He had nurtured the managers' inability to make decisions. Stayer said, "I didn't really want them to make independent decisions. I wanted them to make the decisions I would have made." He ended up replacing three top managers with people who could not read his mind and who were strong enough to call his bluff.[64]

As our economy becomes increasingly based on knowledge work, and as new technologies make it easier for decentralized decision makers to connect, participative decision making will undoubtedly increase.[65] These

participative decision making
Decision making in which individuals who are affected by decisions influence the making of those decisions.

individuals can combine information from anywhere in the world with their own organizational experience and creativity.

Foundations for Participation and Empowerment

Organizational and individual foundations underlie empowerment that enhances task motivation and performance. The organizational foundations for empowerment include a participative, supportive organizational culture and a team-oriented work design. A supportive work environment is essential because of the uncertainty that empowerment can cause within the organization. Empowerment requires that lower-level organizational members be able to make decisions and take action on those decisions. As operational employees become empowered to make decisions, real fear, anxiety, or even terror can be created among middle managers in the organization.[66] Senior leadership must create an organizational culture that is supportive and reassuring for these middle managers as the power dynamics of the system change. If not supported and reassured, the middle managers can become a restraining, disruptive force to participative decision-making efforts.

A second organizational foundation for empowerment concerns the design of work. The old factory system relied on work specialization and narrow tasks with the intent of achieving routinized efficiency.[67] This approach to the design of work had some economic advantages, but it also had some distressing disadvantages leading to monotony and fatigue. This approach to the design of work is inconsistent with participation, because the individual feels absolved of much responsibility for a whole piece of work. Team-oriented work designs are a key organizational foundation, because they lead to broader tasks and a greater sense of responsibility. For example, Volvo builds cars using a team-oriented work design in which each person does many different tasks, and each person has direct responsibility for the finished product.[68] These work designs create a context for effective participation so long as the empowered individuals meet necessary individual prerequisites.

The three individual prerequisites for participation and empowerment are (1) the capability to become psychologically involved in participative activities, (2) the motivation to act autonomously, and (3) the capacity to see the relevance of participation for one's own well-being.[69] First, people must be psychologically equipped to become involved in participative activities if they are to be empowered and become effective team members. Not all people are so predisposed. For example, Germany has an authoritarian tradition that runs counter to participation and empowerment at the individual and group level. General Motors encountered significant difficulties implementing quality circles in its German plants, because workers expected to be directed by supervisors, not to engage in participative problem solving. The German efforts to establish supervisory/worker boards in corporations is an effort to alter this authoritarian tradition.

A second individual prerequisite is the motivation to act autonomously. People with dependent personalities are predisposed to be told what to do and to rely on external motivation rather than internal, intrinsic motivation.[70] These dependent people are not effective contributors to decision making.

Finally, if participative decision making is to work, people must be able to see how it provides a personal benefit to them. The personal payoff for the individual need not be short term. It may be a long-term benefit that results in people receiving greater rewards through enhanced organizational profitability.

What Level of Participation?

Participative decision making is complex, and one of the things managers must understand is that employees can be involved in some, or all, of the stages of the decision-making process. For example, employees could be variously involved in identifying problems, generating alternatives, selecting solutions, planning implementations, or evaluating results. Research shows that greater involvement in all five of these stages has a cumulative effect. Employees who are involved in all five processes have higher satisfaction and performance levels. And, all decision processes are not created equal. If employees can't be provided with full participation in all stages, the highest payoffs seem to come with involvement in generating alternatives, planning implementations, and evaluating results.[71] Styles of participation in decision making may need to change as the company grows, or as its culture changes.

THE GROUP DECISION-MAKING PROCESS

Managers use groups to make decisions for several reasons. One is *synergy*, which occurs when group members stimulate new solutions to problems through the process of mutual influence and encouragement within the group. Another reason for using a group is to gain commitment to a decision. Groups also bring more knowledge and experience to the problem-solving situation.

synergy
A positive force that occurs in groups when group members stimulate new solutions to problems through the process of mutual influence and encouragement within the group.

Group decisions can sometimes be predicted by comparing the views of the initial group members with the final group decision. These simple relationships are known as *social decision schemes*. One social decision scheme is the majority-wins rule, in which the group supports whatever position is taken by the majority of its members. Another scheme, the truth-wins rule, predicts that the correct decision will emerge as an increasing number of members realize its appropriateness. The two-thirds-majority rule means that the decision favored by two-thirds or more of the members is supported. Finally, the first-shift rule states that members support a decision represented by the first shift in opinion shown by a member.

social decision schemes
Simple rules used to determine final group decisions.

Research indicates that these social decision schemes can predict a group decision as much as 80 percent of the time.[72] Current research is aimed at discovering which rules are used in particular types of tasks. For example, studies indicate that the majority-wins rule is used most often in judgment tasks (that is, when the decision is a matter of preference or opinion), whereas the truth-wins rule predicts decisions best when the task is an intellective one (that is, when the decision has a correct answer).[73]

Advantages and Disadvantages of Group Decision Making

Both advantages and disadvantages are associated with group decision making. The advantages include (1) more knowledge and information through the pooling of group member resources; (2) increased acceptance of, and commitment to, the decision, because the members had a voice in it; and (3) greater understanding of the decision, because members were involved in the various stages of the decision process. The disadvantages of group decision making include (1) pressure within the group to conform and fit in; (2) domination of the group by one forceful member or a dominant clique, who may ramrod the decision; and (3) the amount of time required, because a group makes decisions more slowly than an individual.[74]

Given these advantages and disadvantages, should an individual or a group make a decision? Substantial empirical research indicates that whether a group or an individual should be used depends on the type of task involved. For judgment tasks requiring an estimate or a prediction, groups are usually superior to individuals because of the breadth of experience that multiple individuals bring to the problem.[75] On tasks that have a correct solution, other studies have indicated that the most competent individual outperforms the group.[76] This finding has been called into question, however. Much of the previous research on groups was conducted in the laboratory, where group members interacted only for short periods of time. Researchers wanted to know how a longer experience in the group would affect decisions. Their study showed that groups who worked together for longer periods of time outperformed the most competent member 70 percent of the time. As groups gained experience, the best members became less important to the group's success.[77] This study demonstrated that experience in the group is an important variable to consider when evaluating the individual versus group decision-making question.

Given the emphasis on teams in the workplace, many managers believe that groups produce better decisions than do individuals, yet the evidence is mixed. It is evident that more research needs to be conducted in organizational settings to help answer this question.

Two potential liabilities are found in group decision making: groupthink and group polarization. These problems are discussed in the following sections.

Groupthink

One liability of a cohesive group is its tendency to develop **groupthink**, a dysfunctional process. Irving Janis, the originator of the groupthink con-

---

4. Identify the advantages and disadvantages of group decision making.

Experiencing OB

There are both advantages and disadvantages to group decision making, and managers must know what action to take when group decision making is a possibility. Examine some ideas about group decision making at our animated concept and activity site. Choose Decision_Making from the "select a topic" pull-down menu, then Group Decision Making from the "overview tab."

http://www.experiencingob.com

groupthink
A deterioration of mental efficiency, reality testing, and moral judgment resulting from in-group pressures.

cept, describes groupthink as "a deterioration of mental efficiency, reality testing, and moral judgment" resulting from in-group pressures.[78]

Certain conditions favor the development of groupthink. One of the antecedents is high cohesiveness. Cohesive groups tend to favor solidarity because members identify strongly with the group.[79] Other antecedents include directive leadership, high stress, insulation of the group, and lack of methodical procedures for developing and evaluating alternatives. Two other conditions that encourage groupthink are having to make a highly consequential decision and time constraints.[80] A highly consequential decision is one that will have a great impact on the group members and on outside parties. When group members feel that they have a limited time in which to make a decision, they may rush through the process. These antecedents cause members to prefer concurrence in decisions and to fail to evaluate one another's suggestions critically. A group suffering from groupthink shows recognizable symptoms. Table 9.1 presents these symptoms and makes suggestions on how to avoid groupthink.

An incident that has been examined for these symptoms of groupthink is the space shuttle *Challenger* disaster. On January 28, 1986, seventy-three seconds into its flight, the *Challenger* exploded, killing all seven members of its crew. The evidence pointed toward an O-ring seal that was still cold from nighttime temperatures and failed to do its job. A presidential commission was convened, and its investigation cited flawed decision making as a primary cause of the accident.

An analysis of the *Challenger* incident indicated that the negative symptoms of groupthink increased during the twenty-four hours prior to the decision to launch the spacecraft.[81] National Aeronautics and Space Administration (NASA) management officials were warned by engineers that the launch should be canceled because the O-rings would not withstand the temperatures. The engineers were pressured by their bosses to stifle their dissent, and their opinions were devalued. Further, the decision to launch was made by polling managers—engineers were not polled. The decision makers were overconfident because of NASA's record of success. Some managers knew that a redesign of the rocket casings had been ordered, but this information was withheld from other decision makers.

Consequences of groupthink include an incomplete survey of alternatives, failure to evaluate the risks of the preferred course of action, biased information processing, and a failure to work out contingency plans. The overall result of groupthink is defective decision making. This was evident in the *Challenger* situation. The group considered only two alternatives: launch or no launch. They failed to consider the risks of their decision to launch the shuttle, and they did not develop any contingency plans.

Table 9.1 presents Janis's guidelines for avoiding groupthink. Many of these suggestions center around the notion of ensuring that decisions are evaluated completely, with opportunities for discussion from all group members. This strategy helps encourage members to evaluate one another's ideas critically.

5. Discuss the symptoms of groupthink and ways to prevent it.

Symptoms of Groupthink

- *Illusions of invulnerability*. Group members feel they are above criticism. This symptom leads to excessive optimism and risk taking.
- *Illusions of group morality*. Group members feel they are moral in their actions and therefore above reproach. This symptom leads the group to ignore the ethical implications of their decisions.
- *Illusions of unanimity*. Group members believe there is unanimous agreement on the decisions. Silence is misconstrued as consent.
- *Rationalization*. Group members concoct explanations for their decisions to make them appear rational and correct. The results are that other alternatives are not considered, and there is an unwillingness to reconsider the group's assumptions.
- *Stereotyping the enemy*. Competitors are stereotyped as evil or stupid. This leads the group to underestimate its opposition.
- *Self-censorship*. Members do not express their doubts or concerns about the course of action. This prevents critical analysis of the decisions.
- *Peer pressure*. Any members who express doubts or concerns are pressured by other group members, who question their loyalty.
- *Mindguards*. Some members take it upon themselves to protect the group from negative feedback. Group members are thus shielded from information that might lead them to question their actions.

Guidelines for Preventing Groupthink

- Ask each group member to assume the role of the critical evaluator who actively voices objections or doubts.
- Have the leader avoid stating his or her position on the issue prior to the group decision.
- Create several groups that work on the decision simultaneously.
- Bring in outside experts to evaluate the group process.
- Appoint a devil's advocate to question the group's course of action consistently.
- Evaluate the competition carefully, posing as many different motivations and intentions as possible.
- Once consensus is reached, encourage the group to rethink its position by reexamining the alternatives.

Table 9.1
Symptoms of Groupthink and How to Prevent It

SOURCE: Janis, Irving L., *Groupthink: Psychological Studies of Policy Decisions and Fiascoes*, Second Edition. Copyright © 1982 by Houghton Mifflin Company. Used with permission.

Janis has used the groupthink framework to conduct historical analyses of several political and military fiascoes, including the Bay of Pigs invasion, the Vietnam War, and Watergate. One review of the decision situation in the *Challenger* incident proposed that two variables, time and leadership style, are important to include.[82] When a decision must be made quickly, there is more potential for groupthink. Leadership style can either promote groupthink (if the leader makes his or her opinion known up front) or avoid groupthink (if the leader encourages open and frank discussion).

There are few empirical studies of groupthink, and most of these involved students in a laboratory setting. More applied research may be seen in the future, however, as a questionnaire has been developed to measure the constructs associated with groupthink.[83] Janis's work on groupthink has led to several interdisciplinary efforts at understanding policy decisions.[84] The work underscores the need to examine multiple explanations for failed decisions.

Group Polarization

Another group phenomenon was discovered by a graduate student. His study showed that groups made riskier decisions; in fact, the group and each individual accepted greater levels of risk following a group discussion of the issue. Subsequent studies uncovered another shift—toward caution. Thus, group discussion produced shifts both toward more risky positions and toward more cautious positions.[85] Further research revealed that individual group member attitudes simply became more extreme following group discussion. Individuals who were initially against an issue became more radically opposed, and individuals who were in favor of the issue became more strongly supportive following discussion. These shifts came to be known as *group polarization*.[86]

The tendency toward polarization has important implications for group decision making. Groups whose initial views lean a certain way can be expected to adopt more extreme views following interaction.

Several ideas have been proposed to explain why group polarization occurs. One explanation is the social comparison approach. Prior to group discussion, individuals believe they hold better views than the other members. During group discussion, they see that their views are not so far from average, so they shift to more extreme positions.[87] A second explanation is the persuasive arguments view. It contends that group discussion reinforces the initial views of the members, so they take a more extreme position.[88] Both explanations are supported by research. It may be that both processes, along with others, cause the group to develop more polarized attitudes.

Group polarization leads groups to adopt extreme attitudes. In some cases, this can be disastrous. For instance, if individuals are leaning toward a dangerous decision, they are likely to support it more strongly following discussion. Both groupthink and group polarization are potential liabilities of group decision making, but several techniques can be used to help prevent or control these two liabilities.

group polarization
The tendency for group discussion to produce shifts toward more extreme attitudes among members.

TECHNIQUES FOR GROUP DECISION MAKING

Once a manager has determined that a group decision approach should be used, he or she can determine the technique that is best suited to the decision situation. Seven techniques will be briefly summarized: brainstorming, nominal group technique, Delphi technique, devil's advocacy, dialectical inquiry, quality circles and quality teams, and self-managed teams.

6. Evaluate the strengths and weaknesses of several group decision-making techniques.

Brainstorming

Brainstorming is a good technique for generating alternatives. The idea behind *brainstorming* is to generate as many ideas as possible, suspending

brainstorming
A technique for generating as many ideas as possible on a given subject, while suspending evaluation until all the ideas have been suggested.

evaluation until all of the ideas have been suggested. Participants are encouraged to build upon the suggestions of others, and imagination is emphasized. Groups that use brainstorming have been shown to produce significantly more ideas than groups that do not.[89] Evidence suggests, however, that group brainstorming is less effective than a comparable number of individuals working alone.[90]

One recent trend is the use of electronic brainstorming instead of verbal brainstorming in groups. Electronic brainstorming overcomes two common problems that can produce group brainstorming failure: production blocking and evaluation apprehension. In verbal brainstorming, individuals are exposed to the inputs of others. While listening to others, individuals are distracted from their own ideas. This is referred to as production blocking. When ideas are recorded electronically, participants are free from hearing the interruptions of others; thus, production blocking is reduced. Some individuals suffer from evaluation apprehension in brainstorming groups. They fear that others might respond negatively to their ideas. In electronic brainstorming, input is anonymous, so evaluation apprehension is reduced. Studies indicate that anonymous electronic brainstorming groups outperform face-to-face brainstorming groups in the number of ideas generated.[91]

Nominal Group Technique

nominal group technique (NGT)
A structured approach to group decision making that focuses on generating alternatives and choosing one.

A structured approach to decision making that focuses on generating alternatives and choosing one is called *nominal group technique (NGT)*. NGT involves the following discrete steps:

1. Individuals silently list their ideas.
2. Ideas are written on a chart one at a time until all ideas are listed.
3. Discussion is permitted, but only to clarify the ideas. No criticism is allowed.
4. A written vote is taken.

NGT is a good technique to use in a situation where group members fear criticism from others.[92]

Delphi Technique

Delphi technique
Gathering the judgments of experts for use in decision making.

The *Delphi technique*, which originated at the Rand Corporation, involves gathering the judgments of experts for use in decision making. Experts at remote locations respond to a questionnaire. A coordinator summarizes the responses to the questionnaire, and the summary is sent back to the experts. The experts then rate the various alternatives generated, and the coordinator tabulates the results. The Delphi technique is valuable in its ability to generate a number of independent judgments without the requirement of a face-to-face meeting.[93]

Devil's Advocacy

devil's advocacy
A technique for preventing groupthink in which a group or individual is given the role of critic during decision making.

In the *devil's advocacy* decision method, a group or individual is given the role of critic. This devil's advocate has the task of coming up with the potential problems of a proposed decision. This helps organizations avoid costly mistakes in decision making by identifying potential pitfalls in advance.[94] As we discussed in Chapter 8, a devil's advocate who challenges the CEO and top management team can help sustain the vitality and performance of the upper echelon.

Dialectical Inquiry

Dialectical inquiry is essentially a debate between two opposing sets of recommendations. Although it sets up a conflict, it is a constructive approach, because it brings out the benefits and limitations of both sets of ideas.[95] When using this technique, it is important to guard against a win–lose attitude and to concentrate on reaching the most effective solution for all concerned. Research has shown that the way a decision is framed (that is, win–win versus win–lose) is very important. A decision's outcome could be viewed as a gain or a loss, depending on the way the decision is framed.[96]

Quality Circles and Quality Teams

As you recall from Chapter 8, quality circles are small groups that voluntarily meet to provide input for solving quality or production problems. Quality circles are also a way of extending participative decision making into teams. Managers often listen to recommendations from quality circles and implement the suggestions. The rewards for the suggestions are intrinsic—involvement in the decision-making process is the primary reward.

Quality circles are often generated from the bottom up; that is, they provide advice to managers, who still retain decision-making authority. As such, quality circles are not empowered to implement their own recommendations. They operate in parallel fashion to the organization's structure, and they rely on voluntary participation.[97] In Japan, quality circles have been integrated into the organization instead of added on. This may be one reason for Japan's success with this technique. In contrast, the U.S. experience is not as positive. It has been estimated that 60 to 75 percent of the quality circles have failed. Reasons for the failures have included lack of top management support and lack of problem-solving skills among quality circle members.[98]

Quality teams, in contrast, are included in total quality management and other quality improvement efforts as part of a change in the organization's structure. Quality teams are generated from the top down and are empowered to act on their own recommendations. Whereas quality circles emphasize the generation of ideas, quality teams make data-based decisions about improving product and service quality. Various decision-making techniques are employed in quality teams. Brainstorming, flow charts, and cause-and-effect diagrams help pinpoint problems that affect quality.

Some organizations have moved toward quality teams, but Toyota has stuck with quality circles. The company has used them since 1963 and was the second company in the world to do so. Toyota's quality circles constitute

dialectical inquiry
A debate between two opposing sets of recommendations.

a limited form of empowerment—and they like it that way. The members want to participate but don't have the desire to be self-directed. They would rather leave certain decisions to managers, who are trusted to take good care of them. Toyota attributes its success with quality circles to the longevity of their use and to its view of them as true methods of participation.[99]

Quality circles and quality teams are methods for using groups in the decision-making process. Self-managed teams take the concept of participation one step further.

Self-Managed Teams

Another group decision-making method is the use of self-managed teams, which we also discussed in Chapter 8. The decision-making activities of self-managed teams are more broadly focused than those of quality circles and quality teams, which usually emphasize quality and production problems. Self-managed teams make many of the decisions that were once reserved for managers, such as work scheduling, job assignments, and staffing. Unlike quality circles, whose role is an advisory one, self-managed teams are delegated authority in the organization's decision-making process.

Many organizations have claimed success with self-managed teams. At Northern Telecom (now Nortel Networks), revenues rose 63 percent and sales increased 26 percent following the implementation of self-managed teams.[100] Preliminary research evidence is also encouraging. An analysis of seventy studies concluded that self-managed teams positively affected productivity and attitudes toward self-management. However, the analysis indicated no significant effects of self-managed teams on job satisfaction, absenteeism, or turnover.[101]

Self-managed teams, like any cohesive group, can fall victim to groupthink. The key to stimulating innovation and better problem solving in these groups is welcoming dissent among members. Dissent breaks down complacency and sets in motion a process that results in better decisions. Team members must know that dissent is permissible so that they won't fear embarrassment or ridicule.[102] Before choosing a group decision-making technique, the manager should carefully evaluate the group members and the decision situation. Then the best method for accomplishing the objectives of the group decision-making process can be selected. If the goal is generating a large number of alternatives, for example, brainstorming would be a good choice. If group members are reluctant to contribute ideas, the nominal group technique would be appropriate. The need for expert input would be best facilitated by the Delphi technique. To guard against groupthink, devil's advocacy or dialectical inquiry would be effective. Decisions that concern quality or production would benefit from the advice of quality circles or the empowered decisions of quality teams. Finally, a manager who wants to provide total empowerment to a group should consider self-managed teams.

CULTURAL ISSUES IN DECISION MAKING

Styles of decision making vary greatly among cultures. Many of the dimensions proposed by Hofstede that were presented in Chapter 2 affect decision making. Uncertainty avoidance, for example, can affect the way people view decisions. In the United States, a culture with low uncertainty avoidance, decisions are seen as opportunities for change. In contrast, cultures such as those of Indonesia and Malaysia attempt to accept situations as they are rather than to change them.[103] Power distance also affects decision making. In more hierarchical cultures, such as India, top-level managers make decisions. In countries with low power distance, lower level employees make many decisions. The Swedish culture exemplifies this type.

The individualist/collectivist dimension has implications for decision making. Japan, with its collectivist emphasis, favors group decisions. The United States has a more difficult time with group decisions because it is an individualistic culture. Time orientation affects the frame of reference of the decision. In China, with its long-term view, decisions are made with the future in mind. In the United States, many decisions are made considering only the short term.

The masculine/feminine dimension can be compared to the Jungian thinking/feeling preferences for decision making. Masculine cultures, as in many Latin American countries, value quick, assertive decisions. Feminine cultures, as in many Scandinavian countries, value decisions that reflect concern for others.

Managers should learn as much as possible about the decision processes in other cultures. NAFTA, for example, has eliminated many barriers to trade with Mexico. In Mexican organizations, decision-making authority is centralized, autocratic, and retained in small groups of top managers. As a consequence, Mexican employees are reluctant to participate in decision making and often wait to be told what to do rather than take a risk. In addition, joint ventures with family-owned *grupos* (large groups of businesses) can be challenging. It may be difficult to identify the critical decision maker in the family and to determine how much decision-making authority is held by the *grupo's* family board.[104]

TECHNOLOGICAL AIDS TO DECISION MAKING

Many computerized decision tools are available to managers. These systems can be used to support the decision-making process in organizations.

7. Describe the effects that expert systems and group decision support systems have on decision-making organizations.

Expert Systems

Artificial intelligence is used to develop an expert system, which is a programmed decision tool. The system is set up using decision rules, and the effectiveness of the expert system is highly dependent on its design. Because expert systems are sources of knowledge and experience and not just passive software, the organization must decide who is responsible for the decisions made by expert systems. Organizations must therefore be concerned about the liability for using the recommendations of expert systems.

Campbell Soup Company, like other organizations in the food industry, faces intense competition. Production downtime must be minimized. One particular problem Campbell Soup faced was that its hydrostatic canned food product sterilizers, seventy feet tall and packed with equipment, incurred a lot of downtime because of malfunctions, which affected the bottom line. The pending retirement of the company's forty-four-year veteran expert diagnostician forced Campbell to do something before his expertise walked out the door with him. The company enlisted the help of Texas Instruments to design an expert system that would "clone" the diagnostician's expertise.

The design team watched the diagnostician perform his job and conducted extensive interviews with him over a period of several weeks. From his expertise, a series of rules was devised and built into the expert system. TI's project team used knowledge of engineering and careful selection of expert system hardware and software to develop "COOKER." The expert system reduced equipment downtime from days to hours.[105]

Expert systems hold great potential for affecting managerial decisions. Thus, managers must carefully scrutinize the expert system rather than simply accepting its decisions.

Decision Support Systems

Managers use decision support systems (DSS) as tools to enhance their ability to make complex decisions. DSS are computer and communication systems that process incoming data and synthesize pertinent information for managers to use. One example is the Fire Management Information System (FMIS) developed by a team of five partners from companies representing four European countries. Fire managers who are in charge of emergencies are bombarded with information and stress as situations change. The team sought to design a system that would help the fire managers in their decision-making tasks during forest fires. Although emergencies can take different forms, managers do not require radically different plans for dealing with them. This makes it possible to develop and store skeletal plans that can be accessed using the DSS instead of starting from scratch with each forest fire.

The team combined five decision support services in putting together the system:

- Weather monitoring synthesized information from remote meteorological stations.
- Fire risk rating assessed risk using an expert system.
- Fighting adviser proposed plans for preventing and fighting the fire.

- Fire detection used a network of imaging sensors for early detection of fires.
- Fire modeling simulated the fire's pattern and spread, taking into account vegetation, topography, and weather.

The fire manager uses the system in two modes. In standby mode, the system constantly updates databases and maps. In operational mode, the fire manager navigates through different functions when an emergency arises. In this way, the FMIS integrates all the decision support tools the manager needs to make the quick decisions needed to fight forest fires.[106]

Group Decision Support Systems

Another tool for decision making focuses on helping groups make decisions. A group decision support system (GDSS) uses computer support and communication facilities to support group decision-making processes in either face-to-face meetings or dispersed meetings. The GDSS has been shown to affect conflict management within a group by depersonalizing the issue and by forcing the group to discuss its conflict management process.[107] It has been suggested that team decisions should improve by using a GDSS, because the use of software pushes team members to structure a decision that otherwise would have been made ad hoc.[108]

Boeing is one company that has seen the benefits of GDSS. By using new network software called *groupware*, Boeing has reduced the time needed to complete team projects by 91 percent. The company was interested in groupware because of its experience in team meetings: 20 percent of the members did 80 percent of the talking, and potentially valuable team members kept quiet. Groupware eliminated the problem. Meetings are now held in a conference room with a computer at every place. Everyone can speak at once via the computer. Ideas accumulate on each screen, and comments are anonymous, which encourages even shy team members to contribute.[109]

The success of GDSS as an aid to decision making depends on a number of factors. Organizations in which people are open to change and in which managers attach importance to flexible and creative decision processes are more likely to benefit. Evidence also shows that a GDSS that encourages full participation and promotes raising questions and expressing concerns is more likely to be successful. Further, managers should carefully consider the group's size and the type of task in planning for a GDSS. In the initial stages of decision making, such as generating alternatives, larger groups may work well with a GDSS. For more complex problem solving and choice making, however, small groups (fifteen members or fewer) are more effective.[110]

The effects of GDSS need further investigation. In a study that involved making investment decisions, minority opinion holders expressed their views most frequently using a GDSS. However, these minority views were more influential under face-to-face communication. This means that GDSS may facilitate the expression of minority viewpoints, but GDSS may also diminish their influence on group decisions.[111]

Decision Making in the Virtual Workplace

Managers today are working in flexible organizations—so flexible in fact that many workplaces are unconstrained by geography, time, and organizational boundaries. Virtual teams are emerging as a new form of working arrangement. Virtual teams are groups of geographically dispersed coworkers who work together using a combination of telecommunications and information technologies to accomplish a task. Virtual teams seldom meet face to face, and membership often shifts according to the project at hand.

How are decisions made in virtual teams? These teams require advanced technologies for communication and decision making. Three basic technologies aid virtual teams in decision making: desktop videoconferencing systems (DVCS); group decision support systems (GDSS), as described in the previous section; and Internet/intranet systems.[112]

Desktop videoconferencing systems are the major technologies that form the basis for other virtual team technologies. DVCS re-create the face-to-face interactions of teams and go one step beyond by supporting more complex levels of communication among virtual team members. Small cameras on top of computer monitors provide video feeds, and voice transmissions are made possible through earpieces and microphones. High-speed data connections are used for communication. All team members can be connected, and outside experts can even be added. A local group can connect with up to fifteen different individuals or groups. Users can simultaneously work on documents, analyze data, or map out ideas.

GDSS make real-time decision making possible in the virtual team. They are ideal systems for brainstorming, focus groups, and group decisions. By using support tools within the GDSS, users can turn off their individual identities and interact with anonymity, and can poll participants and assemble statistical information relevant to the decision being made. GDSS are thus the sophisticated software that makes collaboration possible in virtual teams.

Internal internets, or intranets, are adaptations of Internet technologies for use within a company. For virtual teams, the Internet and intranets can be rich communication and decision-making resources. These tools allow virtual teams to archive text, visual, audio, and data files for use in decision making. They permit virtual teams to inform other organization members about the team's progress and enable the team to monitor other projects within the organization.

By using DVCS, GDSS, and Internet/intranet technologies, virtual teams can capitalize on a rich communications environment for decision making. It is difficult, however, to duplicate the face-to-face environment. The effectiveness of a virtual team's decision making depends on its members' ability to use the tools that are available. Collaborative systems can enhance virtual teams' decision quality if they are used well.[113]

ETHICAL ISSUES IN DECISION MAKING

One criterion that should be applied to decision making is the ethical implications of the decision. Ethical decision making in organizations is influenced by many factors, including individual differences and organizational rewards and punishments.

Kenneth Blanchard and Norman Vincent Peale proposed an "ethics check" for decision makers in their book *The Power of Ethical Management*.[114] They contend that the decision maker should ponder three questions:

1. Is it legal? (Will I be violating the law or company policy?)

2. Is it balanced? (Is it fair to all concerned in the short term and long term? Does it promote win–win relationships?)

3. How will it make me feel about myself? (Will it make me proud of my actions? How will I feel when others become aware of the decision?)

Groups can also make decisions that are unethical. Beech-Nut, for example, admitted selling millions of jars of "phony" apple juice that contained cheap, adulterated concentrate. Groupthink may have been responsible for this unethical decision. Beech-Nut was losing money, and its managers believed that other companies were selling fake juice. They were convinced that their fake juice was safe for consumers and that no laboratory test could conclusively distinguish real juice from artificial ingredients. Normally a reputable company, Beech-Nut ignored caution and conscience in favor of bottom-line mentality, ignored dissent, and thus suffered damage to its reputation because of unethical practices.[115]

Unethical group decisions like the one at Beech-Nut can be prevented by using the techniques for overcoming groupthink. Appointing a devil's advocate who constantly questions the group's course of action can help bring ethical issues to the surface. Setting up a dialectical inquiry between two subgroups can head off unethical decisions by leading the group to question its course of action.

In summary, all decisions, whether made by individuals or by groups, must be evaluated for their ethics. Organizations should reinforce ethical decision making among employees by encouraging and rewarding it. Socialization processes should convey to newcomers the ethical standards of behavior in the organization. Groups should use devil's advocates and dialectical methods to reduce the potential for groupthink and the unethical decisions that may result. Effective and ethical decisions are not mutually exclusive.

8. Utilize an "ethics check" for examining managerial decisions.

MANAGERIAL IMPLICATIONS: DECISION MAKING IS A CRITICAL ACTIVITY

Decision making is important at all levels of every organization. At times managers may have the luxury of optimizing (selecting the best alternative), but more often they are forced to satisfice (select the alternative that is good enough). And, at times, the decision process can even seem unpredictable and random.

Individuals differ in their preferences for risk, as well as in their styles of gathering information and making judgments. Understanding individual differences can help managers maximize strengths in employee decision styles and build teams that capitalize on strengths. Creativity is one such strength. It can be encouraged by providing employees with a supportive environment that nourishes innovative ideas. Creativity training has been used in some organizations with positive results.

Some decisions are best made by individuals and some by teams or groups. The task of the manager is to diagnose the situation and implement the appropriate level of participation. To do this effectively, managers should know the advantages and disadvantages of various group decision-making techniques and should minimize the potential for groupthink. Finally, decisions made by individuals or groups should be analyzed to see whether they are ethical.

Looking Back

Starbucks Makes the Chicago Decision Work

In 1990, Starbucks hired Howard Behar to run its retail operations. In Chicago, experienced managers were hired, and prices were raised to reflect the higher rents and labor charges in Chicago. The first store in Chicago was a disaster because it faced the street. To operate successfully in Chicago's Loop, a store must open into a lobby. In cold and windy Chicago winters, no one will wait outside for a cup of coffee. The Loop store was shut down, but the other Starbucks stores remained open.

Part of the problem was simply time. Starbucks took a while to develop a critical mass of customers in Chicago who liked its taste profile. Many customers switched from drip coffee, which they deemed too strong, to cappuccinos and caffe lattes, which were more appealing on first taste. Today, Starbucks is so popular that many Chicagoans think it is a local company.

Howard Schultz's decision was a risky one that finally paid off. He hung on to the decision in the face of discouraging words from experts and financial losses. What made the decision work was not only perseverance, but also follow-through in analyzing why the Chicago operations were not working and taking steps to make things right.

CHAPTER SUMMARY

1. Bounded rationality assumes that there are limits to how rational managers can be.

2. The garbage can model shows that under high uncertainty, decision making in organizations can be an unsystematic process.

3. Jung's cognitive styles can be used to help explain individual differences in gathering information and evaluating alternatives.

4. Intuition and creativity are positive influences on decision making and should be encouraged in organizations.

5. Empowerment and teamwork require specific organizational design elements and individual characteristics and skills.

6. Techniques such as brainstorming, nominal group technique, Delphi technique, devil's advocacy, dialectical inquiry, quality circles and teams, and self-managed teams can help managers reap the benefits of group methods while limiting the possibilities of groupthink and group polarization.

7. Technology is providing assistance to managerial decision making, especially through expert systems and group decision support systems. More research is needed to determine the effects of these technologies.

8. Managers should carefully weigh the ethical issues surrounding decisions and encourage ethical decision making throughout the organization.

KEY TERMS

programmed decision   247

nonprogrammed decision   247

effective decision   248

rationality   249

bounded rationality   249

satisfice   249

heuristics   249

garbage can model   250

risk aversion   252

escalation of commitment   252

cognitive style   253

intuition   258

creativity   259

participative decision making   263

synergy   265

social decision schemes   265

groupthink   266

group polarization   269

brainstorming   269

nominal group technique (NGT)   270

Delphi technique   270

devil's advocacy   270

dialectical inquiry   271

REVIEW QUESTIONS

1. Compare the garbage can model with the bounded rationality model. Compare the usefulness of these models in today's organizations.

2. List and describe Jung's four cognitive styles. How does the Z problem-solving model capitalize on the strengths of the four preferences?

3. What are the individual and organizational influences on creativity?

4. What are the organizational foundations of empowerment and teamwork? The individual foundations?

5. Describe the advantages and disadvantages of group decision making.

6. Describe the symptoms of groupthink, and identify actions that can be taken to prevent it.

7. What techniques can be used to improve group decisions?

DISCUSSION AND COMMUNICATION QUESTIONS

1. Why is identification of the real problem the first and most important step in the decision-making process? How does attribution theory explain mistakes that can be made as managers and employees work together to explain why the problem occurred?

2. How can organizations effectively manage both risk taking and escalation of commitment in the decision-making behavior of employees?

3. How will you most likely make decisions based on your cognitive style? What might you overlook using your preferred approach?

4. How can organizations encourage creative decision making?

5. What are some organizations that use expert systems? Group decision support systems? How will these two technologies affect managerial decision making?

6. How do the potential risks associated with participating in quality circles differ from those associated with participating in quality teams? If you were a member of a quality circle, how would management's decisions to reject your recommendations affect your motivation to participate?

7. (communication question) Form a team of four persons. Find two examples of recent decisions made in organizations: one that you consider a good decision, and one that you consider a bad decision. Two members should work on the good decision, and two on the bad decision. Each pair should write a brief description of the decision. Then write a summary of what went right, what went wrong, and what could be done to improve the decision process. Compare and contrast your two examples in a presentation to the class.

8. (comunication question) Reflect on your own experiences in groups with groupthink. Describe the situation in which you encountered groupthink, the symptoms that were present, and the outcome. What remedies for groupthink would you prescribe? Summarize your answers in a memo to your instructor.

ETHICS QUESTIONS

1. Think of a decision made by a group that you feel was an unethical one. What factors led to the unethical decision? Evaluate whether groupthink may have been a factor by examining the antecedents, symptoms, and consequences of groupthink.

2. How can organizations encourage ethical decision making?

3. How do cultural differences affect ethical decision making?

4. Describe groupthink as an ethical problem.

5. Whose responsibility is it to ensure that employees make ethical decisions?

6. Using the "ethics check," evaluate the decision to launch the *Challenger*. How could a knowledge of ethical decision making have aided the individuals who made this decision?

Experiential Exercises

9.1 Making a Layoff Decision

Purpose

In this exercise, you will examine how to weigh a set of facts and make a difficult personnel decision about laying off valued employees during a time of financial hardship. You will also examine your own values and criteria used in the decision-making process.

The Problem

Walker Space (WSI) is a medium-sized firm located in Connecticut. The firm essentially has been a subcontractor on many large space contracts that have been acquired by firms like Alliant Techsystems and others.

With the cutback in many of the National Aeronautics and Space Administration programs, Walker has an excess of employees. Stuart Tartaro, the head of one of the sections, has been told by his superior that he must reduce his section of engineers from nine to six. He is looking at the following summaries of their vitae and pondering how he will make this decision:

1. *Roger Allison*, age twenty-six, married, two children. Allison has been with WSI for a year and a half. He is a very good engineer, with a degree from Rensselaer Polytech. He has held two prior jobs and lost both of them because of cutbacks in the space program. He moved to Connecticut from California to take this job. Allison is well liked by his coworkers.

2. *Dave Jones*, age twenty-four, single. Jones is an African American, and the company looked hard to get him because of affirmative action pressure. He is not very popular with his coworkers. Because he has been employed less than a year, not too much is known about his work. On his one evaluation (which was average), Jones accused his supervisor of bias against African Americans. He is a graduate of the Detroit Institute of Technology.

3. *William Foster*, age fifty-three, married, three children. Foster is a graduate of "the school of hard knocks." After serving in the Vietnam War, he started to go to school but dropped out because of high family expenses. Foster has worked at the company for twenty years. His ratings were excellent for fifteen years. The last five years they have been average. Foster feels his supervisor grades him down because he does not "have sheepskins covering his office walls."

4. *Donald Boyer*, age thirty-two, married, no children. Boyer is well liked by his coworkers. He has been at WSI five years, and he has a B.S. and M.S. in engineering from Purdue University. Boyer's ratings have been mixed. Some supervisors rated him high and some average. Boyer's wife is an M.D.

5. *Ann Shuster*, age twenty-nine, single. Shuster is a real worker, but a loner. She has a B.S. in engineering from the University of California. She is working on her M.S. at night, always trying to improve her technical skills. Her performance ratings have been above average for the three years she has been at WSI.

6. *Sherman Soltis*, age thirty-seven, divorced, two children. He has a B.S. in engineering from Ohio State University. Soltis is very active in community affairs: Scouts, Little League, and United Way. He is a friend of the vice-president through church

work. His ratings have been average, although some recent ones indicate that he is out of date. He is well liked and has been employed at WSI for fourteen years.

7. *Warren Fortuna*, age forty-four, married, five children. He has a B.S. in engineering from Georgia Tech. Fortuna headed this section at one time. He worked so hard that he had a heart attack. Under doctor's orders, he resigned from the supervisory position. Since then he has done good work, though because of his health, he is a bit slower than the others. Now and then he must spend extra time on a project, because he did get out of date during the eight years he headed the section. His performance evaluations for the last two years have been above average. He has been employed at WSI for fourteen years.

8. *Robert Treharne*, age forty-seven, single. He began an engineering degree at MIT but had to drop out for financial reasons. He tries hard to stay current by regular reading of engineering journals and taking all the short courses the company and nearby colleges offer. His performance evaluations have varied, but they tend to be average to slightly above average. He is a loner, and Tartaro thinks this has negatively affected Treharne's performance evaluations. He has been employed at WSI sixteen years.

9. *Sandra Rosen*, age twenty-two, single. She has a B.S. in engineering technology from the Rochester Institute of Technology. Rosen has been employed less than a year. She is enthusiastic, a very good worker, and well liked by her coworkers. She is well regarded by Tartaro.

Tartaro does not quite know what to do. He sees the good points of each of his section members. Most have been good employees. They all can pretty much do one another's work. No one has special training.

He is fearful that the section will hear about the downsizing and morale will drop. Work would fall off. He does not even want to talk to his wife about it, in case she would let something slip. Tartaro has come to you, Edmund Graves, personnel manager at WSI, for some guidelines on this decision—legal, moral, and best personnel practice.

Assignment

You are Edmund Graves. Write a report with your recommendations for termination and a careful analysis of the criteria for the decision. You should also carefully explain to Tartaro how you would go about the terminations and what you would consider reasonable termination pay. You should also advise him about the pension implications of this decision. Generally, fifteen years' service entitles you to at least partial pension.

SOURCE: W. F. Glueck, *Cases and Exercises in Personnel* (Dallas: Business Publications, 1978), 24–26.

9.2 The Wilderness Experience

Try to imagine yourself in the situation depicted. Assume that you are alone and have a minimum of equipment, except where specified. The season is fall. The days are warm and dry, but the nights are cold. Circle the letter beside the best answer.

1. You have strayed from your party in a trackless timber. You have no special signaling equipment. The best way to attempt to contact your friends is to:
   a. call "help" loudly but in a low register.
   b. yell or scream as loud as you can.
   c. whistle loudly and shrilly.

2. You are in "snake country." Your best action to avoid snakes is to:
   a. make a lot of noise with your feet.
   b. walk softly and quietly.
   c. travel at night.

3. You are hungry and lost in wild country. The best rule for determining which plants are safe to eat (those you don't recognize) is to:
   a. try anything you see the birds eat.
   b. eat anything except plants with bright red berries.
   c. put a bit of the plant on your lower lip for five minutes; if it seems all right, try a little.

4. The day becomes dry and hot. You have a full canteen of water (about 1 liter) with you. You should:
   a. ration it—about a cupful a day.
   b. not drink until you stop for the night, then drink what you think you need.
   c. drink as much as you think you need when you need it.

5. Your water is gone; you become very thirsty. You finally come to a dried-up watercourse. Your best chance of finding water is to:
   a. dig anywhere in the stream bed.
   b. dig up plant and tree roots near the bank.
   c. dig in the stream bed at the outside of a bend.

6. You decide to walk out of the wild country by following a series of ravines where a water supply is available. Night is coming on. The best place to make camp is:
   a. next to the water supply in the ravine.
   b. high on a ridge.
   c. midway up the slope.

7. Your flashlight glows dimly as you are about to make your way back to your campsite after a brief foraging trip. Darkness comes quickly in the woods and the surroundings seem unfamiliar. You should:
   a. head back at once, keeping the light on, hoping the light will glow enough for you to make landmarks.
   b. put the batteries under your armpits to warm them, and then replace them in the flashlight.
   c. shine your light for a few seconds, try to get the scene in mind, move in the darkness, and repeat the process.

8. An early snow confines you to your small tent. You doze with your small stove going. There is danger if the flame is:
   a. yellow.
   b. blue.
   c. red.

9. You must ford a river that has a strong current, large rocks, and some white water. After carefully selecting your crossing spot, you should:
   a. leave your boots and pack on.
   b. take your boots and pack off.
   c. take off your pack, but leave your boots on.

10. In waist-deep water with a strong current, when crossing the stream, you should face:
    a. upstream.
    b. across the stream.
    c. downstream.

11. You find yourself rimrocked; your only route is up. The way is mossy, slippery rock. You should try it:
    a. barefoot.
    b. with boots on.
    c. in stocking feet.

12. Unarmed and unsuspecting, you surprise a large bear prowling around your campsite. As the bear rears up about ten meters from you, you should:

    a. run.
    b. climb the nearest tree.
    c. freeze, but be ready to back away slowly.

After you have completed the worksheet, your instructor will help you form groups of five or six members. Then each group should go through the worksheet and agree on a correct answer for each question.

SOURCE: "The Wilderness Experience" from *The 1976 Annual*. Copyright 1976 Pfeiffer/Jossey-Bass. Reprinted by permission of Jossey-Bass, Inc., a subsidiary of John Wiley & Sons, Inc.

Learning Objectives

After reading this chapter, you should be able to do the following:

1. Distinguish between power, influence, and authority. *p. 285*

2. Describe the interpersonal and intergroup sources of power. *p. 286*

3. Understand the ethical use of power. *p. 288*

4. Explain power analysis, an organizational-level theory of power. *p. 291*

5. Identify symbols of power and powerlessness in organizations. *p. 293*

6. Define organizational politics and understand the major influence tactics. *p. 295*

7. Develop a plan for managing employee–boss relationships. *p. 300*

8. Discuss how managers can empower others. *p. 302*

10

Power and Political Behavior

Thinking Ahead

Texas Cattle Ranchers versus Harpo Productions: The Real Issue Is Power and Influence

The entertainment industry is full of powerful companies—Disney and Universal Studios, for example. Entertainment can shape our worldview and influence our attitudes. Just how much influence can a company and its founder have?

Oprah Winfrey is considered by some to be the most powerful woman in business today, and she consistently lands at the top of the "most admired" polls. She is only the third woman (behind Mary Pickford and Lucille Ball) in the television and film industry to own her own production company (Harpo Productions), and she is the first black woman to do so. She is on her way to becoming the first African American billionaire.

Almost 33 million people watch *The Oprah Winfrey Show* daily. The show has garnered thirty Emmys and has been TV's number one talk show for fourteen consecutive seasons. Oprah's Book Club, aimed at increasing literacy, encourages the audience to read serious literary fiction and to discuss it once a month on her show. When a book club selection is announced, readers are invited to e-mail or write with thoughts on the book. Four letter-writers are then invited to dine with Winfrey and the book's author, and the gathering is featured on the show. Books by unknown authors have been catapulted to the top of the best-seller list by being an Oprah's Book Club selection.

Harpo Productions landed in court over a show about dangerous foods. News outlets had reported that ten people in Britain had died of mad cow disease from eating beef from cattle that had consumed protein supplements produced from the wastes of slaughtered cattle. An official with the Humane Society appeared on Oprah's program and speculated that mad cow disease would become rampant among cattle in the United States. Four ranching families in Amarillo, Texas, filed suit, claiming that comments made during the program caused cattle prices to fall, costing them around $11 million. Specifically, Oprah had said that the practice of feeding supplements made from slaughtered cattle "has just stopped me cold from eating another hamburger." The suit was considered to be a test of the constitutionality of the "veggie libel" law in Texas and other states that protects perishable agricultural products from unsubstantiated comments about their safety.

Was this case really about "veggie libel," or was it about power and influence? Could TV's most powerful woman really cause cattle prices to plummet? For the verdict, and more on the power and politics of entertainment, see the Looking Back feature at the end of the chapter.[1]

THE CONCEPT OF POWER

Power is the ability to influence someone else. As an exchange relationship, it occurs in transactions between an agent and a target. The agent is the person using the power, and the target is the recipient of the attempt to use power.[2]

Because power is an ability, individuals can learn to use it effectively. *Influence* is the process of affecting the thoughts, behavior, and feelings of another person. *Authority* is the right to influence another person.[3] It is important to understand the subtle differences among these terms. For instance, a manager may have authority but no power. She may have the right, by virtue of her position as boss, to tell someone what to do. But she may not have the skill or ability to influence other people.

In a relationship between the agent and the target, there are many influence attempts that the target considers legitimate. Working forty hours per week, greeting customers, solving problems, and collecting bills are actions that, when requested by the manager, are considered legitimate by a customer service representative. Requests such as these fall within the employee's *zone of indifference*—the range in which attempts to influence the employee are perceived as legitimate and are acted on without a great deal of thought.[4] The employee accepts that the manager has the authority to request such behaviors and complies with the requests. Some requests, however, fall outside the zone of indifference, so the manager must work to enlarge the employee's zone of indifference. Enlarging the zone is accomplished with power (an ability) rather than with authority (a right).

1. Distinguish between power, influence, and authority.

power
The ability to influence another person.

influence
The process of affecting the thoughts, behavior, and feelings of another person.

authority
The right to influence another person.

zone of indifference
The range in which attempts to influence a person will be perceived as legitimate and will be acted on without a great deal of thought.

Suppose the manager asks the employee to purchase a birthday gift for the manager's wife or to overcharge a customer for a service call. The employee may think that the manager has no right to ask these things. These requests fall outside the zone of indifference; they're viewed as extraordinary, and the manager has to operate from outside the authority base to induce the employee to fulfill them. In some cases, no power base is enough to induce the employee to comply, especially if the behaviors requested by the manager are considered unethical by the employee.

Failures to understand power and politics can be costly in terms of your career. Managers must learn as much as possible about power and politics to be able to use them effectively and to manage the inevitable political behavior in organizations.

FORMS AND SOURCES OF POWER IN ORGANIZATIONS

Individuals have many forms of power to use in their work settings. Some of them are interpersonal—used in interactions with others. One of the earliest and most influential theories of power comes from French and Raven, who tried to determine the sources of a power a manager uses to influence other people.

Interpersonal Forms of Power

French and Raven identified five forms of interpersonal power that managers use. They are reward, coercive, legitimate, referent, and expert power.[5]

Reward power is power based on the agent's ability to control rewards that a target wants. For example, managers control the rewards of salary increases, bonuses, and promotions. Reward power can lead to better performance, but only as long as the employee sees a clear and strong link between performance and rewards. To use reward power effectively, then, the manager should be explicit about the behavior being rewarded and should make the connection clear between the behavior and the reward.

Coercive power is power that is based on the agent's ability to cause the target to have an unpleasant experience. To coerce someone into doing something means to force the person to do it, often with threats of punishment. Managers using coercive power may verbally abuse employees or withhold support from them.

Legitimate power, which is similar to authority, is power that is based on position and mutual agreement. The agent and target agree that the agent has the right to influence the target. It doesn't matter that a manager thinks he has the right to influence his employees; for legitimate power to be effective, the employees must also believe the manager has the right to tell them what to do. In Native American societies, the chieftain has legitimate power; tribe members believe in his right to influence the decisions in their lives.

---

2. Describe the interpersonal and intergroup sources of power.

reward power
Power based on an agent's ability to control rewards that a target wants.

coercive power
Power that is based on an agent's ability to cause an unpleasant experience for a target.

legitimate power
Power that is based on position and mutual agreement; agent and target agree that the agent has the right to influence the target.

Referent power is an elusive power that is based on interpersonal attraction. The agent has referent power over the target because the target identifies with or wants to be like the agent. Charismatic individuals are often thought to have referent power. Interestingly, the agent need not be superior to the target in any way. People who use referent power well are most often individualistic and respected by the target.

Expert power is the power that exists when the agent has information or knowledge that the target needs. For expert power to work, three conditions must be in place. First, the target must trust that the information given is accurate. Second, the information involved must be relevant and useful to the target. Third, the target's perception of the agent as an expert is crucial. As a manager, you may believe you are an expert, but if your employees do not share this view, then your expert power will not be effective.

Which type of interpersonal power is most effective? Research has focused on this question since French and Raven introduced their five forms of power. Some of the results are surprising. Reward power and coercive power have similar effects.[6] Both lead to compliance. That is, employees will do what the manager asks them to, at least temporarily, if the manager offers a reward or threatens them with punishment. Reliance on these sources of power is dangerous, however, because it may require the manager to be physically present and watchful in order to apply rewards or punishment when the behavior occurs. Constant surveillance creates an uncomfortable situation for managers and employees and eventually results in a dependency relationship. Employees will not work unless the manager is present.

Legitimate power also leads to compliance. When told "Do this because I'm your boss," most employees will comply. However, the use of legitimate power has not been linked to organizational effectiveness or to employee satisfaction.[7] In organizations where managers rely heavily on legitimate power, organizational goals are not necessarily met.

Referent power is linked with organizational effectiveness. It is the most dangerous power, however, because it can be too extensive and intensive in altering the behavior of others. Charismatic leaders need an accompanying sense of responsibility for others. Magic Johnson's referent power has made him a powerful spokesman for AIDS prevention, especially among young people.

Expert power has been called the power of the future.[8] Of the five forms of power, it has the strongest relationship with performance and satisfaction. It is through expert power that vital skills, abilities, and knowledge are passed on within the organization. Employees internalize what they observe and learn from managers they perceive to be experts.

The results on the effectiveness of these five forms of power pose a challenge in organizations. The least effective power bases—legitimate, reward, and coercive—are the ones most likely to be used by managers.[9] Managers inherit these power bases as part of the position when they take

referent power
An elusive power that is based on interpersonal attraction.

expert power
The power that exists when an agent has information or knowledge that the target needs.

Experiencing OB

Power comes from many sources including personal as well as organizational sources. To learn more about sources of power, visit our animated concept and activity site. Choose Power&Politics from the "select a topic" pull-down menu, then Organizational Sources of Power from the "overview tab."

http://www.experiencingob.com

a supervisory job. In contrast, the most effective power bases—referent and expert—are ones that must be developed and strengthened through interpersonal relationships with employees.

Using Power Ethically

3.■ Understand the ethical use of power.

Managers can work at developing all five of these forms of power for future use. The key to using them well is using them ethically, as Table 10.1 shows.

Table 10.1

Guidelines for the Ethical Use of Power

Form of Power	Guidelines for Use
Reward power	Verify compliance.
	Make feasible, reasonable requests.
	Make only ethical requests.
	Offer rewards desired by subordinates.
	Offer only credible rewards.
Coercive power	Inform subordinates of rules and penalties.
	Warn before punishing.
	Administer punishment consistently and uniformly.
	Understand the situation before acting.
	Maintain credibility.
	Fit punishment to the infraction.
	Punish in private.
Legitimate power	Be cordial and polite.
	Be confident.
	Be clear and follow up to verify understanding.
	Make sure request is appropriate.
	Explain reasons for request.
	Follow proper channels.
	Exercise power consistently.
	Enforce compliance.
	Be sensitive to subordinates' concerns.
Referent power	Treat subordinates fairly.
	Defend subordinates' interests.
	Be sensitive to subordinates' needs and feelings.
	Select subordinates similar to oneself.
	Engage in role modeling.
Expert power	Maintain credibility.
	Act confident and decisive.
	Keep informed.
	Recognize employee concerns.
	Avoid threatening subordinates' self-esteem.

SOURCE: *Leadership in Organizations* by Gary A. Yukl. Copyright © 1981. Reprinted by permission of Prentice-Hall, Upper Saddle River, NJ.

Coercive power, for example, requires careful administration if it is to be used in an ethical manner. Employees should be informed of the rules in advance, and any punishment should be used consistently, uniformly, and privately. The key to using all five types of interpersonal power ethically is to be sensitive to employees' concerns and to communicate well.

Determining whether a power-related behavior is ethical is complex. Another way to look at the ethics surrounding the use of power is to ask three questions that show the criteria for examining power-related behaviors:[10]

1. *Does the behavior produce a good outcome for people both inside and outside the organization?* This question represents the criterion of *utilitarian outcomes*. The behavior should result in the greatest good for the greatest number of people. If the power-related behavior serves only the individual's self-interest and fails to help the organization reach its goals, it is considered unethical. A salesperson might be tempted to discount a product deeply in order to make a sale that would win a contest. Doing so would be in her self-interest but would not benefit the organization.

2. *Does the behavior respect the rights of all parties?* This question emphasizes the criterion of *individual rights*. Free speech, privacy, and due process are individual rights that are to be respected, and power-related behaviors that violate these rights are considered unethical.

3. *Does the behavior treat all parties equitably and fairly?* This question represents the criterion of *distributive justice*. Power-related behavior that treats one party arbitrarily or benefits one party at the expense of another is unethical. Granting a day of vacation to one employee in a busy week in which coworkers must struggle to cover for him might be considered unethical.

To be considered ethical, power-related behavior must meet all three criteria. If the behavior fails to meet the criteria, then alternative actions should be considered. Unfortunately, most power-related behaviors are not easy to analyze. Conflicts may exist among the criteria; for example, a behavior may maximize the greatest good for the greatest number of people but may not treat all parties equitably. Individual rights may need to be sacrificed for the good of the organization. A CEO may need to be removed from power for the organization to be saved. Still, these criteria can be used on a case-by-case basis to sort through the complex ethical issues surrounding the use of power.

Two Faces of Power: One Positive, One Negative

We turn now to a theory of power that takes a strong stand on the "right" versus "wrong" kind of power to use in organizations. David McClelland has spent a great deal of his career studying the need for power and the ways managers use power. As was discussed in Chapter 5, he believes that there are two distinct faces of power, one negative and one positive.[11] The

personal power
Power used for personal gain.

social power
Power used to create motivation or to accomplish group goals.

negative face of power is *personal power*—power used for personal gain. Managers who use personal power are commonly described as "power hungry." Personal power is a win–lose form of power in which the manager tends to treat others as objects to be utilized to get ahead. It is based on the traditional notion of power as domination over others.

The positive face of power is *social power*—power used to create motivation or to accomplish group goals. McClelland clearly favors the use of social power by managers. He has found that the best managers are those who have a high need for social power coupled with a relatively low need for affiliation. In addition, he has found that managers who use power successfully have four power-oriented characteristics:

1. *Belief in the authority system.* They believe that the institution is important and that its authority system is valid. They are comfortable influencing and being influenced. The source of their power is the authority system of which they are a part.

2. *Preference for work and discipline.* They like their work and are very orderly. They have a basic value preference for the Protestant work ethic, believing that work is good for a person over and beyond its income-producing value.

3. *Altruism.* They publicly put the company and its needs before their own needs. They are able to do this because they see their own well-being as integrally tied to the corporate well-being.

4. *Belief in justice.* They believe justice is to be sought above all else. People should receive that to which they are entitled and that which they earn.

McClelland takes a definite stand on the proper use of power by managers. When power is used for the good of the group, rather than for individual gain, it is positive. McClelland's approach to power is basically psychological in nature, focusing on the needs and drives of the individual.

Intergroup Sources of Power

Groups or teams within an organization can also use power from several sources. One source of intergroup power is control of *critical resources.*[12] When one group controls an important resource that another group desires, the first group holds power. Controlling resources needed by another group allows the power-holding group to influence the actions of the less powerful group.

Salancik and Pfeffer, who proposed this resource dependency model, conducted a study of university budgeting decisions. Various departments within a university have power by virtue of their national ranking, their ability to win outside grant monies, and their success in attracting promising graduate students. Departments that obtain these critical outside resources are awarded more internal resources from within the university.[13] Thus, one source of group power is control over valued resources.

Groups also have power to the extent that they control *strategic contingencies*—activities that other groups depend on in order to complete their tasks.[14] The dean's office, for example, may control the number of faculty positions to be filled in each department of a college. The departmental hiring plans are thus contingent on approval from the dean's office. In this case, the dean's office controls the strategic contingency of faculty hiring, and thus has power.

Three factors can give a group control over a strategic contingency.[15] One is the *ability to cope with uncertainty*. If a group can help another group deal with uncertainty, it has power. One organizational group that has gained power in recent years is the legal department. Faced with increasing government regulations and fears of litigation, many other departments seek guidance from the legal department.

Another factor that can give a group control power is a *high degree of centrality* within the organization. If a group's functioning is important to the organization's success, it has high centrality. The sales force in a computer firm, for example, has power because of its immediate effect on the firm's operations and because other groups (accounting and servicing groups, for example) depend on its activities.

The third factor that can give a group power is *nonsubstitutability*—the extent to which a group performs a function that is indispensable to an organization. A team of computer specialists may be powerful because of its expertise with a system. It may have specialized experience that another team cannot provide.

The strategic contingencies model thus shows that groups hold power over other groups when they can reduce uncertainty, when their functioning is central to the organization's success, and when the group's activities are difficult to replace.[16] The key to all three of these factors, as you can see, is dependency. When one group controls something that another group needs, it creates a dependent relationship—and gives one group power over the other.

strategic contingencies
Activities that other groups depend on in order to complete their tasks.

POWER ANALYSIS: A BROADER VIEW

Amitai Etzioni takes a more sociological orientation to power. Etzioni has developed a theory of power analysis.[17] He says that there are three types of organizational power and three types of organizational involvement, or membership, that will lead to either congruent or incongruent uses of power. The three types of organizational power are the following:

1. *Coercive power*—influencing members by forcing them to do something under threat of punishment, or through fear and intimidation.
2. *Utilitarian power*—influencing members by providing them with rewards and benefits.
3. *Normative power*—influencing members by using the knowledge that they want very much to belong to the organization and by letting them know that what they are expected to do is the "right" thing to do.

4. Explain power analysis, an organizational-level theory of power.

Along with these three types of organizational power, Etzioni proposes that we can classify organizations by the type of membership they have:

1. *Alienative membership.* The members have hostile, negative feelings about being in the organization. They don't want to be there. Prisons are a good example of alienative memberships.
2. *Calculative membership.* Members weigh the benefits and limitations of belonging to the organization. Businesses are good examples of organizations with calculative memberships.
3. *Moral membership.* Members have such positive feelings about organizational membership that they are willing to deny their own needs. Organizations with many volunteer workers, such as the American Heart Association, are examples of moral memberships. Religious groups are another example.

Etzioni argues that the type of organizational power should be matched to the type of membership in the organization in order to achieve congruence. Figure 10.1 shows the matches in his power analysis theory.

In an alienative membership, members have hostile feelings. In prisons, for example, Etzioni would contend that coercive power is the appropriate type to use.

A calculative membership is characterized by an analysis of the good and bad aspects of being in the organization. In a business partnership, for example, each partner weighs the benefits from the partnership against the costs entailed in the contractual arrangement. Utilitarian, or reward-based, power is the most appropriate type to use.

In a moral membership, the members have strong positive feelings about the particular cause or goal of the organization. Normative power is the most appropriate to use because it capitalizes on the members' desires to belong.

Etzioni's power analysis is an organizational-level theory. It emphasizes that the characteristics of an organization play a role in determining the

Figure 10.1
Etzioni's Power Analysis

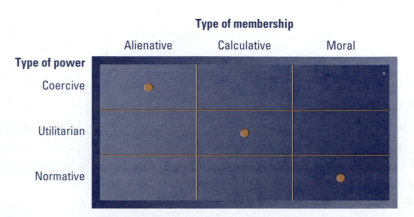

SOURCE: Adapted from Amitai Etzioni, *Modern Organizations* (Upper Saddle River, N.J.: Prentice-Hall, 1964), 59–61.

type of power appropriate for use in the organization. Etzioni's theory is controversial in its contention that a single type of power is appropriate in any organization.

SYMBOLS OF POWER

Organization charts show who has authority, but they do not reveal much about who has power. We'll now look at two very different ideas about the symbols of power. The first one comes from Rosabeth Moss Kanter. It is a scholarly approach to determining who has power and who feels powerless. The second is a semiserious look at the tangible symbols of power by Michael Korda.

5. Identify symbols of power and powerlessness in organizations.

Kanter's Symbols of Power

Kanter provides several characteristics of powerful people in organizations:[18]

1. *Ability to intercede for someone in trouble.* An individual who can pull someone out of a jam has power.
2. *Ability to get placements for favored employees.* Getting a key promotion for an employee is a sign of power.
3. *Exceeding budget limitations.* A manager who can go above budget limits without being reprimanded has power.
4. *Procuring above-average raises for employees.* One faculty member reported that her department head distributed 10 percent raises to the most productive faculty members although the budget allowed for only 4 percent increases. "I don't know how he did it; he must have pull," she said.
5. *Getting items on the agenda at meetings.* If a manager can raise issues for action at meetings, it's a sign of power.
6. *Access to early information.* Having information before anyone else does is a signal that a manager is plugged in to key sources.
7. *Having top managers seek out their opinion.* When top managers have a problem, they may ask for advice from lower-level managers. The managers they turn to have power.

A theme that runs through Kanter's list is doing things for others: for people in trouble, for employees, for bosses. There is an active, other-directed element in her symbols of power.

You can use Kanter's symbols of power to identify powerful people in organizations. They can be particularly useful in finding a mentor who can effectively use power.

Kanter's Symbols of Powerlessness

Kanter also wrote about symptoms of *powerlessness*—a lack of power—in managers at different levels of the organization. First-line supervisors, for

powerlessness
A lack of power.

example, often display three symptoms of powerlessness: overly close supervision, inflexible adherence to the rules, and a tendency to do the job themselves rather than training their employees to do it. Staff professionals such as accountants and lawyers display different symptoms of powerlessness. When they feel powerless, they tend to resist change and try to protect their turf. Top executives can also feel powerless. They show symptoms such as focusing on budget cutting, punishing others, and using dictatorial, top-down communication.

Employees at any level can feel powerless. When caught in powerless jobs, they may react passively and display overdependence on their boss.[19] In contrast, they may become frustrated and disrupt the work group.[20] What can you do when you recognize that employees are feeling powerless? The key to overcoming powerlessness is to share power and delegate decision-making authority to employees.

Korda's Symbols of Power

Michael Korda takes a different look at symbols of power in organizations.[21] He discusses three unusual symbols: office furnishings, time power, and standing by.

Furniture is not just physically useful; it also conveys a message about power. Locked file cabinets are signs that the manager has important and confidential information in the office. A rectangular (rather than round) conference table enables the most important person to sit at the head of the table. The size of one's desk may convey the amount of power. Most executives prefer large, expensive desks.

Time power means using clocks and watches as power symbols. Korda says that the biggest compliment a busy executive can pay a visitor is to remove his watch and place it face down on the desk, thereby communicating "my time is yours." He also notes that the less powerful the executive, the more intricate the watch; moreover, managers who are really secure in their power wear no watch at all, since they believe nothing important can happen without them. A full calendar is also proof of power. Personal planners are left open on the desk to display busy schedules.

Standing by is a game in which people are obliged to keep their cell phones, pagers, etc. with them at all times so executives can reach them. The idea is that the more you can impose your schedule on other people, the more power you have. In fact, Korda defines *power* as follows: There are more people who inconvenience themselves on your behalf than there are people on whose behalf you would inconvenience yourself. Closely tied to this is the ability to make others perform simple tasks for you, such as getting your coffee or fetching the mail.

You can use both Kanter's and Korda's perspectives to identify people who hold power in organizations. By identifying powerful people and learning from their modeled behavior, you can learn the keys to power use in the organization.

POLITICAL BEHAVIOR IN ORGANIZATIONS

Like power, the term politics in organizations may conjure up a few negative images. However, *organizational politics* is not necessarily negative; it is the use of power and influence in organizations. As people try to acquire power and expand their power base, they use various tactics and strategies. Some are sanctioned (acceptable to the organization); others are not. *Political behavior* refers to actions not officially sanctioned by an organization that are taken to influence others in order to meet one's personal goals.[22]

Politics is a controversial topic among managers. Some managers take a favorable view of political behavior; others see it as detrimental to the organization. In one study of managers, 53 percent reported that politics had a positive impact on the achievement of the organization's goals.[23] In contrast, 44 percent reported that politics distracted organization members from focusing on goal achievement. In a different study, managers displayed conflicting attitudes toward politics in organizations. More than 89 percent agreed that workplace politics was common in most organizations and that successful executives must be good politicians. However, 59 percent indicated that workplaces that were free of politics were more satisfying to work in.[24] These studies point out the controversial nature of political behavior in organizations.

Many organizational conditions encourage political activity. Among them are unclear goals, autocratic decision making, ambiguous lines of authority, scarce resources, and uncertainty.[25] Even supposedly objective activities may involve politics. One such activity is the performance appraisal process. A study of sixty executives who had extensive experience in employee evaluation indicated that political considerations were nearly always part of the performance appraisal process.[26]

The effects of political behavior in organizations can be quite negative when the political behavior is strategically undertaken to maximize self-interest. If people within the organization are competitively pursuing selfish ends, they're unlikely to be attentive to the concerns of others. The workplace can seem less helpful, more threatening, and more unpredictable. People focus on their own concerns rather than on organizational goals. This represents the negative face of power described earlier by David McClelland as personal power. If employees view the organization's political climate as extreme, they experience more anxiety, tension, fatigue, and burnout. The are also dissatisfied with their jobs and are more likely to leave.[27] There are ways to avoid this negative climate, as discussed later in this chapter.

Influence Tactics

Influence is the process of affecting the thoughts, behavior, or feelings of another person. That other person could be the boss (upward influence), an employee (downward influence), or a coworker (lateral influence). There

organizational politics
The use of power and influence in organizations.

political behavior
Actions not officially sanctioned by an organization that are taken to influence others in order to meet one's personal goals.

6. Define organizational politics and understand the major influence tactics.

are eight basic types of influence tactics. They are listed and described in Table 10.2.[28]

Research has shown that the four tactics used most frequently are consultation, rational persuasion, inspirational appeals, and ingratiation,

Table 10.2

Influence Tactics Used in Organizations

Tactics	Description	Examples
Pressure	The person uses demands, threats, or intimidation to convince you to comply with a request or to support a proposal.	If you don't do this, you're fired. You have until 5:00 to change your mind, or I'm going without you.
Upward appeals	The person seeks to persuade you that the request is approved by higher management, or appeals to higher management for assistance in gaining your compliance with the request.	I'm reporting you to my boss. My boss supports this idea.
Exchange	The person makes an explicit or implicit promise that you will receive rewards or tangible benefits if you comply with a request or support a proposal, or reminds you of a prior favor to be reciprocated.	You owe me a favor. I'll take you to lunch if you'll support me on this.
Coalition	The person seeks the aid of others to persuade you to do something or uses the support of others as an argument for you to agree also.	All the other supervisors agree with me. I'll ask you in front of the whole committee.
Ingratiation	The person seeks to get you in a good mood or to think favorably of him or her before asking you to do something.	Only you can do this job right. I can always count on you, so I have another request.
Rational persuasion	The person uses logical arguments and factual evidence to persuade you that a proposal or request is viable and likely to result in the attainment of task objectives.	This new procedure will save us $150,000 in overhead. It makes sense to hire John; he has the most experience.
Inspirational appeals	The person makes an emotional request or proposal that arouses enthusiasm by appealing to your values and ideals, or by increasing your confidence that you can do it.	Being environmentally conscious is the right thing. Getting that account will be tough, but I know you can do it.
Consultation	The person seeks your participation in making a decision or planning how to implement a proposed policy, strategy, or change.	This new attendance plan is controversial. How can we make it more acceptable? What do you think we can do to make our workers less fearful of the new robots on the production line?

SOURCE: First two columns from G. Yukl and C. M. Falbe, "Influence Tactics and Objectives in Upward, Downward, and Lateral Influence Attempts," *Journal of Applied Psychology* 75 (1990): 132–140. Copyright © 1990 by the American Psychological Association. Reprinted with permission.

regardless of the target of the influence attempt. Thus, individuals do not differentiate among bosses, subordinates, and peers in terms of the tactic they choose. Upward appeals and coalition tactics are used moderately. Exchange tactics are used least often.

Some of the influence tactics are used for impression management, which was described in Chapter 3. In impression management, individuals use influence tactics to control others' impressions of them. One way in which people engage in impression management is through image building. The Workshoppe, a Silicon Valley consulting firm, helps "technogeeks" present a better image by training them in etiquette, as described in Organizational Reality 10.1.

Ingratiation is an example of one tactic often used for impression management. Ingratiation can take many forms, including flattery, opinion conformity, and subservient behavior.[29] Exchange is another influence tactic that may be used for impression management. Offering to do favors for someone in an effort to create a favorable impression is an exchange tactic.

Experiencing OB

Learn more about influence tactics and their uses at our animated concept and activity site. Choose Power&Politics from the "select a topic" pull-down menu, then Effective Influence Tactics from the "overview tab."

http://www.experiencingob.com

ORGANIZATIONAL REALITY 10.1

Etiquette Training for "Technogeeks"

Suppose you are a Silicon Valley "technogeek" who has an idea that is sure to generate billions of dollars. You must look for venture capital to launch the idea—but how can you ensure that your "dirt-under-the-fingernails" image will not interfere with the merits of your idea or your ability to sell it? One thing you could do is to get a manicure. Better yet, you might invest a mere $150 to attend a Workshoppe, Silicon Valley's finishing school for techies.

Sue Fox, a former marketer for Apple Computer, and Lyndy Janes, a retired fashion model, founded Workshoppe to help technophiles with their image management skills. They also have a line of videotapes on such topics as formal table settings and honing social skills. Companies such as Adobe, Sun, Netscape, and AT&T have used their services.

At a typical Workshoppe, techies learn to get rid of behaviors like licking sauce from their knives and leaving cell phone ringers turned on during lunch—both are mammoth *faux pas.* Groups of participants meet at a chic restaurant, and Janes coaches them through every aspect of the meal. Often, attendees arrive late to the session, and Janes knows that she has a tough task to perform. One of the most glaring errors in etiquette is being late for appointments. Most of the instruction is remedial and helps rid the techies of old habits. Participants learn how to correctly eat the palate-cleansing sorbet, how to properly use finger bowls, which fork to use, and how to discreetly excuse themselves from the table. "We don't need to know about your potty runs," says Janes. "And ladies, do you really expect anyone to believe that you're going to powder your nose?"

Business is brisk for the Workshoppe. Attendees give the training high marks, because it beats having to ask which fork to use in front of business associates or potential investors. That image might cause them to blow the big deal.

Discussion Question

1. How do training and etiquette and social skills relate to power? To influence?

SOURCE: E. Brown, "Etiquette Training for Geeks," *Fortune* (June 22, 1998): 148–149.

Which influence tactics are most effective? It depends on the target of the influence attempt and the objective. Individuals use different tactics for different purposes, and they use different tactics for different people. Influence attempts with subordinates, for example, usually involve assigning tasks or changing behavior. With peers, the objective is often to request assistance. With superiors, influence attempts are often made to request approval, resources, political support, or personal benefits. Rational persuasion and coalition tactics are used most often to get support from peers and superiors to change company policy. Consultation and inspirational appeals are particularly effective for gaining support and resources for a new project.[30] Overall, the most effective tactic in terms of achieving objectives is rational persuasion, while pressure seems to be the least effective.

One way in which subordinates often use influence attempts is in trying to convince their supervisors of their promotability. Evidence indicates that rational persuasion has a positive effect on supervisors' assessments of promotability. Ingratiation, a softer tactic, has a negative effect on promotability—supervisors may see their subordinate's ingratiation attempts as self-serving attempts to get ahead.[31] When supervisors believe an employee's motive for doing favors for the boss is simply to be a good citizen, they are likely to reward that employee. However, when the motive is seen as brown-nosing (ingratiation), supervisors respond negatively.[32] And, as it becomes more obvious that the employee has something to gain by impressing the boss, the likelihood that ingratiation will succeed decreases.

Still, a well-disguised ingratiation is hard to resist. Attempts that are not obvious usually succeed in increasing the target's liking for the ingratiator.[33] Most people have trouble remaining neutral when someone flatters them or agrees with them. However, witnesses to the ingratiation are more likely to question the motive behind the flattery or agreement. Observers are more skeptical than the recipients of the ingratiation.

There is evidence that men and women view politics and influence attempts differently. Men tend to view political behavior more favorably than do women. When both men and women witness political behavior, they view it more positively if the agent is of their gender and the target is of the opposite gender.[34]

There is also some preliminary evidence that different cultures prefer different influence tactics at work. One study found that American managers dealing with a tardy employee tended to rely on pressure tactics such as "If you don't start reporting on time for work, I will have no choice but to start docking your pay." In contrast, Japanese managers relied on influence tactics that either appealed to the employee's sense of duty ("It is your duty as a responsible employee of this company to begin work on time") or emphasized a consultative approach ("Is there anything I can do to help you overcome the problems that are preventing you from coming to work on time?").[35]

It is important to note that influence tactics do have some positive effects. The influencer can gain self-esteem, the target can feel positive about himself or herself, and work can get done through influence attempts.[36] However, some influence tactics, such as pressure, coalition building, and exchange, have strong ethical implications. There is a fine line between being an impression manager and being seen as a manipulator.

How can a manager use influence tactics well? First, a manager can develop and maintain open lines of communication in all directions: upward, downward, and lateral. Then, the manager can treat the targets of influence attempts—whether managers, employees, or peers—with basic respect. Finally, the manager can understand that influence relationships are reciprocal—they are two-way relationships. As long as the influence attempts are directed toward organizational goals, the process of influence can be advantageous to all involved.

Managing Political Behavior in Organizations

Politics cannot and should not be eliminated from organizations. Managers can, however, take a proactive stance and manage the political behavior that inevitably occurs.[37]

Open communication is one key to managing political behavior. Uncertainty tends to increase political behavior, and communication that reduces the uncertainty is important. One form of communication that will help is to clarify the sanctioned and nonsanctioned political behaviors in the organization. For example, you may want to encourage social power as opposed to personal power.[38]

Another key is to clarify expectations regarding performance. This can be accomplished through the use of clear, quantifiable goals and through the establishment of a clear connection between goal accomplishment and rewards.[39]

Participative management is yet another key. Often, people engage in political behavior when they feel excluded from decision-making processes in the organization. By including them, you will encourage positive input and eliminate behind-the-scenes maneuvering.

Encouraging cooperation among work groups is another strategy for managing political behavior. Managers can instill a unity of purpose among work teams by rewarding cooperative behavior and by implementing activities that emphasize the integration of team efforts toward common goals.[40]

Managing scarce resources well is also important. An obvious solution to the problem of scarce resources is to increase the resource pool, but few managers have this luxury. Clarifying the resource allocation process and making the connection between performance and resources explicit can help discourage dysfunctional political behavior.

Providing a supportive organizational climate is another way to manage political behavior effectively. A supportive climate allows employees to discuss controversial issues promptly and openly. This prevents the issue from festering and potentially causing friction among employees.[41]

Managing political behavior at work is important. The perception of dysfunctional political behavior can lead to dissatisfaction.[42] When employees

Experiencing OB

Learn more about approaches for managing dysfunctional political behaviors by interacting with these approaches at our animated concept and activity site. Choose Power&Politics from the "select a topic" pulldown menu, then Managing Political Behavior from the "overview tab."

http://www.experiencingob.com

perceive that there are dominant interest groups or cliques at work, they are less satisfied with pay and promotions. When they believe that the organization's reward practices are influenced by political behavior, they are less satisfied with their supervisors. In addition, when employees believe that their coworkers are exhibiting increased political behavior, they are less satisfied with their coworkers. Open communication, clear expectations about performance and rewards, participative decision-making practices, work group cooperation, effective management of scarce resources, and a supportive organizational climate can help managers prevent the negative consequences of political behavior.

MANAGING UP: MANAGING THE BOSS

7. Develop a plan for managing employee–boss relationships.

One of the least discussed aspects of power and politics is the relationship between you and your boss. This is a crucial relationship, because your boss is your most important link with the rest of the organization.[43] The employee–boss relationship is one of mutual dependence; you depend on your boss to give you performance feedback, provide resources, and supply critical information. She depends on you for performance, information, and support. Because it's a mutual relationship, you should take an active role in managing it. Too often, the management of this relationship is left to the boss; but if the relationship doesn't meet your needs, chances are you haven't taken the responsibility to manage it proactively.

Table 10.3 shows the basic steps to take in managing your relationship with your boss. The first step is to try to understand as much as you can about your boss. What are the person's goals and objectives? What kind of pressures does the person face in the job? Many individuals naively expect the boss to be perfect and are disappointed when they find that this is not the case. What are the boss's strengths, weaknesses, and blind spots? Because this is an emotionally charged relationship, it is difficult to be objective; but this is a critical step in forging an effective working relationship. What is the boss's preferred work style? Does the person prefer everything in writing or hate detail? Does the boss prefer that you make appointments, or is dropping in at the boss's office acceptable? The point is to gather as much information about your boss as you can and to try to put yourself in that person's shoes.

The second step in managing this important relationship is to assess yourself and your own needs much in the same way you analyzed your boss's. What are your strengths, weaknesses, and blind spots? What is your work style? How do you normally relate to authority figures? Some of us have tendencies toward counterdependence; that is, we rebel against the boss as an authority and view the boss as a hindrance to our performance. Or, in contrast, we might take an overdependent stance, passively accepting the employee–boss relationship and treating the boss as an all-wise, protective parent. What is your tendency? Knowing how you react to authority figures can help you understand your interactions with your boss.

Table 10.3
Managing Your Relationship with Your Boss

Make Sure You Understand Your Boss and Her Context, Including:

Her goals and objectives.
The pressures on her.
Her strengths, weaknesses, blind spots.
Her preferred work style.

Assess Yourself and Your Needs, Including:

Your own strengths and weaknesses.
Your personal style.
Your predisposition toward dependence on authority figures.

Develop and Maintain a Relationship that:

Fits both your needs and styles.
Is characterized by mutual expectations.
Keeps your boss informed.
Is based on dependability and honesty.
Selectively uses your boss's time and resources.

SOURCE: Reprinted by permission of Harvard Business Review. From J. J. Gabarro and J. P. Kotter, "Managing Your Boss," *Harvard Business Review* (January–February 1980): 92–100. Copyright © 1980 by the President and Fellows of Harvard College. All rights reserved.

Once you have done a careful self-analysis and tried to understand your boss, the next step is to work to develop an effective relationship. Both parties' needs and styles must be accommodated. A fundraiser for a large volunteer organization related a story about a new boss, describing him as cold, aloof, unorganized, and inept. She made repeated attempts to meet with him and clarify expectations, and his usual reply was that he didn't have the time. Frustrated, she almost looked for a new job. "I just can't reach him!" was her refrain. Then she stepped back to consider her boss's and her own styles. Being an intuitive-feeling type of person, she prefers constant feedback and reinforcement from others. Her boss, an intuitive-thinker, works comfortably without feedback from others and has a tendency to fail to praise or reward others. She sat down with him and cautiously discussed the differences in their needs. This discussion became the basis for working out a comfortable relationship. "I still don't like him, but I understand him better," she said.

Another aspect of managing the relationship involves working out mutual expectations. One key activity is to develop a plan for work objectives and have the boss agree to it.[44] It is important to do things right, but it is also important to do the right things. Neither party to the relationship is a mind reader, and clarifying the goals is a crucial step.

Keeping the boss informed is also a priority. No one likes to be caught off guard, and there are several ways to keep the boss informed. Give the boss a weekly to-do list as a reminder of the progress towards goals. When you read something pertaining to your work, clip it out for the boss. Most busy executives appreciate being given materials they don't have time to find for themselves. Give the boss interim reports, and let the boss know if the work schedule is slipping. Don't wait until it's too late to take action.

The employee–boss relationship must be based on dependability and honesty. This means giving and receiving positive and negative feedback. Most of us are reluctant to give any feedback to the boss, but positive feedback is welcomed at the top. Negative feedback, while tougher to initiate, can clear the air. If given in a problem-solving format, it can even bring about a closer relationship.[45]

One university professor was constantly bombarded by the department head's requests that she serve on committees. When she complained about this to a colleague, she was told, "It's your fault; you need to learn how to say no." She went to the department head, explained that the committee work was keeping her from being an effective researcher and teacher, and asked that he reassign other faculty members to the committees. The department head was astonished that he had relied on her so heavily. "I just didn't realize that you were on so many committees already. Thanks for pointing it out. We need to spread these responsibilities around better."

Another point about negative feedback is that it is better to give it directly, rather than behind the boss's back. If the boss never gets the information, how can the problem be corrected?

Being considerate of the boss's time is important. Before running into the person's office, ask yourself if the meeting is necessary at that particular time. Does the boss need the information right now? Could you supply the information in a note? Is it a matter you could handle yourself? Another good time management technique is to submit an agenda before your meeting with the boss; that way, the boss can select an appropriate time slot and will have time to think about the items.

Finally, remember that the boss is on the same team you are. The golden rule is to make the boss look good, because you expect the boss to do the same for you.

SHARING POWER: EMPOWERMENT

8. Discuss how managers can empower others.

empowerment
Sharing power within an organization.

Another positive strategy for managing political behavior is **empowerment**—sharing power within an organization. As modern organizations grow flatter, eliminating layers of management, empowerment becomes more and more important. Jay Conger defines *empowerment* as "creating conditions for heightened motivation through the development of a strong sense of personal self-efficacy."[46] This means sharing power in such a way that individuals learn to believe in their ability to do the job. The driving idea of empowerment is that the individuals closest to the work and to the customers should make the decisions and that this makes the best use of employees' skills and talents. You can empower yourself by developing your sense of self-efficacy. Challenge 10.1 helps you assess your progress in terms of self-empowerment.

Challenge 10.1

Are You Self-Empowered?

Check either a or b to indicate how you usually are in these situations:

1. If someone disagrees with me in a class or a meeting, I
   a. immediately back down
   b. explain my position further
2. When I have an idea for a project, I
   a. typically take a great deal of time to start it
   b. get going on it fairly quickly
3. If my boss or teacher tells me to do something that I think is wrong, I
   a. do it anyway, telling myself he or she is "the boss"
   b. ask for clarification and explain my position
4. When a complicated problem arises, I usually tell myself
   a. I can take care of it
   b. I will not be able to solve it
5. When I am around people of higher authority, I often
   a. feel intimidated and defer to them
   b. enjoy meeting important people
6. As I awake in the morning, I usually feel
   a. alert and ready to conquer almost anything
   b. tired and have a hard time getting myself motivated
7. During an argument I
   a. put a great deal of energy into "winning"
   b. try to listen to the other side and see if we have any points of agreement
8. When I meet new people, I
   a. always wonder what they are "really" up to
   b. try to learn what they are about and give them the benefit of the doubt until they prove otherwise
9. During the day I often
   a. criticize myself on what I am doing or thinking
   b. think positive thoughts about myself

10. When someone else does a great job, I
    a. find myself picking apart that person and looking for faults
    b. often give a sincere compliment
11. When I am working in a group, I try to
    a. do a better job than the others
    b. help the group function more effectively
12. If someone pays me a compliment, I typically
    a. try not to appear boastful and I downplay the compliment
    b. respond with a positive "thank you" or similar response
13. I like to be around people who
    a. challenge me and make me question what I do
    b. give me respect
14. In love relationships I prefer the other person to
    a. have his/her own selected interests
    b. do pretty much what I do
15. During a crisis I try to
    a. resolve the problem
    b. find someone to blame
16. After seeing a movie with friends, I
    a. wait to see what they say before I decide whether I liked it
    b. am ready to talk about my reactions right away
17. When work deadlines are approaching, I typically
    a. get flustered and worry about completion
    b. buckle down and work until the job is done
18. If a job comes up I am interested in, I
    a. go for it and apply
    b. tell myself I am not qualified enough
19. When someone treats me unkindly or unfairly, I
    a. try to rectify the situation
    b. tell other people about the injustice
20. If a difficult conflict situation or problem arises, I
    a. try not to think about it, hoping it will resolve itself
    b. look at various options and may ask others for advice before I figure out what to do

Scoring:

Score one point for each of the following circled: 1b, 2b, 3b, 4a, 5b, 6a, 7b, 8b, 9b, 10b, 11b, 12b, 13a, 14a, 15a, 16b, 17b, 18a, 19a, 20b.

Analysis of Scoring

16–20 You are a take-charge person and generally make the most of opportunities. When others tell you something cannot be done, you may take this as a challenge and do it anyway. You see the world as an oyster with many pearls to harvest.

11–15 You try hard, but sometimes your negative attitude prevents you from getting involved in productive projects. Many times you take responsibility, but there are situations where you look to others to take care of problems.

0–10 You complain too much and are usually focused on the "worst case scenario." To you the world is controlled by fate and no matter what you do it seems to get you nowhere, so you let other people develop opportunities. You need to start seeing the positive qualities in yourself and in others and see yourself as the "master of your fate."

For more practice exercises, consult the fifth edition of *Organizational Behavior: Experiences and Cases* by Dorothy Marcic and Joseph Seltzer (South-Western, 1998).

Experiencing OB

Interact with the model of empowerment and its four dimensions at our animated concept and activity site. Choose Power&Politics from the "select a topic" pull-down menu, then Sharing Power from the "overview tab."

http://www.experiencingob.com

Four dimensions comprise the essence of empowerment: meaning, competence, self-determination, and impact.[47] *Meaning* is a fit between the work role and the employee's values and beliefs. It is the engine of empowerment through which employees become energized about their jobs. If employees' hearts are not in their work, they cannot feel empowered. *Competence* is the belief that one has the ability to do the job well. Without competence, employees will feel inadequate and lack a sense of empowerment. *Self-determination* is having control over the way one does his or her work. Employees who feel they're just following orders from the boss cannot feel empowered. *Impact* is the belief that one's job makes a difference within the organization. Without a sense of contributing to a goal, employees cannot feel empowered.

Employees need to experience all four of the empowerment dimensions in order to feel truly empowered. Only then will organizations reap the hoped-for rewards from empowerment efforts. The rewards sought are increased effectiveness, higher job satisfaction, and less stress.

Empowerment is easy to advocate but difficult to put into practice. Conger offers some guidelines on how leaders can empower others.

First, managers should express confidence in employees and set high performance expectations. Positive expectations can go a long way toward enabling good performance, as the Pygmalion effect shows (Chapter 3).

Second, managers should create opportunities for employees to participate in decision making. This means participation in the forms of both voice and choice. Employees should not just be asked to contribute their opinions about any issue; they should also have a vote in the decision that is made. One method for increasing participation is using self-managed teams, as we discussed in Chapter 8.

Third, managers should remove bureaucratic constraints that stifle autonomy. Often, companies have antiquated rules and policies that prevent employees from managing themselves. An example is a collection agency where a manager's signature was once required to approve long-term payment arrangements for delinquent customers. Collectors, who spoke directly with customers, were the best judges of whether the payment arrangements were workable, and having to consult a manager made them feel closely supervised and powerless. The rule was dropped, and collections increased.

Fourth, managers should set inspirational or meaningful goals. When individuals feel they "own" a goal, they are more willing to take personal responsibility for it.

Empowerment is a matter of degree. Jobs can be thought of in two dimensions: job content and job context. Job content consists of the tasks and procedures necessary for doing a particular job. Job context is broader. It is the reason the organization needs the job and includes the way the job fits into the organization's mission, goals, and objectives. These two dimensions are depicted in Figure 10.2, the employee empowerment grid.

Figure 10.2
Employee Empowerment Grid

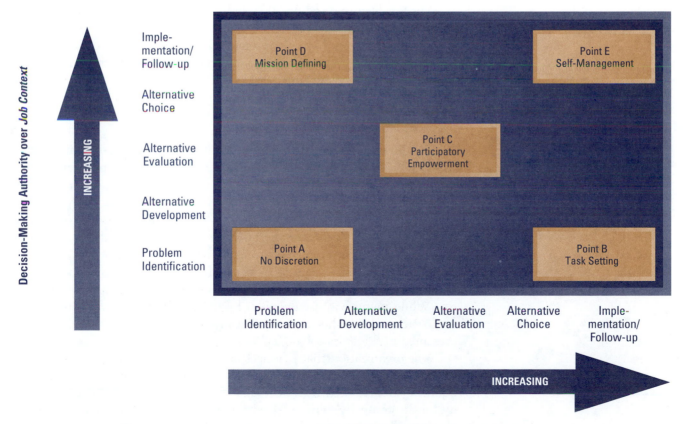

Both axes of the grid contain the major steps in the decision-making process. As shown on the horizontal axis, decision-making authority over job content increases in terms of greater involvement in the decision-making process. Similarly, the vertical axis shows that authority over job context increases with greater involvement in that decision-making process. Combining job content and job context authority in this way produces five points that vary in terms of the degree of empowerment.[48]

No Discretion (point A) represents the traditional, assembly-line job: highly routine and repetitive, with no decision-making power. Recall from Chapter 7 that if these jobs have a demanding pace and if workers have no discretion, distress will result.

Task Setting (point B) is the essence of most empowerment programs in organizations today. In this case, the worker is empowered to make decisions about the best way to get the job done, but has no decision responsibility for the job context.

Participatory Empowerment (point C) represents a situation that is typical of autonomous work groups that have some decision-making power over both job content and job context. Their involvement is in problem identification, developing alternatives, and evaluating alternatives, but the actual choice of alternatives is often beyond their power. Participatory empowerment can lead to job satisfaction and productivity.

Mission Defining (point D) is an unusual case of empowerment and is seldom seen. Here, employees have power over job context but not job content. An example would be a unionized team that is asked to decide whether their jobs could be better done by an outside vendor. Deciding to outsource would dramatically affect the mission of the company, but would not affect job content, which is specified in the union contract. Assuring these employees of continued employment regardless of their decision would be necessary for this case of empowerment.

Self-Management (point E) represents total decision-making control over both job content and job context. It is the ultimate expression of trust. One example is Chaparral Steel (part of Texas Industries), where employees redesign their own jobs to add value to the organization.

Empowerment should begin with job content and proceed to job context. Because the workforce is so diverse, managers should recognize that some employees are more ready for empowerment than others. Managers must diagnose situations and determine the degree of empowerment to extend to employees. Eaton Corporation has learned this through trial and error. While many Eaton employees loved empowerment, some resisted it, and some even left the company. Eaton's experience with empowerment is presented in Organizational Reality 10.2.

One organization that practices empowerment successfully is Square D Company, an electronics technology company of 16,000 employees.[49] Square D created Vision College in 1987 to focus on personal accountability for the company's vision: "Dedicated to growth, committed to quality." Vision College provides an opportunity for Square D employees to compare

ORGANIZATIONAL REALITY 10.2

"Empowerment Is Not for Everybody"

At Eaton Corporation's small forge plant in South Bend, Indiana, empowerment is a near-religion. Like many American businesses, Eaton latched onto empowerment by creating self-directed work teams and moving responsibilities down to workers on the factory floor. The hope was to tap into workers' brains, instill a greater sense of professionalism, encourage self-motivation, and increase commitment to Eaton's success. Sounds good, doesn't it? To most workers, it does. Many prefer empowerment to old-style management and narrowly defined jobs.

For some, however, empowerment is not a good fit. One factory worker liked the idea of being her own boss, but hated having to fix broken machines and having to learn a wide ranges of jobs. She felt her teammates were constantly watching her and found that experience stressful. After nine months, she quit.

Eaton's work teams are empowered to enforce policies themselves. If someone has excessive absences or doesn't get along with coworkers, the other members of the team are quick to take action. It can feel like having a hundred bosses. Workers at Eaton even tried the extreme measure of putting offenders in front of the workforce and having a vote on whether to keep them. In one case, the offenders were abusing the overtime guidelines, and both kept their jobs, but the meetings to vote on whether to fire people were dropped. Plant manager Tom Gothard says, "You run self-direction by trial and error."

One employee, a ten-year veteran from a unionized auto plant, lasted only six months at Eaton. Coworkers said he was constantly in conflict with other workers. The employee claimed he did like certain things about empowerment: the absence of time clocks and self-reporting of hours worked and overtime. He did not, however, like the emphasis on communication, interaction with teammates, and frequent meetings. He felt that coworkers acted quietly to fire him, and without a protective union, they were able to do so easily.

Eaton's plant has an employee turnover rate of 10 percent per year, and most are people who quit. Part of the turnover may be due to a distaste for empowerment, but part is also due to the nature of the work, which is hot, heavy, dirty, and noisy. The turnover is remarkable given the elaborate hiring process used. Only one in ten applicants is offered a job, and applicants can go through as many as thirteen interviews before being hired. Workers are careful about endorsing an applicant, because they fear that if the new hire fails, it will reflect badly on themselves.

Eaton's experience shows that some people are simply not suited for empowerment. They may simply want to put in their eight hours and go home. Plant manager Gothard sums it up by saying, "It takes a huge amount of maturity to be a self-directed worker." Empowerment can be taught, but the employee has to want to learn it.

Discussion Question

1. What type of individual responds best to empowerment? If an employee resists empowerment, what can a manager do?

SOURCE: T. Aeppel, "Missing the Boss: Not All Workers Find Idea of Empowerment as Neat As It Sounds," *The Wall Street Journal*, September 8, 1997, A1. Permission conveyed through Copyright Clearance Center, Inc.

their current state with their vision, or desired state. All Square D employees participate in two-day Vision College sessions, in which the employees provide information about what works, what doesn't work, and what needs improvement in the company. They also discuss and define their own role in that improvement process. The establishment of Vision College to promote empowerment has moved accountability to the lowest levels of the organization.

At Oregon Cutting Systems (a subsidiary of Blount, Inc.), empowerment is a key element of the quality process. Oregon Cutting designs and manufactures cutting tools and holds half of the world's market for chains for saws. At Oregon Cutting, machine operators use statistical process control to improve product quality. Operators are empowered to gather their own data, find the causes of problems, make decisions, and act to fix the problems. Managers at Oregon Cutting prefer that employees ask for forgiveness rather than permission. Empowerment is essential to an organizational culture that supports quality.

The empowerment process also carries with it a risk of failure. When you delegate responsibility and authority, you must be prepared to allow employees to fail; and failure is not something most managers tolerate well. At Levi Strauss, an employee failed to order enough fabric to meet a production run on jeans. The manager sat down with the employee and found out what had gone wrong and how to prevent that problem in the future. She did this in a nonthreatening way, without blaming or fingerpointing.[50] Coaching and counseling following a failure can turn it into a learning experience.

MANAGERIAL IMPLICATIONS: USING POWER EFFECTIVELY

Managers must depend on others to get things done. John Kotter argues that managers therefore need to develop power strategies to operate effectively.[51] Kotter offers some guidelines for managing dependence on others and for using power successfully:

- *Use power in ethical ways.* People make certain assumptions about the use of power. One way of using the various forms of power ethically is by applying the criteria of utilitarian outcomes, individual rights, and distributive justice.

- *Understand and use all of the various types of power and influence.* Successful managers diagnose the situation, understand the people involved, and choose a compatible influence method.

- *Seek jobs that allow you to develop your power skills.* Recognize that managerial positions are dependent ones, and look for positions that allow you to focus on a critical issue or problem.

- *Use power tempered by maturity and self-control.* Power for its own sake should not be a goal, nor should power be used for self-aggrandizement.

- *Accept that influencing people is an important part of the management job.* Power means getting things accomplished; it is not a dirty word. Acquiring and using power well is a key to managerial success.

You can use these guidelines to enhance your own power skills. Mastering the power and politics within an organization takes respect and patience. When all people are treated as important, the total amount of power within the organization will increase.

Looking Back

Harpo, Oprah, and Power

Did Harpo Productions, Inc., Oprah Winfrey, and Howard Lyman, a guest on her show, hurt Amarillo ranching families and the cattle industry by their comments? Do Harpo and its spokesperson, Oprah, have enough power to damage an entire industry?

The judge in the case determined that the cattle ranchers could not use the food disparagement ("veggie libel") law because live cattle are not a perishable food and are thus not covered by the law. That meant the ranchers had to pursue the case as basic business defamation; that is, they had to show that Harpo and Oprah deliberately and recklessly made untrue statements, not just that the ranchers suffered financial losses.

While on the stand in Amarillo, Oprah was asked about her power and her ability to influence her audience. Her reply was, "I believe people I speak to are intelligent enough to make decisions for themselves." She added that everyone at Harpo Productions bears the responsibility of making sure the show is fair. Harpo's mission is "to inform, enlighten, uplift and entertain; to use our lives and voices as a means of service to the viewing public." In other contexts, Oprah has remarked on power: "Unless you choose to do great things with it, it makes no difference . . . how much power you have."

In the end, the Texas jury threw out the lawsuit. The jurors decided that the real power that was relevant in the case was the power of free speech guaranteed by the First Amendment.[52]

CHAPTER SUMMARY

1. Power is the ability to influence others. Influence is the process of affecting the thoughts, behavior, and feelings of others. Authority is the right to influence others.

2. French and Raven's five forms of interpersonal power are reward, coercive, legitimate, referent, and expert power.

3. The key to using all of these types of power well is to use them ethically.

4. McClelland believes personal power is negative and social power is positive.

5. Intergroup power sources include control of critical resources and strategic contingencies.

6. According to Etzioni's power analysis, the characteristics of the organization are an important factor in deciding the type of power to use.

7. Recognizing symbols of both power and powerlessness is a key diagnostic skill for managers.

8. Organizational politics is an inevitable feature of work life. Political behavior consists of actions not officially sanctioned that are taken to influence others in order to meet personal goals. Managers should take a proactive role in managing politics.

9. The employee–boss relationship is an important political relationship. Employees can use their skills to develop more effective working relationships with their bosses.

10. Empowerment is a positive strategy for sharing power throughout the organization.

KEY TERMS

power   285

influence   285

authority   285

zone of indifference   285

reward power   286

coercive power   286

legitimate power   286

referent power   287

expert power   287

personal power   290

social power   290

strategic contingencies   291

powerlessness   293

organizational politics   295

political behavior   295

empowerment   302

REVIEW QUESTIONS

1. What are the five types of power according to French and Raven? What are the effects of these types of power?
2. What are the intergroup sources of power?
3. Distinguish between personal and social power. What are the four power-oriented characteristics of the best managers?
4. According to Rosabeth Moss Kanter, what are the symbols of power? The symptoms of powerlessness?
5. How do organizations encourage political activity?
6. Which influence tactics are most effective?
7. What are some of the characteristics of an effective relationship between you and your boss?
8. What are some ways to empower people at work?

DISCUSSION AND COMMUNICATION QUESTIONS

1. Who is the most powerful person you know personally? What is it that makes the person so powerful?
2. Why is it hard to determine if power has been used ethically?
3. What kinds of membership (alienative, calculative, moral) do you currently have? Is the power used in these relationships congruent?
4. As a student, do you experience yourself as powerful, powerless, or both? On what symbols or symptoms are you basing your perception?
5. How does attribution theory explain the reactions supervisors can have to influence tactics? How can managers prevent the negative consequences of political behavior?
6. Are people in your work environment empowered? How could they become more empowered?
7. Chapter 2 discussed power distance as a dimension of cultural differences. How would empowerment efforts be different in a country with high power distance?
8. (*communication question*) Think of a person you admire. Write a newspaper feature analyzing the person's use of power in terms of the ideas presented in the chapter.

ETHICS QUESTIONS

1. Which of French and Raven's five types of power has the most potential for abuse? How can the abuse be prevented?

2. Under what circumstances is it ethical to manipulate people for the good of the organization?

3. Are moral memberships the only ethical organizational memberships? That is, can alienative and calculative memberships be ethical? Explain.

4. What are the most common forms of political behavior that you see in your work or school environment? Are they ethical or unethical? Explain.

5. Is it possible to have an organization where all power is equally shared, or is the unequal distribution of power a necessary evil in organizations? Explain.

Experiential Exercises

10.1 Social Power Role Plays

1. Divide the class into five groups of equal size, each of which is assigned one of the French and Raven types of power.

2. Read the following paragraph and prepare an influence plan using the type of power that has been assigned to your group. When you have finished your planning, select one member to play the role of instructor. Then choose from your own or another group a "student" who is to be the recipient of the "instructor's" efforts.

You are an instructor in a college class and have become aware that a potentially good student has been repeatedly absent from class and sometimes is unprepared when he is there. He seems to be satisfied with the grade he is getting, but you would like to see him attend regularly, be better prepared, and thus do better in the class. You even feel that the student might get really turned on to pursuing a career in this field, which is an exciting one for you. You are respected and liked by your students, and it irritates you that this person treats your dedicated teaching with such a cavalier attitude. You want to influence the student to start attending regularly.

3. Role-playing.
   a. Each group role-plays its influence plan.
   b. During the role-playing, members in other groups should think of themselves as the student being influenced. Fill out the following "Reaction to Influence Questionnaire" for each role-playing episode, including your own.

4. Tabulate the results of the questionnaire within your group. For each role-playing effort, determine how many people thought the power used was reward, coercive, and so on; then add up each member's score for item 2, then for items 3, 4, and 5.

5. Group discussion.
   a. As a class, discuss which influence strategy is the most effective in compliance, long-lasting effect, acceptable attitude, and enhanced relationships.
   b. What are the likely side effects of each type of influence strategy?

Reaction to Influence Questionnaire

Role-Play #1

1. Type of power used (mark one):

   Reward—Ability to influence because of potential reward.

   Coercive—Ability to influence because of capacity to coerce or punish.

   Legitimate—Stems from formal position in organization.

   Referent—Comes from admiration and liking.

   Expert—Comes from superior knowledge or ability to get things done.

Think of yourself on the receiving end of the influence attempt just described and record your own reaction with an "X" in the appropriate box.

2. As a result of this influence attempt I will . . .

   definitely not comply   definitely comply
   1   2   3   4   5

3. Any change that does come about will be . . .

   temporary   long-lasting
   1   2   3   4   5

4. My own personal reaction is . . .

   resistant   accepting
   1   2   3   4   5

5. As a result of this influence attempt, my relationship with the instructor will probably be . . .

   worse   better
   1   2   3   4   5

Role-Plays

1	2	3	4	5

1	2	3	4	5

SOURCE: Gib Akin, *Exchange* 3, No. 4 (1978): 38–39. Reprinted by permission of Gib Akin, McIntire School of Commerce, University of Virginia.

10.2 Empowerment in the Classroom

1. Divide the class into groups of six people.

2. Each group is to brainstorm ways in which students might be more empowered in the classroom. The ideas do not have to be either feasible or reasonable. They can be as imaginative as possible.

3. Each group should now analyze each of the empowerment ideas for feasibility, paying attention to administrative or other constraints that may hamper implementation. This feasibility discussion might include ideas about how the college or university could be altered.

4. Each group should present its empowerment ideas along with its feasibility analysis. Questions of clarification for each group should follow each presentation.

5. Discuss the following questions as a class:
    a. Who is threatened by the power changes caused by empowerment?
    b. Are there unintended or adverse consequences of empowerment? Explain.

Learning Objectives

After reading this chapter, you should be able to do the following:

1. Define *leadership* and *followership*. *p. 315*

2. Discuss the differences between leadership and management. *p. 315*

3. Distinguish among transformational, transactional, and charismatic leaders. *p. 319*

4. Compare autocratic, democratic, and laissez-faire leadership styles. *p. 322*

5. Explain initiating structure and consideration, leader behaviors, and the Managerial Grid. *p. 324*

6. Explain Fiedler's contingency theory of leadership. *p. 328*

7. Distinguish among the path–goal theory, the Vroom-Yetton-Jago theory, and the situational leadership model. *p. 331*

8. Discuss the characteristics of effective and dynamic followers. *p. 336*

11

Leadership and Followership

Thinking Ahead

Howard Schultz's Leadership Role in Changing Starbucks Coffee

Leaders may trigger organizational transformations when they create a new business vision for a company. Howard Schultz triggered this type of transformation and changed the game at Starbucks Coffee beginning in the late 1980s. Change may create one of three kinds of organizational transformations.[1] Growth may trigger organizational transformations of the first kind—a change from an entrepreneurship to a professionally managed company. Decline may trigger organizational transformations of the second kind—a revitalization of an established company, such as the "new" Chrysler Corporation (now part of DaimlerChrysler) under Lee Iacocca. New business visions like Schultz's trigger organizational transformations of the third kind—a metamorphosis from one kind of business to another.

Founded in 1971 as a purveyor of whole bean coffee, Starbucks was a successful entrepreneurial venture for well over a decade. A year after joining the company in 1982, Schultz took a business trip to Milan where he marveled at the romantic and ubiquitous Italian

314

coffee bars. From this experience he developed the vision to change the basic business of Starbucks from that of a purveyor of coffee to an American version of the Italian coffee bar. Starbucks Coffee's owners were reluctant to pursue the new business vision. Therefore, Schultz left Starbucks in 1985, founding *Il Giornale* as the company through which to pursue his business vision. In 1987 he returned to buy Starbucks Coffee, beginning its transformation into a new organization. As they say, the rest is history. Well, not quite. Starbucks's change in business vision beginning in the late 1980s led to significant national and international growth, triggering an organizational transformation of the first kind. Starbucks Coffee's transformation from an entrepreneurial venture to a professionally managed company is discussed in the Looking Back feature at the end of the chapter.

Leadership in organizations is the process of guiding and directing the behavior of people in the work environment. The first section of the chapter distinguishes leadership from management. *Formal leadership* occurs when an organization officially bestows on a leader the authority to guide and direct others in the organization. *Informal leadership* occurs when a person is unofficially accorded power by others in the organization and uses influence to guide and direct their behavior. Leadership is among the most researched topics in organizational behavior and one of the least understood social processes in organizations.

Sections two through five examine four types of leadership theories: Type I (universal trait) theories, Type II (universal behavior) theories, Type III (situational trait) theories, and Type IV (situational behavior) theories. The sixth section summarizes guidelines for leadership in organizations. The final section of the chapter focuses on the process of followership. *Followership* in organizations is the process of being guided and directed by a leader in the work environment. Leaders and followers are companions in these processes. Herb Kelleher's leadership style, which inspires his followers at Southwest Airlines, is described in Organizational Reality 11.1. Kelleher's transformational style of leadership and his followers' positive responses have benefited everyone at Southwest Airlines as well as its customers.

1. Define *leadership* and *followership*.

leadership
The process of guiding and directing the behavior of people in the work environment.

formal leadership
Officially sanctioned leadership based on the authority of a formal position.

informal leadership
Unofficial leadership accorded to a person by other members of the organization.

followership
The process of being guided and directed by a leader in the work environment.

LEADERSHIP AND MANAGEMENT

John Kotter suggests that leadership and management are two distinct, yet complementary systems of action in organizations.[2] Specifically, he believes that effective leadership produces useful change in organizations (as exemplified by Lee Iacocca at Chrysler Corporation in the early 1980s) and that good management controls complexity in the organization and its environment (as exemplified by Jack Welch at General Electric). Healthy organizations need both effective leadership and good management.

For Kotter, the management process involves (1) planning and budgeting, (2) organizing and staffing, and (3) controlling and problem solv-

2. Discuss the differences between leadership and management.

ORGANIZATIONAL REALITY 11.1

Kelleher's Inspiring Leadership at Southwest Airlines

Herb Kelleher is chairman and CEO of Southwest Airlines, one of the "100 Best Companies to Work for in America" in 1998. Kelleher's business life is focused on inspiring his employees through a transformational style of leadership that enables them to achieve levels of performance beyond all expectations. A lawyer by profession, Kelleher learned airline operations and led Southwest to the top tier of an industry that became savagely competitive following the 1978 Airline Deregulation Act. Though he smokes, armwrestles, drinks Wild Turkey, and raps in music videos, it is only slight hyperbole to say Kelleher inspires all his employees to worship the ground he walks on. His behavior is charismatic, and he intellectually stimulates and empowers people at work, giving individual and personal consideration to all Southwest employees. His followers at Southwest have the self-respect, self-confidence, creativity, and sense of purpose that have led to numerous awards and recognitions for performance excellence within the service and airline industries. From the founding of the company in 1967, Kelleher has emphasized a vision for Southwest Airlines that enabled him and his followers to overcome significant legal obstacles in the first four years of incorporation, to successfully do battle with now defunct airlines, and to lift off their first flight in Texas during 1971. Kelleher's inspiring and transforming style of leadership has been the wind under the wings of his followers at Southwest Airlines, enabling these companions in the leader–follower duet at work to create a productive environment that is the best of the best in America.

Discussion Questions

1. What are the potential downsides to Kelleher's style of leadership, if any?

2. What leadership challenges, dilemmas, or problems is Kelleher's successor at Southwest Airlines likely to face?

SOURCE: R. B. Lieber, "100 Best Companies to Work for in America," *Fortune* (January 12, 1998): 72+.

Experiencing OB

Learn how a leader's use of power affects employee behavior and productivity. Visit our animated concept and activity site. Choose Leadership from the "select a topic" pull-down menu, then Power from the "overview tab."

http://www.experiencingob.com

ing. The management process reduces uncertainty and stabilizes an organization. Alfred P. Sloan's integration and stabilization of General Motors after its early growth years are an example of good management.

In contrast, the leadership process involves (1) setting a direction for the organization; (2) aligning people with that direction through communication; and (3) motivating people to action, partly through empowerment and partly through basic need gratification. The leadership process creates uncertainty and change in an organization. Donald Peterson's championing of a quality revolution at Ford Motor Company is an example of effective leadership. Leadership is not necessarily limited to one person; for example, General Electric Medical Systems Group (GEMS) uses the Global Leadership Program to train leaders for global operations, focusing on cross-cultural and language skills.[3] GEMS is just one of many companies focusing on leadership training for global operations. This training requires different skills from traditional leadership training, and the privatization of government services requires still different skills.

All managers have a leadership role and management responsibility, and this chapter addresses the leadership role. We have organized the many theories of leadership into four categories using Jago's typology shown in Figure 11.1.[4] The two dimensions of the typology are (1) the attribute of the leader (i.e., personality trait or behavior) considered most important in the theory and (2) the generalizability of the leader's traits or behaviors across situations or contexts. Universal theories do not give much emphasis to the specific situation or context in which the leader exercises influence, whereas contingency theories believe that the specific situation or context is important. The four categories of leadership theories that result when these two dimensions are considered together are Type I universal trait theories, Type II universal behavior theories, Type III situational trait theories, and Type IV situational behavioral theories. The theories within this four-category framework offer the student or manager a toolkit of alternatives for fulfilling their leadership role in organizations. Cultural diversity should be considered in the international or global applications of any of the theories discussed in the chapter.

Jay Conger finds qualitative leadership studies to be among the richest, yet rarest in leadership research.[5] Biographical studies that offer insight into the leadership context also fall in this category. For example, George C. Marshall, World War II general and later secretary of state, comes to mind as a great leader whose traits enabled him to be successful in the military and as a statesman. In contrast, John DeLorean was a very successful automotive executive who rose to the top ranks of General Motors Corporation only to fail as an entrepreneur designing and building his own cars. These examples suggest that some individuals may be good leaders in different situations and some individuals may not. Hence, the situation and the leader may be important considerations in leadership.

All leadership theories in one way or another address the issue of how followers receive necessary guidance and respond positively to their leaders.

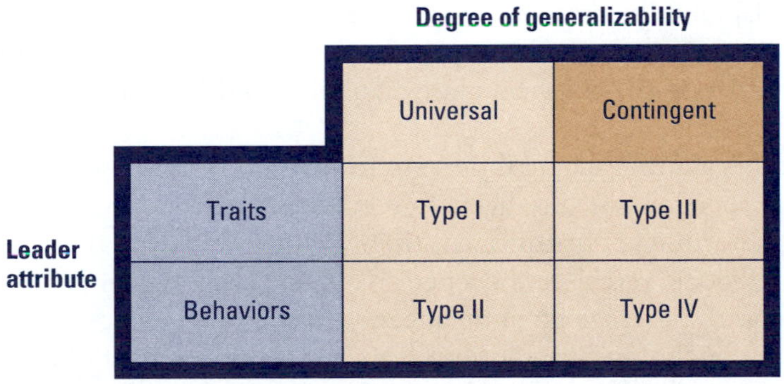

Degree of generalizability

		Universal	Contingent
Leader attribute	Traits	Type I	Type III
	Behaviors	Type II	Type IV

Figure 11.1
A Typology for Leadership Theories

SOURCE: Reprinted by permission, A. G. Jago, "Leadership: Perspectives in Theory and Research," *Management Science* 28 (1982):316. Copyright © 1982, The Institute of Management Sciences (currently INFORMS), 901 Elkridge Landing Road, Suite 400, Linthicum, Maryland 21090–2909 USA.

The theories assume the leader is the primary source of guidance and positive influence. Possibly, however, followers receive the necessary guidance and positive influence from alternative sources in the work environment. Task substitutes for leadership include unambiguous, routine work. Organizational substitutes for task-oriented behavior include formal rules, regulations, and procedures. Organizational substitutes for relationship-oriented behavior include a closely knit, cohesive work group. Alternatively, followers may exercise self-leadership, one important part of individual self-control systems at work.[6]

TYPE I UNIVERSAL TRAIT THEORIES

Type I theories of leadership were the first attempts at understanding leadership. These theories of leadership attempt to identify the traits and/or inherent attributes of leaders, regardless of the leaders' situation or circumstances, as well as the impact of these traits and/or styles on the followers. Early Type I theories focused on a leader's physical attributes, personality, and abilities. Recently, a renewed interest in Type I theories has focused attention on the distinctions between leaders and managers, as well as on charismatic leadership. The implications of Type I theories for organizations involve selection issues rather than training and development issues.

Physical Attributes, Personality, and Abilities

The first studies of leadership attempted to identify what physical attributes, personality characteristics, and abilities distinguished leaders from other members of a group.[7] The physical attributes considered have been height, weight, physique, energy, health, appearance, and even age. This line of research yielded some interesting findings. However, very few valid generalizations emerged from this line of inquiry. Therefore, there is insufficient evidence to conclude that leaders can be distinguished from followers on the basis of physical attributes.

Leader personality characteristics that have been examined include originality, adaptability, introversion–extroversion, dominance, self-confidence, integrity, conviction, mood optimism, and emotional control. There is some evidence that leaders may be more adaptable and self-confident than the average group member.

With regard to leader abilities, attention has been devoted to such constructs as social skills, intelligence, scholarship, speech fluency, cooperativeness, and insight. In this area, there is some evidence that leaders are more intelligent, verbal, and cooperative and have a higher level of scholarship than the average group member.

These conclusions suggest traits leaders possess, but the findings are neither strong nor uniform. For each attribute or trait claimed to distinguish leaders from followers, there were always at least one or two studies with contradictory findings. For some, the trait theories are invalid, though interesting and intuitively of some relevance. The trait theories have had very limited success in being able to identify universal, distinguishing attributes of leaders.

Transformational Leadership

Transformational leaders inspire and excite followers to high levels of performance.[8] They rely on their personal attributes instead of their official position to manage followers. For example, the late Sam Walton may be considered the transformational leader and the visionary heart of Wal-Mart. Certainly, he changed the way the U.S. retailing business operated. As in the case of Wal-Mart, however, it becomes an organizational challenge to figure out a way to institutionalize a transformational leader's style and vision.[9]

There is some evidence that leaders may learn transformational leadership and benefit from its power to inspire followers to perform beyond expectations.[10] As a young student at Texas A&M University, for example, Henry Cisneros began developing the leadership skills that would later enable him to inspire his diverse followers as mayor of San Antonio and cochair of the National Hispanic Leadership Agenda. Cisneros believes that studying the history and biographies of great leaders can enable a person to develop transformational leadership skills.[11] Early successful development as a leader does not immunize one against subsequent problems. As U.S. corporations increasingly operate in a global economy, there is a greater demand for leaders who can practice transformational leadership by converting their visions into reality.[12]

Jerry C. Wofford and his colleagues have focused attention on the unique cognitions of transformational leaders that distinguish their thinking from the thinking of transactional leaders and managers. The research results have important implications for leadership development, suggesting that those who aspire to being transformational leaders should learn to think differently about themselves, their followers, and the work in which they are engaged with their followers. As transformational leaders think, so do they act, and research by others has demonstrated that transformational leadership influences organizational citizenship behaviors through followers' trust in their leader. The findings validate the basic notion that transformational leader behaviors influence followers to perform "above and beyond the call of duty."[13]

Unfortunately, organizations often do not encourage the development of transformational leaders within their ranks. In fact, bureaucratic organizations foster the development of managers to the exclusion of leaders, leaving a leadership gap in organizations and society.[14] Because leaders challenge established ways of working, they are a source of uncertainty, anxiety, and discomfort to the organization, and they challenge its stability. Leaders want to change the established order to improve the system. While at General Motors, John DeLorean never fully accepted the GM way of doing things; he was a leader who agitated for improvements in the system. DeLorean was less concerned with appearances, which were important at

3. ▪ Distinguish among transformational, transactional, and charismatic leaders.

GM, than he was with substance in automotive manufacturing. However, too much agitation led to his early departure from General Motors. The dilemma for an organization is how to draw on the strengths and contributions of each type of personality without alienating either type.

Leaders as Distinct Personalities

Abraham Zaleznik proposes that leaders have distinct personalities that stand in contrast to the personalities of manager.[15] Zaleznik suggests that both leaders and managers make a valuable contribution to an organization and that each one's contribution is different. Whereas **leaders** agitate for change and new approaches, **managers** advocate stability and the status quo. There is a dynamic tension between leaders and managers that makes it difficult for each to understand the other. Leaders and managers differ along four separate dimensions of personality: attitudes toward goals, conceptions of work, relationships with other people, and sense of self. The differences between these two personality types are summarized in Table 11.1. Zaleznik's distinction between leaders and managers is similar to the distinction made between transactional and transformational leaders, or between leadership and supervision. Transactional leaders use formal rewards and punishment to engage in deal making and contractual obligations.

leader
An advocate for change and new approaches to problems.

manager
An advocate for stability and the status quo.

Table 11.1
Leaders and Managers

Personality Dimension	Manager	Leader
Attitudes toward goals	Has an impersonal, passive, functional attitude; believes goals arise out of necessity and reality	Has a personal and active attitude; believes goals arise from desire and imagination
Conceptions of work	Views work as an enabling process that combines people, ideas, and things; seeks moderate risk through coordination and balance	Looks for fresh approaches to old problems; seeks high-risk positions, especially with high payoffs
Relationships with others	Avoids solitary work activity, preferring to work with others; avoids close, intense relationships; avoids conflict	Is comfortable in solitary work activity; encourages close, intense working relationships; is not conflict averse
Sense of self	Is once born; makes a straightforward life adjustment; accepts life as it is	Is twice born; engages in a struggle for a sense of order in life; questions life

SOURCE: A. Zaleznik, "Managers and Leaders: Are They Different?" *Harvard Business Review* 55 (1977): 67–77.

Women Leaders

An important, emergent leadership question is this: Do women and men lead differently? Historical stereotypes persist, and people characterize successful managers as having more male-oriented attributes than female-oriented attributes.[16] Although legitimate gender differences may exist, the same leadership traits may be interpreted differently in a man and a woman because of stereotypes. The real issue should be leader behaviors that are not bound by gender stereotypes.

Recent research on women's leadership suggests that female leaders form a unique relationship with each of their employees that is independent of their group membership.[17] Further, this research did not find that women systematically used transformational or transactional leadership more frequently in their working relationships. These findings imply that female leaders act out leadership as an individualized, interpersonal process.

Charismatic Leadership

Anita Roddick (founder of The Body Shop), Sam Walton, and Herb Kelleher are charismatic leaders who created a vision and sold it to customers and followers alike, motivating their followers to fulfill the vision. ***Charismatic leadership*** results when a leader uses the force of personal abilities and talents to have profound and extraordinary effects on followers.[18] Some scholars see transformational leadership and charismatic leadership as very similar, but others believe they are different. *Charisma* is a Greek word meaning "gift"; the charismatic leader's unique and powerful gifts are the source of the leader's great influence with followers.[19] In fact, followers often view the charismatic leader as one who possesses superhuman, or even mystical, qualities.[20] Charismatic leaders rely heavily on referent power, discussed in Chapter 10. Followers often accept unconditionally the mission and directions of the leader, suspending their own discriminatory judgment. Hence, charismatic leadership carries with it not only great potential for high levels of achievement and performance on the part of followers but also shadowy risks of destructive courses of action that might harm followers or other people.

Charismatic leadership falls to those who are chosen (are born with the "gift" of charisma) or who cultivate that gift. Some say charismatic leaders are born, and others say they are taught.

Several researchers have attempted to demystify charismatic leadership and distinguish its two faces.[21] The ugly face of charisma is revealed in the personalized power motivations of Adolf Hitler in Nazi Germany and David Koresh of the Branch Davidian cult in Waco, Texas. Both men led their followers into struggle, conflict, and death. The brighter face of charisma is revealed in the socialized power motivations of U.S. President Franklin D. Roosevelt and of Cable News Network (CNN) entrepreneur Ted Turner, who built a large business empire. Peter Drucker has thoughtfully described President Roosevelt and other leaders' styles from firsthand experience.

charismatic leadership
The use, by a leader, of personal abilities and talents in order to have profound and extraordinary effects on followers.

Whereas charismatic leaders with socialized power motivation are concerned about the collective well-being of their followers, charismatic leaders with a personalized power motivation are driven by the need for personal gain and glorification. The former are constructive forces for organizational improvement, whereas the latter may be narcissistic leaders who abuse their power by manipulating and taking advantage of their followers.[22]

Charismatic leadership, like other Type I theories, does not address attributes of the situation that may create contingencies for the exercise of leadership. Whereas the early Type I theories focused on a leader's physical attributes, personality, and abilities, subsequent Type I theories examined leaders from psychodynamic and power motivation perspectives. All Type I theories are concerned with inherent attributes of leaders. Type II theories of leadership shift the focus from traits and attributes to actions and behaviors.

TYPE II UNIVERSAL BEHAVIOR THEORIES

Type II theories of leadership are concerned with describing leaders' actions and behaviors, often from the perspective of the followers. Like Type I theories, Type II theories exclusively emphasize the leader, as opposed to situational characteristics. Although Type II theories depend in some cases on the descriptions by followers of their leaders, these theories do not consider characteristics of the followers themselves or of the leadership situation in understanding the leadership process. The first Type II theory classified leaders according to one of three basic leadership styles, whereas subsequent Type II theories examined common behavioral dimensions of all leaders. Type II theories help organizations train and develop leaders rather than select them.

Leadership Style and Emotional Climate at Work

4. Compare autocratic, democratic, and laissez-faire leadership styles.

autocratic style
A style of leadership in which the leader uses strong, directive, controlling actions to enforce the rules, regulations, activities, and relationships in the work environment.

democratic style
A style of leadership in which the leader takes collaborative, responsive, interactive actions with followers concerning the work and work environment.

laissez-faire style
A style of leadership in which the leader fails to accept the responsibilities of the position.

The earliest research on leadership style, conducted by Kurt Lewin and his students, identified three basic styles: autocratic, democratic, and laissez-faire.[23] Each leader uses one of these three basic styles when approaching a group of followers in a leadership situation. The specific situation is not an important consideration, because the leader's style does not vary with the situation. Rather, the leader's style is a universal trait taken into all situations. The *autocratic style* is directive, strong, and controlling in relationships. Leaders with an autocratic style use rules and regulations to run the work environment. Followers have little discretionary influence over the nature of the work, its accomplishment, or other aspects of the work environment. The leader with a *democratic style* is collaborative, responsive, and interactive in relationships and emphasizes rules and regulations less than the autocratic leader. Followers have a high degree of discretionary influence, although the leader has ultimate authority and responsibility. The leader with a *laissez-faire style* leads through nonleadership. A laissez-faire leader abdicates the authority and responsibility of the position.

Subsequent leadership research has used somewhat different terminology for the same leadership styles: an autocratic style has been labeled boss-centered, job-centered, authoritarian, and even dictatorial.[24] All these labels refer to the same basic traits of autocratic leadership. Likewise, a democratic style has been labeled subordinate-centered, employee-centered, and participative. All these labels refer to the same basic traits of democratic leadership. The laissez-faire style of leadership has not had a comparable alternative set of labels. It is uniformly referred to as laissez-faire leadership.

This approach to the study of leadership, developed at the University of Michigan, suggests that the leader's style has very important implications for the emotional atmosphere of the work environment and, therefore, for the followers who work under that leader. Comparing the work environments under autocratic and democratic leadership is easier than comparing either with the work environment under laissez-faire leadership. The most pronounced consequence of laissez-faire leadership tends to be chaos in the work environment, although there are exceptions.

An autocratic leadership style leads to a work environment characterized by constant influence attempts on the part of the leader, either through direct, close supervision or through the use of many written and unwritten rules and regulations for behavior. The resulting restrictive work environment can create high levels of tension for followers. High tension may affect followers in one of two ways in the work environment. Either the followers strongly inhibit their tension and suppress any conflict at work (which leads to a superficially calm atmosphere), or they express their tension (which results in periodic outbursts of intense conflict and aggression). The pathway the followers choose is in part determined by the strength of the leader. In either case, the autocratic style leads to a restriction of the physical and psychological discretion that followers feel. Finally, leader–follower relationships are often rigid in authoritarian environments. When not taken to an extreme, autocratic leadership can provide structure in the work environment and direction for followers who need clear, explicit guidelines for action.

In comparison with an autocratic leadership style, a democratic leadership style leads to a work environment characterized by fewer influence attempts by the leader. The leader exhibits less direct or less close supervision and establishes fewer written or unwritten rules and regulations for behavior. This pattern of influence leads to lower levels of tension among followers. Nonetheless, tension may still exist and be manifested in expressed conflict, usually over ideas and issues. The conflict tends not to be personalized. Followers in a democratic work environment are less inhibited and experience a much greater sense of physical and psychological freedom than followers in an autocratic work environment. Finally, the relationships between the leader and followers in the democratic work environment exhibit flexibility and spontaneity. For those who need more structure, however, a democratic work environment may elicit uncertainty and anxiety.

5. Explain initiating structure and consideration, leader behaviors, and the Managerial Grid.

initiating structure
Leader behavior aimed at defining and organizing work relationships and roles, as well as establishing clear patterns of organization, communication, and ways of getting things done.

consideration
Leader behavior aimed at nurturing friendly, warm working relationships, as well as encouraging mutual trust and interpersonal respect within the work unit.

P-oriented behavior
Leader behavior that encourages a fast work pace, emphasizes good quality and high accuracy, works toward high-quantity production, and demonstrates concern for rules and regulations.

M-oriented behavior
Leader behavior that is sensitive to employees' feelings, emphasizes comfort in the work environment, works to reduce stress levels, and demonstrates appreciation for follower contributions.

Leadership Behaviors

The leadership research program at Ohio State University measured several specific leader behaviors as an alternative to a generalized leader style, such as autocratic, as was done at Michigan. The initial Ohio State research studied aircrews and pilots.[25] The aircrew members, as followers, were asked a wide range of questions about their lead pilots using the Leader Behavior Description Questionnaire (LBDQ). The results using the LBDQ suggested that there were two important underlying dimensions of leader behaviors.[26] These were labeled initiating structure and consideration.

Initiating structure is leader behavior aimed at defining and organizing work relationships and roles, as well as establishing clear patterns of organization, communication, and ways of getting things done. *Consideration* is leader behavior aimed at nurturing friendly, warm working relationships, as well as encouraging mutual trust and interpersonal respect within the work unit. These two leader behaviors are independent of each other. That is, a leader may be high on both, low on both, or high on one while low on the other. The Ohio State studies were intended to describe leader behavior, not to evaluate or judge behavior.

The Ohio State approach to the study of leadership suggested that leader behavior was open to change and modification, because it was not an enduring trait or attribute. In a study at International Harvester Company (now Navistar International Corporation), Edwin Fleishman found that consideration behaviors could be improved through a training program for the company's supervisors.[27] Although the training resulted in changes in both initiating structure and consideration, the changes were not permanent in either attitude or behavior. When back in the work environment, the supervisors tended toward increased initiating structure behavior and less consideration. The conclusion was that the leadership climate at the company was a more important determinant of leader behaviors than was the training. Therefore, upper management's influence on the behaviors of middle managers and supervisors is important. This logic led some corporations (for example, General Electric) to establish desired leader behaviors directly at the top of the organization.[28]

Leadership Styles in Japan

Shortly after World War II, a program of research was begun in Japan to examine whether U.S. leadership approaches could be generalized in Japanese organizations. This led to a thirty-year program of research that was labeled the Performance-Maintenance (PM) theory of leadership; *P-oriented behavior* and *M-oriented behavior* are characterized in Table 11.2. Although not exactly the same, initiating structure and P-oriented leader behavior are similar, as are consideration and M-oriented leader behavior. According to the Japanese researchers, autocratic leaders are those who emphasize P-oriented behavior to the exclusion of M-oriented behavior, whereas democratic leaders are those who emphasize M-oriented behavior, though not necessarily to the exclusion of P-oriented behavior. Laissez-faire leaders are those who do not exhibit either P-oriented or M-oriented behaviors.

The Japanese researchers studied leadership styles in private enterprises, local government, the postal service, secondary school classrooms, family systems, and sports groups. Their findings suggest that the leadership styles of lower- and middle-level managers affect employee performance in Japan more than in the United States. In addition, the researchers concluded that autocratic leadership may be less successful in Japanese companies than in some U.S. companies.

What distinguishes the Japanese application of Kurt Lewin's original theory is the use of two independent aspects of a leader's behavior as the basis for classifying the leader into an autocratic, democratic, or laissez-faire style. The measurement of two or more dimensions of a leader's behavior is very similar to the Ohio State leader behavior studies begun during the 1950s. Before we turn to a discussion of these studies, take a few minutes to complete Challenge 11.1. This exercise gives you an opportunity to examine your supervisor's or professor's P-oriented and M-oriented behaviors.

The Leadership Grid

The Ohio State leadership studies and the subsequent Japanese leadership approaches focused on behaviors. Robert Blake and Jane Mouton's **Leadership Grid**, originally called the Managerial Grid, was developed with a focus on attitudes. The two underlying dimensions of the Grid are labeled Concern for Results and Concern for People. These two attitudinal dimensions are independent of each other and in different combinations form various leadership styles. Blake and Mouton originally identified five distinct managerial styles, and further development of the Grid has led to the seven distinct leadership styles shown in Figure 11.2.

The **organization man manager (5,5)** is a middle-of-the-road leader who has a medium concern for people and production. This leader attempts to balance a concern for both people and production without a commitment to either. The **authority-compliance manager (9,1)** has great con-

Leadership Grid
An approach to understanding a leader's or manager's concern for results (production) and concern for people.

organization man manager (5,5)
A middle-of-the-road leader.

authority-compliance manager (9,1)
A leader who emphasizes efficient production.

P-Oriented Leadership

Encourages fast work pace
Emphasizes good quality and high accuracy
Works toward high-quantity production
Demonstrates concern for rules and regulations

M-Oriented Leadership

Is sensitive to employees' feelings
Emphasizes comfort in the work environment
Works to reduce stress levels
Demonstrates appreciation for follower contributions

Table 11.2
Characteristics of P-Oriented and M-Oriented Leadership

SOURCE: Reprinted from "The Performance-Maintenance (PM) Theory of Leadership: Review of a Japanese Research Program" by J. Misumi and M. F. Peterson published in *Administrative Science Quarterly* 30 (1985): 207 by permission of Administrative Science Quarterly © 1985.

Challenge 11.1

How Does Your Supervisor Lead?

Answer the following sixteen questions concerning your supervisor's (or professor's) leadership behaviors using the seven-point Likert scale. Then complete the summary to examine your supervisor's behaviors.

	Not at All				Very Much		
1. Is your superior strict about observing regulations?	1	2	3	4	5	6	7
2. To what extent does your superior give you instructions and orders?	1	2	3	4	5	6	7
3. Is your superior strict about the amount of work you do?	1	2	3	4	5	6	7
4. Does your superior urge you to complete your work by the time he or she has specified?	1	2	3	4	5	6	7
5. Does your superior try to make you work to your maximum capacity?	1	2	3	4	5	6	7
6. When you do an inadequate job, does your superior focus on the inadequate way the job was done instead of on your personality?	1	2	3	4	5	6	7
7. Does your superior ask you for reports about the progress of your work?	1	2	3	4	5	6	7
8. Does your superior work out precise plans for goal achievement each month?	1	2	3	4	5	6	7
9. Can you talk freely with your superior about your work?	1	2	3	4	5	6	7
10. Generally, does your superior support you?	1	2	3	4	5	6	7
11. Is your superior concerned about your personal problems?	1	2	3	4	5	6	7
12. Do you think your superior trusts you?	1	2	3	4	5	6	7
13. Does your superior give you recognition when you do your job well?	1	2	3	4	5	6	7
14. When a problem arises in your workplace, does your superior ask your opinion about how to solve it?	1	2	3	4	5	6	7
15. Is your superior concerned about your future benefits like promotions and pay raises?	1	2	3	4	5	6	7
16. Does your superior treat you fairly?	1	2	3	4	5	6	7

Add up your answers to Questions 1 through 8. This total indicates your supervisor's performance orientation:

P-orientation = ————

Add up your answers to Questions 9 through 16. This total indicates your supervisor's maintenance orientation:

M-orientation = ————

A score above 40 is high, and a score below 20 is low.

SOURCE: From J. Misumi and M. F. Peterson, "The Performance-Maintenance (PM) Theory of Leadership," *Administrative Science Quarterly* 30 (1985): 207. Reprinted by permission of the Administrative Science Quarterly.

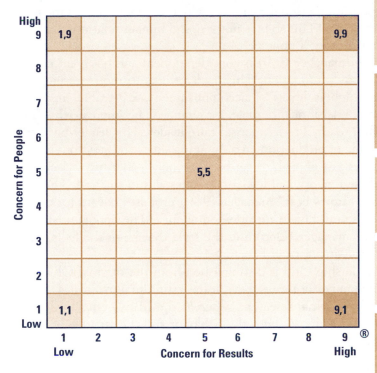

1,9 Country Club Management:
Thoughtful attention to the needs of the people for satisfying relationships leads to a comfortable, friendly organization atmosphere and work tempo.

9,9 Team Management:
Work accomplishment is from committed people; interdependence through a "common stake" in organization purpose leads to relationships of trust and respect.

5,5 Middle-of-the-Road Management:
Adequate organization performance is possible through balancing the necessity to get work out while maintaining morale of people at a satisfactory level.

1,1 Impoverished Management:
Exertion of minimum effort to get required work done is appropriate to sustain organization membership.

9,1 Authority-Compliance Management:
Efficiency in operations results from arranging conditions of work in such a way that human elements interfere to a minimum degree.

In Opportunisitic Management, people adapt and shift to any grid style needed to gain the maximum advantage. Performance occurs according to a system of selfish gain. Effort is given only for an advantage for personal gain.

9+9: Paternalism/Maternalism Management:
Reward and approval are bestowed to people in return for loyalty and obedience; failure to comply leads to punishment.

SOURCE: The Leadership Grid® figure, Paternalism Figure and Opportunism from *Leadership Dilemmas—Grid Solutions*, by Robert R. Blake and Anne Adams McCanse (Formerly the Managerial Grid by Robert R. Blake and Jane S. Mouton). Houston: Gulf Publishing Company, (Grid Figure: p. 29, Paternalism Figure: p. 30, Opportunism Figure: p. 31). Copyright 1991 by Blake and Mouton, and Scientific Methods, Inc. Reproduced by permission of the owners.

Figure 11.2
The Leadership Grid

cern for production and little concern for people. This leader desires tight control in order to get tasks done efficiently and considers creativity and human relations unnecessary. The **country club manager (1,9)** has great concern for people and little concern for production, attempts to avoid con-

country club manager (1,9)
A leader who creates a happy, comfortable work environment.

team manager (9,9)
A leader who builds a highly productive team of committed people.

impoverished manager (1,1)
A leader who exerts just enough effort to get by.

paternalistic "father knows best" manager (9+9)
A leader who promises reward and threatens punishment.

opportunistic "what's in it for me" manager (Opp)
A leader whose style aims to maximize self-benefit.

Experiencing OB

Interact with Fiedler's Contingency Theory and test your understanding by visiting our animated concept and activity site. Choose Leadership from the "select a topic" pull-down menu, then Contingency Leadership from the "overview tab."

http://www.experiencingob.com

6. Explain Fiedler's contingency theory of leadership.

flict, and seeks to be well liked. This leader's goal is to keep people happy through good interpersonal relations, which are more important to him or her than the task. (This style is not a sound human relations approach but rather a soft Theory X approach.)

The **team manager (9,9)** is considered ideal and has great concern for both people and production. This leader works to motivate employees to reach their highest levels of accomplishment, is flexible, responsive to change, and understands the need for change. The **impoverished manager (1,1)** is often referred to as a laissez-faire leader. This leader has little concern for people or production, avoids taking sides, and stays out of conflicts; he or she does just enough to get by. Two new leadership styles have been added to these five original leadership styles within the grid. The **paternalistic "father knows best" manager (9+9)** promises reward for compliance and threatens punishment for non-compliance. The **opportunistic "what's in it for me" manager (Opp)** uses the style that he or she feels will return him or her the greatest self-benefits.

The Leadership Grid is distinguished from the original Ohio State research in two important ways. First, it has attitudinal overtones that are not present in the original research. Whereas the LBDQ aims to describe behavior, the grid addresses both the behavior and the attitude of the leader. Second, the Ohio State approach is fundamentally descriptive and nonevaluative, whereas the grid is normative and prescriptive. Specifically, the grid evaluates the team manager (9,9) as the very best style of managerial behavior. This is the basis on which the grid has been used for team building and leadership training in organizational development, which are discussed in Chapter 16. As an organizational development method, the grid aims to transform the leadership structure of the organization and the manner in which teams throughout the organization are led and managed.

TYPE III SITUATIONAL TRAIT THEORIES

Type III theories of leadership are concerned with identifying the situationally specific conditions in which leaders with particular traits are effective. These contingency theories also focus on leaders' traits or attributes, as do Type I theories. However, Type III theories are contingency theories, as opposed to universal theories. They have a dual focus: the leader and the situation in which the leader works. The central concern of Type III theories is how the leader's traits interact with situational factors in determining team effectiveness in task performance. Fiedler's contingency theory is the one Type III leadership theory developed to date. Its implications for organizations concern how to select the right leader for the situation.

Fiedler's Contingency Theory

Fiedler's contingency theory of leadership proposes that the fit between the leader's need structure and the favorableness of the leader's situation determine the team's effectiveness in work accomplishment. This theory assumes that leaders are either task oriented or relationship oriented, depending upon how the leaders obtain their primary need gratification.[30] Task-oriented leaders are primarily gratified by accomplishing tasks and getting work done. Relationship-oriented leaders are primarily gratified by developing good, comfortable interpersonal relationships. Accordingly, the effectiveness of both types of leaders depends on the favorableness of their situation. The theory classifies the favorableness of the leader's situation according to the leader's position power, the structure of the team's task, and the quality of the leader–follower relationships.

The Least Preferred Coworker Fiedler classifies leaders using the Least Preferred Coworker (LPC) Scale.[31] The LPC Scale is a projective technique through which a leader is asked to think about the person with whom he or she can work least well (the *least preferred coworker*, or **LPC**). This is not necessarily the person the leader likes least; rather, it is the person with whom the leader had the most difficulty getting the job done.

The leader is asked to describe this least preferred coworker using sixteen eight-point bipolar adjective sets. Three of these bipolar adjective sets follow (the leader marks the blank most descriptive of the least preferred coworker):

Pleasant	:	:	:	:	:	:	:	:	Unpleasant
Efficient	:	:	:	:	:	:	:	:	Inefficient
Gloomy	:	:	:	:	:	:	:	:	Cheerful

Leaders who describe their least preferred coworker in positive terms (that is, pleasant, efficient, cheerful, and so on) are classified as high LPC, or relationship-oriented, leaders. Those who describe their least preferred coworker in negative terms (that is, unpleasant, inefficient, gloomy, and so on) are classified as low LPC, or task-oriented, leaders.

The LPC score is a controversial element in contingency theory.[32] The LPC score has been critiqued conceptually and methodologically because it is a projective technique with low measurement reliability.

Situational Favorableness The leader's situation has three dimensions: task structure, position power, and leader–member relations. Based on these three dimensions, the situation is either favorable or unfavorable for the leader. *Task structure* refers to the number and clarity of rules, regulations, and procedures for getting the work done. *Position power* refers to the leader's legitimate authority to evaluate and reward performance, punish errors, and demote group members.

The quality of *leader–member relations* is measured by the Group-Atmosphere Scale, composed of nine eight-point bipolar adjective sets. Three of these bipolar adjective sets follow:

Friendly	:	:	:	:	:	:	:	:	Unfriendly
Accepting	:	:	:	:	:	:	:	:	Rejecting
Warm	:	:	:	:	:	:	:	:	Cold

A favorable leadership situation is one with a structured task for the work group, strong position power for the leader, and good leader–member rela-

least preferred coworker (LPC)
The person a leader has least preferred to work with over his or her career.

task structure
The degree of clarity, or ambiguity, in the work activities assigned to the group.

position power
The authority associated with the leader's formal position in the organization.

leader–member relations
The quality of interpersonal relationships among a leader and the group members.

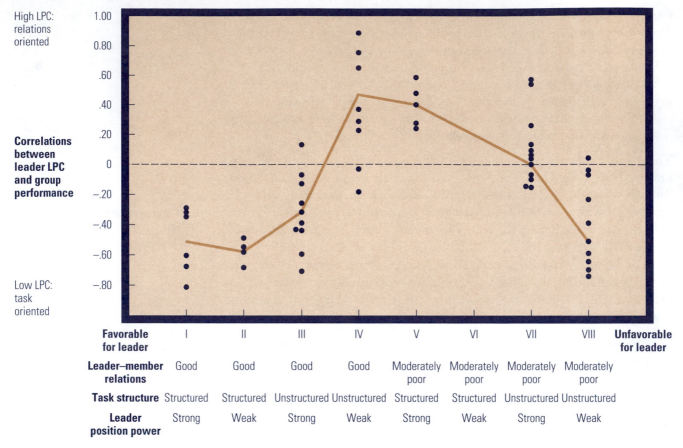

High LPC: relations oriented

Low LPC: task oriented

Correlations between leader LPC and group performance

	I	II	III	IV	V	VI	VII	VIII	
	Favorable for leader							Unfavorable for leader	
Leader–member relations	Good	Good	Good	Good	Moderately poor	Moderately poor	Moderately poor	Moderately poor	
Task structure	Structured	Structured	Unstructured	Unstructured	Structured	Structured	Unstructured	Unstructured	
Leader position power	Strong	Weak	Strong	Weak	Strong	Weak	Strong	Weak	

Figure 11.3
Leadership Effectiveness in the Contingency Theory

SOURCE: F. E. Fiedler, *A Theory of Leader Effectiveness* (New York: McGraw-Hill, 1964). Reprinted with permission of the author.

tions. In contrast, an unfavorable leadership situation is one with an unstructured task, weak position power for the leader, and moderately poor leader–member relations. Between these two extremes, the leadership situation has varying degrees of moderate favorableness for the leader.

Leadership Effectiveness

The contingency theory suggests that low and high LPC leaders are each effective if placed in the right situation.[33] Specifically, low LPC (task-oriented) leaders are most effective in either very favorable or very unfavorable leadership situations. In contrast, high LPC (relationship-oriented) leaders are most effective in situations of intermediate favorableness. Figure 11.3 shows the nature of these relationships and suggests that leadership effectiveness is determined by the degree of fit between the leader and the situation.

What, then, is to be done if there is a misfit? That is, what happens when a low LPC leader is in a moderately favorable situation or when a high LPC leader is in a highly favorable or highly unfavorable situation? It is unlikely that the leader can be changed, according to the theory, because the leader's need structure is an enduring trait requiring intense psychological intervention to alter. This leaves the situation as the preferred point of intervention. Specifically, Fiedler recommends that the leader's situation be reengineered to fit the leader's basic predisposition.[34] Hence, a moderately favorable situation would be reengineered to be more favorable and therefore more suitable for the low LPC leader. The highly favorable or highly unfavorable situation would be changed to one that is moderately favorable, and therefore more suitable for the high LPC leader.

Fiedler's contingency theory is a Type III theory because he considers the leaders' inherent traits, not their behaviors, in considering a fit with the leadership situation. His theory makes an important contribution in drawing our attention to the leader's situation.

TYPE IV SITUATIONAL BEHAVIOR THEORIES

Type IV theories of leadership are concerned with identifying the specific leader behaviors that are most effective in specific leadership situations. A number of leader behaviors are considered important by different Type IV theories. Like Type III theories, Type IV theories are considered contingency theories, as opposed to universal theories. The central concern in the Type IV theories is the behavioral contingencies of the leader that yield the most effective performance by the followers. This section considers three specific Type IV theories: Robert House's path–goal theory, the Vroom-Yetton-Jago normative decision theory, and the situational leadership model developed by Paul Hersey and Kenneth Blanchard. As with Type II theories, the implications for organizations of Type IV theories concern how to train and develop leaders rather than how to select them.

7. Distinguish among the path–goal theory, the Vroom-Yetton-Jago theory, and the situational leadership model.

The Path–Goal Theory

Robert House advocates a path–goal theory of leader effectiveness based on an expectancy theory of motivation.[35] From the perspective of path–goal theory, the basic role of the leader is to enhance follower motivation so that the followers are able to experience need gratification. The leader uses the most appropriate of four leader behavior styles to help followers clarify the paths that lead them to work and personal goals. The key concepts in the theory are shown in Figure 11.4.

The path–goal theory is based on the following two propositions:

- *Proposition 1.* Leader behavior is acceptable and satisfying to followers to the extent that they see it as an immediate source of satisfaction or as instrumental to future satisfaction.
- *Proposition 2.* Leader behavior is motivational to the extent that (1) it makes followers' need satisfaction contingent on effective performance and (2) it complements the followers' environment by pro-

viding the coaching, guidance, support, and rewards necessary for effective performance—rewards that are not otherwise available.

A leader selects from the four leader behavior styles, shown in Figure 11.4, the one that is most helpful to followers at a given time. The directive style is used when the leader must give specific guidance about work tasks, schedule work, maintain performance standards, and let followers know what is expected. The supportive style is used when the leader needs to express concern for followers' well-being and social status. The participative style is used when the leader must engage in problem solving and mutual decision-making activities with followers. The achievement-oriented style is used when the leader must set challenging goals for followers, expect very high levels of performance, and show strong confidence in the followers.

In selecting the appropriate leader behavior style, the leader must consider characteristics of the followers and the work environment. A few characteristics are included in Figure 11.4. Let us look at four examples. In Example 1, the followers are inexperienced and working on an ambiguous, unstructured task. The leader in this situation might best use a directive style. In Example 2, the task is structured, and the followers are experienced and able. Here the leader might better use a supportive style. In Example 3, the followers are experienced and able, but the task is confusing and unstructured. The leader in this situation may be most helpful by using a participative style. In Example 4, the followers are highly trained professionals, and the task is a difficult, yet achievable one. The leader in this situation might best use an achievement-oriented style. The leader always chooses the leader behavior style that helps followers achieve their goals.

The path–goal theory assumes that leaders adapt their behavior and style to fit the characteristics of the followers and the environment in which they work. Actual tests of the path–goal theory and its propositions provide conflicting evidence.[36] Hence, it is premature either to fully accept or fully reject the theory at this point. The path–goal theory does have intuitive

Figure 11.4
The Path–Goal Theory of Leadership

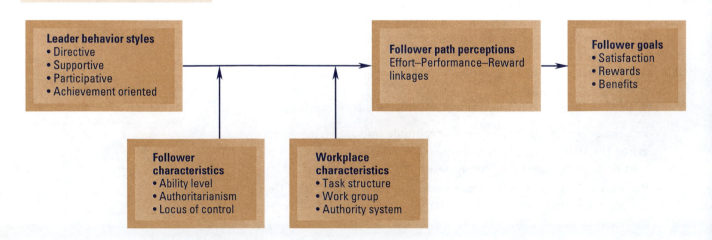

appeal and offers a number of constructive ideas for leaders who lead a variety of followers in a variety of work environments.

Vroom-Yetton-Jago Normative Decision Model

The Vroom-Yetton-Jago normative decision model helps leaders and managers know when to have employees participate in the decision-making process. Victor Vroom, Phillip Yetton, and Arthur Jago developed and refined the normative decision model, which helps managers determine the appropriate decision-making strategy to use. The model recognizes the benefits of authoritative, democratic, and consultive styles of leader behavior.[37] Five forms of decision making are described in the model: two autocratic forms (AI and AII), two consultative forms (CI and CII), and a group method (G). The five forms of decision making follow:

- *The AI form.* The manager makes the decision alone, using whatever information is available at the time. This is the most authoritarian method.
- *The AII form.* The manager seeks information from employees or peers and then makes the decision. Employees may or may not know what the problem is before providing the information to the manager.
- *The CI form.* The manager explains the problem to appropriate peers or employees in a one-on-one format. The manager makes the decision, which may or may not reflect the others' inputs.
- *The CII form.* The manager explains the problem to employees or peers as a group. The manager makes the decision, which may or may not reflect the others' inputs.
- *The G form.* The manager explains the problem to employees and peers as a group, and the group makes the final decision.

The key to the normative decision model is that a manager should use the decision method most appropriate for a given decision situation. The manager arrives at the proper method by working through the decision tree shown in Figure 11.5. Each node in the decision tree asks the manager to answer a question about the decision situation. The questions reflect key attributes of the decision situation: time, quality, commitment, and information. Working through the decision tree leads to a prescribed decision style at the end of the path.

Although the model offers very explicit predictions, as well as prescriptions, for leaders, its utility is limited to the leader decision situation. The model offers no guidance for leaders in nondecision situations where interaction with followers is required for task accomplishment.

One test of the normative decision model supported it based on leader perceptions of a recent decision process but failed to support the model based on follower perceptions of the same process.[38] Vroom and Jago created a new model that substantially improves the original by adding a number of objectives that leaders may choose to seek, such as cost reduction.[39]

QR	Quality requirement	How important is the technical quality of this decision?
CR	Commitment requirement	How important is employee commitment to the decision?
LI	Leader's information	Do you have sufficient information to make a high-quality decision?
ST	Problem structure	Is the problem well structured?
CP	Commitment probability	If you were to make the decision by yourself, is it reasonably certain that your employees would be commited to the decision?
GC	Goal congruence	Do employees share the organizational goals to be attained in solving this problem?
CO	Employee conflict	Is conflict among employees over preferred solutions likely?
SI	Employee information	Do employees have sufficient information to make a high-quality decision?

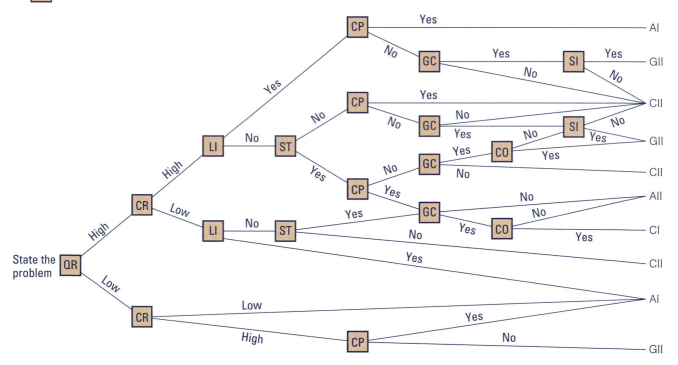

Figure 11.5
*The Vroom-Yetton-Jago
Normative Decision Model*

SOURCE: Adapted and reprinted from *Leadership and Decision-making*, by Victor H. Vroom and Philip W. Yetton, by permission of the University of Pittsburgh Press. © 1973 by University of Pittsburgh Press.

The Situational Leadership Model

The situational leadership model, developed by Paul Hersey and Kenneth Blanchard, suggests that the leader's behavior should be adjusted to the maturity level of the followers.[40] The model employs two dimensions of leader behavior as used in the Ohio State studies; one dimension is task or production oriented, and the other is relationship or people oriented. Follower maturity is categorized into four levels, as shown in Figure 11.6. Follower maturity is determined by the ability and willingness of the followers to accept responsibility for completing their work. Followers who are unable and

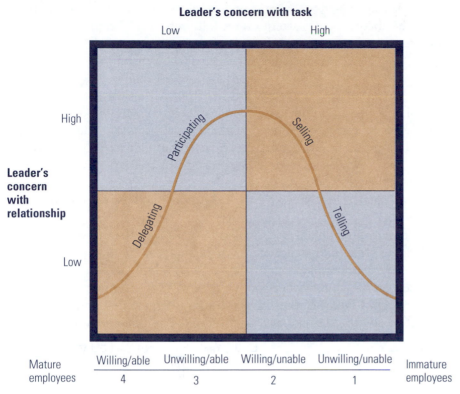

Leader's concern with task

Low   High

High

Leader's concern with relationship

Low

Participating   Selling

Delegating   Telling

Mature employees	Willing/able	Unwilling/able	Willing/unable	Unwilling/unable	Immature employees
	4	3	2	1	

SOURCE: Adapted from P. Hersey and K. H. Blanchard, *Management of Organizational Behavior: Utilizing Human Resources*, 3d ed. (Upper Saddle River, N.J.: Prentice-Hall, 1977), 170.

Figure 11.6
The Situational Leadership Model: The Hersey-Blanchard Model

unwilling are the least mature, and those who are both able and willing are the most mature. The four styles of leader behavior associated with each level of follower maturity are depicted in the figure as well.

According to the situational leadership model, a leader should use a telling style of leadership with immature followers who are unable and unwilling to take responsibility for completing their work. This style is characterized by high concern with the task and strong initiating structure behavior, coupled with low concern with relationships and little consideration behavior. As followers mature to the second level, the leader should use a selling style, in which there is high concern with both the task and relationships. The able but unwilling followers are the next most mature and require a participating style from the leader. This style is characterized by high concern with relationships and low concern with the task. Finally, the most mature followers are ones who are both able and willing, thus requiring a delegating style of leadership. The leader employing this style of leadership shows low concern with the task and relationships, because the followers accept responsibility.

One key limitation of the situational leadership model is the absence of central hypotheses that could be tested, which would make it a more valid, reliable theory of leadership.[41] However, the theory has intuitive ap-

Experiencing OB

You may learn more about Hersey and Blanchard's Situational Theory by examining the model and completing the activities at our animated concept and activity site. Choose Leadership from the "select a topic" pull-down menu, then Situational Leadership from the "overview tab."

http://www.experiencingob.com

peal and is widely used for training and development in corporations. In addition, the theory focuses attention on followers as important participants, if not determinants, of the leadership process.

GUIDELINES FOR LEADERSHIP

Leadership is a key to influencing organizational behavior and achieving organizational effectiveness. When artifacts are eliminated, studies of leadership succession show a moderately strong leader influence on organizational performance.[42] With this said, it is important to recognize that other factors also influence organizational performance. These include environmental factors (such as general economic conditions) and technological factors (such as efficiency).

Corporate leaders play a central role in setting the ethical tone and moral values for their organizations. For example, as chairman and CEO of Johnson & Johnson, James Burke played a pivotal role in modeling ethical leadership at the company in the 1970s and 1980s. Further, Johnson & Johnson ranked No. 1 in the *Fortune* list of most admired corporations in corporate leadership, in part due to the ethical and moral values reflected in the J&J culture and credo.[43]

Five useful guidelines appear to emerge from the extensive leadership research of the past sixty years:

- First, leaders and organizations should appreciate the unique attributes, predispositions, and talents of each leader. No two leaders are the same, and there is value in this diversity.
- Second, although there appears to be no single best style of leadership, there are organizational preferences in terms of style. Leaders should be chosen who challenge the organizational culture, when necessary, without destroying it.
- Third, participative, considerate leader behaviors that demonstrate a concern for people appear to enhance the health and well-being of followers in the work environment. This does not imply, however, that a leader must ignore the team's work tasks.
- Fourth, different leadership situations call for different leadership talents and behaviors. This may result in different individuals taking the leader role, depending on the specific situation in which the team finds itself.
- Fifth, good leaders are likely to be good followers. Although there are distinctions between their social roles, the attributes and behaviors of leaders and followers may not be as distinct as is sometimes thought.

FOLLOWERSHIP

8. Discuss the characteristics of effective and dynamic followers.

In contrast to leadership, the topic of followership has not been extensively researched. Much of the leadership literature suggests that leader and follower roles are highly differentiated. The traditional view casts followers as passive, whereas a more contemporary view casts the follower role as an active one with potential for leadership.[44] The follower role has alternatively been cast as one of self-leadership in which the follower assumes responsibility for influencing his or her own performance.[45] This approach emphasizes the follower's individual responsibility and self-control. Self-led followers perform naturally motivating tasks and do work that must be done but that is not naturally motivating. Self-leadership enables followers to be disciplined and effective, essential first steps if one is to become a leader. Organizational programs such as empowerment and self-managed work teams may be used to further activate the follower role.[46]

It is increasingly difficult to think of followers as passive agents of willful leaders. One study of leader–follower dynamics over a three-month period actually found leaders responding to follower performance rather than causing or initiating it.[47] Leaders have a responsibility to provide feedback to followers on poor performance so that the followers have an opportunity to take corrective action. Followers are an active component of the leadership process, and we need to expand our core knowledge about followership even further.

This section examines different types of followers and the characteristics of a dynamic subordinate. As we examine the follower role, keep in mind that blind, unquestioning followership may lead to destructive, and even antisocial, behavior.[48]

Types of Followers

Contemporary work environments are ones in which followers recognize their interdependence with leaders and learn to challenge them while at the same time respecting the leaders' authority.[49] Effective followers are active, responsible, and autonomous in their behavior and critical in their thinking without being insubordinate or disrespectful. Effective followers and four other types of followers are identified based on two dimensions: (1) activity versus passivity and (2) independent, critical thinking versus dependent, uncritical thinking.[50] Figure 11.7 shows these follower types.

Alienated followers think independently and critically, yet are very passive in their behavior. As a result, they become psychologically and emotionally distanced from their leaders. Alienated followers are potentially disruptive and a threat to the health of the organization. Sheep are followers who do not think independently or critically and are passive in their behavior. They simply do as they are told by their leaders. In a sense, they are slaves to the system. Yes people are followers who also do not think independently or critically, yet are very active in their behavior. They uncritically reinforce the thinking and ideas of their leaders with enthusiasm, never questioning or challenging the wisdom of the leaders' ideas and proposals. Yes people are the most dangerous to a leader because they are the most likely to give a false positive reaction and give no warning of potential pitfalls. Survivors are the least disruptive and the lowest risk followers in an organization. They perpetually sample the wind, and their motto is "Better safe than sorry."

Effective followers are the most valuable to a leader and an organization because of their active contributions. Effective followers share

Figure 11.7
Five Types of Followers

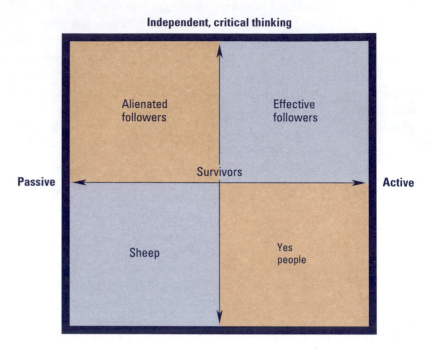

SOURCE: Reprinted by permission of *Harvard Business Review*. From "In Praise of Followers" by R. E. Kelley, Vol. 66, 1988, p. 145. Copyright © 1988 by Harvard Business School Publishing Corporation.

Experiencing OB

Learn how a leader's qualities, such as vision and charisma, influence followers to become more cohesive, empowered, and energized, by visiting our animated concept and activity site. Choose Leadership from the "select a topic" pull-down menu, then Transformational Leadership from the "overview tab."

http://www.experiencingob.com

four essential qualities. First, they practice self-management and self-responsibility. A leader can delegate to an effective follower without anxiety about the outcome. Second, they are committed to both the organization and a purpose, principle, or person outside themselves. Effective followers are not self-centered or self-aggrandizing. There is a risk, however, when the follower is committed to a purpose or principle at odds with the organization. Third, effective followers invest in their own competence and professionalism and focus their energy for maximum impact. Effective followers look for challenges and ways in which to add to their talents or abilities. Fourth, they are courageous, honest, and credible. Challenge 11.2 gives you an opportunity to consider your effectiveness as a follower.

Effective followers might be thought of as self-leaders who do not require close supervision.[51] The notion of self-leadership, or superleadership, blurs the distinction between leaders and followers. There is a complementary concept of caring leadership.[52] Caring leadership focuses attention on the followers, demonstrating concern for their development and well-being. Caring leadership is follower centered, not self-centered. The caring leader is able to develop dynamic followers.

The Dynamic Follower

The traditional stereotype of the follower or employee is of someone in a powerless, dependent role rather than in a potent, active, significant role.

Challenge 11.2

Are You an Effective Follower?

To determine whether you are an effective follower, read the text section on "Types of Followers," look back at your self-reliance results on Challenge 7.2, and work through the following four steps. Answer each question in the four steps yes or no.

Step 1. Self-Management and Self-Responsibility
____ Do you take the initiative at work?
____ Do you challenge the system at work when appropriate?
____ Do you ask questions when you need more information?
____ Do you successfully bring your projects to completion?

Step 2. Commitment beyond Yourself
____ Are you committed to your boss's and company's success?
____ Is there a higher purpose in life that you value deeply?
____ Is there a principle(s) that you will not compromise?
____ Is there a person at work or elsewhere you admire greatly?

Step 3. Self-Development
____ Do you attend a professional development class annually?
____ Do you have a program of self-study or structured learning?
____ Do you take at least one class each semester in the year?

____ Have you identified new skills to learn for your job?

Step 4. Courage and Honesty
____ Have you disagreed with your boss twice this year?
____ Have you taken two unpopular positions at work this year?
____ Have you given critical feedback to someone, kindly?
____ Have you taken one risk at work to do a better job?

Scoring:
Count the number of "yes" answers in Steps 1 through 4: _____

If you have 10 to 16 "yes" answers, this would suggest that you are an effective follower. If you have 7 or fewer "yes" answers, this may suggest that you fall into one of the other four categories of followers.

People who are self-reliant may also be effective followers, and effective followers may also be self-reliant. If you are an effective follower, were you also self-reliant in Challenge 7.2? If you were not self-reliant in Challenge 7.2, did you fall into a category other than the effective follower category?

SOURCE: Reprinted by permission of *Harvard Business Review*. From "In Praise of Followers" by R. E. Kelley, Vol. 66, 1988, p. 145. Copyright © 1988 by Harvard Business School Publishing Corporation.

The latter, in which the follower is dynamic, is a more contemporary, healthy role.[53] The *dynamic follower* is a responsible steward of his or her job, is effective in managing the relationship with the boss, and practices responsible self-management.

A responsible job steward is one who masters the content of his or her work and possesses or develops the skills required to do a good job. Once prepared, a dynamic follower then does a good job without being led. The dynamic follower is a self-starter.

The dynamic follower becomes a trusted adviser to the boss by keeping the supervisor well informed and building trust and dependability into the

dynamic follower
A follower who is a responsible steward of his or her job, is effective in managing the relationship with the boss, and practices self-management.

relationship. He or she is open to constructive criticism and solicits performance feedback. The dynamic follower shares needs and is responsible.

Self-management requires acquiring self-awareness and control of one's own feelings and behavior. It means being nondefensive and taking risks by challenging the supervisor and the organization.

A dynamic follower is effective in managing the relationship with the boss along the lines discussed in Chapter 10, aiming to achieve the best possible results for the follower, the boss, and the organization. It takes time and patience to nurture a good relationship between a follower and a supervisor. Once this relationship has been developed, it is a valuable resource for both. Therefore, the follower should be selective in the use of the supervisor's time and resources while always keeping the supervisor informed about work.

CULTURAL DIFFERENCES IN LEADERSHIP

In Chapter 5 we noted a number of cultural differences in several motivation theories. Parallel differences do not appear to exist in the area of leadership. Earlier in this chapter we noted similar findings when applying American leadership studies in Japan, along with some differences. The People's Republic of China is another country in which American leadership theories have been said to apply.[54] However, some of the groundbreaking research on leadership and culture concluded that ethnic differences were more important than national or industrial ones.[55] For example, in the early 1980s, David Kearns, then the CEO of Xerox Corporation, became convinced that the Japanese copier industry had targeted Xerox for elimination from that industry.[56] Convinced he was in a battle for Xerox's life, Kearns introduced Leadership-through-Quality to Xerox after learning from Fuji Xerox that quality improvements would not increase real costs.[57] Kearns's leadership came at the right time to revolutionize Xerox's culture. The situational approaches to leadership would lead to the conclusion that a leader must factor in culture as an important situational variable when exercising influence and authority. Thus, global leaders should expect to be flexible enough to alter their approaches when crossing national boundaries and working with people from foreign cultures.[58]

MANAGERIAL IMPLICATIONS: LEADERS AND FOLLOWERS AS PARTNERS

The chapter includes guidelines for leaders and followers, because both affect the quality of work performed and the success, and even survival, of the organization. The actions of national and international competitors and government regulations also affect the success of the organization.

There is no one best leadership theory. Many theories have been proposed, because not one of them works in every situation. One theory may be useful in one firm, whereas another may be more useful in another firm.

The many theories of leadership can be thought of as tools of the trade to be applied selectively by the leader in the most appropriate way. Properly applied, each theory is of some value to the user.

The 1990s was a period of significant transition for American industries. They must increasingly learn from other countries and cultures about leadership and followership. Some concepts appear to be cross-culturally applicable, whereas others may not be. Leadership within American corporations is changing, too, as more women assume positions of leadership. Women may lead differently than men, and both men and women can benefit from building on their unique strengths and talents.

Followers are equally important partners in the leadership process, for without followers, who would leaders lead? The role of the follower deserves greater respect, dignity, and understanding than it currently receives. Effective followers keep leaders out of trouble and advance the cause of leaders with vision and imagination.

Looking Back

Focusing the Shooting Stars

When Howard Schultz triggered an organizational transformation of the third kind at Starbucks Coffee with his new business vision, the company began a growth spurt that triggered an organizational transformation of the first kind. The transformation of any organization from an entrepreneurship to a professionally managed company can be painful and difficult, requiring strong leadership. As Starbucks began to grow in response to Schultz's challenge for the future, the company began to experience growing pains.[59] For example, during the three-year period from 1989 to 1991, Starbucks lost more than $3 million. People often felt overburdened, out of focus, and insecure about their place at the new Starbucks; the organization was short of good managers; and plans were made without actions being taken. Such growing pains were symptoms of deeper systemic problems resulting from the company's growth. Schultz had led Starbucks into an organizational transformation of the third kind by setting a new direction and motivating its people to action; now he needed to lead Starbucks through an organizational transformation of the first kind.[60] Starbucks needed good management to complement its effective leadership. To ensure that this transformation would succeed, Schultz led Starbucks to develop planning and professional management systems that enabled the newly national and international company to plan and budget, organize and staff, control and problem solve in a way that had never been required during Starbucks Coffee's entrepreneurship years. Schultz helped Starbucks grow up and come of age by enabling men like Howard Behar in retail operations and Orin Smith in finance to complement his own effective, visionary leadership for the company with their professional management skills and expertise.

CHAPTER SUMMARY

1. Leadership is the process of guiding and directing the behavior of followers in organizations. Followership is the process of being guided and directed by a leader. Leaders and followers are companions in these processes.
2. A leader creates meaningful change in organizations, whereas a manager controls complexity. Charismatic leaders have a profound impact on their followers.
3. Autocratic leaders create high pressure for followers, whereas democratic leaders create healthier environments for followers.
4. Two distinct dimensions of leader behavior are labeled initiating structure and consideration, alternatively called P-oriented behavior and M-oriented behavior, respectively, in Japan.
5. The five styles in the Managerial Grid are organization man manager, authority-obedience manager, country club manager, team manager, and impoverished manager.
6. According to the contingency theory, task-oriented leaders are most effective in highly favorable or highly unfavorable leadership situations, and relationship-oriented leaders are most effective in moderately favorable leadership situations.
7. The path–goal theory, Vroom-Yetton-Jago theory, and situational leadership model say that a leader should adjust his or her behavior to the situation and should appreciate diversity among followers.
8. Effective, dynamic followers are competent and active in their work, assertive, independent thinkers, sensitive to their bosses' needs and demands, and responsible self-managers. Caring leadership and dynamic followership go together.

KEY TERMS

leadership   315
formal leadership   315
informal leadership   315
followership   315
leader   320
manager   320
charismatic leadership   321
autocratic style   322
democratic style   322
laissez-faire style   322

initiating structure   324
consideration   324
P-oriented behavior   324
M-oriented behavior   324
Leadership Grid   325
organization man manager (5,5)   325
authority-compliance manager (9,1)   325
country club manager (1,9)   327
team manager (9,9)   328
impoverished manager (1,1)   328

paternalist "father knows best" manager (9+9)   328
opportunistic "what's in it for me" manager (Opp)   328
least preferred coworker (LPC)   329
task structure   329
position power   329
leader–member relations   329
dynamic follower   339

REVIEW QUESTIONS

1. Define *leadership* and *followership*. Distinguish between formal leadership and informal leadership.
2. Discuss transformational and charismatic leadership. Would you expect these styles of leadership to exist in all cultures? Differ across cultures?
3. Describe the differences between autocratic and democratic work environments. How do they differ from a laissez-faire workplace?
4. Define *initiating structure* and *consideration* as leader behaviors. How do they compare with P-oriented behavior and M-oriented behavior?
5. Describe the organization man manager, author-ity-obedience manager, country club manager, team manager, and impoverished manager.
6. How does the LPC scale measure leadership style? What are the three dimensions of the leader's situation?
7. Describe the alternative decision strategies used by a leader in the Vroom-Yetton-Jago normative decision theory.
8. Compare House's path–goal theory of leadership with the situational leadership model.
9. Describe alienated followers, sheep, yes people, survivors, and effective followers.

DISCUSSION AND COMMUNICATION QUESTIONS

1. Do you (or would you want to) work in an autocratic, democratic, or laissez-faire work environment? What might be the advantages of each work environment? The disadvantages?
2. Is your supervisor or professor someone who is high in concern for production? High in concern for people? What is his or her Managerial Grid style?
3. What decision strategies does your supervisor use to make decisions? Are they consistent or inconsistent with the Vroom-Yetton-Jago model?
4. Discuss the similarities and differences between effective leadership and dynamic followership. Are you dynamic?
5. Describe the relationship you have with your supervisor or professor. What is the best part of the relationship? The worst part? What could you do to make the relationship better?
6. (communication question) Who is the leader you admire the most? Write a description of this person including his or her characteristics and attributes that you admire. Note any aspects of this leader or his or her behavior that you find less than wholly admirable.
7. (communication question) Refresh yourself on the distinction between leaders (also called transformational leaders) and managers (also called transactional leaders) in the text. Then read about four contemporary business leaders. Prepare a brief summary of each and classify them as leaders or managers.
8. (communication question) Interview a supervisor or manager about the best follower the supervisor or manager has worked with. Ask questions about the characteristics and behaviors that made this person such a good follower. Note in particular how this follower responds to change. Be prepared to present your interview results in class.

ETHICS QUESTIONS

1. Is it ethical for leaders to tell followers unilaterally what to do without asking their opinions or getting any input from them?
2. Is it acceptable for a leader to take credit for the work of followers for whom he or she has responsibility?
3. If a leader is using a delegating leadership style and big problems develop in the team's work, is the leader still responsible for what happens?
4. If a follower disagrees with the supervisor's directions, is the follower obligated to follow those directions anyway? Or is the follower obligated to be disobedient while adhering to a moral principle?
5. What should you do if your supervisor acts in an unethical or illegal manner? Talk with the supervisor? Immediately report the action to the company's ethics committee?

Experiential Exercises

11.1 National Culture and Leadership

Effective leadership often varies by national culture, as Hofstede's research has shown. This exercise gives you the opportunity to examine your own and your group's leadership orientation compared to norms from ten countries, including the United States.

Exercise Schedule

1. Preparation (before class)
Complete the 29-item questionnaire.

2. Individual and Group Scoring
Your instructor will lead you through the scoring of the questionnaire, both individually and as a group.

3. Comparison of Effective Leadership Patterns by Nation. Your instructor leads a discussion on Hofstede's value system and presents the culture dimension scores for the ten countries.

In the questionnaire below, indicate the extent to which you agree or disagree with each statement. For example, if you strongly agree with a particular statement, circle the 5 next to the statement.

1 = strongly disagree
2 = disagree
3 = neither agree nor disagree
4 = agree
5 = strongly agree

QUESTIONNAIRE

	STRONGLY DISAGREE				STRONGLY AGREE

1. It is important to have job instructions spelled out in detail so that employees always know what they are expected to do.　　1　2　3　4　5

2. Managers expect employees to closely follow instructions and procedures.　　1　2　3　4　5

3. Rules and regulations are important because they inform employees what the organization expects of them.　　1　2　3　4　5

4. Standard operating procedures are helpful to employees on the job.　　1　2　3　4　5

5. Instructions for operations are important for employees on the job.　　1　2　3　4　5

6. Group welfare is more important than individual rewards.　　1　2　3　4　5

7. Group success is more important than individual success.　　1　2　3　4　5

8. Being accepted by the members of your work group is very important.　　1　2　3　4　5

9. Employees should pursue their own goals only after considering the welfare of the group.　　1　2　3　4　5

10. Managers should encourage group loyalty even if individual goals suffer.　　1　2　3　4　5

11. Individuals may be expected to give up their goals in order to benefit group success.　　1　2　3　4　5

12. Managers should make most decisions without consulting subordinates.　　1　2　3　4　5

QUESTIONNAIRE	STRONGLY DISAGREE				STRONGLY AGREE
13. Managers should frequently use authority and power when dealing with subordinates.	1	2	3	4	5
14. Managers should seldom ask for the opinions of employees.	1	2	3	4	5
15. Managers should avoid off-the-job social contacts with employees.	1	2	3	4	5
16. Employees should not disagree with management decisions.	1	2	3	4	5
17. Managers should not delegate important tasks to employees.	1	2	3	4	5
18. Managers should help employees with their family problems.	1	2	3	4	5
19. Managers should see to it that employees are adequately clothed and fed.	1	2	3	4	5
20. A manager should help employees solve their personal problems.	1	2	3	4	5
21. Management should see that all employees receive health care.	1	2	3	4	5
22. Management should see that children of employees have an adequate education.	1	2	3	4	5
23. Management should provide legal assistance for employees who get into trouble with the law.	1	2	3	4	5
24. Managers should take care of their employees as they would their children.	1	2	3	4	5
25. Meetings are usually run more effectively when they are chaired by a man.	1	2	3	4	5
26. It is more important for men to have a professional career than it is for women to have a professional career.	1	2	3	4	5
27. Men usually solve problems with logical analysis; women usually solve problems with intuition.	1	2	3	4	5
28. Solving organizational problems usually requires an active, forcible approach, which is typical of men.	1	2	3	4	5
29. It is preferable to have a man, rather than a woman, in a high-level position.	1	2	3	4	5

SOURCE: By Peter Dorfman, *Advances in International Comparative Management*, vol. 3, pages 127–150, 1988. Reprinted by permission of JAI Press Inc. D. Marcic and S. M. Puffer, "Dimensions of National Culture and Effective Leadership Patterns: Hofstede Revisited," *Management International* (Minneapolis/St. Paul: West Publishing, 1994), 10–15. All rights reserved. May not be reproduced without written permission of the publisher.

11.2 Leadership and Influence

To get a better idea of what your leadership style is and how productive it would be, fill out the questionnaire below. If you are currently a manager or have been a manager, answer the questions considering "members" to be your employees. If you have never been a manager, think of situations when you were a leader in an organization and consider "members" to be people working for you.

Response choices for each item:

A = always   B = often   C = occasionally
D = seldom   E = never

                                          A B C D E

1. I would act as the spokesperson of the group.

2. I would allow the members complete freedom in their work.

3. I would encourage overtime work.

4. I would permit the members to use their own judgment in solving problems.

5. I would encourage the use of uniform procedures.

6. I would needle members for greater effort.

7. I would stress being ahead of competing groups.

8. I would let the members do their work the way they think best.

9. I would speak as the representative of the group.

10. I would be able to tolerate postponement and uncertainty.

11. I would try out my ideas in the group.

                                          A B C D E

12. I would turn the members loose on a job, and let them go on it.

13. I would work hard for a promotion.

14. I would get swamped by details.

15. I would speak for the group when visitors are present.

16. I would be reluctant to allow the members any freedom of action.

17. I would keep the work moving at a rapid pace.

18. I would let some members have authority that I should keep.

19. I would settle conflicts when they occur in the group.

20. I would allow the group a high degree of initiative.

21. I would represent the group at outside meetings.

22. I would be willing to make changes.

23. I would decide what will be done and how it will be done.

24. I would trust the members to exercise good judgment.

25. I would push for increased production.

26. I would refuse to explain my actions.

27. Things usually turn out as I predict.

28. I would permit the group to set its own pace.

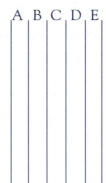

29. I would assign group members to particular tasks.

30. I would act without consulting the group.

31. I would ask the members of the group to work harder.

32. I would schedule the work to be done.

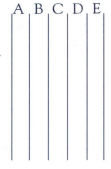

33. I would persuade others that my ideas are to their advantage.

34. I would urge the group to beat its previous record.

35. I would ask that group members follow standard rules and regulations.

Scoring

People oriented: Place a check mark by the number if you answered either A or B to any of these questions:

Question # 2 ____   10 ____   22 ____
           4 ____   12 ____   24 ____
           6 ____   18 ____   28 ____
           8 ____   20 ____

Place a check mark by the number if you answered either D or E to any of these questions:

14 ____   16 ____   26 ____   30 ____

Count your check marks to get your total people-oriented score. ——

Task oriented: Place a check mark by the number if you answered either A or B to any of these questions:

3 ____   7 ____   11 ____   13 ____
17 ____   25 ____   29 ____   31 ____
34 ____

Place a check mark by the number if you answered C or D to any of these questions:

1 ____   5 ____   9 ____   15 ____
19 ____   21 ____   23 ____   27 ____
32 ____   33 ____   35 ____

Count your check marks to get your total task-oriented score. ____

Range	Range		
People 0–7;	Task 0–10	You are not involved enough in either the task or the people.	Uninvolved
People 0–7;	Task 10–20	You tend to be autocratic, a whip-snapper. You get the job done, but at a high emotional cost.	Task-oriented
People 8–15;	Task 0–10	People are happy in their work, but sometimes at the expense of productivity.	People-oriented
People 8–15;	Task 10–20	People enjoy working for you and are productive. They naturally expend energy because they get positive reinforcement for doing a good job.	Balanced

As a leader, most people tend to be more task-oriented or more people-oriented. Task-orientation is concerned with getting the job done, while people-orientation focuses on group interactions and the needs of individual workers.

Effective leaders, however, are able to use both styles, depending on the situation. There may be times when a rush job demands great attention placed on task completion. During a time of low morale, though, sensitivity to workers' problems would be more appropriate. The best managers are able to balance both task and people concerns. Therefore a high score on both would show this balance. Ultimately, you will gain respect, admiration, and productivity from your workers.

Exercise Schedule

1. Preparation (before class)
Complete and score inventory.

2. Group discussion
The class should form four groups based on the scores on the Leadership Style Inventory. Each group will be given a separate task.

Uninvolved: Devise strategies for developing task-oriented and people-oriented styles.

Task-oriented: How can you develop a more people-oriented style? What problems might occur if you do not do so?

People-oriented: How can you develop a more task-oriented style? What problems might occur if you do not do so?

Balanced: Do you see any potential problems with your style? Are you a fully developed leader?

SOURCE: From Thomas Sergiovanni, Richard Metzcus, and Larry Burden, "Toward a Particularistic Approach to Leadership Style: Some Findings," *American Educational Research Journal*, vol. 6(1), January 1969. Copyright 1969 The American Educational Research Association. Reprinted with permission of AERA.

For more practice exercises, consult the fifth edition of *Organizational Behavior: Experiences and Cases* by Dorothy Marcic and Joseph Seltzer (South-Western, 1998).

Learning Objectives

After reading this chapter, you should be able to do the following:

1. Diagnose functional versus dysfunctional conflict. *p. 350*

2. Identify the causes of conflict in organizations. *p. 352*

3. Identify the different forms of conflict. *p. 357*

4. Understand the defense mechanisms that individuals exhibit when they engage in interpersonal conflict. *p. 363*

5. Construct an action plan for dealing with difficult behavior at work. *p. 365*

6. Describe effective and ineffective techniques for managing conflict. *p. 369*

7. Understand five styles of conflict management, and diagnose your own preferred style. *p. 371*

12

Conflict at Work

Thinking Ahead

Conflict Management Pays Off at Ford

Union–management relationships in the automotive industry are a study in contrasts. Strikes at two parts plants in Flint, Michigan, that lasted fifty-four days cost General Motors nearly $3 billion in earnings in 1998. The strikes forced the shutdown of nearly all of GM's North American manufacturing operations. Details of the settlement called for the leaders of GM and the United Auto Workers (UAW) to meet periodically to discuss their differences, and this was seen as a monumental accomplishment—a sign of how poorly the two sides get along. And few people on either side expect the years of bitter conflict to end just because the two parties say they'll do more talking.

By contrast, Ford Motor Company has not had a strike from the UAW since 1986. In fact, the company considers its cordial, cooperative relationship with the union a competitive advantage. This relationship has evolved over several years. In 1982, Ford engineered a contract with the UAW that included concessions from the union and rescued Ford from financial disaster. In 1987, Ford crafted an unprecedented deal guaranteeing continued employment for UAW members who might otherwise have been laid off (with the important exception of an industry-wide sales slump). This agreement was negotiated during a three-day contract extension during which Ford employees continued to work. UAW members threw aside the "no contract, no work" rule, reflecting a new, more cooperative relationship between the union and Ford.

In 1993, Ford agreed to hire thousands of new workers in exchange for an agreement that would allow automakers to pay the new workers 70 percent of regular UAW wages. This unprecedented agreement broke the union's long-time policy of equal wages for all union members.

Over time, Ford has turned an adversarial, rancorous relationship with the union into a cooperative one. How has Ford accomplished this? The Looking Back feature at the end of the chapter will fill you in on Ford's secrets to managing conflict with the UAW.[1]

THE NATURE OF CONFLICTS IN ORGANIZATIONS

conflict
Any situation in which incompatible goals, attitudes, emotions, or behaviors lead to disagreement or opposition between two or more parties.

All of us have experienced conflict of various types, yet we probably fail to recognize the variety of conflicts that occur in organizations. **Conflict** is defined as any situation in which incompatible goals, attitudes, emotions, or behaviors lead to disagreement or opposition between two or more parties.[2]

Today's organizations may face greater potential for conflict than ever before in history. The marketplace, with its increasing competition and globalization, magnifies differences among people in terms of personality, values, attitudes, perceptions, languages, cultures, and national backgrounds.[3] With the increasing diversity of the workforce, furthermore, comes the potential for incompatibility and conflict.

Importance of Conflict Management Skills for the Manager

Estimates show that managers spend about 21 percent of their time dealing with conflict.[4] That is the equivalent of one day every week. And conflict management skills are a major predictor of managerial success.[5] Emotional intelligence (EQ) relates to the ability to manage conflict. It is the power to control one's emotions and perceive emotions in others, adapt to change, and manage adversity. Conflict management skills may be more a reflection of EQ than of IQ. People who lack emotional intelligence, especially empathy or the ability to see life from another person's perspective, are more likely to be causes of conflict than managers of conflict.[6] EQ seems to be valid across cultures. It is common among successful people not only in North America, but also in Nigeria, India, Argentina, and France.

Functional versus Dysfunctional Conflict

1. Diagnose functional versus dysfunctional conflict.

Not all conflict is bad. In fact, some types of conflict encourage new solutions to problems and enhance creativity in the organization. In these cases, managers will want to encourage the conflicts. Thus, the key to conflict management is to stimulate functional conflict and prevent or resolve dysfunctional conflict. The difficulty, however, is to distinguish between dysfunctional and functional conflicts. The consequences of conflict can be positive or negative, as shown in Table 12.1.

Functional conflict is a healthy, constructive disagreement between two or more people. Functional conflict can produce new ideas, learning, and growth among individuals. When individuals engage in constructive conflict, they develop a better awareness of themselves and others. In addition, functional conflict can improve working relationships: when two parties work through their disagreements, they feel they have accomplished something together. By releasing tensions and solving problems in working together, morale is improved.[7] Functional conflict can lead to innovation and positive change for the organization.[8] Because it tends to encourage creativity among individuals, this positive form of conflict can translate into increased productivity.[9] A key to recognizing functional conflict is that it is often cognitive in origin; that is, it arises from someone challenging old policies or thinking of new ways to approach problems.

functional conflict
A healthy, constructive disagreement between two or more people.

Dysfunctional conflict is an unhealthy, destructive disagreement between two or more people. Its danger is that it takes the focus away from the work to be done and places the focus on the conflict itself and the parties involved. Excessive conflict drains energy that could be used more productively. A key to recognizing a dysfunctional conflict is that its origin is often emotional or behavioral. Disagreements that involve personalized anger and resentment directed at specific individuals rather than specific ideas are dysfunctional.[10] Individuals involved in dysfunctional conflict tend to act before thinking, and they often rely on threats, deception, and verbal abuse to communicate. In dysfunctional conflict, the losses to both parties may exceed any potential gain from the conflict.

dysfunctional conflict
An unhealthy, destructive disagreement between two or more people.

Diagnosing conflict as good or bad is not easy. The manager must look at the issue, the context of the conflict, and the parties involved. The

Positive Consequences	Negative Consequences
• Leads to new ideas	• Diverts energy from work
• Stimulates creativity	• Threatens psychological well-being
• Motivates change	• Wastes resources
• Promotes organizational vitality	• Creates a negative climate
• Helps individuals and groups establish identities	• Breaks down group cohesion
• Serves as a safety valve to indicate problems	• Can increase hostility and aggressive behaviors

Table 12.1
Consequences of Conflict

following questions can be used to diagnose the nature of the conflict a manager faces:

- Are the parties approaching the conflict from a hostile standpoint?
- Is the outcome likely to be a negative one for the organization?
- Do the potential losses of the parties exceed any potential gains?
- Is energy being diverted from goal accomplishment?

If the majority of the answers to these questions are yes, then the conflict is probably dysfunctional. Once the manager has diagnosed the type of conflict, he or she can either work to resolve it (if it is dysfunctional) or to stimulate it (if it is functional).

One occasion when managers should work to stimulate conflict is when they suspect their group is suffering from groupthink, discussed in Chapter 9.[11] When a group fails to consider alternative solutions and becomes stagnant in its thinking, it might benefit from healthy disagreements. Teams exhibiting symptoms of groupthink should be encouraged to consider creative problem solving and should appoint a devil's advocate to point out opposing perspectives. These actions can help stimulate constructive conflict in a group.

CAUSES OF CONFLICT IN ORGANIZATIONS

2. Identify the causes of conflict in organizations.

Conflict is pervasive in organizations. To manage it effectively, managers should understand the many sources of conflict. They can be classified into two broad categories: structural factors, which stem from the nature of the organization and the way in which work is organized, and personal factors, which arise from differences among individuals. Figure 12.1 summarizes the causes of conflict within each category.

Structural Factors

The causes of conflict related to the organization's structure include specialization, interdependence, common resources, goal differences, authority relationships, status inconsistencies, and jurisdictional ambiguities.

Specialization When jobs are highly specialized, employees become experts at certain tasks. For example, one software company has one specialist for

Figure 12.1
Causes of Conflict in Organizations

Structural Factors
- Specialization
- Interdependence
- Common resources
- Goal differences
- Authority relationships
- Status inconsistencies
- Jurisdictional ambiguities

Conflict

Personal Factors
- Skills and abilities
- Personalities
- Perceptions
- Values and ethics
- Emotions
- Communication barriers
- Cultural differences

databases, one for statistical packages, and another for expert systems. Highly specialized jobs can lead to conflict, because people have little awareness of the tasks that others perform.

A classic conflict of specialization may occur between salespeople and engineers. Engineers are technical specialists responsible for product design and quality. Salespeople are marketing experts and liaisons with customers. Salespeople are often accused of making delivery promises to customers that engineers cannot keep because the sales force lacks the technical knowledge necessary to develop realistic delivery deadlines.

Interdependence Work that is interdependent requires groups or individuals to depend on one another to accomplish goals.[12] Depending on other people to get work done is fine when the process works smoothly. When there is a problem, however, it becomes very easy to blame the other party, and conflict escalates. In a garment manufacturing plant, for example, when the fabric cutters get behind in their work, the workers who sew the garments are delayed as well. Considerable frustration may result when the workers at the sewing machines feel their efforts are being blocked by the cutters' slow pace.

Common Resources Any time multiple parties must share resources, there is potential for conflict.[13] This potential is enhanced when the shared resources become scarce. For example, managers often share secretarial support. Not uncommonly, one secretary supports ten or more managers, each of whom believes his or her work is most important. This puts pressure on the secretary and leads to potential conflicts in prioritizing and scheduling work.

Goal Differences When work groups have different goals, these goals may be incompatible. For example, in one cable television company, the salesperson's goal was to sell as many new installations as possible. This created problems for the service department, because its goal was timely installations. With increasing sales, the service department's workload became backed up, and orders were delayed. Often these types of conflicts occur because individuals do not have knowledge of another department's objectives.

Authority Relationships A traditional boss–employee relationship is hierarchical in nature with a boss who is superior to the employee. For many employees, such a relationship is not a comfortable one, because another individual has the right to tell them what to do. Some people resent authority more than others, and obviously this creates conflicts. In addition, some bosses are more autocratic than others; this compounds the potential for conflict in the relationship. As organizations move toward the team approach and empowerment, there should be less potential for conflict from authority relationships.

Status Inconsistencies Some organizations have a strong status difference between management and nonmanagement workers. Managers may enjoy

Experiencing OB

Learn more about structural and personal sources of conflict at our animated concept and activity site. Choose Conflict&Negotiation from the "select a topic" pull-down menu, then Causes of Conflict from the "overview tab."

http://www.experiencingob.com

jurisdictional ambiguity
The presence of unclear lines of responsibility within an organization.

privileges—such as flexible schedules, personal telephone calls at work, and longer lunch hours—that are not available to nonmanagement employees. This may result in resentment and conflict.

Jurisdictional Ambiguities Have you ever telephoned a company with a problem and had your call transferred through several different people and departments? This situation illustrates *jurisdictional ambiguity*—that is, unclear lines of responsibility within an organization.[14] When there is no definite source of responsibility for a problem, workers tend to "pass the buck," or avoid dealing with the problem. Conflicts emerge over responsibility for the problem.

The factors just discussed are structural in that they arise from the ways in which work is organized. Other conflicts come from differences among individuals.

Personal Factors

The causes of conflict that arise from individual differences include skills and abilities, personalities, perceptions, values and ethics, emotions, communication barriers, and cultural differences.

Skills and Abilities The workforce is composed of individuals with varying levels of skills and ability. Diversity in skills and abilities may be positive for the organization, but it also holds potential for conflict, especially when jobs are interdependent. Experienced, competent workers may find it difficult to work alongside new and unskilled recruits. Workers can become resentful when their new boss, fresh from college, knows a lot about managing people but is unfamiliar with the technology with which they are working.

Personalities Individuals do not leave their personalities at the doorstep when they enter the workplace. Personality conflicts are realities in organizations. To expect that you will like all of your coworkers may be a naive expectation, as would be the expectation that they will all like you.

One personality trait that many people find difficult to deal with is abrasiveness.[15] An abrasive person ignores the interpersonal aspects of work and the feelings of colleagues. Abrasive individuals are often achievement oriented and hardworking, but their perfectionist, critical style often leaves others feeling unimportant. This style creates stress and strain for those around the abrasive person.[16] Organizational Reality 12.1 shows that success comes at a high price when it involves alienating others.

Perceptions Differences in perception can also lead to conflict. For example, managers and workers may not have a shared perception of what motivates people. In this case, the reward system can create conflicts if managers provide what they think employees want rather than what employees really want.

Values and Ethics Differences in values and ethics can be sources of disagreement. Older workers, for example, value company loyalty and proba-

---

ORGANIZATIONAL REALITY 12.1

"By the Way . . . Your Staff Hates You!!!!!"

Few interpersonal conflicts are as painful as those between a manager and his or her staff. Interestingly, most managers have no idea how their employees perceive them. Some who do know how they're perceived simply don't care how employees feel.

Take the case of Scott Rudin, the producer of *The Truman Show* and *In and Out*, who has a reputation for being notoriously unpleasant. Rudin is famous for throwing telephones, verbally abusing employees, and demanding sixteen-hour workdays and seven-day workweeks of staffers. While expressing admiration for Rudin's work, an ex-assistant has said, "I think the people that work there—most of them hate him. Nobody likes him. Everybody's miserable."

How does Rudin get away with this behavior? First, he offers staffers rare opportunities in the highly competitive film industry, but expects "the better part of their lives while they are here." He pays enormous salaries, $70,000 to $100,000 per year. And, he welcomes turnover, believing that it's too hot an environment for employees to stay more than two years.

What can you learn from Rudin? It's okay to abuse your workers, only if you're in a field that has 100 applicants for every job, have the luxury of shelling out huge salaries, and don't mind losing your entire staff every two years. But for just about every other manager, Rudin's style would be career suicide. In the developing knowledge-based economy, recruiting and retaining talented workers are a company's top priority. It pays, therefore, to treat workers with respect.

Even Scott Rudin, relentless and unrepenting, has paid a price. Ex-assistants recall with glee the time they scratched up his prized CD collection. They relish the memory of a team of assistants that drove to Rudin's house and urinated in his swimming pool.

An astute manager can spot several indicators that the staff loathes him or her. If machinery keeps breaking, that's a sign. High turnover is a sign, as are stress claims. Little things like the general mood in the office, or people not being willing to go the extra mile, are indicators. Finally, you might find out your nickname among employees. If people won't tell you, that's a sign. And, if you hear that you are "The Pig" or some similarly unaffectionate term, watch out. Being despised is a luxury you can't afford.

Discussion Question

1. What are the consequences of being viewed negatively by your employees? How can a manager find out what the staff thinks of him or her?

SOURCE: T. Carvell, "By the Way, Your Staff Hates You," *Fortune* (September 28, 1998): 200–212.

---

bly would not take a sick day when they were not really ill. Younger workers, valuing mobility, like the concept of "mental health days," or calling in sick to get away from work. This may not be true for all workers, but it illustrates that differences in values can lead to conflict.

Most people have their own sets of values and ethics. The extent to which they apply these ethics in the workplace varies. Some people have strong desires for approval from others and will work to meet others' ethical standards. Some people are relatively unconcerned about approval from others and strongly apply their own ethical standards. Still others operate seemingly without regard to ethics or values.[17] When conflicts about values or ethics do arise, heated disagreement is common because of the personal nature of the differences.

Emotions   The moods of others can be a source of conflict in the workplace. Problems at home often spill over into the work arena, and the related moods can be hard for others to deal with.

Communication Barriers   Communication barriers such as physical separation and language can create distortions in messages, and these can lead to conflict. Another communication barrier is value judgment, in which a listener assigns a worth to a message before it is received. For example, suppose a team member is a chronic complainer. When this individual enters the manager's office, the manager is likely to devalue the message before it is even delivered. Conflict can then emerge.

Cultural Differences   Although cultural differences are assets in organizations, sometimes they can be seen as sources of conflict. Often, these conflicts stem from a lack of understanding of another culture. In one MBA class, for example, Indian students were horrified when American students challenged the professor. Meanwhile, the American students thought the students from India were too passive. Subsequent discussions revealed that professors in India expected to be treated deferentially and with great respect. While students might challenge an idea vigorously, they would rarely challenge the professor. Diversity training that emphasizes education on cultural differences can make great strides in preventing misunderstandings.

GLOBALIZATION AND CONFLICT

Large transnational corporations employ many different ethnic and cultural groups. In these multiethnic corporations, the widely differing cultures represent vast differences among individuals, so the potential for conflict increases.[18] As indicated in Chapter 2, Hofstede has identified five dimensions along which cultural differences may emerge: individualism/collectivism, power distance, uncertainty avoidance, masculinity/femininity, and long-term/short-term orientation.[19] These cultural differences have many implications for conflict management in organizations.

Individualism means that people believe that their individual interests take priority over society's interests. Collectivism, in contrast, means that people put the good of the group first. For example, the United States is a highly individualistic culture, whereas Japan is a very collectivist culture. The individualism/collectivism dimension of cultural differences strongly influences conflict management behavior. People from collectivist cultures tend to display a more cooperative approach to managing conflict.[20]

Hofstede's second dimension of cultural differences is power distance. In cultures with high power distance, individuals accept that people in organizations have varying levels of power. In contrast, in cultures with low power distance, individuals do not automatically respect those in positions of authority. For example, the United States is a country of low power distance, whereas Brazil is a country with a high power distance. Differences in power distance can lead to conflict. Imagine a U.S. employee managed by a Brazilian supervisor who expects deferential behavior. The supervisor would expect automatic respect based on legitimate power. When this respect was not given, conflict would arise.

Uncertainty avoidance also varies by culture. In the United States, employees can tolerate high levels of uncertainty, whereas employees in Israel tend to prefer certainty in their work settings. A U.S.-based multinational firm might run into conflicts operating in Israel. Suppose such a firm is installing a new technology. Its expatriate workers from the United States would tolerate the uncertainty of the technological transition better than would their Israeli coworkers, and this might lead to conflicts among the employees.

Masculinity versus femininity illustrates the contrast between preferences for assertiveness and material goods versus preferences for human capital and quality of life. The United States is a masculine society, whereas Sweden is considered a feminine society. Adjustment to the assertive interpersonal style of U.S. workers may be difficult for Swedish coworkers.

Conflicts can also arise between cultures that vary in their time orientation of values. China, for example, has a long-term orientation; the Chinese prefer values that focus on the future, such as saving and persistence. The United States and Russia, in contrast, have short-term orientations. These cultures emphasize values in the past and present, such as respect for tradition and fulfillment of social obligations. Conflicts can arise when managers fail to understand the nature of differences in values.

An organization whose workforce consists of multiple ethnicities and cultures holds potential for many types of conflict because of the sheer volume of individual differences among workers. The key to managing conflict in a multicultural workforce is understanding cultural differences and appreciating their value.

FORMS OF CONFLICT IN ORGANIZATIONS

Conflict can take on any of several different forms in an organization, including interorganizational, intergroup, interpersonal, and intrapersonal conflicts. It is important to note that the prefix *inter* means "between," whereas the prefix *intra* means "within."

3. Identify the different forms of conflict.

Interorganizational Conflict

Conflict that occurs between two or more organizations is called ***interorganizational conflict***. Competition can heighten interorganizational conflict. The ongoing rivalries between U.S. and Japanese automakers reflect this competition. Corporate takeovers, mergers, and acquisitions can also produce interorganizational conflict.

Conflicts between organizations abound. Some of these conflicts can be functional, as when firms improve the quality of their products and services

interorganizational conflict
Conflict that occurs between two or more organizations.

in the spirit of healthy competition. Other interorganizational conflicts can have dysfunctional results. Organizational Reality 12.2 describes a conflict between two rival hospitals in Denver, Colorado. Whether this conflict will have positive or negative consequences is yet to be seen; given the behavior of the people involved, however, there are hints that the conflict may turn nasty.

ORGANIZATIONAL REALITY 12.2

Physicians Open New Hospital and Old Wounds

A turf war has begun in Denver between Columbia-HealthONE and a group of its former physicians who have formed Precedent Health Center, a new sixty-bed hospital. Accusations are flying, mainly that Columbia-HealthONE is trying to sabotage the new hospital's success. The physicians who started Precedent felt Columbia forgot the importance of doctors. Their project was a reaction to managed care, which they feel undermines the physician's decision-making authority and doctor/patient relationships.

Precedent is a boutique hospital that offers amenities like a concierge, private rooms for each patient, a day care center for children of sick parents, a tenth floor suite overlooking a city park (for $350 extra per day), and rooms equipped with computers, faxes, televisions, and VCRs. Pagers are provided to family members who don't want to be stuck in waiting rooms. Despite these frills, Precedent doesn't intend to charge more than other hospitals. To cut costs, Precedent rents out several floors to other health care providers. One floor is even donated to Hospice of Metro Denver. Because doctors own the hospital, they'll make the tough calls when money and medicine collide.

Not surprisingly, Columbia is not happy that the competing facility is only eighteen blocks away. And, Columbia isn't happy that Precedent is targeting profitable services like medical imaging and ambulatory surgery, while leaving other hospitals the costlier services like trauma and emergency care. Columbia fears that the money-losing services Precedent doesn't offer will be sent to them.

So, Columbia is fighting back. Columbia urged health plans to boycott Predecent, and offered PacifiCare, the state's second largest insurer, deep discounts if it refused to do business with Precedent. Precedent, however, says it tried to work with Columbia by making a number of offers for involvement, which were rejected.

Some people may question why Columbia is spending so much energy fighting Precedent. Linda Howell, president of Health Quest Consulting, sees it differently. "Columbia-HealthONE is the gem of Columbia. It is the most beautiful network that they have in their whole organization. The physicians are happy . . . there are multiple hospitals involved, multiple clinics . . . they're very proud of it. So, losing business to Precedent is more than losing business to Precedent. It's losing the power of the gem that they can put up on the pedestal for the rest of the nation to say 'look at what we've done in Denver.' To have a little mosquito come along—and that's what Precedent is considered—and buzz around your ear is embarassing."

Discussion Question

1. What effects might the conflict between Columbia and Precedent have on customers? On employees of each hospital? How would you go about formulating a win–win solution to the conflict?

SOURCE: S. Campbell, "Former Columbia/HCA Physicians Open New Hospital and Old Wounds." Reprinted with permission from *Health Care Strategic Management*, 16 (1998): 14–15. Copyright, The Business Word Inc.(800-328-3211). All rights reserved.

Intergroup Conflict

When conflict occurs between groups or teams, it is known as *intergroup conflict*. Conflict between groups can have positive effects within each group, such as increased group cohesiveness, increased focus on tasks, and increased loyalty to the group. There are, however, negative consequences as well. Groups in conflict tend to develop an "us against them" mentality whereby each sees the other team as the enemy, becomes more hostile, and decreases its communication with the other group. The existence of a number of negative relationships between members of two different groups heightens the potential for conflict between the groups.[21]

Competition between groups must be managed carefully so that it does not escalate into dysfunctional conflict. Research has shown that when groups compete for a goal that only one group can achieve, negative consequences like territoriality, aggression, and prejudice toward the other group can result.[22] Managers should encourage and reward cooperative behaviors across groups. Some effective ways of doing this include modifying performance appraisals to include assessing intergroup behavior and using an external supervisor's evaluation of intergroup behavior. Group members will be more likely to help other groups when they know that the other group's supervisor will be evaluating their behavior, and that they will be rewarded for cooperation.[23] In addition, managers should encourage social interactions across groups so that trust can be developed. Trust allows individuals to exchange ideas and resources with members of other groups and results in innovation when members of different groups cooperate.[24]

intergroup conflict
Conflict that occurs between groups or teams in an organization.

Interpersonal Conflict

Conflict between two or more people is *interpersonal conflict*. Conflict between people can arise from many individual differences, including personalities, attitudes, values, perceptions, and the other differences we discussed in Chapters 3 and 4. Later in this chapter, we look at defense mechanisms that individuals exhibit in interpersonal conflict and at ways to cope with difficult people.

interpersonal conflict
Conflict that occurs between two or more individuals.

Intrapersonal Conflict

When conflict occurs within an individual, it is called *intrapersonal conflict*. There are several types of intrapersonal conflict, including interrole, intrarole, and person–role conflicts. A role is a set of expectations placed on an individual by others.[25] The person occupying the focal role is the role incumbent, and the individuals who place expectations on the person are role senders. Figure 12.2 depicts a set of role relationships.

Interrole conflict occurs when a person experiences conflict among the multiple roles in his or her life. One interrole conflict that many employees experience is work/home conflict, in which their role as worker clashes with their role as spouse or parent.[26] For example, when a child gets sick at school, the parent often must leave work to care for the child.

intrapersonal conflict
Conflict that occurs within an individual.

interrole conflict
A person's experience of conflict among the multiple roles in his or her life.

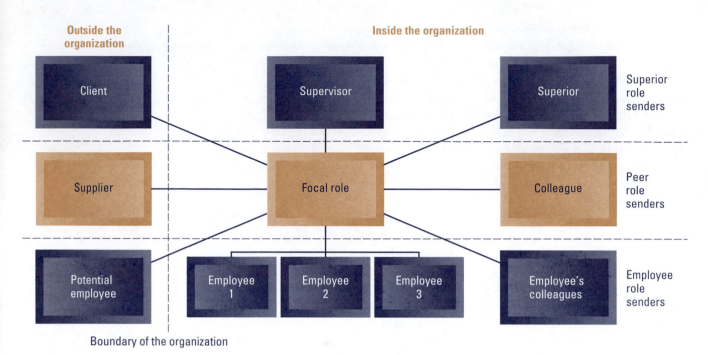

Outside the organization

Inside the organization

Client

Supervisor

Superior — Superior role senders

Supplier

Focal role

Colleague — Peer role senders

Potential employee

Employee 1

Employee 2

Employee 3

Employee's colleagues — Employee role senders

Boundary of the organization

Figure 12.2
An Organization Member's Role Set

SOURCE: J. C. Quick, J. D. Quick, D. L. Nelson, & J. J. Hurrell, Jr. *Preventive Stress Management in Organizations*, 1997. Copyright © 1997 by the American Psychological Association. Reprinted with permission.

intrarole conflict
Conflict that occurs within a single role, such as when a person receives conflicting messages from role senders about how to perform a certain role.

Intrarole conflict is conflict within a single role. It often arises when a person receives conflicting messages from role senders about how to perform a certain role. Suppose a manager receives counsel from her department head that she needs to socialize less with the nonmanagement employees. She also is told by her project manager that she needs to be a better team member, and that she can accomplish this by socializing more with the other nonmanagement team members. This situation is one of intrarole conflict.

person–role conflict
Conflict that occurs when an individual is expected to perform behaviors in a certain role that conflict with his or her personal values.

Person–role conflict occurs when an individual in a particular role is expected to perform behaviors that clash with his or her values.[27] Salespeople, for example, may be required to offer the most expensive item in the sales line first to the customer, even when it is apparent that the customer does not want or cannot afford the item. A computer salesman may be required to offer a large, elaborate system to a student he knows is on a tight budget. This may conflict with the salesman's values, and he may experience person–role conflict.

Intrapersonal conflicts can have positive consequences. Often, professional responsibilities clash with deeply held values. A budget shortfall may force you to lay off a loyal, hardworking employee. Your daughter may have a piano recital on the same day your largest client is scheduled to be in town visiting the office. In such conflicts, we often have to choose between right and right; that is, there's no correct response. These may be thought of as *defining moments* that challenge us to choose between two or more things in which we believe.[28] Character is formed in defining moments because they cause us to shape our identities. They help us crystallize our values and serve as opportunities for personal growth.

INTRAPERSONAL CONFLICT

Intrapersonal conflict can be managed with careful self-analysis and diagnosis of the situation. Two actions in particular can help prevent or resolve intrapersonal conflicts.

First, when seeking a new job, you should find out as much as possible about the values of the organization.[29] Many person–role conflicts center around differences between the organization's values and the individual's values. Research has shown that when there is a good fit between the values of the individual and the organization, the individual is more satisfied and committed and is less likely to leave the organization.[30]

Second, to manage intrarole or interrole conflicts, role analysis is a good tool.[31] In role analysis, the individual asks the various role senders what they expect of him or her. The outcomes are clearer work roles and the reduction of conflict and ambiguity.[32] Role analysis is a simple tool that clarifies the expectations of both parties in a relationship and reduces the potential for conflict within a role or between roles.

All these forms of conflict can be managed. An understanding of the many forms is a first step. The next section focuses more extensively on interpersonal conflict because of its pervasiveness in organizations.

INTERPERSONAL CONFLICT

When a conflict occurs between two or more people, it is known as interpersonal conflict. To manage interpersonal conflict, it is helpful to understand power networks in organizations, defense mechanisms exhibited by individuals, and ways to cope with difficult people.

Power Networks

According to Mastenbroek, individuals in organizations are organized in three basic types of power networks.[33] Based on these power relationships, certain kinds of conflict tend to emerge. Figure 12.3 illustrates three basic kinds of power relationships in organizations.

The first relationship is equal versus equal, in which there is a horizontal balance of power among the parties. An example of this type of relationship would be a conflict between individuals from two different project teams. The behavioral tendency is toward suboptimization; that is, the

Experiencing OB

Test your understanding of intrapersonal conflict at our animated concept and activity site. Choose Conflict&Negotiation from the "select a topic" pull-down menu, then Role Conflict from the "overview tab."

http://www.experiencingob.com

Figure 12.3
Power Relationships in Organizations

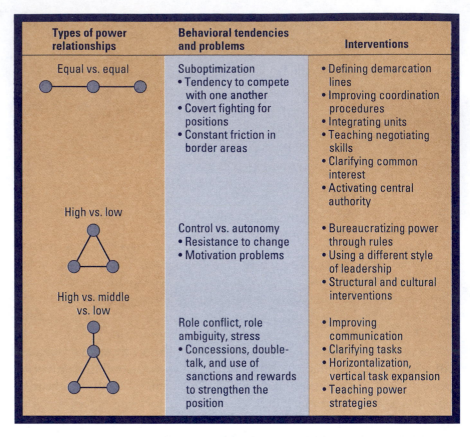

Types of power relationships	Behavioral tendencies and problems	Interventions
Equal vs. equal	Suboptimization • Tendency to compete with one another • Covert fighting for positions • Constant friction in border areas	• Defining demarcation lines • Improving coordination procedures • Integrating units • Teaching negotiating skills • Clarifying common interest • Activating central authority
High vs. low	Control vs. autonomy • Resistance to change • Motivation problems	• Bureaucratizing power through rules • Using a different style of leadership • Structural and cultural interventions
High vs. middle vs. low	Role conflict, role ambiguity, stress • Concessions, double-talk, and use of sanctions and rewards to strengthen the position	• Improving communication • Clarifying tasks • Horizontalization, vertical task expansion • Teaching power strategies

SOURCE: W. F. G. Mastenbroek, *Conflict Management and Organization Development*, 1987. Copyright John Wiley & Sons Limited. Reproduced with permission.

focus is on a win–lose approach to problems, and each party tries to maximize its power at the expense of the other party. Interventions like improving coordination between the parties and working toward common interests can help manage these conflicts.

The second power network is high versus low, or a powerful versus a less powerful relationship. Conflicts that emerge here take the basic form of the powerful individuals trying to control others, with the less powerful people trying to become more autonomous. Organizations typically respond to these conflicts by tightening the rules. However, the more successful ways of managing these conflicts are to try a different style of leadership, such as a coaching and counseling style, or to change the structure to a more decentralized one.

The third power network is high versus middle versus low. This power network illustrates the classic conflicts felt by middle managers. Two particular conflicts are evident for middle managers: role conflict, in which conflicting expectations are placed on the manager from bosses and employees, and role ambiguity, in which the expectations of the boss are unclear. Improved communication among all parties can reduce role conflict and ambiguity. In addition, middle managers can benefit from training in positive ways to influence others.

Knowing the typical kinds of conflicts that arise in various kinds of relationships can help a manager diagnose conflicts and devise appropriate ways to manage them.

Defense Mechanisms

When individuals are involved in conflict with another human being, frustration often results.[34] Conflicts can often arise within the context of a performance appraisal session. Most people do not react well to negative feedback, as was illustrated in a classic study.[35] In this study, when employees were given criticism about their work, over 50 percent of their responses were defensive.

When individuals are frustrated, as they often are in interpersonal conflict, they respond by exhibiting defense mechanisms.[36] Defense mechanisms are common reactions to the frustration that accompanies conflict. Table 12.2 describes several defense mechanisms seen in organizations.

Aggressive mechanisms, such as fixation, displacement, and negativism, are aimed at attacking the source of the conflict. In *fixation*, an individual fixates on the conflict, or keeps up a dysfunctional behavior that obviously will not solve the conflict. An example of fixation occurred in a university, where a faculty member became embroiled in a battle with the dean because the faculty member felt he had not received a large enough salary increase. He persisted in writing angry letters to the dean, whose hands were tied because of a low budget allocation to the college. *Displacement* means directing anger toward someone who is not the source of the conflict. For example, a manager may respond harshly to an employee after a telephone confrontation with an angry customer. Another aggressive defense mechanism is *negativism*, which is active or passive resistance. Negativism is illustrated by a manager who, when appointed to a committee on which she did not want to serve, made negative comments throughout the meeting.

Compromise mechanisms, such as compensation, identification, and rationalization, are used by individuals to make the best of a conflict situation. *Compensation* occurs when an individual tries to make up for an inadequacy by putting increased energy into another activity. Compensation can be seen when a person makes up for a bad relationship at home by spending more time at the office. *Identification* occurs when one individual patterns his or her behavior after another's. One supervisor at a construction firm, not wanting to acknowledge consciously that she was not likely to be promoted, mimicked the behavior of her boss, even going so far as to buy a car just like the boss's. *Rationalization* is trying to justify one's behavior by constructing bogus reasons for it. Employees may rationalize unethical behavior like padding their expense accounts because "everyone else does it."

Withdrawal mechanisms are exhibited when frustrated individuals try to flee from a conflict using either physical or psychological means. Flight,

4. Understand the defense mechanisms that individuals exhibit when they engage in interpersonal conflict.

fixation
An aggressive mechanism in which an individual keeps up a dysfunctional behavior that obviously will not solve the conflict.

displacement
An aggressive mechanism in which an individual directs his or her anger toward someone who is not the source of the conflict.

negativism
An aggressive mechanism in which a person responds with pessimism to any attempt at solving a problem.

compensation
A compromise mechanism in which an individual attempts to make up for a negative situation by devoting himself or herself to another pursuit with increased vigor.

identification
A compromise mechanism whereby an individual patterns his or her behavior after another's.

rationalization
A compromise mechanism characterized by trying to justify one's behavior by constructing bogus reasons for it.

Table 12.2
Common Defense Mechanisms

Defense Mechanism	Psychological Process
Aggressive Mechanisms	
• Fixation	Person maintains a persistent, nonadjustive reaction even though all the cues indicate the behavior will not cope with the problem.
• Displacement	Individual redirects pent-up emotions toward persons, ideas, or objects other than the primary source of the emotion.
• Negativism	Person uses active or passive resistance, operating unconsciously.
Compromise Mechanisms	
• Compensation	Individual devotes himself or herself to a pursuit with increased vigor to make up for some feeling of real or imagined inadequacy.
• Identification	Individual enhances own self-esteem by patterning behavior after another's, frequently also internalizing the values and beliefs of the other person; also vicariously shares the glories or suffering in the disappointments of other individuals or groups.
• Rationalization	Person justifies inconsistent or undesirable behavior, beliefs, statements, and motivations by providing acceptable explanations for them.
Withdrawal Mechanisms	
• Flight or withdrawal	Through either physical or psychological means, person leaves the field in which frustration, anxiety, or conflict is experienced.
• Conversion	Emotional conflicts are expressed in muscular, sensory, or bodily symptoms of disability, malfunctioning, or pain.
• Fantasy	Person daydreams or uses other forms of imaginative activity to obtain an escape from reality and obtain imagined satisfactions.

SOURCE: Timothy W. Costello and Sheldon S. Zalkind, adapted table from "Psychology in Administration: A Research Orientation" from *Journal of Conflict Resolution* III 1959, pp. 148–149. Reprinted by permission of Sage Publications, Inc.

flight/withdrawal
A withdrawal mechanism that entails physically escaping a conflict (flight) or psychologically escaping (withdrawal).

conversion
A withdrawal mechanism in which emotional conflicts are expressed in physical symptoms.

conversion, and fantasy are examples of withdrawal mechanisms. Physically escaping a conflict is *flight*. An employee who takes a day off after a blowup with the boss is an example. *Withdrawal* may take the form of emotionally leaving a conflict, such as exhibiting an "I don't care anymore" attitude. *Conversion* is a process whereby emotional conflicts become expressed in physical symptoms. Most of us have experienced the conversion reaction of a headache following an emotional exchange with another person. *Fantasy* is an escape by daydreaming. An excellent example of fantasy occurred in the movie *9 to 5*, in which Dolly Parton, Lily Tomlin, and Jane Fonda played characters who fantasized about torturing their boss because he was such a tyrant.

Knowledge of these defense mechanisms can be extremely beneficial to a manager. By understanding the ways in which people typically react to interpersonal conflict, managers can be prepared for employees' reactions and help them uncover their feelings about a conflict.

Coping with Difficult Behavior

Many interpersonal conflicts arise when one person finds another person's behavior uncomfortable, irritating, or bothersome in one way or another. Robert Bramson has identified seven basic types of difficult behavior that may cause interpersonal conflict at work.[37] Table 12.3 presents the seven types of difficult behavior, along with suggestions for coping with them.

Hostile-aggressive behavior occurs when individuals bully other people by bombarding them with cutting remarks or by throwing a tantrum when things do not go their way. Their focus is on attacking the other party in a conflict. Openly emotional, they use these displays to create discomfort or surprise in their adversaries. Underlying their behavior is a strong sense of "shoulds," internal rules about the way things ought to be. A key to dealing with hostile-aggressive behavior is to recognize the behavior and not to be drawn into it yourself.

Complainers gripe constantly but never take action about what they complain about, usually because they feel powerless or do not want to take responsibility. You may want to hear complainers out and let them know you understand their feelings, but do not get drawn into pitying them. Use a problem-solving stance. For instance, a manager might say, "Joan, what do you want the outcome of our meeting to be? What action needs to be taken?" This focuses the complainer on solutions, not complaints.

Clams are silent and unresponsive when asked for opinions. They react to conflict by closing up (like their namesakes) and refusing to discuss problems. The challenge in coping with clams is getting them to open up and talk. Open-ended questions are invaluable, as is patience in allowing them their silence for a reasonable time. If a coworker is avoiding you and has refused to talk, "Are you angry with me?" may not be a good question. "Why are you avoiding me?" may be better. If no response is forthcoming, you might try direct action. "Since you won't discuss this, I'm going to assume that there's nothing wrong and sign us both up for the company volleyball team."

Superagreeable behavior is often exhibited by charming individuals who are sincere and helpful to your face, but fail to do what they promise when you leave. A service manager at an auto dealership may listen attentively to the problems you report with your new car, dutifully write them down, and assure you that they will be taken care of. When you pick up the car, however, none of the problems are resolved. Does this sound familiar? These people are often conflict avoiders and make unrealistic promises to avoid a

fantasy
A withdrawal mechanism that provides an escape from a conflict through daydreaming.

5. Construct an action plan for dealing with difficult behavior at work.

Table 12.3
Coping Tactics for Dealing with Difficult Behavior

Hostile-Aggressives:

- Stand up for yourself.
- Give them time to run down.
- Use self-assertive language.
- Avoid a direct confrontation.

Complainers:

- Listen attentively.
- Acknowledge their feelings.
- Avoid complaining with them.
- State the facts without apology.
- Use a problem-solving mode.

Clams:

- Ask open-ended questions.
- Be patient in waiting for a response.
- Ask more open-ended questions.
- If no response occurs, tell clams what you plan to do, because no discussion has taken place.

Superagreeables:

- In a nonthreatening manner, work hard to find out why they will not take action.
- Let them know you value them as people.
- Be ready to compromise and negotiate, and do not allow them to make unrealistic commitments.
- Try to discern the hidden meaning in their humor.

Negativists:

- Do not be dragged into their despair.
- Do not try to cajole them out of their negativism.
- Discuss the problem thoroughly, without offering solutions.
- When alternatives are discussed, bring up the negative side yourself.
- Be ready to take action alone, without their agreement.

Know-It-Alls:

Bulldozers:

- Prepare yourself.
- Listen and paraphrase their main points.
- Use the questioning form to raise problems.

Balloons:

- State facts or opinions as your own perceptions of reality.
- Find a way for balloons to save face.
- Confront balloons alone, not in public.

Indecisive Stallers:

- Raise the issue of why they are hesitant.
- If you are the problem, ask for help.
- Keep the action steps in your own hands.
- Possibly remove the staller from the situation.

confrontation. Be prepared to compromise on a solution, and make sure it is workable. Finally, if you get a humorous response from a superagreeable, look for the hidden meaning in it.

Negativists respond to any attempts to solve a problem with pessimism. Their behavior is dangerous, because their negativism is contagious, and you may lose your optimism about solving the problem in interacting with them. A problem-solving mode is appropriate in this case; let the negativist bring up alternative solutions. Play devil's advocate, bringing up the negative aspects yourself. You may also want to ask, "What is the worst that might happen?" When the negativists are convinced that they can handle even the worst-case scenario, they may feel more in control.

Know-it-alls display superior attitudes, wanting you to know that they know everything there is to know about everything. If they really know what they are talking about, they are bulldozers. Bulldozers overrun individuals with their blustery style, and they are most aggravating because they are always right. To cope with bulldozers, you need to be prepared. They will respect you if you have done your homework. Phony experts are known as balloons. Balloons only think they know everything. To deal with balloon behavior, state your position as your own perception of the situation. It is also important to allow the balloon to save face when deflated, so confront the balloon in private. A new professor, when asked to explain a particular statistical technique to his new colleagues, provided a faulty explanation. This new professor was a balloon, eager to display his expertise. A wise, seasoned professor took the newcomer aside after the presentation and said, "I think my old pal Professor Windbag at State U. misinformed you on that statistic. Let me show you a book I have that explains it." The new professor's face was saved and his factual knowledge enhanced.

Indecisive stallers put off decisions until they have no choice, or they fail to come to a decision at all. Stallers often are genuinely concerned about others and are afraid that no matter what they decide, they will alienate or fail to please someone. The key in coping with stallers is to uncover the reasons for their hesitation. You must take responsibility to ensure that the staller follows through. If stallers are too disruptive, you may want to remove them from the decision situation.

In coping with difficult behavior, it is important to identify the reasons you perceive the behavior as difficult. Bramson's framework helps accompish this. In addition, you should analyze your response to the difficult person.

CONFLICT MANAGEMENT STRATEGIES AND TECHNIQUES

The overall approach (or strategy) you use in a conflict is important in determining whether the conflict will have a positive or negative outcome.

These overall strategies are competitive versus cooperative strategies. Table 12.4 depicts the two strategies and four different conflict scenarios.

Table 12.4
Win–Lose versus Win–Win Strategies

Strategy	Department A	Department B	Organization
Competitive	Lose	Lose	Lose
	Lose	Win	Lose
	Win	Lose	Lose
Cooperative	Win–	Win–	Win

The competitive strategy is founded on assumptions of win–lose and entails dishonest communication, mistrust, and a rigid position from both parties.[38] The cooperative strategy is founded on different assumptions: the potential for win–win outcomes, honest communication, trust, openness to risk and vulnerability, and the notion that the whole may be greater than the sum of the parts.

To illustrate the importance of the overall strategy, consider the case of two groups competing for scarce resources. Suppose budget cuts have to be made at an insurance company. The claims manager argues that the sales training staff should be cut, because agents are fully trained. The sales training manager argues that claims personnel should be cut, because the company is processing fewer claims. This could turn into a dysfunctional brawl, with both sides refusing to give ground. This would constitute a win–lose, lose–win, or lose–lose scenario. Personnel cuts could be made in only one department, or in both departments. In all three cases, with the competitive approach the organization winds up in a losing position.

Even in such intense conflicts as those over scarce resources, a win–win strategy can lead to an overall win for the organization. In fact, conflicts over scarce resources can be productive if the parties have cooperative goals—a strategy that seeks a winning solution for both parties. To achieve a win–win outcome, the conflict must be approached with open-minded discussion of opposing views. Through open-minded discussion, both parties integrate views and create new solutions that facilitate productivity and strengthen their relationship; the result is feelings of unity rather than separation.[39]

In the example of the conflict between the claims manager and sales training manager, open-minded discussion might reveal that there are ways to achieve budget cuts without cutting personnel. Sales support might surrender part of its travel budget, and claims might cut out overtime. This represents a win–win situation for the company. The budget has been reduced, and relationships between the two departments have been preserved. Both parties have given up something (note the "win–" in Table 12.4), but the conflict has been resolved with a positive outcome.

You can see the importance of the broad strategy used to approach a conflict. We now move from broad strategies to more specific techniques.

Experiencing OB

Conflict management often involves negotiating with others to decide the allocation of resources. You can learn more about negotiation approaches by visiting our animated concept and activity site. Choose Conflict&Negotiation from the "select a topic" pull-down menu, then Negotiation from the "overview tab."

http://www.experiencingob.com

Ineffective Techniques

There are many specific techniques for dealing with conflict. Before turning to techniques that work, it should be recognized that some actions commonly taken in organizations to deal with conflict are not effective.[40]

Nonaction is doing nothing in hopes that the conflict will disappear. Generally, this is not a good technique, because most conflicts do not go away, and the individuals involved in the conflict react with frustration.

Secrecy, or trying to keep a conflict out of view of most people, only creates suspicion. An example is an organizational policy of pay secrecy. In some organizations, discussion of salary is grounds for dismissal. When this is the case, employees suspect that the company has something to hide.

Administrative orbiting is delaying action on a conflict by buying time, usually by telling the individuals involved that the problem is being worked on or that the boss is still thinking about the issue. Like nonaction, this technique leads to frustration and resentment.

Due process nonaction is a procedure set up to address conflicts that is so costly, time-consuming, or personally risky that no one will use it. Some companies' sexual harassment policies are examples of this technique. To file a sexual harassment complaint, detailed paperwork is required, the accuser must go through appropriate channels, and the accuser risks being branded a troublemaker. Thus, the company has a procedure for handling complaints (due process), but no one uses it (nonaction).

Character assassination is an attempt to label or discredit an opponent. In the confirmation hearings of Supreme Court Justice Clarence Thomas, for example, attempts at character assassination were made upon Anita Hill by referring to her as a spurned woman and by saying she lived in fantasy. Justice Thomas was also a victim of character assassination; he was portrayed as a womanizer and a perpetrator of sexual harassment. Character assassination can backfire and make the individual who uses it appear dishonest and cruel.

Effective Techniques

Fortunately, there are effective conflict management techniques. These include appealing to superordinate goals, expanding resources, changing personnel, changing structure, and confronting and negotiating.

Superordinate Goals An organizational goal that is more important to both parties in a conflict than their individual or group goals is a *superordinate goal*.[41] Superordinate goals cannot be achieved by an individual or by one group alone. The achievement of these goals requires cooperation by both parties.

One effective technique for resolving conflict is to appeal to a superordinate goal—in effect, to focus the parties on a larger issue on which they both agree. This helps them realize their similarities rather than their differences.

---

nonaction
Doing nothing in hopes that a conflict will disappear.

secrecy
Attempting to hide a conflict or an issue that has the potential to create conflict.

administrative orbiting
Delaying action on a conflict by buying time.

due process nonaction
A procedure set up to address conflicts that is so costly, time-consuming, or personally risky that no one will use it.

character assassination
An attempt to label or discredit an opponent.

6. Describe effective and ineffective techniques for managing conflict.

superordinate goal
An organizational goal that is more important to both parties in a conflict than their individual or group goals.

In the conflict between service representatives and cable television installers that was discussed earlier, appealing to a superordinate goal would be an effective technique for resolving the conflict. Both departments can agree that superior customer service is a goal worthy of pursuit and that this goal cannot be achieved unless cables are installed properly and in a timely manner, and customer complaints are handled effectively. Quality service requires that both departments cooperate to achieve the goal.

Expanding Resources One conflict resolution technique is so simple that it may be overlooked. If the conflict's source is common or scarce resources, providing more resources may be a solution. Of course, managers working with tight budgets may not have the luxury of obtaining additional resources. Nevertheless, it is a technique to be considered. In the example earlier in this chapter, one solution to the conflict among managers over secretarial support would be to hire more secretaries.

Changing Personnel Sometimes a conflict is prolonged and severe, and efforts at resolution fail. In such cases, it may be appropriate to change personnel. Transferring or firing an individual may be the best solution, but only after due process.

Changing Structure Another way to resolve a conflict is to change the structure of the organization. One way of accomplishing this is to create an integrator role. An integrator is a liaison between groups with very different interests. In severe conflicts, it may be best that the integrator be a neutral third party.[42] Creating the integrator role is a way of opening dialogue between groups that have difficulty communicating.

Using cross-functional teams is another way of changing the organization's structure to manage conflict. In the old methods of designing new products in organizations, many departments had to contribute, and delays resulted from difficulties in coordinating the activities of the various departments. Using a cross-functional team made up of members from different departments improves coordination and reduces delays by allowing many activities to be performed at the same time rather than sequentially.[43] The team approach allows members from different departments to work together and reduces the potential for conflict.

Confronting and Negotiating Some conflicts require confrontation and negotiation between the parties. Both these strategies require skill on the part of the negotiator and careful planning before engaging in negotiations. The process of negotiating involves an open discussion of problem solutions, and the outcome often is an exchange in which both parties work toward a mutually beneficial solution.

Negotiation is a joint process of finding a mutually acceptable solution to a complex conflict. Negotiating is a useful strategy under the following conditions:

- There are two or more parties. Negotiation is primarily an interpersonal or intergroup process.

- There is a conflict of interest between the parties such that what one party wants is not what the other party wants.

- The parties are willing to negotiate because each believes it can use its influence to obtain a better outcome than by simply taking the side of the other party.

- The parties prefer to work together than to fight openly, give in, break off contact, or take the dispute to a higher authority.

There are two major negotiating approaches: distributive bargaining and integrative negotiation.[44] *Distributive bargaining* is an approach in which the goals of one party are in direct conflict with the goals of the other party. Resources are limited, and each party wants to maximize its share of the resources (get its part of the pie). It is a competitive or win–lose approach to negotiations. Sometimes distributive bargaining causes negotiators to focus so much on their differences that they ignore their common ground. In these cases, distributive bargaining can become counterproductive. The reality is, however, that some situations are distributive in nature, particularly when the parties are interdependent. If a negotiator wants to maximize the value of a single deal and is not worried about maintaining a good relationship with the other party, distributive bargaining may be an option.

In contrast, *integrative negotiation* is an approach in which the parties' goals are not seen as mutually exclusive and in which the focus is on making it possible for both sides to achieve their objectives. Integrative negotiation focuses on the merits of the issues and is a win–win approach. (How can we make the pie bigger?) For integrative negotiation to be successful, certain preconditions must be present. These include having a common goal, faith in one's own problem-solving abilities, a belief in the validity of the other party's position, motivation to work together, mutual trust, and clear communication.

distributive bargaining
A negotiation approach in which the goals of the parties are in conflict, and each party seeks to maximize its resources.

integrative negotiation
A negotiation approach that focuses on the merits of the issues and seeks a win–win solution.

CONFLICT MANAGEMENT STYLES

Managers have at their disposal a variety of conflict management styles: avoiding, accommodating, competing, compromising, and collaborating. One way of classifying styles of conflict management is to examine the styles' assertiveness (the extent to which you want your goals met) and cooperativeness (the extent to which you want to see the other party's concerns met).[45] Figure 12.4 graphs the five conflict management styles using these two dimensions. Table 12.5 lists appropriate situations for using each conflict management style.

7. Understand five styles of conflict management, and diagnose your own preferred style.

Avoiding

Avoiding is a style low on both assertiveness and cooperativeness. Avoiding is a deliberate decision to take no action on a conflict or to stay out of a conflict situation. An example of an organization avoiding conflict oc-

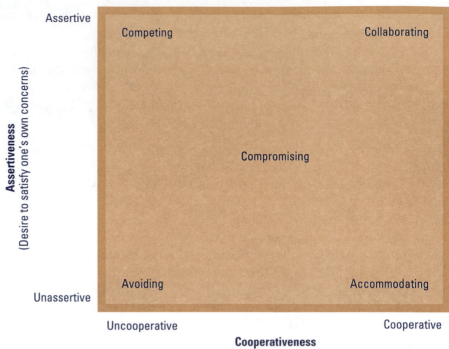

Figure 12.4
Conflict Management Styles

SOURCE: K. W. Thomas, "Conflict and Conflict Management," in M. D. Dunnette, *Handbook of Industrial and Organizational Psychology* (Chicago: Rand McNally, 1976), 900. Used with permission of M. D. Dunnette.

Experiencing OB

You many interact with this model of conflict management styles at our animated concept and activity site. Choose Conflict&Negotiation from the "select a topic" pull-down menu, then Conflict Management Styles from the "overview tab."

http://www.experiencingob.com

curred in 1973 and 1974, when officials at Exxon (now ExxonMobil) quietly withdrew their executives from Argentina because of the increased rate of kidnapping of U.S. executives.[46] In certain situations, it may be appropriate to avoid a conflict. For example, when the parties are angry and need time to cool down, it may be best to use avoidance. There is a potential danger in using an avoiding style too often, however. Research shows that overuse of this style results in negative evaluations from others in the workplace.[47]

Accommodating

A style in which you are concerned that the other party's goals be met but relatively unconcerned with getting your own way is called accommodating. It is cooperative but unassertive. Appropriate situations for accommodating include times when you find you are wrong, when you want to let the other party have his or her way so that that individual will owe you similar treatment later, or when the relationship is important. Overreliance on accommodating has its dangers. Managers who constantly defer to others may find that others lose respect for them. In addition, accommodating managers may become frustrated because their own needs are never met, and they may lose self-esteem.[48]

Conflict-Handling Style	Appropriate Situation
Competing	1. When quick, decisive action is vital (e.g., emergencies).
	2. On important issues where unpopular actions need implementing (e.g., cost cutting, enforcing unpopular rules, discipline).
	3. On issues vital to company welfare when you know you are right.
	4. Against people who take advantage of noncompetitive behavior.
Collaborating	1. To find an integrative solution when both sets of concerns are too important to be compromised.
	2. When your objective is to learn.
	3. To merge insights from people with different perspectives.
	4. To gain commitment by incorporating concerns into a consensus.
	5. To work through feelings that have interfered with a relationship.
Compromising	1. When goals are important, but not worth the effort or potential disruption of more assertive modes.
	2. When opponents with equal power are committed to mutually exclusive goals.
	3. To achieve temporary settlements to complex issues.
	4. To arrive at expedient solutions under time pressure.
	5. As a backup when collaboration or competition is unsuccessful.
Avoiding	1. When an issue is trivial, or more important issues are pressing.
	2. When you perceive no chance of satisfying your concerns.
	3. When potential disruption outweighs the benefits of resolution.
	4. To let people cool down and regain perspective.
	5. When gathering information supersedes immediate decision.
	6. When others can resolve the conflict more effectively.
	7. When issues seem tangential or symptomatic of other issues.
Accommodating	1. When you find you are wrong—to allow a better position to be heard, to learn, and to show your reasonableness.
	2. When issues are more important to others than to yourself—to satisfy others and maintain cooperation.
	3. To build social credits for later issues.
	4. To minimize loss when you are outmatched and losing.
	5. When harmony and stability are especially important.
	6. To allow employees to develop by learning from mistakes.

Table 12.5
Uses of Five Styles of Conflict Management

SOURCE: *The Conflict Positive Organization*, by Tjsovold, © 1991. Reprinted by permission of Prentice-Hall, Inc., Upper Saddle River, N.J.

Competing

Competing is a style that is very assertive and uncooperative. You want to satisfy your own interests and are willing to do so at the other party's expense. In an emergency or in situations where you know you are right, it may be appropriate to put your foot down. For example, environmentalists forced Shell Oil Company (part of Royal Dutch Petroleum) to scrap its plans to build a refinery in Delaware after a bitter "To Hell with Shell" campaign.[49] Relying solely on competing strategies is dangerous, though. Managers who do so may become reluctant to admit when they are wrong and may find themselves surrounded by people who are afraid to disagree with them.

Compromising

The compromising style is intermediate in both assertiveness and cooperativeness, because each party must give up something to reach a solution to the conflict. Compromises are often made in the final hours of union–management negotiations, when time is of the essence. Compromise may be an effective backup style when efforts toward collaboration are not successful.[50]

It is important to recognize that compromises are not optimal solutions. Compromise means partially surrendering one's position for the sake of coming to terms. Often, when people compromise, they inflate their demands to begin with. The solutions reached may only be temporary, and often compromises do nothing to improve relationships between the parties in the conflict.

Collaborating

A win–win style that is high on both assertiveness and cooperativeness is known as collaborating. Working toward collaborating involves an open and thorough discussion of the conflict and arriving at a solution that is satisfactory to both parties. Situations where collaboration may be effective include times when both parties need to be committed to a final solution or when a combination of different perspectives can be formed into a solution. Collaborating requires open, trusting behavior and sharing information for the benefit of both parties. Long term, it leads to improved relationships.[51]

Research on the five styles of conflict management indicates that although most managers favor a certain style, they have the capacity to change styles as the situation demands.[52] A study of project managers found that managers who used a combination of competing and avoiding styles were seen as ineffective by the engineers who worked on their project teams.[53] In another study of conflicts between R&D project managers and technical staff, competing and avoiding styles resulted in more frequent conflict and lower performance, whereas the collaborating style resulted in less frequent conflict and better performance.[54] Use Challenge 12.1 to assess your dominant conflict management style.

Cultural differences also influence the use of different styles of conflict management. For example, one study compared Turkish and Jordan-

Challenge 12.1

What Is Your Conflict-Handling Style?

Instructions:

For each of the fifteen items, indicate how often you rely on that tactic by circling the appropriate number.

	Rarely Always
1. I argue my case with my coworkers to show the merits of my position.	1—2—3—4—5
2. I negotiate with my coworkers so that a compromise can be reached.	1—2—3—4—5
3. I try to satisfy the expectations of my coworkers.	1—2—3—4—5
4. I try to investigate an issue with my coworkers to find a solution acceptable to us.	1—2—3—4—5
5. I am firm in pursuing my side of the issue.	1—2—3—4—5
6. I attempt to avoid being "put on the spot" and try to keep my conflict with my coworkers to myself.	1—2—3—4—5
7. I hold on to my solution to a problem.	1—2—3—4—5
8. I use "give and take" so that a compromise can be made.	1—2—3—4—5
9. I exchange accurate information with my coworkers to solve a problem together.	1—2—3—4—5
10. I avoid open discussion of my differences with my coworkers.	1—2—3—4—5
11. I accommodate the wishes of my coworkers.	1—2—3—4—5
12. I try to bring all our concerns out in the open so that the issues can be resolved in the best possible way.	1—2—3—4—5
13. I propose a middle ground for breaking deadlocks.	1—2—3—4—5
14. I go along with the suggestions of my coworkers.	1—2—3—4—5
15. I try to keep my disagreements with my coworkers to myself in order to avoid hard feelings.	1—2—3—4—5

Scoring Key:

Collaborating		Accommodating		Competing		Avoiding		Compromising	
Item	**Score**	**Item**	**Score**	**Item**	**Score**	**Item**	**Score**	**Item**	**Score**
4.	___	3.	___	1.	___	6.	___	2.	___
9.	___	11.	___	5.	___	10.	___	8.	___
12.	___	14.	___	7.	___	15.	___	13.	___
Total = ___		Total = ___		Total = ___		Total = ___		Total = ___	

Your primary conflict-handling style is: _____   Your backup conflict-handling style is: _____
 (The category with the highest total.)   (The category with the second highest total.)

ian managers with U.S. managers. All three groups preferred the collaborating style. Turkish managers also reported frequent use of the competing style, whereas Jordanian and U.S. managers reported that it was one of their least used styles.[55]

The human resources manager of one U.S. telecommunications company's office in Singapore engaged a consultant to investigate the conflict in the office.[56] Twenty-two expatriates from the United States and Canada and thirty-eight Singaporeans worked in the office. The consultant used the Thomas model (Figure 12.4) and distributed questionnaires to all managers to determine their conflict management styles. The results were not surprising: The expatriate managers preferred the competing, collaborating, and compromising styles, while the Asians preferred the avoiding and accommodating styles.

Workshops were conducted within the firm to develop an understanding of the differences and how they negatively affected the firm. The Asians interpreted the results as reflecting the tendency of Americans to "shout first and ask questions later." They felt that the Americans had an arrogant attitude and could not handle having their ideas rejected. The Asians attributed their own styles to their cultural background. The Americans attributed the results to the stereotypical view of Asians as unassertive and timid, and they viewed their own results as reflecting their desire to "get things out in the open."

The process opened a dialogue between the two groups, who began to work on the idea of harmony through conflict. They began to discard the traditional stereotypes in favor of shared meanings and mutual understanding.

It is important to remember that preventing and resolving dysfunctional conflict is only half the task of effective conflict management. Stimulating functional conflict is the other half.

MANAGERIAL IMPLICATIONS: CREATING A CONFLICT-POSITIVE ORGANIZATION

Dean Tjosvold argues that well-managed conflict adds to an organization's innovation and productivity.[57] He discusses procedures for making conflict positive. Too many organizations take a win–lose, competitive approach to conflict or avoid conflict altogether. These two approaches view conflict as negative. A positive view of conflict, in contrast, leads to win–win solutions. Figure 12.5 illustrates these three approaches to conflict management.

Four interrelated steps are involved in creating a conflict-positive organization:

1. *Value diversity and confront differences.* Differences should be seen as opportunities for innovation, and diversity should be celebrated. Open and honest confrontations bring out differences, and they are essential for positive conflict.

2. *Seek mutual benefits, and unite behind cooperative goals.* Conflicts have to be managed together. Through conflict, individuals learn how much they depend on one another. Even when employees share goals, they may differ on how to accomplish the goals. The important point is that they are

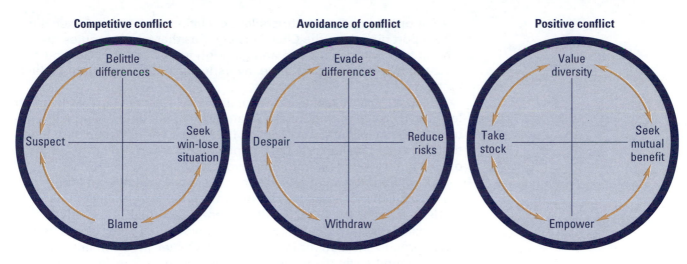

Competitive conflict

- Belittle differences
- Seek win-lose situation
- Blame
- Suspect

Avoidance of conflict

- Evade differences
- Reduce risks
- Withdraw
- Despair

Positive conflict

- Value diversity
- Seek mutual benefit
- Empower
- Take stock

SOURCE: *The Conflict Positive Organization*, by Tjosvold, © 1991. Reprinted by permission of Prentice-Hall, Inc., Upper Saddle River, N.J.

Figure 12.5
Three Organization Views of Conflict

moving toward the same objectives. Joint rewards should be given to the whole team for cooperative behavior.

3. *Empower employees to feel confident and skillful.* People must be made to feel that they control their conflicts and that they can deal with their differences productively. When they do so, they should be recognized.

4. *Take stock to reward success and learn from mistakes.* Employees should be encouraged to appreciate one another's strengths and weaknesses and to talk directly about them. They should celebrate their conflict managment successes and work out plans for ways they can improve in the future.

Tjosvold believes that a conflict-positive organization has competitive advantages for the future.

Looking Back

The Secrets to Ford's Success in Managing Relationships with the United Auto Workers

As you recall from the Thinking Ahead feature, Ford considers its cooperative relationship with the United Auto Workers union a key to its competitive advantage. The relationship has developed over time through carefully crafted joint agreements, with each side making concessions. The UAW's relationships with other automakers are not as cooperative; in fact, some are downright adversarial. How does Ford maintain smooth relations with the union?

For one thing, Ford entrusts labor relations to top-level executives who report directly to the CEO. This ensures that labor disputes quickly land in the chairman's office and get high-level attention. General Motors' top labor manager is three layers lower in the management hierarchy.

Second, Ford executives maintain close relationships with union leaders. Because of these close relationships, the union negotiated national agreements first with Ford in 1993 and 1996, and then demanded that GM and Chrysler accept the same agreements. Ford has used these opportunities to put GM at a disadvantage.

Third, Ford does not tolerate managers who cannot get along with workers. Such managers are removed from the factory. In contrast, GM tends to transfer the managers to different factories.

Finally, Ford promotes high levels of worker involvement in its factories around the nation. High levels of worker involvement produce more committed and satisfied workers, which in turn leads to better union–management relationships.

Trust and communication are the hallmarks of Ford's approach. To illustrate this, consider GM's announcement that it planned to spin off its huge Delphi Automotive Systems unit as an independent company. Union leaders remarked, "We weren't advised of Delphi, we were told of Delphi . . . that shows exactly what's wrong with GM." The company told the union of its plans after the decision was made. Just the week before, agreements had been reached with the union that included a "no strike, no sales" clause applying to some Delphi plants.

Amid rumors that Ford might make its Visteon parts division independent, top union officials expressed less concern. "I don't think Ford would take action on Visteon without talking to [the union]. We will have long conversations with them."[58]

CHAPTER SUMMARY

1. Conflict management skills are keys to management success. The manager's task is to stimulate functional conflict and prevent or resolve dysfunctional conflict.

2. Structural causes of conflict include specialization, interdependence, common resources, goal differences, authority relationships, status inconsistencies, and jurisdictional ambiguities.

3. Personal factors that lead to conflict include differences in skills and abilities, personalities, perceptions, or values and ethics; emotions; communication barriers; and cultural differences. The increasing diversity of the workforce and globalization of business have potential to increase conflict arising from these differences.

4. The levels of conflict include interorganizational, intergroup, interpersonal, and intrapersonal.

5. Individuals engaged in interpersonal conflict often display aggressive, compromise, or withdrawal defense mechanisms.

6. In coping with difficult behavior, it is important to identify the reasons the behavior is perceived as difficult and to analyze the response to the difficult behavior.

7. Ineffective techniques for managing conflict include nonaction, secrecy, administrative orbiting, due process nonaction, and character assassination.

8. Effective techniques for managing conflict include appealing to superordinate goals, expanding resources, changing personnel, changing structure, and confronting and negotiating.

9. In negotiating, managers can use a variety of conflict management styles, including avoiding, accommodating, competing, compromising, and collaborating.

10. Managers should strive to create a conflict-positive organization—one that values diversity, empowers employees, and seeks win–win solutions to conflicts.

KEY TERMS

conflict   350

functional conflict   351

dysfunctional conflict   351

jurisdictional ambiguity   354

interorganizational conflict   357

intergroup conflict   359

interpersonal conflict   359

intrapersonal conflict   359

interrole conflict   359

intrarole conflict   360

person–role conflict   360

fixation   363

displacement   363

negativism   363

compensation   363

identification   363

rationalization   363

flight/withdrawal   364

conversion   364

fantasy   364

nonaction   369

secrecy   369

administrative orbiting   369

due process nonaction   369

character assassination   369

superordinate goal   369

distributive bargaining   371

integrative negotiation   371

REVIEW QUESTIONS

1. Discuss the differences between functional and dysfunctional conflict. Why should a manager understand conflict?

2. Identify the structural and personal factors that contribute to conflict.

3. Discuss the four major forms of conflict in organizations.

4. What defense mechanisms do people use in interpersonal conflict?

5. Characterize the different types of difficult behavior that may cause conflict at work.

6. What are the most effective techniques for managing conflict at work? What are some ineffective techniques?

7. Identify and discuss five styles of conflict management.

DISCUSSION AND COMMUNICATION QUESTIONS

1. What causes you the most conflict at work or school?

2. Identify the different interrole, intrarole, and person–role conflicts that you experience.

3. What methods have you found most personally helpful in dealing with difficult people at school or work? At home? In social situations?

4. Are you comfortable with your preferred conflict management style? Would you consider modifying it?

5. (communication question) Think of a person with whom you have had a recent conflict. Write a letter to this person, attempting to resolve the conflict. Use the concepts from the chapter to accomplish your objective. Be sure to address whether the conflict is functional or dysfunctional, what styles each party has used, effective strategies for resolving the conflict, and ineffective strategies that should be avoided.

ETHICS QUESTIONS

1. What kind of ethical conflicts have you experienced at school or work? At home?
2. Is it ethical to avoid a conflict?
3. How can you stimulate conflict in an ethical manner?
4. Evaluate the following techniques in terms of their implications for ethical behavior: nonaction, secrecy, administrative orbiting, and changing personnel.
5. Suppose an employee comes to you with a sexual harassment complaint. You know that your company has a policy in place, but the policy is so complicated and risky that it is hardly worth using. What should you do?
6. In what situations is the competing style of conflict management appropriate? What unethical behaviors might be associated with this style? How can these behaviors be avoided?

Experiential Exercises

12.1 Conflicts over Unethical Behavior

Many conflicts in work organizations arise over differences in beliefs concerning what constitutes ethical versus unethical behavior. The following questionnaire provides a list of behaviors that you or your coworkers might engage in when working for a company. Go over each item, and circle the number that best indicates the frequency with which you personally would (or do, if you work now) engage in that behavior. Then put an X over the number you think represents how often your coworkers would (or do) engage in that behavior. Finally, put a check mark beside the item (in the "Needs Control" column) if you believe that management should control that behavior.

	At Every Opportunity	Often	About Half the Time	Seldom	Never	Needs Control
1. Passing blame for errors to an innocent coworker.	5	4	3	2	1	_____
2. Divulging confidential information.	5	4	3	2	1	_____
3. Falsifying time/quality/ quantity reports.	5	4	3	2	1	_____
4. Claiming credit for someone else's work.	5	4	3	2	1	_____
5. Padding an expense account by over 10 percent.	5	4	3	2	1	_____
6. Pilfering company materials and supplies.	5	4	3	2	1	_____
7. Accepting gifts/favors in exchange for preferential treatment.	5	4	3	2	1	_____
8. Giving gifts/favors in exchange for preferential treatment.	5	4	3	2	1	_____
9. Padding an expense account by up to 10 percent.	5	4	3	2	1	_____
10. Authorizing a subordinate to violate company rules.	5	4	3	2	1	_____

	At Every Opportunity	Often	About Half the Time	Seldom	Never	Needs Control
11. Calling in sick to take a day off.	5	4	3	2	1	_____
12. Concealing one's errors.	5	4	3	2	1	_____
13. Taking longer than necessary to do a job.	5	4	3	2	1	_____
14. Using company services for personal use.	5	4	3	2	1	_____
15. Doing personal business on company time.	5	4	3	2	1	_____
16. Taking extra personal time (lunch hour, breaks, early departure, and so forth).	5	4	3	2	1	_____
17. Not reporting others' violations of company policies and rules.	5	4	3	2	1	_____
18. Overlooking a superior's violation of policy to prove loyalty to the boss.	5	4	3	2	1	_____

Discussion Questions

1. Would (do) your coworkers seem to engage in these behaviors more often than you would (do)? Why do you have this perception?

2. Which behaviors tend to be most frequent?

3. How are the most frequent behaviors different from the behaviors engaged in less frequently?

4. What are the most important items for managers to control? How should managers control these behaviors?

5. Select a particular behavior from the list. Have two people debate whether the behavior is ethical or not.

6. What types of conflicts could emerge if the behaviors in the list occurred frequently?

SOURCE: Excerpt from *The Managerial Experience: Cases, Exercises, and Readings*, Third Edition by Sally Coltrin and Lawrence R. Jauch, copyright © 1983 by The Dryden Press, reprinted by permission of the publisher.

12.2 The World Bank Game: An Intergroup Negotiation

The purposes of this exercise are to learn about conflict and trust between groups and to practice negotiation skills. In the course of the exercise, money will be won or lost. Your team's objective is to win as much money as it can. Your team will be paired with another team, and both teams will receive identical instructions. After reading these instructions, each team will have ten minutes to plan its strategy.

Each team is assumed to have contributed $50 million to the World Bank. Teams may have to pay more or may receive money from the World Bank, depending on the outcome.

Each team will receive twenty cards. These cards are the weapons. Each card has a marked side (X) and an unmarked side. The marked side signifies that the weapon is armed; the unmarked side signifies that the weapon is unarmed.

At the beginning, each team will place ten of its twenty weapons in their unarmed position (marked side up) and the remaining ten in their unarmed position (marked side down). The weapons will remain in the team's possession and out of sight of the other team at all times.

The game will consist of *rounds* and *moves*. Each round will be composed of seven moves by each team. There will be two or more rounds in the game, depending on the time available. Payoffs will be determined and recorded after each round. The rules are as follows:

1. A move consists of turning two, one, or none of the team's weapons from armed to unarmed status, or vice versa.

2. Each team has one and a half minutes for each move. There is a thirty-second period between each move. At the end of the one and a half minutes, the team must have turned two, one, or none of its weapons from armed to unarmed status or from unarmed to armed status. If the team fails to move in the allotted time, no change can be made in weapon status until the next move.

3. The two-minute length of the period between the beginning of one move and the beginning of the next is unalterable.

Finances

The funds each team has contributed to the World Bank are to be allocated in the following manner: $30 million will be returned to each team to be used as the team's treasury during the course of the game, and $20 million will be retained for the operation of the World Bank.

Payoffs

1. If there is an attack:
   a. Each team may announce an attack on the other team by notifying the banker during the thirty seconds following any minute-and-a-half period used to decide upon the move (including the seventh, or final, decision period in any round). The choice of each team during the decision period just ended counts as a move. An attack may not be made during negotiations.
   b. If there is an attack by one or both teams, two things happen: (1) the round ends, and (2) the World Bank assesses a penalty of $2.5 million on each team.
   c. The team with the greater number of armed weapons wins $1.5 million for each armed weapon it has over and above the number of armed weapons of the other team. These funds are paid directly from the treasury of the losing team to the treasury of the winning team. The banker will manage the transfer of funds.

2. If there is no attack:

   At the end of each round (seven moves), each team's treasury will receive from the World Bank $1 million for each of its weapons that is at that point unarmed; and each team's treasury will pay to the World Bank $1 million for each of its weapons remaining armed.

Negotiations

Between moves, each team will have the opportunity to communicate with the other team through its negotiations. Either team may call for negotiations by notifying the banker during any of the thirty-second periods between decisions. A team is free to accept or reject any invitation to negotiate.

Negotiators from both teams are required to meet after the third and sixth moves (after the thirty-second period following the move, if there is no attack).

Negotiations can last no longer than three minutes. When the two negotiators return to their teams, the minute-and-a-half decision period for the next move will begin once again.

Negotiators are bound only by (a) the three-minute time limit for negotiations and (b) their required appearance after the third and sixth moves. They are always free to say whatever is necessary to benefit themselves or their teams. The teams are not bound by agreements made by their negotiators, even when those agreements are made in good faith.

Special Roles

Each team has ten minutes to organize itself and plan team strategy. During this period, before the first round begins, each team must choose persons to fill the following roles:

- A *negotiator*—activities stated above.
- A *representative*—to communicate the team's decisions to the banker.
- A *recorder*—to record the moves of the team and to keep a running balance of the team's treasury.
- A *treasurer*—to execute all financial transactions with the banker.

The instructor will serve as the banker for the World Bank and will signal the beginning of each of the rounds.

At the end of the game, each participant should complete the following questionnaire, which assesses reactions to the World Bank Game.

World Bank Questionnaire

1. To what extent are you satisfied with your team's strategy?

| Highly dissatisfied | 1 2 3 4 5 6 7 | Highly satisfied |

2. To what extent do you believe the other team is trustworthy?

| Highly untrustworthy | 1 2 3 4 5 6 7 | Highly trustworthy |

3. To what extent are you satisfied with the performance of your negotiator?

| Highly dissatisfied | 1 2 3 4 5 6 7 | Highly satisfied |

4. To what extent was there a consensus on your team regarding its moves?

| Very little | 1 2 3 4 5 6 7 | A great deal |

5. To what extent do you trust the other members of your team?

| Very little | 1 2 3 4 5 6 7 | A great deal |

6. Select one word that describes how you feel about your team: _____ .

7. Select one word that describes how you feel about the other team: _____ .

Negotiators only:

How did you see the other team's negotiator?

| Phony and insincere | 1 2 3 4 5 6 7 | Authentic and sincere |

At the end of the game, the class will reconvene and discuss team members' responses to the World Bank Questionnaire. In addition, the following questions are to be addressed:

1. What was each team's strategy for winning? What strategy was most effective?

2. Contrast the outcomes in terms of win–win solutions to conflict versus win–lose solutions.

SOURCE: Adapted by permission from N. H. Berkowitz and H. A. Hornstein, "World Bank: An Intergroup Negotiation," in J. W. Pfeiffer and J. E. Jones, eds., *The 1975 Handbook for Group Facilitators* (San Diego: Pfeiffer), 58–62. Copyright © 1975 by Pfeiffer & Company, San Diego, CA.

WORLD BANK RECORD SHEET

	Round One		Round Two		Round Three		Round Four	
	Armed	Unarmed	Armed	Unarmed	Armed	Unarmed	Armed	Unarmed
Move	10	10	10	10	10	10	10	10
1								
2								
3								
Required Negotiation 4								
5								
6								
Required Negotiation 7								

Funds in Team Treasury	$30 million				
Funds of Other Treasury	$30 million				
Funds in World Bank	$40 million				

PART 4

Organizational Processes and Structure

13. Jobs and the Design of Work   386

14. Organizational Design and Structure   416

15. Organizational Culture   447

16. Managing Change   476

Learning Objectives

After reading this chapter, you should be able to do the following:

1. Define the term *job*, and identify six patterns of defining *work*. *p. 387*

2. Discuss the four traditional approaches to job design. *p. 390*

3. Describe the job characteristics model. *p. 393*

4. Compare the social information-processing (SIP) model with traditional job design approaches. *p. 398*

5. Explain the interdisciplinary approach to job design. *p. 399*

6. Compare Japanese, German, and Scandinavian approaches to work. *p. 401*

7. Explain how job control, uncertainty, and conflict can be managed for employee well-being. *p. 403*

8. Discuss five emerging issues in the design of work. *p. 405*

13

Jobs and the Design of Work

Thinking Ahead

Jobs, Work Rules, and the Airline Industry

Jobs and work rules are central concerns in labor–management negotiations at many airlines, as in many other industries. While labor is interested in protecting jobs and ensuring fair pay, benefits, and working conditions, management is interested in efficiency, flexibility, and maximum productivity to meet and beat the competition. The competing interests of labor and management have resulted in pilot, flight attendant, and mechanic strikes at various times since deregulation.

Even though the industry is deregulated, the Federal Aviation Administration (FAA) continues to establish work rules and regulations for airlines' flight crews, including pilots and flight engineers, to ensure the safety of the traveling public.[1] FAA work rules limit a flight crew's scheduled and actual flying hours each day and their time on duty. FAA rules also specify how much ground time and rest a crew is entitled to following a trip. Thus, flight crew jobs are limited by FAA safety rules. Airline pilot and engineer unions strive to further improve working conditions for their members, beyond the FAA maximums, while guarding member pay and benefits.

Although not governed by FAA rules, airline fleet service personnel, such as baggage handlers and food service personnel, are often unionized. Jobs and job descriptions are important bargaining chips in these cases. For example, aircraft mechanics may guard their job definitions to ensure they do not handle baggage on the ramp. When scheduling trips around bad weather conditions or mechanical problems, airline schedulers may ask flight crews to perform beyond their work rules. Technically, this can be a contract violation and grounds for a grievance. If a union really wants to cause management serious problems, its members can simply "work to rule." Although job descriptions and work rules may limit personnel at some airlines, Southwest Airlines employees, even though unionized, appear to work with expanded flexibility, as we see in the Looking Back feature at the chapter's end.

Jobs may be narrowly defined as suggested in the opening vignette while being flexibly executed as we see in the Looking Back feature. A *job* is defined as an employee's specific work and task activities in an organization. A job is not the same as an organizational position or a career. *Organizational position* identifies a job in relation to other parts of the organization; *career* refers to a sequence of job experiences over time.

This chapter focuses on jobs and the design of work as elements of the organization's structure. Jobs help people define their work and become integrated into the organization. The first section in the chapter examines the meaning of work in organizations. The second major section addresses four traditional approaches to job design developed between the late 1800s and the 1970s. The third major section examines four alternative approaches to job design developed over the past couple of decades. The final section addresses emerging issues in job design.

job
A set of specified work and task activities that engage an individual in an organization.

1. Define the term *job*, and identify six patterns of defining *work*.

WORK IN ORGANIZATIONS

Work is effortful, productive activity resulting in a product or a service. Work is one important reason why organizations exist. A job is composed of a set of specific tasks, each of which is an assigned piece of work to be done in a specific time period. Work is an especially important human endeavor because it has a powerful effect in binding a person to reality. Through work, people become securely attached to reality and securely connected in human relationships.

work
Mental or physical activity that has productive results.

Work has different meanings for different people. For all people, work is organized into jobs, and jobs fit into the larger structure of an organization. The structure of jobs is the concern of this chapter, and the structure of the organization is the concern of the next chapter. Both chapters emphasize organizations as sets of task and authority relationships through which people get work done.

The Meaning of Work

The *meaning of work* differs from person to person, and from culture to culture. In an increasingly global workplace, it is important to understand and appreciate differences among individuals and between cultures with regard to the meaning of work. One study found six patterns people follow in defining *work*, and these help explain the cultural differences in people's motivation to work.[2] Pattern A people define *work* as an activity in which value comes from performance and for which a person is accountable. It is generally self-directed and devoid of negative affect. Pattern B people define *work* as an activity that provides a person with positive personal affect and identity. Work contributes to society and is not unpleasant. Pattern C people define *work* as an activity from which profit accrues to others by its performance and that may be done in various settings other than a working place. Work is usually physically strenuous and somewhat compulsive. Pattern D people define *work* as primarily a physical activity a person must do that is directed by others and generally performed in a working place. Work is usually devoid of positive affect and is unpleasantly connected to performance. Pattern E people define *work* as a physically and mentally strenuous activity. It is generally unpleasant and devoid of positive affect. Pattern F people define *work* as an activity constrained to specific time periods that does not bring positive affect through its performance.

These six patterns were studied in six different countries: Belgium, the former Federal Republic of Germany, Israel, Japan, the Netherlands, and the United States. Table 13.1 summarizes the percentage of workers in each

Table 13.1
Work Definition Patterns by Nation

Sample	Pattern[a]					
	A	B	C	D	E	F
Total Sample (N = 4,950)	11%	28%	18%	22%	11%	12%
Nation						
Belgium	8%	40%	13%	19%	11%	9%
Federal Republic of Germany	8	26	13	28	11	14
Israel	4	22	33	23	9	9
Japan	21	11	13	29	10	17
The Netherlands	15	43	12	11	9	9
United States	8	30	19	19	12	11

Note: $X^2 = 680.98$ (25 degrees of freedom). $P<.0001$ Significance level

[a]In Pattern A, work is valued for its performance. The person is accountable and generally self-directed. In Pattern B, work provides a person with positive affect and identity. It contributes to society. In Pattern C, work provides profit to others by its performance. It is physical and not confined to a working place. In Pattern D, work is a required physical activity directed by others and generally unpleasant. In Pattern E, work is physically and mentally strenuous. It is generally unpleasant. In Pattern F, work is constrained to specific time periods. It does not bring positive affect through performance.

SOURCE: From G. W. England and I. Harpaz, "How Working Is Defined: National Contexts and Demographic and Organizational Role Influences," from *Journal of Organizational Behavior*, 11, 1990. Copyright John Wiley & Sons, Limited. Reproduced with permission.

country who defined *work* according to each of the six patterns. An examination of the table shows that a small percentage of workers in all six countries used either Pattern E or Pattern F to define *work*. Furthermore, there are significant differences among countries in how *work* is defined. In the Netherlands, *work* is defined most positively and with the most balanced personal and collective reasons for doing it. *Work* is defined least positively and with the most collective reason for doing it in Germany and Japan. Belgium, Israel, and the United States represent a middle position between these two. Future international studies should include Middle Eastern countries, India, Central and South American countries, and other Asian countries to better represent the world's cultures.

In another international study, 5,550 people across ten occupational groups in twenty different countries completed the Work Value Scales (WVS).[3] The WVS is composed of thirteen items measuring various aspects of the work environment, such as responsibility and job security. The study found two common basic work dimensions across cultures. Work content is one dimension, measured by items such as "the amount of responsibility on the job." Job context is the other dimension, measured by items such as "the policies of my company." This finding suggests that people in many cultures distinguish between the nature of the work itself and elements of the context in which work is done. This supports Herzberg's two-factor theory of motivation (see Chapter 5) and his job enrichment method discussed later in this chapter. Thus, although the meaning of *work* differs among countries, similarities exist across countries in understanding the structure in which work is done.

Jobs in Organizations

Task and authority relationships define an organization's structure. Jobs are the basic building blocks of this task–authority structure and are considered the micro-structural element to which employees most directly relate. Jobs are usually designed to complement and support other jobs in the organization. Isolated jobs are rare, although one was identified at Coastal Corporation during the early 1970s. Shortly after Oscar Wyatt moved the company from Corpus Christi, Texas, to Houston, Coastal developed organizational charts and job descriptions because the company had grown so large. In the process of charting the organization's structure, it was discovered that the beloved corporate economist reported to no one. Everyone assumed he worked for someone else. Such peculiarities are rare, however.

Jobs in organizations are interdependent and designed to make a contribution to the organization's overall mission and goals. For salespeople to be successful, the production people must be effective. For production people to be effective, the material department must be effective. These interdependencies require careful planning and design so that all of the "pieces of work" fit together into a whole. For example, if an envelope salesperson takes an order for 1 million envelopes from John Hancock Life Insurance Company and promises a two-week delivery date without knowing that the production department cannot meet that deadline, the salesperson dooms the company to failure in meeting John Hancock's expectations. The central concerns of this chapter are designing work and structuring jobs to prevent such problems and to ensure employee well-being.

Chapter 14 addresses the larger issues in the design of organizations. In particular, it examines the competing processes of differentiation and integration in organizations. Differentiation is the process of subdividing and departmentalizing the work of an organization. Jobs result from differentiation, which is necessary because no one can do it all (contrary to the famous statement made by Harold Geneen, former chairman of ITT: "If I had enough arms and legs and time, I'd do it all myself"). Even small organizations must divide work so that each person is able to accomplish a manageable piece of the whole. At the same time the organization divides up the work, it must also integrate those pieces back into a whole. Integration is the process of connecting jobs and departments into a coordinated, cohesive whole. For example, if the envelope salesperson had coordinated with the production manager before finalizing the order with John Hancock, the company could have met the customer's expectations, and integration would have occurred.

TRADITIONAL APPROACHES TO JOB DESIGN

2. Discuss the four traditional approaches to job design.

Failure to differentiate, integrate, or both may result in badly designed jobs, which in turn cause a variety of performance problems in organizations. Good job design helps avoid these problems, improves productivity, and enhances employee well-being. Four approaches to job design that were developed during the twentieth century are scientific management, job enlargement/job rotation, job enrichment, and the job characteristics theory. Each approach offers unique benefits to the organization, the employee, or both, but each also has limitations and drawbacks. Furthermore, an unthinking reliance on a traditional approach can be a serious problem in any company. The later job design approaches were developed to overcome the limitations of traditional job design approaches. For example, job enlargement was intended to overcome the problem of boredom associated with scientific management's narrowly defined approach to jobs.

Scientific Management

work simplification
Standardization and the narrow, explicit specification of task activities for workers.

Scientific management, an approach to work design advocated by Frederick Taylor from the late 1800s through 1915, emphasized work simplification. **Work simplification** is the standardization and the narrow, explicit specification of task activities for workers.[4] Jobs designed through scientific management have a limited number of tasks, and each task is scientifically specified so that the worker is not required to think or deliberate. According to Taylor, the role of management and the industrial engineer is to calibrate and define each task carefully. The role of the worker is to execute the task. The elements of scientific management, such as time and motion studies, differential piece rate systems of pay, and the scientific selection of workers, all focus on the efficient use of labor to the economic benefit of the corporation. Employees who are satisfied with various aspects of repetitive work may like scientifically designed jobs.

Two arguments supported the efficient and standardized job design approach of scientific management in the early days of the American industrial revolution. The first argument was that work simplification allowed workers of diverse ethnic and skill backgrounds to work together in a systematic way. Large industrial organizations had to find ways to blend the large waves of European immigrants of the late 1800s into a productive workforce. With work simplification, workers did not have to engage in problem-solving or decision-making activities, which would have been difficult, because no one language united all the various immigrants. Germans, Scots, Hungarians, and Poles might have a difficult time in a quality circle without a common language.[5] Taylor's unique approach to work standardization allowed immigrants of various linguistic and ethnic origins to be blended into a functional workforce.

The second argument for scientific management was that work simplification led to production efficiency in the organization and, therefore, to higher profits. This economic argument for work simplification tended to treat labor as a means of production and dehumanized it.

A fundamental limitation of scientific management is that it undervalues the human capacity for thought and ingenuity. Jobs designed through scientific management use only a portion of a person's capabilities. This underutilization makes work boring, monotonous, and understimulating. The failure to fully utilize the workers' capacity in a constructive fashion may cause a variety of work problems. A contemporary example of a work problem resulting from underutilization and boredom is the intentional installation of Coke bottles in car doors on an automobile assembly line.

Job Enlargement/Job Rotation

Job enlargement proposes to overcome the limitations of overspecialized work, such as boredom.[6] *Job enlargement* is a method of job design that increases the number of tasks in a job. *Job rotation*, a variation of job enlargement, exposes a worker to a variety of specialized job tasks over time. The reasoning behind these approaches to the problems of overspecialization is as follows. First, the core problem with overspecialized work was believed to be lack of variety. That is, jobs designed by scientific management were too narrow and limited in the number of tasks and activities assigned to each worker. Second, a lack of variety led to understimulation and underutilization of the worker. Third, the worker would be more stimulated and better utilized by increasing the variety in the job. Variety could be increased by increasing the number of activities or by rotating the worker through different jobs. For example, job enlargement for a lathe operator in a steel plant might include selecting the steel pieces to be turned and performing all of the maintenance work on the lathe. As

job enlargement
A method of job design that increases the number of activities in a job to overcome the boredom of overspecialized work.

job rotation
A variation of job enlargement in which workers are exposed to a variety of specialized jobs over time.

an example of job rotation, an employee at a small bank might take new accounts one day, serve as a cashier another day, and process loan applications on a third day.

One of the first studies of the problem of repetitive work was conducted at IBM after World War II. The company implemented a job enlargement program during the war and evaluated the effort after six years.[7] The two most important results were a significant increase in product quality and a reduction in idle time, both for people and for machines. Less obvious and measurable are the benefits of job enlargement to IBM through enhanced worker status and improved manager–worker communication. Thus, job enlargement does counter the problems of work specialization.

A later study examined the effects of mass production jobs on assembly-line workers in the automotive industry.[8] Mass production jobs have six characteristics: mechanically controlled work pace, repetitiveness, minimum skill requirements, predetermined tools and techniques, minute division of the production process, and a requirement for surface mental attention, rather than thoughtful concentration. The researchers conducted 180 private interviews with assembly-line workers and found generally positive attitudes toward pay, security, and supervision. They concluded that job enlargement and job rotation would improve other job aspects, such as repetition and a mechanical work pace.

cross-training
A variation of job enlargement in which workers are trained in different specialized tasks or activities.

Job rotation and **cross-training** programs are variations of job enlargement. Pharmaceutical company Eli Lilly has found that job rotation can be a proactive means for enhancing work experiences for career development and can have tangible benefits for employees in the form of salary increases and promotions.[9] In cross-training, workers are trained in different specialized tasks or activities. All three kinds of programs horizontally enlarge jobs; that is, the number and variety of an employee's tasks and activities are increased. Graphic Controls Corporation (now a subsidiary of Tyco International) used cross-training to develop a flexible workforce that enabled the company to maintain high levels of production.[10]

Job Enrichment

Whereas job enlargement increases the number of job activities through horizontal loading, job enrichment increases the amount of job responsibility through vertical loading. Both approaches to job design are intended, in part, to increase job satisfaction for employees. A study to test whether job satisfaction results from characteristics of the job or of the person found that an interactionist approach is most accurate and that job redesign can contribute to increased job satisfaction for some employees. Another two-year study found that intrinsic job satisfaction and job perceptions are reciprocally related to each other.[11]

job enrichment
Designing or redesigning jobs by incorporating motivational factors into them.

Job enrichment is a job design or redesign method aimed at increasing the motivational factors in a job. Job enrichment builds on Herzberg's two-factor theory of motivation, which distinguished between motivational and hygiene factors for people at work. Whereas job enlargement recommends increasing and varying the number of activities a person does, job enrichment recommends increasing the recognition, responsibility, and opportunity for achievement. For example, enlarging the lathe operator's job means adding maintenance activities, and enriching the job means having the operator meet with customers who buy the products.

Herzberg believes that only certain jobs should be enriched and that the first step is to select the jobs appropriate for job enrichment.[12] He recognizes that some people prefer simple jobs. Once jobs are selected for enrichment, management should brainstorm about possible changes, revise the list to include only specific changes related to motivational factors, and screen out generalities and suggestions that would simply increase activities or numbers of tasks. Those whose jobs are to be enriched should not participate in this process because of a conflict of interest. Two key problems can arise in the implementation of job enrichment. First, an initial drop in performance can be expected as workers accommodate to the change. Second, first-line supervisors may experience some anxiety or hostility as a result of employees' increased responsibility.

A seven-year implementation study of job enrichment at AT&T found the approach beneficial.[13] Job enrichment required a big change in management style, and AT&T found that it could not ignore hygiene factors in the work environment just because it was enriching existing jobs. Although the AT&T experience with job enrichment was positive, a critical review of job enrichment did not find that to be the case generally.[14] One problem with job enrichment as a strategy for work design is that it is based on an oversimplified motivational theory. Another problem is the lack of consideration for individual differences among employees. Job enrichment, like scientific management's work specialization and job enlargement/job rotation, is a universal approach to the design of work and thus does not differentiate among individuals.

Job Characteristics Theory

The job characteristics theory, which was initiated during the mid-1960s, is a traditional approach to the design of work that makes a significant departure from the three earlier approaches. It emphasizes the interaction between the individual and specific attributes of the job; therefore, it is a person–job fit model rather than a universal job design model. It originated in a research study of 470 workers in forty-seven different jobs across eleven industries.[15] The study measured and classified relevant task characteristics for these forty-seven jobs and found four core job characteristics: job variety, autonomy, responsibility, and interpersonal interaction. The study also found that core job characteristics did not affect all workers in the same way. A worker's values, religious beliefs, and ethnic background influenced how the worker responded to the job. Specifically, workers with rural values and strong religious beliefs preferred jobs high in core characteristics, and workers with urban values and weaker religious beliefs preferred jobs low in core characteristics.

3. Describe the job characteristics model.

Job Characteristics Model
A framework for understanding person–job fit through the interaction of core job dimensions with critical psychological states within a person.

Job Diagnostic Survey (JDS)
The survey instrument designed to measure the elements in the Job Characteristics Model.

Richard Hackman and his colleagues modified the original model by including three critical psychological states of the individual and refining the measurement of core job characteristics. The result is the **Job Characteristics Model** shown in Figure 13.1.[16] The **Job Diagnostic Survey (JDS)** was developed to diagnose jobs by measuring the five core job characteristics and three critical psychological states shown in the model. The core job characteristics stimulate the critical psychological states in the manner shown in Figure 13.1. This results in varying personal and work outcomes, as identified in the figure.

The five core job characteristics are defined as follows:

1. *Skill variety.* The degree to which a job includes different activities and involves the use of multiple skills and talents of the employee.

2. *Task identity.* The degree to which the job requires completion of a whole and identifiable piece of work—that is, doing a job from beginning to end with a tangible outcome.

3. *Task significance.* The degree to which the job has a substantial impact on the lives or work of other people, whether in the immediate organization or in the external environment.

Figure 13.1
The Job Characteristics Model

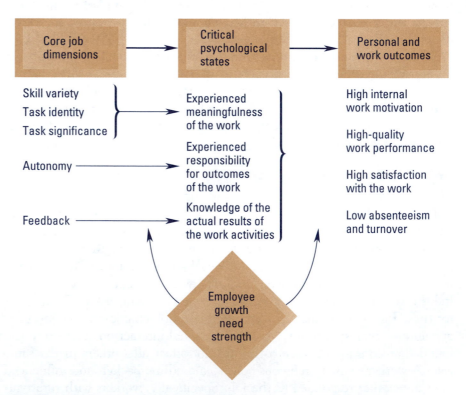

SOURCE: J. R. Hackman and G. R. Oldham, "The Relationship Among Core Job Dimensions, the Critical Psychological States, and On-the-Job Outcomes," *The Job Diagnostic Survey: An Instrument for the Diagnosis of Jobs and the Evaluation of Job Redesign Projects*, 1974. Reprinted by permission of Greg R. Oldham.

4. *Autonomy*. The degree to which the job provides the employee with substantial freedom, independence, and discretion in scheduling the work and in determining the procedures to be used in carrying it out.

5. *Feedback from the job itself*. The degree to which carrying out the work activities results in the employee's obtaining direct and clear information about the effectiveness of his or her performance.

Hackman and his colleagues say that the five core job characteristics interact to determine an overall Motivating Potential Score (MPS) for a specific job. The MPS indicates a job's potential for motivating incumbents. An individual's MPS is determined by the following equation:

$$\text{MPS} = \frac{\left[\begin{array}{c}\text{Skill}\\\text{variety}\end{array}\right] + \left[\begin{array}{c}\text{Task}\\\text{identity}\end{array}\right] + \left[\begin{array}{c}\text{Task}\\\text{significance}\end{array}\right]}{3} \times [\text{Autonomy}] \times [\text{Feedback}].$$

Challenge 13.1 enables you to answer five questions from the JDS short form to get an idea about the motivating potential of your present job or any job you have held.

The Job Characteristics Model includes *growth need strength* (the desire to grow and fully develop one's abilities) as a moderator. People with a high growth need strength respond favorably to jobs with high MPSs, and individuals with low growth need strength respond less favorably to such jobs. The job characteristics theory further suggests that core job dimensions stimulate three critical psychological states according to the relationships specified in the model. These critical psychological states are defined as follows:

1. *Experienced meaningfulness of the work*, or the degree to which the employee experiences the job as one that is generally meaningful, valuable, and worthwhile.

2. *Experienced responsibility for work outcomes*, or the degree to which the employee feels personally accountable and responsible for the results of the work he or she does.

3. *Knowledge of results*, or the degree to which the employee knows and understands, on a continuous basis, how effectively he or she is performing the job.

In one early study, Hackman and Oldham administered the JDS to 658 employees working on sixty-two different jobs in seven business organizations.[17] The JDS was useful for job redesign efforts through one or more of five implementing concepts: (1) combining tasks into larger jobs, (2) forming natural work teams to increase task identity and task significance, (3) establishing relationships with customers, (4) loading jobs vertically with more responsibility, and/or (5) opening feedback channels for the job incumbent. For example, if an automotive mechanic received little feedback on the quality of repair work performed, one redesign strategy would be to solicit customer feedback one month after each repair.

Challenge 13.1

Diagnosing Your Job

This questionnaire challenges you to examine the motivating potential in your job. If you are not currently working, complete the questionnaire for any job you have ever held for which you want to examine the motivating potential. For each of the following five questions, circle the number of the most accurate description of the job. Be as objective as you can in describing the job by answering these questions.

1. How much *autonomy* is there in the job? That is, to what extent does the job permit a person to decide *on his or her own* how to go about doing the work?

1	2	3	4	5	6	7

Very little; the job gives a person almost no personal say about how and when the work is done.

Moderate autonomy; many things are standardized and not under the control of the person, but he or she can make some decisions about the work.

Very much; the job gives the person almost complete responsibility for deciding how and when the work is done.

2. To what extent does the job involve doing a "*whole*" and *identifiable piece of work*? That is, is the job a complete piece of work that has an obvious beginning and end? Or is it a small part of the overall piece of work, which is finished by other people or by automatic machines?

1	2	3	4	5	6	7

The job is only a tiny part in the overall piece of work; the results of the person's activities cannot be seen in the final product or service.

The job is a moderate-sized "chunk" of the overall piece of work; the person's own contribution can be seen in the final outcome.

The job involves doing the whole piece of work, from start to finish; the results of the person's activities are easily seen in the final product or service.

3. How much *variety* is there in the job? That is, to what extent does the job require a person to do many different things at work, using a variety of his or her skills and talents?

1	2	3	4	5	6	7

Very little; the job requires the person to do the same routine things over and over again.

Moderate variety.

Very much; the job requires the person to do many different things, using a number of different skills and talents.

4. In general, how *significant* or *important* is the job? That is, are the results of the person's work likely to affect significantly the lives or well-being of other people?

1	2	3	4	5	6	7

Not at all significant; the outcome of the work is *not* likely to affect anyone in any important way.

Moderately significant.

Highly significant; the outcome of the work can affect other people in very important ways.

5. To what extent *does doing the job itself* provide the person with information about his or her work performance? That is, does the actual work itself provide clues about how well the person is doing—aside from any feedback coworkers or supervisors may provide?

1	2	3	4	5	6	7

Very little; the job itself is set up so a person could work forever without finding out how well he or she was doing.

Moderately; sometimes doing the job provides feedback to the person; sometimes it does not.

Very much; the job is set up so that a person gets almost constant feedback as he or she works about how well he or she is doing.

To score your questionnaire, place your responses to Questions 3, 2, 4, 1, and 5, respectively, in the blank spaces in the following equation:

$$\text{Motivating Potential Score (MPS)} = \frac{\overset{\text{Q\#3}}{[\quad]} + \overset{\text{Q\#2}}{[\quad]} + \overset{\text{Q\#4}}{[\quad]}}{3} \times \overset{\text{Q\#1}}{[\quad]} \times \overset{\text{Q\#5}}{[\quad]} = \underline{\quad}.$$

If the MPS for the job you rated is between

- 200 and 343, it is high in motivating potential.
- 120 and 199, it is moderate in motivating potential.
- 0 and 119, it is low in motivating potential.

SOURCE: J. R. Hackman and G. R. Oldham, "The Job Diagnostic Survey: An Instrument for the Diagnosis of Jobs and the Evaluation of Job Redesign Projects," *Technical Report No. 4*, 1974, 2–3 of the Short Form. Reprinted by permission of Greg R. Oldham.

In an international study, the Job Characteristics Model was tested in a sample of fifty-seven jobs from thirty-seven organizations in Hong Kong.[18] Job incumbents each completed the JDS, and their supervisors completed the Job Rating Form (JRF).[19] The JRF, a supervisory version of the JDS, asks the supervisor to rate the employee's job. The study supported the model in general. However, task significance was not a reliable core job dimension in this study, which suggests either national differences in the measurement of important job dimensions or cultural biases about work. This result may also suggest value differences between American and Asian people with regard to jobs.

An alternative to the Job Characteristics Model is the Job Characteristics Inventory (JCI) developed by Henry Sims and Andrew Szilagyi.[20] The

JCI primarily measures core job characteristics. It is not as comprehensive as the JDS, because it does not incorporate critical psychological states, personal and work outcomes, or employee needs. The JCI does give some consideration to structural and individual variables that affect the relationship between core job characteristics and the individual.[21] One comparative analysis of the two models found similarities in the measures and in the models' predictions.[22] The comparative analysis also found two differences. First, the variety scales in the two models appear to have different effects on performance. Second, the autonomy scales in the two models appear to have different effects on employee satisfaction. Overall, the two models together support the usefulness of a person–job fit approach to the design of work over the earlier, universal theories.

ALTERNATIVE APPROACHES TO JOB DESIGN

Because each of the traditional job design approaches has limitations, several alternative approaches to job design have emerged over the past couple of decades. This section examines four of these alternatives that are in the process of being tried and tested. First, it examines the social information-processing model. Second, it reviews the interdisciplinary approach of Michael Campion and Paul Thayer. Their approach builds on the traditional job design approaches. Third, this section examines the international perspectives of the Japanese, the Germans, and the Scandinavians. Finally, it focuses on the health and well-being aspects of work design. An emerging fifth approach to the design of work through teams and autonomous work groups was addressed in Chapter 8. George Fisher, chairman of Eastman Kodak, believes that jobs in today's workplace must be designed for a world that has moved beyond the industrial age of mass production.

Social Information Processing

4. Compare the social information-processing (SIP) model with traditional job design approaches.

social information-processing (SIP) model
A model that suggests that the important job factors depend in part on what others tell a person about the job.

The traditional approaches to the design of work emphasize objective core job characteristics. In contrast, the *social information-processing (SIP) model* emphasizes the interpersonal aspects of work design. Specifically, the SIP model says that what others tell us about our jobs is important.[23] The SIP model has four basic premises about the work environment.[24] First, other people provide cues we use to understand the work environment. Second, other people help us judge what is important in our jobs. Third, other people tell us how they see our jobs. Fourth, other people's positive and negative feedback helps us understand our feelings about our jobs.

People's perceptions and reactions to their jobs are shaped by information from other people in the work environment.[25] In other words, what others believe about a person's job may be important to understanding the person's perceptions of, and reactions to, the job. This does not mean that objective job characteristics are unimportant; rather, it means that others can modify the way these characteristics affect us. For example, one study of task complexity found that the objective complexity of a task must be distinguished from the subjective task complexity experienced by the employee.[26] While objective task complexity may be a motivator, the presence of others in the work environment, social interaction, or even daydreaming may be important additional sources of motivation. The SIP model makes an important contribution to the design of work by emphasizing the importance of other people and the social context of work. In some cases, these aspects of the work environment may be more important than objective core job characteristics. For example, the subjective feedback of other people about how difficult a particular task is may be more important to a person's motivation to perform than an objective probability estimate of the task's difficulty.

Interdisciplinary Approach

The interdisciplinary approach to job design of Michael Campion and Paul Thayer builds on the traditional job design approaches and does not emphasize the social aspects of the work environment. Four approaches—the mechanistic, motivational, biological, and perceptual/motor approaches—are necessary, they say, because no one approach can solve all performance problems caused by poorly designed jobs. Each approach has its benefits, as well as its limitations.

5. Explain the interdisciplinary approach to job design.

The interdisciplinary approach allows the job designer or manager to consider trade-offs and alternatives among the approaches based on desired outcomes. If a manager finds poor performance a problem, for example, the manager should analyze the job to ensure a design aimed at improving performance. The interdisciplinary approach is important because badly designed jobs cause far more performance problems than managers realize.[27]

Table 13.2 summarizes the positive and negative outcomes of each job design approach. The mechanistic and motivational approaches to job design are very similar to scientific management's work simplification and to the Job Characteristics Model, respectively. Because these were discussed earlier in the chapter, they are not further elaborated here.

The biological approach to job design emphasizes the person's interaction with physical aspects of the work environment and is concerned with the amount of physical exertion, such as lifting and muscular effort, required by the position. For example, an analysis of medical claims at Chaparral Steel Company (part of Texas Industries) identified lower back problems as the most common physical problem experienced by steel workers and managers alike. As a result, the company instituted an education and exercise program under expert guidance to improve care of the lower back. Program graduates received back cushions for their chairs with "Chaparral Steel Company" embossed on them. Herman Miller designed an office chair to support the lower back and other parts of the human body.[28] The chair is being tested in several offices including that of the director of human resources for Valero Energy Corporation. Lower back problems associated with improper lifting may be costly, but they are not fatal. Campion describes the potentially catastrophic problem that occurred at Three Mile Island, when

Job Design Approach (Discipline)	Positive Outcomes	Negative Outcomes
Mechanistic Approach (mechanical engineering)	Decreased training time Higher personnel utilization levels Lower likelihood of error Less chance of mental overload Lower stress levels	Lower job satisfaction Lower motivation Higher absenteeism
Motivational Approach (industrial psychology)	Higher job satisfaction Higher motivation Greater job involvement Higher job performance Lower absenteeism	Increased training time Lower personnel utilization levels Greater chance of errors Greater chance of mental overload and stress
Biological Approach (biology)	Less physical effort Less physical fatigue Fewer health complaints Fewer medical incidents Lower absenteeism Higher job satisfaction	Higher financial costs because of changes in equipment or job environment
Perceptual Motor Approach (experimental psychology)	Lower likelihood of error Lower likelihood of accidents Less chance of mental stress Decreased training time Higher personnel utilization levels	Lower job satisfaction Lower motivation

Table 13.2

Summary of Outcomes from Various Job Design Approaches

SOURCE: Reprinted from *Organizational Dynamics*, Winter/1987 copyright © 1987, with permission from Elsevier Science.

nuclear materials contaminated the surrounding area and threatened disaster. Campion concluded that poor design of the control room operator's job caused the problem.

The perceptual/motor approach to job design also emphasizes the person's interaction with physical aspects of the work environment and is based on engineering that considers human factors such as strength or coordination, ergonomics, and experimental psychology. This approach addresses how people mentally process information acquired from the physical work environment through perceptual and motor skills. The approach emphasizes perception and fine motor skills, as opposed to the gross motor skills and muscle strength emphasized in the mechanistic approach. The perceptual/motor approach is more likely to be relevant to operational and technical work, such as keyboard operations and data entry jobs, which may tax a person's concentration and attention, than to managerial, administrative, and custodial jobs, which are less likely to strain concentration and attention.

One study using the interdisciplinary approach to improve jobs evaluated 377 clerical, 80 managerial, and 90 analytical positions.[29] The jobs were improved by combining tasks and adding ancillary duties. The improved jobs provided greater motivation for the incumbents and were better from a perceptual/motor standpoint. The jobs were poorly designed from a mechanical engineering standpoint, however, and they were unaffected from a biological standpoint. Again, the interdisciplinary approach considers trade-offs and alternatives when evaluating job redesign efforts.

International Perspectives on the Design of Work

Each nation or ethnic group has a unique way of understanding and designing work.[30] As organizations become more global and international, an appreciation of the perspectives of other nations is increasingly important. The Japanese, Germans, and Scandinavians in particular have distinctive perspectives on the design and organization of work. Each country's perspective is forged within its unique cultural and economic system, and each is distinct from the approaches used in North America.

The Japanese Approach The Japanese began harnessing their productive energies during the 1950s by drawing on the product quality ideas of W. Edwards Deming.[31] In addition, the central government became actively involved in the economic resurgence of Japan, and it encouraged companies to conquer industries rather than to maximize profits.[32] Such an industrial policy, which built on the Japanese cultural ethic of collectivism, has implications for how work is done. Whereas Frederick Taylor and his successors in the United States emphasized the job of an individual worker, the Japanese work system emphasizes the strategic level and encourages collective and cooperative working arrangements.[33] As Table 13.1 shows, the Japanese emphasize performance, accountability, and other- or self-directedness in defining work, whereas Americans emphasize the positive affect, personal identity, and social benefits of work.

The Japanese success with lean production has drawn the attention of managers. *Lean production* methods are similar to the production concept of *sociotechnical systems (STS)*, although there are some differences.[34] In particular, STS gives greater emphasis to teamwork and self-managed and autonomous work groups, to the ongoing nature of the design process, and to human values in the work process. The approaches are similar, however, in that both differ from Taylor's scientific management and both emphasize job variety, feedback to work groups and teams, support of human resources, and control of production variance close to the point of origin. Hence, the Japanese emphasis on lean production has led to a renewed consideration of the STS concept.

The German Approach The German approach to work has been shaped by Germany's unique educational system, cultural values, and economic system. The Germans are a highly educated and well-organized people. For example, their educational system has a multitrack design with technical and

6. Compare Japanese, German, and Scandinavian approaches to work.

lean production
Using committed employees with ever-expanding responsibilities to achieve zero waste, 100 percent good product, delivered on time, every time.

sociotechnical systems (STS)
Giving equal attention to technical and social considerations in job design.

university alternatives. The German economic system puts a strong emphasis on free enterprise, private property rights, and management–labor cooperation. A comparison of voluntary and mandated management–labor cooperation in Germany found that productivity was superior under voluntary cooperation.[35] The Germans value hierarchy and authority relationships and, as a result, are generally disciplined.[36] Germany's workers are highly unionized, and their discipline and efficiency have enabled Germany to be highly productive while its workers labor substantially fewer hours than do Americans.

technocentric

Placing technology and engineering at the center of job design decisions.

anthropocentric

Placing human considerations at the center of job design decisions.

The traditional German approach to work design was **technocentric**, an approach that placed technology and engineering at the center of job design decisions. Recently, German industrial engineers have moved to a more **anthropocentric** approach, which places human considerations at the center of job design decisions. The former approach uses a natural scientific process in the design of work, whereas the latter relies on a more humanistic process, as shown in Figure 13.2. In the anthropocentric approach, work is evaluated using the criteria of practicability and worker satisfaction at the individual level and the criteria of endurability and acceptability at the group level. Figure 13.2 also identifies problem areas and disciplines concerned with each aspect of the work design.

The Scandinavian Approach The Scandinavian cultural values and economic system stand in contrast to the German system. The social democratic tradition in Scandinavia has emphasized social concern rather than

Figure 13.2
Hierarchical Model of Criteria for the Evaluation of Human Work

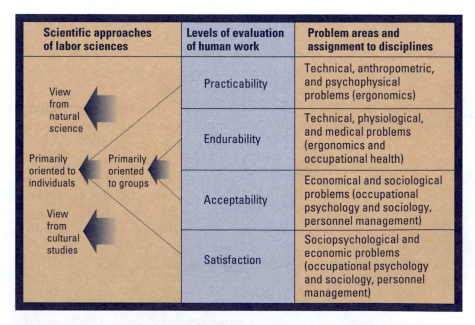

Scientific approaches of labor sciences	Levels of evaluation of human work	Problem areas and assignment to disciplines
View from natural science	Practicability	Technical, anthropometric, and psychophysical problems (ergonomics)
Primarily oriented to individuals / Primarily oriented to groups	Endurability	Technical, physiological, and medical problems (ergonomics and occupational health)
	Acceptability	Economical and sociological problems (occupational psychology and sociology, personnel management)
View from cultural studies	Satisfaction	Sociopsychological and economic problems (occupational psychology and sociology, personnel management)

SOURCE: H. Luczak, "'Good Work' Design: An Ergonomic, Industrial Engineering Perspective," in J. C. Quick, L. R. Murphy, and J. J. Hurrell, eds., *Stress and Well-Being at Work* (Washington, D.C.: American Psychological Association). Reprinted by permission.

industrial efficiency. The Scandinavians place great emphasis on a work design model that encourages a high degree of worker control and good social support systems for workers.[37] Lennart Levi believes that circumstantial and inferential scientific evidence provides a sufficiently strong basis for legislative and policy actions for redesigns aimed at enhancing worker well-being. An example of such an action for promoting good working environments and occupational health was Swedish Government Bill 1976/77:149, which stated, "Work should be safe both physically and mentally, *but also* provide opportunities for involvement, job satisfaction, and personal development." In 1991, the Swedish Parliament set up the Swedish Working Life Fund to fund research, intervention programs, and demonstration projects in work design. For example, a study of Stockholm police on shift schedules found that going from a daily, counterclockwise rotation to a clockwise rotation was more compatible with human biology and resulted in improved sleep, less fatigue, lower systolic blood pressure, and lower blood levels of triglycerides and glucose.[38] Hence, the work redesign improved the police officers' health.

Work Design and Well-Being

American social scientists have had concerns like those of the Scandinavians with regard to the effects of work and job design on health and well-being. This issue was discussed briefly in Chapter 7. Economic and industry-specific upheavals in the United States during the 1980s and 1990s led to job loss and unemployment, and the adverse health impact of these factors has received attention.[39] Attention has also been devoted to the effects of specific work design parameters on psychological health.[40] Frank Landy believes that organizations should redesign jobs to increase worker control and reduce worker uncertainty, while at the same time managing conflict and task/job demands. These objectives can be achieved in several ways.

7. ■ Explain how job control, uncertainty, and conflict can be managed for employee well-being.

Control in work organizations can be increased by (1) giving workers the opportunity to control several aspects of the work and the workplace; (2) designing machines and tasks with optimal response times and/or ranges; and (3) implementing performance-monitoring systems as a source of relevant feedback to workers. Uncertainty can be reduced by (1) providing employees with timely and complete information needed for their work; (2) making clear and unambiguous work assignments; (3) improving communication at shift change time, and (4) increasing employee access to information sources. Conflict at work can be managed through (1) participative decision making to reduce conflict; (2) using supportive supervisory styles to resolve conflict; and (3) having sufficient resources available to meet work demands, thus preventing conflict. Task/job design can be improved by enhancing core job characteristics and not patterning service work after assembly-line work.

Task uncertainty was shown to have an adverse effect on morale in a study of 629 employment security work units in California and Wisconsin.[41] More important, the study showed that morale was better predicted by considering both the overall design of the work unit and the task uncertainty. This study suggests that if one work design parameter, such as task uncertainty, is a problem in a job, its adverse effects on people may be mitigated by other work design parameters. For example, higher pay may offset an employee's frustration with a difficult coworker, or a friendly, supportive working environment may offset frustration with low pay. Challenge 13.2 provides you with an opportunity to evaluate how psychologically healthy your work environment is.

Challenge 13.2

Is Your Work Environment a Healthy One?

To determine whether your work environment is a healthy one, read the text section on "Work Design and Well-Being," then complete the following four steps. Answer each question in the five steps "yes" or "no."

Step 1. Control and Influence

_____ Do you have influence over the pace of your work?

_____ Are system response times neither too fast nor too slow?

_____ Do you have a say in your work assignments and goals?

_____ Is there an opportunity for you to comment on your performance appraisal?

Step 2. Information and Uncertainty

_____ Do you receive timely information to complete your work?

_____ Do you receive complete information for your work assignments?

_____ Is there adequate planning for changes that affect you at work?

_____ Do you have access to all the information you need at work?

Step 3. Conflict at Work

_____ Does the company apply policies clearly and consistently?

_____ Are job descriptions and task assignments clear and unambiguous?

_____ Are there adequate policies and procedures for the resolution of conflicts?

_____ Is your work environment an open, participative one?

Step 4. Job Scope and Task Design

_____ Is there adequate variety in your work activities and/or assignments?

_____ Do you receive timely, constructive feedback on your work?

_____ Is your work important to the overall mission of the company?

_____ Do you work on more than one small piece of a big project?

Scoring:

Count the number of "yes" answers in Steps 1 through 4: _____

If you have 10 to 16 "yes" answers, this suggests that your work environment is a psychologically healthy one.

If you have 7 or fewer "yes" answers, this may suggest that your work environment is not as psychologically healthy as it could be.

EMERGING ISSUES IN THE DESIGN OF WORK

A number of issues related to specific aspects of the design of work have emerged during the past several years. Rather than addressing job design or worker well-being in a comprehensive way, these issues address one or another aspect of a job. The issues include telecommuting, alternative work patterns, technostress, task revision, and skill development. Telecommuting and alternative work patterns such as job sharing can increase flexibility for employees, as illustrated in Organizational Reality 13.1. Baxter Export uses these and other approaches to the design of work as ways to manage a growing business while contributing to a better balance of work and family life for employees.

8. Discuss five emerging issues in the design of work.

ORGANIZATIONAL REALITY 13.1

Telecommuting, Job Sharing, and Flexibility at Baxter Export

Many employees experience difficulty balancing work and family life, often being confronted with work–family chaos. Flexibility is the norm at Baxter Export Corporation, the international logistics unit of Baxter International, Inc., where 30 percent of the 85 employees telecommute, job-share, or work part-time. The work–family balance challenge starts at the top with President Harry M. Kraemer, Jr., who often relates personal tales about his dual-career, three-child family life to communicate to employees that everyone is in the same boat. Employee Debbie DeBree also has a dual-career, three-child family life; her workday begins at 4:30 A.M. when she arises to start breakfast for her children while husband Mark is finishing the second of two night jobs. Operations analyst Jackie Demo's workday begins at 6:30 A.M. and includes looking in on her mother-in-law who lives in a basement apartment of the Demos' home, where the senior Mrs. Demo requires round-the-clock attention as she battles cancer with care from her family and the hospice agency. A Baxter International study of 1,000 employees revealed that among salaried employees, most work–life tension was driven by the need for greater work–family balance and by the desire for flexibility.

Baxter Export is in a growth period with business expanding between 12 and 15 percent annually. Because the company cannot always add people, Baxter Export manages growth and work–family balance through job redesign, the elimination of unnecessary tasks, and the rethinking of its work processes. Automation with new technologies helps too. For example, the company expects an automated allocation system to standardize procedures across 120 countries by 2002; overseas customers will be required to prepare demand forecasts and enter orders, thus reducing workloads for Baxter Export analysts like Jackie Demo. The average workweek at Baxter Export is down to fifty hours from sixty hours.

Discussion Questions

1. What are the limitations in the use of telecommuting, job sharing, and part-time work?

2. What specific work–family balance challenges do you, or your friends, face?

SOURCE: Keith H. Hammonds, "Case Study: One Company's Delicate Balancing Act," *Business Week* (September 15, 1997): 102.

Telecommuting

Telecommuting, as noted in Chapter 2, is when employees work at home or in other locations geographically separate from their company's main location. Telecommuting may entail working in a combination of home, satellite office, and main office locations. This flexible arrangement is designed to achieve a better fit between the needs of the individual employee and the organization's task demands.

Executives have practiced forms of telecommuting for years. For example, Jonathan Fielding, while serving as a professor at UCLA and working for Johnson & Johnson, telecommuted between offices in Berkeley, California; Brunswick, New Jersey; and other locations throughout the country and the world. A number of companies, such as AT&T in Phoenix and Bell Atlantic (now part of Verizon Communications), started pilot programs in telecommuting for a wide range of employees. These flexible arrangements help some companies respond to changing demographics and a shrinking labor pool. The Travelers Companies (now part of Citigroup) was one of the first companies to try telecommuting and was considered an industry leader in telecommuting. Because of its confidence in its employees, Travelers reaped rewards from telecommuting, including higher productivity, reduced absenteeism, expanded opportunities for disabled workers, and an increased ability to attract and retain talent.[42]

Pacific Bell (now part of SBC Communications) tried telecommuting on a large scale.[43] In 1990, Pacific Bell had 1,500 managers who telecommuted. For example, an employee might work at home four days a week as an information systems designer and spend one day a week at the main office location in meetings, work exchanges, and coordination with others. Of 3,000 Pacific Bell managers responding to a mail survey, 87 percent said telecommuting would reduce employee stress, 70 percent said it would increase job satisfaction while reducing absenteeism, and 64 percent said it would increase productivity.

Telecommuting is neither a cure-all nor a universally feasible alternative. Many telecommuters feel a sense of social isolation. Furthermore, not all forms of work are amenable to telecommuting. For example, firefighters and police officers must be at their duty stations to be successful in their work. Employees for whom telecommuting is not a viable option within a company may feel jealous of those able to telecommute. In addition, telecommuting may have the potential to create the sweatshops of the twenty-first century. Thus, telecommuting is a novel, emerging issue.

Alternative Work Patterns

Job sharing is an alternative work pattern in which more than one person occupies a single job. Job sharing may be an alternative to telecommuting for addressing demographic and labor pool concerns. Job sharing is found throughout a wide range of managerial and professional jobs, as well as in production and service jobs. It is not common among senior executives.

job sharing
An alternative work pattern in which more than one person occupies a single job.

The four-day workweek is a second type of alternative work schedule. Information systems personnel at the United Services Automobile Association (USAA) in San Antonio, Texas, work four ten-hour days and enjoy a three-day weekend. This arrangement provides the benefit of more time for those who want to balance work and family life through weekend travel. However, the longer workdays may be a drawback for employees with many family or social activities on weekday evenings. Hence, the four-day workweek has both benefits and limitations.

Flextime is a third alternative work pattern. Flextime, in which employees can set their own daily work schedules, has been applied in numerous ways in work organizations. For example, many companies in highly concentrated urban areas, like Houston, Los Angeles, and New York City, allow employees to set their own daily work schedules as long as they start their eight hours at any thirty-minute interval from 6:00 A.M. to 9:00 A.M. This arrangement is designed to ease traffic and commuting pressures. It also is somewhat responsive to individual biorhythms, allowing early risers to go to work early and nighthawks to work late. Typically, 9:00 A.M. to 3:00 P.M. is the required core working time for everyone in the company. Flextime options take many forms in organizations, depending on the nature of the work and the coordination requirements in various jobs. Even in companies without formal flextime programs, flextime may be an individual option arranged between supervisor and subordinate. For example, a first-line supervisor who wants to complete a college degree may negotiate a work schedule accommodating both job requirements and course schedules at the university. Flextime options may be more likely for high performers who assure their bosses that work quality and productivity will not suffer.[44]

flextime
An alternative work pattern that enables employees to set their own daily work schedules.

Technology at Work

New technologies are changing the face of work environments, dramatically in some cases. As forces for change, new technologies are a double-edged sword that can be used to improve job performance, or to create stress. On the positive side, modern technologies are helping to revolutionize the way jobs are designed and the way work gets done. The *virtual office* is a mobile platform of computer, telecommunication, and information technology and services that allows mobile workforce members to conduct business virtually anywhere, anytime, globally. While virtual offices have benefits, they may also lead to a lack of social connection or to technostress.

virtual office
A mobile platform of computer, telecommunication, and information technology and services.

Technostress is stress caused by new and advancing technologies in the workplace, most often information technologies.[45] For example, the widespread use of electronic bulletin boards as a forum for rumors of layoffs may cause feelings of uncertainty and anxiety (technostress). However, the same electronic bulletin boards can be an important source of information and thus reduce uncertainty for workers.

technostress
The stress caused by new and advancing technologies in the workplace.

New information technologies enable organizations to monitor employee work performance, even when the employee is not aware of the monitoring.[46] These new technologies also allow organizations to tie pay to performance as it is electronically monitored.[47] The Office of Technology Assessment suggests three guidelines for making electronic workplace monitoring, especially of performance, less distressful.[48] First, workers should participate in the introduction of the monitoring system. Second, performance standards should be seen as fair. Third, performance records should be used to improve performance, not to punish the performer.

Task Revision

task revision
The modification of incorrectly specified roles or jobs.

A new concept in the design of work is *task revision*.[49] Task revision is an innovative way to modify an incorrectly specified role or job. Task revision assumes that organizational roles and job expectations may be correctly or incorrectly defined. Furthermore, a person's behavior in a work role has very different performance consequences depending on whether the role is correctly or incorrectly defined. Table 13.3 sets out the performance consequences of three categories of role behaviors based on the definition of the role or job. As indicated in the table, standard role behavior leads to good performance if the role is correctly defined, and it leads to poor performance if the role is incorrectly defined. These performances go to the extreme when incumbents exhibit extreme behavior in their jobs.[50] Going to extremes leads one to exceed expectations and display extraordinary behavior (extrarole behavior); this results in either excellent performance or very poor performance, depending on the accuracy of the defined role.

counter-role behavior
Deviant behavior in either a correctly or incorrectly defined job or role.

Counter-role behavior is when the incumbent acts contrary to the expectations of the role or exhibits deviant behavior. This is a problem if the role is correctly defined. For example, poor performance occurred on a hospital ward when the nursing supervisor failed to check the administration of all medications for the nurses she was supervising, resulting in one near fatality because a patient was not given required medication by a charge nurse. The nursing supervisor exhibited counter-role behavior in believing she could simply trust the nurses and did not have to double-check their

Table 13.3
Performance Consequences of Role Behaviors

Role Characteristics	Standard Role Behavior (Meets Expectations)	Extra Role Behavior (Goes beyond Expectations)	Counter-Role Behavior (Differs from Expected)
Correctly specified role	Ordinary good performance	Excellent performance (organizational citizenship and prosocial behavior)	Poor performance (deviance, dissent, and grievance)
Incorrectly specified role	Poor performance (bureaucratic behavior)	Very poor performance (bureaucratic zeal)	Excellent performance (task revision and redirection, role innovation)

SOURCE: Republished with permission of Academy of Management, PO Box 3020, Briar Cliff Manor, NY 10510-8020. "Task Revision: A Neglected Form of Work Performance," (Table), R. M. Staw & R. D. Boettger, *Academy of Management Journal*, 1990, Vol. 33. Reproduced by permission of the publisher via Copyright Clearance Center, Inc.

actions. The omission was caught on the next shift. When a role or task is correctly defined (for example, double-checking medication administration), counter-role behavior leads to poor performance.

Task revision is counter-role behavior in an incorrectly specified role and is a useful way to correct for the problem in the role specification (see Table 13.3). Task revision is a form of role innovation that modifies the job to achieve a better performance. Task revision is the basis for long-term adaptation when the current specifications of a job are no longer applicable.[51] For example, the traditional role for a surgeon is to complete surgical procedures in an accurate and efficient manner. Based on this definition, socio-emotional caregiving is counter-role behavior on the part of the surgeon. However, if the traditional role were to be labeled incorrect, the surgeon's task revision through socio-emotional caregiving would be viewed as leading to much better medical care for patients.

Skill Development

Problems in work system design are often seen as the source of frustration for those dealing with technostress.[52] However, system and technical problems are not the only sources of technostress in new information technologies. Some experts see a growing gap between the skills demanded by new technologies and the skills possessed by employees in jobs using these technologies.[53] Although technical skills are important and are emphasized in many training programs, the largest sector of the economy is actually service-oriented, and service jobs require interpersonal skills. Managers also need a wide range of nontechnical skills to be effective in their work.[54] Therefore, any discussion of jobs and the design of work must recognize the importance of incumbent skills and abilities to meet the demands of the work. Organizations must consider the talents and skills of their employees when they engage in job design efforts. The two issues of employee skill development and job design are interrelated. The knowledge and information requirements for jobs of the future are especially high.

MANAGERIAL IMPLICATIONS: THE CHANGING NATURE OF WORK

Work is an important aspect of a healthy life. The two central needs in human nature are to engage in productive work and to form healthy relationships with others. Work means different things to different ethnic and national groups. Therefore, job design efforts must be sensitive to cultural values and beliefs.

In crafting work tasks and assignments, managers should make an effort to fit the jobs to the people who are doing them. There are no universally accepted ways to design work, and early efforts to find them have been replaced by a number of alternatives. Early approaches to job design were valuable for manufacturing and administrative jobs of the mid-1900s. Now, however, the changing nature of work in the United States and the Americans with Disabilities Act (ADA) challenge managers to find new ways to define work and design jobs.

The distinguishing feature of job design in the foreseeable future is flexibility. Dramatic global, economic, and organizational changes dictate that managers be flexible in the design of work in their organizations. Jobs must be designed to fit the larger organizational structures discussed in Chapter 14. Organizations must ask, does the job support the organization's mission? Employees must ask, does the job meet my short- and long-term needs?

Technology is one of the distinguishing features of the modern workplace. Advances in information, mechanical, and computer technology are transforming work into a highly scientific endeavor demanding employees who are highly educated, knowledgeable workers. American workers can expect these technological advances to continue during their lifetimes and should expect to meet the challenge through continuous skill development and enhancement.

Looking Back

Good Relations and Job Flexibility at Southwest Airlines

Although Southwest Airlines has unionized workers, the company has also enjoyed excellent labor–management relations through the years. Whereas other airlines have experienced periods of strife resulting in strikes, such has not been the story at Southwest. Southwest's flight crews are subject to the same FAA work rules as other airlines' flight crews, and its employees work within established union contracts just as other airlines' workers do. Nevertheless, there are several differences at Southwest Airlines. First, Southwest's flying routes are often shorter than those of many other major airlines, and none are international. Second, Southwest has a unique culture that permeates the way the company does business.[55] While the company has a traditional hierarchical structure and people work very hard at their jobs, Southwest employees also enjoy a unique spirit of teamwork, flexibility in shouldering multiple job responsibilities (think of it as nontraditional job sharing), a supportive work culture, an air of mutual respect, and appreciation for fellow workers. Rather than working to rule, Southwest pilots can be seen picking up trash and flight attendants helping to load baggage. Southwest's flexible approach to jobs, work rules, and job responsibilities has made the company a leader in the industry in many measures of performance and productivity, such as employees per plane (89 versus 110 or more at other airlines) and revenue passengers per employee (2,246 versus 1,489 or fewer at other airlines). The flexibility and spontaneity of the Southwest work culture may result in a celebration on the ramp, complete with "high fives," when a ground crew turns a plane within fifteen minutes. While the work and jobs at

Southwest are no less demanding nor less important than at other airlines, the unique Southwest approach to jobs and work rules leads to
a spirit of teamwork, mutual support, and collaboration that helps lift
the load for everyone.

CHAPTER SUMMARY

1. Different countries have different preferences for one or more of six distinct patterns of defining *work*.
2. Scientific management, job enlargement/job rotation, job enrichment, and the job characteristics theory are traditional American approaches to the design of work and the management of workforce diversity.
3. The social information-processing (SIP) model suggests that information from others and the social context are important in a job.
4. The interdisciplinary approach draws on mechanical engineering, industrial psychology, experimental psychology, and biology in consider-

ing the advantages and disadvantages of job design efforts.
5. The cultural values and social organizations in Japan, Germany, and Scandinavia lead to unique approaches to the design of work.
6. Control, uncertainty, conflict, and job/task demands are important job design parameters to consider when designing work for the well-being of the workers.
7. Telecommuting, alternative work patterns, technostress, task revision, and skill development are emerging issues in the design of work and the use of information technology.

KEY TERMS

job   387

work   387

meaning of work   388

work simplification   390

job enlargement   391

job rotation   391

cross-training   392

job enrichment   392

Job Characteristics Model   394

Job Diagnostic Survey (JDS)   394

social information-processing (SIP) model   398

lean production   401

sociotechnical systems (STS)   401

technocentric   402

anthropocentric   402

job sharing   406

flextime   407

virtual office   407

technostress   407

task revision   408

counter-role behavior   408

REVIEW QUESTIONS

1. Define a job in its organizational context.
2. Describe six patterns of working that have been studied in different countries.
3. Describe four traditional approaches to the design of work in America.
4. Identify and define the five core job dimensions and the three critical psychological states in the Job Characteristics Model.
5. What are the salient features of the social information-processing (SIP) model of job design?
6. List the positive and negative outcomes of the four job design approaches considered by the interdisciplinary model.
7. How do the Japanese, German, and Scandinavian approaches to work differ from one another and from the American approach?
8. Describe the key job design parameters considered when examining the effects of work design on health and well-being.
9. What are five emerging issues in jobs and the design of work?

DISCUSSION AND COMMUNICATION QUESTIONS

1. Is there ever one best way to design a particular job?

2. What should managers learn from the traditional approaches to the design of work used in the United States?

3. It is possible for American companies to apply approaches to the design of work that were developed in other countries?

4. What is the most important emerging issue in the design of work?

5. *(communication question)* Read about new approaches to jobs, such as job sharing. Prepare a memo comparing what you have learned from your reading to one or more approaches to job design discussed in the chapter. What changes in approaches to jobs and job design do you notice from this comparison?

6. *(communication question)* Interview an employee in your organization or another organization and develop an oral presentation about how the job the employee is doing could be enriched. Make sure you ask questions about all aspects of the employee's work (e.g., what specific tasks are done and with whom the employee interacts on the job).

7. *(communication question)* Based on the materials in the chapter, prepare a memo detailing the advantages and disadvantages of flextime job arrangements. In a second part of the memo, identify the specific conditions and characteristics required for a successful flextime program. Would you like to work under a flextime arrangement?

ETHICS QUESTIONS

1. Assume that a company is planning to redesign all of the jobs in one department based on the advice of a major consulting firm. Should the company discuss the job redesign plans with employees before implementing them? Should the employees have been consulted prior to hiring the consulting firm?

2. Assume that a company is aware of certain psychological or physical risks associated with a job, such as respiratory problems and cancer risk associated with the installation of asbestos. Assume also that the medical costs for workers will not be too great. Is it ethical not to warn employees about the possible health risks? Would it make a differ-

ence if the risks were less permanent, such as lower back tension or temporarily altered vision?

3. Suppose that the design of a particular job exposes employees to a health or safety risk and that redesigning the job would cost the company more than paying the medical claims if an employee is injured or hurt. Should the company tell employees doing the job about its decision not to redesign the job to make it safer? Is it ethical for the company not to redesign the job?

4. Assume that a company has many older, mature workers. Rather than retrain them in new technologies, the company wants to replace the older workers with younger ones. Should this be allowed?

Experiential Exercises

13.1 Chaos and the Manager's Job

Managers' jobs are increasingly chaotic as a result of high rates of change, uncertainty, and turbulence. Some managers thrive on change and chaos, but others have a difficult time responding to high rates of

change and uncertainty in a positive manner. This questionnaire gives you an opportunity to evaluate how you would react to a manager's job that is rather chaotic.

Exercise Schedule

1. Preparation (preclass)
   Complete the questionnaire.

2. Individual Scoring
   Give yourself 4 points for each A, 3 points for each B, 2 points for each C, 1 point for each D, and 0 points for each E. Compute the total, divide by 24, and round to one decimal place.

3. Group Discussion
   Your instructor may have you discuss your scores in groups of six students. The higher your score, the more you respond positively to change and chaos; the lower your score, the more difficulty you would have responding to this manager's job in a positive manner. In addition, answer the following questions.
   a. If you could redesign this manager's job, what are the two or three aspects of the job that you would change first?
   b. What are the two or three aspects of the job that you would feel no need to change?

SOURCE: "Chaos and the Manager's Job" in D. Marcic, "Option B. Quality and the New Management Paradigm," *Organizational Behavior: Experiences and Cases*, 4th ed. (Minneapolis/St. Paul: West Publishing, 1995): 296–297. Reprinted by permission.

A Manager's Job[a]

Listed below are some statements a 37-year-old manager made about his job at a large and successful corporation. If your job had these characteristics, how would you react to them? After each statement are five letters, A–E. Circle the letter that best describes how you would react according to the following scale:

A. I would enjoy this very much; it's completely acceptable.
B. This would be enjoyable and acceptable most of the time.
C. I'd have no reaction one way or another, or it would be about equally enjoyable and unpleasant.
D. This feature would be somewhat unpleasant for me.
E. This feature would be very unpleasant for me.

1. I regularly spend 30–40 percent of my time in meetings.   A B C D E

2. A year and a half ago, my job did not exist, and I have been essentially inventing it as I go along.   A B C D E

3. The responsibilities I either assume or am assigned consistently exceed the authority I have for discharging them.   A B C D E

4. At any given moment in my job, I average about a dozen phone calls to be returned.   A B C D E

5. There seems to be very little relation in my job between the quality of my performance and my actual pay and fringe benefits.   A B C D E

6. I need about two weeks of management training a year to stay current in my job.   A B C D E

7. Because we have very effective equal employment opportunity in my company and because it is thoroughly multinational, my job consistently brings me into close contact at a professional level with people of many races, ethnic groups, and nationalities and of both sexes.   A B C D E

8. There is no objective way to measure my effectiveness.   A B C D E

9. I report to three different bosses for different aspects of my job, and each has an equal say in my performance appraisal.   A B C D E

10. On average, about a third of my time is spent dealing with unexpected emergencies that force all scheduled work to be postponed.   A B C D E

11. When I need to meet with the people who report to me, it takes my secretary most of a day to find a time when we are all available, and even then I have yet to have a meeting where everyone is present for the entire meeting.   A B C D E

12. The college degree I earned in preparation for this type of work is now obsolete, and I probably should return for another degree.   A B C D E

13. My job requires that I absorb about 100–200 pages a week of technical material.   A B C D E

14. I am out of town overnight at least one night a week.   A B C D E

15. My department is so interdependent with several other departments in the company that all distinctions about which department is responsible for which tasks are quite arbitrary.   A B C D E

16. I will probably get a promotion in about a year to a job in another division that has most of these same characteristics.   A B C D E

17. During the period of my employment here, either the entire company or the division I worked in has been reorganized every year or so.   A B C D E

18. While I face several possible promotions, I have no real career path.   A B C D E

19. While there are several possible promotions I can see ahead of me, I think I have no realistic chance of getting to the top levels of the company.   A B C D E

20. While I have many ideas about how to make things work better, I have no direct influence on either the business policies or the personnel policies that govern my division.   A B C D E

21. My company has recently put in an "assessment center" where I and other managers must go through an extensive battery of psychological tests to assess our potential.   A B C D E

22. My company is a defendant in an antitrust suit, and if the case comes to trial, I will probably have to testify about some decisions that were made a few years ago.   A B C D E

23. Advanced computer and other electronic office technology is continually being introduced into my division, necessitating constant learning on my part.   A B C D E

24. The computer terminal and screen I have in my office can be monitored in my boss's office without my knowledge.   A B C D E

[a]"A Manager's Job" by Peter B. Vaill in *Managing as a Performing Art: New Ideas for a World of Chaotic Change*, 1989. Reprinted by permission of Jossey-Bass Inc., Publishers.

13.2 A Job Redesign Effort

This activity will help you consider ways in which work can be redesigned to improve its impact on people and its benefit to the organization. Consider the following case:

Eddie is a quality control inspector for an automotive assembly line. His job is to inspect the body, interior, and engine of cars as they roll off the assembly line. Eddie's responsibility is to identify quality problems that either hinder the functioning of these parts of the car or noticeably mar the car's appearance. He is to report the problem so that it can be corrected. Sometimes late in the day, especially on Thursdays and Fridays, Eddie lets assembly problems slip past him. In addition, Eddie's back feels sore at the end of the day, and sometimes he is very stiff in the morning. There are times when he is not sure whether he is seeing a serious problem or just a glitch.

As a five-person team, your job is to evaluate two alternative approaches to redesigning Eddie's job using theories presented in the chapter. Answer the following questions as a team. Your team should be prepared to present its recommendations to the class as a whole.

Discussion Questions
Your instructor will lead a class discussion of each of the following questions:

1. For this particular job, which are the two best models to use in a redesign effort? Why?

2. Does your team need any additional information before it begins to redesign Eddie's job? If so, what information do you need?

3. Using the two models you chose in Question 1, what would your team specifically recommend to redesign Eddie's job?

For more practice exercises, consult the fifth edition of *Organizational Behavior: Experiences and Cases* by Dorothy Marcic and Joseph Seltzer (South-Western, 1998).

Learning Objectives

After reading this chapter, you should be able to do the following:

1. Define *differentiation* and *integration* as organizational design processes. *p. 417*

2. Discuss six basic design dimensions of an organization. *p. 423*

3. Briefly describe five structural configurations for organizations. *p. 424*

4. Describe four contextual variables for an organization. *p. 427*

5. Explain the four forces reshaping organizations. *p. 436*

6. Discuss emerging organizational structures. *p. 440*

7. Identify two cautions about the effect of organizational structures on people. *p. 440*

14

Organizational Design and Structure

Thinking Ahead

Organizing for Emergencies, Crises, and Disaster Relief

The original and most visible mission of the American Red Cross is disaster relief. Disasters can be either natural, as in the case of hurricanes, tornadoes, or floods, or human-made, as in the case of industrial accidents, railroad train derailments, or public utility accidents. The challenge for the American Red Cross is to have a flexible, responsive, and mobile organization that is able to meet disaster relief needs when and where they occur. With a national volunteer staff to paid staff ratio of 45:1, traditionally only one paid staff member per Red Cross chapter is responsible for emergency and disaster services. This paid emergency services director plans and implements procedures for volunteers.[1] Specifically, the emergency services director creates, reviews, and annually updates an area disaster action plan in conjunction with city emergency management teams. In addition, the director establishes shelter agreements with churches, schools, and other large facilities to be used in the event of a large disaster. These agreements are updated every two years. Finally, the emergency services director arranges for motels, clothing stores, and grocery stores to accept Red Cross disbursing orders from disaster clients during an emergency.

A Red Cross organizational chart for disaster services specifies an overall organizational structure and possible job functions to be performed during a disaster operation, though it does not specify lines of authority, communication, or reporting relationships. The paid emergency services director is neither on the chart nor part of the disaster response organization structure that springs into action once a call for emergency services or disaster relief is received by a Red Cross volunteer. Red Cross disaster relief organizations are managed, staffed, and run by an all-volunteer force of trained professionals. Training is a key to the successful execution of disaster relief by the American Red Cross. We look more closely at these flexible, mobile field organizations in the Looking Back feature at the end of this chapter.

Organizational design is the process of constructing and adjusting an organization's structure to achieve its goals. The design process begins with the organization's goals, as illustrated by the American Red Cross disaster relief mission just discussed. The organization's goals are broken into tasks as the basis for jobs, as discussed in Chapter 13. Jobs are grouped into departments, and departments are linked to form the *organizational structure*. Neither the organizational design nor the organizational structure of SAS Institute is standard for the highly competitive software industry, as discussed in Organizational Reality 14.1. Rather, Dr. James H. Goodnight has designed a unique organizational structure on a highly effective business model at closely held SAS. SAS's family-friendly values and amenities build employee loyalty.

The first section of the chapter examines the design processes of differentiation and integration. The second section addresses the six basic design dimensions of an organization's structure. The organization's structure gives it the form to fulfill its function in the environment. As Louis Sullivan, the father of the skyscraper, said, "Form ever follows function." The third section of the chapter presents five structural configurations for organizations. Based on its mission and purpose, an organization determines the best structural configuration for its unique situation. The fourth section examines size, technology, environment, and strategy and goals as *contextual variables* influencing organizational design. When the organization's contextual variables change, the organization must redesign itself to meet new demands and functions. The fifth section examines five forces shaping organizations today. The final section notes several areas where managers should be cautious with regard to structural weaknesses and dysfunctional structural constellations.

organizational design

The process of constructing and adjusting an organization's structure to achieve its goals.

organizational structure

The linking of departments and jobs within an organization.

contextual variables

A set of characteristics that influence the organization's design processes.

KEY ORGANIZATIONAL DESIGN PROCESSES

Differentiation is the design process of breaking the organizational goals into tasks. Integration is the design process of linking the tasks together to form

1. Define *differentiation* and *integration* as organizational design processes.

ORGANIZATIONAL REALITY 14.1

Family Values at the SAS Institute

The SAS Institute is the world's largest closely held software company and a very unique organization. Though many employees find family-friendly SAS an idyllic, utopian workplace, a few former employees regard it as a gilded cage. Professor Jeffrey Pfeffer, who has studied SAS, says the institute is built on an enormously effective business model even though it appears paternalistic at first glance. Co-founder and current CEO Dr. James H. Goodnight has designed a hugely profitable statistical software company, in which he has 67 percent ownership. It is organized like a large family and insulated on a 200-acre wooded campus on the outskirts of Raleigh, North Carolina. Goodnight's home is on the grounds. SAS uses a very unusual organizational design in a highly competitive industry, leasing its software with a 98 percent renewal rate rather than selling its software outright.

SAS instills employee loyalty through an array of family-friendly amenities, including a free health clinic, two day-care centers, flexible thirty-five-hour workweeks, an elder-care program, year-end bonuses and profit sharing, private offices for everyone, and a pianist in the subsidized cafeteria. The annual bonus may be 125 percent or more of annual salary. Quaintly, the institute has a choir. Over 50 percent of the employees are women, and the institute's turnover rate is 4 percent in an industry whose norm is typically 20 percent. The very low turnover rate saves SAS about $50 million annually, and while the free health clinic costs $1 million annually to operate, the institute would likely pay $1.5 million annually for treatment costs offsite. Goodnight spurns perks that enhance employee mobility, such as tuition reimbursement and stock options. He also spurns sales commissions, believing they lead to high-pressure sales tactics. For many employees, Goodnight has designed a good workplace and organization at SAS.

Discussion Questions

1. What elements of Goodnight's SAS model are most applicable to other organizations?

2. What are the costs to employees of the strong, directive management culture at SAS?

SOURCE: T. D. Schellhardt, "An Idyllic Workplace under a Tycoon's Thumb," *The Wall Street Journal,* November 23, 1998, B1. Permission conveyed through Copyright Clearance Center, Inc.

Experiencing OB

You may test your knowledge of some basic principles of organizational design by visiting our animated concept and activity site. Choose Organizational_Design from the "select a topic" pull-down menu, then Principles of Coordination from the "overview tab."

http://www.experiencingob.com

a structure that supports goal accomplishment. These two processes are the keys to successful organizational design. The organizational structure is designed to prevent chaos through an orderly set of reporting relationships and communication channels. Understanding the key design processes and organizational structure helps a person understand the larger working environment and may prevent confusion in the organization.

The organization chart is the most visible representation of the organization's structure and underlying components. Most organizations have a series of organization charts showing reporting relationships throughout the system. The underlying components are (1) formal lines of authority and responsibility (the organizational structure designates reporting relationships by the way jobs and departments are grouped) and (2) formal systems of communication, coordination, and integration (the organizational structure designates the expected patterns of formal interaction among employees).[2]

Differentiation

Differentiation is the process of deciding how to divide the work in an organization.[3] Differentiation ensures that all essential organizational tasks are assigned to one or more jobs and that the tasks receive the attention they need. Many dimensions of differentiation have been considered in organizations. Lawrence and Lorsch found four dimensions of differentiation in one study: (1) manager's goal orientation, (2) time orientation, (3) interpersonal orientation, and (4) formality of structure.[4] Table 14.1 shows some typical differences in orientation for various functional areas of an organization. Three different forms of differentiation are horizontal, vertical, and spatial.

Horizontal differentiation is the degree of differentiation between organizational subunits and is based on employees' specialized knowledge, education, or training. For example, two university professors who teach specialized subjects in different academic departments are subject to horizontal differentiation. Horizontal differentiation increases with specialization and departmentation.

Specialization refers to the particular grouping of activities performed by an individual.[5] The degree of specialization or the division of labor in the organization gives an indication of how much training is needed, what the scope of a job is, and what individual characteristics are needed for job holders. Specialization can also lead to the development of a specialized vocabulary, as well as other behavioral norms. As the two college professors specialize in their subjects, abbreviations or acronyms take on unique meanings. For example, OB means "organizational behavior" to a professor of management but "obstetrics" to a professor of medicine.

Usually, the more specialized the jobs within an organization, the more departments are differentiated within that organization (the greater the departmentation). Departmentation can be by function, product, service, client, geography, process, or some combination of these. A large organization may departmentalize its structure using all or most of these methods at different levels of the organization.

Vertical differentiation is the difference in authority and responsibility in the organizational hierarchy. Vertical differentiation occurs, for example, between a chief executive and a maintenance supervisor. Tall, narrow organizations have greater vertical differentiation, and flat, wide organizations have less vertical differentiation. The height of the organization is also

differentiation
The process of deciding how to divide the work in an organization.

Experiencing OB

Learn why managers may prefer one or another of these departmentation approaches at our animated concept and activity site. Choose Organizational_Design from the "select a topic" pull-down menu, then Departmentalization from the "overview tab."

http://www.experiencingob.com

Basis for Difference	Marketing	Engineering
Goal orientation	Sales volume	Design
Time orientation	Long run	Medium run
Interpersonal orientation	People oriented	Task oriented
Structure	Less formal	More formal

Table 14.1
Differentiation between Marketing and Engineering

influenced by level of horizontal differentiation and span of control. The span of control defines the number of subordinates a manager can and should supervise.[6]

Tall structures—those with narrow spans of control—tend to be characterized by closer supervision and tighter controls. In addition, the communication becomes more burdensome, since directives and information must be passed through more layers. The banking industry has often had tall structures. Flat structures—those with wider spans of control—have simpler communication chains and reduced promotion opportunities due to fewer levels of management. Sears is an example of an organization that has gone to a flat structure. With the loss of more than a million middle management positions in organizations during the 1980s, many organizations are now flatter. The degree of vertical differentiation affects organizational effectiveness, but there is no consistent finding that flatter or taller organizations are better.[7] Organizational size, type of jobs, skills and personal characteristics of employees, and degree of freedom must all be considered in determining organizational effectiveness.[8]

Spatial differentiation is the geographic dispersion of an organization's offices, plants, and personnel. A Boise-Cascade salesperson in New York and one in Portland experience spatial differentiation. An increase in the number of locations increases the complexity of organizational design but may be necessary for organizational goal achievement or organizational protection. For example, if an organization wants to expand into a different country, it may be in its best interest to form a separate subsidiary that is partially owned and managed by citizens of that country. Few U.S. citizens think of Shell Oil Company as being a subsidiary of Royal Dutch Petroleum/ Shell Transport and Trading Group, a company whose international headquarters is in the Netherlands.

Spatial differentiation may give an organization political and legal advantages in a country because it will be identified as a local company. Distance is as important as political and legal issues in making spatial differentiation decisions. For example, a salesperson in Lubbock, Texas, would have a hard time servicing accounts in Beaumont, Texas (over 500 miles away), whereas a salesperson in Delaware might be able to cover all of that state, as well as parts of one or two others.

Horizontal, vertical, and spatial differentiation indicate the amount of width, height, and breadth an organizational structure needs. Just because an organization is highly differentiated along one of these dimensions does not mean it must be highly differentiated along the others. The university environment, for example, is generally characterized by great horizontal differentiation but relatively little vertical and spatial differentiation. A company such as Coca-Cola is characterized by a great deal of all three types of differentiation. The more structurally differentiated an organization is, the more complex it is.[9]

Complexity refers to the number of activities, subunits, or subsystems within the organization. Lawrence and Lorsch suggest that an organization's complexity should mirror the complexity of its environment. As the complexity of an organization increases, its need for mechanisms to link and coordinate the differentiated parts also increases. If these links do not exist, the departments or differentiated parts of the organization can lose sight of the organization's larger mission, and the organization runs the risk of chaos. Designing and building linkage and coordination mechanisms is known as *integration*.

Integration

Integration is the process of coordinating the different parts of an organization. Integration mechanisms are designed to achieve unity among individuals and groups in various jobs, departments, and divisions in the accomplishment of organizational goals and tasks.[10] Integration helps keep the organization in a state of dynamic equilibrium, a condition in which all the parts of the organization are interrelated and balanced.

integration
The process of coordinating the different parts of an organization.

Vertical linkages are used to integrate activities up and down the organizational chain of command. A variety of structural devices can be used to achieve vertical linkage. These include hierarchical referral, rules and procedures, plans and schedules, positions added to the structure of the organization, and management information systems.[11]

The vertical lines on an organization chart indicate the lines of hierarchical referral up and down the organization. When employees do not know how to solve a problem, they can refer it up the organization for consideration and resolution. Work that needs to be assigned is usually delegated down the chain of command as indicated by the vertical lines.

Rules and procedures, as well as plans and schedules, provide standing information for employees without direct communication. These vertical integrators, such as an employee handbook, communicate to employees standard information or information that they can understand on their own. These integrators allow managers to have wider spans of control, because the managers do not have to inform each employee of what is expected and when it is expected. Vertical integrators encourage managers to use management by exception—to make decisions when employees bring problems up the hierarchy. Military organizations depend heavily on vertical linkages. The army, for example, has a well-defined chain of command. Certain duties are expected to be carried out, and proper paperwork is to be in place. In times of crisis, however, much more information is processed, and the proper paperwork becomes secondary to "getting the job done." Vertical linkages help individuals understand their roles in the organization, especially in times of crisis.

Adding positions to the hierarchy is used as a vertical integrator when a manager becomes overloaded by hierarchical referral or problems arise in the chain of command. Positions such as "assistant to" may be added or another level may be added. Adding levels to the hierarchy often reflects growth and increasing complexity. This action tends to reduce the span of control, thus allowing more communication and closer supervision.

Management information systems that are designed to process information up and down the organization also serve as a vertical linkage mechanism. With the advent of computers and network technology, it has become easier for managers and employees to communicate through written reports that are entered into a network and then electronically compiled for managers in the hierarchy. Electronic mail systems allow managers and employees greater access to one another without having to be in the same place at the same time or even attached by telephone. These types of systems make information processing up and down the organization more efficient.

Generally, the taller the organization, the more vertical integration mechanisms are needed. This is because the chains of command and communication are longer. Additional length requires more linkages to minimize the potential for misunderstandings and miscommunications.

Horizontal integration mechanisms provide the communication and coordination that are necessary for links across jobs and departments in the organization. The need for horizontal integration mechanisms increases as the complexity of the organization increases. The horizontal linkages are built into the design of the organization by including liaison roles, task forces, integrator positions, and teams.

A liaison role is created when a person in one department or area of the organization has the responsibility for coordinating with another department (for example, a liaison between the engineering and production departments). Task forces are temporary committees composed of representatives from multiple departments who assemble to address a specific problem affecting these departments.[12]

A stronger device for integration is to develop a person or department designed to be an integrator. In most organizations, the integrator has a good deal of responsibility, but not much authority. Such an individual must have the ability to get people together to resolve differences within the perspective of organizational goals.[13]

The strongest method of horizontal integration is through teams. Horizontal teams cut across existing lines of organizational structure to create new entities that make organizational decisions. An example of this may occur in product development with the formation of a team that includes marketing, research, design, and production personnel. Ford used such a cross-functional team, discussed in detail in Chapter 8, to develop the Taurus automobile, which was designed to regain market share in the United States. The information exchanged by such a product development team should lead to a product that is acceptable to a wider range of organizational groups, as well as to customers.[14]

The use of these linkage mechanisms varies from organization to organization, as well as within areas of the same organization. In general, the flatter the organization, the more necessary horizontal integration mechanisms are.

Experiencing OB

The need to equate responsibility to authority is examined at our animated concept and activity site. Choose Organizational_Design from the "select a topic" pull-down menu, then Delegation from the "overview tab."

http://www.experiencingob.com

BASIC DESIGN DIMENSIONS

Differentiation, then, is the process of dividing work in the organization, and integration is the process of coordinating work in the organization. From a structural perspective, every manager and organization look for the best combination of differentiation and integration for accomplishing the goals of the organization. There are many ways to approach this process. One way is to establish a desired level of each structural dimension on a high to low continuum and then develop a structure that meets the desired configuration. These structural dimensions include the following:[15]

1. *Formalization*: The degree to which an employee's role is defined by formal documentation (procedures, job descriptions, manuals, and regulations).

2. *Centralization*: The extent to which decision-making authority has been delegated to lower levels of an organization. An organization is centralized if the decisions are made at the top of the organization and decentralized if decision making is pushed down to lower levels in the organization.

3. *Specialization*: The degree to which organizational tasks are subdivided into separate jobs. The division of labor and the degree to which formal job descriptions spell out job requirements indicate the level of specialization in the organization.

4. *Standardization*: The extent to which work activities are described and performed routinely in the same way. Highly standardized organizations have little variation in the defining of jobs.

5. *Complexity*: The number of activities within the organization and the amount of differentiation needed within the organization.

6. *Hierarchy of authority*: The degree of vertical differentiation through reporting relationships and the span of control within the structure of the organization.

An organization that is high on formalization, centralization, specialization, standardization, and complexity and has a tall hierarchy of authority is said to be highly bureaucratic. Bureaucracies are not in and of themselves bad; however, they are often tainted by abuse and red tape. The Internal Revenue Service is often described as bureaucratic. An organization that is on the opposite end of each of these continua is very flexible and loose. Control is very hard to implement and maintain in such an organization, but at certain times such an organization is appropriate. The research and development departments in many organizations are often more flexible than other departments in order to stimulate creativity. An important organizational variable, which is not included in the structural dimensions, is trust.

Another approach to the process of accomplishing organizational goals is to describe what is and is not important to the success of the organization

2. Discuss six basic design dimensions of an organization.

formalization
The degree to which the organization has official rules, regulations, and procedures.

centralization
The degree to which decisions are made at the top of the organization.

specialization
The degree to which jobs are narrowly defined and depend on unique expertise.

standardization
The degree to which work activities are accomplished in a routine fashion.

complexity
The degree to which many different types of activities occur in the organization.

hierarchy of authority
The degree of vertical differentiation across levels of management.

rather than worry about specific characteristics. Henry Mintzberg feels that the following questions can guide managers in designing formal structures that fit each organization's unique set of circumstances:[16]

1. How many tasks should a given position in the organization contain, and how specialized should each task be?
2. How standardized should the work content of each position be?
3. What skills, abilities, knowledge, and training should be required for each position?
4. What should be the basis for the grouping of positions within the organization into units, departments, divisions, and so on?
5. How large should each unit be, and what should the span of control be (that is, how many individuals should report to each manager)?
6. How much standardization should be required in the output of each position?
7. What mechanisms should be established to help individuals in different positions and units to adjust to the needs of other individuals?
8. How centralized or decentralized should decision-making power be in the chain of authority? Should most of the decisions be made at the top of the organization (centralized) or be made down in the chain of authority (decentralized)?

The manager who can answer these questions has a good understanding of how the organization should implement the basic structural dimensions. These basic design dimensions act in combination with one another and are not entirely independent characteristics of an organization. Challenge 14.1 gives you (or a friend) an opportunity to consider how decentralized your company is.

FIVE STRUCTURAL CONFIGURATIONS

3. Briefly describe five structural configurations for organizations.

Differentiation, integration, and the basic design dimensions combine to yield various structural configurations. Mintzberg proposes five structural configurations: the simple structure, the machine bureaucracy, the professional bureaucracy, the divisionalized form, and the adhocracy.[17] Table 14.2 summarizes the prime coordinating mechanism, the key part of the organization, and the type of decentralization for each of these structural configurations. The five fundamental elements of the organization, for Mintzberg, are the upper echelon; the middle level; the operating core, where work is accomplished; the technical staff; and the support staff. Each configuration affects people in the organization somewhat differently.

Simple Structure

simple structure
A centralized form of organization that emphasizes the upper echelon and direct supervision.

The *simple structure* is an organization with little technical and support staff, strong centralization of decision making in the upper echelon, and

Challenge 14.1

How Decentralized Is Your Company?

Decentralization is one of the key design dimensions in an organization. It is closely related to several behavioral dimensions of an organization, such as leadership style, degree of participative decision making, and the nature of power and politics within the organization.

The following questionnaire allows you to get an idea about how decentralized your organization is. (If you do not have a job, have a friend who does work complete the questionnaire to see how decentralized his or her organization is.) Which level in your organization has the authority to make each of the following eleven decisions? Answer the questionnaire by circling one of the following:

0 = The board of directors makes the decision.
1 = The CEO makes the decision.
2 = The division/functional manager makes the decision.
3 = A subdepartment head makes the decision.
4 = The first-level supervisor makes the decision.
5 = Operators on the shop floor make the decision.

Decision Concerning:	Circle Appropriate Level					
a. The number of workers required.	0	1	2	3	4	5
b. Whether to employ a worker.	0	1	2	3	4	5
c. Internal labor disputes.	0	1	2	3	4	5
d. Overtime worked at shop level.	0	1	2	3	4	5
e. Delivery dates and order priority.	0	1	2	3	4	5
f. Production planning.	0	1	2	3	4	5
g. Dismissal of a worker.	0	1	2	3	4	5
h. Methods of personnel selection.	0	1	2	3	4	5
i. Method of work to be used.	0	1	2	3	4	5
j. Machinery or equipment to be used.	0	1	2	3	4	5
k. Allocation of work among workers.	0	1	2	3	4	5

Add up all your circled numbers. Total = ————. The higher your number (for example, 45 or more), the more decentralized your organization. The lower your number (for example, 25 or less), the more centralized your organization.

SOURCE: From D. Miller and C. Droge, "Psychological and Traditional Determinants of Structure," *Administrative Science Quarterly* 31 (1986): 558. Reprinted by permission of the Administrative Science Quarterly.

a minimal middle level. This structure has a minimum of vertical differentiation of authority and minimal formalization. It achieves coordination through direct supervision, often by the chief executive in the upper echelon. An example of a simple structure is a small, independent landscape practice in which one or two landscape architects supervise the vast

Structural Configuration	Prime Coordinating Mechanism	Key Part of Organization	Type of Decentralization
Simple structure	Direct supervision	Upper echelon	Centralization
Machine bureaucracy	Standardization of work processes	Technical staff	Limited horizontal decentralization
Professional bureaucracy	Standardization of skills	Operating level	Vertical and horizontal decentralization
Divisionalized form	Standardization of outputs	Middle level	Limited vertical decentralization
Adhocracy	Mutual adjustment	Support staff	Selective decentralization

SOURCE: H. Mintzberg, *The Structuring of Organizations*, © 1979, 301. Reprinted by permission of Prentice-Hall, Inc., Upper Saddle River, NJ.

Table 14.2
Five Constructural Configurations of Organizations

majority of work with no middle-level managers. Even an organization with as few as thirty people can become dysfunctional as a simple structure after an extended period.

Machine Bureaucracy

machine bureaucracy
A moderately decentralized form of organization that emphasizes the technical staff and standardization of work processes.

The *machine bureaucracy* is an organization with a well-defined technical and support staff differentiated from the line operations of the organization, limited horizontal decentralization of decision making, and a well-defined hierarchy of authority. The technical staff is powerful in a machine bureaucracy. There is strong formalization through policies, procedures, rules, and regulations. Coordination is achieved through the standardization of work processes. An example of a machine bureaucracy is an automobile assembly plant, with routinized operating tasks. The strength of the machine bureaucracy is efficiency of operation in stable, unchanging environments. The weakness of the machine bureaucracy is its slow responsiveness to external changes and to individual employee preferences and ideas.

Professional Bureaucracy

professional bureaucracy
A decentralized form of organization that emphasizes the operating level and standardization of skills.

The *professional bureaucracy* emphasizes the expertise of the professionals in the operating core of the organization. The technical and support staffs serve the professionals. There is both vertical and horizontal differentiation in the professional bureaucracy. Coordination is achieved through the standardization of the professionals' skills. Examples of professional bureaucracies are hospitals and universities. The doctors, nurses, and professors are given wide latitude to pursue their work based on professional training and indoctrination through professional training programs. Large accounting firms may fall into the category of professional bureaucracies.

Divisionalized Form

divisionalized form
A moderately decentralized form of organization that emphasizes the middle level and standardization of outputs.

The *divisionalized form* is a loosely coupled, composite structural configuration.[18] It is a configuration composed of divisions, each of which may have its own structural configuration. Each division is designed to respond to the market in which it operates. There is vertical decentralization from the upper echelon to the middle of the organization, and the middle level of management is the key part of the organization. This form of organization may have one division that is a machine bureaucracy, one that is an adhocracy, and one that is a simple structure. An example of this form of organization is Valero Energy Corporation, headquartered in San Antonio, Texas, with oil refining operations throughout the country. The divisionalized organization uses standardization of outputs as its coordinating mechanism.

Adhocracy

The *adhocracy* is a highly organic, rather than mechanistic, configuration with minimal formalization and order. It is designed to fuse interdisciplinary experts into smoothly functioning ad hoc project teams. Liaison devices are the primary mechanism for integrating the project teams through a process of mutual adjustment. There is a high degree of horizontal specialization based on formal training and expertise. Selective decentralization of the project teams occurs within the adhocracy. An example of this form of organization is the National Aeronautics and Space Administration (NASA), which is composed of many talented experts who work in small teams on a wide range of projects related to America's space agenda. New high-technology businesses also often select an adhocracy design. Paradoxically, though, some new high-tech ventures choose bureaucratic design strategies as antidotes for the uncertainty, anxiety, and stress of their typically turbulent operating environments.

adhocracy
A selectively decentralized form of organization that emphasizes the support staff and mutual adjustment among people.

CONTEXTUAL VARIABLES

The basic design dimensions and the resulting structural configurations play out in the context of the organization's internal and external environments. Four contextual variables influence the success of an organization's design: size, technology, environment, and strategy and goals. These variables provide a manager with challenges in considering an organizational design, although they are not necessarily determinants of structure. As the content of the organization changes, so should the structural design. Also, the amount of change in the contextual variables throughout the life of the organization influences the amount of change needed in the basic dimensions of the organization's structure.[19]

4. Describe four contextual variables for an organization.

Size

The total number of employees is the appropriate definition of size when discussing the design of organizational structure. This is logical, because people and their interactions are the building blocks of structure. Other measures, such as net assets, production rates, and total sales, are usually highly correlated with the total number of employees but may not reflect the actual number of interpersonal relationships that are necessary to effectively structure an organization.

Electronic Data Systems (EDS) began as an entrepreneurial venture of H. Ross Perot and had grown into an internationally prominent provider of information technology services when it was bought by General Motors Corporation (GM) in the early 1980s. Nearly half of EDS's revenues came from GM at the time of the buyout. The early culture of EDS placed a premium on technical competence, high achievement drive, an entrepreneurial attitude, and a maverick spirit. EDS has continued to grow and to change. In 1996, it was spun off by GM and became an autonomous company once again.

Although there is some argument over the degree of influence that size has on organizational structure, there is no argument that it does influence design options. In one study, Meyer found size of the organization to be the most important of all variables considered in influencing the organization's structure and design, whereas other researchers argue that the decision to expand the organization's business causes an increase in size as the structure is adjusted to accommodate the planned growth.[20] Downsizing is a planned strategy to reduce the size of an organization, and is often accompanied by related restructuring and revitalization activities.[21]

How much influence size exerts on the organization's structure is not as important as the relationship between size and the design dimensions of structure. In other words, when exploring structural alternatives, what should the manager know about designing structures for large and small organizations?

Table 14.3 illustrates the relationships among each of the design dimensions and organizational size. Formalization, specialization, and standardization all tend to be greater in larger organizations, because they are necessary to control activities within the organization. For example, larger organizations are more likely to use documentation, rules, written policies and procedures, and detailed job descriptions than to rely on personal observation by the manager. The more relationships that have to be managed by the structure, the more formalized and standardized the processes need to be. McDonald's has several volumes that describe how to make all its products, how to greet customers, how to maintain the facilities, and so on.

Table 14.3

Relationship between Organizational Size and Basic Design Dimensions

Basic Design Dimensions	Small Organizations	Large Organizations
Formalization	Less	More
Centralization	High	Low
Specialization	Low	High
Standardization	Low	High
Complexity	Low	High
Hierarchy of authority	Flat	Tall

This level of standardization, formalization, and specialization helps Mc-Donald's maintain the same quality of product no matter where a restaurant is located. In contrast, at a small, locally owned café, your hamburger and french fries may taste a little different every time you visit. This is evidence of a lack of standardization.

Formalization and specialization also help a large organization decentralize decision making. Because of the complexity and number of decisions in a large organization, formalization and specialization are used to set parameters for decision making at lower levels. Can you imagine the chaos if Donald Carty, CEO of American Airlines, had to make every decision about flights, food, or ticketing procedures for the airline? By decentralizing decision making, the larger organization adds horizontal and vertical complexity, but not necessarily spatial complexity. However, it is more common for a large organization to have more geographic dispersion.

Another dimension of design, hierarchy of authority, is related to complexity. As size increases, complexity increases; thus, more levels are added to the hierarchy of authority. This keeps the span of control from getting too large. However, there is a balancing force, because formalization and specialization are added. The more formalized, standardized, and specialized the roles within the organization, the wider the span of control can be.

Although some have argued that the future belongs to small, agile organizations, others argue that size will continue to be an advantage. To take advantage of size, organizations must become centerless corporations with a global core.[22] The global core provides strategic leadership, helps distribute and provide access to the company's capabilities and knowledge, creates the corporate identity, ensures access to low cost capital, and exerts control over the enterprise as a whole.

Technology

An organization's technology is an important contextual variable in determining the organization's structure, as noted in Chapter 2.[23] Technology is defined as the tools, techniques, and actions used by an organization to transform inputs into outputs.[24] The inputs of the organization include human resources, machines, materials, information, and money. The outputs are the products and services that the organization offers to the external environment. Determining the relationship between technology and structure is complicated, because different departments may employ very different technologies. As organizations become larger, there is greater variation in technologies across units in the organization. Joan Woodward, Charles Perrow, and James Thompson have developed ways to understand traditional organizational technologies. More work is needed to better understand the contemporary engineering, research and development, and knowledge-based technologies of the information age.

Woodward introduced one of the best-known classification schemes for technology, identifying three types: unit, mass, or process production. Unit technology is small-batch manufacturing technology and, sometimes, made-to-order production. Examples include Smith and Wesson's arms manufacture and the manufacture of fine furniture. Mass technology is large-batch manufacturing technology. Examples include American automotive assembly lines and latex glove production. Process production is continuous-production processes. Examples include oil refining and beer making. Woodward classified unit technology as the least complex, mass technology as more complex, and process technology as the most complex. The more complex the organization's technology, the more complex the administrative component or structure of the organization needs to be.

Perrow proposed an alternative to Woodward's scheme based on two variables: task variability and problem analyzability. Task variability considers the number of exceptions encountered in doing the tasks within a job. Problem analyzability examines the types of search procedures followed to find ways to respond to task exceptions. For example, for some exceptions encountered while doing a task, the appropriate response is easy to find. If you are driving down a street and see a sign that says, "Detour—Bridge Out," it is very easy to respond to the task variability. When Thomas Edison was designing the first electric light bulb, however, the problem analyzability was very high for his task.

Perrow went on further to identify the four key aspects of structure that could be modified to the technology. These structural elements are (1) the amount of discretion that an individual can exercise to complete a task, (2) the power of groups to control the unit's goals and strategies, (3) the level of interdependence among groups, and (4) the extent to which organizational units coordinate work using either feedback or planning. Figure 14.1 summarizes Perrow's findings about types of technology and basic design dimensions.[25]

technological interdependence
The degree of interrelatedness of the organization's various technological elements.

Thompson offered yet another view of technology and its relationship to organizational design. This view is based on the concept of **technological interdependence** (i.e., the degree of interrelatedness of the organization's various technological elements) and the pattern of an organization's work flows. Thompson's research suggests that greater technological interdependence leads to greater organizational complexity and that the problems of this greater complexity may be offset by decentralized decision making.[26]

The research of these three early scholars on the influence of technology on organizational design can be combined into one integrating concept—routineness in the process of changing inputs into outputs in an organization. This routineness has a very strong relationship with organizational structure. The more routine and repetitive the tasks of the organization, the higher the degree of formalization that is possible; the more centralized, specialized, and standardized the organization can be; and the more hierarchical levels with wider spans of control that are possible.

Since the work of Woodward, Perrow, and Thompson, however, an important caveat to the discussion of technology has emerged: the advance of information technology has influenced how organizations transform inputs

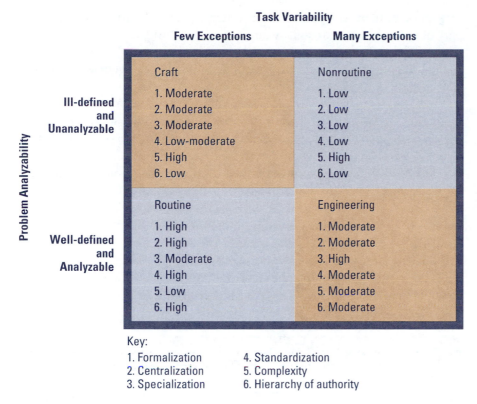

Task Variability

	Few Exceptions	Many Exceptions
Ill-defined and Unanalyzable	Craft 1. Moderate 2. Moderate 3. Moderate 4. Low-moderate 5. High 6. Low	Nonroutine 1. Low 2. Low 3. Low 4. Low 5. High 6. Low
Well-defined and Analyzable	Routine 1. High 2. High 3. Moderate 4. High 5. Low 6. High	Engineering 1. Moderate 2. Moderate 3. High 4. Moderate 5. Moderate 6. Moderate

Problem Analyzability

Key:
1. Formalization   4. Standardization
2. Centralization   5. Complexity
3. Specialization   6. Hierarchy of authority

SOURCE: Built from C. Perrow, "A Framework for the Comparative Analysis of Organizations," *American Sociological Review* (April 1967): 194–208.

Figure 14.1
Summary of Perrow's Findings about the Relationship between Technology and Basic Design Dimensions

into outputs. The introduction of computer-integrated networks, CAD/CAM systems, and computer-integrated manufacturing has broadened the span of control, flattened the organizational hierarchy, decentralized decision making, and lowered the amount of specialization and standardization.[27] Advances in information technology have allowed for other advances in manufacturing, such as mass customization. Hewlett-Packard has found a key to mass customization in postponing the task of differentiating a product for a specific customer until the latest possible time.[28]

Environment

The third contextual variable for organizational design is *environment*. The environment of an organization is most easily defined as anything outside the boundaries of that organization. Different aspects of the environment have varying degrees of influence on the organization's structure. The general environment includes all conditions that may have an impact on the organization. These conditions could include economic factors, political considerations, ecological changes, sociocultural demands, and governmental regulation.

When aspects of the general environment become more focused in areas of direct interest to the organization, those aspects become part of the

environment
Anything outside the boundaries of an organization.

task environment

The elements of an organization's environment that are related to its goal attainment.

task environment, or specific environment. The task environment is that part of the environment that is directly relevant to the organization. Typically, this level of environment includes stakeholders such as unions, customers, suppliers, competitors, government regulatory agencies, and trade associations. Organizational Reality 14.2 looks at environmental protection in the task environment of Florida agriculture. Three years after the Florida legislature passed the Everglades Forever Act, farmers were found to be much more effective than the state's government bureaucracy in cleaning up the Everglades Protection Area.

The domain of the organization refers to the area the organization claims for itself with respect to how it fits into its relevant environments. The domain is particularly important because it is defined by the organization, and it influences how the organization perceives and acts within its environments.[29] For example, Wal-Mart and Neiman-Marcus both sell clothing apparel, but their domains are very different.

The organization's perceptions of its environment and the actual environment may not be the same. The environment that the manager per-

---

ORGANIZATIONAL REALITY 14.2

The Everglades—An Environmental Treasure Cleanup

In 1994, the Florida state legislature passed the Everglades Forever Act as a plan for cleaning up one of the nation's premier environmental treasures. This environmental cleanup effort became a case study in the use of private industry incentives versus traditional government bureaucracy as mechanisms for environmental protection. The private industry coalition in this case was agriculture, and the government bureaucracy was the South Florida Water Management District, which, before beginning work, projected a budget shortfall as high as $180 million by 1997. Although many environmentalists preferred a traditional bureaucratic model for environmental protection, farmers in the Everglades Agricultural Area were given incentives and a timetable for meeting environmental goals as well as the freedom to choose the most efficient means for achieving those goals. Three years after passage of the 1994 cleanup act, private industry was seven years ahead of schedule. Using a combination of high-technology and common-sense techniques, the farmers had achieved a 68 percent reduction in phosphorus from the water running off

their land, which was more than two times better than the goal of a 25 percent reduction. One environmentally-friendly scientist testified that 97 percent of the Everglades Protection Area had achieved the year 2003 phosphorus target levels by 1997 and that almost all of the positive results were attributable to the farmers' private industry incentive program as opposed to the state government's bureaucratic efforts. Giving private business organizations the flexibility to achieve socially desirable goals seems to have achieved great results in Florida.

Discussion Questions

1. Under what conditions might a traditional government bureaucracy be more effective than private industry?

2. What limitations might there be to the agriculture industry's environmental protection efforts?

SOURCE: R. W. Hahn, "Incentive Outpaces Bureaucracy in Everglades Cleanup," *The Wall Street Journal*, May 15, 1997, A22. Permission conveyed through Copyright Clearance Center, Inc.

ceives is the environment that the organization responds to and organizes for.[30] Therefore, two organizations may be in relatively the same environment from an objective standpoint, but if the managers perceive differences, the organizations may enact very different structures to deal with this same environment.

The perception of *environmental uncertainty* or the perception of the lack of environmental uncertainty is how the contextual variable of environment most influences organizational design. Some organizations have relatively static environments with little uncertainty, whereas others are so dynamic that no one is sure what tomorrow may bring. Binney and Smith, for example, has made relatively the same product for more than fifty years with very few changes in the product design or packaging. The environment for its Crayola products is relatively static. In fact, customers rebelled when the company tried to get rid of some old colors and add new ones. In contrast, in the last two decades, competitors in the airline industry have encountered deregulation, mergers, bankruptcies, safety changes, changes in cost and price structures, changes in customer and employee demographics, and changes in global competition. The uncertainty of the environment of the major airlines has been relatively high during this period.

The amount of uncertainty in the environment influences the structural dimensions. Burns and Stalker labeled two structural extremes that are appropriate for the extremes of environmental uncertainty—mechanistic structure and organic structure.[31] Table 14.4 compares the structural dimensions of these two extremes. The mechanistic and organic structures are opposite ends of a continuum of organizational design possibilities. Although the general premise of environmental uncertainty and structural dimensions has been upheld by research, the organization must make adjustments for the realities of its perceived environment when designing its structure.[32]

The question for those trying to design organizational structures is how to determine environmental uncertainty. Dess and Beard defined three dimensions of environment that should be measured in assessing the degree of uncertainty: capacity, volatility, and complexity.[33] The capacity of the environment reflects the abundance or scarcity of resources. If resources abound, the environment supports expansion, mistakes, or both. In contrast, in times of scarcity, the environment demands survival of the fittest. Volatility is the degree of instability. The airline industry is in a volatile

environmental uncertainty
The amount and rate of change in the organization's environment.

Basic Design Dimensions	Mechanistic	Organic
Formalization	High	Low
Centralization	High	Low
Specialization	High	Low
Standardization	High	Low
Complexity	Low	High
Hierarchy of authority	Strong, tall	Weak, flat

Table 14.4
Mechanistic and Organic Organizational Forms

environment. This makes it difficult for managers to know what needs to be done. The complexity of the environment refers to the differences and variability among environmental elements.

If the organization's environment is uncertain, dynamic, and complex and resources are scarce, the manager needs an organic structure that is better able to adapt to its environment. Such a structure allows the manager to monitor the environment from a number of internal perspectives, thus helping the organization maintain flexibility in responding to environmental changes.[34]

Strategy and Goals

The fourth contextual variable that influences how the design dimensions of structure should be enacted is the strategies and goals of the organization. Strategies and goals provide legitimacy to the organization, as well as employee direction, decision guidelines, and criteria for performance.[35] In addition, strategies and goals help the organization fit into its environment.

As more understanding of the contextual influence of strategies and goals has developed, several strategic dimensions that influence structure have been defined. One of these definitions was put forth by Danny Miller.[36] His framework for these strategic dimensions and their implications for organizational structure is shown in Table 14.5.

For example, when Apple Computer introduced personal computers to the market, its strategies were very innovative. The structure of the organization was relatively flat and very informal. Apple had Friday afternoon beer and popcorn discussion sessions, and eccentric behavior was easily accepted. As the personal computer market became more competitive, however, the structure of Apple changed to help it differentiate its products and to help control costs. The innovative strategies and structures devised by Steve Jobs, one of Apple's founders, were no longer appropriate. The board of directors recruited John Scully, a marketing expert from PepsiCo, to help

Table 14.5
Miller's Integrative Framework of Structural and Strategic Dimensions

Strategic Dimension	Predicted Structural Characteristics
Innovation—to understand and manage new processes and technologies	Low formalization Decentralization Flat hierarchy
Market differentiation—to specialize in customer preferences	Moderate to high complexity Moderate to high formalization Moderate centralization
Cost control—to produce standardized products efficiently	High formalization High centralization High standardization Low complexity

SOURCE: D. Miller, "The Structural and Environmental Correlates of Business Strategy," *Strategic Management Journal* 8 (1987): 55–76. Copyright © John Wiley & Sons Limited. Reproduced with permission.

Apple better compete in the market it had created. In 1996 and 1997, Apple reinvented itself again and brought back Jobs to try to restore its innovative edge.

Limitations exist, however, on how much strategies and goals influence structure. Because the structure of the organization includes the formal information-processing channels in the organization, it stands to reason that the need to change strategies may not be communicated throughout the organization. In such a case, the organization's structure influences its strategic choice.

The inefficiency of the structure to perceive environmental changes may even lead to organizational failure. In the airline industry, several carriers failed to adjust quickly enough to deregulation and the highly competitive marketplace. Only those airlines that were generally viewed as lean structures with good information-processing systems have flourished in the turbulent years since deregulation. Examples of how different design dimensions can affect the strategic decision process are listed in Table 14.6.

Formalization
As the level of formalization increases, so does the probability of the following:
1. The strategic decision process will become reactive to crisis rather than proactive through opportunities.
2. Strategic moves will be incremental and precise.
3. Differentiation in the organization will not be balanced with integrative mechanisms.
4. Only environmental crises that are in areas monitored by the formal organizational systems will be acted upon.
Centralization
As the level of centralization increases, so does the probability of the following:
1. The strategic decision process will be initiated by only a few dominant individuals.
2. The decision process will be goal-oriented and rational.
3. The strategic process will be constrained by the limitations of top managers.
Complexity
As the level of complexity increases, so does the probability of the following:
1. The strategic decision process will become more politicized.
2. The organization will find it more difficult to recognize environmental opportunities and threats.
3. The constraints on good decision processes will be multiplied by the limitations of each individual within the organization.

Table 14.6
Examples of How Structure Affects the Strategic Decision Process

SOURCE: Republished with permission of Academy of Management, PO Box 3020, Briar Cliff Manor, NJ 10510-8020. "The Strategic Decision Process and Organizational Structure" (Table), J. Fredrickson, *Academy of Management Review* (1986): 284. Reproduced by permission of the publisher via Copyright Clearance Center, Inc.

The four contextual variables—size, technology, environment, and strategy and goals—combine to influence the design process. However, the existing structure of the organization influences how the organization interprets and reacts to information about each of the variables. Each of the contextual variables has management researchers who claim that it is the most important variable in determining the best structural design. Because of the difficulty in studying the interactions of the four contextual dimensions and the complexity of organizational structures, the argument about which variable is most important continues.

What is apparent is that there must be some level of fit between the structure and the contextual dimensions of the organization. The better the fit, the more likely the organization will achieve its short-run goals. In addition, the better the fit, the more likely the organization will process information and design appropriate organizational roles for long-term prosperity, as indicated in Figure 14.2.

FORCES RESHAPING ORGANIZATIONS

5. Explain the four forces reshaping organizations.

Managers and researchers traditionally examine organizational design and structure within the framework of basic design dimensions and contextual variables. Several forces reshaping organizations are causing managers to go beyond the traditional frameworks and to examine ways to make organizations more responsive to customer needs. Some of these forces include shorter life cycles within the organization, globalization, and rapid changes in information technology. These forces together increase the demands on process capabilities within the organization and emerging organizational structures.

Life Cycles in Organizations

organizational life cycle
The differing stages of an organization's life from birth to death.

Organizations are dynamic entities. As such, they ebb and flow through different stages. Usually, researchers think of these stages as *organizational life cycles*. The total organization has a life cycle that begins at birth, moves through growth and maturity to decline, and possibly experiences revival.[37]

Organizational subunits may have very similar life cycles. Because of changes in technology and product design, many organizational subunits, especially those that are product based, are experiencing shorter life cycles. Hence, the subunits that compose the organization are changing more rapidly than in the past. These shorter life cycles enable the organization to respond quickly to external demands and changes.

When a new organization or subunit is born, the structure is organic and informal. If the organization or subunit is successful, it grows and matures. This usually leads to formalization, specialization, standardization, complexity, and a more mechanistic structure. If the environment changes, however, the organization must be able to respond. A mechanistic structure is not able to respond to a dynamic environment as well as an organic one. If the organization or subunit does respond, it becomes more organic and revives; if not, it declines and possibly dies.

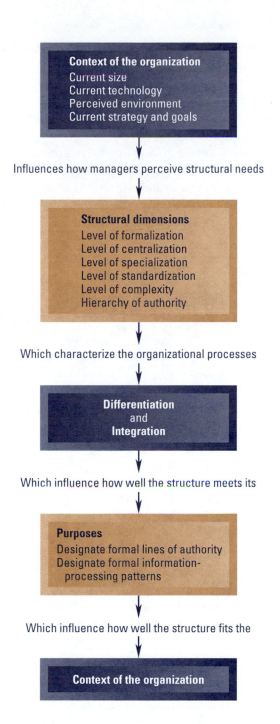

Figure 14.2
*The Relationship among Key
Organizational Design
Elements*

Shorter life cycles put more pressure on the organization to be both flexible and efficient at the same time. Further, as flexible organizations use design to their competitive advantage, discrete organizational life cycles may give way to a kaleidoscope of continuously emerging, efficiency-seeking organizational designs.[38] The manager's challenge in this context becomes one of creating congruency among various organizational design dimensions to fit continuously changing markets and locations.

Globalization

Another force that is reshaping organizations is the globalization of organizations and markets. In other words, organizations operate worldwide rather than in just one country or region. Such globalization makes spatial differentiation even more of a reality for organizations. Besides the obvious geographic differences, there may be deep cultural and value system differences. This adds another type of complexity to the structural design process and necessitates the creation of integrating mechanisms so that people are able to understand and interpret one another, as well as coordinate with one another.

The choice of structure for managing an international business is generally based on choices concerning the following three factors:

1. *The level of vertical differentiation*. A hierarchy of authority must be created that clarifies the responsibilities of both domestic and foreign managers.

2. *The level of horizontal differentiation*. Foreign and domestic operations should be grouped in such a way that the company effectively serves the needs of all customers.

3. *The degree of formalization, specialization, standardization, and centralization*. The global structure must allow decisions to be made in the most appropriate area of the organization. However, controls must be in place that reflect the strategies and goals of the parent firm.[39]

Changes in Information-Processing Technologies

Many of the changes in information-processing technologies have allowed organizations to move into new product and market areas more quickly. However, just as shorter life cycles and globalization have caused new concerns for designing organizational structures, so has the increased availability of advanced information-processing technologies.

Organizational structures are already feeling the impact of advanced information-processing technologies. More integration and coordination are evident, because managers worldwide can be connected through computerized networks. The basic design dimensions have also been affected as follows:

1. The hierarchy of authority has been flattened.

2. The basis of centralization has been changed. Now managers can use technology to acquire more information and make more decisions, or they can use technology to push information and decision making lower in the hierarchy and thus decrease centralization.

3. Less specialization and standardization are needed, because people using advanced information-processing technologies have more sophisticated jobs that require a broader understanding of how the organization gets work done.[40]

Advances in information processing are leading to knowledge-based organizations, the outlines of which are now only seen dimly. Some of the hallmarks of these new organizational forms are virtual enterprising, dynamic teaming, and knowledge networking.[41] This fifth generation of management thought and practice leads to co-creation of products and services. Future organizations may well be defined by networks of overlapping teams.

Demands on Organizational Processes

Because of the forces reshaping organizations, managers find themselves trying to meet what seem to be conflicting goals: an efficiency orientation that results in on-time delivery *and* a quality orientation that results in customized, high-quality goods or services.[42] Traditionally, managers have seen efficiency and customization as conflicting demands.

To meet these conflicting demands, organizations need to become "dynamically stable."[43] To do so, an organization must have managers who see their roles as architects who clearly understand the "how" of the organizing process. Managers must combine long-term thinking with flexible and quick responses that help improve process and know-how. The organizational structure must help define, at least to some degree, roles for managers who hope to successfully address the conflicting demands of dynamic stability. The differences between the structural roles of managers today and managers of the future are illustrated in Table 14.7.

Roles of Managers Today
1. Strictly adhering to boss–employee relationships.
2. Getting things done by giving orders.
3. Carrying messages up and down the hierarchy.
4. Performing a prescribed set of tasks according to a job description.
5. Having a narrow functional focus.
6. Going through channels, one by one by one.
7. Controlling subordinates.

Roles of Future Managers
1. Having hierarchical relationships subordinated to functional and peer relationships.
2. Getting things done by negotiating.
3. Solving problems and making decisions.
4. Creating the job by developing entrepreneurial projects.
5. Having broad cross-functional collaboration.
6. Emphasizing speed and flexibility.
7. Coaching their workers.

Table 14.7
Structural Roles of Managers Today versus Managers of the Future

SOURCE: Reprinted by permission of the publisher, from *Management Review*, January 1991 © 1991. Thomas R. Horton. American Management Association, New York. All rights reserved.

Emerging Organizational Structures

6. Discuss emerging organizational structures.

The demands on managers and on process capabilities place demands on structures. The emphasis in tomorrow's organizations will be on organizing around processes, a key tenet of total quality management (TQM). This process orientation emerges from the combination of three streams of applied organizational design: high-performance, self-managed teams; managing processes rather than functions; and the evolution of information technology.

Horizontal companies are an emerging organizational structure. Frank Ostroff and Doug Smith of McKinsey and Company developed a ten-step blueprint for a horizontal company.[44] The steps are as follows: (1) organize primarily around process, not task; (2) flatten the hierarchy by minimizing subdivision of processes and arranging teams in parallel; (3) make senior managers responsible for processes and process performance; (4) use customer satisfaction as the basic link to performance objectives and evaluation; (5) make teams the focus of organizational performance and design; (6) break down vertical barriers in the organization; (7) encourage employees to develop multiple competencies; (8) inform and train people on a just-in-time, need-to-perform basis; (9) maximize contacts with suppliers and customers for everyone in the organization; and (10) reward both individual skills and team performance. Horizontal organization can be applied to all sectors of the economy.

The modular corporation is an alternative to the vertically integrated company. Companies that focus on their distinctive competence and on the distinctive value they add to a product or service can outsource (i.e., allow external suppliers to provide) a wide range of activities that are not part of their core business. These companies become modular corporations and exploit their distinctive expertise.[45] For example, Nike considers its competitive strengths to be the design and marketing of fine athletic shoes. Nike outsources the production of shoes it designs to non-Nike-owned factories worldwide.

CAUTIONARY NOTES ABOUT STRUCTURE

7. Identify two cautions about the effect of organizational structures on people.

This chapter has identified the purposes of structure, the processes of organizational design, and the dimensions and contexts that must be considered in structure. In addition, it has looked at forces and trends in organizational design. Two cautionary notes are important for the student of organizational behavior. First, an organizational structure may be weak or deficient. In general, if the structure is out of alignment with its contextual variables, one or more of the following four symptoms appears. First, decision making is delayed because the hierarchy is overloaded and too much information is being funneled through one or two channels. Second, decision making lacks quality, because information linkages are not providing the correct information to the right person in the right format. Third, the organization does not respond innovatively to a changing environment, especially when coordinated effort is lacking across departments. Fourth, a great deal of conflict is evident when departments are working against one another rather than working for the strategies and goals of the organization as a whole; the structure is often at fault.

The second caution is that the personality of the chief executive may adversely affect the structure of the organization.[46] Five dysfunctional combinations of personality and organization have been identified: the paranoid, the depressive, the dramatic, the compulsive, and the schizoid.[47] Each of these personality–organization constellations can create problems for the people who work in the organization. For example, in a paranoid constellation, people are suspicious of each other, and distrust in working relationships may interfere with effective communication and task accomplishment. For another example, in a depressive constellation, people feel depressed and inhibited in their work activities, which can lead to low levels of productivity and task accomplishment.

MANAGERIAL IMPLICATIONS: FITTING PEOPLE AND STRUCTURES TOGETHER

Organizations are complex social systems composed of numerous interrelated components. They can be complicated to understand. Managers who design, develop, and improve organizations must have a mastery of the basic concepts related to the anatomy and processes of organizational functioning. It is essential for executives at the top to have a clear concept of how the organization can be differentiated and then integrated into a cohesive whole.

People can work better in organizations if they understand how their jobs and departments relate to other jobs and teams in the organization. An understanding of the whole organization enables people to better relate their contribution to the overall mission of the organization and to compensate for structural deficiencies that may exist in the organization.

Different structural configurations place unique demands on the people who work within them. The diversity of people in work organizations suggests that some people are better suited for a simple structure, others are better suited to a professional bureaucracy, and still others are most productive in an adhocracy. Organizational structures are not independent of the people who work within them. This is especially true as organizations become more global in their orientation.

Managers must pay attention to the technology of the organization's work, the amount of change occurring in the organization's environment, and the regulatory pressures created by governmental agencies as the managers design effective organizations and subunits to meet emerging international demands and a diverse, multicultural workforce.

Looking Back

American Red Cross Disaster Response Field Organizations

American Red Cross volunteers are on twenty-four-hour call for disaster duty and are required to work one twelve-hour shift (5 A.M. to 5 P.M. or 5 P.M. to 5 A.M.) per month. Volunteers spring into action every time the disaster duty volunteer receives a call from a fire department or emergency operation center because of a natural or human-made disaster. A Red Cross volunteer captain then builds a disaster response field organization to address the specific emergency or disaster. The field organization's basic functions are management, direct services, internal support services, and external support services.[48] The Red Cross captain is the volunteer in charge of disaster field operations who calls up the required force of trained volunteers, drives the American Red Cross emergency response vehicle to the scene, and serves as liaison with the commander of the emergency operation.

Volunteers must be trained in disaster relief functions before they can be part of a disaster response field organization. Regularly scheduled training covers the administration and management of disaster operations; delivery of direct services including disaster health services, disaster mental health services, disaster welfare inquiry, family services, and mass care; internal support services such as accounting, building and repair, communication, damage assessment, logistics, records and reports, and disaster computer operations; and external support services such as fund-raising, public affairs, and liaison activities with government, labor, and other volunteer agencies. The captain and other volunteers provide assistance to emergency workers and clothes, food, and shelter for families; they stay on the scene until all needs are met. Once the captain determines that the operation is complete, he or she releases other Red Cross volunteers and files the appropriate reports and paperwork. At that point, this Red Cross disaster response field organization designed, built, and operated for a specific emergency or disaster no longer exists.

CHAPTER SUMMARY

1. Three basic types of differentiation occur in organizations: horizontal, vertical, and spatial.
2. The greater the complexity of an organization because of its degree of differentiation, the greater the need for integration.
3. Formalization, centralization, specialization, standardization, complexity, and hierarchy of authority are the six basic design dimensions in an organization.
4. Simple structure, machine bureaucracy, professional bureaucracy, divisionalized form, and adhocracy are five structural configurations of an organization.
5. The contextual variables important to organizational design are size, technology, environment, and strategy and goals.
6. Life cycles, globalization, changes in information-processing technologies, and demands on

process capabilities are forces reshaping organizations today.

7. New, emerging organizational structures differ from the traditional ones.

8. Organizational structures may be inherently weak, or chief executives may create personality–organization constellations that adversely affect employees.

KEY TERMS

organizational design   417

organizational structure   417

contextual variables   417

differentiation   419

integration   421

formalization   423

centralization   423

specialization   423

standardization   423

complexity   423

hierarchy of authority   423

simple structure   424

machine bureaucracy   426

professional bureaucracy   426

divisionalized form   426

adhocracy   427

technological interdependence   430

environment   431

task environment   432

environmental uncertainty   433

organizational life cycle   436

REVIEW QUESTIONS

1. Define the processes of differentiation and integration.
2. Describe the six basic dimensions of organizational design.
3. Discuss five structural configurations from the chapter.
4. Discuss the effects of the four contextual variables on the basic design dimensions.

5. Identify four forces that are reshaping organizations today.
6. Discuss the nature of emerging organizational structures.
7. List four symptoms of structural weakness and five unhealthy personality–organization combinations.

DISCUSSION AND COMMUNICATION QUESTIONS

1. How would you describe the organization you work for (or your college) on each of the basic design dimensions? For example, is it a very formal organization or an informal organization?
2. Do the size, technology, and mission of your organization directly affect you? How?
3. Who are your organization's competitors? What changes do you see in information technology where you work?
4. Does your company show any one or more of the four symptoms of structural deficiency discussed at the end of the chapter?
5. (communication question) Write a memo classifying and describing the structural configuration of

your university based on the five choices in Table 14.2. Do you need more information than you have to be comfortable with your classification and description? Where could you get the information?

6. (communication question) Interview an administrator in your college or university about possible changes in size (Will the college or university get bigger? smaller?) and technology (Is the college or university making a significant investment in information technology?). What effects does the administrator anticipate from these changes? Be prepared to present your results orally to the class.

ETHICS QUESTIONS

1. For what types of individual behavior is it ethical for an organization to have formal rules and regulations? For what types of individual behavior is it unethical for an organization to have formal rules and regulations?

2. Should legal limits be set to prevent large companies from engaging in very competitive behavior to drive small companies out of business?

3. As an organization changes its structure over time, how much commitment should it show to employees who need to be retrained to fit into the new system? Or is it acceptable for the organization to hire new people to fit the new structure?

4. Suppose an employee complains about organizational design problems and suggests a solution. The organization is redesigned accordingly, but that employee's department is eliminated. Is it ethical for the company to terminate the employee? Should the company always make room for a person who has a beneficial idea for the organization?

Experiential Exercises

14.1 Words-in-Sentences Company

Purpose: To design an organization for a particular task and carry through to production; to compare design elements with effectiveness.

Group Size: Any number of groups of six to fourteen persons.

Time Required: Fifty to ninety minutes.

Related Topics: Dynamics within groups, work motivation.

Background

You are a small company that manufactures words and then packages them in meaningful English-language sentences. Market research has established that sentences of at least three words but not more than six words are in demand. Therefore, packaging, distribution, and sales should be set up for three- to six-word sentences.

The "words-in-sentences" (WIS) industry is highly competitive; several new firms have recently entered what appears to be an expanding market. Since raw materials, technology, and pricing are all standard for the industry, your ability to compete depends on two factors: (1) volume and (2) quality.

Your Task

Your group must design and participate in running a WIS company. You should design your organization to be as efficient as possible during each ten-minute production run. After the first production run, you will have an opportunity to reorganize your company if you want.

Raw Materials

For each production you will be given a "raw material word or phrase." The letters found in the word or phrase serve as raw materials available to produce new words in sentences. For example, if the raw material word is "organization," you could produce the words and sentence: "Nat ran to a zoo."

Production Standards

Several rules must be followed in producing "words-in-sentences." If these rules are not followed, your output will not meet production specifications and will not pass quality-control inspection.

1. The same letter may appear only as often in a manufactured word as it appears in the raw material word or phrase; for example, "organization" has two o's. Thus, "zoo" is legitimate, but not "zoonosis." It has too many o's and s's.

2. Raw material letters can be used again in different manufactured words.

3. A manufactured word may be used only once in a sentence and in only one sentence during a production run; if a word—for example, "a"—is used once in a sentence, it is out of stock.

4. A new word may not be made by adding "s" to form the plural of an already manufactured word.

5. A word is defined by its spelling, not its meaning.

6. Nonsense words or nonsense sentences are unacceptable.

7. All words must be in the English language.

8. Names and places are acceptable.

9. Slang is not acceptable.

Measuring Performance

The output of your WIS company is measured by the total number of acceptable words that are packaged in sentences. The sentences must be legible, listed on no more than two sheets of paper, and handed to the Quality Control Review Board at the completion of each production run.

Delivery

Delivery must be made to the Quality Control Review Board thirty seconds after the end of each production run, or else all points are lost.

Quality Control

If any word in a sentence does not meet the standards set forth above, all the words in the sentence will be rejected. The Quality Control Review Board (composed of one member from each company) is the final arbiter of acceptability. In the event of a tie on the Review Board, a coin toss will determine the outcome.

Exercise Schedule	Unit Time	Total Time
1. Form groups, organizations, and assign workplaces Groups should have between six and fourteen members (if there are more than eleven or twelve persons in a group, assign one or two observers). Each group is a company.	2–5 min	2–5 min
2. Read "Background" Ask the instructor about any points that need clarification.	5 min	10 min
3. Design organizations Design your organizations using as many members as you see fit to produce your "words-in-sentences." You may want to consider the following. a. What is your objective? b. What technology would work here? c. What type of division of labor is effective? Assign one member of your group to serve on the Quality Review Board. This person may also take part in production runs.	7–15 min	14–25 min
4. Production Run #1 The instructor will hand each WIS company a sheet with a raw material word or pharase. When the instructor announces "Begin production," you are to manufacture as many words as possible and package them in sentences for delivery to the Quality Control Review Board. You will have ten minutes. When the instructor announces "Stop production," you will have thirty seconds to deliver your output to the Quality Control Review Board. Output received after thirty seconds does not meet the delivery schedule and will not be counted.	7–10 min	21–35 min
5. Quality Review Board meets, evaulates output While that is going on, groups discuss what happened during the previous production run.	5–10 min	26–45 min
6. Companies evaluate performance and type of organization Groups may choose to restructure and reorganize for the next production run.	5–10 min	31–55 min
7. Production run #2 (same as Production Run #1)	7–10 min	38–65 min
8. Quality Review Board meets Quality Review Board evaluates output while groups draw their organization charts (for Runs #1 and #2) on the board.	5–10 min	43–75 min

	Unit Time	Total Time
	7–15 min	50–90 min

9. **Class discussion**

Instructor leads discussion of exercise as a whole. Discuss the following questions:

a. What were the companies' scores for Runs #1 and #2?

b. What type of structure did the "winning" company have? Did it reorganize for Run #2?

c. What type of task was there? Technology? Environment?

d. What would Joan Woodward, Henry Mintzberg, Frederick Taylor, Lawrence and Lorsch, or Burns and Stalker say about WIS Company organization?

SOURCE: "Words-in-Sentences Company" in Dorothy Marcic, *Organizational Behavior: Experiences and Cases*, 4th ed. (St. Paul: West, 1995), 303–305. Reprinted by permission.

14.2 Design and Build a Castle

This exercise is intended to give your group an opportunity to design an organization and produce a product.

Your group is one of three product-development teams working within the research and development division of the GTM (General Turret and Moat) Corporation. GTM has decided to enter new markets by expanding the product line to include fully designed and produced castles, rather than selling components to other companies, as it has in the past.

Each of the three teams has been asked to design a castle for the company to produce and sell. Given its limited resources, the company cannot put more than one design on the market. Therefore, the company will have to decide which of the three designs it will use and will discard the other two designs.

Your task is to develop and design a castle. You will have forty-five minutes to produce a finished product. At the end of this period, several typical consumers, picked by scientific sampling techniques, will judge which is the best design. Before the consumers make their choice, each group will have one to two minutes to make a sales presentation.

Step 1. Each group is designated either 1, 2, or 3. The instructor will provide group members a memorandum

appropriate for their group. One (or two for larger groups) observer is selected for each group. Observers read their materials.

Step 2. Groups design their organization in order to complete their goal.

Step 3. Each group designs its own castle and draws it on newsprint.

Step 4. "Typical consumers" (may be observers) tour building locations and hear sales pitches. Judges caucus to determine winner.

Step 5. Groups meet again and write up their central goal statement. They also write the organization chart on newsprint with the goal written beneath. These are posted around the room.

Step 6. Instructor leads a class discussion on how the different memos affected organization design. Which design seemed most effective for this task?

NOTE: Your instructor may allow more time and actually have you *build* the castles.

SOURCE: "Design and Build a Castle" from Dorothy Marcic and Richard C. Housley, *Organizational Behavior: Experiences and Cases* (St. Paul: West, 1989), 221–225. Reprinted by permission.

For more practice exercises, consult the fifth edition of *Organizational Behavior: Experiences and Cases* by Dorothy Marcic and Joseph Seltzer (South-Western, 1998).

Learning Objectives

After reading this chapter, you should be able to do the following:

1. Define *organizational culture* and explain its three levels. *p. 448*

2. Identify the four functions of culture within an organization. *p. 455*

3. Explain the relationship between organizational culture and performance. *p. 456*

4. Contrast the characteristics of adaptive and non-adaptive cultures. *p. 457*

5. Describe five ways leaders reinforce organizational culture. *p. 458*

6. Describe the three stages of organizational socialization and the ways culture is communicated in each step. *p. 460*

7. Identify ways of assessing organizational culture. *p. 463*

8. Explain actions managers can take to change organizational culture. *p. 466*

15

Organizational Culture

Thinking Ahead

A Culture of Family, Fun, and Luv

When you fly Southwest Airlines, chances are that you will hear the traditional instructions to passengers sung to the tune of "Under the Boardwalk" or "I Heard It through the Grapevine." An in-flight contest may be held to see which passenger's socks display the most holes. Fun serves a function at Southwest. Harried travelers can become anxious and cranky. Humor keeps them calm and happy.

You may see CEO Herb Kelleher dressed up like a chicken or as Elvis Presley. He is a kisser and a hugger and believes so strongly in affection that Southwest's ticker symbol is LUV. He's also been known to load baggage and serve peanuts to passengers. Herb also arm-wrestled a potential litigant to forestall a possible lawsuit.

Love is the way Southwest's employees are encouraged to treat each other and passengers. Family, fun, and altruism are key values. The walls of corporate headquarters are covered with snapshots of people at parties—all of them Southwest family. To its employees, Southwest conveys the message that work is important, and it shouldn't be spoiled by seriousness. Preserving Southwest's culture is serious business, though—fifty managers from all over the company join Colleen Barrett, executive vice-president–customers, in approving plans designed to maintain Southwest's culture and values.

Teamwork is another value. It takes efficient teams to turn two out of three flights around in twenty minutes or less with fewer gate attendants than its competitors. And Southwest flies around 2,300 flights per day. Teamwork also extends to Southwest's favorite charity, Ronald McDonald houses for children, where groups of employees donate hours of their time to help.

Southwest's corporate culture is highly visible and translates into unsurpassed customer service. It yields another bonus as well. Southwest ranked No. 1 in *Fortune*'s 1998 list of America's 100 Best Companies to work for.[1]

THE KEY ROLE OF ORGANIZATIONAL CULTURE

1. Define *organizational culture* and explain its three levels.

The concept of organizational culture has its roots in cultural anthropology. Just as there are cultures in larger human society, there seem to be cultures within organizations. These cultures are similar to societal cultures. They are shared, communicated through symbols, and passed down from generation to generation of employees.

The concept of cultures in organizations was alluded to as early as the Hawthorne studies, which described work group culture. The topic came into its own during the early 1970s, when managers and researchers alike began to search for keys to survival for organizations in a competitive and turbulent environment. Then, in the early 1980s, several books on corporate culture were published, including Deal and Kennedy's *Corporate Cultures*,[2] Ouchi's *Theory Z*,[3] and Peters and Waterman's *In Search of Excellence*.[4] These books found wide audiences, and research began in earnest on the elusive topic of organizational cultures. Executives indicated that these cultures were real and could be managed.[5]

Culture and Its Levels

organizational (corporate) culture
A pattern of basic assumptions that are considered valid and that are taught to new members as the way to perceive, think, and feel in the organization.

Many definitions of *organizational culture* have been proposed. Most of them agree that there are several levels of culture and that these levels differ in terms of their visibility and their ability to be changed. The definition adopted in this chapter is that *organizational (corporate) culture* is a pattern of basic assumptions that are considered valid and that are taught to new members as the way to perceive, think, and feel in the organization.[6]

Edgar Schein, in his comprehensive book on organizational culture and leadership, suggests that organizational culture has three levels. His view of culture is presented in Figure 15.1. The levels range from visible artifacts and creations to testable values to invisible and even preconscious basic assumptions. To achieve a complete understanding of an organization's culture, all three levels must be studied.

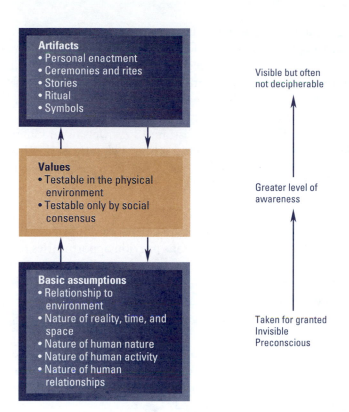

SOURCE: From Edgar H. Schein, *Organizational Culture and Leadership: A Dynamic View*. Copyright © 1985 Jossey-Bass Inc. Reprinted by permission of Jossey-Bass, Inc., a subsidiary of John Wiley & Sons, Inc.

Artifacts

Symbols of culture in the physical and social work environment are called *artifacts*. They are the most visible and accessible level of culture. The key to understanding culture through artifacts lies in figuring out what they mean. Artifacts are also the most frequently studied manifestation of organizational culture, perhaps because of their accessibility. Among the artifacts of culture are personal enactment, ceremonies and rites, stories, rituals, and symbols.[7]

Personal Enactment   Culture can be understood, in part, through an examination of the behavior of organization members. Personal enactment is behavior that reflects the organization's values. In particular, personal enactment by the top managers provides insight into these values. If, for example, customer service is highly valued, then the CEO may be seen going the extra mile for the customer, as did the late Sam Walton of Wal-Mart. He reinforced quality service by visiting stores often and recognizing individual employees. The CEO transmits values to others in the organization through modeling appropriate behavior.

During the 1980s, when Boone Pickens was CEO of Mesa Petroleum (now part of Pioneer Natural Resources), he valued physical fitness for its

artifacts
Symbols of culture in the physical and social work environment.

psychological and spiritual benefits and believed a physically fit workforce would lead to economic benefits for the company. He established a fitness center for employees and was a regular participant at the center. His presence resulted in fitness participation by three-quarters of Mesa's employees—and cost savings for the company.[8]

Modeled behavior is a powerful learning tool for employees, as Bandura's social learning theory demonstrated.[9] As we saw in Chapter 5, individuals learn vicariously by observing others' behavior and patterning their own behavior similarly. The values reflected in that behavior can permeate the entire employee population.

Ceremonies and Rites Relatively elaborate sets of activities that are enacted time and again on important occasions are known as organizational ceremonies and rites.[10] These occasions provide opportunities to reward and recognize employees whose behavior is congruent with the values of the company. Ceremonies and rites send a message that individuals who both espouse and exhibit corporate values are heroes to be admired.

The ceremonies also bond organization members together. Southwestern Bell (now part of SBC Communications) emphasized the importance of management training to the company. Training classes were kicked off by a high-ranking executive (a rite of renewal), and completion of the classes was signaled by a graduation ceremony (a rite of passage). Six kinds of rites in organizations have been identified:[11]

1. *Rites of passage* show that an individual's status has changed. Retirement dinners are an example.
2. *Rites of enhancement* reinforce the achievement of individuals. An example is the awarding of certificates to sales contest winners.
3. *Rites of renewal* emphasize change in the organization and commitment to learning and growth. An example is the opening of a new corporate training center.
4. *Rites of integration* unite diverse groups or teams within the organization and renew commitment to the larger organization. Company functions such as annual picnics fall into this category.
5. *Rites of conflict reduction* focus on dealing with conflicts or disagreements that arise naturally in organizations. Examples are grievance hearings and the negotiation of union contracts.
6. *Rites of degradation* are used by some organizations to visibly punish persons who fail to adhere to values and norms of behavior. Some CEOs, for example, are replaced quite publicly for unethical conduct or for failure to achieve organizational goals. In some Japanese organizations, employees who perform poorly are given ribbons of shame as punishment.

Wal-Mart's annual meeting is an important cultural ceremony. Almost 20,000 shareholders, associates (the company's preferred term for employees), and analysts attend the Wal-Mart annual meeting. Celebrities such as Nolan Ryan, Trisha Yearwood, Joe Montana, and Barbara Bush are featured.

Although the meeting doesn't begin until 10 A.M., people start arriving at 7 A.M. for the extravaganza held for the benefit of the associates. Because it is the primary vehicle for perpetuating Wal-Mart's culture, videos of the meeting are played in Wal-Mart stores to motivate associates who are unable to attend.

The annual meeting is like a big family reunion. Patriotism is a common theme. The associates hear stories and watch videos about Wal-Mart's "Buy American" program, which has rescued jobs in small towns and created new ones. Associates who go the "extra mile" for customers are recognized and rewarded. One associate delivered a Sega Genesis on his own time on Christmas Eve, and another group of employees replaced presents for a family whose home was burglarized. Each example points to the generosity and compassion of Wal-Mart associates.[12]

Stories Some researchers have argued that the most effective way to reinforce organizational values is through stories.[13] As they are told and retold, stories give meaning and identity to organizations and are especially helpful in orienting new employees. Part of the strength of organizational stories is that the listeners are left to draw their own conclusions—a powerful communication tool.[14]

Stories reinforce such values as customer service. IBM once had a client company whose machine went down one afternoon in the midst of payroll processing. Paychecks were to be distributed the following day. As the story goes, IBM flew in another machine and personnel, who worked all night to ensure that the client's payroll was distributed on time.[15]

Research by Joanne Martin and her colleagues has indicated that certain themes appear in stories across different types of organizations:[16]

1. *Stories about the boss.* These stories may reflect whether the boss is "human" or how the boss reacts to mistakes.

2. *Stories about getting fired.* Events leading to employee firings are recounted.

3. *Stories about how the company deals with employees who have to relocate.* These stories relate to the company's actions toward employees who have to move—whether the company is helpful and takes family and other personal concerns into account.

4. *Stories about whether lower-level employees can rise to the top.* Often, these stories describe a person who started out at the bottom and eventually became the CEO.

5. *Stories about how the company deals with crisis situations.* The example of the client crisis at IBM shows how the company overcomes obstacles.

6. *Stories about how status considerations work when rules are broken.* When Tom Watson, Sr., was CEO of IBM, he was once confronted by a security guard because he was not wearing an ID badge.

These are the themes that can emerge when stories are passed down. The information from these stories serves to guide the behavior of organization members.

To be effective cultural tools, stories must be credible. You can't tell a story about your flat corporate hierarchy and then have reserved parking spaces for managers. Stories that aren't backed by reality can lead to cynicism and mistrust.

Effective stories, however, can reinforce culture and create renewed energy. Industrial Light and Magic is the home of director and producer George Lucas and the birthplace of such blockbusters as *Star Wars* and *Forrest Gump.* Stories of the company's legendary accomplishments are used to reinforce the creative culture and to rally the troops. When Gail Currey, head of the company's digital division, finds her 300 designers are grumbling, she reminds them of how they did *Gump* when everyone else said it was impossible and what a hit the film was. The geniuses head back to their computers to add to the company's success.[17]

Rituals Everyday organizational practices that are repeated over and over are rituals. They are usually unwritten, but they send a clear message about "the way we do things around here." While some companies insist that people address each other by their titles (Mr., Mrs., Ms., Miss) and surnames to reinforce a professional image, others prefer that employees operate on a first-name basis—from the top manager on down. Hewlett-Packard values open communication, so its employees address one another by first names only.

The Charles Machine Works, producer of Ditch Witch underground excavation equipment, values informality, teamwork, and a flat organizational structure. One ritual practiced in the company is that workers are referred to as employees or team members, not subordinates. The idea is that implying that one person is lower than others is in opposition to the value placed on teamwork.

As everyday practices, rituals reinforce the organizational culture. Insiders who commonly practice the rituals may be unaware of their subtle influence, but outsiders recognize it easily.

Symbols Symbols communicate organizational culture by unspoken messages. Southwest Airlines has used symbols in several ways. During its early years, the airline emphasized its customer service value by using the heart symbol (the "Love" airline) and love bites (peanuts). More recently, the airline has taken on the theme of fun. Flight attendants wear casual sports clothes in corporate colors. Low fares are "fun fares," and weekend getaways are "fun packs." Some aircraft are painted to resemble Shamu the whale, underscoring the fun image.

Symbols are representative of organizational identity and membership to employees. Nike's trademark "swoosh" is proudly tattooed above the ankles of some Nike employees. Apple Computer employees readily identify themselves as "Apple People." Symbols are used to build solidarity in the organizational culture.[18]

Symbols may be only mental images. At Southwestern Bell, company loyalty was valued. Longtime company employees were referred to as "bleeding blue and gold" (company colors).

Personal enactment, rites and ceremonies, stories, rituals, and symbols serve to reinforce the values that are the next level of culture.

Values

Values are the second, and deeper, level of culture. They reflect a person's underlying beliefs of what should be or should not be. Values are often consciously articulated, both in conversation and in a company's mission statement or annual report. However, there may be a difference between a company's *espoused values* (what the members say they value) and its *enacted values* (values reflected in the way the members actually behave).[19] Values also may be reflected in the behavior of individuals, which is an artifact of culture.

One company that emphasizes values is Levi Strauss. Its values are espoused in a formal aspirations statement and are enacted by its employees from the CEO down. At Levi Strauss, the values include diversity, ethical behavior, recognition for individuals and teams, and empowerment, among others. The result of practicing these values has been positive. Employees' work is more creative and entrepreneurial. Business has never been better. One-third of the reward package for managers depends on their ability to manage "aspirationally"—based on the company's aspirations.

Values underlie the adaptable and innovative culture at Levi Strauss. As guides for behavior, they are reinforced in the aspirations statement and in the reward system of the organization. Workforce diversity is valued at Levi Strauss. A former strong supporter of the Boy Scouts of America, the company discontinued its funding after the Scouts were shown to discriminate on the basis of sexual orientation. Mary Gross, a Levi Strauss spokesperson, expressed the company's position on valuing diversity: "One of the family values of this company is treating people who are different from you the same as you'd like to be treated. Tolerance is a pretty important family value."[20]

Some organizational cultures are characterized by values that support healthy lifestyle behaviors. When the workplace culture values worker health and psychological needs, there is enhanced potential for high performance and improved well-being.[21] One such culture is that of Clif Bar, Inc., a maker of energy bars. Clif Bar's culture may represent the extreme in terms of promoting fitness. It attracts and hires individuals who are sports enthusiasts, and provides them with a culture that shares those values. Organizational Reality 15.1 shows the lengths that Clif Bar goes to in order to maintain its fitness-oriented culture.

Assumptions

Assumptions are the deeply held beliefs that guide behavior and tell members of an organization how to perceive and think about things. As the deepest and most fundamental level of an organization's culture, according to Edgar Schein, they are the essence of culture. They are so strongly held that a member behaving in any fashion that would violate them would be

espoused values
What members of an organization say they value.

enacted values
Values reflected in the way individuals actually behave.

assumptions
Deeply held beliefs that guide behavior and tell members of an organization how to perceive and think about things.

ORGANIZATIONAL REALITY 15.1

A Culture of Climbers

At noon or on breaks, you'll find the workers at Clif Bar, Inc., an energy-bar maker, climbing the walls—literally. There is a twenty-two-foot artificial rock climbing wall in the office, along with a corporate gym. The company's sixty-five workers enjoy fitness perks like the assistance of three part-time fitness trainers and long midafternoon breaks for "spinning" classes, weightlifting, and other workout activities. Clif Bar also pays for spa, ski, and camping weekends for employees and their families. The company has trained forty-two staffers and flown them all over the country to bicycle in AIDS Rides.

Commitment to fitness is corporate culture at Clif Bar. The company began as Kali Sport-Naturals in 1986, and Clif Bar was developed as an alternative to PowerBar, the market leading energy bar. Founder Gary Erickson added a strategic marketing twist by focusing on Clif Bar's "all-natural" ingredients, as opposed to the refined sugar and processed foods in PowerBar. The twist worked—the company has projected sales of $22 million and is so busy that employees are finding it tougher to take breaks for wall climbing.

The "jock shop" culture is attractive to many and is a boon to recruiting in the worker-friendly San Francisco Bay area. The company is a haven for bikers, climbers, and runners. "People come in here pretty excited about the culture," says Sheryl O'Loughlin, a marathon runner who left Quaker Oats to become marketing manager at Clif Bar. In addition to fitness, Clif Bar's culture promotes the value of self-esteem. Cofounder Lisa Thomas says, "If you have high self-esteem, you're more productive because you feel good about yourself."

Employees will need both fitness and self-esteem to tackle the competition in the energy-bar market. Clif Bar is number three behind PowerBar and Balance Bar. Clif Bar's answer has been rapid expansion; nevertheless, the founders insist the corporate culture is more important than how big the company wants to be. The climbing wall symbolizes pushing your limits—a nice tie-in with Clif Bar's packaging, which shows a climber on a mountainside.

Discussion Question

1. What are the advantages of Clif Bar's culture? The disadvantages?

SOURCES: J. S. Lublin, "Climbing Walls on Company Time," *The Wall Street Journal*, December 1, 1998, B1, B14; J. Rosenbloom, "Follow the Leader," *Inc.* 19 (1997): 83–84. Permission conveyed through Copyright Clearance Center, Inc.

unthinkable. Another characteristic of assumptions is that they are often unconscious. Organization members may not be aware of their assumptions and may be reluctant or unable to discuss them or change them.

Chaparral Steel (part of Texas Industries) is a small steel manufacturer that outperforms all other domestic and foreign steel companies in amount of steel produced per person. Located in Midlothian, Texas, the company has fewer than 1,000 employees. Its success is due, in large part, to its assumptions about people. Chaparral Steel's values reflect three basic assumptions: (1) that people are basically good, which is reflected in the company's emphasis on trust; (2) that people want opportunities to learn and grow, which is seen in the value placed on education and training; and (3) that people are motivated by opportunities to learn and by work that is challenging and enjoyable, which is reflected in Chaparral's goal-setting program.

FUNCTIONS AND EFFECTS OF ORGANIZATIONAL CULTURE

In an organization, culture serves four basic functions. First, culture provides a sense of identity to members and increases their commitment to the organization.[22] When employees internalize the values of the company, they find their work intrinsically rewarding and identify with their fellow workers. Motivation is enhanced, and employees are more committed.[23]

Second, culture is a sense-making device for organization members. It provides a way for employees to interpret the meaning of organizational events.[24]

Third, culture reinforces the values in the organization. During the 1980s, for example, at the Commercial Nuclear Fuel Division of the former Westinghouse Electric Corporation, a cultural change was undertaken to achieve total quality as the number one value. All employees were involved in creating the quality plan, which won the coveted Baldrige National Quality Award.[25]

Finally, culture serves as a control mechanism for shaping behavior. Norms that guide behavior are part of culture. At Westinghouse, employee suggestions increased fivefold following the emphasis on total quality. It became a norm to think of ways to improve processes at the division.

The effects of organizational culture are hotly debated by organizational behaviorists and researchers. It seems that managers attest strongly to the positive effects of culture in organizations, but it is difficult to quantify these effects. John Kotter and James Heskett have reviewed three theories about the relationship between organizational culture and performance and the evidence that either supports or refutes these theories.[26] The three are the strong culture perspective, the fit perspective, and the adaptation perspective.

The Strong Culture Perspective

The strong culture perspective states that organizations with "strong" cultures perform better than other organizations.[27] A **strong culture** is an organizational culture with a consensus on the values that drive the company and with an intensity that is recognizable even to outsiders. Thus, a strong culture is deeply held and widely shared. It also is highly resistant to change. One example of a strong culture is IBM's. Its culture is one we are all familiar with: conservative, with a loyal workforce and an emphasis on customer service.

Strong cultures are thought to facilitate performance for three reasons. First, these cultures are characterized by goal alignment; that is, all employees share common goals. Second, strong cultures create a high level of motivation because of the values shared by the members. Third, strong cultures provide control without the oppressive effects of a bureaucracy.

To test the strong culture hypothesis, Kotter and Heskett selected 207 firms from a wide variety of industries. They used a questionnaire to calcu-

2. Identify the four functions of culture within an organization.

strong culture
An organizational culture with a consensus on the values that drive the company and with an intensity that is recognizable even to outsiders.

late a culture strength index for each firm, and they correlated that index with the firm's economic performance over a twelve-year period. They concluded that strong cultures were associated with positive long-term economic performance, but only modestly.

3. Explain the relationship between organizational culture and performance.

There are also two perplexing questions about the strong culture perspectives. First, what can be said about evidence showing that strong economic performance can create strong cultures, rather than the reverse? Second, what if the strong culture leads the firm down the wrong path? Sears, for example, is an organization with a strong culture, but in the 1980s, it focused inward, ignoring competition and consumer preferences and damaging its performance. Changing Sears' strong but stodgy culture has been a tough task, with financial performance only recently showing an upward trend.[28]

The Fit Perspective

The "fit" perspective argues that a culture is good only if it fits the industry's or the firm's strategy. For example, a culture that values a traditional hierarchical structure and stability would not work well in the computer manufacturing industry, which demands fast response and a lean, flat organization. Three particular characteristics of an industry may affect culture: the competitive environment, customer requirements, and societal expectations.[29] In the computer industry, firms face a highly competitive environment, customers who require highly reliable products, and a society that expects state-of-the-art technology and high-quality service. These characteristics affect the culture in computer manufacturing companies.

A study of twelve large U.S. firms indicated that cultures consistent with industry conditions help managers make better decisions. It also indicated that cultures need not change as long as the industry doesn't change. If the industry does change, however, many cultures change too slowly to avoid negative effects on firms' performance.[30]

The fit perspective is useful in explaining short-term performance but not long-term performance. It also indicates that it is difficult to change culture quickly, especially if the culture is widely shared and deeply held. But it doesn't explain how firms can adapt to environmental change.

The Adaptation Perspective

adaptive culture
An organizational culture that encourages confidence and risk taking among employees, has leadership that produces change, and focuses on the changing needs of customers.

The third theory about culture and performance is the adaptation perspective. Its theme is that only cultures that help organizations adapt to environmental change are associated with excellent performance. An *adaptive culture* is a culture that encourages confidence and risk taking among employees,[31] has leadership that produces change,[32] and focuses on the changing needs of customers.[33] 3M is a company with an adaptive culture, in that it encourages new product ideas from all levels within the company.

To test the adaptation perspective, Kotter and Heskett interviewed industry analysts about the cultures of twenty-two firms. The contrast between adaptive cultures and nonadaptive cultures was striking. The results of the study are summarized in Table 15.1.

	Adaptive Organizational Cultures	Nonadaptive Organizational Cultures
Core values	Most managers care deeply about customers, stockholders, and employees. They also strongly value people and processes that can create useful change (e.g., leadership up and down the management hierarchy).	Most managers care mainly about themselves, their immediate work group, or some product (or technology) associated with that work group. They value the orderly and risk-reducing management process much more highly than leadership initiatives.
Common behavior	Managers pay close attention to all their constituencies, especially customers, and initiate change when needed to serve their legitimate interests, even if that entails taking some risks.	Managers tend to behave somewhat insularly, politically, and bureaucratically. As a result, they do not change their strategies quickly to adjust to or take advantage of changes in their business environments.

Table 15.1
Adaptive versus Nonadaptive Organizational Cultures

Adaptive cultures facilitate change to meet the needs of three groups of constituents: stockholders, customers, and employees. Nonadaptive cultures are characterized by cautious management that tries to protect its own interests. Adaptive firms showed significantly better long-term economic performance in Kotter and Heskett's study. One contrast that can be made is between Hewlett-Packard (HP), a high performer, and Xerox, a lower performer. The industry analysts viewed HP as valuing excellent leadership more than Xerox did and as valuing all three key constituencies more than Xerox did. Economic performance from 1977 through 1988 suported this difference: HP's index of annual net income growth was 40.2, as compared to Xerox's 13.1. Kotter and Heskett concluded that the cultures that promote long-term performance are those that are most adaptive.

Given that high-performing cultures are adaptive ones, it is important to know how managers can develop adaptive cultures. In the next section, we will examine the leader's role in managing organizational culture.

4. Contrast the characteristics of adaptive and nonadaptive cultures.

THE LEADER'S ROLE IN SHAPING AND REINFORCING CULTURE

5. Describe five ways leaders reinforce organizational culture.

According to Edgar Schein, leaders play crucial roles in shaping and reinforcing culture.[34] The five most important elements in managing culture are (1) what leaders pay attention to; (2) how leaders react to crises; (3) how leaders behave; (4) how leaders allocate rewards; and (5) how leaders hire and fire individuals.

What Leaders Pay Attention To

Leaders in an organization communicate their priorities, values, and beliefs through the themes that consistently emerge from what they focus on. These themes are reflected in what they notice, comment on, measure, and control. The late Ray Kroc, founder of McDonald's, paid attention to detail. He built the company on the basis of a vision of providing identical, high-quality hamburgers at low cost.[35] Through careful training, quality control, and even special measuring cups, he honed his company's expertise so that the Big Mac in Miami would be the same as the Big Mac in Moscow.

If leaders are consistent in what they pay attention to, measure, and control, employees receive clear signals about what is important in the organization. If, however, leaders are inconsistent, employees spend a lot of time trying to decipher and find meaning in the inconsistent signals.

How Leaders React to Crises

The way leaders deal with crises communicates a powerful message about culture. Emotions are heightened during a crisis, and learning is intense. When Lee Iacocca began his effort to turn Chrysler around, the company perceived itself to be in crisis. Iacocca appealed for a government bailout, framing his argument in such a way that a refusal would be seen as a lack of commitment to businesses and to America's competitive position.[36] Iacocca had articulated Chrysler's mission as protecting America's jobs, and his reaction to the crisis underscored Chrysler's value that the free enterprise system should be protected.

Difficult economic times present crises for many companies and illustrate their different values. Some organizations do everything possible to prevent laying off workers. Others may claim that employees are important but quickly institute major layoffs at the first signal of an economic downturn. Employees may perceive that the company shows its true colors in a crisis and thus may pay careful attention to the reactions of their leaders.

How Leaders Behave

Through role modeling, teaching, and coaching, leaders reinforce the values that support the organizational culture. Employees often emulate leaders' behavior and look to the leaders for cues to appropriate behavior. Many companies are encouraging employees to be more entrepreneurial—to take more initiative and be more innovative in their jobs. A study showed that if managers want employees to be more entrepreneurial, they must demonstrate such behaviors themselves.[37] This is the case with any cultural value. Employees observe the behavior of leaders to find out what the organization values.

How Leaders Allocate Rewards

To ensure that values are accepted, leaders should reward behavior that is consistent with the values. Some companies, for example, may claim that they use a pay-for-performance system that distributes rewards on the basis of performance. When the time comes for raises, however, the increases are awarded according to length of service with the company. Imagine the feelings of a high-performing newcomer who has heard leaders espouse the value of rewarding individual performance and then receives only a tiny raise.

Some companies may value teamwork. They form cross-functional teams and empower these teams to make important decisions. However, when performance is appraised, the criteria for rating employees focus on individual performance. This sends a confusing signal to employees about the company's culture: Is individual performance valued, or is teamwork the key?

How Leaders Hire and Fire Individuals

A powerful way that leaders reinforce culture is through the selection of newcomers to the organization. Leaders often unconsciously look for individuals who are similar to current organizational members in terms of values and assumptions. Some companies hire individuals on the recommendation of a current employee; this tends to perpetuate the culture because the new employees typically hold similar values. Promotion-from-within policies also serve to reinforce organizational culture.

The way a company fires an employee and the rationale behind the firing also communicate the culture. Some companies deal with poor performers by trying to find a place within the organization where they can perform better and make a contribution. Other companies seem to operate under the philosophy that those who cannot perform are out quickly.

The reasons for terminations may not be directly communicated to other employees, but curiosity leads to speculation. An employee who displays unethical behavior and is caught may simply be reprimanded even though such behavior is clearly against the organization's values. Other employees may view this as a failure to reinforce the values within the organization.

All of these elements are ways leaders shape the culture within the organization. From the Looking Ahead feature, you'll recall that Herb Kelleher, leader of Southwest Airlines, displays behavior that shapes Southwest's unique culture. A story of Kelleher's interaction with another airline's CEO vividly shows how his behavior helps form the company's culture. When Robert Crandall, then the CEO of American Airlines (and a Rhode Island native), asked him what he was going to do with the whale droppings from Southwest's freshly painted Shamu airplane, Kelleher's response was, "I am going to turn it into chocolate mousse and feed it to Yankees from Rhode

Island." To follow up, he sent a tub of chocolate mousse to Crandall's office, along with a king-size Shamu spoon. Kelleher's leadership has made humor and altruism two key values at Southwest Airlines.[38]

ORGANIZATIONAL SOCIALIZATION

organizational socialization
The process by which newcomers are transformed from outsiders to participating, effective members of the organization.

We have seen that leaders play key roles in shaping an organization's culture. Another process that perpetuates culture is the way it is handed down from generation to generation of employees. Newcomers learn the culture through *organizational socialization*—the process by which newcomers are transformed from outsiders to participating, effective members of the organization.[39] The process is also a vehicle for bringing newcomers into the organizational culture. As we saw earlier, cultural socialization begins with the careful selection of newcomers who are likely to reinforce the organizational culture.[40] Once selected, newcomers pass through the socialization process.

The Stages of the Socialization Process

6. Describe the three stages of organizational socialization and the ways culture is communicated in each step.

The organizational socialization process is generally described as having three stages: anticipatory socialization, encounter, and change and acquisition. Figure 15.2 presents a model of the process and the key concerns at

Figure 15.2
The Organizational Socialization Process: Stages and Outcomes

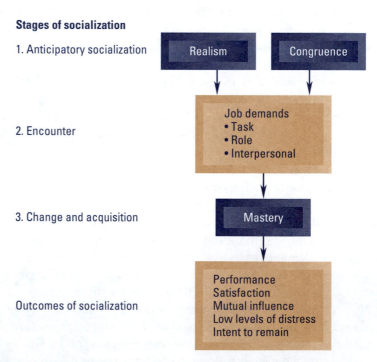

SOURCE: From "An Ethical Weather Report: Assessing the Organization's Ethical Climate" by John B. Cullen, et al. in "Organizational Dynamics," Autumn 1989. Copyright © 1989, with permission from Elsevier Science.

each stage of it.[41] It also describes the outcomes of the process, which will be discussed in the next section of the chapter.

Anticipatory Socialization *Anticipatory socialization*, the first stage, encompasses all of the learning that takes place prior to the newcomer's first day on the job. It includes the newcomer's expectations. The two key concerns at this stage are realism and congruence.

Realism is the degree to which a newcomer holds realistic expectations about the job and about the organization. One thing newcomers should receive information about during entry into the organization is the culture. Information about values at this stage can help newcomers begin to construct a scheme for interpreting their organizational experiences. A deeper understanding of the organization's culture will be possible through time and experience in the organization.

There are two types of *congruence* between an individual and an organization: congruence between the individual's abilities and the demands of the job, and the fit between the organization's values and the individual's values. Value congruence is particularly important for organizational culture. It is also important in terms of newcomer adjustment. Newcomers whose values match the company's values are more satisfied with their new jobs, adjust more quickly, and say they intend to remain with the firm longer.[42]

It has even been suggested that employees should be hired to fit the culture of the organization, not just the requirements of the job. This is practiced extensively in Korean chaebols, which are conglomerate groups. Each chaebol has a unique culture and selects newcomers in part on the basis of personality criteria. The Hanjin group, for example, looks for newcomers who exhibit patriotism and a desire to be of service to others. Korean Airlines (KAL) is a member of the Hanjin group, which also has other transportation subsidiaries. At KAL, employees are expected to act as civilian diplomats; they are required to master a foreign language and to go abroad at least once. Polished manners and refined language are required, and female employees are forbidden to wear jeans even off duty.[43]

Encounter The second stage of socialization, *encounter*, is when newcomers learn the tasks associated with the job, clarify their roles, and establish new relationships at work. This stage commences on the first day at work and is thought to encompass the first six to nine months on the new job. Newcomers face task demands, role demands, and interpersonal demands during this period.

Task demands involve the actual work performed. Learning to perform tasks is related to the organization's culture. In some organizations, newcomers are given considerable latitude to experiment with new ways to do the job, and creativity is valued. In others, newcomers are expected to learn the established procedures for their tasks. Newcomers may also need guidance from the culture about work hours. Is a value placed on putting in long hours, or is leaving work at 5 P.M. to spend time with family more the norm?

anticipatory socialization
The first socialization stage, which encompasses all of the learning that takes place prior to the newcomer's first day on the job.

encounter
The second socialization stage, in which the newcomer learns the tasks associated with the job, clarifies roles, and establishes new relationships at work.

Role demands involve the expectations placed on newcomers. Newcomers may not know exactly what is expected of them (role ambiguity) or may receive conflicting expectations from other individuals (role conflict). The way newcomers approach these demands depends in part on the culture of the organization. Are newcomers expected to operate with considerable uncertainty, or is the manager expected to clarify the newcomers' roles? Some cultures even put newcomers through considerable stress in the socialization process, including humility-inducing experiences, so newcomers will be more open to accepting the firm's values and norms. Long hours, tiring travel schedules, and an overload of work are part of some socialization practices.

Interpersonal demands arise from relationships at work. Politics, leadership style, and group pressure are interpersonal demands. All of them reflect the values and assumptions that operate within the organization. Most organizations have basic assumptions about the nature of human relationships. The Korean chaebol Lucky-Goldstar strongly values harmony in relationships and in society, and its decision-making policy emphasizes unanimity.

In the encounter stage, the expectations formed in anticipatory socialization may clash with the realities of the job. It is a time of facing the task, role, and interpersonal demands of the new job.

change and acquisition
The third socialization stage, in which the newcomer begins to master the demands of the job.

Change and Acquisition In the third and final stage of socialization, **change and acquisition**, newcomers begin to master the demands of the job. They become proficient at managing their tasks, clarifying and negotiating their roles, and engaging in relationships at work. The time when the socialization process is completed varies widely, depending on the individual, the job, and the organization. The end of the process is signaled by newcomers being considered by themselves and others as organizational insiders.

Outcomes of Socialization

Newcomers who are successfully socialized should exhibit good performance, high job satisfaction, and the intention to stay with the organization. In addition, they should exhibit low levels of distress symptoms.[44] High levels of organizational commitment are also marks of successful socialization.[45] This commitment is facilitated throughout the socialization process by the communication of values that newcomers can buy into. Successful socialization is also signaled by mutual influence; that is, the newcomers have made adjustments in the job and organization to accommodate their knowledge and personalities. Newcomers are expected to leave their mark on the organization and not be completely conforming.

When socialization is effective, newcomers understand and adopt the organization's values and norms. This ensures that the company's culture, including its central values, survives. It also provides employees a context for interpreting and responding to things that happen at work, and it ensures a shared framework of understanding among employees.[46]

Socialization as Cultural Communication

Socialization is a powerful cultural communication tool. While the transmission of information about cultural artifacts is relatively easy, the transmission of values is more difficult. The communication of organizational assumptions is almost impossible, since organization members themselves may not be consciously aware of them.

The primary purpose of socialization is the transmission of core values to new organization members.[47] Newcomers are exposed to these values through the role models they interact with, the training they receive, and the behavior they observe being rewarded and punished. Newcomers are vigilant observers, seeking clues to the organization's culture and consistency in the cultural messages they receive. If they are expected to adopt these values, it is essential that the message reflect the underlying values of the organization.

One company known for its culture is the Walt Disney Company. Disney transmits its culture to employees though careful selection, socialization, and training. The Disney culture is built around customer service, and its image serves as a filtering process for applicants. Peer interviews are used to learn how applicants interact with each other. Disney tries to secure a good fit between employee values and the organization's culture. To remind employees of the image they are trying to project, employees are referred to as "cast members" and they occupy a "role." They work either "on stage" or "backstage" and wear "costumes," rather than uniforms. Disney operates its own "universities," which are attended by all new employees. Once trained at a Disney university, cast members are paired with role models to continue their learning on-site.

Companies such as Disney use the socialization process to communicate messages about organizational culture. Both individuals and organizations can take certain actions to ensure the success of the socialization process.

ASSESSING ORGANIZATIONAL CULTURE

Although some organizational scientists argue for assessing organizational culture with quantitative methods, others say that organizational culture must be assessed with qualitative methods.[48] Quantitative methods, such as questionnaires, are valuable because of their precision, comparability, and objectivity. Qualitative methods, such as interviews and observations, are valuable because of their detail, descriptiveness, and uniqueness.

7. Identify ways of assessing organizational culture.

Two widely used quantitative assessment instruments are the Organizational Culture Inventory (OCI) and the Kilmann-Saxton Culture-Gap Survey. Both assess the behavioral norms of organizational cultures, as opposed to the artifacts, values, or assumptions of the organization.

Organizational Culture Inventory

The OCI focuses on behaviors that help employees fit into the organization and meet the expectations of coworkers. Using Maslow's motivational need hierarchy as its basis, it measures twelve cultural styles. The two underlying dimensions of the OCI are task/people and security/satisfaction. There are four satisfaction cultural styles and eight security cultural styles.

A self-report instrument, the OCI contains 120 questions. It provides an individual assessment of culture and may be aggregated to the work group and to the organizational level.[49] It has been used in firms throughout North America, Western Europe, New Zealand, and Thailand, as well as in U.S. military units, the Federal Aviation Administration, and nonprofit organizations.

Kilmann-Saxton Culture-Gap Survey

The Kilmann-Saxton Culture-Gap Survey focuses on what actually happens and on the expectations of others in the organization.[50] Its two underlying dimensions are technical/human and time (the short term versus the long term). With these two dimensions, the actual operating norms and the ideal norms in four areas are assessed. The areas are task support (short-term technical norms), task innovation (long-term technical norms), social relationships (short-term human orientation norms), and personal freedom (long-term human orientation norms). Significant gaps in any of the four areas are used as a point of departure for cultural change to improve performance, job satisfaction, and morale.

A self-report instrument, the Gap Survey provides an individual assessment of culture and may be aggregated to the work group. It has been used in firms throughout the United States and in nonprofit organizations.

Triangulation

triangulation
The use of multiple methods to measure organizational culture.

A study of a rehabilitation center in a 400-bed hospital incorporated *triangulation* (the use of multiple methods to measure organizational culture) to improve inclusiveness and accuracy in measuring the organizational culture.[51] Triangulation has been used by anthropologists, sociologists, and other behavioral scientists to study organizational culture. Its name comes from the navigational technique of using multiple reference points to locate an object. In the rehabilitation center study, the three methods used to triangulate on the culture were (1) obtrusive observations by eight trained observers, which provided an outsider perspective; (2) self-administered questionnaires, which provided quantitative insider information; and (3) personal interviews with the center's staff, which provided qualitative contextual information.

The study showed that each of the three methods made unique contributions toward the discovery of the rehabilitation center's culture. The complete picture could not have been drawn with just a single technique. Triangulation can lead to a better understanding of the phenomenon of culture and is the best approach to assessing organizational culture.

CHANGING ORGANIZATIONAL CULTURE

Changing situations may require changes in the existing culture of an organization. With rapid environmental changes such as globalization, workforce diversity, and technological innovation, the fundamental assumptions and basic values that drive the organization may need to be altered. One particular situation that may require cultural change is a merger or acquisition. The blending of two distinct organizational cultures may prove difficult.

One merger worth keeping an eye on is that between Exxon, with its tiger, and Mobil, with the flying horse. Organizational Reality 15.2 describes what may turn out to be a clash of cultures in combining these two energy industry giants. Exxon, with its more conservative style, and Mobil, with a

---

ORGANIZATIONAL REALITY 15.2

The Stalking Tiger Meets the Flying Horse

The chairmen of Exxon Corporation and Mobil Corporation agreed that combining the two huge operations would be a success because their assets—refineries, gas stations, oil fields all over the world—were a good fit. The deal promised to yield $2.8 million in savings. The real question, however, was not the fit of assets but the fit between the two corporate cultures.

Even though they were in the same industry, Exxon's and Mobil's cultures were as different as night and day, and their corporate symbols reflected the differences. Exxon's stalking tiger became an icon for the company, representing power. The tiger also represented Exxon's huge size, tight-lipped business approach, and conservative style. Mobil's flying horse, a more whimsical mascot, was more open to the public and to new ideas.

Exxon, well known for its *Exxon Valdez* oil spill in 1989, has been publicity shy. Its chairman once said a good day is when Exxon stays out of the news. Mobil, however, wore its image on its sleeve and had no qualms about being outspoken. The company went to battle with the media in the 1970s over the media's (in Mobil's view) biased coverage of the oil embargoes. Mobil was also the first oil company to push energy conservation in the United States.

Exxon's decision making has been slow and deliberate. Its culture involves lots of reviews and lots of steps before decisions are made. The mix of its oil assets has been conservative, and its production strategy has focused on the North Sea and North America. Mobil, in contrast, was always a risk taker, venturing into natural gas in the 1980s before it became the thing to do among oil companies. It also moved boldly into Central Asia, taking advantage of the dissolution of the Soviet Union. Not all of Mobil's risk taking worked, which may be one reason the company joined Exxon.

Mobil's top management is now working for Exxon's leadership. Will Exxon's corporate culture effectively use Mobil's risk-taking talent? Will Mobil's corporate culture and identity survive? Only time will tell.

Discussion Question

1. What are some actions Exxon and Mobil can take to avoid culture conflict?

SOURCE: S. Liesman and A. Sullivan, "Tight-Lipped Exxon, Outspoken Mobil Face Image, Culture Differences," *The Wall Street Journal*, December 2, 1998, A10. Permission conveyed through Copyright Clearance Center, Inc.

bolder style, joined forces in 1999 to form ExxonMobil. The challenge of working through the clash of cultures will ultimately decide the success of the venture.

Alterations in culture may also be required when an organization employs people from different countries. Research indicates that some organizational cultures actually enhance differences in national cultures.[52] One study compared foreign employees working in a multinational organization with employees working in different organizations within their own countries. The assumption was that the employees from various countries working for the same multinational organization would be more similar than employees working in diverse organizations in their native countries. The results were surprising, in that there were significantly greater differences between the employees of the multinational than between managers working for different companies within their native countries. In the multinational, Swedes became more Swedish, Americans became more American, and so forth. It appears that employees enhance their national culture traditions even when working within a single organizational culture.[53]

Changing an organization's culture is feasible but difficult.[54] One reason for the difficulty is that assumptions—the deepest level of culture—are often unconscious. As such, they are often nonconfrontable and nondebatable. Another reason for the difficulty is that culture is deeply ingrained and behavioral norms and rewards are well learned.[55] In a sense, employees must unlearn the old norms before they can learn new ones. Managers who want to change the culture should look first to the ways culture is maintained.

A model for cultural change that summarizes the interventions managers can use is presented in Figure 15.3. In this model, the numbers represent the actions managers can take. There are two basic approaches to changing the existing culture: (1) helping current members buy into a new set of values (actions 1, 2, and 3); or (2) adding newcomers and socializing them into the organization, and removing current members as appropriate (actions 4 and 5).[56]

The first action is to change behavior in the organization. Even if behavior does change, however, this change is not sufficient for cultural change to occur. Behavior is an artifact (level 1) of culture. Individuals may change their behavior but not the values that drive it. They may rationalize, "I'm only doing this because my manager wants me to."

Therefore, managers must use action 2, which is to examine the justifications for the changed behavior. Are employees buying into the new set of values, or are they just complying?

The third action, cultural communication, is extremely important. All of the artifacts (personal enactment, stories, rites and ceremonies, rituals, and symbols) must send a consistent message about the new values and beliefs. It is crucial that the communication be credible; that is, managers must live the new values and not just talk about them. The communication must also be persuasive. Individuals may resist cultural change and may have to be persuaded to try the new behavior by someone they respect and can identify with.

8. Explain actions managers can take to change organizational culture.

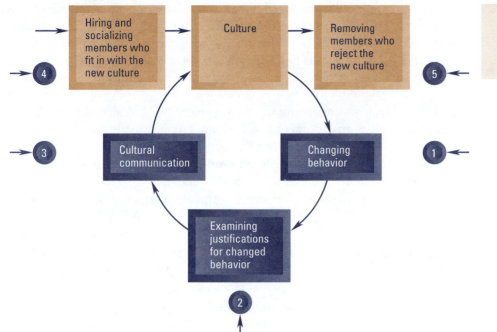

Figure 15.3
Interventions for Changing Organizational Culture

→ Managers seeking to create cultural change must intervene at these points.

SOURCE: From Vijay Sathe "How to Decipher and Change Corporate Culture," Chap. 13 in Gaining Control of the Corporate Culture (R. H. Kilmann et al., Eds.) Fig. 1, p. 245. Copyright © 1985 Jossey-Bass, Inc. Reprinted by permission of Jossey-Bass, Inc., a subsidiary of John Wiley & Sons, Inc.

The two remaining actions (4 and 5) involve shaping the workforce to fit the intended culture. First, the organization can revise its selection strategies to more accurately reflect the new culture. Second, the organization can identify individuals who resist the cultural change or who are no longer comfortable with the values in the organization. Reshaping the workforce should not involve a ruthless pursuit of nonconforming employees; it should be a gradual and subtle change that takes considerable time. Changing personnel in the organization is a lengthy process; it cannot be done effectively in a short period of time without considerable problems.

Evaluating the success of cultural change may be best done by looking at behavior. Cultural change can be assumed to be successful if the behavior is intrinsically motivated—on "automatic pilot." If the new behavior would persist even if rewards were not present, and if the employees have internalized the new value system, then the behavior is probably intrinsically motivated. If employees automatically respond to a crisis in ways consistent with the corporate culture, then the cultural change effort can be deemed successful.

One organization that has changed its culture is AT&T. In 1984, the courts ordered the breakup of AT&T. Prior to the breakup, the company operated in a stable environment with low levels of uncertainty. The organization was a highly structured bureaucracy. The culture emphasized lifetime employment, promotion from within, and loyalty. AT&T faced minimal competition, and it offered individual security. When the courts ordered AT&T to divest its Bell operating companies, the old culture was no longer effective. The company had to move toward a culture that holds individuals accountable for their performance. Change at AT&T was painful and slow, but it was necessary for the company to be able to operate in the new competitive environment.[57] Changing environments may bring about changes in organizational culture.

Given the current business environment, managers may want to focus on three particular cultural modifications. They are (1) support for a global view of business, (2) reinforcement of ethical behavior, and (3) empowerment of employees to excel in product and service quality.

Developing a Global Organizational Culture

The values that drive the organizational culture should support a global view of the company and its efforts. To do so, the values should be clear to everyone involved so that everyone understands them. The values should also be strongly supported at the top. Management should embody the shared values and reward employees who support the global view. Finally, the values should be consistent over time. Consistent values give an organization a unifying theme that competitors may be unable to emulate.[58]

Global corporations suffer from the conflicting pressures of centralization and decentralization. An overarching corporate culture that integrates the decentralized subsidiaries in locations around the world can be an asset in the increasingly competitive global marketplace.

Following are six specific guidelines for managers who want to create a global culture:[59]

1. Create a clear and simple mission statement. A shared mission can unite individuals from diverse cultural backgrounds.

2. Create systems that ensure an effective flow of information. Coordination councils and global task forces can be used to ensure that information flows throughout the geographically dispersed organization are consistent.

3. Create "matrix minds" among managers; that is, broaden managers' minds to allow them to think globally. IBM does this through temporary overseas assignments. Managers with international experience share that experience when they return to the home organization.

4. Develop global career paths. This means ensuring not only that home country executives go overseas but also that executives from other countries rotate into service in the home office.

5. Use cultural differences as a major asset. The former Digital Equipment Corporation (now part of Compaq Computer), for example, transferred its research and development functions to Italy to take advantage of the

free-flowing Italian management style that encouraged creativity. Its manufacturing operations went to Germany, which offered a more systematic management style.

6. Implement worldwide management education and team development programs. Unified training efforts that emphasize corporate values can help establish a shared identity among employees.

These guidelines are specifically aimed at multinational organizations that want to create a global corporate culture, but other organizations can also benefit from them. Companies that want to broaden employees' views or to use the diversity of their workforce as a resource will find several of these recommendations advantageous.

Developing an Ethical Organizational Culture

The organizational culture can have profound effects on the ethical behavior of organization members.[60] When a company's culture promotes ethical norms, individuals behave accordingly. Managers can encourage ethical behavior by being good role models for employees. They can institute the philosophy that ethical behavior makes good business sense and puts the company in congruence with the larger values of the society.[61] Managers can also communicate that rationalizations for unethical behavior are not tolerated. For example, some salespersons justify padding their expense accounts because everyone else does it. Declaring these justifications illegitimate sends a clear message about the lack of tolerance for such behavior.

Trust is another key to effectively managing ethical behavior, especially in cultures that encourage whistle-blowing (as we saw in Chapter 2). Employees must trust that whistle-blowers will be protected, that procedures used to investigate ethical problems will be fair, and that management will take action to solve problems that are uncovered.

Cummins Engine Company is proud of its values-driven culture and its emphasis on ethics. One summer, a Cummins engineer received an innocuous looking package in the mail from Illinois. When he opened it, he realized that it contained partial plans for a new engine that was being designed by Cummins's arch rival, Caterpillar. The plans were vital corporate intelligence slipped to the engineer by an obviously disgruntled Caterpillar employee. (At that time, Caterpillar was facing long and difficult strikes by employees.) The engineer reported the package to Cummins's legal department, who rewrapped the package and sent it back to Caterpillar. Three more packages arrived, which were sent back to Illinois. Caterpillar's legal counsel got wind of the event and sent a note of thanks to Cummins. "I find it gratifying," the Caterpillar executive wrote, "when ethical behavior overshadows the temptation for a competitive edge."[62]

The reasons most often cited for unethical corporate conduct are interesting.[63] They include the belief that a behavior is not really unethical, that it is in the organization's best interest, that it will not be discovered, and that the organization will support it because it offers a good outcome for the organization. An ethical corporate culture can eliminate the viability of these excuses by clearly communicating the boundaries of ethical conduct, selecting employees who support the ethical culture, rewarding organization members who exhibit ethical behavior, and conspicuously punishing members who engage in unethical behavior.

Organizations that seek to encourage ethical behavior can do so by using their organizational culture. By completing Challenge 15.1, you can assess the ethical culture of an organization you're familiar with.

Challenge 15.1

Organizational Culture and Ethics

Think about the organization you currently work for or one you know something about and complete the following Ethical Climate Questionnaire.

Use the scale below and write the number that best represents your answer in the space next to each item.

To what extent are the following statements true about your company?

Completely false	Mostly false	Somewhat false	Somewhat true	Mostly true	Completely true
0	1	2	3	4	5

____ **1.** In this company, people are expected to follow their own personal and moral beliefs.
____ **2.** People are expected to do anything to further the company's interests.
____ **3.** In this company, people look out for each other's good.
____ **4.** It is very important here to follow the company's rules and procedures strictly.
____ **5.** In this company, people protect their own interests above other considerations.
____ **6.** The first consideration is whether a decision violates any law.
____ **7.** Everyone is expected to stick by company rules and procedures.
____ **8.** The most efficient way is always the right way in this company.
____ **9.** Our major consideration is what is best for everyone in the company.
____ **10.** In this company, the law or ethical code of the profession is the major consideration.
____ **11.** It is expected at this company that employees will always do what is right for the customer and the public.

To score the questionnaire, first add up your responses to questions 1, 3, 6, 9, 10, and 11. This is subtotal number 1. Next, reverse the scores on questions 2, 4, 5, 7, and 8 (5 = 0, 4 = 1, 3 = 2, 2 = 3, 1 = 4, 0 = 5). Add the reverse scores to form subtotal number 2. Add subtotal number 1 to subtotal number 2 for an overall score.

Subtotal 1 _____ + Subtotal 2 _____ = Overall Score _____.

Overall scores can range from 0 to 55. The higher the score, the more the organization's culture encourages ethical behavior.

SOURCE: "An Ethical Weather Report: Assessing the Organization's Ethical Climate" by J. B. Cullen, B. Victor, and C. Stephens, from *Organizational Dynamics*, Autumn 1989. Copyright © 1989 American Management Association International. Reprinted by permission of American Management Association International, New York, NY. All rights reserved. http://www.amanet.org.

Developing a Culture of Empowerment and Quality

Throughout this book, we have seen that successful organizations promote a culture that empowers employees and excels in product and service quality. Empowerment serves to unleash employees' creativity and productivity. It requires eliminating traditional hierarchical notions of power. Cultures that emphasize empowerment and quality are preferred by employees. A large-scale survey showed that employees who worked in cultures characterized by empowerment and recognition were more satisfied with their jobs.[64]

General Motors' Cadillac division experienced a massive cultural change. The company installed state-of-the-art robotics technology at its Hamtramck Assembly Center.[65] The idea was to use tomorrow's technology to build the Cadillac of the future. The plant, intended to be a technology showcase, turned into a technology disaster. Robots went haywire, spray-painting one another, smashing windshields, and destroying cars. Computer systems had bugs that led to body parts being installed on the wrong cars.

The new technology was considered a total failure, and the reason cited for the failure was that "people issues" had not been addressed. The technology was yanked. The plant was redesigned to develop a balance between technology and people. Extensive employee involvement and a teamwork approach to design were used to empower employees throughout the Cadillac division.

Managers decided to incorporate input from assemblers in the product design process.[66] Designers, product development engineers, and assembly workers came together in teams to design the new car models. Once the cars were designed, the rest of the assembly workers were consulted a year and a half prior to the scheduled date of production. The designs were then revised to improve the cars' quality. More than 300 modifications were made on the Seville and El Dorado models alone.

Teams were also used to improve quality once a model went into production. A team made up of engineers, assemblers, and supervisors worked on a continuous quality improvement process that targeted electrical system problems. The team effort reduced defects by 90 percent. Employee involvement was the key to the turnaround of Cadillac's culture. The original culture, emphasizing technology as the means for success, was replaced with a culture that emphasizes empowerment and product quality. One of the results was the Malcolm Baldrige National Quality Award.

Small companies can also have cultures that support quality. Texas Nameplate makes metal product identification tags that are found on computers, refrigerators, and military equipment. Employees entered that Baldrige award competition never dreaming they would win; they just wanted to get feedback from the Baldrige judges on how to make their product and service quality better. On the third time, they won—the smallest company (fifty-seven employees) ever to win the award. The judges noted that Texas Nameplate employees visit customers to identify opportunities to improve products. In addition, employees are empowered to make decisions, and as a result, product rejects were reduced to less than 1 percent. Because of its culture, Texas Nameplate was able to eliminate its quality control department.[67]

Managers can learn from the experience of Cadillac that employee empowerment is a key to achieving quality. Involving employees in decision making, removing obstacles to their performance, and communicating the value of product and service quality reinforce the values of empowerment and quality in the organizational culture.

MANAGERIAL IMPLICATIONS: THE ORGANIZATIONAL CULTURE CHALLENGE

Managing organizational culture is a key challenge for leaders in today's organizations. With the trend toward downsizing and restructuring, maintaining an organizational culture in the face of change is difficult. In addition, such challenges as globalization, workforce diversity, technology, and managing ethical behavior often require that an organization change its culture. Adaptive cultures that can respond to changes in the environment can lead the way in terms of organizational performance.

Managers have at their disposal many techniques for managing organizational culture. These techniques range from manipulating the artifacts of culture, such as ceremonies and symbols, to communicating the values that guide the organization. The socialization process is a powerful cultural communication process. Managers are models who communicate the organizational culture to employees through personal enactment. Their modeled behavior sets the norms for the other employees to follow. Their leadership is essential for developing a culture that values diversity, supports empowerment, fosters innovations in product and service quality, and promotes ethical behavior.

Looking Back

Culture and Performance at Southwest Airlines

Southwest's culture has served it well as the airline has grown. Three decades ago, the company started with three Boeing 737s in Texas. The company's initial objective was to enable Texas travelers to get from Dallas to Houston or San Antonio quickly and with low fares. By 2000, Southwest had a fleet of 275 aircraft and was providing service to fifty-five cities in twenty-nine states. Southwest is the only major U.S. airline to remain consistently profitable since 1972. And it has become the fifth largest U.S. airline in terms of domestic passengers boarded.

While Southwest's cultural hallmark is fun, the airline is deadly serious about customer service. It is not a culture of nonperformance.

One Christmas, Southwest was forced to cancel 141 flights on December 23 and Christmas Eve because of an apparent flu outbreak among flight attendants. Later, however, Southwest found out that although many employees were ill, several flight attendants who called in sick were not really sick. After thorough investigations, more than a dozen flight attendants were fired.

Southwest is devoted to delivering maximum value to its customers, or "Positively Outrageous Service." It repeatedly achieves the highest ratings for on-time service, fewest complaints, and fewest baggage errors, along with an unparalleled safety record. Part of the reason for this service is the freedom and support Southwest gives its employees to do everything possible to provide excellent service. If a passenger has a restricted ticket valid only for a certain flight and has an emergency, agents are empowered to make exceptions. By encouraging employees to be creative and empowering them to demonstrate extraordinary customer care, Southwest puts its culture to work to deliver Positively Outrageous Service.[68]

CHAPTER SUMMARY

1. Organizational (corporate) culture is a pattern of basic assumptions that are considered valid and that are taught to new members as the way to perceive, think, and feel in the organization.

2. The most visible and accessible level of culture is artifacts, which include personal enactment, ceremonies and rites, stories, rituals, and symbols.

3. Organizational culture has four functions: giving members a sense of identity and increasing their commitment, serving as a sense-making device for members, reinforcing organizational values, and serving as a control mechanism for shaping behavior.

4. Three theories about the relationship between culture and performance are the strong culture perspective, the fit perspective, and the adaptation perspective.

5. Leaders shape and reinforce culture by what they pay attention to, how they react to crises, how they behave, how they allocate rewards, and how they hire and fire individuals.

6. Organizational socialization is the process by which newcomers become participating, effective members of the organization. Its three stages are anticipatory socialization, encounter, and change and acquisition. Each stage plays a unique role in communicating organizational culture.

7. The Organizational Culture Inventory and Kilmann-Saxton Culture-Gap Survey are two quantitative instruments for assessing organizational culture. Triangulation, using multiple methods for assessing culture, is an effective measurement strategy.

8. It is difficult but not impossible to change organizational culture. Managers can do so by helping current members buy into a new set of values, by adding newcomers and socializing them into the organization, and by removing current members as appropriate.

KEY TERMS

organizational (corporate) culture   448

artifacts   449

espoused values   453

enacted values   453

assumptions   453

strong culture   455

adaptive culture   456

organizational socialization   460

anticipatory socialization   461

encounter   461

change and acquisition   462

triangulation   464

REVIEW QUESTIONS

1. Explain the three levels of organizational culture. How can each level of culture be measured?
2. Describe five artifacts of culture and give an example of each.
3. Explain three theories about the relationship between organizational culture and performance. What does the research evidence say about each one?
4. Contrast adaptive and nonadaptive cultures.
5. How can leaders shape organizational culture?
6. Describe the three stages of organizational socialization. How is culture communicated in each stage?
7. How can managers assess the organizational culture? What actions can they take to change the organizational culture?
8. How does a manager know that cultural change has been successful?
9. What can managers do to develop a global organizational culture?

DISCUSSION AND COMMUNICATION QUESTIONS

1. Name a company with a visible organizational culture. What do you think are the company's values? Has the culture contributed to the organization's performance? Explain.
2. Name a leader you think manages organizational culture well. How does the leader do this? Use Schein's description of how leaders reinforce culture to analyze the leader's behavior.
3. Suppose you want to change your organization's culture. What sort of resistance would you expect from employees? How would you deal with this resistance?
4. Given Schein's three levels, can we ever truly understand an organization's culture? Explain.
5. To what extent is culture manageable? Changeable?
6. (communication question) Select an organization that you might like to work for. Learn as much as you can about that company's culture, using library resources, online sources, contacts within the company, and as many creative means as you can. Prepare a brief presentation to the class summarizing the culture.

ETHICS QUESTIONS

1. Are rites of degradation ethical?
2. Is it ethical to influence an individual's values through the organizational culture? If culture shapes behavior, is managing culture a manipulative tactic? Explain.
3. How can leaders use organizational culture as a vehicle for encouraging ethical behavior?
4. Korean chaebols hire individuals to fit their cultures. To what extent might this practice be considered unethical in the United States?
5. One way of changing culture is to remove members who do not change with the culture. How can this be done ethically?

Experiential Exercises

15.1 Identifying Behavioral Norms

This exercise asks you to identify campus norms at your university. Every organization or group has a set of norms that help determine individuals' behavior. A norm is an unwritten rule for behavior in a group.

When a norm is not followed, negative feedback is given. It may include negative comments, stares, harassment, and exclusion.

1. As a group, brainstorm all the norms you can think of in the following areas:

Dress	Classroom behavior
Studying	Weekend activities
Living arrangements	Campus activities
Dating (who asks whom)	Relationships with faculty
Eating on campus versus off campus	Transportation

2. How did you initially get this information?

3. What happens to students who don't follow these norms?

4. What values can be inferred from these norms?

SOURCE: "Identifying Behavioral Norms" by Dorothy Marcic, *Organizational Behavior: Experiences and Cases* (St. Paul, Minn.: West Publishing, 1989). Reprinted by permission.

15.2 Contrasting Organizational Cultures

To complete this exercise, groups of four or five students should be formed. Each group should select one of the following pairs of organizations:

> American Airlines and Northwest Airlines
> Anheuser-Busch and Coors
> Hewlett-Packard and Xerox
> Albertson's and Winn-Dixie
> Target and J. C. Penney

Using resources found at your university library or online, gather information about the companies' cultures.

Contrast the cultures of the two organizations using the following dimensions:

- Strength of the culture.
- Fit of the culture with the industry's environment.
- Adaptiveness of the culture.

Which of the two is the better performer? On what did you base your conclusion? How does the performance of each relate to its organizational culture?

SOURCE: Adapted with the permission of The Free Press, a Division of Simon & Schuster, Inc. from *Corporate Culture and Performance* by John P. Kotter and James L. Heskett. Copyright © 1992 by Kotter Associates, Inc. and James L. Heskett.

For more practice exercises, consult the fifth edition of *Organizational Behavior: Experiences and Cases* by Dorothy Marcic and Joseph Seltzer (South-Western, 1998).

Managing Change

Learning Objectives

After reading this chapter, you should be able to do the following:

1. Identify the major external and internal forces for change in organizations. *p. 477*

2. Define the terms *incremental change*, *strategic change*, *transformational change*, and *change agent*. *p. 483*

3. Describe the major reasons individuals resist change, and discuss methods organizations can use to manage resistance. *p. 485*

4. Apply force field analysis to a problem. *p. 491*

5. Explain Lewin's organizational change model. *p. 494*

6. Describe the use of organizational diagnosis and needs analysis as a first step in organizational development. *p. 495*

7. Discuss the major organization development interventions. *p. 496*

8. Identify the ethical issues that must be considered in organization development efforts. *p. 503*

Thinking Ahead

Transformation of the American Red Cross Biomedical Services

The American Red Cross has been helping millions of people for more than 120 years. It has a long and proud history of providing assistance to victims of disasters such as hurricanes, tornadoes, fires, and bombings. Its symbol is known worldwide as a sign of help and hope. Yet, even with its lengthy history and strong traditions, the American Red Cross has not been untouched by change.

Elizabeth Dole, former president of the American Red Cross, led an intensive effort to modernize the American Red Cross Biomedical Services so that it would be on the leading edge of developments in health care. The Red Cross is the largest supplier of blood, plasma, and tissue products in the United States—it provides almost half of the nation's blood supply. Dole explained the change process by saying, "We let go of what we knew in search of what we hoped to find."

Biomedical Services needed to become a more customer-oriented organization. Surveys were conducted to determine what customers needed and wanted, and customers were defined in the broadest sense, including blood donors, individuals donating money, volunteers, and recipients of Red Cross services. These surveys yielded important suggestions on needed changes—and those suggestions were acted on.

Technology needed to be updated, so $169 million was invested in a new computer system. The financial management system was consolidated so that data can be accessed instantaneously. Programs were developed to train senior managers in leadership skills. A state-of-the-art system for collecting, processing, and testing blood was installed, with sophisticated equipment located in areas most likely to be hit by disasters. A command operations center monitors current and future threats twenty-four hours a day, seven days a week, and then moves people where they are needed. As a result, the number of people ready to help with disasters has increased from 3,000 to 20,000.

Dole says that none of these changes was as wrenching as the cultural change the American Red Cross faced. There was initially resistance to becoming a more strategic, business-oriented organization. The people issues are the toughest, and they are constantly discussed at conventions, meetings, and seminars. Dole summarized the challenge: "It is important to recognize that the organization may be very highly respected—it doesn't matter how venerable they are, how large, how old. Unless they understand the importance of taking advantage of change, they won't be here in the next century. We see that with many businesses today. I think that our people are alert to the fact that this is important, but obviously we have to keep working at this."[1]

FORCES FOR CHANGE IN ORGANIZATIONS

Change has become the norm in most organizations. Plant closings, business failures, mergers and acquisitions, and downsizing have become experiences common to American companies. *Adaptiveness*, *flexibility*, and *responsiveness* are characteristics of the organizations that will succeed in meeting the competitive challenges that businesses face.[2] In the past, organizations could succeed by claiming excellence in one area—quality, reliability, or cost, for example—but this is not the case today. The current environment demands excellence in all areas.

As we saw in Chapter 1, change is what's on managers' minds. The pursuit of organizational effectiveness through downsizing, restructuring, reengineering, productivity management, cycle-time reduction, and other efforts is paramount. Organizations are in a state of tremendous turmoil and transition, and all members are affected. The downsizing spree of the 1990s may have left firms leaner but not necessarily richer. Though downsizing can increase shareholder value by better aligning costs with revenues, the effective organizations are the ones that excel at new product innovation—the systematic innovators.[3]

Organizations must also deal with ethical, environmental, and other social issues. Competition is fierce, and companies can no longer afford to rest on their laurels. American Airlines has developed a series of programs to constantly reevaluate and change its operating methods to prevent the

1. Identify the major external and internal forces for change in organizations.

company from stagnating. General Electric holds off-site WorkOut sessions with groups of managers and employees whose goal is to make GE a faster, less complex organization that can respond effectively to change. In the WorkOut sessions, employees recommend specific changes, explain why they are needed, and propose ways the changes can be implemented. Top management must make an immediate response: an approval, a disapproval (with an explanation), or a request for more information. The GE WorkOut sessions eliminate the barriers that keep employees from contributing to change.

planned change
Change resulting from a deliberate decision to alter the organization.

unplanned change
Change that is imposed on the organization and is often unforeseen.

There are two basic forms of change in organizations. *Planned change* is change resulting from a deliberate decision to alter the organization. Companies that wish to move from a traditional hierarchical structure to one that facilitates self-managed teams must use a proactive, carefully orchestrated approach. Not all change is planned, however. *Unplanned change* is imposed on the organization and is often unforeseen. Changes in government regulations and changes in the economy, for example, are often unplanned. Responsiveness to unplanned change requires tremendous flexibility and adaptability on the part of organizations. Managers must be prepared to handle both planned and unplanned forms of change in organizations.

Forces for change can come from many sources. Some of these are external, arising from outside the company, whereas others are internal, arising from sources within the organization.

External Forces

The four major managerial challenges we have described throughout the book are major external forces for change. Globalization, workforce diversity, technological change, and managing ethical behavior are challenges that precipitate change in organizations.

Globalization   The power players in the global market are the multinational and transnational organizations. Conoco, for example, formed a joint venture with Arkhangelskgeologia, a Russian firm, to develop a new oil field in Russia. This partnership, named Polar Lights, was the first of its kind. It is exploring a geographic area where there is no existing production, and its investment could total $3 billion.[4] Expanding into such ventures requires extreme adaptability and flexibility on the part of both parties to the agreement.

New opportunities are not limited to the former Soviet Union, however, and the United States is but one nation in the drive to open new markets. Japan and Germany are responding to global competition in powerful ways, and the emergence of the European Union as a powerful trading group will have a profound impact on world markets. By joining with their European neighbors, companies in smaller countries will begin to make major progress in world markets, thus increasing the fierce competition that already exists.

All of these changes, along with others, have led companies to rethink the borders of their markets and to encourage their employees to think globally. Jack Welch of GE called for a boundaryless company, in which there are no mental distinctions between domestic and foreign operations or between managers and employees.[5] The thought that drives the boundaryless company is that barriers that get in the way of people's working together should be removed. Globalizing an organization means rethinking the most efficient ways to use resources, disseminate and gather information, and develop people. It requires not only structural changes but also changes in the minds of employees.

The Hartford Financial Services Group is globalizing but finding some challenges along the way. When the company attempted to enter the lucrative British and Dutch insurance markets by acquiring British and Dutch companies, the overseas staff resisted changes suggested by Hartford, such as using laptops and introducing new financial products. The introduction of such U.S. business practices is often referred to as "economic imperialism" by employees who feel they are being forced to substitute corporate values for personal or national values.

Hartford needed its European staff to understand that they were part of a transnational company. Its solution was to offer a stock ownership plan that tied the personal fortunes of the staff to the company. This gave employees a considerable interest in Hartford's success and helped them identify with the company.[6]

Workforce Diversity Related to globalization is the challenge of workforce diversity. As we have seen throughout this book, workforce diversity is a powerful force for change in organizations. Let us recap the demographic trends contributing to workforce diversity that we discussed at length in Chapter 2. First, the workforce will see increased participation from females, as the majority of new workers will be female.[7] Second, the workforce will be more culturally diverse than ever. Part of this is attributable to globalization, but in addition, U.S. demographics are changing. The participation of African Americans and Hispanic Americans is increasing in record numbers. Third, the workforce is aging. There will be fewer young workers and more middle-aged Americans working.[8]

A few years ago, Denny's, the restaurant chain, was a name synonymous with racism. In 1994, the company paid $54.4 million to settle two lawsuits brought by black customers who claimed some restaurants refused to seat or serve them. Advantica, Denny's parent company, undertook radical changes led by a new blunt-talking CEO in 1995. Because Denny's responded quickly, decisively, and sincerely, it weathered the crisis. Performance appraisals are now based on valuing diversity. A top manager who doesn't do so can have up to 25 percent of his or her bonus withheld. Minorities now own 35 percent of the Denny's franchises. Nearly half of its officers and managers are minorities. The commitment to diversity has moved the company to the number two spot in *Fortune*'s 1998 list of the 50 Best Companies for Asians, blacks, and Hispanics.[9]

Technological Change Rapid technological innovation is another force for change in organizations, and those that fail to keep pace can quickly fall behind. Even small businesses are dramatically affected by technological advances. Cushing & Company is a small reprographics company in Chicago that started out producing blueprints in 1929. The reprographics industry is threatened by the powerful printers used in-house by contractors, architects, and engineers and by copying services provided by chains like Kinko's. Cushing has managed to survive by embracing technological change and helping customers adopt new technologies rather than viewing the innovations as the enemy.

The company got ahead of its competition by teaching construction companies how to use computers before it was popular to do so. Because Cushing staffers used computers, they advised customers to use them and even taught them to use computer-aided design—free of charge. Technical wizards were sent along on sales calls to valued customers. Soon, Cushing got a reputation for knowing how to use computers in an industry that really didn't understand how to use them yet. Later, when color graphics arrived on the scene, Cushing employees educated customers about how to use them. Now, rather than running around with blueprints under their arms, employees take scanned plans from customers or scan them on site and move the plans around the company as computer files. Cushing doesn't hire technology specialists. It looks for good people skills and then builds technical expertise in-house. And the approach works. Cushing's annual revenues of more than $8 million are well above the industry average.[10]

Technological innovations bring about profound change because they are not just changes in the way work is performed. Instead, the innovation process promotes associated changes in work relationships and organizational structures.[11] The team approach adopted by many organizations leads to flatter structures, decentralized decision making, and more open communication between leaders and team members.

Managing Ethical Behavior Recent ethical scandals have brought ethical behavior in organizations to the forefront of public consciousness. Ethical issues, however, are not always public and monumental. Employees face ethical dilemmas in their daily work lives. The need to manage ethical behavior has brought about several changes in organizations. Most center around the idea that an organization must create a culture that encourages ethical behavior.

One company that undertook a massive campaign to move to a more ethical organizational culture was the former Sundstrand Corporation, which was a major defense contractor in the aerospace industry until 1999 when it was acquired by United Technologies. Earlier, however, Sundstrand had faced charges of ethical violations by Pentagon officials that resulted in a $227 million penalty. The company's stock dropped substantially as well.

Sundstrand took immediate steps to emphasize ethical conduct in its culture, including encouraging whistle-blowing by employees. A corporate director of business conduct and ethics was hired. A code of conduct was written. Employees were given thirty days to read it and sign a card obligating them to follow the code. Extensive ethics training sessions were conducted with all 8,000 aerospace division employees. Hotlines were established for employees to report ethical violations or to simply ask questions. Each hotline call was answered within twenty-four hours. The most critical ingredient in Sundstrand's change was encouraging whistle-blowing. Employees were made aware that appropriate action would be taken and that whistle-blowers would be protected. Extensive follow-up by the company indicated that the program worked. The company committed no more ethical violations, employees reported satisfaction with the program, and hotline calls resulted in actions against those who violated Sundstrand's ethics policy.[12]

Society expects organizations to maintain ethical behavior both internally and in relationships with other organizations. Ethical behavior is expected in relationships with customers, the environment, and society. These expectations may be informal, or they may come in the form of increased legal requirements.

These four challenges are forces that place pressures to change on organizations. There are other forces as well. Legal developments, changing stakeholder expectations, and shifting consumer demands can also lead to change.[13] Other powerful forces for change originate from within the organization.

Internal Forces

Pressures for change that originate inside the organization are generally recognizable in the form of signals indicating that something needs to be altered.

Declining effectiveness is a pressure to change. A company that experiences its third quarterly loss within a fiscal year is undoubtedly motivated to do something about it. Some companies react by instituting layoffs and massive cost-cutting programs, whereas others look at the bigger picture, view the loss as symptomatic of an underlying problem, and seek the cause of the problem. Organizational Reality 16.1 describes how Continental Airlines dealt with its financial problems.

A crisis may also stimulate change in an organization. Strikes or walkouts may lead management to change the wage structure. The resignation of a key decision maker may cause the company to rethink the composition of its management team and its role in the organization. A much-publicized crisis that led to change at Exxon (now ExxonMobil) was the oil spill caused by the *Exxon Valdez* oil tanker. The accident brought about many changes in Exxon's environmental policies.

Changes in employee expectations can also trigger change in organizations. A company that hires a group of young newcomers may find that their expectations are very different from those expressed by older workers. The workforce is more educated than ever before. Although this has

ORGANIZATIONAL REALITY 16.1

Continental's New Flight Plan

Not too many years ago, Continental Airlines was on its way out of business. It had had two bankruptcies in nine years, no profits since 1978, and a reputation for lousy service. It ranked tenth of ten large U.S. airlines in terms of on-time arrivals, baggage handling, customer complaints, and involuntary denied boardings (aka "getting bumped"). Internally, the company was dysfunctional. Managers were paralyzed by anxiety, and employees were so embarrassed to be working for Continental that they tore the company's logo off their shirts. The company went through ten presidents in ten years.

Then, former consultant Greg Brenneman joined the airline as president and chief operating officer and worked with CEO Gordon Bethune in engineering a phenomenal turnaround. The Go Forward Plan had four elements: Fly to Win (marketing plan), Fund the Future (financial plan), Make Reliability a Reality (product plan), and Working Together (the people plan).

Continental's new flight plan was not without pain—7,000 employees, including managers, were let go. Members of the old management team were too busy trying to knock each other off, so they were replaced, humanely and with dignity. Continental also began a forgiveness campaign, distributing angry letters from customers among company officers, who called to apologize and explain what they were doing to fix the company. The advertising budget was cut in half. Managers asked customers what they wanted and delivered on it. Planes were painted, interiors were refurbished. The "meatball," Continental's

ugly, round, red logo, was replaced with a blue globe with gold lettering. To improve reliability, two groups were asked to coordinate with each other: those who wrote the flight schedules and those who ran the flight and airport operations. Putting the two groups in charge of their own destiny made them work together.

In the past, employees learned what was going on at Continental through the press. The communication philosophy changed from "Don't tell anyone anything unless absolutely required" to "Tell everybody everything." Employees were liberated. The nine-inch-thick "Thou Shalt Not" book was thrown into a fifty-five-gallon drum and burned in the parking lot. Employee compensation was aligned with the company objectives.

As a result, the airline is flying high again. Turnover, sick leave, injuries, and worker's compensation claims have declined. Employees no longer tear patches off their shirts—they buy Continental logo merchandise for themselves and friends. COO Brenneman says he learned three turnaround lessons: (1) Fly your flight plan and track your progress; (2) clean house; and (3) think "money in," not "money out."

Discussion Question

1. What was the scope of change at Continental Airlines?

SOURCE: Reprinted by permission of *Harvard Business Review.* From "Right Away and All at Once: How We Saved Continental" by G. Brenneman, Vol. 76, 1998, pp. 162–179. Copyright © 1998 by Harvard Business School Publishing Corporation.

its advantages, workers with more education demand more of employers. Today's workers are also concerned with career and family balance issues, such as dependent care. The many sources of workforce diversity hold potential for a host of differing expectations among employees.

Changes in the work climate at an organization can also stimulate change. A workforce that seems lethargic, unmotivated, and dissatisfied is a symptom that must be addressed. This symptom is common in organizations that have experienced layoffs. Workers who have escaped a layoff may grieve for those who have lost their jobs and may find it hard to continue to be productive. They may fear that they will be laid off as well, and many feel insecure in their jobs.

CHANGE IS INEVITABLE

We have seen that organizations face substantial pressures to change from both external and internal sources. Change in organizations is inevitable, but change is a process that can be managed. The scope of change can vary from small to quantum.

The Scope of Change

Change can be of a relatively small scope, such as a modification in a work procedure (an *incremental change*). Such changes, in essence, are a fine-tuning of the organization, or the making of small improvements. Change can also be of a larger scale, such as the restructuring of an organization (a *strategic change*).[14] In strategic change, the organization moves from an old state to a known new state during a controlled period of time. Strategic change usually involves a series of transition steps.

The most massive scope of change is *transformational change*, in which the organization moves to a radically different, and sometimes unknown, future state.[15] In transformational change, the organization's mission, culture, goals, structure, and leadership may all change dramatically.[16]

Sears is a company that has undergone transformational change. Sears's culture had become an 800-pound gorilla that impaired performance and stifled change. It was an in-bred culture of "salute and obey," and Sears was bleeding red ink because of it. Regions were fragmented, and competition from Wal-Mart was not being taken seriously. The company was in a state of denial and complacency.

Art Martinez, the new CEO of Sears, began telling the hard truth. He generated a sense of urgency by setting difficult goals. He worked from the bottom up with town hall meetings and a straightforward style of communication. Attention to improvement became a daily discipline. The catalog, which lost money, was given up, and 113 stores were closed. Sears's image was rebuilt with better merchandise and catchy advertisements. After a long period of severe difficulties, its revenues are in the black. The company's transformation process, however, is not complete. It is an ongoing struggle to change to a more competitive organization.[17]

The Change Agent's Role

The individual or group that undertakes the task of introducing and managing a change in an organization is known as a *change agent*. Change agents can be internal, such as managers or employees who are appointed to oversee the change process. In her book *The Change Masters*, Rosabeth Moss Kanter notes that at companies like Hewlett-Packard and Polaroid,

incremental change
Change of a relatively small scope, such as making small improvements.

strategic change
Change of a larger scale, such as organizational restructuring.

transformational change
Change in which the organization moves to a radically different, and sometimes unknown, future state.

2. Define the terms *incremental change*, *strategic change*, *transformational change*, and *change agent*.

change agent
The individual or group that undertakes the task of introducing and managing a change in an organization.

managers and employees alike are developing the needed skills to produce change and innovation in the organization.[18] Change agents can also be external, such as outside consultants.

Internal change agents have certain advantages in managing the change process. They know the organization's past history, its political system, and its culture. Because they must live with the results of their change efforts, internal change agents are likely to be very careful about managing change. There are disadvantages, however, to using internal change agents. They may be associated with certain factions within the organization and may easily be accused of favoritism. Furthermore, internal change agents may be too close to the situation to have an objective view of what needs to be done.

In a recent study, interviews were conducted with 150 internal change agents at thirty organizations. The researchers focused on middle managers as change agents because to make large-scale changes, organizations need a critical mass of change leaders in the middle of the company. Change leaders, as the researchers call them, tend to be young, in the twenty-five to forty age range. They are more flexible than ordinary general managers and much more people oriented. A high number of change leaders are women. The change leaders have a balance of technical and interpersonal skills. They are tough decision makers who focus on performance results. They also know how to energize people and get them aligned in the same direction. They get more out of people than ordinary managers can. In addition, they have the ability to operate in more than one leadership style and can shift from a team mode to command and control, depending on the situation. They are also comfortable with uncertainty.[19]

External change agents bring an outsider's objective view to the organization. They may be preferred by employees because of their impartiality. External change agents face certain problems, however; not only is their knowledge of the organization's history limited, but they may also be viewed with suspicion by organization members. External change agents have more power in directing changes if employees perceive the change agents as being trustworthy, possessing important expertise, having a track record that establishes credibility, and being similar to them.[20]

THE PROCESS OF CHANGE IN ORGANIZATIONS

Once an organization has made the decision to change, careful planning and analysis must take place. Change processes such as business process reengineering cannot ensure the success of the change. The people aspects of change are the most critically important for successful transformations.[21] If people are not taken into account, a change process will be negatively affected or may even fail.

The challenge of managing the change process involves harnessing the energy of diverse individuals who hold a variety of views of change. It is important to recognize that most changes will be met with varying degrees of resistance and to understand the basis of resistance to change.

Resistance to Change

People often resist change in a rational response based on self-interest. However, there are countless other reasons people resist change. Many of these center around the notion of reactance—that is, a negative reaction that occurs when individuals feel that their personal freedom is threatened.[22] Some of the major reasons for resisting change follow.

Fear of the Unkown Change often brings with it substantial uncertainty. Employees facing a technological change, such as the introduction of a new computer system, may resist the change simply because it introduces ambiguity into what was once a comfortable situation for them. This is especially a problem when there has been little communication about the change.

Fear of Loss When a change is impending, some employees may fear losing their jobs; this fear is particularly acute when an advanced technology like robotics is introduced. Employees may also fear losing their status because of a change.[23] Computer systems experts, for example, may feel threatened when they feel their expertise is eroded by the installation of a more user-friendly networked information system. Another common fear is that changes may diminish the positive qualities the individual enjoys in the job. Computerizing the customer service positions at Southwestern Bell (now part of SBC Communications), for example, threatened the autonomy that representatives previously enjoyed.

Fear of Failure Some employees fear changes because they fear their own failure. Introducing computers into the workplace often arouses individuals' self-doubts about their ability to interact with the computer.[24] Resistance can also stem from a fear that the change itself will not really take place. In one large library that was undergoing a major automation effort, employees were doubtful that the vendor could really deliver the state-of-the-art system that was promised. In this case, the implementation never became a reality—the employees' fears were well founded.[25]

Disruption of Interpersonal Relationships Employees may resist change that threatens to limit meaningful interpersonal relationships on the job. Librarians facing the automation effort described previously feared that once the computerized system was implemented, they would not be able to interact as they did when they had to go to another floor of the library to get help finding a resource. In the new system, with the touch of a few buttons on the computer, they would get their information without consulting another librarian.

Personality Conflicts When the change agent's personality engenders negative reactions, employees may resist the change. A change agent who appears insensitive to employee concerns and feelings may meet considerable resistance, because employees perceive that their needs are not being taken into account.

Politics Organizational change may also shift the existing balance of power in the organization. Individuals or groups who hold power under the current

3. Describe the major reasons individuals resist change, and discuss methods organizations can use to manage resistance.

Experiencing OB

Learn more about resistance to change and how managers may overcome that resistance by interacting with these ideas at our animated concept and activity site. Choose Innovation&Change from the "select a topic" pull-down menu, then Resistance to Change and also Overcoming Resistance from the "overview tab."

http://www.experiencingob.com

arrangement may be threatened with losing these political advantages in the advent of change.

Cultural Assumptions and Values   Sometimes cultural assumptions and values can be impediments to change, particularly if the assumptions underlying the change are alien to employees. This form of resistance can be very difficult to overcome, because some cultural assumptions are unconscious. As we discussed in Chapter 2, some cultures tend to avoid uncertainty. In Mexican and Greek cultures, for example, change that creates a great deal of uncertainty may be met with great resistance.

Some individuals are more tolerant of ambiguity than others. You can assess your own attitude toward ambiguity in Challenge 16.1.

Challenge 16.1

Tolerance for Ambiguity

Tolerance for Ambiguity Survey Form

Read each of the following statements carefully. Then rate each of them in terms of the extent to which you either agree or disagree with the statement using the following scale:

Completely Disagree			Neither Agree nor Disagree			Completely Agree
1	2	3	4	5	6	7

Place the number that best describes your degree of agreement or disagreement in the blank to the left of each statement.

____   **1.** An expert who doesn't come up with a definite answer probably doesn't know much.

____   **2.** I would like to live in a foreign country for a while.

____   **3.** The sooner we all acquire similar values and ideals the better.

____   **4.** A good teacher is one who makes you wonder about your way of looking at things.

____   **5.** I like parties where I know most of the people more than ones where all or most of the people are complete strangers.

____   **6.** Teachers or supervisors who hand out vague assignments give a chance for one to show initiative and originality.

____   **7.** A person who leads an even, regular life in which few surprises or unexpected happenings arise really has a lot to be grateful for.

____   **8.** Many of our most important decisions are based upon insufficient information.

____   **9.** There is really no such thing as a problem that can't be solved.

____   **10.** People who fit their lives to a schedule probably miss most of the joy of living.

____   **11.** A good job is one where what is to be done and how it is to be done are always clear.

____   **12.** It is more fun to tackle a complicated problem than to solve a simple one.

____   **13.** In the long run, it is possible to get more done by tackling small, simple problems rather than large and complicated ones.

____   **14.** Often the most interesting and stimulating people are those who don't mind being different and original.

____   **15.** What we are used to is always preferable to what is unfamiliar.

Scoring: For even-numbered questions, add the total points.
For odd-numbered questions, use reverse scoring and add the total points.
Your score is the total of the even- and odd-numbered questions.

Norms Using the Tolerance for Ambiguity Scale

Source: The Tolerance for Ambiguity Scale

Basis: The survey asks 15 questions about personal and work-oriented situations with ambiguity. You were asked to rate each situation on a scale from one (tolerant) to seven (intolerant). (Alternating questions have the response scale reversed.) The index scores the items. A perfectly tolerant person would score 15 and a perfectly intolerant person 105. Scores between 20 and 80 are reported, with means of 45. The responses to the even-numbered questions with 7 minus the score are added to the response for the odd-numbered questions.

The Scale:

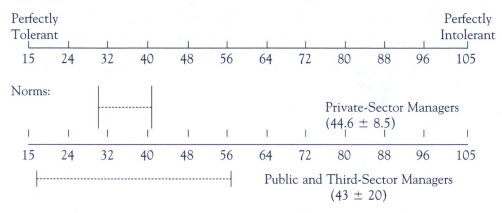

SOURCE: "Tolerance for Ambiguity" from D. Marcic, *Organizational Behavior: Experiences and Cases* (St. Paul, Minn.: West Publishing, 1992), 339–340. Adapted from Paul Nutt. Used with permission.

We have described several sources of resistance to change. The reasons for resistance are as diverse as the workforce itself and vary with different individuals and organizations. The challenge for managers is introducing change in a positive manner and managing employee resistance.

Managing Resistance to Change

The traditional view of resistance to change treated it as something to be overcome, and many organizational attempts to reduce the resistance have only served to intensify it. The contemporary view holds that resistance is simply a form of feedback and that this feedback can be used very productively to manage the change process.[26] One key to managing resistance is to plan for it and to be ready with a variety of strategies for using the resistance as feedback and helping employees negotiate the transition. Three key strategies for managing resistance to change are communication, participation, and empathy and support.[27]

Communication about impending change is essential if employees are to adjust effectively. The details of the change should be provided, but equally important is the rationale behind the change. Employees want to know why change is needed. If there is no good reason for it, why should they favor the change? Providing accurate and timely information about the change can help prevent unfounded fears and potentially damaging rumors from developing. Delaying the announcement of a change and handling information in a secretive fashion can serve to fuel the rumor mill. Open communication in a culture of trust is a key ingredient for successful change.[28] It is also beneficial to inform people about the potential consequences of the change. Educating employees on new work procedures is often helpful. Studies on the introduction of computers in the workplace indicate that providing employees with opportunities for hands-on practice helps alleviate fears about the new technology. Employees who have experience with computers display more positive attitudes and greater efficacy—a sense that they can master their new tasks.[29]

There is substantial research support underscoring the importance of participation in the change process. Employees must be engaged and involved in order for change to work—as supported by the notion "That which we create, we support." GE's WorkOut process, which was mentioned earlier in this chapter, is a good illustration of how to get a large group together in a free-form, open-ended meeting. The outcome is a change to which everyone is committed. The group comes together later, after the change is implemented, to see what has been learned and to look for what is happening on the horizon. Participation by a large group can move change further along.[30] Participation helps employees become involved in the change and establish a feeling of ownership in the process. When employees are allowed to participate, they are more committed to the change.

Another strategy for managing resistance is providing empathy and support to employees who have trouble dealing with the change. Active listening is an excellent tool for identifying the reasons behind resistance and for uncovering fears. An expression of concerns about the change can provide important feedback that managers can use to improve the change process. Emotional support and encouragement can help an employee deal with the anxiety that is a natural response to change. Employees who experience severe reactions to change can benefit from talking with a counselor. Some companies provide counseling through their employee assistance plans.

Open communication, participation, and emotional support can go a long way toward managing resistance to change. Managers must realize that some resistance is inevitable, however, and should plan ways to deal with resistance early in the change process.

Managing resistance to change is a long and often arduous process. GTE Mobilnet (later GTE Wireless and now part of Verizon Communications) faced substantial resistance to change when it implemented its customer connection initiative, with the goal of building a cellular-phone network that ranked first in customer service. The change agent, Ben Powell, and his teammates tried to persuade staffers at Mobilnet's 350 service centers to send new cellular phones out the door with fully charged batteries in them. The salespeople liked the idea—they could tell customers that their phones were ready to use immediately. Service workers, however, balked at the idea because they were the ones who had to install the batteries.

Powell and his team essentially repeated the following dialogue 350 times: "You can't see why you need to bother with installing the batteries? Here are sales figures showing how much revenue we lose by making customers wait to use their phones. The average customer calls everybody he knows when he first gets the thing, like a kid with a new toy—but only if it has a charged battery in it. Don't have room to stock all those batteries? We'll help you redesign your workspace to accommodate them. Can't predict how many of which battery you'll need on hand at any given time? We'll provide data to help you with those projections. Can't afford any of this to come out of your operating budget? We'll fund it for you."

As Powell said, "When you meet this kind of resistance, the only thing you can do is keep plugging away. . . . Finally, in the last six months or so we have been getting to the point where we're really changing how we do business. But it's taken years. Not weeks. Not months. On a day-to-day basis, it feels like bowling in sand."[31]

Behavioral Reactions to Change

In spite of attempts to minimize the resistance to change in an organization, some reactions to change are inevitable. Negative reactions may be manifested in overt behavior or through more passive resistance to change. People show four basic, identifiable reactions to change: disengagement, disidentification, disenchantment, and disorientation.[32] Managers can use interventions to deal with these reactions, as shown in Table 16.1.

Disengagement is psychological withdrawal from change. The employee may appear to lose initiative and interest in the job. Employees who disengage may fear the change but approach it by doing nothing and simply hoping for the best. Disengaged employees are physically present but mentally absent. They lack drive and commitment, and they simply comply without real psychological investment in their work. Disengagement can be recognized by behaviors such as being hard to find or doing only the basics to get the job done. Typical disengagement statements include "No problem" or "This won't affect me."

disengagement
Psychological withdrawal from change.

Reaction	Expression	Managerial Intervention
Disengagement	Withdrawal	Confront, identify
Disidentification	Sadness, worry	Explore, transfer
Disenchantment	Anger	Neutralize, acknowledge
Disorientation	Confusion	Explain, plan

Table 16.1
Reactions to Change and Managerial Interventions

SOURCE: Table adapted from H. Woodward and S. Buchholz, *Aftershock: Helping People through Corporate Change*, p. 15. Copyright © 1987 John Wiley & Sons, Inc. Reprinted by permission of John Wiley & Sons, Inc.

The basic managerial strategy for dealing with disengaged individuals is to confront them with their reaction and draw them out so that they can identify the concerns that need to be addressed. Disengaged employees may not be aware of the change in their behavior, and they need to be assured of your intentions. Drawing them out and helping them air their feelings can lead to productive discussions. Disengaged people seldom become cheerleaders for the change, but they can be brought closer to accepting and working with a change by open communication with an empathetic manager who is willing to listen.

disidentification
Feeling that one's identify is being threatened by a change.

Another reaction to change is **disidentification**. Individuals reacting in this way feel that their identity has been threatened by the change, and they feel very vulnerable. Many times they cling to a past procedure because they had a sense of mastery over it, and it gave them a sense of security. "My job is completely changed" and "I used to . . ." are verbal indications of disidentification. Disidentified employees often display sadness and worry. They may appear to be sulking and dwelling on the past by reminiscing about the old ways of doing things.

Because disidentified employees are so vulnerable, they often feel like victims in the change process. Managers can help them through the transition by encouraging them to explore their feelings and helping them transfer their positive feelings into the new situation. One way to do this is to help them identify what they liked in the old situation and then show them how it is possible to have the same positive experience in the new situation. Disidentified employees need to see that work itself and emotion are separable—that is, that they can let go of old ways and experience positive reactions to new ways of performing their jobs.

disenchantment
Feeling negativity or anger toward a change.

Disenchantment is also a common reaction to change. It is usually expressed as negativity or anger. Disenchanted employees realize that the past is gone, and they are mad about it. They may try to enlist the support of other employees by forming coalitions. Destructive behaviors like sabotage and backstabbing may result. Typical verbal signs of disenchantment are "This will never work" and "I'm getting out of this company as soon as I can." The anger of a disenchanted person may be directly expressed in organizational cultures where it is permissible to do so. This behavior tends to get the issues out in the open. More often, however, cultures view the expression of emotion at work as improper and unbusinesslike. In these cultures, the anger is suppressed and emerges in more passive-aggressive ways, such as badmouthing and starting rumors. One of the particular dangers of disenchantment is that it is quite contagious in the workplace.

It is often difficult to reason with disenchanted employees. Thus, the first step in managing this reaction is to bring these employees from their highly negative, emotionally charged state to a more neutral state. To neutralize the reaction does not mean to dismiss it; rather, it means to allow the individuals to let off the necessary steam so that they can come to terms with their anger. The second part of the strategy for dealing with disenchanted employees is to acknowledge that their anger is normal and that you do not hold it against them. Sometimes disenchantment is a mask for one of the other three reactions, and it must be worked through to get to the core of the employee's reaction. Employees may also become cynical about change and lose faith in the leaders of change.

A final reaction to change is *disorientation*. Disoriented employees are lost and confused, and often they are unsure of their feelings. They waste energy trying to figure out what to do instead of how to do things. Disoriented individuals ask a lot of questions and become very detail oriented. They may appear to need a good deal of guidance and may leave their work undone until all of their questions have been answered. "Analysis paralysis" is characteristic of disoriented employees. They feel that they have lost touch with the priorities of the company, and they may want to analyze the change to death before acting on it. Disoriented employees may ask questions like "Now what do I do?" or "What do I do first?"

Disorientation is a common reaction among people who are used to clear goals and unambiguous directions. When change is introduced, it creates uncertainty and a lack of clarity. The managerial strategy for dealing with this reaction is to explain the change in a way that minimizes the ambiguity that is present. The information about the change needs to be put into a framework or an overall vision so that the disoriented individual can see where he or she fits into the grand scheme of things. Once the disoriented employee sees the broader context of the change, you can plan a series of steps to help this employee adjust. The employee needs a sense of priorities to work on.

Managers need to be able to diagnose these four reactions to change. Because each reaction brings with it significant and different concerns, no single universal strategy can help all employees adjust. By recognizing each reaction and applying the appropriate strategy, it is possible to help even strong resisters work through a transition successfully.

Lewin's Change Model

Kurt Lewin developed a model of the change process that has stood the test of time and continues to influence the way organizations manage planned change. Lewin's model is based on the idea of force field analysis.[33] Figure 16.1 shows a force field analysis of a decision to engage in exercise behavior.

This model contends that a person's behavior is the product of two opposing forces; one force pushes toward preserving the status quo, and the other force pushes for change. When the two opposing forces are approximately equal, current behavior is maintained. For behavioral change to occur, the forces maintaining the status quo must be overcome. This can be accomplished by increasing the forces for change, by weakening the forces for the status quo, or by a combination of these actions. Challenge 16.2 asks you to apply force field analysis to a problem in your life.

Lewin's change model is a three-step process, as shown in Figure 16.2. The process begins with *unfreezing*, which is a crucial first hurdle in the change process. Unfreezing involves encouraging individuals to discard old

disorientation
Feelings of loss and confusion due to a change.

4. Apply force field analysis to a problem.

unfreezing
The first step in Lewin's change model, in which individuals are encouraged to discard old behaviors by shaking up the equilibrium state that maintains the status quo.

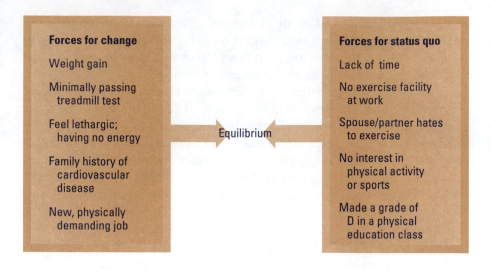

Figure 16.1
Force Field Analysis of a Decision to Engage in Exercise

Forces for change

Weight gain

Minimally passing treadmill test

Feel lethargic; having no energy

Family history of cardiovascular disease

New, physically demanding job

Equilibrium

Forces for status quo

Lack of time

No exercise facility at work

Spouse/partner hates to exercise

No interest in physical activity or sports

Made a grade of D in a physical education class

Challenge 16.2

Applying Force Field Analysis

Think of a problem you are currently facing. An example would be trying to increase the amount of study time you devote to a particular class.

1. Describe the problem, as specifically as possible.
2. List the forces driving change on the arrows at the left side of the diagram.
3. List the forces restraining change on the arrows at the right side of the diagram.
4. What can you do, specifically, to remove the obstacles to change?
5. What can you do to increase the forces driving change?
6. What benefits can be derived from breaking a problem down into forces driving change and forces restraining change?

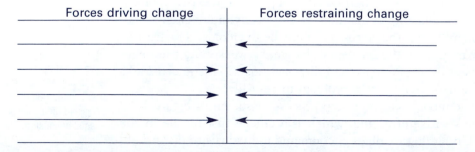

Forces driving change | Forces restraining change

Unfreezing	Moving	Refreezing
Reducing forces for status quo	Developing new attitudes, values, and behaviors	Reinforcing new attitudes, values, and behaviors

Figure 16.2
Lewin's Change Model

behaviors by shaking up the equilibrium state that maintains the status quo. Organizations often accomplish unfreezing by eliminating the rewards for current behavior and showing that current behavior is not valued. By unfreezing, individuals accept that change needs to occur. In essence, individuals surrender by allowing the boundaries of their status quo to be opened in preparation for change.[34]

The second step in the change process is *moving*. In the moving stage, new attitudes, values, and behaviors are substituted for old ones. Organizations accomplish moving by initiating new options and explaining the rationale for the change, as well as by providing training to help employees develop the new skills they need. Employees should be given the overarching vision for the change so that they can establish their roles within the new organizational structure and processes.[35]

Refreezing is the final step in the change process. In this step, new attitudes, values, and behaviors are established as the new status quo. The new ways of operating are cemented in and reinforced. Managers should ensure that the organizational culture and formal reward systems encourage the new behaviors and avoid rewarding the old ways of operating. Changes in the reward structure may be needed to ensure that the organization is not rewarding the old behaviors and merely hoping for the new behaviors. A study by Exxon Research and Engineering showed that framing and displaying a mission statement in managers' offices may eventually change the behavior of 2 percent of the managers. In contrast, changing managers' evaluation and reward systems will change the behavior of 55 percent of the managers almost overnight.[36]

The approach used by Monsanto (now part of Pharmacia Corporation) to increase opportunities for women within the company is an illustration of how to use Lewin's model effectively. First, Monsanto emphasized unfreezing by helping employees debunk negative stereotypes about women in business. This also helped overcome resistance to change. Second, Monsanto moved employees' attitudes and behaviors by diversity training in which differences were emphasized as positive, and supervisors learned ways of training and developing female employees. Third, Monsanto changed its reward system so that managers were evaluated and paid according to how they coached and promoted women, which helped refreeze the new attitudes and behaviors.

Lewin's model proposes that for change efforts to be successful, the three-stage process must be completed. Failures in efforts to change can be traced back to one of the three stages. Successful change thus requires that old behaviors be discarded, new behaviors be introduced, and these new behav-

moving
The second step in Lewin's change model, in which new attitudes, values, and behaviors are substituted for old ones.

refreezing
The final step in Lewin's change model, in which new attitudes, values, and behaviors are established as the new status quo.

Experiencing OB

A model of change that emphasizes unfreezing current behaviors, changing and refreezing new behaviors is presented at our animated concept and activity site. Choose Innovation&Change from the "select a topic" pull-down menu, then Managing Change from the "overview tab."

http://www.experiencingob.com

5. Explain Lewin's organizational change model.

iors be institutionalized and rewarded. This is a learning process, and the learning theories discussed in Chapter 6 certainly apply. Skinner's work helps us understand how to encourage new behaviors and extinguish old ones by using reinforcers. Bandura's social learning theory points out the importance of modeling. Managers should model appropriate behavior, because employees look to them to pattern their own behavior.

Organizations that wish to change can select from a variety of methods to make a change become reality. Organization development is a method that consists of various programs for making organizations more effective.

ORGANIZATION DEVELOPMENT INTERVENTIONS

organization development (OD)
A systematic approach to organizational improvement that applies behavioral science theory and research in order to increase individual and organizational well-being and effectiveness.

Organization development (OD) is a systematic approach to organizational improvement that applies behavioral science theory and research in order to increase individual and organizational well-being and effectiveness.[37] This definition implies certain characteristics. First, OD is a systematic approach to planned change. It is a structured cycle of diagnosing organizational problems and opportunities and then applying expertise to them. Second, OD is grounded in solid research and theory. It involves the application of our knowledge of behavioral science to the challenges that organizations face. Third, OD recognizes the reciprocal relationship between individuals and organizations. It acknowledges that for organizations to change, individuals must change. Finally, OD is goal oriented. It is a process that seeks to improve both individual and organizational well-being and effectiveness.

Organization development has a rich history. Some of the early work in OD was conducted by Kurt Lewin and his associates during the 1940s. This work was continued by Rensis Likert, who pioneered the use of attitude surveys in OD. During the 1950s, Eric Trist and his colleagues at the Tavistock Institute in London focused on the technical and social aspects of organizations and how they affect the quality of work life. These programs on the quality of work life migrated to the United States during the 1960s. During this time, a 200-member OD network was established, and it has grown to more than 2,000 members today. As the number of practitioners has increased, so has the number of different OD methods. One compendium of organizational change methods estimates that more than 300 different methods have been used.[38]

Organization development is also being used internationally. OD has been applied in Canada, Sweden, Norway, Germany, Japan, Australia, Israel, and Mexico, among others. Some OD methods are difficult to implement in other cultures. As OD becomes more internationally widespread, we will increase our knowledge of how culture affects the success of different OD approaches.

Prior to deciding on a method of intervention, managers must carefully diagnose the problem they are attempting to address. Diagnosis and needs analysis is a critical first step in any OD intervention. Following this, an intervention method is chosen and applied. Finally, a thorough follow-up of the OD process is conducted. Figure 16.3 presents the OD cycle, a contin-

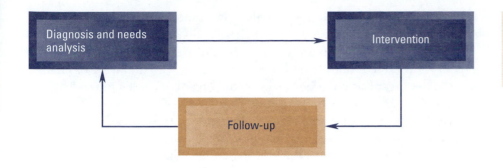

Figure 16.3
The Organization Development Cycle

uous process of moving the organization and its employees toward effective functioning.

Diagnosis and Needs Analysis

Before any intervention is planned, a thorough organizational diagnosis should be conducted. Diagnosis is an essential first step for any organization development intervention.[39] The term *diagnosis* comes from *dia* (through) and *gnosis* (knowledge of). Thus, the diagnosis should pinpoint specific problems and areas in need of improvement. Problems can arise in any part of the organization. Six areas to examine carefully are the organization's purpose, structure, reward system, support systems, relationships, and leadership.[40]

Harry Levinson's diagnostic approach asserts that the process should begin by identifying where the pain (the problem) in the organization is, what it is like, how long it has been happening, and what has already been done about it.[41] Then a four-part, comprehensive diagnosis can begin. The first part of the diagnosis involves achieving an understanding of the organization's history. In the second part, the organization as a whole is analyzed to obtain data about its structure and processes. In the third part, interpretive data about attitudes, relationships, and current organizational functioning are gathered. In the fourth part of the diagnosis, the data are analyzed and conclusions are reached. In each stage of the diagnosis, the data can be gathered using a variety of methods, including observation, interviews, questionnaires, and archival records.

The diagnostic process may yield the conclusion that change is necessary. As part of the diagnosis, it is important to address the following issues:

- What are the forces for change?
- What are the forces preserving the status quo?
- What are the most likely sources of resistance to change?
- What are the goals to be accomplished by the change?

This information constitutes a force field analysis, as discussed earlier in the chapter.

A needs analysis is another crucial step in managing change. This is an analysis of the skills and competencies that employees must have to achieve

6. Describe the use of organizational diagnosis and needs analysis as a first step in organizational development.

the goals of the change. A needs analysis is essential because interventions such as training programs must target these skills and competencies.

Hundreds of alternative OD intervention methods exist. One way of classifying these methods is by the target of change. The target of change may be the organization, groups within the organization, or individuals.

Organization- and Group-Focused Techniques

Some OD intervention methods emphasize changing the organization itself or changing the work groups within the organization. Intervention methods in this category include survey feedback, management by objectives, product and service quality programs, team building, and process consultation.

Survey Feedback *Survey feedback* is a widely used intervention method whereby employee attitudes are solicited using a questionnaire. Once the data are collected, they are analyzed and fed back to the employees to diagnose problems and plan other interventions. Survey feedback is often used as an exploratory tool and then is combined with some other intervention. The effectiveness of survey feedback in actually improving outcomes (absenteeism or productivity, for example) increases substantially when this method is combined with other interventions.[42]

Some surveys are developed by managers within the organization and tailored to a specific problem or issue. Well-established and widely used surveys also are available for use. Two such surveys are the Survey of Organizations and the Michigan Organizational Assessment Questionnaire, both of which were developed at the University of Michigan's Institute for Social Research.[43] A large body of research indicates that these surveys have good reliability and validity, and they are useful tools for gathering employees' perceptions of their work environments.

For survey feedback to be an effective method, certain guidelines should be used. Employees must be assured that their responses to the questionnaire will be confidential and anonymous. Unless this assurance is given, the responses may not be honest. Feedback should be reported in a group format; that is, no individual responses should be identified. Employees must be able to trust that there will be no negative repercussions from their responses. Employees should be informed of the purpose of the survey. Failing to do this can set up unrealistic expectations about the changes that might come from the surveys.

In addition, management must be prepared to follow up on the survey results. If some things cannot be changed, the rationale (for example, prohibitive cost) must be explained to the employees. Without appropriate follow-through, employees will not take the survey process seriously the next time.

Management by Objectives As an organization-wide technique, *management by objectives (MBO)* involves joint goal setting between employees and managers. The MBO process includes the setting of initial objectives, periodic progress reviews, and problem solving to remove any obstacles to

---

7. Discuss the major organization development interventions.

survey feedback
A widely used method of intervention whereby employee attitudes are solicited using a questionnaire.

management by objectives (MBO)
An organization-wide intervention technique that involves joint goal setting between employees and managers.

goal achievement.[44] All these steps are joint efforts between managers and employees.

MBO is a valuable intervention because it meets three needs. First, it clarifies what is expected of employees. This reduces role conflict and ambiguity. Second, MBO provides knowledge of results, an essential ingredient in effective job performance. Finally, MBO provides an opportunity for coaching and counseling by the manager. The problem-solving approach encourages open communication and discussion of obstacles to goal achievement.[45]

Companies that have used MBO successfully include the former Tenneco, Mobil (now part of ExxonMobil), and General Electric. The success of MBO in effecting organizational results hinges on the linking of individual goals to the goals of the organization. MBO is usually tailored to the organization; as such, MBO programs may appear to differ widely across organizations.[46] Nevertheless, the programs all focus on joint goal setting and evaluation. MBO programs should be used with caution, however. An excessive emphasis on goal achievement can result in cutthroat competition among employees, falsification of results, and striving for results at any cost. In addition, top management support is essential if the program aspires to be more than just an exercise in red tape.

Product and Service Quality Programs *Quality programs*—programs that embed product and service quality excellence in the organizational culture—are assuming key roles in the organization development efforts of many companies. For example, the success or failure of a service company may depend on the quality of customer service it provides.[47] The quality revolution consists of programs that entail two steps. The first step is to raise aspirations about the product and service quality, both within the company and among its customers. If the organization is to improve, employees must be committed to product and service quality excellence, and customers must expect it. The second step is to embed product and service quality excellence in the organizational culture, using continual improvement tools such as benchmarking to change habits, attitudes, skills, and knowledge. Benchmarking involves comparing products and processes with those of other companies in order to imitate and improve on them. Xerox uses benchmarking to improve the product quality of its copiers. Service quality improvement programs can lead to competitive advantage, increased productivity, enhanced employee morale, and word-of-mouth advertising from satisfied customers. Gateway, Inc., provides toll-free technical support for the life of the customer's Gateway computer system, and it is reputed to have the best qualified technical support staff in the industry.

The Ritz-Carlton Hotel Company (now part of Marriott International) integrated its comprehensive service quality program into marketing and business objectives. The Atlanta-based company, which managed twenty-eight luxury hotels, won the Malcolm Baldrige Award for service quality. Key elements of Ritz-Carlton's quality program included participatory executive leadership, thorough information gathering, coordinated execution,

quality program
A program that embeds product and service quality excellence in the organizational culture.

and employees who were empowered to "move heaven and earth" to satisfy customers.[48]

At Ritz-Carlton, the company president and thirteen senior executives made up the senior quality management team, which met weekly to focus on service quality. Quality goals were established at all levels of the company. The crucial product and service requirements of travel consumers were translated into Ritz-Carlton Gold Standards, which included a credo, a motto, three steps of service, and twenty Ritz-Carlton Basics. These standards guided service quality throughout the organization.

Employees were required to act on a customer complaint at once and were empowered to provide "instant pacification," no matter what it took. Quality teams set action plans at all levels of the company. Each hotel had a quality leader, who served as a resource to the quality teams. Daily quality production reports provided an early warning system for identifying areas that needed quality improvement.

The Ritz-Carlton program had all of the hallmarks of an excellent service quality program: committed leadership, empowered teams and employees, carefully researched standards and goals, and constant monitoring. The company reaped rewards from its excellent service; it received hundreds of quality-related awards, along with best-in-industry rankings from all three major hotel-ranking organizations.

After celebrating an award as the best hotel in the world, Ritz-Carlton did not stop its quality improvement process. At one hotel, the chief complaint was that room service was always late. A quality team was put together, including a cook, a waiter, and a room service order taker. They studied how the process flowed. When they discovered that the service elevator was slow, they added an engineer and a representative from the elevator company to the team. They found the elevators worked well. Next they posted a team member in the elevator twenty-four hours a day for a week. Every time the door opened, the team member had to find out why. Finally, a team member noticed that housemen who helped the maids got on the elevator a lot. It turned out that the housemen were stealing towels from other floors because their maids needed more. The problem with room service was that the hotel didn't own enough towels. Ritz-Carlton bought more towels, and room service complaints fell 50 percent.[49]

team building
An intervention designed to improve the effectiveness of a work group.

Team Building As an organization development intervention, *team building* can improve the effectiveness of work groups. Team building usually begins with a diagnostic process through which team members identify problems, and it continues with the team's planning actions to take in order to resolve those problems. The OD practitioner in team building serves as a facilitator, and the work itself is completed by team members.[50]

Team building is a very popular OD method. A survey of Fortune 500 companies indicated that human resource managers considered team building the most successful OD technique.[51] Four areas in team building are critical to the success of the intervention:

1. Team building should develop communication that facilitates respect for other members' input and the desire to work for the good of the team.
2. Team building should encourage member interaction and mutual inter-dependence.
3. Team building should emphasize team goals. Team members should learn one another's responsibilities so that the team can deal adaptively with crisis situations.
4. Team building must provide examples of effective and ineffective team-work, and it should stress flexibility.[52]

One popular technique for team building is the use of outdoor challenges. Participants go through a series of outdoor activities, such as climbing a fourteen-foot wall. Similar physical challenges require the participants to work as a team and focus on trust, communication, decision making, and leadership. GE and Weyerhaeuser use outdoor challenges at the beginning of their team-building courses, and later in the training, team members apply what they have learned to actual business situations.[53]

Because team building is a relatively new intervention, it is difficult to assess its effectiveness. Preliminary studies, however, indicate that team building can improve group processes.[54]

Large Group Interventions Among the newer techniques on the horizon for managing change are large group interventions, which bring all of the key members of a group together in one room for an extended period of time. Prior to the event, consultants work with the organization to determine who will participate and what the goal of the event should be. Large group interventions are intended to create a critical mass of people within an organization to support a change. These individuals then become internal change agents who implement the changes that are designed by the large group. One such intervention is FutureSearch, which uses a set format. It works with self-managed teams, lasts three days, and includes forty to eighty participants. The advantage of large group interventions is that they can quickly have an impact because they involve many people at once.[55]

Process Consultation Pioneered by Edgar Schein, *process consultation* is an OD method that helps managers and employees improve the processes that are used in organizations.[56] The processes most often targeted are communication, conflict resolution, decision making, group interaction, and leadership.

One of the distinguishing features of the process consultation approach is that an outside consultant is used. The role of the consultant is to help employees help themselves. The consultant guides the organization members in examining the processes in the organization and in refining them. The steps in process consultation are entering the organization, defining the relationship, choosing an approach, gathering data and diagnosing problems, intervening, and gradually leaving the organization.

Process consultation is an interactive technique between employees and an outside consultant, so it is seldom used as a sole OD method. Most often, it is used in combination with other OD interventions.

process consultation
An OD method that helps managers and employees improve the processes that are used in organizations.

All the preceding OD methods focus on changing the organization or the work group. Other OD methods are aimed at facilitating change within individuals.

Individual-Focused Techniques

Organization development efforts that are targeted toward individuals include skills training, sensitivity training, management development training, role negotiation, job redesign, stress management programs, and career planning.

Skills Training The key question addressed by *skills training* is "What knowledge, skills, and abilities are necessary to do this job effectively?" Skills training is accomplished either in formal classroom settings or on the job. The challenge of integrating skills training into organization development is the rapid change that most organizations face. The job knowledge in most positions requires continual updates to keep pace with rapid change.

FedEx depends on 107,000 full- and part-time employees in more than 200 countries to deliver 100 percent customer satisfaction. The company is constantly changing its products and services, sometimes at the rate of 1,700 changes per year. FedEx decided to accomplish its mission using interactive video training and job skills testing. The video training consists of twenty-five laser disks updated with a CD-ROM every six weeks. Employees find the interactive video training easy to use, convenient, and individualized. FedEx has found it to be economical as well because it eliminates travel expenses and the need for instructors. In job skills testing, every customer service employee takes a test every six months via computer. The test generates a unique prescription that informs employees what they do well and how they need to improve. It also directs employees to the interactive video lesson they need to practice to improve their skills.[57]

Sensitivity Training Also called T-group training, *sensitivity training* is designed to help individuals understand how their behavior affects others. In a typical session, groups of ten to twelve strangers (T-groups) are formed. Participants from the same organization are placed in different T-groups. The trainer serves as a resource person but does not engage in structuring behaviors. The members are left on their own to work out the interaction in the group, and they are encouraged to concentrate on the "here and now" of the experience and on openness with other group members. It is important that the trainer be well qualified to monitor the group's progress. The trainer intervenes only to help move the group forward.[58]

The outcome of sensitivity training should be an increased sensitivity to others, and in some cases this has been demonstrated. In other cases, however, the new and better ways of dealing with others did not persist on the job. When people returned to their jobs, which rewarded the old behaviors, the new behavior patterns were quickly extinguished. There are also side effects from T-groups. Because they result in emotional exposure, some participants feel vulnerable and react negatively to the extreme personal nature of the interactions.

---

skills training
Increasing the job knowledge, skills, and abilities that are necessary to do a job effectively.

sensitivity training
An intervention designed to help individuals understand how their behavior affects others.

Sensitivity training is less popular today than it was in the early 1980s.[59] It can still be used, however, to help managers deal with current challenges like cultural, gender, age, and ability diversity. T-groups can help employees understand others better, become aware of their own feelings and perceptions, and improve communication.

Management Development Training *Management development* encompasses a host of techniques designed to enhance a manager's skills on the job. Management development training generally focuses on four types of learning: verbal information, intellectual skills, attitudes, and development. Verbal information that is disseminated in training, such as information on leadership theory, can be assessed with objective measures like tests. Intellectual skills, such as how to conduct a performance appraisal in a specific format, can be evaluated by performance demonstrations. Attitudes, such as attitudes toward workforce diversity, can be assessed via questionnaires. Development—a change in self-knowledge and behavior—is more difficult to evaluate. It can be assessed, however, by descriptive reports from the manager, performance appraisals from the manager's supervisor, and organizational outcomes.[60]

management development
A host of techniques for enhancing managers' skills in an organization.

Development as a manager requires an integration of classroom learning with on-the-job experiences. One way of accomplishing development is through the use of action learning, a technique that was pioneered in Europe.[61] In action learning, managers take on unfamiliar problems or familiar problems in unfamiliar settings. The managers work on the problems and meet weekly in small groups made up of individuals from different organizations. The outcome of action learning is that managers learn about themselves through the challenges of their comrades. Other techniques that provide active learning for participants are simulation, business games, role-playing, and case studies.[62]

Management development can be conducted in a formal classroom setting or consist of on-the-job training. If a classroom setting is used, it is essential that follow-up be done to ensure that the skills transfer to the job.

Management development should be based on a careful needs assessment. The content of the program should focus on the skills that managers must possess to be successful in the future.

Role Negotiation Individuals who work together sometimes have differing expectations of one another within the working relationship. *Role negotiation* is a simple technique whereby individuals meet and clarify their psychological contract. In doing this, the expectations of each party are clarified and negotiated. The outcome of role negotiation is a better understanding between the two parties of what each can be expected to give and receive in the reciprocal relationship. When both parties have a mutual agreement on expectations, there is less ambiguity in the process of working together.

role negotiation
A technique whereby individuals meet and clarify their psychological contract.

Job Redesign As an OD intervention method, *job redesign* emphasizes the fit between individual skills and the demands of the job. Chapter 13 outlined several approaches to job design. Many of these methods are used as

job redesign
An OD intervention method that alters jobs to improve the fit between individual skills and the demands of the job.

OD techniques for realigning task demands and individual capabilities, or for redesigning jobs to fit new techniques or organizational structures better.

One company that has undergone tremendous change is Harley-Davidson. The motorcycle manufacturer was close to financial disaster when it engaged in a radical restructuring effort. The company essentially threw out the old hierarchies and traditional jobs, opted for a leaner organization, and redesigned jobs to allow employees more participation and control. The company credits its renewed success, in part, to its redesign efforts.[63]

Steelcase, the world's leading designer and manufacturer of office furniture, used job redesign as a key component of its comprehensive change from a traditional manufacturing system to a "factory within a factory" design. In the old system, jobs were designed around the principle of task simplicity and specialization. In the new design, operations are arranged by products, with each factory run by a self-managed team. Employees' jobs are now flexible, team oriented, and characterized by high levels of empowerment.

Health Promotion Programs As organizations have become increasingly concerned with the costs of distress in the workplace, health promotion programs have become a part of larger organization development efforts. In Chapter 7, we examined stress and strain at work. Companies that have successfully integrated health promotion programs into their organizations include AT&T, Caterpillar, Kimberly-Clark, and Johnson & Johnson.

The components of health promotion and stress management programs vary widely. They can include education about stress and coping, diagnosis of the causes of stress, relaxation training, company-provided exercise programs, and employee assistance programs. These efforts all focus on helping employees manage stress before it becomes a problem.

Career Planning Matching an individual's career aspirations with the opportunities in the organization is career planning. This proactive approach to career management is often part of an organization's development efforts. Career planning is a joint responsibility of organizations and individuals. Companies like IBM, Travelers Insurance (part of Citigroup), and 3M have implemented career-planning programs.

Career-planning activities benefit the organization, as well as its individuals. Through counseling sessions, employees identify their skills and skill deficiencies. The organization then can plan its training and development efforts based on this information. In addition, the process can be used to identify and nurture talented employees for potential promotion.

Managers can choose from a host of organization development techniques to facilitate organizational change. Some of these techniques are aimed toward organizations or groups, and others focus on individuals. Large-scale changes in organizations require the use of multiple techniques. For example, implementing a new technology like robotics may require simultaneous changes in the structure of the organization, the configuration of work groups, and individual attitudes.

We should recognize at this point that the organization development methods just described are means to an end. Programs do not drive change; business needs do. The OD methods are merely vehicles for moving the organization and its employees in a more effective direction.

ETHICAL CONSIDERATIONS IN ORGANIZATION DEVELOPMENT

Organization development is a process of helping organizations improve. It may involve resistance to change, shifts in power, losses of control, and redefinition of tasks.[64] These are all sensitive issues. Further, the change agent, whether a manager from within the organization or a consultant from outside, is in a position of directing the change. Such a position carries the potential for misuse of power. The ethical concerns surrounding the use of organization development center around four issues.[65]

The first issue is the selection of the OD method to be used. Every change agent has inherent biases about particular methods, but these biases must not enter into the decision process. The OD method used must be carefully chosen in accordance with the problem as diagnosed, the organization's culture, and the employees concerned. All alternatives should be given fair consideration in the choice of a method. In addition, the OD practitioner should never use a method he or she is not skilled in delivering. Using a method you are not an expert in is unethical, because the client assumes you are.

The second ethical issue is voluntary participation. No employee should be forced to participate in any OD intervention.[66] To make an informed decision about participation, employees should be given information about the nature of the intervention and what will be expected of them. They should also be afforded the option to discontinue their participation at any time they so choose.

The third issue of ethical concern is confidentiality. Change agents gather a wealth of information during organizational diagnoses and interventions. Successful change agents develop a trusting relationship with employees. They may receive privileged information, sometimes unknowingly. It is unethical for a change agent to reveal information in order to give some group or individual political advantage or to enhance the change agent's own standing. Consultants should not reveal information about an organization to its competitors. The use of information gathered from OD efforts is a sensitive issue and presents ethical dilemmas.

A final ethical concern in OD is the potential for manipulation by the change agent. Because any change process involves influence, some individuals may feel manipulated. The key to alleviating the potential for manipulation is open communication. Participants should be given complete knowledge of the rationale for change, what they can expect of the change process, and what the intervention will entail. No actions should be taken that limit the participants' freedom of choice.[67]

8. Identify the ethical issues that must be considered in organization development efforts.

ARE ORGANIZATION DEVELOPMENT EFFORTS EFFECTIVE?

Because organization development is designed to help organizations manage change, it is important to evaluate the effectiveness of these efforts. The success of any OD intervention depends on a host of factors, including the technique used, the competence of the change agent, the organization's readiness for change, and top management commitment. No single method of OD is effective in every instance. Instead, multiple-method OD approaches are recommended, because they allow organizations to capitalize on the benefits of several approaches.[68]

Efforts to evaluate OD efforts have focused on outcomes such as productivity. One review of more than 200 interventions indicated that worker productivity improved in 87 percent of the cases.[69] A separate analysis of 98 of these interventions revealed impressive productivity increases.[70] We can conclude that when properly applied and managed, organization development programs have positive effects on performance.[71]

MANAGERIAL IMPLICATIONS: MANAGING CHANGE

Several guidelines can be used to facilitate the success of management change efforts.[72] First, managers should recognize the forces for change. These forces can come from a combination of sources both internal and external to the organization.

A shared vision of the change should be developed that includes participation by all employees in the planning process. Top management must be committed to the change and should visibly demonstrate support, because employees look to these leaders to model appropriate behavior. A comprehensive diagnosis and needs analysis should be conducted. The company then must ensure that there are adequate resources for carrying out the change.

Resistance to change should be planned for and managed. Communication, participation, and empathetic support are ways of helping employees adjust. The reward system within the organization must be carefully evaluated to ensure that new behaviors, rather than old ones, are being reinforced. Participation in the change process should also be recognized and rewarded.

The organization development technique used should be carefully selected to meet the goals of the change. Finally, organization development efforts should be managed in an ethical manner and should preserve employees' privacy and freedom of choice. By using these guidelines, managers can meet the challenges of managing change while enhancing productivity in their organizations.

Experiencing OB

One of the main productivity outcomes that results from changing organizational processes is the enhancement of employee creativity. Learn more about creativity in organizations at our animated concept and activity site. Choose Innovation&Change from the "select a topic" pull-down menu, then Fostering Innovation from the "overview tab."

http://www.experiencingob.com

Looking Back

Technology Keeps the American Red Cross Running Smoothly

Charities are often ranked by how efficiently they spend your money. By this criterion, the American Red Cross is the number one charity on most rankings. It dedicates an average of 92 percent of its income to programs. Led by its 1.4 million volunteers, the Red Cross not only assists in disasters, but also teaches first aid and swimming, keeps American troops in touch with loved ones, and provides half of the U.S. blood supply, as you saw in the Thinking Ahead feature. It has a record of successful operations that many businesses envy.

You may not know that the American Red Cross is quite a high-tech organization.[73] Internet commerce is a hot prospect among nonprofit organizations and charities as well as businesses. The Red Cross has a Web site (www.redcross.org) so that people motivated by a disaster can instantly donate money. Web site donations, like other donations, peak during December, when people are in a giving mood and because December is the last chance for tax write-offs. Web site receipts average $100,000 for the Red Cross. The Web site is also an excellent way to recruit volunteers and to educate people about the Red Cross's mission, which is to "provide relief to victims of disasters and help people prevent, prepare for, and respond to emergencies."

A sophisticated monitoring system forecasts and tracks disasters so that volunteers and equipment can be mobilized into action. Wireless local-area network (LAN) technology eases the costs and hassles of setting up the temporary warehouses that the Red Cross uses to stock emergency disaster services operations. The organization needs to set up temporary communications and data networks in donated space, and it is impossible to lay wires in those situations. The wireless LANs also reduce the cost of providing relief services because it takes less time to track supplies.

Technology allows the American Red Cross to respond quickly and effectively to the world's crises. Relief operations require the speed and efficiency of modern technologies, and by staying at the forefront of change, the Red Cross puts the technologies to good use.

CHAPTER SUMMARY

1. Organizations face many pressures to change. Some forces are external, including globalization, workforce diversity, technological innovation, and ethics. Other forces are internal, such as declining effectiveness, crises, changing employee expectations, and a changing work climate.

2. Organizations face both planned and unplanned change. Change can be of an incremental, strategic, or transformational nature. The individual who directs the change, known as a change agent, can be internal or external to the organization.

3. Individuals resist change for many reasons, and many of these reasons are rooted in fear. Organizations can help manage resistance by educating workers and openly communicating the change, encouraging worker participation in the change efforts, and providing empathy and support to those who have difficulty dealing with change.

4. Reactions to change may be manifested in behaviors reflecting disengagement, disidentification, disenchantment, and disorientation. Managers can use separate interventions targeted toward each reaction.

5. Force field analysis states that when the forces for change are balanced by the forces restraining change, an equilibrium state exists. For change to occur, the forces for change must increase, or the restraining forces must decrease.

6. Lewin's change model proposes three stages of change: unfreezing, moving, and refreezing.

7. A thorough diagnosis and needs analysis is a critical first step in any organization development (OD) intervention.

8. OD interventions targeted toward organizations and groups include survey feedback, management by objectives, product and service quality programs, team building, and process consultation.

9. OD interventions that focus on individuals include skills training, sensitivity training, management development training, role negotiation, job redesign, stress management programs, and career planning.

10. OD efforts should be managed ethically and should preserve individual freedom of choice and privacy.

11. When properly conducted, organization development can have positive effects on performance.

KEY TERMS

planned change   478
unplanned change   478
incremental change   483
strategic change   483
transformational change   483
change agent   483
disengagement   489
disidentification   490

disenchantment   490
disorientation   491
unfreezing   491
moving   493
refreezing   493
organization development (OD)   494
survey feedback   496
management by objectives (MBO)   496

quality program   497
team building   498
process consultation   499
skills training   500
sensitivity training   500
management development   501
role negotiation   501
job redesign   501

REVIEW QUESTIONS

1. What are the major external and internal forces for change in organizations?

2. Contrast incremental, strategic, and transformational change.

3. What is a change agent? Who plays this role?

4. What are the major reasons individuals resist change? How can organizations deal with resistance?

5. Name the four behavioral reactions to change. Describe the behavioral signs of each reaction, and identify an organizational strategy for dealing with each reaction.

6. Describe force field analysis and its relationship to Lewin's change model.

7. What is organization development? Why is it undertaken by organizations?

8. Name six areas to be critically examined in any comprehensive organizational diagnosis.

9. What are the major organization-focused and group-focused OD intervention methods? The major individual-focused methods?

10. Which OD intervention is most effective?

DISCUSSION AND COMMUNICATION QUESTIONS

1. What are the major external forces for change in today's organizations?
2. What are the advantages of using an external change agent? An internal change agent?
3. Review Challenge 16.1. What can you learn from this challenge about how individuals' tolerance for ambiguity can lead to resistance?
4. Can organizations prevent resistance to change? If so, how?
5. What organization development techniques are the easiest to implement? What techniques are the most difficult to implement? Why?
6. Suppose your organization experiences a dramatic increase in turnover. How would you diagnose the underlying problem?
7. Downsizing has played a major role in changing U.S. organizations. Analyze the internal and external forces for change regarding downsizing an organization.
8. If you were in charge of designing the ideal management development program, what topics would you include? Why?
9. *(communication question)* Find an article that describes an organization that has gone through change and managed it well. Develop an "Organizational Reality" feature of your own about the example you find using the format in this book. Prepare a brief oral presentation of your Organizational Reality for your class.
10. *(communication question)* Think of a change you would like to make in your life. Using Figure 16.1 as a guide, prepare your own force field analysis for that change. How will you overcome the forces for the status quo? How will you make sure to "refreeze" following the change? Summarize your analysis in an action plan.

ETHICS QUESTIONS

1. What constitutes abuse of a change agent's power? How can organizations prevent this?
2. Is it ethical for an organization to coerce individuals to change?
3. You are leading a management development seminar, and the supervisor of one of the participants asks how his employee is performing in the seminar. Should you reveal this information?
4. Suppose you are a consultant, and an organization asks you to deliver a team-building intervention. You know a little about team building, but not a lot. You do know that a competitor will probably get the job if you do not do it. What should you do?
5. Suppose you are a consultant, and a company asks you to assist in rewriting its policies and procedures manual to help eliminate the company's excessive absenteeism. From your limited knowledge about the company, you suspect that the problem lies elsewhere, and that changing the manual will not solve the problem. What should you do?

Experiential Exercises

16.1 Organizational Diagnosis of the University

The purpose of this exercise is to give you experience in organizational diagnosis. Assume that your team has been hired to conduct a diagnosis of problem areas in your university and to make preliminary recommendations for organization development interventions.

Each team member should complete the following University Profile. Then, as a team, evaluate the strengths and weaknesses within each area (academics, teaching, social, cultural, and administrative) using the accompanying University Diagnosis form. Finally, make recommendations concerning organization development interventions for each area. Be as specific as possible in both your diagnosis and your recommendations. Each team should then present its diagnosis to the class.

UNIVERSITY PROFILE

Not True   1   2   3   4   5   Very True

I. Academics

1 2 3 4 5   1. There is a wide range of courses to choose from.

1 2 3 4 5   2. Classroom standards are too easy.

1 2 3 4 5   3. The library is adequate.

1 2 3 4 5   4. Textbooks are helpful.

II. Teachers

1 2 3 4 5   1. Teachers here are committed to quality instruction.

1 2 3 4 5   2. We have a high-quality faculty.

III. Social

1 2 3 4 5   1. Students are friendly to one another.

1 2 3 4 5   2. It is difficult to make friends.

1 2 3 4 5   3. Faculty get involved in student activities.

1 2 3 4 5   4. Too much energy goes into drinking and goofing off.

IV. Cultural Events

1 2 3 4 5   1. There are ample activities on campus.

1 2 3 4 5   2. Student activities are boring.

1 2 3 4 5   3. The administration places a high value on student activities.

1 2 3 4 5   4. Too much emphasis is placed on sports.

1 2 3 4 5   5. We need more "cultural" activities.

V. Organizational/Management

1 2 3 4 5   1. Decision making is shared at all levels of the organization.

1 2 3 4 5   2. There is unity and cohesiveness among departments and units.

1 2 3 4 5   3. Too many departmental clashes hamper the organization's effectiveness.

1 2 3 4 5   4. Students have a say in many decisions.

1 2 3 4 5   5. The budgeting process seems fair.

1 2 3 4 5   6. Recruiting and staffing are handled thoughtfully, with student needs in mind.

University Diagnosis

	STRENGTH	WEAKNESS	INTERVENTION
1. Academic			
2. Teaching			
3. Social			
4. Cultural			
5. Administrative			

SOURCE: "Organizational Diagnosis of the University" by D. Marcic, *Organizational Behavior: Experiences and Cases* (St. Paul, Minn.: West Publishing Company, 1989), 326–329. Reprinted by permission.

16.2 Team Building for Team Effectiveness

This exercise will allow you and your team to engage in an organization development activity for team building. The two parts of the exercise are diagnosis and intervention.

Part 1. Diagnosis

Working as a team, complete the following four steps:

1. Describe how you have worked together this semester as a team.

2. What has your team done especially well? What has enabled this?

3. What problems or conflicts have you had as a team? (Be specific.) What was the cause of the problems your team experienced? Have the conflicts been over ideas, methods, or people?

4. Would you assess the overall effectiveness of your team as excellent, good, fair, poor, or a disaster? Explain your effectiveness rating.

Part 2. Intervention

A diagnosis provides the basis for intervention and action in organization development. Team building is a way to improve the relationships and effectiveness of teams at work. It is concerned with the results of work activities and the relationships among the members of the team. Complete the following three steps as a team.

Step 1. Answer the following questions with regard to the relationships within the team:
  a. How could conflicts have been handled better?
  b. How could specific relationships have been improved?
  c. How could the interpersonal atmosphere of the team have been improved?

Step 2. Answer the following questions with regard to the results of the team's work:
  a. How could the team have been more effective?
  b. Are there any team process changes that would have improved the team's effectiveness?
  c. Are there any team structure changes that would have improved the team's effectiveness?

Step 3. Answer the following questions with regard to the work environment in your place of employment:
  a. What have you learned about team building that you can apply there?
  b. What have you learned about team building that would not be applicable there?

For more practice exercises, consult the fifth edition of *Organizational Behavior: Experiences and Cases* by Dorothy Marcic and Joseph Seltzer (South-Western, 1998).

Endnotes

Chapter 1

1. E. A. Schein, "Reassessing the 'Divine Rights' of Managers," *Sloan Management Review* 30 (1989): 63–68

2. H. Schwartz, "The Clockwork or the Snakepit: An Essay on the Meaning of Teaching Organizational Behavior," *Organizational Behavior Teaching Review* 11, No. 2 (1987): 19–26.

3. K. Lewin, "Field Theory in Social Science," selected theoretical papers (edited by Dorin Cartwright) (New York: Harper, 1951).

4. L. R. Offermann and M. K. Gowing, guest eds., "Special Issue: Organizational Psychology," *American Psychologist* 45 (1990): 95–283.

5. R. M. Yerkes, "The Relation of Psychology to Military Activities," *Mental Hygiene* 1 (1917): 371–376.

6. R. K. Merton, "The Role Set," *British Journal of Sociology* 8 (1957): 106–120.

7. N. Gross, W. Mason, and A. McEachen, *Explorations in Role Analysis: Studies of the School Superintendency Role* (New York: Wiley, 1958)

8. F. W. Taylor, *The Principles of Scientific Management* (New York: Norton, 1911).

9. E. A. Locke and G. P. Latham, *A Theory of Goal Setting and Task Performance* (Englewood Cliffs, N.J.: Prentice-Hall, 1990).

10. A. L. Wilkins and W. G. Ouchi, "Efficient Cultures: Exploring the Relationship between Culture and Organizational Performance," *Administrative Science Quarterly* 28 (1983): 468–481.

11. M. F. R. Kets de Vries and D. Miller, "Personality, Culture, and Organization," *Academy of Management Review* 11 (1986): 266–279.

12. H. Schwartz, *Narcissistic Process and Corporate Decay: The Theory of the Organizational Ideal* (New York: NYU Press, 1990).

13. J. G. March and H. A. Simon, *Organizations* (New York: Wiley, 1958).

14. H. B. Elkind, *Preventive Management: Mental Hygiene in Industry* (New York: B. C. Forbes, 1931).

15. J. C. Quick, "Occupational Health Psychology: Historical Roots and Future Directions," *Health Psychology* 18 (1999).

16. K. R. Pelletier, *Mind as Healer, Mind as Slayer: A Holistic Approach to Preventing Stress Disorders* (New York: Delacorte, 1977).

17. D. R. Ilgen, "Health Issues at Work," *American Psychologist* 45 (1990): 273–283.

18. R. L. A. Sterba, "The Organization and Management of the Temple Corporations in Ancient Mesopotamia," *Academy of Management Review* 1 (1976): 16–26; S. P. Dorsey, *Early English Churches in America* (New York: Oxford University Press, 1952).

19. Sir I. Moncreiffe of That Ilk, *The Highland Clans: The Dynastic Origins, Chiefs, and Background of the Clans and of Some Other Families Connected to Highland History*, rev. ed. (New York: C. N. Potter, 1982).

20. D. Shambaugh, "The Soldier and the State in China: The Political Work System in the People's Liberation Army," *Chinese Quarterly* 127 (1991): 527–568.

21. L. L'Abate, ed., *Handbook of Developmental Family Psychology and Psychopathology* (New York: Wiley, 1993).

22. J. A. Hostetler, *Communitarian Societies* (New York: Holt, Rinehart & Winston, 1974).

23. J. M. Lewis, "The Family System and Physical Illness," in *No Single Thread: Psychological Health in Family Systems* (New York: Brunner/Mazel, 1976).

24. H. J. Leavitt, "Applied Organizational Change in Industry: Structural, Technological, and Humanistic Approaches," in J. G. March, ed., *Handbook of Organizations* (Chicago: Rand McNally, 1965), 1144–1170.

25. J. D. Thompson, *Organizations in Action* (New York: McGraw-Hill, 1967).

26. F. J. Roethlisberger and W. J. Dickson, *Management and the Worker* (Cambridge, Mass.: Harvard University Press, 1939).

27. R. J. Selfridge and S. L. Sokolik, "A Comprehensive View of Organizational Development," *MSU Business Topics*, Winter 1975, 47.

28. W. L. French and C. H. Bell, *Organization Development*, 4th ed. (Englewood Cliffs, N.J.: Prentice-Hall, 1990).

29. J. P. Kotter, "Managing External Dependence," *Academy of Management Review* 4 (1979): 87–92.

30. P. Kepos, ed., "Ford Motor Company," *International Directory of Company Histories*, vol. 11 (New York: St James Press/ITP, 1988), 136–140; R. L. Shook, *Turn Around: The New Ford Motor Company* (New York: Prentice-Hall, 1990); *Moody's Company Data Report on Ford Motor Co.*, April 1998.

31. P. Kepos, ed., "Gateway 2000, Inc.," *International Directory of Company Histories*, vol. 10 (New York: St James Press/ITP, 1988), 307–309; *Hoover's Handbook of American Business 1998* (Austin, Tex.: Hoover's, 1998), 642–643; *Moody's Company Data Report on Gateway 2000 Inc.*, April 1998.

32. P. Kepos, ed., "Southwest Airlines Co.," *International Directory of Company Histories*, vol. 6 (Detroit: St James Press/ITP, 1988), 119–121; A. Haasen and G. F. Shea, *A Better Place to Work: A New Sense of Motivation Leading to High Productivity* (New York: American Management Association, 1997); *Moody's Company Data Report on Southwest Airlines Co.*, April 1998.

33. E. G. Flamholtz and Y. Randle, *Changing the Game* (New York: Oxford, 1998); T. Grant, ed., "Starbucks Corporation," *International Directory of Company Histories*, vol. 13 (New York: St James Press/ITP, 1988), 493–494; *Hoover's Handbook of Emerging Companies 1998* (Austin, Tex.: Hoover's, 1998), 662–663; *Moody's Company Data Report on Starbucks Corp.*, April 1998.

34. http://www.hoovers.com; P. Newcomb and L. Gubernick, "The Top 40," *Forbes*, September 27, 1993, 97–104; "The Hot 100," *Success*, May 1, 1998, 50.

35. American Red Cross, *FACTS 1997* (Falls Church, Va.: Author, 1997); *Hoover's Company Profile Database—American Private Enterprise* (Austin, Tex.: Hoover's, 1998).

36. M. K. Gowing, J. D. Kraft, and J. C. Quick, *The New Organizational Reality: Downsizing, Restructuring and Revitalization* (Washington, D.C.: American Psychological Association, 1998); T. Tang and R. M. Fuller, "Corporate Downsizing: What Managers Can Do to Lessen the Negative Effects of Layoffs," *SAM Advanced Management Journal*, 60 (1995): 12–15, 31.

37. L. E. Thurow, *Head to Head: The Coming Economic Battle among Japan, Europe, and America* (New York: William Morrow, 1992).

38. J. E. Patterson, *Acquiring the Future: America's Survival and Success in the Global Economy* (Homewood, Ill.: Dow Jones-Irwin, 1990) and H. B. Stewart, *Recollecting the Future: A View of Business, Technology, and Innovation in the Next 30 Years* (Homewood, Ill.: Dow Jones-Irwin, 1989).

39. L. R. Offermann and M. K. Gowing, "Organizations of the Future," *American Psychologist* 45 (1990): 95–108.

40. R. S. Fosler, W. Alonso, J. A. Meyer, and R. Kern, *Demographic Change and the American Future* (Pittsburgh, Pa.: University of Pittsburgh Press, 1990).

41. D. Ciampa, *Total Quality* (Reading, Mass.: Addison-Wesley, 1992).

42. American Management Association, *Blueprints for Service Quality: The Federal Express Approach* (New York: American Management Association, 1991) and P. R. Thomas, L. J. Gallace, and K. R. Martin, *Quality Alone Is Not Enough* (New York: American Management Association, 1992).

43. J. A. Edosomwan, "Six Commandments to Empower Employees for Quality Improvement," *Industrial Engineering* 24 (1992): 14–15.

44. See also the five articles in the Special Research Forum on Teaching Effectiveness in the Organizational Sciences, *The Academy of Management Journal* 40 (1997): 1265–1398.

45. R. M. Steers, L. W. Porter, and G. A. Bigley, *Motivation and Leadership at Work* (New York: McGraw-Hill, 1996).

46. H. Levinson, *Executive Stress* (New York: New American Library, 1975).

47. D. L. Whetzel, "The Department of Labor Identifies Workplace Skills," *Industrial/Organizational Psychologist* 29 (1991): 89–90.

48. D. A. Whetten and K. S. Cameron, *Developing Management Skills*, 3rd ed. (New York: HarperCollins, 1995).

49. C. Argyris and D. A. Schon, *Organizational Learning: A Theory of Action Perspective* (Reading, Mass.: Addison-Wesley, 1978).

50. E. E. Lawler III, "From Job-Based to Competency-Based Organizations," *Journal of Organizational Behavior* 15 (1994): 3–15.

51. http://www.gateway.com

Chapter 2

1. S. Zesiger, "Jac Nasser Is Car Crazy," *Fortune* (June 22, 1998): 79–82; I. Picker, "Alex Trotman of Ford Motor Co.: The $10 Billion Man," *Institutional Investor* (October 1997): 23–27.

2. M. A. Hitt, R. E. Hoskisson, and J. S. Harrison, "Strategic Competitiveness in the 1990s: Challenges and Opportunities for U.S. Executives," *Academy of Management Executive* 5 (1991): 7–22.

3. "Competitiveness Survey: *HBR* Readers Respond," *Harvard Business Review* 65 (1987): 8–11.

4. S. C. Harper, "The Challenges Facing CEOs: Past, Present, and Future," *Academy of Management Executive* 6 (1992): 7–25.

5. T. R. Mitchell and W. G. Scott, "America's Problems and Needed Reforms: Confronting the Ethic of Personal Advantage," *Academy of Management Executive* 4 (1990): 23–25.

6. D. Jamieson and J. O'Mara, *Managing Workforce 2000* (San Francisco: Jossey-Bass, 1991).

7. K. Sera, "Corporate Globalization: A New Trend," *Academy of Management Executive* 6 (1992): 89–96.

8. K. Ohmae, *Borderless World: Power and Strategies in the Interlinked Economy* (New York: Harper & Row, 1990).

9. C. A. Bartlett and S. Ghoshal, *Managing across Borders: The Transnational Solution* (Boston: Harvard Business School Press, 1989).

10. K. R. Xin and J. L. Pearce, "Guanxi: Connections as Substitutes for Formal Institutional Support," *Academy of Management Journal* 39 (1996): 1641–1658.

11. P. S. Chan, "Franchise Management in East Asia," *Academy of Management Executive* 4 (1990): 75–85.

12. H. Weihrich, "Europe 1992: What the Future May Hold," *Academy of Management Executive* 4 (1990): 7–18.

13. R. Sharpe, "Hi-Tech Taboos," *The Wall Street Journal*, October 31, 1995, A1.

14. G. Hofstede, *Culture's Consequences: International Differences in Work-Related Values* (Beverly Hills, Calif.: Sage Publications, 1980).

15. G. Hofstede, "Motivation, Leadership, and Organization: Do American Theories Apply Abroad?" *Organizational Dynamics* (Summer 1980): 42–63.

16. R. Buda and S. M. Elsayed-Elkhouly, "Cultural Differences between Arabs and Americans," *Journal of Cross-Cultural Psychology* 29 (1998): 487–492.

17. G. Hofstede, "Gender Stereotypes and Partner Preferences of Asian Women in Masculine and Feminine Countries," *Journal of Cross-Cultural Psychology* 27 (1996): 533–546.

18. G. Hofstede, "Cultural Constraints in Management Theories," *Academy of Management Executive* 7 (1993): 81–94.

19. G. M. Spreitzer, M. W. McCall, Jr., and J. D. Mahoney, "Early Identification of International Executive Potential," *Journal of Applied Psychology* 82 (1997): 6–29.

20. A. J. Michel, "Goodbyes Can Cost Plenty in Europe," *Fortune*, April 6, 1992, 16.

21. M. Adams, "Building a Rainbow One Stripe at a Time," *HR Magazine*, vol. 9 (August 1999): 72–79.

22. E. Brandt, "Global HR," *Personnel Journal* 70 (1991): 38–44.

23. Towers Perrin and Hudson Institute, *Workforce 2000: Competing in a Seller's Market* (Valhalla, N.Y.: Towers Perrin, 1990).

24. R. W. Judy and C. D'Amico, *Workforce 2020* (Indianapolis, Ind.: Hudson Institute, 1997).

25. L. S. Gottfredson, "Dilemmas in Developing Diversity Programs," in S. E. Jackson, ed., *Diversity in the Workplace: Human Resources Initiatives* (New York: Guilford Press, 1992), 279–305.

26. U.S. Bureau of the Census, *Statistical Abstract of the United States: 1999* (Washington, D.C.: Government Printing Office, 1999).

27. Catalyst (1999). *Catalyst Census of Women Corporate Officers and Top Earners*.

28. S. W. Wellington, *Women in Corporate Leadership: Progress and Prospects* (New York: Catalyst, 1996.)

29. U.S. Department of Labor (1998), "Usual Weekly Earnings Summary," *Labor Force Statistics from the Current Population Survey* (Washington, DC: U.S. Government, 1998).

30. A. M. Morrison, R. P. White, E. Van Velsor, and the Center for Creative Leadership, *Breaking the Glass Ceiling: Can Women Reach the Top of America's Largest Corporations?* (Reading, Mass.: Addison-Wesley, 1987).

31. N. J. Adler, "Global Leadership: Women Leaders," *Management International Review* 37 (1997): 171–196.

32. A. Eyring and B. A. Stead, "Shattering the Glass Ceiling: Some Successful Corporate Practices," *Journal of Business Ethics* 17 (1998): 245–251.

33. Catalyst, *Advancing Women in Business: The Catalyst Guide* (San Francisco: Jossey-Bass, 1998).

34. D. L. Nelson and M. A. Hitt, "Employed Women and Stress: Implications for Enhancing Women's Mental Health in the Workplace," in J. C. Quick, L. R. Murphy, and J. J. Hurrell, Jr., eds., *Stress and Well-Being at Work* (Washington, D.C.: American Psychological Association, 1992), 164–177.

35. L. E. Atwater and D. D. Van Fleet, "Another Ceiling: Can Males Compete for Traditionally Female Jobs?" *Journal of Management* 23 (1997): 603–626.

36. U.S. Department of Health and Human Services, *Profile of Older Americans* (Washington, DC: U.S. Government, 1997).

37. W. B. Johnston, "Global Workforce 2000: The New World Labor Market," *Harvard Business Review* 69 (1991): 115–127.

38. S. E. Jackson and E. B. Alvarez, "Working through Diversity as a Strategic Imperative," in S. E. Jackson, ed., *Diversity in the Workplace: Human Resources Initiatives* (New York: Guilford Press, 1992), 13–36.

39. "Managing Generational Diversity," *HR Magazine* 36 (1991): 91–92.

40. C. M. Solomon, "Managing the Baby Busters," *Personnel Journal* (March 1992): 52–59.

41. S. R. Rhodes, "Age-related Differences in Work Attitudes and Behavior: A Review and

Conceptual Analysis," *Psychological Bulletin* 93 (1983): 338–367.

42. B. L. Hassell and P. L. Perrewe, "An Examination of Beliefs about Older Workers: Do Stereotypes Still Exist?" *Journal of Organizational Behavior* 16 (1995): 457–468.

43. U.S. Bureau of the Census, *Population Profile of the United States, 1997,* U.S. Gov't Printing Office, Washington, D.C.

44. W. J. Rothwell, "HRD and the Americans with Disabilities Act," *Training and Development Journal* (August 1991): 45–47.

45. J. Waldrop, "The Cost of Hiring the Disabled," *American Demographics* (March 1991): 12.

46. Laabs, "The Golden Arches," 52–57.

47. L. Winfield and S. Spielman, "Making Sexual Orientation Part of Diversity," *Training and Development* (April 1995): 50–51.

48. N. E. Day and P. Schoenrade, "Staying in the Closet versus Coming Out: Relationships between Communication about Sexual Orientation and Work Attitudes," *Personnel Psychology* 50 (1997): 147–163.

49. J. Landau, "The Relationship of Race and Gender to Managers' Ratings of Promotion Potential," *Journal of Organizational Behavior* 16 (1995): 391–400.

50. P. Barnum, "Double Jeopardy for Women and Minorities: Pay Differences with Age," *Academy of Management Journal* 38 (1995): 863–880.

51. J. E. Rigdon, "PepsiCo's KFC Scouts for Blacks and Women for Its Top Echelons," *The Wall Street Journal,* November 13, 1991, A1.

52. P. A. Galagan, "Tapping the Power of a Diverse Workforce," *Training and Development Journal* 26 (1991): 38–44.

53. R. Thomas, "From Affirmative Action to Affirming Diversity," *Harvard Business Review* 68 (1990): 107–117.

54. T. H. Cox, Jr., *Cultural Diversity in Organizations: Theory, Research and Practice* (San Francisco: Berrett-Koehler, 1994).

55. J. Gordon, "Different from What?" *Training* (May 1995): 25–33.

56. Task Force on Management of Innovation, *Technology and Employment: Innovation and Growth in the U.S. Economy* (Washington, D.C.: U.S. Government Research Council, 1987).

57. C. H. Ferguson, "Computers and the Coming of the U.S. Keiretsu," *Harvard Business Review* 68 (1990): 55–70.

58. C. Arnst, "The Networked Corporation," *Business Week,* June 26, 1995, 86–89.

59. J. A. Senn, *Information Systems in Management,* 4th ed. (Belmont, Calif.: Wadsworth, 1990).

60. R. Forsyth, "The Anatomy of Expert Systems," in M. Yazdani and A. Narayanan, eds., *Artificial Intelligence: Human Effects* (Chichester, England: Ellis Horwood, 1984), 186–199.

61. M. T. Damore, "A Presentation and Examination of the Integration of Unlawful Discrimination Practices in the Private Business Sector with Artificial Intelligence" (Thesis, Oklahoma State University, 1992).

62. A. Tanzer and R. Simon, "Why Japan Loves Robots and We Don't," *Forbes,* April 16, 1990, 148–153.

63. E. Fingleton, "Jobs for Life: Why Japan Won't Give Them Up," *Fortune,* March 20, 1995, 119–125.

64. B. Wysocki, Jr., "Pulling the Plug: Some Firms, Let Down by Costly Computers, Opt to De-Engineer," *The Wall Street Journal,* April 30, 1998, A1.

65. M. B. W. Fritz, S. Narasimhan, and H. Rhee, "Communication and Coordination in the Virtual Office," *Journal of Management Information Systems* 14 (1998): 7–28.

66. M. Apgar IV, "The Alternative Workplace: Changing Where and How People Work," *Harvard Business Review* (May–June 1998): 121–136.

67. D. L. Nelson, "Individual Adjustment to Information-driven Technologies: A Critical Review," *MIS Quarterly* 14 (1990): 79–98.

68. M. Allen, "Legislation Could Restrict Bosses from Snooping on Their Workers," *The Wall Street Journal,* September 24, 1991, B1–B8.

69. K. D. Hill and S. Kerr, "The Impact of Computer-integrated Manufacturing Systems on the First Line Supervisor," *Journal of Organizational Behavior Management* 6 (1984): 81–87.

70. J. Anderson, "How Technology Brings Blind People into the Workplace," *Harvard Business Review* 67 (1989): 36–39.

71. D. L. Nelson and M. G. Kletke, "Individual Adjustment during Technological Innovation: A Research Framework," *Behaviour and Information Technology* 9 (1990): 257–271.

72. D. Mankin, T. Bikson, B. Gutek, and C. Stasz, "Managing Technological Change: The Process Is the Key," *Datamation* 34 (1988): 69–80.

73. M. R. Fusilier, C. D. Aby, Jr., J. K. Worley, and S. Elliott, "Perceived Seriousness of Business Ethics Issues," *Business and Professional Ethics Journal* 15 (1996): 67–78.

74. J. S. Mill, *Utilitarianism, Liberty, and Representative Government* (London: Dent, 1910).

75. K. H. Blanchard and N. V. Peale, *The Power of Ethical Management* (New York: Morrow, 1988).

76. C. Fried, *Right and Wrong* (Cambridge, Mass.: Harvard University Press, 1978).

77. I. Kant, *Groundwork of the Metaphysics of Morals,* trans. H. J. Paton (New York: Harper & Row, 1964).

78. A. Smith, *An Inquiry into the Nature and Causes of the Wealth of Nations,* vol. 10 of The Harvard Classics, ed. C. J. Bullock (New York: P. F. Collier & Son, 1909).

79. H. W. Lane and J. J. DiStefano, *International Management Behavior,* 2d ed. (Boston: PWS-Kent, 1992).

80. L. R. Smeltzer and M. M. Jennings, "Why an International Code of Business Ethics Would Be Good for Business," *Journal of Business Ethics* 17 (1998): 57–66.

81. D. Kemp, "Employers and AIDS: Dealing with the Psychological and Emotional Issues of AIDS in the Workplace," *American Review of Public Administration* 25 (1995): 263–278.

82. J. J. Koch, "Wells Fargo's and IBM's HIV Policies Help Protect Employees' Rights," *Personnel Journal* (April 1990): 40–48.

83. A. Arkin, "Positive HIV and AIDS Policies at Work," *Personnel Management* (December 1994): 34–37.

84. S. J. Adler, "Lawyers Advise Concerns to Provide Precise Written Policy to Employees," *The Wall Street Journal,* October 9, 1991, B1.

85. L. F. Fitzgerald, F. Drasgow, C. L. Hulin, M. J. Gelfand, and V. J. Magley, "Antecedents and Consequences of Sexual Harassment in Organizations: A Test of an Integrated Model," *Journal of Applied Psychology* 82 (1997): 578–589.

86. E. Felsenthal, "Rulings Open Way for Sex-Harass Cases," *The Wall Street Journal,* June 29, 1998, A10.

87. K. T. Schneider, S. Swan, and L. F. Fitzgerald, "Job-Related and Psychological Effects of Sexual Harassment in the Workplace: Empirical Evidence from Two Organizations," *Journal of Applied Psychology* 82 (1997): 401–415.

88. C. S. Piotrkowski, "Gender Harassment, Job Satisfaction and Distress Among Employed White and Minority Women," *Journal of Occupational Health Psychology* 3 (1998): 33–42.

89. L. M. Goldenhar, N. G. Swanson, J. J. Hurrell, Jr., A. Ruder, and J. Deddens, "Stressors and Adverse Outcomes for Female Construction Workers," *Journal of Occupational Health Psychology* 3 (1998): 19–32.

90. G. N. Powell and S. Foley, "Something to Talk About: Romantic Relationships in Organizational Settings," *Journal of Management* 24 (1998): 421–448.

91. J. Greenberg and R. Folger, "Procedural Justice, Participation, and the Fair Process Effect in Groups and Organizations," in P. B. Paulus, ed., *Basic Group Processes* (New York: Springer-Verlag, 1983), 235–256.

92. H. L. Laframboise, "Vile Wretches and Public Heroes: The Ethics of Whistleblowing in Government," *Canadian Public Administration* (Spring 1991): 73–78.

93. L. Gomes, "A Whistle-Blower Finds Jackpot at the End of His Quest," *The Wall Street Journal*, April 27, 1998, B1.

94. D. B. Turban and D. W. Greening, "Corporate Social Performance and Organizational Attractiveness to Prospective Employees," *Academy of Management Journal* 40 (1996): 658–672.

Chapter 3

1. A. Oldenburg, "Winfrey Spars Over Her Power," *USA Today*, February 5, 1998, 2D.

2. K. Lewin, "Formalization and Progress in Psychology," in D. Cartwright, ed., *Field Theory in Social Science* (New York: Harper, 1951).

3. N. S. Endler and D. Magnusson, "Toward an Interactional Psychology of Personality," *Psychological Bulletin* 83 (1976): 956–974.

4. J. R. Terborg, "Interactional Psychology and Research on Human Behavior in Organizations," *Academy of Management Review* 6 (1981): 561–576.

5. T. J. Bouchard, Jr., "Twins Reared Together and Apart: What They Tell Us about Human Diversity," in S. W. Fox, ed., *Individuality and Determinism* (New York: Plenum Press, 1984).

6. R. D. Arvey, T. J. Bouchard, Jr., N. L. Segal, and L. M. Abraham, "Job Satisfaction: Environmental and Genetic Components," *Journal of Applied Psychology* 74 (1989): 235–248.

7. G. Allport, *Pattern and Growth in Personality* (New York: Holt, 1961).

8. R. B. Cattell, *Personality and Mood by Questionnaire* (San Francisco: Jossey-Bass, 1973).

9. J. M. Digman, "Personality Structure: Emergence of a Five-Factor Model," *Annual Review of Psychology* 41 (1990): 417–440.

10. T. A. Judge, J. J. Martocchio, and C. J. Thoresen, "Five-Factor Model of Personality and Employee Absence," *Journal of Applied Psychology* 82 (1997): 745–755.

11. J. F. Salgado, "The Five Factor Model of Personality and Job Performance," *Journal of Applied Psychology* 82 (1997): 30–43.

12. M. R. Barrick and M. K. Mount, "The Big Five Personality Dimensions and Job Performance: A Meta-Analysis," *Personnel Psychology* 44 (1991): 1–26.

13. S. Freud, *An Outline of Psychoanalysis* (New York: Norton, 1949).

14. C. Rogers, *On Becoming a Person: A Therapist's View of Psychotherapy*, 2d ed. (Boston: Houghton Mifflin, 1970).

15. D. D. Clark and R. Hoyle, "A Theoretical Solution to the Problem of Personality-Situational Interaction," *Personality and Individual Differences* 9 (1988): 133–138.

16. D. Byrne and L. J. Schulte, "Personality Dimensions as Predictors of Sexual Behavior," in J. Bancroft, ed., *Annual Review of Sexual Research*, vol. 1 (Philadelphia: Society for the Scientific Study of Sex, 1990).

17. J. B. Rotter, "Generalized Expectancies for Internal vs. External Control of Reinforcement," *Psychological Monographs* 80, whole No. 609 (1966).

18. T. R. Mitchell, C. M. Smyser, and S. E. Weed, "Locus of Control: Supervision and Work Satisfaction," *Academy of Management Journal* 18 (1975): 623–631.

19. P. Spector, "Behavior in Organizations as a Function of Locus of Control," *Psychological Bulletin* 93 (1982): 482–497.

20. B. W. Pelham and W. B. Swann, Jr., "From Self-Conceptions to Self-Worth: On the Sources and Structure of Global Self-Esteem," *Journal of Personality and Social Psychology* 57 (1989): 672–680.

21. A. H. Baumgardner, C. M. Kaufman, and P. E. Levy, "Regulating Affect Interpersonally: When Low Esteem Leads to Greater Enhancement," *Journal of Personality and Social Psychology* 56 (1989): 907–921.

22. P. Tharenou and P. Harker, "Moderating Influences of Self-Esteem on Relationships between Job Complexity, Performance, and Satisfaction," *Journal of Applied Psychology* 69 (1984): 623–632.

23. R. A. Ellis and M. S. Taylor, "Role of Self-Esteem within the Job Search Process," *Journal of Applied Psychology* 68 (1983): 632–640.

24. J. Brockner and T. Hess, "Self-Esteem and Task Performance in Quality Circles," *Academy of Management Journal* 29 (1986): 617–623.

25. B. R. Schlenker, M. F. Weingold, and J. R. Hallam, "Self-Serving Attributions in Social Context: Effects of Self-Esteem and Social Pressure," *Journal of Personality and Social Psychology* 57 (1990): 855–863.

26. M. Snyder and S. Gangestad, "On the Nature of Self-Monitoring: Matters of Assessment, Matters of Validity," *Journal of Personality and Social Psychology* 51 (1986): 123–139.

27. M. Kilduff and D. V. Day, "Do Chameleons Get Ahead? The Effects of Self-Monitoring on Managerial Careers," *Academy of Management Journal* 37 (1994): 1047–1060.

28. A. H. Church, "Managerial Self-Awareness in High-Performing Individuals in Organizations," *Journal of Applied Psychology* 82 (1997): 281–292.

29. A. M. Isen and R. A. Baron, "Positive Affect and Organizational Behavior," in B. M. Staw and L. L. Cummings, eds., *Research in Organizational Behavior*, vol. 12 (Greenwich, Conn.: JAI Press, 1990).

30. D. Watson and L. A. Clark, "Negative Affectivity: The Disposition to Experience Aversive Emotional States," *Psychological Bulletin* 96 (1984): 465–490.

31. R. A. Baron, "Interviewer's Moods and Reactions to Job Applicants: The Influence of Affective States on Applied Social Judgments," *Journal of Applied Social Psychology* 16 (1987): 16–28.

32. J. M. George, "Mood and Absence," *Journal of Applied Psychology* 74 (1989): 287–324.

33. M. J. Burke, A. P. Brief and J. M. George, "The Role of Negative Affectivity in Understanding Relations between Self-Reports of Stressors and Strains: A Comment on the Applied Psychology Literature," *Journal of Applied Psychology* 78 (1993): 402–412.

34. J. M. George, "Personality, Affect, and Behavior in Groups," *Journal of Applied Psychology* 75 (1990): 107–116.

35. W. Mischel, "The Interaction of Person and Situation," in D. Magnusson and N. S. Endler, eds., *Personality at the Crossroads: Current Issues in Interactional Psychology* (Hillsdale, N.J.: Erlbaum, 1977).

36. H. Rorschach, *Psychodiagnostics* (Bern: Hans Huber, 1921).

37. C. G. Jung, *Psychological Types* (New York: Harcourt & Brace, 1923).

38. Consulting Psychologists Press.

39. R. Benfari and J. Knox, *Understanding Your Management Style* (Lexington, Mass.: Lexington Books, 1991).

40. O. Kroeger and J. M. Thuesen, *Type Talk* (New York: Delacorte Press, 1988).

41. S. Hirsch and J. Kummerow, *Life Types* (New York: Warner Books, 1989).

42. I. B. Myers and M. H. McCaulley, *Manual: A Guide to the Development and Use of the Myers-Briggs Type Indicator* (Palo Alto, Calif.: Consulting Psychologists Press, 1990).

43. G. P. Macdaid, M. H. McCaulley, and R. I. Kainz, *Myers-Briggs Type Indicator: Atlas of Type Tables* (Gainesville, Fla.: Center for Application of Psychological Type, 1987).

44. J. B. Murray, "Review of Research on the Myers-Briggs Type Indicator," *Perceptual and Motor Skills* 70 (1990): 1187–1202.

45. J. G. Carlson, "Recent Assessment of the Myers-Briggs Type Indicator," *Journal of Personality Assessment* 49 (1985): 356–365.

46. C. Walck, "Training for Participative Management: Implications for Psychological Type," *Journal of Psychological Type* 21 (1991): 3–12.

47. E. C. Webster, *The Employment Interview: A Social Judgment Process* (Schomberg, Canada: SIP, 1982).

48. N. Adler, *International Dimensions of Organizational Behavior*, 2d ed. (Boston: PWS-Kent, 1991).

49. L. R. Offerman and M. K. Gowing, "Personnel Selection in the Future: The Impact of

Changing Demographics and the Nature of Work," in Schmitt, Borman & Associates, eds., *Personnel Selection in Organizations* (San Francisco: Jossey-Bass, 1993).

50. A. M. Isen and R. Baron, "Positive Affect as a Factor in Organizational Behavior," in B. M. Staw and L. L. Cummins, eds., *Research in Organizational Behavior* 13 (1991): 1–54.

51. M. W. Levine and J. M. Shefner, *Fundamentals of Sensation and Perception* (Reading, Mass.: Addison-Wesley, 1981).

52. R. L. Dipboye, H. L. Fromkin, and K. Willback, "Relative Importance of Applicant Sex, Attractiveness, and Scholastic Standing in Evaluations of Job Applicant Resumes," *Journal of Applied Psychology* 60 (1975): 39–43.

53. I. H. Frieze, J. E. Olson, and J. Russell, "Attractiveness and Income for Men and Women in Management," *Journal of Applied Social Psychology* 21 (1991): 1039–1057.

54. P. Ekman and W. Friesen, *Unmasking the Face* (Englewood Cliffs, N.J.: Prentice-Hall, 1975).

55. J. E. Rehfeld, "What Working for a Japanese Company Taught Me," *Harvard Business Review*, (November–December 1990): 167–176.

56. M. W. Morris and R. P. Larrick, "When One Cause Casts Doubt on Another: A Normative Analysis of Discounting in Causal Attribution," *Psychological Review* 102 (1995): 331–355.

57. L. Copeland, "Learning to Manage a Multicultural Workforce," *Training*, May 1988, 48–56.

58. S. Ferrari, "Human Behavior in International Groups," *Management International Review* 7 (1972): 31–35.

59. A. Feingold, "Gender Differences in Effects of Physical Attractiveness on Romantic Attraction: A Comparison across Five Research Paradigms," *Journal of Personality and Social Psychology* 59 (1990): 981–993.

60. M. Snyder, "When Belief Creates Reality," *Advances in Experimental Social Psychology* 18 (1984): 247–305.

61. E. Burnstein and Y. Schul, "The Informational Basis of Social Judgments: Operations in Forming an Impression of Another Person," *Journal of Experimental Social Psychology* 18 (1982): 217–234.

62. J. Bruner, D. Shapiro, and R. Tagiuri, "The Meaning of Traits in Isolation and in Combination," in R. Tagiuri and L. Petrullo, eds., *Person Perception and Interpersonal Behavior* (Stanford, Calif.: Stanford University Press, 1958).

63. S. T. Fiske and S. E. Taylor, *Social Cognition* (Reading, Mass.: Addison-Wesley, 1984).

64. R. Rosenthal and L. Jacobson, *Pygmalion in the Classroom: Teacher Expectations and Pupils' Intellectual Development* (New York: Holt, Rinehart & Winston, 1968).

65. D. Eden and Y. Zuk, "Seasickness as a Self-Fulfilling Prophecy: Raising Self-Efficacy to Boost Performance at Sea," *Journal of Applied Psychology* 80 (1995): 628–635.

66. D. Eden, *Pygmalion in Management: Productivity as a Self-Fulfilling Prophecy* (Lexington, Mass.: Lexington Books, 1990).

67. D. Eden, "Pygmalion without Interpersonal Contrast Effects: Whole Groups Gain from Raising Manager Expectations," *Journal of Applied Psychology* 75 (1990): 394–398.

68. R. A. Giacolone and P. Rosenfeld, eds., *Impression Management in Organizations* (Hillsdale, N.J.: Erlbaum, 1990); J. Tedeschi and V. Melburg, "Impression Management and Influence in the Organization," in S. Bacharach and E. Lawler, eds., *Research in the Sociology of Organizations* (Greenwich, Conn.: JAI Press, 1984), 31–58.

69. T. E. Becker and S. L. Martin, "Trying to Look Bad at Work: Methods and Motives for Managing Poor Impressions in Organizations," *Academy of Management Journal* 38 (1995): 174–199.

70. D. C. Gilmore and G. R. Ferris, "The Effects of Applicant Impression Management Tactics on Interviewer Judgments," *Journal of Management* (December 1989): 557–564.

71. C. K. Stevens and A. L. Kristof, "Making the Right Impression: A Field Study of Applicant Impressions Management during Job Interviews," *Journal of Applied Psychology* 80 (1995): 587–606.

72. S. J. Wayne and R. C. Liden, "Effects of Impression Management on Performance Ratings: A Longitudinal Study," *Academy of Management Journal* 38 (1995): 232–260.

73. R. A. Baron, "Impression Management by Applicants during Employment Interviews: The 'Too Much of a Good Thing' Effect," in R. W. Eder and G. R. Ferris, eds., *The Employment Interview: Theory, Research, and Practice* (Newbury Park, Calif.: Sage Publications, 1989).

74. F. Heider, *The Psychology of Interpersonal Relations* (New York: Wiley, 1958).

75. B. Weiner, "An Attributional Theory of Achievement Motivation and Emotion," *Psychological Review* (October 1985): 548–573.

76. P. D. Sweeney, K. Anderson, and S. Bailey, "Attributional Style in Depression: A Meta-Analytic Review," *Journal of Personality and Social Psychology* 51 (1986): 974–991.

77. J. Silvester, "Spoken Attributions and Candidate Success in Graduate Recruitment Interviews," *Journal of Occupational and Organizational Psychology* 70 (1997): 61–71.

78. L. Ross, "The Intuitive Psychologist and His Shortcomings: Distortions in the Attribution Process," in L. Berkowitz, ed., *Advances in Experimental Social Psychology* (New York: Academic Press, 1977).

79. D. T. Miller and M. Ross, "Self-Serving Biases in the Attribution of Causality: Fact or Fiction?" *Psychological Bulletin* 82 (1975): 313–325.

80. J. R. Schermerhorn, Jr., "Team Development for High-Performance Management," *Training and Development Journal* 40 (1986): 38–41.

81. J. G. Miller, "Culture and the Development of Everyday Causal Explanation," *Journal of Personality and Social Psychology* 46 (1984): 961–978.

82. G. Si, S. Rethorst, and K. Willimczik, "Causal Attribution Perception in Sports Achievement: A Cross-Cultural Study on Attributional Concepts in Germany and China," *Journal of Cross-Cultural Psychology* 26 (1995): 537–553.

83. B. Adler, ed., *The Uncommon Wisdom of Oprah Winfrey* (Secaucus, N.J.: Birch Lane Publishing).

Chapter 4

1. H. Schwartz and D. J. Yang, *Pour Your Heart into It* (New York: Hyperion, 1997).

2. A. H. Eagly and S. Chaiken, *The Psychology of Attitudes* (Orlando, Fla.: Harcourt Brace Jovanovich, 1993).

3. M. J. Rosenberg, C. I. Hovland, W. J. McGuire, R. P. Abelson, and J. H. Brehm, *Attitude Organization and Change* (New Haven: Yale University Press, 1960).

4. L. Festinger, *A Theory of Cognitive Dissonance* (Evanston, Ill.: Row, Peterson, 1957).

5. R. H. Fazio and M. P. Zanna, "On the Predictive Validity of Attitudes: The Roles of Direct Experience and Confidence," *Journal of Personality* 46 (1978): 228–243.

6. A. Tversky and D. Kahneman, "Judgment under Uncertainty: Heuristics and Biases," in D. Kahneman, P. Slovic, and A. Tversky, eds., *Judgment under Uncertainty* (New York: Cambridge University Press, 1982), 3–20.

7. D. Rajecki, *Attitudes*, 2d ed. (Sunderland, Mass.: Sinauer Associates, 1989).

8. I. Ajzen and M. Fishbein, "Attitude–Behavior Relations: A Theoretical Analysis and Review of Empirical Research," *Psychological Bulletin* 84 (1977): 888–918.

9. B. T. Johnson and A. H. Eagly, "Effects of Involvement on Persuasion: A Meta-Analysis," *Psychological Bulletin* 106 (1989): 290–314.

10. K. G. DeBono and M. Snyder, "Acting on One's Attitudes: The Role of History of Choosing Situations," *Personality and Social Psychology Bulletin* 21 (1995): 629–636.

11. I. Ajzen and M. Fishbein, *Understanding Attitudes and Predicting Social Behavior* (Englewood Cliffs, N.J.: Prentice-Hall, 1980).

12. I. Ajzen, "From Intentions to Action: A Theory of Planned Behavior," in J. Kuhl and J. Beckmann, eds., *Action-Control: From Cognition to Behavior* (Heidelberg: Springer, 1985).

13. I. Ajzen, "The Theory of Planned Behavior," *Organizational Behavior and Human Decision Processes* 50 (1991): 1–33.

14. D. A. Garvin, "Quality Problems, Policies, and Attitudes in the United States and Japan: An Exploratory Study," *Academy of Management Journal* 29 (1986): 653–673.

15. E. A. Locke, "The Nature and Causes of Job Satisfaction," in M. Dunnette, ed., *Handbook of Industrial and Organizational Psychology* (Chicago: Rand McNally, 1976).

16. P. C. Smith, L. M. Kendall, and C. L. Hulin, *The Measurement of Satisfaction in Work and Retirement* (Skokie, Ill.: Rand McNally, 1969).

17. D. J. Weiss, R. V. Davis, G. W. England, and L. H. Lofquist, *Manual for the Minnesota Satisfaction Questionnaire* (Minneapolis: Industrial Relations Center, University of Minnesota, 1967).

18. M. T. Iaffaldano and P. M. Muchinsky, "Job Satisfaction and Job Performance: A Meta-Analysis," *Psychological Bulletin* 97 (1985): 251–273.

19. D. W. Organ and M. Konovsky, "Cognitive versus Affective Determinants of Organizational Citizenship Behavior," *Journal of Applied Psychology* 74 (1989): 157–164; R. H. Moorman, "The Influence of Cognitive and Affective Based Job Satisfaction Measures on the Relationship between Satisfaction and Organizational Citizenship Behavior," *Human Relations* 46 (1993): 759–776.

20. D. W. Organ, *Organizational Citizenship Behavior: The Good Soldier Syndrome* (Lexington, Mass.: Lexington Books, 1988).

21. P. M. Podsakoff, S. B. Mackenzie, and C. Hui, "Organizational Citizenship Behaviors and Managerial Evaluations of Employee Performance: A Review and Suggestions for Future Research," in *Research in Personnel and Human Resources Management*, ed. G. Ferris (Greenwich, Conn.: JAI Press, 1993), 1–40.

22. C. Ostroff, "The Relationship between Satisfaction, Attitudes and Performance: An Organizational Level Analysis," *Journal of Applied Psychology* 77 (1992): 963–974.

23. R. Griffin and T. Bateman, "Job Satisfaction and Organizational Commitment," in C. Cooper and I. Robertson, eds., *International Review of Industrial and Organizational Psychology* (New York: Wiley, 1986).

24. J. R. Lincoln, "Employee Work Attitudes and Management Practice in the U.S. and Japan: Evidence from a Large Comparative Survey," *California Management Review* (Fall 1989): 89–106.

25. I. A. McCormick and C. L. Cooper, "Executive Stress: Extending the International Comparison," *Human Relations* 41 (1988): 65–72.

26. A. Krishnan and R. Krishnan, "Organizational Variables and Job Satisfaction," *Psychological Research Journal* 8 (1984): 1–11.

27. R. T. Mowday, L. W. Porter, and R. M. Steers, *Employee-Organization Linkages: The Psychology of Commitment* (New York: Academic Press, 1982).

28. H. S. Becker, "Notes on the Concept of Commitment," *American Journal of Sociology* 66 (1960): 32–40.

29. J. P. Meyer, N. J. Allen, and C. A. Smith, "Commitment to Organizations and Occupations: Extension and Test of a Three-Component Model," *Journal of Applied Psychology* 78 (1993): 538–551.

30. J. P. Curry, D. S. Wakefield, J. L. Price, and C. W. Mueller, "On the Causal Ordering of Job Satisfaction and Organizational Commitment," *Academy of Management Journal* 29 (1986): 847–858.

31. B. Benkhoff, "Ignoring Commitment Is Costly: New Approaches Establish the Missing Link between Commitment and Performance," *Human Relations* 50 (1997): 701–726; N. J. Allen and J. P. Meyer, "Affective, Continuance and Normative Commitment to the Organization: An Examination of Construct Validity," *Journal of Vocational Behavior* 49 (1996): 252–276.

32. M. J. Somers, "Organizational Commitment, Turnover, and Absenteeism: An Examination of Direct and Interaction Effects," *Journal of Organizational Behavior* 16 (1995): 49–58; L. Lum, J. Kervin, K. Clark, F. Reid, and W. Sirola, "Explaining Nursing Turnover Intent: Job Satisfaction, Pay Satisfaction, or Organizational Commitment?" *Journal of Organizational Behavior* 19 (1998): 305–320.

33. A. al-Meer, "Organizational Commitment: A Comparison of Westerners, Asians, and Saudis," *International Studies of Management and Organization* 19 (1989): 74–84.

34. F. Luthans, H. S. McCaul, and N. C. Dodd, "Organizational Commitment: A Comparison of American, Japanese, and Korean Employees," *Academy of Management Journal* 28 (1985): 213–219.

35. J. Cooper and R. T. Croyle, "Attitudes and Attitude Change," *Annual Review of Psychology* 35 (1984): 395–426.

36. D. M. Mackie and L. T. Worth, "Processing Deficits and the Mediation of Positive Affect in Persuasion," *Journal of Personality and Social Psychology* 57 (1989): 27–40.

37. J. W. Brehm, *Responses to Loss of Freedom: A Theory of Psychological Reactance* (New York: General Learning Press, 1972).

38. R. E. Petty and J. T. Cacioppo, *Communication and Persuasion: Central and Peripheral Routes to Attitude Change* (New York: Springer-Verlag, 1985).

39. R. Petty, D. T. Wegener, and L. R. Fabrigar, "Attitudes and Attitude Change," *Annual Review of Psychology* 48 (1997): 609–647.

40. M. Rokeach, *The Nature of Human Values* (New York: Free Press, 1973).

41. L. Bruce, "Exporting Tandem's Californiaesque Corporate Culture," *International Management* (July–August 1987): 35.

42. M. Rokeach and S. J. Ball-Rokeach, "Stability and Change in American Value Priorities, 1968–1981," *American Psychologist* 44 (1989): 775–784.

43. G. W. England, "Organizational Goals and Expected Behavior of American Managers," *Academy of Management Journal* 10 (1967): 107–117.

44. E. C. Ravlin and B. M. Meglino, "Effects of Values on Perception and Decision Making: A Study of Alternative Work Values Measures," *Journal of Applied Psychology* 72 (1987): 666–673.

45. E. C. Ravlin and B. M. Meglino, "The Transitivity of Work Values: Hierarchical Preference Ordering of Socially Desirable Stimuli," *Organizational Behavior and Human Decision Processes* 44 (1989): 494–508.

46. B. M. Meglino, E. C. Ravlin, and C. L. Adkins, "A Work Values Approach to Corporate Culture: A Field Test of the Value Congruence Process and Its Relationship to Individual Outcomes," *Journal of Applied Psychology* 74 (1989): 424–432.

47. T. A. Judge and R. D. Bretz, Jr., "Effects of Work Values on Job Choice Decisions," *Journal of Applied Psychology* 77 (1992): 261–271.

48. A. Weiss, "The Value System," *Personnel Administrator* (July 1989): 40–41.

49. R. H. Doktor, "Asian and American CEOs: A Comparative Study," *Organizational Dynamics* 18 (1990): 46–56.

50. R. L. Tung, "Handshakes across the Sea: Cross-Cultural Negotiating for Business Success," *Organizational Dynamics* (Winter 1991): 30–40.

51. S. E. Peterson, "3M Company Announces the Establishment of Wholly Owned Subsidiary in Moscow," *Minneapolis Star Tribune*, January 30, 1992, 1–2.

52. R. Neale and R. Mindel, "Rigging Up Multicultural Teamworking," *Personnel Management* (January 1992): 27–30.

53. K. Hodgson, "Adapting Ethical Decisions to a Global Marketplace," *Management Review* 81 (1992): 53–57.

54. F. Navran, "Your Role in Shaping Ethics," *Executive Excellence* 9 (1992): 11–12.

55. K. Labich, "The New Crisis in Business Ethics," *Fortune*, April 20, 1992, 167–176.

56. W. H. Wagel, "A New Focus on Business Ethics at General Dynamics," *Personnel* (August 1987): 4–8.

57. G. Flynn, "Make Employee Ethics Your Business," *Personnel Journal* (June 1995): 30–40.

58. M. S. Baucus and D. A. Baucus, "Paying the Piper: An Empirical Examination of Longer-Term Financial Consequences of Illegal Corporate Behavior," *Academy of Management Journal* 40 (1997): 129–151.

59. J. O. Cherrington and D. J. Cherrington, "A Menu of Moral Issues: One Week in the Life of *The Wall Street Journal*," *Journal of Business Ethics* 11 (1992): 255–265.

60. L. K. Trevino, "Ethical Decision Making in Organizations: A Person-Situation Interactionist Model," *Academy of Management Review* 11 (1986): 601–617.

61. K. R. Andrews, "Ethics in Practice," *Harvard Business Review* (September–October 1989): 99–104.

62. A. Bhide and H. H. Stevens, "Why Be Honest if Honesty Doesn't Pay?" *Harvard Business Review* (September–October 1990): 121–129.

63. J. B. Rotter, "Generalized Expectancies for Internal versus External Control of Reinforcement," *Psychological Monographs* 80 (1966): 1–28.

64. L. K. Trevino and S. A. Youngblood, "Bad Apples in Bad Barrels: A Causal Analysis of Ethical Decision-Making Behavior," *Journal of Applied Psychology* 75 (1990): 378–385.

65. H. M. Lefcourt, *Locus of Control: Current Trends in Theory and Research*, 2d ed. (Hillsdale, N.J.: Erlbaum, 1982).

66. N. Machiavelli, *The Prince*, trans. George Bull (Middlesex, England: Penguin Books, 1961).

67. R. Christie and F. L. Geis, *Studies in Machiavellianism* (New York: Academic Press, 1970).

68. R. A. Giacalone and S. B. Knouse, "Justifying Wrongful Employee Behavior: The Role of Personality in Organizational Sabotage," *Journal of Business Ethics* 9 (1990): 55–61.

69. S. B. Knouse and R. A. Giacalone, "Ethical Decision-Making in Business: Behavioral Issues and Concerns," *Journal of Business Ethics* 11 (1992): 369–377.

70. L. Kohlberg, "Stage and Sequence: The Cognitive Developmental Approach to Socialization," in D. A. Goslin, ed., *Handbook of Socialization Theory and Research* (Chicago: Rand McNally, 1969), 347–480.

71. C. I. Malinowski and C. P. Smith, "Moral Reasoning and Moral Conduct: An Investigation Prompted by Kohlberg's Theory," *Journal of Personality and Social Psychology* 49 (1985): 1016–1027.

72. M. Brabeck, "Ethical Characteristics of Whistleblowers," *Journal of Research in Personality* 18 (1984): 41–53.

73. W. Y. Penn and B. D. Collier, "Current Research in Moral Development as a Decision Support System," *Journal of Business Ethics* 4 (1985): 131–136.

74. Trevino and Youngblood, "Bad Apples in Bad Barrels."

75. C. Gilligan, *In a Different Voice: Psychological Theory and Women's Development* (Cambridge, Mass.: Harvard University Press, 1982).

76. G. R. Franke, D. F. Crown, and D. F. Spake, "Gender Differences in Ethical Perceptions of Business Practices: A Social Role Theory Perspective," *Journal of Applied Psychology* 82 (1997): 920–934.

77. S. A. Goldman and J. Arbuthnot, "Teaching Medical Ethics: The Cognitive-Developmental Approach," *Journal of Medical Ethics* 5 (1979): 171–181.

78. Schwartz and Yang, *Pour Your Heart into It*; S. Kravetz, "These People Search for a Cup That Suits the Coffee It Holds," *The Wall Street Journal*, March 24, 1998, A1; The Washington Department of Community Trade and Economic Development.

Chapter 5

1. American Red Cross, *National Office of Volunteers Fact Sheet* (Falls Church, Va.: Author, 1997).

2. R. M. Steers and L. W. Porter, *Motivation and Work Behavior*, 5th ed. (New York: McGraw-Hill, 1991).

3. J. P. Campbell and R. D. Pritchard, "Motivation Theory in Industrial and Organizational Psychology," in M. D. Dunnette, ed., *Handbook of Industrial and Organizational Psychology* (Chicago: Rand McNally, 1976), 63–130.

4. M. Weber, *The Protestant Ethic and the Spirit of Capitalism* (London: Talcott Parson, tr., 1930).

5. S. Freud, *Civilization and Its Discontents*, trans. and ed. J. Strachey (New York: Norton, 1961).

6. D. Mangelsdorff, ed., *Proceedings of the 7th Stress Conference: Training for Psychic Trauma* (San Antonio: U.S. Army Health Services Command, 1989).

7. B. S. Frey, *Not Just for the Money: An Economic Theory of Personal Motivation* (Brookfield, Vt.: Edgar Elger, 1997).

8. F. J. Roethlisberger, *Management and Morale* (Cambridge, Mass.: Harvard University Press, 1941).

9. A. Smith, *An Inquiry into the Nature and Causes of the Wealth of Nations*, vol. 10 of *The Harvard Classics*, ed. C. J. Bullock (New York: Collier, 1909).

10. F. W. Taylor, *The Principles of Scientific Management* (New York: Norton, 1911).

11. Hearings before Special Committee of the House of Representatives to Investigage the Taylor and Other Systems of Shop Management under Authority of House Resolution 90, vol. 3, 1377–1508, contains Taylor's testimony before the committee from Thursday, January 25, through Tuesday, January 30, 1912.

12. A. H. Maslow, "A Theory of Human Motivation," *Psychological Review* 50 (1943): 370–396.

13. W. James, *The Principles of Psychology* (New York: H. Holt & Co., 1890; Cambridge, Mass.: Harvard University Press, 1983).

14. J. Dewey, *Human Nature and Conduct: An Introduction to Social Psychology* (New York: Holt, 1922).

15. S. Freud, *A General Introduction to Psycho-Analysis: A Course of Twenty-Eight Lectures Delivered at the University of Vienna* (New York: Liveright, 1963); A. Adler, *Understanding Human Nature* (Greenwich, Conn.: Fawcett, 1927).

16. L. W. Porter, "A Study of Perceived Need Satisfactions in Bottom and Middle Management Jobs," *Journal of Applied Psychology* 45 (1961): 1–10.

17. E. E. Lawler III and J. L. Suttle, "A Causal Correlational Test of the Need Hierarchy Concept," *Organizational Behavior and Human Performance* 7 (1973): 265–287.

18. D. M. McGregor, *The Human Side of Enterprise* (New York: McGraw-Hill, 1960).

19. D. M. McGregor, "The Human Side of Enterprise," *Management Review* (November 1957): 22–28, 88–92.

20. D. E. Petersen and J. Hillkirk, *A Better Idea: Redefining the Way Americans Work* (Boston: Houghton Mifflin, 1991).

21. G. E. Forward, D. E. Beach, D. A. Gray, and J. C. Quick, "Mentofacturing: A Vision for American Industrial Excellence," *Academy of Management Executive* 5 (1991): 32–44.

22. C. P. Alderfer, *Human Needs in Organizational Settings* (New York: Free Press, 1972).

23. B. Schneider and C. P. Alderfer, "Three Studies of Need Satisfactions in Organizations," *Administrative Science Quarterly* 18 (1973): 489–505.

24. H. A. Murray, *Explorations in Personality: A Clinical and Experimental Study of Fifty Men of College Age* (New York: Oxford University Press, 1938).

25. D. C. McClelland, *Motivational Trends in Society* (Morristown, N.J.: General Learning Press, 1971).

26. J. P. Chaplin and T. S. Krawiec, *Systems and Theories of Psychology* (New York: Holt, Rinehart & Winston, 1960).

27. F. Herzberg, B. Mausner, and B. Snyderman, *The Motivation to Work* (New York: Wiley, 1959).

28. F. Herzberg, *Work and the Nature of Man* (Cleveland: World, 1966).

29. R. J. House and L. Wigdor, "Herzberg's Dual-Factor Theory of Job Satisfaction and Motivation: A Review of the Evidence and a Criticism," *Personnel Psychology* 20 (1967): 369–389.

30. D. C. McClelland, "Achievement Motivation Can Be Learned," *Harvard Business Review* 43 (1965): 6–24.

31. E. A. Ward, "Multidimensionality of Achievement Motivation among Employed Adults," *Journal of Social Psychology* 134 (1997): 542–544.

32. A. Sagie, D. Elizur, and H. Yamauchi, "The Structure and Strength of Achievement Motivation: A Cross-Cultural Comparison," *Journal of Organizational Behavior* 17 (1996): 431–444.

33. D. C. McClelland and D. Burnham, "Power Is the Great Motivator," *Harvard Business Review* 54 (1976): 100–111; J. Hall and J. Hawker, *Power Management Inventory* (The Woodlands, Tex.: Teleometrics International, 1988).

34. F. Luthans, "Successful versus Effective Real Managers," *Academy of Management Executive* 2 (1988): 127–131.

35. S. Schachter, *The Psychology of Affiliation* (Stanford, Calif.: Stanford University Press, 1959).

36. P. M. Blau, *Exchange and Power in Social Life* (New York: Wiley, 1964).

37. A. Etzioni, "A Basis for Comparative Analysis of Complex Organizations," in A. Etzioni, ed., *A Sociological Reader on Complex Organizations*, 2d ed., (New York: Holt, Rinehart & Winston, 1969), 59–76.

38. J. P. Campbell, M. D. Dunnette, E. E. Lawler III, and K. E. Weick, Jr., *Managerial Behavior, Performance and Effectiveness* (New York: McGraw-Hill, 1970).

39. J. S. Adams, "Inequity in Social Exchange," in L. Berkowitz, ed., *Advances in Experimental Social Psychology*, vol. 2 (New York: Academic Press, 1965), 267–299.

40. J. S. Adams, "Toward an Understanding of Inequity," *Journal of Abnormal and Social Psychology* 67 (1963): 422–436.

41. J. Nelson-Horchler, "The Best Man for the Job Is a Man," *Industry Week*, January 7, 1991, 50–52.

42. P. D. Sweeney, D. B. McFarlin, and E. J. Inderrieden, "Using Relative Deprivation Theory to Explain Satisfaction with Income and Pay Level: A Multistudy Examination," *Academy of Management Journal* 33 (1990): 423–436.

43. R. C. Huseman, J. D. Hatfield, and E. A. Miles, "A New Perspective on Equity Theory: The Equity Sensitivity Construct," *Academy of Management Review* 12 (1987): 222–234.

44. D. McLoughlin and S. C. Carr, "Equity and Sensitivity and Double Demotivation," *Journal of Social Psychology* 137 (1997): 668–670.

45. K. E. Weick, M. G. Bougon, and G. Maruyama, "The Equity Context," *Organizational Behavior and Human Performance* 15 (1976): 32–65.

46. R. Coles, *Privileged Ones* (Boston: Little, Brown, 1977).

47. J. Greenberg, "Equity and Workplace Status: A Field Experiment," *Journal of Applied Psychology* 73 (1988): 606–613.

48. R. A. Cosier and D. R. Dalton, "Equity Theory and Time: A Reformulation," *Academy of Management Review* 8 (1983): 311–319.

49. J. E. Martin and M. W. Peterson, "Two-Tier Wage Structures: Implications for Equity Theory," *Academy of Management Journal* 30 (1987): 297–315.

50. V. H. Vroom, *Work and Motivation* (New York: Wiley, 1964/1970).

51. U. R. Larson, "Supervisor's Performance Feedback to Subordinates: The Effect of Performance Valence and Outcome Dependence," *Organizational Behavior and Human Decision Processes* 37 (1986): 391–409.

52. M. F. Fadden and B. L. Smith, *High Performance Flying* (Houston: Tenneco Chemicals, 1976).

53. M. C. Kernan and R. G. Lord, "Effects of Valence, Expectancies, and Goal-Performance Discrepancies in Single and Multiple Goal Environments," *Journal of Applied Psychology* 75 (1990): 194–203.

54. W. VanEerde and H. Thierry, "Vroom's Expectancy Models and Work-Related Criteria: A Meta-Analysis," *Journal of Applied Psychology* 81 (1996): 575–586.

55. E. D. Pulakos and N. Schmitt, "A Longitudinal Study of a Valence Model Approach for the Prediction of Job Satisfaction of New Employees," *Journal of Applied Psychology* 68 (1983): 307–312.

56. F. J. Landy and W. S. Becker, "Motivation Theory Reconsidered," in L. L. Cummings and B. M. Staw, eds., *Research in Organizational Behavior* 9 (Greenwich, Conn.: JAI Press, 1987), 1–38.

57. L. Kohlberg, "The Cognitive-Developmental Approach to Socialization," in D. A. Goslin, ed., *Handbook of Socialization Theory and Research* (Chicago: Rand McNally, 1969).

58. N. J. Adler, *International Dimensions of Organizational Behavior* (Boston: PWS-KENT, 1991).

59. G. Hofstede, "Motivation, Leadership, and Organization: Do American Theories Apply Abroad?" *Organizational Dynamics* 9 (1980): 42–63.

60. G. H. Hines, "Cross-Cultural Differences in Two-Factor Theory," *Journal of Applied Psychology* 58 (1981): 313–317.

Chapter 6

1. www.oprah.com; G. Wilkinson, "Leaders and Success: Talk Show Host Oprah Winfrey," *Investor's Business Daily*, June 1, 1998, A1; S. Rebello, "Brand Oprah," *Success* 45 (1998): 64–65.

2. I. P. Pavlov, *Conditioned Reflexes* (New York: Oxford University Press, 1927).

3. Bradford Cannon, "Walter B. Cannon: Reflections on the Man and His Contributions," *Centennial Session*, American Psychological Association Centennial Convention, Washington, D.C., 1992.

4. B. F. Skinner, *The Behavior of Organisms: An Experimental Analysis* (New York: Appleton-Century-Crofts, 1938).

5. B. F. Skinner, *Science and Human Behavior* (New York: Free Press, 1953).

6. F. Luthans and R. Kreitner, *Organizational Behavior Modification and Beyond* (Glenview, Ill.: Scott, Foresman, 1985).

7. J. Hale, "Strategic Rewards: Keeping Your Best Talent from Walking out the Door," *Compensation & Benefits Management* 14 (1998): 39–50.

8. B. F. Skinner, *Contingencies of Reinforcement: A Theoretical Analysis* (New York: Appleton-Century-Crofts, 1969).

9. J. P. Chaplin and T. S. Krawiec, *Systems and Theories of Psychology* (New York: Holt, Rinehart & Winston, 1960).

10. A. Bandura, *Social Learning Theory* (Englewood Cliffs, N.J.: Prentice-Hall, 1977); A. Bandura, "Self-Efficacy: Toward a Unifying Theory of Behavioral Change," *Psychological Review* 84 (1977): 191–215.

11. A. Bandura, "Regulation of Cognitive Processes through Perceived Self-Efficacy," *Developmental Psychology* (September 1989): 729–735.

12. J. M. Phillips and S. M. Gully, "Role of Goal Orientation, Ability, Need for Achievement, and Locus of Control in the Self-Efficacy and Goal-Setting Process," *Journal of Applied Psychology* 82 (1997): 792–802.

13. A. D. Stajkkovic and F. Luthans, "Social Cognitive Theory and Self-Efficacy: Going Beyond Traditional Motivational and Behavioral Approaches," *Organizational Dynamics* (Spring 1998): 62–74.

14. V. Gecas, "The Social Psychology of Self-Efficacy," *Annual Review of Sociology* 15 (1989): 291–316.

15. O. Isachsen and L. V. Berens, *Working Together: A Personality Centered Approach to Management* (Coronado, Calif.: Neworld Management Press, 1988); O. Krueger and J. M. Thuesen, *Type Talk* (New York: Tilden Press, 1988).

16. E. A. Locke and G. P. Latham, *A Theory of Goal Setting and Task Performance* (Englewood Cliffs, N.J.: Prentice-Hall, 1990).

17. T. O. Murray, *Management by Objectives: A Systems Approach to Management* (Fort Worth, Tex.: Western Company, n.d.).

18. W. T. Brooks and T. W. Mullins, *High Impact Time Management* (Englewood Cliffs, N.J.: Prentice-Hall, 1989).

19. E. A. Locke, "Toward a Theory of Task Motivation and Incentives," *Organizational Behavior and Human Performance* 3 (1968): 157–189.

20. J. C. Quick, "Dyadic Goal Setting within Organizations: Role Making and Motivational Considerations," *Academy of Management Review* 4 (1979): 369–380.

21. D. McGregor, "An Uneasy Look at Performance Appraisal," *Harvard Business Review* 35 (1957): 89–94.

22. H. Garland, "Influence of Ability, Assigned Goals, and Normative Information on Personal Goals and Performance: A Challenge to the Goal Attainability Assumption," *Journal of Applied Psychology* 68 (1982): 20–30.

23. J. R. Hollenbeck, C. R. Williams, and H. J. Klein, "An Empirical Examination of the Antecedents of Commitment to Difficult Goals," *Journal of Applied Psychology* 74 (1989): 18–23.

24. R. C. Rodgers and J. E. Hunter, "The Impact of Management by Objectives on Organizational Productivity," unpublished paper (Lexington: University of Kentucky, 1989).

25. E. A. Locke, K. N. Shaw, L. M. Saari, and G. P. Latham, "Goal Setting and Task Performance: 1969–1980," *Psychological Bulletin* 90 (1981): 125–152.

26. J. C. Quick, "Dyadic Goal Setting and Role Stress," *Academy of Management Journal* 22 (1979): 241–252.

27. G. S. Odiorne, *Management by Objectives: A System of Managerial Leadership* (New York: Pitman, 1965).

28. American Management Association, *Blueprints for Service Quality: The Federal Express Approach* (New York: American Management Association, 1991).

29. G. P. Latham and G. A. Yukl, "A Review of Research on the Application of Goal Setting in Organizations," *Academy of Management Journal* 18 (1975): 824–845.

30. P. F. Drucker, *The Practice of Management* (New York: Harper & Bros., 1954).

31. R. D. Prichard, P. L. Roth, S. D. Jones, P. J. Galgay, and M. D. Watson, "Designing a Goal-Setting System to Enhance Performance: A Practical Guide," *Organizational Dynamics* 17 (1988): 69–78.

32. C. L. Hughes, *Goal Setting: Key to Individual and Organizational Effectiveness* (New York: American Management Association, 1965).

33. M. E. Tubbs and S. E. Ekeberg, "The Role of Intentions in Work Motivation: Implications for Goal-Setting Theory and Research," *Academy of Management Review* 16 (1991): 180–199.

34. J. M. Ivancevich, J. T. McMahon, J. W. Streidl, and A. D. Szilagyi, "Goal Setting: The Tenneco Approach to Personnel Development and Management Effectiveness," *Organizational Dynamics* 7 (1978): 58–80.

35. J. R. Hollenbeck and A. P. Brief, "The Effects of Individual Differences and Goal Origin on Goal Setting and Performance," *Organizational Behavior and Human Decision Processes* 40 (1987): 392–414.

36. Locke and Latham, *A Theory of Goal Setting and Task Performance*.

37. R. A. Katzell and D. E. Thompson, "Work Motivation: Theory and Practice," *American Psychologist* 45 (1990): 144–153; M. W. McPherson, "Is Psychology the Science of Behavior?" *American Psychologist* 47 (1992): 329–335.

38. E. A. Locke, "The Ideas of Frederick W. Taylor: An Evaluation," *Academy of Management Review* 7 (1982): 15–16; R. M. Yerkes and J. D. Dodson, "The Relation of Strength of Stimulus to Rapidity of Habit-Formation," *Journal of Comparative Neurology and Psychology* 18 (1908): 459–482.

39. P. Cappelli and N. Rogovsky, "Employee Involvement and Organizational Citizenship: Implications for Labor Law Reform and 'Lean Production,'" *Industrial & Labor Relations Review* 51 (1998): 633–653.

40. I. M. Jawahar and C. R. Williams, "Where All the Children Are Above Average: The Performance Appraisal Purpose Effect," *Personnel Psychology* 50 (1997): 905–925.

41. D. A. Gioia and C. O. Longenecker, "Delving into the Dark Side: The Politics of Executive Appraisal," *Organizational Dynamics* 22 (1994): 47–58.

42. H. H. Meyer, E. Kay, and J. R. P. French, "Split Roles in Performance Appraisal," *Harvard Business Review* 43 (1965): 123–129.

43. W. A. Fisher, J. C. Quick, L. L. Schkade, and G. W. Ayers, "Developing Administrative Personnel through the Assessment Center Technique," *Personnel Administrator* 25 (1980): 44–46, 62.

44. M. B. DeGregorio and C. D. Fisher, "Providing Performance Feedback: Reactions to Alternative Methods," *Journal of Management* 14 (1988): 605–616.

45. G. C. Thornton, "The Relationship between Supervisory and Self-Appraisals of Executive Performance," *Personnel Psychology* 21 (1968): 441–455.

46. L. L. Cummings and D. P. Schwab, *Performance in Organizations* (Glenview, Ill.: Scott, Foresman, 1973).

47. L. Hirschhorn, "Leaders and Followers in a Postindustrial Age: A Psychodynamic View," *Journal of Applied Behavioral Science* 26 (1990): 529–542.

48. F. M. Jablin, "Superior-Subordinate Communication: The State of the Art," *Psychological Bulletin* 86 (1979): 1201–1222.

49. J. Pfeffer, "Six Dangerous Myths about Pay," *Harvard Business Review* 76 (1998): 108–119.

50. M. Erez, "Work Motivation from a Cross-Cultural Perspective," in A. M. Bouvy, F. J. R. Van de Vijver, P. Boski, and P. G. Schmitz, eds., *Journeys into Cross-Cultural Psychology* (Amsterdam, Netherlands: Swets & Zeitlinger, 1994), 386–403.

51. George T. Milkovich and Jerry M. Newman, *Compensation*, 4th ed. (Homewood, Ill.: Irwin, 1993).

52. S. Kerr, "On the Folly of Rewarding A, While Hoping for B," *Academy of Management Journal* 18 (1975): 769–783.

53. J. M. Bardwick, *Danger in the Comfort Zone* (New York: American Management Association, 1991).

54. M. J. Martinko and W. L. Gardner, "The Leader/Member Attributional Process," *Academy of Management Review* 12 (1987): 235–249.

55. K. N. Wexley, R. A. Alexander, J. P. Greenawalt, and M. A. Couch, "Attitudinal Congruence and Similarity as Related to Interpersonal Evaluations in Manager-Subordinate Dyads," *Academy of Management Journal* 23 (1980): 320–330.

56. H. H. Kelley, *Attribution in Social Interaction* (New York: General Learning Press, 1971).

57. H. H. Kelley, "The Processes of Causal Attribution," *American Psychologist* 28 (1973): 107–128.

58. A. G. Athos and J. J. Gabarro, *Interpersonal Behavior: Communication and Understanding in Relationships* (Englewood Cliffs, N.J.: Prentice-Hall, 1978).

59. K. Doherty, "The Good News about Depression," *Business and Health* 3 (1989): 1–4.

60. K. E. Kram, "Phases of the Mentor Relationship," *Academy of Management Journal* 26 (1983): 608–625.

61. T. N. Bauer and S. G. Green, "Development of Leader–Member Exchange: A Longitudinal Test," *Academy of Management Journal* 39 (1996): 1538–1567.

62. K. E. Kram and L. A. Isabella, "Mentoring Alternatives: The Role of Peer Relationships in Career Development," *Academy of Management Journal* 28 (1985): 110–132.

Chapter 7

1. B. Adrangi, G. Chow, and K. Raffiee, "Airline Deregulation, Safety, and Profitability in the U.S.," *Transportation Journal* 36 (Summer 1997): 44–52.

2. J. C. Quick and J. D. Quick, *Organizational Stress and Preventive Management* (New York: McGraw-Hill, 1984).

3. S. Benison, A. C. Barger, and E. L. Wolfe, *Walter B. Cannon: The Life and Times of a Young Scientist* (Cambridge, Mass.: Harvard University Press, 1987).

4. W. B. Cannon, "Stresses and Strains of Homeostasis," *American Journal of the Medical Sciences* 189 (1935): 1–14.

5. W. B. Cannon, *The Wisdom of the Body* (New York: Norton, 1932).

6. R. S. Lazarus, *Psychological Stress and the Coping Process* (New York: McGraw-Hill, 1966).

7. D. Katz and R. L. Kahn, *The Social Psychology of Organizations*, 2d ed. (New York: Wiley, 1978), 185–221.

8. H. Levinson, "A Psychoanalytic View of Occupational Stress," *Occupational Mental Health* 3 (1978): 2–13.

9. F. J. Landy, "Work Design and Stress," in G. P. Keita and S. L. Sauter, eds., *Work and Well-Being: An Agenda for the 1990s* (Washington, D.C.: American Psychological Association, 1992), 119–158.

10. T. Theorell and R. A. Karasek, "Current Issues Relating to Psychosocial Job Strain and Cardiovascular Disease," *Journal of Occupational Health Psychology* 1 (1996): 9–26.

11. D. T. Hall and J. Richter, "Career Gridlock: Baby Boomers Hit the Wall," *Academy of Management Executive* 4 (1990): 7–22.

12. S. Zuboff, *In the Age of the Smart Machine: The Future of Work and Power* (New York: Basic Books, 1988).

13. R. L. Kahn, D. M. Wolfe, R. P. Quinn, J. D. Snoek, and R. A. Rosenthal, *Organizational Stress: Studies in Role Conflict and Ambiguity* (New York: Wiley, 1964).

14. M. F. Peterson, et al., "Role Conflict, Ambiguity, and Overload: A 21-Nation Study," *Academy of Management Journal* 38 (1995): 429–452.

15. Y. Fried, H. A. Ben-David, R. B. Tiegs, N. Avital, and U. Yeverechyahu, "The Interactive Effect of Role Conflict and Role Ambiguity on Job Performance," *Journal of Occupational & Organizational Psychology* 71 (1998): 19–27.

16. L. T. Hosmer, "Trust: The Connecting Link between Organizational Theory and Philosophical Ethics," *Academy of Management Review* 20 (1995): 379–403; V. J. Doby and R. D. Caplan, "Organizational Stress as Threat to Reputation: Effects on Anxiety at Work and at Home," *Academy of Management Journal* 38 (1995): 1105–1123.

17. M. F. Peterson and P. B. Smith, "Does National Culture or Ambient Temperature Explain Cross-National Differences in Role Stress? No Sweat!" *Academy of Management Journal* 40 (1997): 930–946.

18. K. K. Gillingham, "High-G Stress and Orientational Stress: Physiologic Effects of Aerial Maneuvering," *Aviation, Space, and Environmental Medicine* 59 (1988): A10–A20.

19. R. S. Bhagat, S. J. McQuaid, S. Lindholm, and J. Segovis, "Total Life Stress: A Multimethod Validation of the Construct and Its Effect on Organizationally Valued Outcomes and Withdrawal Behaviors," *Journal of Applied Psychology* 70 (1985): 202–214.

20. J. C. Quick, J. R. Joplin, D. A. Gray, and E. C. Cooley, "The Occupational Life Cycle and the Family," in L. L'Abate, ed., *Handbook of Developmental Family Psychology and Psychopathology* (New York: John Wiley, 1993).

21. S. Shellenbarger, "Work & Family," *The Wall Street Journal*, January 31, 1996, B1.

22. S. A. Lobel, "Allocation of Investment in Work and Family Roles: Alternative Theories and Implications for Research," *Academy of Management Review* 16 (1991): 507–521.

23. J. W. Pennebaker, C. F. Hughes, and R. C. O'Heeron, "The Psychophysiology of Confession: Linking Inhibitory and Psychosomatic Processes," *Journal of Personality and Social Psychology* 52 (1987): 781–793.

24. "Stress: The Test Americans Are Failing," *Business Week* (April 18, 1988).

25. J. D. Quick, R. S. Horn, and J. C. Quick, "Health Consequences of Stress," *Journal of Organizational Behavior Management* 8 (1986): 19–36.

26. R. M. Yerkes and J. D. Dodson, "The Relation of Strength of Stimulus to Rapidity of Habit-Formation," *Journal of Comparative Neurology and Psychology* 18 (1908): 459–482.

27. J. E. McGrath, "Stress and Behavior in Organizations," in M. D. Dunnette, ed., *Handbook of Industrial and Organizational Psychology* (Chicago: Rand McNally, 1976), 1351–1395.

28. W. B. Cannon, *Bodily Changes in Pain, Hunger, Fear, and Rage* (New York: Appleton, 1915).

29. P. A. Herbig and F. A. Palumbo, "Karoshi: Salaryman Sudden Death Syndrome," *Journal of Managerial Psychology* 9 (1994): 11–16.

30. S. Sauter, L. R. Murphy, and J. J. Hurrell, Jr., "Prevention of Work-Related Psychological Distress: A National Strategy Proposed by the National Institute for Occupational Safety and Health," *American Psychologist* 45 (1990): 1146–1158.

31. H. Selye, *Stress in Health and Disease* (Boston: Butterworth, 1976).

32. B. G. Ware and D. L. Block, "Cardiovascular Risk Intervention at a Work Site: The Ford Motor Company Program," *International Journal of Mental Health* 11 (1982): 68–75.

33. B. S. Siegel, *Love, Medicine, and Miracles* (New York: Harper & Row, 1986).

34. N. Bolger, A. DeLongis, R. C. Kessler, and E. A. Schilling, "Effects of Daily Stress on Negative Mood," *Journal of Personality and Social Psychology* 57 (1989): 808–818.

35. B. A. Macy and P. H. Mirvis, "A Methodology for Assessment of Quality of Work Life and Organizational Effectiveness in Behavioral-Economic Terms," *Administrative Science Quarterly* 21 (1976): 212–226.

36. J. M. Ivancevich, M. T. Matteson, and E. Richards, "Who's Liable for Stress on the Job?" *Harvard Business Review* 64 (1985): 60–72.

37. *Frank S. Deus v. Allstate Insurance Company*, civil action no. 88-2099, U.S. District Court, Western District of Louisiana.

38. R. S. DeFrank and J. M. Ivancevich, "Stress on the Job: An Executive Update," *Academy of Management Executive* 12 (1998): 55–66.

39. E. Ramey, "Gender Differences in Cardiac Disease: The Paradox of Heart Disease in Women." Paper delivered at the Healing the Heart Conference, Boston, May 3–5, 1990.

40. D. L. Nelson and J. C. Quick, "Professional Women: Are Distress and Disease Inevitable?" *Academy of Management Review* 10 (1985): 206–218; T. D. Jick and L. F. Mitz, "Sex Differences in Work Stress," *Academy of Management Review* 10 (1985): 408–420.

41. L. Verbrugge, "Recent, Present, and Future Health of American Adults," *Annual Review of Public Health* 10 (1989): 333–361.

42. M. D. Friedman and R. H. Rosenman, *Type A Behavior and Your Heart* (New York: Knopf, 1974).

43. L. Wright, "The Type A Behavior Pattern and Coronary Artery Disease," *American Psychologist* 43 (1988): 2–14.

44. J. M. Ivancevich and M. T. Matteson, "A Type A-B Person-Work Environment Interaction Model for Examining Occupational Stress and Consequences," *Human Relations* 37 (1984): 491–513.

45. S. O. C. Kobasa, "Conceptualization and Measurement of Personality in Job Stress Research," in J. J. Hurrell, Jr., L. R. Murphy, S. L. Sauter, and C. L. Cooper, eds., *Occupational Stress: Issues and Developments in Research* (New York: Taylor & Francis, 1988), 100–109.

46. J. Borysenko, "Personality Hardiness," Lectures in Behavioral Medicine (Boston: Harvard Medical School, 1985).

47. J. S. House, K. R. Landis, and D. Umberson, "Social Relationships and Health," *Science* 241 (1988): 540–545.

48. J. Bowlby, *A Secure Base* (New York: Basic Books, 1988).

49. C. Hazan and P. Shaver, "Love and Work: An Attachment-Theoretical Perspective," *Journal of Personality and Social Psychology* 59 (1990): 270–280.

50. D. L. Nelson and J. C. Quick, "Social Support and Newcomer Adjustment in Organization: Attachment Theory at Work?" *Journal of Organizational Behavior* 12 (1991): 543–554; J. C. Quick, J. R. Joplin, D. L. Nelson, and J. D. Quick, "Behavioral Responses to Anxiety: Self-Reliance, Counterdependence, and Overdependence," *Anxiety, Stress, and Coping* 5 (1992): 41–54; J. C. Quick, D. L. Nelson, and J. D. Quick, *Stress and Challenge at the Top: The Paradox of the Successful Executive* (Chichester, England: Wiley, 1990).

51. J. C. Quick, J. R. Joplin, D. L. Nelson, and J. D. Quick, "Self-Reliance for Stress and Combat" (Proceedings of the 8th Combat Stress Conference, U.S. Army Health Services Command, Fort Sam Houston, Texas, September 23–27, 1991): 1–5.

52. K. Hickox, "Content and Competitive," *Airman* (January 1994): 31–33.

53. R. W. Griffin, A. O'Leary-Kelly, and J. M. Collins, eds., *Dysfunctional Behavior in Organizations: Violent and Deviant Behavior* (Stamford, Conn.: JAI Press, 1998).

54. W. L. French and C. H. Bell, Jr., *Organizational Development: Behavioral Science Interventions for Organization Improvement*, 4th ed. (Englewood Cliffs, N.J.: Prentice-Hall, 1990).

55. S. A. Lobel and L. St. Clair, "Effects of Family Responsibilities, Gender, and Career Identity Salience on Performance Outcomes of Professionals," *Academy of Management Journal* 35 (1992): 1057–1069.

56. M. E. P. Seligman, *Learned Optimism* (New York: Knopf, 1990).

57. W. T. Brooks and T. W. Mullins, *High-Impact Time Management* (Englewood Cliffs, N.J.: Prentice-Hall, 1989).

58. M. Westman and D. Eden, "Effects of a Respite from Work on Burnout: Vacation Relief and Fade-Out," *Journal of Applied Psychology* 82 (1997): 516–527.

59. K. H. Cooper, *Can Stress Heal?* (Nashville: Nelson, 1997).

60. M. Davis, E. R. Eshelman, and M. McKay, *The Relaxation and Stress Reduction Workbook*, 3d ed. (Oakland, Calif.: New Harbinger, 1988).

61. H. Benson, "Your Innate Asset for Combating Stress," *Harvard Business Review* 52 (1974): 49–60.

62. D. Ornish, *Dr. Dean Ornish's Program for Reversing Cardiovascular Disease* (New York: Random House, 1990).

63. J. W. Pennebaker, *Opening Up: The Healing Power of Confiding in Others* (New York: Morrow, 1990).

64. M. E. Francis and J. W. Pennebaker, "Putting Stress into Words: The Impact of Writing on Physiological, Absentee, and Self-Reported Emotional Well-being Measures," *American Journal of Health Promotion* 6 (1992): 280–287.

65. Z. Solomon, B. Oppenheimer, and S. Noy, "Subsequent Military Adjustment of Combat Stress Reaction Casualties: A Nine-Year Follow-Up Study," in N. A. Milgram, ed., *Stress and Coping in Time of War: Generalizations from the Israeli Experience* (New York: Brunner/Mazel, 1986), 84–90.

66. D. Wegman and L. Fine, "Occupational Health in the 1990s," *Annual Review of Public Health* 11 (1990): 89–103; J. C. Quick, "Occupational Health Psychology: Historical Roots and Future Directions," *Health Psychology* 17 (1999): 82–88.

67. D. Gebhardt and C. Crump, "Employee Fitness and Wellness Programs in the Workplace," *American Psychologist* 45 (1990): 262–272.

68. T. Wolf, H. Randall, and J. Faucett, "A Survey of Health Promotion Programs in U.S. and Canadian Medical Schools," *American Journal of Health Promotion* 3 (1988): 33–36.

69. S. Weiss, J. Fielding, and A. Baum, *Health at Work* (Hillsdale, N.J.: Erlbaum, 1990).

70. D. Rosato, "Today's Issue: Putting Humor to Work in the Workplace. Guest CEO: Herb Kelleher of Southwest Airlines," *USA Today*, February 23, 1998, 5B; J. C. Quick, "Crafting an Organizational Culture: Herb's Hand at Southwest Airlines," *Organizational Dynamics* 21 (1992): 45–56.

Chapter 8

1. G. S. Vasilash, "Quality at Ford Wayne Assembly," *Production* 109 (1997): 60–61.

2. L. Iacocca, *Iacocca: An Autobiography* (New York: Bantam Books, 1984).

3. A. M. Towsend, S. M. DeMarie, and A. R. Hendrickson, "Virtual Teams: Technology and the Workplace of the Future," *Academy of Management Executive* 12 (1998): 17–29.

4. D. M. McGregor, *The Human Side of Enterprise* (New York: McGraw-Hill, 1960).

5. J. R. Katzenbach and D. K. Smith, "The Discipline of Teams," *Harvard Business Review* 71 (1993): 111–120.

6. K. L. Bettenhausen and J. K. Murnighan, "The Development and Stability of Norms in Groups Facing Interpersonal and Structural Challenge," *Administrative Science Quarterly* 36 (1991): 20–35.

7. I. Summers, T. Coffelt, and R. E. Horton, "Work-Group Cohesion," *Psychological Reports* 63 (1988): 627–636.

8. K. H. Price, "Decision Responsibility, Task Responsibility, Identifiability, and Social Loafing," *Organizational Behavior and Human Decision Processes* 40 (1987): 330–345.

9. R. Albanese and D. D. Van Fleet, "Rational Behavior in Groups: The Free-Riding Tendency," *Academy of Management Review* 10 (1985): 244–255.

10. E. Diener, "Deindividuation, Self-Awareness, and Disinhibition," *Journal of Personality and Social Psychology* 37 (1979): 1160–1171.

11. S. Prentice-Dunn and R. W. Rogers, "Deindividuation and the Self-Regulation of Behavior," in P. Paulus, ed., *Psychology of Group Influence* (Hillsdale, N.J.: Erlbaum, 1989), 87–109.

12. B. M. Bass and E. C. Ryterband, *Organizational Psychology*, 2d ed. (Boston: Allyn & Bacon, 1979); B. W. Tuckman, "Developmental Sequences in Small Groups," *Psychological Bulletin* 63 (1963): 384–399.

13. W. G. Bennis and H. A. Shepard, "A Theory of Group Development," *Human Relations* 9 (1956): 415–438.

14. S. Caudron, "Monsanto Responds to Diversity," *Personnel Journal* (November 1990): 72–80.

15. D. L. Fields and T. C. Bloom, "Employee Satisfaction in Work Groups with Different Gender Composition," *Journal of Organizational Behavior* 18 (1997): 181–196.

16. D. C. Lau and J. K. Murnighan, "Demographic Diversity and Faultlines: The Compositional Dynamics of Organizational Groups," *Academy of Management Review* 23 (1998): 325–340.

17. D. Nichols, "Quality Program Sparked Company Turnaround," *Personnel* (October 1991): 24. For a commentary on Wallace's hard times and subsequent emergence from Chapter 11 bankruptcy, see R. C. Hill, "When the Going Gets Tough: A Baldrige Award Winner on the Line," *Academy of Management Executive* 7 (1993): 75–79.

18. M. Hardaker and B. K. Ward, "How to Make a Team Work," *Harvard Business Review* 65 (1987): 112–120.

19. C. R. Gowen, "Managing Work Group Performance by Individual Goals and Group Goals for an Interdependent Group Task," *Journal of Organizational Behavior Management* 7 (1986): 5–27.

20. K. L. Bettenhausen and J. K. Murnighan, "The Emergence of Norms in Competitive Decision-Making Groups," *Administrative Science Quarterly* 30 (1985): 350–372; K. L. Bettenhausen, "Five Years of Groups Research: What We Have Learned and What Needs to Be Addressed," *Journal of Management* 17 (1991): 345–381.

21. J. E. McGrath, *Groups: Interaction and Performance* (Englewood Cliffs, N.J.: Prentice-Hall, 1984).

22. S. E. Seashore, *Group Cohesiveness in the Industrial Work Group* (Ann Arbor, Mich.: University of Michigan, 1954).

23. S. M. Klein, "A Longitudinal Study of the Impact of Work Pressure on Group Cohesive Behaviors," *International Journal of Management* 12 (1996): 68–75.

24. N. Steckler and N. Fondas, "Building Team Leader Effectiveness: A Diagnostic Tool," *Organizational Dynamics* 23 (1995): 20–35.

25. G. Parker, *Team Players and Teamwork* (San Francisco: Jossey-Bass, 1990).

26. N. R. F. Maier, "Assets and Liabilities in Group Problem Solving: The Need for an Integrative Function," *Psychological Review* 74 (1967): 239–249.

27. T. A. Stewart, "The Search for the Organization of Tomorrow," *Fortune*, May 18, 1992, 92–98.

28. J. R. Goktepe and C. E. Schneier, "Role of Sex, Gender Roles, and Attraction in Predicting Emergent Leaders," *Journal of Applied Psychology* 74 (1989): 165–167.

29. B. Dumaine, "The Bureaucracy Busters," *Fortune*, June 17, 1991, 36.

30. P. F. Drucker, "There's More Than One Kind of Team," *The Wall Street Journal*, February 11, 1992, A16.

31. J. H. Sheridan, "A Star in the GM Heavens," *Industry Week* (March 18, 1991): 50–54.

32. P. M. Podsakoff, M. Ahearne, and S. B. MacKenzie, "Organizational Citizenship Behavior and the Quantity and Quality of Work Group Performance," *Journal of Applied Psychology* 82 (1997): 262–270.

33. W. L. Mohr and H. Mohr, *Quality Circles: Changing Images of People at Work* (Reading, Mass.: Addison-Wesley, 1983).

34. R. W. Griffin, "A Longitudinal Assessment of the Consequences of Quality Circles in an Industrial Setting," *Academy of Management Journal* 31 (1988): 338–358.

35. P. Shaver and D. Buhrmester, "Loneliness, Sex-Role Orientation, and Group Life: A Social Needs Perspective," in P. Paulus, ed., *Basic Group Processes* (New York: Springer-Verlag, 1985), 259–288.

36. W. R. Lassey, "Dimensions of Leadership," in W. R. Lassey and R. R. Fernandez, eds., *Leadership and Social Change* (La Jolla, Calif.: University Associates, 1976), 10–15.

37. J. D. Quick, G. Moorhead, J. C. Quick, E. A. Gerloff, K. L. Mattox, and C. Mullins, "Decision Making among Emergency Room Residents: Preliminary Observations and a Decision Model," *Journal of Medical Education* 58 (1983): 117–125.

38. W. J. Duncan and J. P. Feisal, "No Laughing Matter: Patterns of Humor in the Workplace," *Organizational Dynamics* 17 (1989): 18–30.

39. K. W. Thomas and B. A. Velthouse, "Cognitive Elements of Empowerment: An 'Interpretive' Model of Intrinsic Task Motivation," *Academy of Management Review* 15 (1990): 666–681.

40. R. R. Blake, J. S. Mouton, and R. L. Allen, *Spectacular Teamwork: How to Develop the Leadership Skills for Team Success* (New York: Wiley, 1987).

41. American Management Association, *Blueprints for Service Quality: The Federal Express Approach*, AMA Management Briefing (New York: AMA, 1991).

42. W. C. Byham, *ZAPP! The Human Lightning of Empowerment* (Pittsburgh, Pa.: Developmental Dimensions, 1989).

43. F. Shipper and C. C. Manz, "Employee Self-Management without Formally Designated Teams: An Alternative Road to Empowerment," *Organizational Dynamics* (Winter 1992): 48–62.

44. P. Block, *The Empowered Manager: Positive Political Skills at Work* (San Francisco: Jossey-Bass, 1987).

45. V. J. Derlega and J. Grzelak, eds., *Cooperation and Helping Behavior: Theories and Research* (New York: Academic Press, 1982).

46. A. G. Athos and J. J. Gabarro, *Interpersonal Behavior: Communication and Understanding in Relationships* (Englewood Cliffs, N.J.: Prentice-Hall, 1978).

47. J. L. Cordery, W. S. Mueller, and L. M. Smith, "Attitudinal and Behavioral Effects of Autonomous Group Working: A Longitudinal Field Study," *Academy of Management Journal* 34 (1991): 464–476.

48. G. Moorhead, C. P. Neck, and M. S. West, "The Tendency Toward Defective Decision Making within Self-Managing Teams: The Relevance of Groupthink for the 21st Century," *Organizational Behavior & Human Decision Processes* 73 (1998): 327–351.

49. R. M. Robinson, S. L. Oswald, K. S. Swinehart, and J. Thomas, "Southwest Industries: Creating High-Performance Teams for High-Technology Production," *Planning Review* 19, published by the Planning Forum (November–December 1991): 10–47.

50. A. Lienert, "Forging a New Partnership," *Management Review* 83 (1994): 39–43.

51. S. Thiagaraian, "A Game for Cooperative Learning," *Training and Development*, (May 1992), 35–41.

52. D. C. Hambrick and P. Mason, "Upper Echelons: The Organization as a Reflection of Its Top Managers," *Academy of Management Review* 9 (1984): 193–206.

53. D. C. Hambrick, "The Top Management Team: Key to Strategic Success," *California Management Review* 30 (1987): 88–108.

54. D. C. Hambrick and G. D. S. Fukutomi, "The Seasons of a CEO's Tenure," *Academy of Management Review* 16 (1991): 719–742.

55. J. C. Quick, D. L. Nelson, and J. D. Quick, "Successful Executives: How Independent?" *Academy of Management Executive* 1 (1987): 139–145.

56. A. Bennett, "Firms Run by Executive Teams Can Reap Rewards, Incur Risks," *The Wall Street Journal*, February 5, 1991, B1, B2.

57. N. J. Adler, *International Dimensions of Organizational Behavior* (Boston: PWS-Kent, 1991).

58. I. D. Steiner, *Group Process and Productivity* (New York: Academic Press, 1972).

59. A. Taylor III, "The Gentlemen at Ford Are Kicking Butt," *Fortune*, June 22, 1998, 70–75.

60. J. W. Pfeiffer and C. Nolde, eds., *The Encyclopedia of Team-Development Activities* (San Diego: University Associates, 1991).

61. G. S. Vasilash, "Quality at Ford Wayne Assembly," *Production* 109 (1997): 60–61.

Chapter 9

1. H. Schultz and D. J. Yang, *Pour Your Heart into It* (New York: Hyperion, 1997).

2. H. A. Simon, *The New Science of Management Decision* (New York: Harper & Row, 1960).

3. G. Colvin, "The Most Valuable Quality in a Manager," *Fortune*, December 29, 1997, 279–280.

4. G. Huber, *Managerial Decision Making* (Glenview, Ill.: Scott, Foresman, 1980).

5. H. A. Simon, *Administrative Behavior* (New York: Macmillan, 1957).

6. E. F. Harrison, *The Managerial Decision-Making Process* (Boston: Houghton Mifflin, 1981).

7. R. L. Ackoff, "The Art and Science of Mess Management," *Interfaces* (February 1981): 20–26.

8. R. M. Cyert and J. G. March, eds., *A Behavioral Theory of the Firm* (Englewood Cliffs, N.J.: Prentice-Hall, 1963).

9. M. D. Cohen, J. G. March, and J. P. Olsen, "A Garbage Can Model of Organizational Choice," *Administrative Science Quarterly* 17 (1972): 1–25.

10. J. G. March and J. P. Olsen, "Garbage Can Models of Decision Making in Organizations," in J. G. March and R. Weissinger-Baylon, eds., *Ambiguity and Command* (Marshfield, Mass.: Pitman, 1986), 11–53.

11. K. R. MacCrimmon and D. Wehrung, *Taking Risks* (New York: Free Press, 1986).

12. T. S. Perry, "How Small Firms Innovate: Designing a Culture for Creativity," *Research Technology Management* 28 (1995): 14–17.

13. B. M. Staw, "Knee-Deep in the Big Muddy: A Study of Escalating Commitment to a Chosen Course of Action," *Organizational Behavior and Human Performance* 16 (1976): 27–44; B. M. Staw, "The Escalation of Commitment to a Course of Action," *Academy of Management Review* 6 (1981): 577–587.

14. B. M. Staw and J. Ross, "Understanding Behavior in Escalation Situations," *Science* 246 (1989): 216–220.

15. L. Festinger, *A Theory of Cognitive Dissonance* (Evanston, Ill.: Row, Peterson, 1957).

16. B. M. Staw, "The Escalation of Commitment: An Update and Appraisal," in Z. Shapira, ed., *Organizational Decision Making* (Cambridge, England: Cambridge University Press, 1997).

17. G. Whyte, "Diffusion of Responsibility: Effects on the Escalation Tendency," *Journal of Applied Psychology* 76 (1991): 408–415.

18. C. G. Jung, *Psychological Types* (London: Routledge & Kegan Paul, 1923).

19. W. Taggart and D. Robey, "Minds and Managers: On the Dual Nature of Human Information Processing and Management," *Academy of Management Review* 6 (1981): 187–195; D. Hellriegel and J. W. Slocum, Jr., "Managerial Problem-Solving Styles," *Business Horizons* 18 (1975): 29–37.

20. I. I. Mitroff and R. H. Kilmann, "On Organization Stories: An Approach to the Design and Analysis of Organization through Myths and Stories," in R. H. Killman, L. R. Pondy, and D. P. Slevin, eds., *The Management of Organization Design* (New York: Elsevier–North Holland, 1976).

21. B. K. Blaylock and L. P. Rees, "Cognitive Style and the Usefulness of Information," *Decision Sciences* 15 (1984): 74–91; D. L. Davis, S. J. Grove, and P. A. Knowles, "An Experimental Application of Personality Type as an Analogue for Decision-Making Style," *Psychological Reports* 66 (1990): 167–175.

22. I. B. Myers, *Gifts Differing* (Palo Alto, Calif.: Consulting Psychologists Press, 1980).

23. H. Mintzberg, "Planning on the Left Side and Managing on the Right," *Harvard Business Review* 54 (1976): 51–63.

24. D. J. Isenberg, "How Senior Managers Think," *Harvard Business Review* 62 (1984): 81–90.

25. R. N. Beck, "Visions, Values, and Strategies: Changing Attitudes and Culture," *Academy of Managment Executive* 1 (1987): 33–41.

26. C. I. Barnard, *The Functions of the Executive* (Cambridge, Mass.: Harvard University Press, 1938).

27. R. Rowan, *The Intuitive Manager* (New York: Little, Brown, 1986).

28. W. H. Agor, *Intuition in Organizations* (Newbury Park, Calif.: Sage, 1989).

29. Isenberg, "How Senior Managers Think," 81–90.

30. H. A. Simon, "Making Management Decisions: The Role of Intuition and Emotion," *Academy of Management Executive* 1 (1987): 57–64.

31. J. L. Redford, R. H. McPhierson, R. G. Frankiewicz, and J. Gaa, "Intuition and Moral Development," *Journal of Psychology* 129 (1994): 91–101.

32. W. H. Agor, "How Top Executives Use Their Intuition to Make Important Decisions," *Business Horizons* 29 (1986): 49–53.

33. O. Behling and N. L. Eckel, "Making Sense Out of Intuition," *Academy of Management Executive* 5 (1991): 46–54.

34. L. R. Beach, *Image Theory: Decision Making in Personal and Organizational Contexts* (Chichester, England: Wiley, 1990).

35. L. Livingstone, "Person-Environment Fit on the Dimension of Creativity: Relationships with Strain, Job Satisfaction, and Performance" (Ph.D. diss., Oklahoma State University, 1992).

36. M. A. West and J. L. Farr, "Innovation at Work," in M. A. West and J. L. Farr, eds., *Innovation and Creativity at Work: Psychological and Organizational Strategies* (New York: Wiley, 1990), 3–13.

37. G. Morgan, *Riding the Waves of Change* (San Francisco: Jossey-Bass, 1988).

38. G. Wallas, *The Art of Thought* (New York: Harcourt Brace, 1926).

39. M. D. Mumford and S. B. Gustafson, "Creativity Syndrome: Integration, Application, and Innovation," *Psychological Bulletin* 103 (1988): 27–43.

40. T. Poze, "Analogical Connections—The Essence of Creativity," *Journal of Creative Behavior* 17 (1983): 240–241.

41. I. Sladeczek and G. Domino, "Creativity, Sleep, and Primary Process Thinking in Dreams," *Journal of Creative Behavior* 19 (1985): 38–46.

42. F. Barron and D. M. Harrington, "Creativity, Intelligence, and Personality," *Annual Review of Psychology* 32 (1981): 439–476.

43. R. J. Sternberg, "A Three-Faced Model of Creativity," in R. J. Sternberg, ed., *The Nature of Creativity* (London: Cambridge University Press, 1988), 125–147.

44. A. M. Isen, "Positive Affect and Decision Making," in W. M. Goldstein and R. M. Hogarth, eds., *Research on Judgment and Decision Making* (Cambridge, England: Cambridge University Press, 1997).

45. T. Stevens, "Creativity Killers," *Industry Week* (January 23, 1995): 63.

46. S. G. Scott and R. A. Bruce, "Following the Leader in R&D: The Joint Effect of Subordinate Problem-Solving Style and Leader–Member Relations on Innovative Behavior," *IEEE Transactions on Engineering Management* 45 (1998): 3–10.

47. T. M. Amabile, R. Conti, H. Coon, J. Lazenby, and M. Herron, "Assessing the Work Environment for Creativity," *Academy of Management Journal* 39 (1996): 1154–1184.

48. D. M. Harrington, "Creativity, Analogical Thinking, and Muscular Metaphors," *Journal of Mental Imagery* 6 (1981): 121–126; R. M. Kanter, *The Change Masters* (New York: Simon & Schuster, 1983).

49. T. M. Amabile, B. A. Hennessey, and B. S. Grossman, "Social Influences on Creativity: The Effects of Contracted-for Reward," *Journal of Personality and Social Psychology* 50 (1986): 14–23.

50. Livingstone, "Person-Environment Fit."

51. R. L. Firestein, "Effects of Creative Problem-Solving Training on Communication Behaviors in Small Groups," *Small Group Research* (November 1989): 507–521.

52. C. M. Solomon, "What an Idea: Creativity Training," *Personnel Journal* 69 (1990): 64–71.

53. R. Von Oech, *A Whack on the Side of the Head* (New York: Warner, 1983).

54. A. G. Robinson and S. Stern, *How Innovation and Improvement Actually Happen* (San Francisco: Berrett Koehler, 1997).

55. M. F. R. Kets de Vries, R. Branson, and P. Barnevik, "Charisma in Action: The Transformational Abilities of Virgin's Richard Branson and ABBS's Percy Barnevik," *Organizational Dynamics* 26 (1998): 7–21.

56. M. Kostera, M. Proppe, and M. Szatkowski, "Staging the New Romantic Hero in the Old Cynical Theatre: On Managers, Roles, and Change in Poland," *Journal of Organizational Behavior* 16 (1995): 631–646.

57. M. Basadur, "Managing Creativity: A Japanese Model," *Academy of Management Executive* 6 (1992): 29–42.

58. J. Pfeffer, "Seven Practices of Successful Organizations," *California Management Review* 40 (1998): 96–124.

59. P. E. Conner, "Decision-Making Participation Patterns: The Role of Organizational Context," *Academy of Management Journal* 35 (1992): 218–231.

60. M. Sashkin, "Participative Management Is an Ethical Imperative," *Organizational Dynamics* (Spring 1984): 4–22.

61. D. Plunkett, "The Creative Organization: An Empirical Investigation of the Importance of Participation in Decision Making," *Journal of Creative Behavior* 24 (1990): 140–148; J. A. Wagner III and R. Z. Gooding, "Shared Influence and Organizational Behavior: A Meta-Analysis of Situational Variables Expected to Moderate Participation-Outcome Relationships," *Academy of Management Journal* 29 (1987): 524–541.

62. C. R. Leana, E. A. Locke, and D. M. Schweiger, "Fact and Fiction in Analyzing Research on Participative Decision Making: A Critique of Cotton, Vollrath, Froggatt, Lengnick-Hall, and Jennings," *Academy of Management Review* 15 (1990): 137–146; J. L. Cotton, D. A. Vollrath, M. L. Lengnick-Hall, and K. L. Froggatt, "Fact: The Form of Participation Does Matter—A Rebuttal to Leana, Locke, and Schweiger," *Academy of Management Review* 15 (1990): 147–153.

63. D. Collins, R. A. Ross, and T. L. Ross, "Who Wants Participative Management?" *Group and Organization Studies* 14 (1989): 422–445.

64. R. Stayer, "How I Learned to Let My Workers Lead," *Harvard Business Review* (November–December 1990): 66–83.

65. T. W. Malone, "Is Empowerment Just a Fad? Control, Decision Making, and Information Technology," *Sloan Management Review* 38 (1997): 23–35.

66. T. L. Brown, "Fearful of 'Empowerment': Should Managers Be Terrified?" *Industry Week* (June 18, 1990): 12.

67. L. Hirschhorn, "Stresses and Patterns of Adjustment in the Postindustrial Factory," in G. M. Green and F. Baker, eds., *Work, Health, and Productivity* (New York: Oxford University Press, 1991), 115–126.

68. P. G. Gyllenhammar, *People at Work* (Reading, Mass.: Addison-Wesley, 1977).

69. R. Tannenbaum and F. Massarik, "Participation by Subordinates in the Managerial Decision-Making Process," *Canadian Journal of Economics and Political Science* 16 (1950): 408–418.

70. H. Levinson, *Executive* (Cambridge, Mass.: Harvard University Press, 1981).

71. J. S. Black and H. B. Gregersen, "Participative Decision Making: An Integration of Multiple Dimensions," *Human Relations* 50 (1997): 859–878.

72. G. Stasser, L. A. Taylor and C. Hanna, "Information Sampling in Structured and Unstructured Discussion of Three- and Six-Person Groups," *Journal of Personality and Social Psychology* 57 (1989): 67–78.

73. E. Kirchler and J. H. Davis, "The Influence of Member Status Differences and Task Type on Group Consensus and Member Position Change," *Journal of Personality and Social Psychology* 51 (1986): 83–91.

74. R. F. Maier, "Assets and Liabilities in Group Problem Solving," *Psychological Review* 74 (1967): 239–249.

75. M. E. Shaw, *Group Dynamics: The Psychology of Small Group Behavior*, 3d ed. (New York: McGraw-Hill, 1981).

76. P. W. Yetton and P. C. Bottger, "Individual versus Group Problem Solving: An Empirical Test of a Best Member Strategy," *Organizational Behavior and Human Performance* 29 (1982): 307–321.

77. W. Watson, L. Michaelson, and W. Sharp, "Member Competence, Group Interaction, and Group Decision Making: A Longitudinal Study," *Journal of Applied Psychology* 76 (1991): 803–809.

78. I. Janis, *Victims of Groupthink* (Boston: Houghton Mifflin, 1972).

79. M. A. Hogg and S. C. Hains, "Friendship and Group Identification: A New Look at the Role of Cohesiveness in Groupthink," *European Journal of Social Psychology* 28 (1998): 323–341.

80. C. P. Neck and G. Moorhead, "Groupthink Remodeled: The Importance of Leadership, Time Pressure, and Methodical Decision Making Procedures," *Human Relations* 48 (1995): 537–557.

81. J. K. Esser and J. S. Lindoerfer, "Groupthink and the Space Shuttle *Challenger* Accident: Toward a Quantitative Case Analysis," *Journal of Behavioral Decision Making* 2 (1989): 167–177.

82. G. Moorhead, R. Ference, and C. P. Neck, "Group Decision Fiascoes Continue: Space Shuttle *Challenger* and a Revised Groupthink Framework," *Human Relations* 44 (1991): 539–550.

83. J. R. Montanari and G. Moorhead, "Development of the Groupthink Assessment Inventory," *Educational and Psychological Measurement* 49 (1989): 209–219.

84. P. t'Hart, "Irving L. Janis' Victims of Groupthink," *Political Psychology* 12 (1991): 247–278.

85. J. A. F. Stoner, "Risky and Cautious Shifts in Group Decisions: The Influence of Widely Held Values," *Journal of Experimental Social Psychology* 4 (1968): 442–459.

86. S. Moscovici and M. Zavalloni, "The Group as a Polarizer of Attitudes," *Journal of Personality and Social Psychology* 12 (1969): 125–135.

87. G. R. Goethals and M. P. Zanna, "The Role of Social Comparison in Choice of Shifts," *Journal of Personality and Social Psychology* 37 (1979): 1469–1476.

88. A. Vinokur and E. Burnstein, "Effects of Partially Shared Persuasive Arguments on Group-Induced Shifts: A Problem-Solving Approach," *Journal of Personality and Social Psychology* 29 (1974): 305–315.

89. T. Bouchard, "Whatever Happened to Brainstorming?" *Journal of Creative Behavior* 5 (1971): 182–189.

90. L. R. Beach, *The Psychology of Decision Making* (Thousand Oaks, Calif.: Sage, 1997).

91. W. H. Cooper, R. B. Gallupe, S. Pollard, and J. Cadsby, "Some Liberating Effects of Anonymous Electronic Brainstorming," *Small Group Research* 29 (1998): 147–178.

92. A. Van de Ven and A. Delbecq, "The Effectiveness of Nominal, Delphi and Interacting Group Decision-Making Processes," *Academy of Management Journal* 17 (1974): 605–621.

93. A. L. Delbecq, A. H. Van de Ven, and D. H. Gustafson, *Group Techniques for Program Planning: A Guide to Nominal, Group, and Delphi Processes* (Glenview, Ill.: Scott, Foresman, 1975).

94. R. A. Cosier and C. R. Schwenk, "Agreement and Thinking Alike: Ingredients for Poor Decisions," *Academy of Management Executive* 4 (1990): 69–74.

95. D. M. Schweiger, W. R. Sandburg, and J. W. Ragan, "Group Approaches for Improving Strategic Decision Making: A Comparative Analysis of Dialectical Inquiry, Devil's Advocacy, and Consensus," *Academy of Management Journal* 29 (1986): 149–159.

96. G. Whyte, "Decision Failures: Why They Occur and How to Prevent Them," *Academy of Management Executive* 5 (1991): 23–31.

97. E. E. Lawler III and S. A. Mohrman, "Quality Circles: After the Honeymoon," *Organizational Dynamics* (Spring 1987): 42–54.

98. T. L. Tang and E. A. Butler, "Attributions of Quality Circles' Problem-Solving Failure: Differences among Management, Supporting Staff, and Quality Circle Members," *Public Personnel Management* 26 (1997): 203–225.

99. S. R. Olberding, "Toyota on Competition and Quality Circles," *The Journal for Quality and Participation* 21 (1998): 52–54.

100. J. Schilder, "Work Teams Boost Productivity," *Personnel Journal* 71 (1992): 67–72.

101. P. S. Goodman, R. Devadas, and T. L. Griffith-Hughson, "Groups and Productivity: Analyzing the Effectiveness of Self-Managed Teams," in J. P. Campbell, R. J. Campbell, and

Associates, eds., *Productivity in Organizations* (San Francisco: Jossey-Bass, 1988), 295–327.

102. C. J. Nemeth, "Managing Innovation: When Less Is More," *California Management Review* 40 (1997): 59–68.

103. N. Adler, *International Dimensions of Organizational Behavior*, 3d ed. (Cincinnati, Ohio: South-Western, 1997).

104. G. K. Stephens and C. R. Greer, "Doing Business in Mexico: Understanding Cultural Differences," *Organization Dynamics* 24 (1995): 39–55.

105. "How Organizations Are Becoming More Efficient Using Expert Systems," *I/S Analyzer Case Studies* 36 (1995): 2–6.

106. J. Wybo, "FMIS: A Decision Support System for Forest Fire Prevention and Fighting," *IEEE Transactions on Engineering Management* 45 (1998): 127–131.

107. M. S. Poole, M. Holmes, and G. DeSanctis, "Conflict Management in a Computer-Supported Meeting Environment," *Management Science* 37 (1991): 926–953.

108. R. Johansen, *Leading Business Teams: Process, Technology, and Team Effectiveness* (Menlo Park, Calif.: Institute for the Future, 1990).

109. D. Kirkpatrick, "Here Comes the Payoff from PCs," *Fortune*, March 23, 1992, 93–102.

110. A. T. McCartt and J. Rohrbaugh, "Managerial Openness to Change and the Introduction of GDSS: Explaining Initial Success and Failure in Decision Conferencing," *Organization Science* 6 (1995): 569–584.

111. P. L. McLeod, R. S. Baron, M. W. Marti, and K. Yoon, "The Eyes Have It: Minority Influence in Face-to-Face and Computer-Mediated Group Discussion," *Journal of Applied Psychology* 82 (1997): 706–718.

112. A. M. Townsend, S. M. DeMarie, and A. R. Hendrickson, "Virtual Teams: Technology and the Workplace of the Future," *Academy of Management Executive* 12 (1998): 17–29.

113. L. M. Jessup and J. F. George, "Theoretical and Methodological Issues in Group Support Systems," *Small Group Research* 28 (1997): 394–413.

114. K. Blanchard and N. V. Peale, *The Power of Ethical Management* (New York: Fawcett Crest, 1988).

115. R. R. Sims, "Linking Groupthink to Unethical Behavior in Organizations," *Journal of Business Ethics* 11 (1992): 651–662.

Chapter 10

1. P. Mitchell, "Texas Beef Farmers Lose Food Libel Battle with Oprah," *The Lancet* 351 (1998): 814; S. McBride, "Most Admired," *The Wall Street Journal*, December 12, 1997, R2.

2. G. C. Homans, "Social Behavior as Exchange," *American Journal of Sociology* 63 (1958): 597–606.

3. R. D. Middlemist and M. A. Hitt, *Organizational Behavior: Managerial Strategies for Performance* (St. Paul, Minn.: West Publishing, 1988).

4. C. Barnard, *The Functions of the Executive* (Cambridge, Mass.: Harvard University Press, 1938).

5. J. R. P. French and B. Raven, "The Bases of Social Power," in D. Cartwright, ed., *Group Dynamics: Research and Theory* (Evanston, Ill.: Row, Peterson, 1962); T. R. Hinkin and C. A. Schriesheim, "Development and Application of New Scales to Measure the French and Raven (1959) Bases of Social Power," *Journal of Applied Psychology* 74 (1989): 561–567.

6. P. M. Podsakoff and C. A. Schriesheim, "Field Studies of French and Raven's Bases of Power: Critique, Reanalysis, and Suggestions for Future Research," *Psychological Bulletin* 97 (1985): 387–411.

7. M. A. Rahim, "Relationships of Leader Power to Compliance and Satisfaction with Supervision: Evidence from a National Sample of Managers," *Journal of Management* 15 (1989): 545–556.

8. C. Argyris, "Management Information Systems: The Challenge to Rationality and Emotionality," *Management Science* 17 (1971): 275–292; J. Naisbitt and P. Aburdene, *Megatrends 2000* (New York: Morrow, 1990).

9. P. P. Carson, K. D. Carson, E. L. Knight, and C. W. Roe, "Power in Organizations: A Look through the TQM Lens," *Quality Progress* (November 1995): 73–78.

10. M. Velasquez, D. J. Moberg, and G. F. Cavanaugh, "Organizational Statesmanship and Dirty Politics: Ethical Guidelines for the Organizational Politician," *Organizational Dynamics* 11 (1982): 65–79.

11. D. E. McClelland, *Power: The Inner Experience* (New York: Irvington, 1975).

12. J. Pfeffer and G. Salancik, *The External Control of Organizations* (New York: Harper & Row, 1978).

13. G. Salancik and J. Pfeffer, "The Bases and Uses of Power in Organizational Decision Making," *Administrative Science Quarterly* 15 (1971): 216–229.

14. R. H. Miles, *Macro Organizational Behavior* (Glenview, Ill.: Scott, Foresman, 1980).

15. D. Hickson, C. Hinings, C. Lee, R. E. Schneck, and J. M. Pennings, "A Strategic Contingencies Theory of Intraorganizational Power," *Administrative Science Quarterly* 14 (1971): 219–220.

16. C. R. Hinings, D. J. Hickson, J. M. Pennings, and R. E. Schneck, "Structural Conditions of Intraorganizational Power," *Administrative Science Quarterly* 19 (1974): 22–44.

17. A. Etzioni, *Modern Organizations* (Upper Saddle River, N.J.: Prentice-Hall, 1964).

18. R. Kanter, "Power Failure in Management Circuits," *Harvard Business Review* (July–August 1979): 31–54.

19. L. Mainiero, "Coping with Powerlessness: The Relationship of Gender and Job Dependency to Empowerment Strategy Usage," *Administrative Science Quarterly* 31 (1986): 633–653.

20. B. E. Ashforth, "The Experience of Powerlessness in Organizations," *Organizational Behavior and Human Decision Processes* 43 (1989): 207–242.

21. M. Korda, *Power: How to Get It, How to Use It* (New York: Random House, 1975).

22. B. T. Mayes and R. T. Allen, "Toward a Definition of Organizational Politics," *Academy of Management Review* 2 (1977): 672–678.

23. D. L. Madison, R. W. Allen, L. W. Porter, and B. T. Mayes, "Organizational Politics: An Exploration of Managers' Perceptions," *Human Relations* 33 (1980): 92–107.

24. J. Gandz and V. Murray, "The Experience of Workplace Politics," *Academy of Management Journal* 23 (1980): 237–251.

25. D. A. Ralston, "Employee Ingratiation: The Role of Management," *Academy of Management Review* 10 (1985): 477–487; D. R. Beeman and T. W. Sharkey, "The Use and Abuse of Corporate Politics," *Business Horizons* (March–April 1987): 25–35.

26. C. O. Longnecker, H. P. Sims, and D. A. Gioia, "Behind the Mask: The Politics of Employee Appraisal," *Academy of Management Executive* 1 (1987): 183–193.

27. R. Cropanzano, J. C. Howes, A. A. Grandey, and P. Toth, "The Relationship of Organizational Politics and Support to Work Behaviors, Attitudes, and Stress," *Journal of Organizational Behavior* 18 (1997): 159–180.

28. D. Kipnis, S. M. Schmidt, and I. Wilkinson, "Intraorganizational Influence Tactics: Explorations in Getting One's Way," *Journal of Applied Psychology* 65 (1980): 440–452; D. Kipnis, S. Schmidt, C. Swaffin-Smith, and I. Wilkinson, "Patterns of Managerial Influence: Shotgun Managers, Tacticians, and Bystanders," *Organizational Dynamics* (Winter 1984): 60–67; G. Yukl and C. M. Falbe, "Influence Tactics and Objectives in Upward, Downward, and Lateral Influence Attempts," *Journal of Applied Psychology* 75 (1990): 132–140.

29. G. R. Ferris and T. A. Judge, "Personnel/Human Resources Management: A Political Influence Perspective," *Journal of Management* 17 (1991): 447–488.

30. G. Yukl, P. J. Guinan, and D. Sottolano, "Influence Tactics Used for Different Objectives with Subordinates, Peers, and Superiors," *Groups & Organization Management* 20 (1995): 272–296.

31. R. A. Thacker and S. J. Wayne, "An Examination of the Relationship between Upward Influence Tactics and Assessments of Promotability," *Journal of Management* 21 (1995): 739–756.

32. K. K. Eastman, "In the Eyes of the Beholder: An Attributional Approach to Ingratiation and Organizational Citizenship Behavior," *Academy of Management Journal* 37 (1994): 1379–1391.

33. R. A. Gordon, "Impact of Ingratiation on Judgments and Evaluations: A Meta-Analytic Investigation," *Journal of Personality and Social Psychology* 71 (1996): 54–70.

34. A. Drory and D. Beaty, "Gender Differences in the Perception of Organizational Influence Tactics," *Journal of Organizational Behavior* 12 (1991): 249–258.

35. R. Y. Hirokawa and A. Miyahara, "A Comparison of Influence Strategies Utilized by Managers in American and Japanese Organizations," *Communication Quarterly* 34 (1986): 250–265.

36. P. Rosenfeld, R. A. Giacalone, and C. A. Riordan, *Impression Management in Organizations: Theory, Measurement, Practice* (London: Routledge, 1995).

37. K. Kumar and M. S. Thibodeaux, "Organizational Politics and Planned Organizational Change," *Group and Organization Studies* 15 (1990): 354–365.

38. McClelland, *Power*.

39. Beeman and Sharkey, "Use and Abuse of Corporate Politics," 37.

40. C. P. Parker, R. L. Dipboye, and S. L. Jackson, "Perceptions of Organizational Politics: An Investigation of Antecedents and Consequences," *Journal of Management* 21 (1995): 891–912.

41. S. J. Ashford, N. P. Rothbard, S. K. Piderit, and J. E. Dutton, "Out on a Limb: The Role of Context and Impression Management in Selling Gender-Equity Issues," *Administrative Science Quarterly* 43 (1998): 23–57.

42. J. Zhou and G. R. Ferris, "The Dimensions and Consequences of Organizational Politics Perceptions: A Confirmatory Analysis," *Journal of Applied Social Psychology* 25 (1995): 1747–1764.

43. J. J. Gabarro and J. P. Kotter, "Managing Your Boss," *Harvard Business Review* (January–February 1980): 92–100.

44. P. Newman, "How to Manage Your Boss," Peat, Marwick, Mitchell & Company's *Management Focus* (May–June 1980): 36–37.

45. F. Bertolome, "When You Think the Boss Is Wrong," *Personnel Journal* 69 (1990): 66–73.

46. J. Conger and R. Kanungo, *Charismatic Leadership: The Elusive Factor in Organizational Effectiveness* (New York: Jossey-Bass, 1988).

47. G. M. Spreitzer, M. A. Kizilos, and S. W. Nason, "A Dimensional Analysis of the Relationship between Psychological Empowerment and Effectiveness, Satisfaction, and Strain," *Journal of Management* 23 (1997): 679–704.

48. R. C. Ford and M. D. Fottler, "Empowerment: A Matter of Degree," *Academy of Management Executive* 9 (1995): 21–31.

49. J. T. McKenna, "Smart Scarecrows: The Wizardry of Empowerment," *Industry Week*, July 16, 1990, 8–19.

50. B. Dumaine, "The Bureaucracy Busters," *Fortune*, June 17, 1991, 36–50.

51. J. P. Kotter, "Power, Dependence, and Effective Management," *Harvard Business Review* 55 (1977): 125–136; J. P. Kotter, *Power and Influence* (New York: Free Press, 1985).

52. A. Oldenburg, "Winfrey Spars over Her Power: She Says Viewers Can Judge," *USA Today*, February 5, 1998, 2D; B. Adler, ed., *The Uncommon Wisdom of Oprah Winfrey* (Secaucus, N.J.: Birch Lane, 1997).

Chapter 11

1. E. G. Flamholtz and Y. Randle, *Changing the Game: Organizational Transformations of the First, Second, and Third Kinds* (New York: Oxford, 1998).

2. J. P. Kotter, "What Leaders Really Do," *Harvard Business Review* 68 (1990): 103–111.

3. Jennifer J. Laabs, "GE Medical Systems," winner of the 1992 Optimas Award from *Personnel Journal* (January 1992): 55.

4. A. G. Jago, "Leadership: Perspectives in Theory and Research," *Management Science* 28 (1982): 315–336.

5. J. A. Conger, "Qualitative Research as the Cornerstone Methodology for Understanding Leadership," *Leadership Quarterly* 9 (1998): 107–121.

6. C. C. Manz, "Self-Leadership: Toward an Expanded Theory of Self-Influence Processes in Organizations," *Academy of Management Review* 11 (1986): 585–600.

7. R. M. Stogdill, "Personal Factors Associated with Leadership: A Survey of the Literature," *Journal of Psychology* 25 (1948): 35–71.

8. J. M. Burns, *Leadership* (New York: Harper & Row, 1978); T. O. Jacobs, *Leadership and Exchange in Formal Organizations* (Alexandria, Va.: Human Resources Research Organization, 1971).

9. N. Tichy and M. A. DeVanna, *The Transformational Leader* (New York: Wiley, 1986).

10. B. M. Bass, "From Transactional to Transformational Leadership: Learning to Share the Vision," *Organizational Dynamics* 19 (1990): 19–31; B. M. Bass, *Leadership and Performance beyond Expectations* (New York: Free Press, 1985).

11. J. R. Joplin, "Developing Effective Leadership: An Interview with Henry Cisneros," *Academy of Management Executive* 7 (1993): 84–92.

12. W. Bennis, "Managing the Dream: Leadership in the 21st Century," *Training* 27 (1990): 43–48.

13. P. M. Podsakoff, S. B. MacKenzie, R. H. Moorman, and R. Fetter, "Transformational Leader Behaviors and Their Effects on Followers' Trust in Leader, Satisfaction, and Organizational Citizenship Behaviors," *Leadership Quarterly* 1 (1990): 107–142.

14. A. Zaleznik, "The Leadership Gap," *Academy of Management Executive* 4 (1990): 7–22.

15. A. Zaleznik, "HBR Classic—Managers and Leaders: Are They Different?" *Harvard Business Review* 70 (1992): 126–135.

16. M. E. Heilman, C. J. Block, R. F. Martell, and M. C. Simon, "Has Anything Changed? Current Characteristics of Men, Women, and Managers," *Journal of Applied Psychology* 74 (1989): 935–942.

17. F. J. Yammarino, A. J. Dubinsky, L. B. Comer, and M. A. Jolson, "Women and Transformational and Contingent Reward Leadership: A Multiple-Levels-of-Analysis Perspective," *Academy of Management Journal* 40 (1997): 205–222.

18. R. J. House and M. L. Baetz, "Leadership: Some Empirical Generalizations and New Research Directions," in B. M. Staw, ed., *Research in Organizational Behavior*, vol. 1 (Greenwood, Conn.: JAI Press, 1979), 399–401.

19. J. A. Conger and R. N. Kanungo, "Toward a Behavioral Theory of Charismatic Leadership in Organizational Settings," *Academy of Management Review* 12 (1987): 637–647.

20. A. R. Willner, *The Spellbinders: Charismatic Political Leadership* (New Haven, Conn.: Yale University Press, 1984).

21. J. M. Howell, "Two Faces of Charisma: Socialized and Personalized Leadership in Organizations," in J. A. Conger, ed., *Charismatic Leadership: Behind the Mystique of Exceptional Leadership* (San Francisco: Jossey-Bass, 1988).

22. D. Sankowsky, "The Charismatic Leader as Narcissist: Understanding the Abuse of Power," *Organizational Dynamics* 23 (1995): 57–71.

23. K. Lewin, R. Lippitt, and R. K. White, "Patterns of Aggressive Behavior in Experimentally Created 'Social Climates,' " *Journal of Social Psychology* 10 (1939): 271–299.

24. R. Likert, *New Patterns of Management* (New York: McGraw-Hill, 1961); R. Tannenbaum and W. H. Schmidt, "How to Choose a Leadership Pattern," *Harvard Business Review* 51 (1973): 162–180.

25. R. M. Stodgill and A. E. Coons, eds., *Leader Behavior: Its Description and Measurement*, research monograph no. 88 (Columbus, Ohio: Bureau of Business Research, The Ohio State University, 1957).

26. A. W. Halpin and J. Winer, "A Factorial Study of the Leader Behavior Description Questionnaire," in R. M. Stodgill and A. E. Coons, eds., *Leader Behavior: Its Description and Measurement*, research monograph no. 88 (Columbus, Ohio: Bureau of Business Research, The Ohio State University, 1957), 39–51.

27. E. A. Fleishman, "Leadership Climate, Human Relations Training, and Supervisory Behavior," *Personnel Psychology* 6 (1953): 205–222.

28. N. Tichy and R. Charan, "Speed, Simplicity, Self-Confidence: An Interview with Jack Welch," *Harvard Business Review* 67 (1989): 112–121.

29. R. R. Blake and J. S. Mouton, *The Managerial Grid III: The Key to Leadership Excellence* (Houston: Gulf, 1985).

30. F. E. Fiedler, *A Theory of Leader Effectiveness* (New York: McGraw-Hill, 1964).

31. F. E. Fiedler, *Personality, Motivational Systems, and Behavior of High and Low LPC Persons*, tech. rep. no. 70-12 (Seattle: University of Washington, 1970).

32. J. T. McMahon, "The Contingency Theory: Logic and Method Revisited," *Personnel Psychology* 25 (1972): 697–710; L. H. Peters, D. D. Hartke, and J. T. Pohlman, "Fiedler's Contingency Theory of Leadership: An Application of the Meta-analysis Procedures of Schmidt and Hunter," *Psychological Bulletin* 97 (1985): 224–285.

33. F. E. Fiedler, "The Contingency Model and the Dynamics of the Leadership Process," in L. Berkowitz, ed., *Advances in Experimental and Social Psychology*, vol. 11 (New York: Academic Press, 1978).

34. F. E. Fiedler, "Engineering the Job to Fit the Manager," *Harvard Business Review* 43 (1965): 115–122.

35. R. J. House, "A Path–Goal Theory of Leader Effectiveness," *Administrative Science Quarterly* 16 (1971): 321–338; R. J. House and T. R. Mitchell, "Path–Goal Theory of Leadership," *Journal of Contemporary Business* 3 (1974): 81–97.

36. C. A. Schriescheim and V. M. Von Glinow, "The Path–Goal Theory of Leadership: A Theoretical and Empirical Analysis," *Academy of Management Journal* 20 (1977): 398–405; E. Valenzi and G. Dessler, "Relationships of Leader Behavior, Subordinate Role Ambiguity, and Subordinate Job Satisfaction," *Academy of Management Journal* 21 (1978): 671–678; N. R. F. Maier, *Leadership Methods and Skills* (New York: McGraw-Hill, 1963).

37. V. H. Vroom and P. W. Yetton, *Leadership and Decision Making* (Pittsburgh: University of Pittsburgh, 1973).

38. R. H. G. Field and R. J. House, "A Test of the Vroom-Yetton Model Using Manager and Subordinate Reports," *Journal of Applied Psychology* 75 (1990): 362–366.

39. V. H. Vroom and A. G. Jago, *The New Leadership: Managing Participation in Organizations* (Upper Saddle River, N.J.: Prentice-Hall, 1988).

40. P. Hersey and K. H. Blanchard, "Life Cycle Theory of Leadership," *Training and Development Journal* 23 (1969): 26–34; P. Hersey and K. H. Blanchard, *Management of Organizational Behavior: Utilizing Human Resources*, 3d ed. (Upper Saddle River, N.J.: Prentice-Hall, 1977).

41. B. M. Bass, *Bass and Stogdill's Handbook of Leadership: Theory, Research, and Managerial Applications*, 3d ed. (New York: Free Press, 1990).

42. G. A. Yukl, *Leadership in Organizations*, 2d ed. (Upper Saddle River, N.J.: Prentice-Hall, 1989).

43. P. B. Murphy and G. Enderle, "Managerial Ethical Leadership: Examples Do Matter," *Business Ethics Quarterly* 5 (1995): 117–128.

44. E. P. Hollander and L. R. Offerman, "Power and Leadership in Organizations: Relationships in Transition," *American Psychologist* 45 (1990): 179–189.

45. H. P. Sims, Jr., and C. C. Manz, *Company of Heros: Unleashing the Power of Self-Leadership* (New York: John Wiley & Sons, 1996).

46. C. C. Manz and H. P. Sims, "Leading Workers to Lead Themselves: The External Leadership of Self-Managing Work Teams," *Administrative Science Quarterly* 32 (1987): 106–128.

47. C. N. Greene, "The Reciprocal Nature of Influence between Leader and Subordinate," *Journal of Applied Psychology* 60 (1975): 187–193.

48. H. S. Schwartz, "Antisocial Actions of Committed Organizational Participants," in *Narcissistic Process and Corporate Decay* (New York: NYU Press, 1990): 31–45.

49. L. Hirschhorn, "Leaders and Followers in a Postindustrial Age: A Psychodynamic View," *Journal of Applied Behavioral Science* 26 (1990): 529–542.

50. R. E. Kelley, "In Praise of Followers," *Harvard Business Review* 66 (1988): 142–148.

51. C. C. Manz and H. P. Sims, "SuperLeadership: Beyond the Myth of Heroic Leadership," *Organizational Dynamics* 20 (1991): 18–35.

52. J. Chain, General (Retired), former Commander-in-Chief of the Strategic Air Command, in the commissioning address for A.F.R.O.T.C. cadets, Texas Christian University, May 10, 1996.

53. W. J. Crockett, "Dynamic Subordinancy," *Training and Development Journal* (May 1981): 155–164.

54. T. K. Oh, "Theory Y in the People's Republic of China," *California Management Review* 19 (1976): 77–84.

55. M. Haire, E. E. Ghiselli, and L. W. Porter, "Cultural Patterns in the Role of the Manager," *Industrial Relations* 2 (1963): 95–117.

56. D. T. Kearns and D. A. Nadler, *Prophets in the Dark: How Xerox Reinvented Itself and Beat Back the Japanese* (New York: Harper Business, 1992).

57. D. T. Kearns, "Leadership through Quality," *Academy of Management Executive* 4 (1990): 86–89.

58. N. J. Adler, *International Dimensions in Organizational Behavior* (Boston: PWS-Kent, 1991).

59. G. P. Zachary, "Faces of the '90s," *The Wall Street Journal*, September 3, 1997, A1.

60. H. Schultz and D. J. Yang, *Pour Your Heart into It: How Starbucks Built a Company One Cup at a Time* (New York: Hyperion, 1997); Flamholtz and Randle, *Changing the Game*.

Chapter 12

1. R. Blumenstein, G. L. White, and F. Warner, "Can These Adversaries Avoid Another Collision?" *The Wall Street Journal*, July 29, 1998, A2.

2. Definition adapted from D. Hellriegel, J. W. Slocum, Jr., and R. W. Woodman, *Organizational Behavior* (St. Paul: West, 1992), and from R. D. Middlemist and M. A. Hitt, *Organizational Behavior* (St. Paul: West, 1988).

3. D. Tjosvold, *The Conflict-Positive Organization* (Reading, Mass.: Addison-Wesley, 1991).

4. K. Thomas and W. Schmidt, "A Survey of Managerial Interests with Respect to Conflict," *Academy of Management Journal* 19 (1976): 315–318; G. L. Lippitt, "Managing Conflict in Today's Organizations," *Training and Development Journal* 36 (1982): 66–74.

5. M. Rajim, "A Measure of Styles of Handling Interpersonal Conflict," *Academy of Management Journal* 26 (1983): 368–376.

6. D. Goleman, *Emotional Intelligence* (New York: Bantam Books, 1995); J. Stuller, "Unconventional Smarts," *Across the Board* 35 (1998): 22–23.

7. Tjosvold, *The Conflict-Positive Organization*, 4.

8. R. A. Cosier and D. R. Dalton, "Positive Effects of Conflict: A Field Experiment," *International Journal of Conflict Management* 1 (1990): 81–92.

9. D. Tjosvold, "Making Conflict Productive," *Personnel Administrator* 29 (1984): 121–130.

10. A. C. Amason, W. A. Hochwarter, K. R. Thompson, and A. W. Harrison, "Conflict: An Important Dimension in Successful Management

Teams," *Organizational Dynamics* 24 (1995): 25–35.

11. I. Janis, *Groupthink*, 2d ed. (Boston: Houghton Mifflin, 1982).

12. J. D. Thompson, *Organizations in Action* (New York: McGraw-Hill, 1967).

13. G. Walker and L. Poppo, "Profit Centers, Single-Source Suppliers, and Transaction Costs," *Administrative Science Quarterly* 36 (1991): 66–87.

14. R. Miles, *Macro Organizational Behavior* (Glenview, Ill.: Scott, Foresman, 1980).

15. H. Levinson, "The Abrasive Personality," *Harvard Business Review* 56 (1978): 86–94.

16. J. C. Quick and J. D. Quick, *Organizational Stress and Preventive Management* (New York: McGraw-Hill, 1984).

17. F. N. Brady, "Aesthetic Components of Management Ethics," *Academy of Management Review* 11 (1986): 337–344.

18. V. K. Raizada, "Multi-ethnic Corporations and Inter-ethnic Conflict," *Human Resource Management* 20 (1981): 24–27; T. Cox, Jr., "The Multicultural Organization," *Academy of Management Executive* 5 (1991): 34–47.

19. G. Hofstede, *Culture's Consequences: International Differences in Work-related Values* (Beverly Hills, Calif.: Sage, 1980); G. Hofstede and M. H. Bond, "The Confucius Connection: From Cultural Roots to Economic Growth," *Organizational Dynamics* (Spring 1988): 4–21; G. Hofstede, "Cultural Constraints in Management Theories," *Academy of Management Executive* 7 (1993): 81–94.

20. T. H. Cox, S. A. Lobel, and P. L. McLead, "Effects of Ethnic Group Cultural Differences on Cooperative and Competitive Behavior in a Group Task," *Academy of Management Journal* 34 (1991): 827–847.

21. G. LaBianca, D. J. Brass, and B. Gray, "Social Networks and Perceptions of Intergroup Conflict: The Role of Negative Relationships and Third Parties," *Academy of Management Journal* 41 (1998): 55–67.

22. M. Sherif and C. W. Sherif, *Social Psychology* (New York: Harper & Row, 1969).

23. C. Song, S. M. Sommer, and A. E. Hartman, "The Impact of Adding an External Rater on Interdepartmental Cooperative Behaviors of Workers," *International Journal of Conflict Management* 9 (1998): 117–138.

24. W. Tsai and S. Ghoshal, "Social Capital and Value Creation: The Role of Intrafirm Networks," *Academy of Management Journal* 41 (1998): 464–476.

25. D. Katz and R. Kahn, *The Social Psychology of Organizations*, 2d ed. (New York: Wiley, 1978).

26. D. L. Nelson and J. C. Quick, "Professional Women: Are Distress and Disease Inevitable?"

Academy of Management Review 10 (1985): 206–218; D. L. Nelson and M. A. Hitt, "Employed Women and Stress: Implications for Enhancing Women's Mental Health in the Workplace," in J. C. Quick, J. Hurrell, and L. A. Murphy, eds., *Stress and Well-being at Work: Assessments and Interventions for Occupational Mental Health* (Washington, D.C.: American Psychological Association, 1992).

27. R. L. Kahn et al., *Organizational Stress: Studies in Role Conflict and Ambiguity* (New York: Wiley, 1964).

28. J. L. Badaracco, Jr., "The Discipline of Building Character," *Harvard Business Review* (March–April 1998): 115–124.

29. B. Schneider, "The People Make the Place," *Personnel Psychology* 40 (1987): 437–453.

30. C. A. O'Reilly, J. Chatman, and D. F. Caldwell, "People and Organizational Culture: A Profile Comparison Approach to Assessing Person-Organization Fit," *Academy of Management Journal* 34 (1991): 487–516.

31. I. Dayal and J. M. Thomas, "Operation KPE: Developing a New Organization," *Journal of Applied Behavioral Science* 4 (1968): 473–506.

32. R. H. Miles, "Role Requirements as Sources of Organizational Stress," *Journal of Applied Psychology* 61 (1976): 172–179.

33. W. F. G. Mastenbroek, *Conflict Management and Organization Development* (Chichester, England: Wiley, 1987).

34. K. Thomas, "Conflict and Conflict Management," in M. D. Dunnette, ed., *Handbook of Industrial and Organizational Psychology* (New York: Wiley, 1976).

35. H. H. Meyer, E. Kay, and J. R. P. French, "Split Roles in Performance Appraisal," *Harvard Business Review* 43 (1965): 123–129.

36. T. W. Costello and S. S. Zalkind, *Psychology in Administration: A Research Orientation* (Englewood Cliffs, N.J.: Prentice-Hall, 1963).

37. R. Bramson, *Coping with Difficult People* (New York: Dell, 1981).

38. H. S. Baum, "Organizational Politics against Organizational Culture: A Psychoanalytic Perspective," *Human Resource Management* 28 (1989): 191–200.

39. D. Tjosvold and M. Poon, "Dealing with Scarce Resources: Open-Minded Interaction for Resolving Budget Conflicts," *Group and Organization Management* 23 (1998): 237–255.

40. Miles, *Macro Organizational Behavior*; R. Steers, *Introduction to Organizational Behavior*, 4th ed. (Glenview, Ill.: Harper-Collins, 1991).

41. A. Tyerman and C. Spencer, "A Critical Text of the Sherrif's Robber's Cave Experiments: Intergroup Competition and Cooperation between Groups of Well-acquainted Individuals," *Small Group Behavior* 14 (1983): 515–531; R. M.

Kramer, "Intergroup Relations and Organizational Dilemmas: The Role of Categorization Processes," in B. Staw and L. Cummings, eds., *Research in Organizational Behavior* 13 (Greenwich, Conn.: JAI Press, 1991), 191–228.

42. R. Blake and J. Mouton, "Overcoming Group Warefare," *Harvard Business Review* 64 (1984): 98–108.

43. D. G. Ancona and D. Caldwell, "Improving the Performance of New Product Teams," *Research Technology Management* 33 (1990): 25–29.

44. R. J. Lewicki, J. A. Litterer, J. W. Minton, and D. M. Saunders, *Negotiation*, 2d ed. (Burr Ridge, Ill.: Irwin, 1994).

45. K. W. Thomas, "Conflict and Conflict Management," in M. D. Dunnette, ed., *Handbook of Industrial and Organizational Psychology* (Chicago: Rand McNally, 1976), 900.

46. T. N. Gladwin and I. Walter, "How Multinationals Can Manage Social and Political Forces," *Journal of Business Strategy* 1 (1980): 54–68.

47. R. A. Baron, S. P. Fortin, R. L. Frei, L. A. Hauver, and M. L. Shack, "Reducing Organizational Conflict: The Role of Socially Induced Positive Affect," *International Journal of Conflict Management* 1 (1990): 133–152.

48. S. L. Phillips and R. L. Elledge, *The Team Building Source Book* (San Diego: University Associates, 1989).

49. Gladwin and Walter, "How Multinationals Can Manage," 228.

50. K. W. Thomas, "Toward Multidimensional Values in Teaching: The Example of Conflict Behaviors," *Academy of Management Review* 2 (1977): 484–490.

51. P. Graham, "Saying 'No' to Compromise; 'Yes' to Integration," *Journal of Business Ethics* 17 (1998): 1007–1013.

52. W. King and E. Miles, "What We Know and Don't Know about Measuring Conflict," *Management Communication Quarterly* 4 (1990): 222–243.

53. J. Barker, D. Tjosvold, and I. R. Andrews, "Conflict Approaches of Effective and Ineffective Project Managers: A Field Study in a Matrix Organization," *Journal of Management Studies* 25 (1988): 167–178.

54. M. Chan, "Intergroup Conflict and Conflict Management in the R&D Divisions of Four Aerospace Companies," *IEEE Transactions on Engineering Management* 36 (1989): 95–104.

55. M. K. Kozan, "Cultural Influences on Styles of Handling Interpersonal Conflicts: Comparisons among Jordanian, Turkish, and U.S. Managers," *Human Relations* 42 (1989): 787–799.

56. S. McKenna, "The Business Impact of Management Attitudes towards Dealing with

Conflict: A Cross-Cultural Assessment," *Journal of Managerial Psychology* 10 (1995): 22–27.

57. Tjosvold, *The Conflict-Positive Organization*.

58. F. Warner, "UAW Says Its GM Relations Are Still Rocky," *The Wall Street Journal*, August 26, 1998, A4; K. Bradsher, "Lasting Improvement in Labor Relations Is Still Elusive," *New York Times*, July 29, 1998, 1.

Chapter 13

1. Harry Kent, personal communication, December 30, 1998.

2. G. W. England and I. Harpaz, "How Working Is Defined: National Contexts and Demographic and Organizational Role Influences," *Journal of Organizational Behavior* 11 (1990): 253–266.

3. L. R. Gomez-Mejia, "The Cross-Cultural Structure of Task-Related and Contextual Constructs," *Journal of Psychology* 120 (1986): 5–19.

4. F. W. Taylor, *The Principles of Scientific Management* (New York: Norton, 1911).

5. T. Bell, *Out of This Furnace* (Pittsburgh: University of Pittsburgh Press, 1941).

6. N. D. Warren, "Job Simplification versus Job Enlargement," *Journal of Industrial Engineering* 9 (1958): 435–439.

7. C. R. Walker, "The Problem of the Repetitive Job," *Harvard Business Review* 28 (1950): 54–58.

8. C. R. Walker and R. H. Guest, *The Man on the Assembly Line* (Cambridge, Mass.: Harvard University Press, 1952).

9. M. A. Campion, L. Cheraskin, and M. J. Stevens, "Career-Related Antecedents and Outcomes of Job Rotation," *Academy of Management Journal* 37 (1994): 1518–1542.

10. E. Santora, "Keep Up Production Through Cross-Training," *Personnel Journal* (June 1992): 162–166.

11. R. P. Steel and J. R. Rentsch, "The Dispositional Model of Job Attitudes Revisited: Findings of a 10-Year Study," *Journal of Applied Psychology* 82 (1997): 873–879; C.-S. Wong, C. Hui, and K. S. Law, "A Longitudinal Study of the Job Perception–Job Satisfaction Relationship: A Text of the Three Alternative Specifications," *Journal of Occupational & Organizational Psychology* 71 (Part 2, 1998): 127–146.

12. F. Herzberg, "One More Time: How Do You Motivate Employees?" *Harvard Business Review* 46 (1968): 53–62.

13. R. N. Ford, "Job Enrichment Lessons from AT&T," *Harvard Business Review* 51 (1973): 96–106.

14. R. J. House and L. A. Wigdor, "Herzberg's Dual-Factor Theory of Job Satisfaction and Motivation: A Review of the Evidence and a Criticism," *Personnel Psychology* 20 (1967): 369–389.

15. A. N. Turner and P. R. Lawrence, *Industrial Jobs and the Worker* (Cambridge, Mass.: Harvard University Press, 1965).

16. J. R. Hackman and G. R. Oldham, "The Job Diagnostic Survey: An Instrument for the Diagnosis of Jobs and the Evaluation of Job Redesign Projects," *Technical Report No. 4* (New Haven, Conn.: Department of Administrative Sciences, Yale University, 1974).

17. J. R. Hackman and G. R. Oldham, "Development of the Job Diagnostic Survey," *Journal of Applied Psychology* 60 (1975): 159–170.

18. P. H. Birnbaum, J.-L. Farh, and G. Y. Y. Wong, "The Job Characteristics Model in Hong Kong," *Journal of Applied Psychology* 71 (1986): 598–605.

19. J. R. Hackman and G. R. Oldham, *Work Design* (Reading, Mass.: Addison-Wesley, 1980).

20. H. P. Sims, A. D. Szilagyi, and R. T. Keller, "The Measurement of Job Characteristics," *Academy of Management Journal* 19 (1976): 195–212.

21. H. P. Sims and A. D. Szilagyi, "Job Characteristic Relationships: Individual and Structural Moderators," *Organizational Behavior and Human Performance* 17 (1976): 211–230.

22. Y. Fried, "Meta-Analytic Comparison of the Job Diagnostic Survey and Job Characteristic Inventory as Correlates of Work Satisfaction and Performance," *Journal of Applied Psychology* 76 (1991): 690–698.

23. G. R. Salancik and J. Pfeffer, "A Social Information Processing Approach to Job Attitudes and Task Design," *Administrative Science Quarterly* 23 (1978): 224–253.

24. J. Pfeffer, "Management as Symbolic Action: The Creation and Maintenance of Organizational Paradigms," in L. L. Cummings and B. M. Staw, eds., *Research in Organizational Behavior*, vol. 3 (Greenwich, Conn.: JAI Press, 1981), 1–52.

25. J. Thomas and R. Griffin, "The Social Information Processing Model of Task Design: A Review of the Literature," *Academy of Management Review* 8 (1983): 672–682.

26. D. J. Campbell, "Task Complexity: A Review and Analysis," *Academy of Management Review* 13 (1988): 40–52.

27. M. A. Campion and P. W. Thayer, "Job Design: Approaches, Outcomes, and Trade-offs," *Organizational Dynamics* 16 (1987): 66–79.

28. J. Teresko, "Emerging Technologies," *Industry Week* (February 27, 1995): 1–2.

29. M. A. Campion and C. L. McClelland, "Interdisciplinary Examination of the Costs and Benefits of Enlarged Jobs: A Job Design Quasi-Experiment," *Journal of Applied Psychology* 76 (1991): 186–199.

30. B. Kohut, *Country Competitiveness: Organizing of Work* (New York: Oxford University Press, 1993).

31. W. E. Deming, *Out of the Crisis* (Cambridge, Mass.: MIT Press, 1986).

32. L. Thurow, *Head to Head: The Coming Economic Battle among Japan, Europe, and America* (New York: Morrow, 1992).

33. M. A. Fruin, *The Japanese Enterprise System—Competitive Strategies and Cooperative Structures* (New York: Oxford University Press, 1992).

34. W. Niepce and E. Molleman, "Work Design Issue in Lean Production from a Sociotechnical System Perspective: Neo-Taylorism or the Next Step in Sociotechnical Design?" *Human Relations* 51 (1998): 259–287.

35. E. Furubotn, "Codetermination and the Modern Theory of the Firm: A Property-Rights Analysis," *Journal of Business* 61 (1988): 165–181.

36. H. Levinson, Executive: *The Guide to Responsive Management* (Cambridge, Mass.: Harvard University Press, 1981).

37. B. Gardell, "Scandinavian Research on Stress in Working Life" (Paper presented at the IRRA Symposium on Stress in Working Life, Denver, September 1980).

38. L. Levi, "Psychosocial, Occupational, Environmental, and Health Concepts; Research Results; and Applications," in G. P. Keita and S. L. Sauter, eds. *Work and Well-Being: An Agenda for the 1990s* (Washington, D.C.: American Psychological Association, 1992), 199–211.

39. R. L. Kahn, *Work and Health* (New York: Wiley, 1981); M. Gowing, J. Kraft, and J. C. Quick, *The New Organizational Reality: Downsizing, Restructuring, and Revitalization* (Washington, D.C.: American Psychological Association, 1998).

40. F. J. Landy, "Work Design and Stress," in G. P. Keita and S. L. Sauter, eds., *Work and Well-Being: An Agenda for the 1990s* (Washington, D.C.: American Psychological Association, 1992), 119–158.

41. C. Gresov, R. Drazin, and A. H. Van de Ven, "Work-Unit Task Uncertainty, Design, and Morale," *Organizational Studies* 10 (1989): 45–62.

42. S. Caudron, "Working at Home Pays Off," *Personnel Journal* (November 1992): 40–47.

43. D. S. Bailey and J. Foley, "Pacific Bell Works Long Distance," *HRMagazine*, August 1990, 50–52.

44. S. M. Pollan and M. Levine, "Asking for Flextime," *Working Women*, February 1994, 48.

45. S. Zuboff, *In the Age of the Smart Machine: The Future of Work and Power* (New York: Basic Books, 1988).

46. B. A. Gutek and S. J. Winter, "Computer Use, Control over Computers, and Job Satisfaction," in S. Oskamp and S. Spacapan, eds., *People's Reactions to Technology in Factories, Offices, and Aerospace: The Claremont Symposium on Applied Social Psychology* (Newbury Park, Calif.: Sage, 1990), 121–144.

47. L. M. Schleifer and B. C. Amick III, "System Response Time and Method of Pay: Stress Effects in Computer-based Tasks," *International Journal of Human-Computer Interaction* 1 (1989): 23–39.

48. M. J. Smith and P. C. Carayon, "Electronic Monitoring of Worker Performance: A Review of the Potential Effects on Job Design and Stress" (Working paper developed for U.S. Congress, Office of Technology Assessment, Washington, D.C., 1990).

49. B. M. Staw and R. D. Boettger, "Task Revision: A Neglected Form of Work Performance," *Academy of Management Journal* 33 (1990): 534–559.

50. H. S. Schwartz, "Job Involvement as Obsession Compulsion," *Academy of Management Review* 7 (1982): 429–432.

51. C. J. Nemeth and B. M. Staw, "The Tradeoffs of Social Control and Innovation in Groups and Organizations," in L. Berkowitz, ed., *Advances in Experimental Social Psychology*, vol. 22 (New York: Academic Press, 1989), 175–210.

52. M. J. Smith and G. Salvendy, *Work with Computers: Organizational, Management, Stress, and Health Aspects* (New York: Elsevier Press, 1989).

53. D. M. Herold, "Using Technology to Improve Our Management of Labor Market Trends," in M. Greller, ed., "Managing Careers with a Changing Workforce," *Journal of Organizational Change Management* 3 (1990), 44–57.

54. D. A. Whetten and K. S. Cameron, *Developing Management Skills*, 4th ed. (Reading, Mass.: Addison-Wesley, 1998).

55. A. Haasen and G. F. Shea, "Southwest Airlines: The Culture of 'LUV,'" in *A Better Place to Work: A New Sense of Motivation Leading to High Productivity* (New York: American Management Association, 1997).

Chapter 14

1. Anita Foster, personal communication, December 30, 1998.

2. J. Child, *Organization* (New York: Harper & Row, 1984).

3. P. Lawrence and J. Lorsch, "Differentiation and Integration in Complex Organizations," *Administrative Science Quarterly* (June 1967): 1–47.

4. P. Lawrence and J. Lorsch, *Organization and Environment: Managing Differentiation and Integration* (Cambridge, Mass.: Harvard University Press, 1967).

5. J. Hage, "An Axiomatic Theory of Organizations," *Administrative Science Quarterly* (December 1965): 289–320.

6. W. Ouchi and J. Dowling, "Defining the Span of Control," *Administrative Science Quarterly* (September 1974): 357–365.

7. L. Porter and E. Lawler III, "Properties of Organization Structure in Relation to Job Attitudes and Job Behavior," *Psychological Bulletin* (July 1965): 23–51.

8. J. Ivancevich and J. Donnelly, Jr., "Relation of Organization and Structure to Job Satisfaction, Anxiety-Stress, and Performance," *Administrative Science Quarterly* 20 (1975): 272–280.

9. R. Dewar and J. Hage, "Size, Technology, Complexity, and Structural Differentiation: Toward a Theoretical Synthesis," *Administrative Science Quarterly* 23 (1978): 111–136.

10. Lawrence and Lorsch, "Differentiation and Integration," 1–47.

11. J. Galbraith, *Designing Complex Organizations* (Reading, Mass.: Addison-Wesley, 1973).

12. W. Altier, "Task Forces: An Effective Management Tool," *Management Review* (February 1987): 26–32.

13. P. Lawrence and J. Lorsch, "New Managerial Job: The Integrator," *Harvard Business Review* 45 (1967): 142–151.

14. J. Lorsch and P. Lawrence, "Organizing for Product Innovation," *Harvard Business Review* 43 (1965): 110–111.

15. D. Pugh, D. Hickson, C. Hinnings, and C. Turner, "Dimensions of Organization Structure," *Administrative Science Quarterly* (1968): 65–91; R. Daft, *Organization Theory and Design*, 4th ed. (St. Paul, Minn.: West Publishing Company, 1992); B. Reimann, "Dimensions of Structure in Effective Organizations: Some Empirical Evidence," *Academy of Management Journal* (1974): 693–708; S. Robbins, *Organization Theory: The Structure and Design of Organizations*, 3d ed. (Englewood Cliffs, N.J.: Prentice-Hall, 1990).

16. H. Mintzberg, *The Structuring of Organizations* (Englewood Cliffs, N.J.: Prentice-Hall, 1979).

17. Mintzberg, *Structuring of Organizations*.

18. K. Weick, "Educational Institutions as Loosely Coupled Systems," *Administrative Science Quarterly* (1976): 1–19.

19. D. Miller and C. Droge, "Psychological and Traditional Determinants of Structure," *Administrative Science Quarterly* (1986): 540; H. Tosi, Jr., and J. Slocum, Jr., "Contingency Theory: Some Suggested Directions," *Journal of Management* (Spring 1984): 9–26.

20. M. Meyer, "Size and the Structure of Organizations: A Causal Analysis," *American Sociological Review*, (August 1972): 434–441; J. Beyer and H. Trice, "A Reexamination of the Relations between Size and Various Components of Organizational Complexity," *Administrative Science Quarterly* 24 (1979): 48–64; B. Mayhew, R. Levinger, J. McPherson, and T. James, "Systems Size and Structural Differentiation in Formal Organizations: A Baseline Generator for Two Ma-

jor Theoretical Propositions," *American Sociological Review* (October 1972): 26–43.

21. M. Gowing, J. Kraft, and J. C. Quick, *The New Organizational Reality: Downsizing, Restructuring, and Revitalization* (Washington, D.C.: American Psychological Association, 1998).

22. Anonymous, "Organizational Design in the 21st Century," *Journal of Business Strategy* 19 (1998): 33–35.

23. J. Woodward, *Industrial Organization: Theory and Practices* (London: Oxford University Press, 1965).

24. C. Perrow, "A Framework for the Comparative Analysis of Organizations," *American Sociological Review* (April 1967): 194–208; D. Rosseau, "Assessment of Technology in Organizations: Closed versus Open Systems Approaches," *Academy of Management Review* 4 (1979): 531–542.

25. Perrow, "A Framework for the Comparative Analysis of Organizations," 194–208.

26. J. D. Thompson, *Organizations in Action* (New York: McGraw-Hill, 1967).

27. P. Nemetz and L. Fry, "Flexible Manufacturing Organizations: Implication for Strategy Formulation and Organization Design," *Academy of Management Review* 13 (1988): 627–638; G. Huber, "The Nature and Design of Post-Industrial Organizations," *Management Science* 30 (1984): 934.

28. E. Feitzinger and H. L. Lee, "Mass Customization at Hewlett-Packard: The Power of Postponement," *Harvard Business Review* 75 (1997): 116–121.

29. Thompson, *Organizations in Action*.

30. H. Downey, D. Hellriegel, and J. Slocum, Jr., "Environmental Uncertainty: The Construct and Its Application," *Administrative Science Quarterly* 20 (1975): 613–629.

31. T. Burns and G. Stalker, *The Management of Innovation* (London: Tavistock, 1961); Mintzberg, *Structuring of Organizations*.

32. M. Chandler and L. Sayles, *Managing Large Systems* (New York: Harper & Row, 1971).

33. G. Dess and D. Beard, "Dimensions of Organizational Task Environments," *Administrative Science Quarterly* 29 (1984): 52–73.

34. J. Courtright, G. Fairhurst, and L. Rogers, "Interaction Patterns in Organic and Mechanistic Systems," *Academy of Management Journal* 32 (1989): 773–802.

35. R. Daft, *Organization Theory and Design*, 4th ed. (St. Paul, Minn.: West 1992).

36. D. Miller, "The Structural and Environmental Correlates of Business Strategy," *Strategic Management Journal* 8 (1987): 55–76.

37. D. Miller and P. Friesen, "A Longitudinal Study of the Corporate Life Cycle," *Management Science* 30 (1984): 1161–1183.

38. M. H. Overholt, "Flexible Organizations: Using Organizational Design as a Competitive Advantage," *Human Resource Planning* 20 (1997): 22–32; P. W. Roberts and R. Greenwood, "Integrating Transaction Cost and Institutional Theories: Toward a Constrained-Efficiency Framework for Understanding Organizational Design Adoption," *Academy of Management Review* 22 (1997): 346–373.

39. C. Hill and G. Jones, *Strategic Management Theory*, 2d ed. (Boston: Houghton Mifflin, 1992).

40. Daft, *Organization Theory and Design*.

41. C. M. Savage, *5th Generation Management, Revised Edition: Co-Creating through Virtual Enterprising, Dynamic Teaming, and Knowledge Networking* (Boston: Butterworth-Heinemann, 1996).

42. S. Davis, *Future Perfect* (Reading, Mass.: Addison-Wesley, 1987).

43. A. Boynton and B. Victor, "Beyond Flexibility: Building and Managing a Dynamically Stable Organization," *California Management Review* 8 (Fall 1991): 53–66.

44. T. Stewart, "The Search for the Organization of Tomorrow," *Fortune*, May 18, 1992, 92–98.

45. S. Tully, "The Modular Corporation," *Fortune*, February 8, 1993, 106–115; and R. L. Bunning and R. S. Althisar, "Modules: A Team Module for Manufacturing," *Personnel Journal* (1990): 90–96.

46. W. A. Cohen and N. Cohen, *The Paranoid Organization and 8 Other Ways Your Company Can Be Crazy: Advice from an Organizational Shrink* (New York: American Management Association, 1993).

47. M. F. R. Kets de Vries and D. Miller, "Personality, Culture, and Organization," *Academy of Management Review* 11 (1986): 266–279.

48. American Red Cross Poster 916A, revised June 1996.

Chapter 15

1. J. L Heskett and L. A. Schlesinger, "Leading the High Capability Organization: Challenges for the Twenty-First Century," *Human Resource Management* 36 (1997): 105–133; T. A. Stewart, "America's Most Admired Companies: Why Leadership Matters," *Fortune*, March 2, 1998, 70+.

2. T. E. Deal and A. A. Kennedy, *Corporate Cultures* (Reading, Mass.: Addison-Wesley, 1982).

3. W. Ouchi, *Theory Z* (Reading, Mass.: Addison-Wesley, 1981).

4. T. J. Peters and R. H. Waterman, *In Search of Excellence* (New York: Harper & Row, 1982).

5. M. Gardner, "Creating a Corporate Culture for the Eighties," *Business Horizons* (January–February 1985): 59–63.

6. Definition adapted from E. H. Schein, *Organizational Culture and Leadership* (San Francisco: Jossey-Bass, 1985), 9.

7. C. D. Sutton and D. L. Nelson, "Elements of the Cultural Network: The Communicators of Corporate Values," *Leadership and Organization Development* 11 (1990): 3–10.

8. B. Pickens, *Boone* (Boston: Houghton Mifflin, 1987).

9. A. Bandura, *Social Learning Theory* (Englewood Cliffs, N.J.: Prentice-Hall, 1977).

10. J. M. Beyer and H. M. Trice, "How an Organization's Rites Reveal Its Culture," *Organizational Dynamics* 16 (1987): 5–24.

11. H. M. Trice and J. M. Beyer, "Studying Organizational Cultures through Rites and Ceremonials," *Academy of Management Review* 9 (1984): 653–669.

12. M. J. Schneider, "The Wal-Mart Annual Meeting: From Small-Town America to a Global Corporate Culture," *Human Organization* 57 (1998): 292–299.

13. H. Levinson and S. Rosenthal, CEO: *Corporate Leadership in Action* (New York: Basic Books, 1984).

14. V. Sathe, "Implications of Corporate Culture: A Manager's Guide to Action," *Organizational Dynamics* 12 (1987): 5–23.

15. Sutton and Nelson, "Elements of the Cultural Network."

16. J. Martin, M. S. Feldman, M. J. Hatch, and S. B. Sitkin, "The Uniqueness Paradox in Organizational Stories," *Administrative Science Quarterly* 28 (1983): 438–453.

17. B. Durrance, "Stories at Work," *Training and Development* (February 1997): 25–29.

18. R. Goffee and G. Jones, "What Holds the Modern Company Together?" *Harvard Business Review* (November–December 1996): 133–143.

19. C. Argyris and D. A. Schon, *Organizational Learning* (Reading, Mass.: Addison-Wesley, 1978).

20. "Sounds Like a New Woman," *New Woman* (February 1993): 144.

21. M. Peterson, "Work, Corporate Culture, and Stress: Implications for Worksite Health Promotion," *American Journal of Health Behavior* 21 (1997): 243–252.

22. L. Smircich, "Concepts of Culture and Organizational Analysis," *Administrative Science Quarterly* (1983): 339–358.

23. Y. Weiner and Y. Vardi, "Relationships between Organizational Culture and Individual Motivation: A Conceptual Integration," *Psychological Reports* 67 (1990): 295–306.

24. M. R. Louis, "Surprise and Sense Making: What Newcomers Experience in Entering Unfamiliar Organizational Settings," *Administrative Science Quarterly* 25 (1980): 209–264.

25. E. Segalla, "All for Quality and Quality for All," *Training and Development Journal* (September 1989): 36–45.

26. J. P. Kotter and J. L. Heskett, *Corporate Culture and Performance* (New York: Free Press, 1992).

27. Deal and Kennedy, *Corporate Cultures*.

28. D. R. Katz, *The Big Store* (New York: Viking, 1987).

29. G. G. Gordon, "Industry Determinants of Organizational Culture," *Academy of Management Review* 16 (1991): 396–415.

30. G. Donaldson and J. Lorsch, *Decision Making at the Top* (New York: Basic Books, 1983).

31. R. H. Kilman, M. J. Saxton, and R. Serpa, eds., *Gaining Control of the Corporate Culture* (San Francisco: Jossey-Bass, 1986).

32. J. P. Kotter, *A Force for Change: How Leadership Differs from Management* (New York: Free Press, 1990); R. M. Kanter, *The Change Masters* (New York: Simon & Schuster, 1983).

33. T. Peters and N. Austin, *A Passion for Excellence: The Leadership Difference* (New York: Random House, 1985).

34. Schein, *Organizational Culture and Leadership*.

35. W. A. Cohen, *The Art of the Leader* (Englewood Cliffs, N.J.: Prentice-Hall, 1990).

36. J. Conger, "Inspiring Others: The Language of Leadership," *Academy of Management Executive* 5 (1991): 31–45.

37. J. A. Pearce II, T. R. Kramer, and D. K. Robbins, "Effects of Managers' Entrepreneurial Behavior on Subordinates," *Journal of Business Venturing* 12 (1997): 147–160.

38. J. C. Quick, "Crafting an Organizational Culture: Herb's Hand at Southwest Airlines," *Organizational Dynamics* (Autumn 1992): 45–56.

39. D. C. Feldman, "The Multiple Socialization of Organization Members," *Academy of Management Review* 6 (1981): 309–318.

40. R. Pascale, "The Paradox of Corporate Culture: Reconciling Ourselves to Socialization," *California Management Review* 27 (1985): 26–41.

41. D. L. Nelson, "Organizational Socialization: A Stress Perspective," *Journal of Occupational Behavior* 8 (1987): 311–324.

42. J. Chatman, "Matching People and Organizations: Selection and Socialization in Public Accounting Firms," *Administrative Science Quarterly* 36 (1991): 459–484.

43. S. M. Lee, S. Yoo, and T. M. Lee, "Korean Chaebols: Corporate Values and Strategies," *Organizational Dynamics* 19 (1991): 36–50.

44. D. L. Nelson, J. C. Quick, and M. E. Eakin, "A Longitudinal Study of Newcomer Role Adjustment in U.S. Organizations," *Work and Stress* 2 (1988): 239–253.

45. N. J. Allen and J. P. Meyer, "Organizational Socialization Tactics: A Longitudinal Analysis of

Links to Newcomers' Commitment and Role Orientation," *Academy of Management Journal* 33 (1990): 847–858.

46. T. N. Bauer, E. W. Morrison, and R. R. Callister, "Organizational Socialization: A Review and Directions for Future Research," *Research in Personnel and Human Resources Management* 16 (1998): 149–214.

47. M. R. Louis, "Acculturation in the Workplace: Newcomers as Lay Ethnographers," in B. Schneider, ed., *Organizational Climate and Culture* (San Francisco: Jossey-Bass, 1990), 85–129.

48. D. M. Rousseau, "Assessing Organizational Culture: The Case for Multiple Methods," in B. Schneider, ed., *Organizational Climate and Culture* (San Francisco: Jossey-Bass, 1990).

49. R. A. Cooke and D. M. Rousseau, "Behavioral Norms and Expectations: A Quantitative Approach to the Assessment of Organizational Culture," *Group and Organizational Studies* 12 (1988): 245–273.

50. R. H. Kilmann and M. J. Saxton, *Kilmann-Saxton Culture-Gap Survey* (Pittsburgh: Organizational Design Consultants, 1983).

51. W. J. Duncan, "Organizational Culture: 'Getting a Fix' on an Elusive Concept," *Academy of Management Executive* 3 (1989): 229–236.

52. N. J. Adler, *International Dimensions of Organizational Behavior*, 2d ed. (Boston: PWS Kent, 1991).

53. A. Laurent, "The Cultural Diversity of Western Conceptions of Management," *International Studies of Management and Organization* 13 (1983): 75–96.

54. P. Bate, "Using the Culture Concept in an Organization Development Setting," *Journal of Applied Behavior Science* 26 (1990): 83–106.

55. K. R. Thompson and F. Luthans, "Organizational Culture: A Behavioral Perspective," in B. Schneider, ed., *Organizational Climate and Culture* (San Francisco: Jossey-Bass, 1990).

56. V. Sathe, "How to Decipher and Change Corporate Culture," in R. H. Kilman et al., *Managing Corporate Cultures* (San Francisco: Jossey-Bass, 1985).

57. J. B. Shaw, C. D. Fisher, and W. A. Randolph, "From Maternalism to Accountability: The Changing Cultures of Ma Bell and Mother Russia," *Academy of Management Executive* 5 (1991): 7–20.

58. D. Lei, J. W. Slocum, Jr., and R. W. Slater, "Global Strategy and Reward Systems: The Key Roles of Management Development and Corporate Culture," *Organizational Dynamics* 19 (1990): 27–41.

59. S. H. Rhinesmith, "Going Global from the Inside Out," *Training and Development Journal* 45 (1991): 42–47.

60. L. K. Trevino and K. A. Nelson, *Managing Business Ethics: Straight Talk about How to Do It Right* (New York: John Wiley & Sons, 1995).

61. A. Bhide and H. H. Stevenson, "Why Be Honest if Honesty Doesn't Pay?" *Harvard Business Review* (September–October 1990): 121–129.

62. J. L. Cruikshank and D. B. Sicilia, *The Engine That Could* (Boston: Harvard Business School Press, 1997).

63. S. W. Gellerman, "Why Good Managers Make Bad Ethical Choices," *Harvard Business Review* 64 (1986): 85–90.

64. J. J. Johnson and C. L. McIntye, "Organizational Culture and Climate Correlates of Job Satisfaction," *Psychological Reports* 82 (1998): 843–850.

65. J. Teresko, "Best Plants: Cadillac," *Industry Week* (October 21, 1991): 29–32.

66. M. Krebs, "Cadillac Starts Down a New Road," *Industry Week* (August 5, 1991): 18–23.

67. K. L. Alexander, "Texas Nameplate: Company Commitment Pays Off," *USA Today*, November 18, 1998, 5B.

68. L. Sartain, "Why and How Southwest Airlines Uses Consultants," *Journal of Management Consulting* 10 (1998): 12–19; Heskett and Schlesinger, "Leading the High Capability Organization."

Chapter 16

1. J. A. Johnson, "Interview with Elizabeth Dole, President, American Red Cross," *Journal of Healthcare Management* 43 (1998): 3–7.

2. M. A. Verespej, "When Change Becomes the Norm," *Industry Week* (March 16, 1992): 35–38.

3. E. Davis, "What's on American Managers' Minds," *Management Review* (April 1995): 14–20.

4. "Conoco Plans to Develop Oil Fields in Russia: Cost of Up to $3 Billion," *Journal Record* (June 19, 1992): 16.

5. L. Hirschhorn and T. Gilmore, "The New Boundaries of the 'Boundaryless' Company," *Harvard Business Review* (May–June 1992): 104–115.

6. M. Hickins, "Reconcilable Differences," *Management Review* 87 (1998): 54–58.

7. L. R. Offerman and M. Gowing, "Organizations of the Future: Changes and Challenges," *American Psychologist* (February 1990): 95–108.

8. W. B. Johnston, "Global Work Force 2000: The New World Labor Market," *Harvard Business Review*, (March–April 1991): 115–127.

9. A. Faircloth, "Guess Who's Coming to Denny's," *Fortune*, August 3, 1998, 108–110.

10. F. Hapgood, "All Things to All People," *Inc.* 20 (1998): 94–104.

11. R. M. Kanter, "Improving the Development, Acceptance, and Use of New Technology: Organizational and Interorganizational Challenges," in *People and Technology in the Workplace* (Washington, D. C.: National Academy Press, 1991), 15–56.

12. J. A. Benson and D. L. Ross, "Sundstrand: A Case Study in Transformation of Cultural Ethics," *Journal of Business Ethics* 17 (1998): 1517–1527.

13. S. A. Mohrman and A. M. Mohrman, Jr., "The Environment as an Agent of Change," in A. M. Mohrman, Jr., et al., eds., *Large-Scale Organizational Change* (San Francisco: Jossey-Bass, 1989), 35–47.

14. D. Nadler, "Organizational Frame-Bending: Types of Change in the Complex Organization," in R. Kilmann and T. Covin, eds., *Corporate Transformation* (San Francisco: Jossey-Bass, 1988), 66–83.

15. L. Ackerman, "Development, Transition, or Transformation: The Question of Change in Organizations," *OD Practitioner* (December 1986): 1–8.

16. T. D. Jick, *Managing Change* (Homewood, Ill.: Irwin, 1993), 3.

17. R. Pascale, M. Milleman, and L. Gioja, "Changing the Way We Change," *Harvard Business Review* (November–December 1997): 126–139; J. Bardwick, *In Praise of Good Business* (New York: John Wiley & Sons, 1998).

18. R. M. Kanter, *The Change Masters* (New York: Simon & Schuster, 1983).

19. J. R. Katzenbach, *Real Change Leaders* (New York: Times Business, 1995).

20. M. Beer, *Organization Change and Development: A Systems View* (Santa Monica, Calif.: Goodyear, 1980), 78.

21. F. Cheyunski and J. Millard, "Accelerated Business Transformation and the Role of the Organizational Architect," *Journal of Applied Behavioral Science* 34 (1998): 268–285.

22. J. W. Brehm, *A Theory of Psychological Reactance* (New York: Academic Press, 1966).

23. J. A. Klein, "Why Supervisors Resist Employee Involvement," *Harvard Business Review* 62 (1984): 87–95.

24. S. Zuboff, "New Worlds of Computer-Mediated Work," *Harvard Business Review* 60 (1982): 142–152.

25. D. L. Nelson and M. A. White, "Management of Technological Innovation: Individual Attitudes, Stress, and Work Group Attributes," *Journal of High Technology Management Research* 1 (1990): 137–148.

26. D. Klein, "Some Notes on the Dynamics of Resistance to Change: The Defender Role," in W. G. Bennis, K. D. Benne, R. Chin, and K. E. Corey, eds., *The Planning of Change*, 3d ed. (New York: Holt, Rinehart & Winston, 1969), 117–124.

27. T. G. Cummings and E. F. Huse, *Organizational Development and Change* (St. Paul, Minn.: West, 1989).

28. N. DiFonzo and P. Bordia, "A Tale of Two Corporations: Managing Uncertainty during Organizational Change," *Human Resource Management* 37 (1998): 295–303.

29. L. P. Livingstone, M. A. White, D. L. Nelson, and F. Tabak. "Delays in Technological Innovation Implementations: Some Preliminary Results on a Common but Understudied Occurrence," working paper, Oklahoma State University.

30. D. T. Jaffe and C. D. Scott, "Reengineering in Practice: Where Are the People? Where Is the Learning?" *Journal of Applied Behavioral Science* 34 (1998): 250–267.

31. A. B. Fisher, "Making Change Stick," *Fortune*, April 17, 1995, 121–131.

32. J. P. Kotter and L. A. Schlesinger, "Choosing Strategies for Change," *Harvard Business Review* 57 (1979): 109–112; W. Bridges, *Transitions: Making Sense of Life's Changes* (Reading, Mass.: Addison-Wesley, 1980); H. Woodward and S. Buchholz, *Aftershock: Helping People through Corporate Change* (New York: Wiley, 1987).

33. K. Lewin, "Frontiers in Group Dynamics," *Human Relations* 1 (1947): 5–41.

34. W. McWhinney, "Meta-Praxis: A Framework for Making Complex Changes," in A. M. Mohrman, Jr., et al., eds., *Large-Scale Organizational Change* (San Francisco: Jossey-Bass, 1989), 154–199.

35. M. Beer and E. Walton, "Developing the Competitive Organization: Interventions and Strategies," *American Psychologist* 45 (1990): 154–161.

36. B. Bertsch and R. Williams, "How Multinational CEOs Make Change Programs Stick," *Long Range Planning* 27 (1994): 12–24.

37. W. L. French and C. H. Bell, *Organization Development: Behavioral Science Interventions for Organization Improvement*, 4th ed. (Englewood Cliffs, N.J.: Prentice-Hall, 1990); W. W. Burke, *Organization Development: A Normative View* (Reading, Mass.: Addison-Wesley, 1987).

38. A. Huczynski, *Encyclopedia of Organizational Change Methods* (Brookfield, Vt.: Gower, 1987).

39. A. O. Manzini, *Organizational Diagnosis* (New York: AMACOM, 1988).

40. M. R. Weisbord, "Organizational Diagnosis: Six Places to Look for Trouble with or without a Theory," *Group and Organization Studies* (December 1976): 430–444.

41. H. Levinson, *Organizational Diagnosis* (Cambridge, Mass.: Harvard University Press, 1972).

42. J. Nicholas, "The Comparative Impact of Organization Development Interventions," *Academy of Management Review* 7 (1982): 531–542.

43. C. Cammann, M. Fichman, G. D. Jenkins, and J. Klesh, "Assessing the Attitudes and Perceptions of Organization Members," in S. Seashore, E. Lawler III, P. Mirvis, and C. Cammann, eds., *Assessing Organizational Change: A Guide to Methods, Measures, and Practices* (New York: Wiley, 1983), 71–138.

44. G. Odiorne, *Management by Objectives* (Marshfield, Mass.: Pitman, 1965).

45. E. Huse, "Putting in a Management Development Program That Works," *California Management Review* 9 (1966): 73–80.

46. J. P. Muczyk and B. C. Reimann, "MBO as a Complement to Effective Leadership," *Academy of Management Executive* (May 1989): 131–138.

47. L. L. Berry and A. Parasuraman, "Prescriptions for a Service Quality Revolution in America," *Organizational Dynamics* 20 (1992): 5–15.

48. "Five Companies Win 1992 Baldridge Quality Awards," *Business America* (November 2, 1992): 7–16.

49. D. M. Anderson, "Hidden Forces," *Success* (April 1995): 12.

50. W. G. Dyer, *Team Building: Issues and Alternatives*, 2d ed. (Reading, Mass.: Addison-Wesley, 1987).

51. E. Stephan, G. Mills, R. W. Pace, and L. Ralphs, "HRD in the Fortune 500: A Survey," *Training and Development Journal* (January 1988): 26–32.

52. R. Swezey and E. Salas, eds., *Teams: Their Training and Performance* (Norwood, N.J.: Ablex, 1991).

53. M. Whitmire and P. R. Nienstedt, "Lead Leaders into the '90s," *Personnel Journal* (May 1991): 80–85.

54. E. Salas, T. L. Dickinson, S. I. Tannenbaum, and S. A. Converse, *A Meta-Analysis of Team Performance and Training, Naval Training System Center Technical Reports* (Orlando, Fla.: U.S. Government, 1991).

55. B. B. Bunker and B. T. Alban, *Large Group Interventions* (San Francisco: Jossey-Bass, 1997).

56. E. Schein, *Its Role in Organization Development*, vol. 1 of *Process Consultation* (Reading, Mass.: Addison-Wesley, 1988).

57. D. Filipowski, "How Federal Express Makes Your Package Its Most Important," *Personnel Journal* (February 1992): 40–46; P. Galagan, "Training Delivers Results to Federal Express," *Training and Development* (December 1991): 27–33.

58. J. Campbell and M. Dunnette, "Effectiveness of T-Group Experiences in Managerial Training and Development," *Psychological Bulletin* 70 (1968): 73–103.

59. R. T. Golembiewski, *Organization Development* (New Brunswick, N.J.: Transaction Publishers, 1989).

60. N. M. Dixon, "Evaluation and Management Development," in J. Pfeiffer, ed., *The 1991 Annual: Developing Human Resources* (San Diego: University Associates, 1991), 287–296.

61. R. W. Revans, *Action Learning* (London: Blonde & Briggs, 1980).

62. I. L. Goldstein, *Training in Organizations*, 3d ed. (Pacific Grove, Calif.: Brooks/Cole, 1993).

63. C. Steinburg, "Taking Charge of Change," *Training and Development* (March 1992): 26–32.

64. D. A. Nadler, "Concepts for the Management of Organizational Change," in J. R. Hackman, E. E. Lawler III, and L. W. Porter, eds., *Perspectives on Organizational Behavior* (New York: McGraw-Hill, 1983).

65. Cummings and Huse, *Organizational Development*; P. E. Connor and L. K. Lake, *Managing Organizational Change* (New York: Praeger, 1988).

66. R. L. Lowman, "Ethical Human Resource Practice in Organizational Settings," in D. W. Bray, ed., *Working with Organizations* (New York: Guilford Press, 1991).

67. H. Kelman, "Manipulation of Human Behavior: An Ethical Dilemma for the Social Scientist," in W. Bennis, K. Benne, and R. Chin, eds., *The Planning of Change* (New York: Holt, Rinehart, & Winston, 1969).

68. J. B. Nicholas, "The Comparative Impact of Organization Development Interventions on Hard Criteria Measures," *Academy of Management Review* (October 1982): 531–542.

69. R. A. Katzell and R. A. Guzzo, "Psychological Approaches to Worker Productivity," *American Psychologist* 38 (1983): 468–472.

70. R. A. Guzzo, R. D. Jette, and R. A. Katzell, "The Effects of Psychologically Based Intervention Programs on Worker Productivity," *Personnel Psychology* 38 (1985): 275–291.

71. Goldstein, *Training in Organizations*.

72. T. Covin and R. H. Kilmann, "Participant Perceptions of Positive and Negative Influences on Large-Scale Change," *Group and Organization Studies* 15 (1990): 233–248.

73. W. Wong, "Nonprofits Find Funds, Help on Web," *Computerworld* 31 (1997): 37–40.

Glossary

A

adaptive culture An organizational culture that encourages confidence and risk taking among employees, has leadership that produces change, and focuses on the changing needs of customers.

adhocracy A selectively decentralized form of organization that emphasizes the support staff and mutual adjustment among people.

administrative orbiting Delaying action on a conflict by buying time.

affect The emotional component of an attitude.

affective commitment The type of organizational commitment that is based on an individual's desire to remain in an organization.

anthropocentric Placing human considerations at the center of job design decisions.

anthropology The science of the learned behavior of human beings.

anticipatory socialization The first socialization stage, which encompasses all of the learning that takes place prior to the newcomer's first day on the job.

artifacts Symbols of culture in the physical and social work environment.

assumptions Deeply held beliefs that guide behavior and tell members of an organization how to perceive and think about things.

attitude A psychological tendency expressed by evaluating an entity with some degree of favor or disfavor.

attribution theory A theory that explains how individuals pinpoint the causes of their own behavior and that of others.

authority The right to influence another person.

authority-obedience manager (9,1) A manager who emphasizes efficient production.

autocratic style A style of leadership in which the leader uses strong, directive, controlling actions to enforce the rules, regulations, activities, and relationships in the work environment.

B

behavioral measures Personality assessments that involve observing an individual's behavior in a controlled situation.

benevolent An individual who is comfortable with an equity ratio less than that of his or her comparison other.

bounded rationality A theory that suggests that there are limits to how rational a decision maker can actually be.

brainstorming A technique for generating as many ideas as possible on a given subject, while suspending evaluation until all the ideas have been suggested.

C

centralization The degree to which decisions are made at the top of the organization.

challenge The call to competition, contest, or battle.

change The transformation or modification of an organization and/or its stakeholders.

change agent The individual or group that undertakes the task of introducing and managing a change in an organization.

change and acquisition The third socialization stage, in which the newcomer begins to master the demands of the job.

character assassination An attempt to label or discredit an opponent.

charismatic leadership The use, by a leader, of personal abilities and talents in order to have profound and extraordinary effects on followers.

classical conditioning Modifying behavior so that a conditioned stimulus is paired with an unconditioned stimulus and elicits an unconditioned response.

coercive power Power that is based on an agent's ability to cause an unpleasant experience for a target.

cognitive dissonance A state of tension that is produced when an individual experiences conflict between attitudes and behavior.

cognitive moral development The process of moving through stages of maturity in terms of making ethical decisions.

cognitive style An individual's preference for gathering information and evaluating alternatives.

collectivism A cultural orientation in which individuals belong to tightly knit social frameworks and depend strongly on large extended families or clans.

compensation A compromise mechanism in which an individual attempts to make up for a negative situation by devoting himself or herself to another pursuit with increased vigor.

compensation award An organizational cost resulting from court awards for job distress.

complexity The degree to which many different types of activities occur in the organization.

conflict Any situation in which incompatible goals, attitudes, emotions, or behaviors lead to disagreement or opposition between two or more parties.

consensus An informational cue indicating the extent to which peers in the same situation behave in a similar fashion.

consequential theory An ethical theory that emphasizes the consequences or results of behavior.

consideration Leader behavior aimed at nurturing friendly, warm working relationships, as well as encouraging mutual trust and interpersonal respect within the work unit.

consistency An informational cue indicating the frequency of behavior over time.

contextual variables A set of characteristics that influence the organization's design processes.

continuance commitment The type of organizational commitment that is based on the fact that an individual cannot afford to leave.

conversion A withdrawal mechanism in which emotional conflicts are expressed in physical symptoms.

counterdependence An unhealthy, insecure pattern of behavior that leads to separation in relationships with other people.

counter-role behavior Deviant behavior in either a correctly or incorrectly defined job or role.

country club manager (1,9) A manager who creates a happy, comfortable work environment.

creativity A process influenced by individual and organizational factors that results in the production of novel and useful ideas, products, or both.

cross-training A variation of job enlargement in which workers are trained in different specialized tasks or activities.

cultural theory An ethical theory that emphasizes respect for different cultural values.

D

Delphi technique Gathering the judgments of experts for use in decision making.

democratic style A style of leadership in which the leader takes collaborative, reciprocal, interactive actions with followers concerning the work and work environment.

devil's advocacy A technique for preventing groupthink in which a group or individual is given the role of critic during decision making.

dialectical inquiry A debate between two opposing sets of recommendations.

differentiation The process of deciding how to divide the work in an organization.

discounting principle The assumption that an individual's behavior is accounted for by the situation.

disenchantment Feeling negativity or anger toward a change.

disengagement Psychological withdrawal from change.

disidentification Feeling that one's identity is being threatened by a change.

disorientation Feelings of loss and confusion due to a change.

displacement An aggressive mechanism in which an individual directs his or her anger toward someone who is not the source of the conflict.

distinctiveness An informational cue indicating the degree to which an individual behaves the same way in other situations.

distress The adverse psychological, physical, behavioral, and organizational consequences that may arise as a result of stressful events.

distributive bargaining A negotiation approach in which the goals of the parties are in conflict, and each party seeks to maximize its resources.

distributive justice The fairness of the outcomes that individuals receive in an organization.

diversity All forms of individual differences, including culture, gender, age, ability, personality, religious affiliation, economic class, social status, military attachment, and sexual orientation.

divisionalized form A moderately decentralized form of organization that emphasizes the middle level and standardization of outputs.

due process nonaction A procedure set up to address conflicts that is so costly, time-consuming, or personally risky that no one will use it.

dynamic follower A follower who is a responsible steward of his or her job, is effective in managing the relationship with the boss, and practices self-management.

dysfunctional conflict An unhealthy, destructive disagreement between two or more people.

E

effective decision A timely decision that meets a desired objective and is acceptable to those individuals affected by it.

ego-ideal The embodiment of a person's perfect self.

empowerment Sharing power within an organization.

enacted values Values reflected in the way individuals actually behave.

encounter The second socialization stage, in which the newcomer learns the tasks associated with the job, clarifies roles, and establishes new relationships at work.

engineering The applied science of energy and matter.

entitled An individual who is comfortable with an equity ratio greater than that of his or her comparison other.

environment Anything outside the boundaries of an organization.

environmental uncertainty The amount and rate of change in the organization's environment.

equity sensitive An individual who prefers an equity ratio equal to that of his or her comparison other.

escalation of commitment The tendency to continue to commit resources to a losing course of action.

espoused values What members of an organization say they value.

ethical behavior Acting in ways consistent with one's personal values and the commonly held values of the organization and society.

eustress Healthy, normal stress.

expatriate manager A manager who works in a country other than his or her home country.

expectancy The belief that effort leads to performance.

expert power The power that exists when an agent has information or knowledge that the target needs.

expert system A computer-based application that uses a representation of human expertise in a specialized field of knowledge to solve problems.

extinction The attempt to weaken a behavior by attaching no consequences to it.

extraversion A preference indicating that an individual is energized by interaction with other people.

F

fantasy A withdrawal mechanism that provides an escape from a conflict through daydreaming.

feeling Making decisions in a personal, value-oriented way.

femininity The cultural orientation in which relationships and concern for others are valued.

first-impression error The tendency to form lasting opinions about an individual based on initial perceptions.

fixation An aggressive mechanism in which an individual keeps up a dysfunctional behavior that obviously will not solve the conflict.

flextime An alternative work pattern that enables employees to set their own daily work schedules.

flight/withdrawal A withdrawal mechanism that entails physically escaping a conflict (flight) or psychologically escaping (withdrawal).

followership The process of being guided and directed by a leader in the work environment.

formal leadership Officially sanctioned leadership based on the authority of a formal position.

formal organization The part of the organization that has legitimacy and official recognition.

formalization The degree to which the organization has official rules, regulations, and procedures.

functional conflict A healthy, constructive disagreement between two or more people.

fundamental attribution error The tendency to make attributions to internal causes when focusing on someone else's behavior.

G

garbage can model A theory that contends that decisions in organizations are random and unsystematic.

glass ceiling A transparent barrier that keeps women from rising above a certain level in organizations.

goal setting The process of establishing desired results that guide and direct behavior.

group Two or more people with common interests or objectives.

group cohesion The "interpersonal glue" that makes members of a group stick together.

group polarization The tendency for group discussion to produce shifts toward more extreme attitudes among members.

groupthink A deterioration of mental efficiency, reality testing, and moral judgment resulting from in-group pressures.

guanxi The Chinese practice of building networks for social exchange.

H

Hawthorne studies Studies conducted during the 1920s and 1930s that discovered the existence of the informal organization.

heuristics Shortcuts in decision making that save mental activity.

hierarchy of authority The degree of vertical differentiation across levels of management.

homeostasis A steady state of bodily functioning and equilibrium.

humanistic theory The personality theory that emphasizes individual growth and improvement.

hygiene factor A work condition related to dissatisfaction caused by discomfort or pain.

I

identification A compromise mechanism whereby an individual patterns his or her behavior after another's.

implicit personality theory Opinions formed about other people that are based on our own mini-theories about how people behave.

impoverished manager (1,1) A manager who exerts just enough effort to avoid being fired.

impression management The process by which individuals try to control the impression others have of them.

incremental change Change of a relatively small scope, such as making small improvements.

individual differences The way in which factors such as skills, abilities, personalities, perceptions, attitudes, values, and ethics differ from one individual to another.

individualism A cultural orientation in which people belong to loose social frameworks, and their primary concern is for themselves and their families.

inequity The situation in which a person perceives he or she is receiving less than he or she is giving, or is giving less than he or she is receiving.

influence The process of affecting the thoughts, behavior, and feelings of another person.

informal leadership Unofficial leadership accorded to a person by other members of the organization.

informal organization The unofficial part of the organization.

initiating structure Leader behavior aimed at defining and organizing work relationships and roles, as well as establishing clear patterns of organization, communication, and ways of getting things done.

instrumental values Values that represent the acceptable behaviors to be used in achieving some end state.

instrumentality The belief that performance is related to rewards.

integrated involvement Closeness achieved through tasks and activities.

integration The process of coordinating the different parts of an organization.

integrative approach The broad theory that describes personality as a composite of an individual's psychological processes.

integrative negotiation A negotiation approach that focuses on the merits of the issues and seeks a win–win solution.

interactional psychology The psychological approach that emphasizes that in order to understand human behavior, we must know something about the person and about the situation.

intergroup conflict Conflict that occurs between groups or teams in an organization.

interorganizational conflict Conflict that occurs between two or more organizations.

interpersonal conflict Conflict that occurs between two or more individuals.

interrole conflict A person's experience of conflict among the multiple roles in his or her life.

intrapersonal conflict Conflict that occurs within an individual.

intrarole conflict Conflict that occurs within a single role, such as when a person receives conflicting messages from role senders about how to perform a certain role.

introversion A preference indicating that an individual is energized by time alone.

intuiting Gathering information through "sixth sense" and focusing on what could be rather than what actually exists.

intuition A fast, positive force in decision making that is utilized at a level below consciousness and involves learned patterns of information.

J

job A set of specified work and task activities that engage an individual in an organization.

Job Characteristics Model A framework for understanding person–job fit through the interaction of core job dimensions with critical psychological states within a person.

Job Diagnostic Survey (JDS) The survey instrument designed to measure the elements in the Job Characteristics Model.

job enlargement A method of job design that increases the number of activities in a job to overcome the boredom of overspecialized work.

job enrichment Designing or redesigning jobs by incorporating motivational factors into them.

job redesign An OD intervention method that alters jobs to improve the fit between individual skills and the demands of the job.

job rotation A variation of job enlargement in which workers are exposed to a variety of specialized jobs over time.

job satisfaction A pleasurable or positive emotional state resulting from the appraisal of one's job or job experiences.

job sharing An alternative work pattern in which more than one person occupies a single job.

judging Preferring closure and completion in making decisions.

jurisdictional ambiguity The presence of unclear lines of responsibility within an organization.

L

laissez-faire style A style of leadership in which the leader fails to accept the responsibilities of the position.

leader An advocate for change and new approaches to problems.

leader–member relations The quality of interpersonal relationships among a leader and the group members.

leadership The process of guiding and directing the behavior of people in the work environment.

lean production Using committed employees with ever-expanding responsibilities to achieve zero waste, 100 percent good product, delivered on time, every time.

learning A change in behavior acquired through experience.

least preferred coworker (LPC) The person a leader has least preferred to work with over his or her career.

legitimate power Power that is based on position and mutual agreement; agent and target agree that the agent has the right to influence the target.

locus of control An individual's generalized belief about internal control (self-control) versus external control (control by the situation or by others).

loss of individuality A social process in which individual group members lose self-awareness and its accompanying sense of accountability, inhibition, and responsibility for individual behavior.

M

M-oriented behavior Leader behavior that is sensitive to employees' feelings, emphasizes comfort in the work environment, works to reduce stress levels, and demonstrates appreciation for follower contributions.

Machiavellianism A personality characteristic indicating one's willingness to do whatever it takes to get one's own way.

machine bureaucracy A moderately decentralized form of organization that emphasizes the technical staff and standardization of work processes.

maintenance function An activity essential to effective, satisfying interpersonal relationships within a team or group.

management The study of overseeing activities and supervising people in organizations.

management by objectives (MBO) A goal-setting program based on interaction and negotiation between employees and managers.

management development A host of techniques for enhancing managers' skills in an organization.

manager An advocate for stability and the status quo.

Managerial Grid An approach to understanding a manager's concern for production and concern for people.

masculinity The cultural orientation in which assertiveness and materialism are valued.

meaning of work The way a person interprets and understands the value of work as part of life.

medicine The applied science of healing or treatment of diseases to enhance an individual's health and well-being.

mentoring A work relationship that encourages development and career enhancement for people moving through the career cycle.

moral maturity The measure of a person's cognitive moral development.

motivation The process of arousing and sustaining goal-directed behavior.

motivation factor A work condition related to satisfaction of the need for psychological growth.

moving The second step in Lewin's change model, in which new attitudes, values, and behaviors are substituted for old ones.

Myers-Briggs Type Indicator (MBTI) An instrument developed to measure Carl Jung's theory of individual differences.

N

need for achievement A manifest (easily perceived) need that concerns individuals' issues of excellence, competition, challenging goals, persistence, and overcoming difficulties.

need for affiliation A manifest (easily perceived) need that concerns an individual's need to establish and maintain warm, close, intimate relationships with other people.

need for power A manifest (easily perceived) need that concerns an individual's need to make an impact on others, influence others, change people or events, and make a difference in life.

need hierarchy The theory that behavior is determined by a progression of physical, social, and psychological needs.

negative affect An individual's tendency to accentuate the negative aspects of himself or herself, other people, and the world in general.

negative consequences Results of a behavior that a person finds unattractive or aversive.

negativism An aggressive mechanism in which a person responds with pessimism to any attempt at solving a problem.

nominal group technique (NGT) A structured approach to group decision making that focuses on generating alternatives and choosing one.

nonaction Doing nothing in hopes that a conflict will disappear.

nonprogrammed decision A new, complex decision that requires a creative solution.

normative commitment A perceived obligation to remain with the organization.

norms of behavior The standards that a work group uses to evaluate the behavior of its members.

O

objective knowledge Knowledge that results from research and scholarly activities.

operant conditioning Modifying behavior through the use of positive or negative consequences following specific behaviors.

organization development (OD) A systematic approach to organizational improvement that applies behavioral science theory and research in order to increase individual and organizational well-being and effectiveness.

organization man manager (5,5) A manager who maintains the status quo.

organizational behavior The study of individual behavior and group dynamics in organizational settings.

organizational citizenship behavior Behavior that is above and beyond the call of duty.

organizational commitment The strength of an individual's identification with an organization.

organizational (corporate) culture A pattern of basic assumptions that are considered valid and that are taught to new members as the way to perceive, think, and feel in the organization.

organizational design The process of constructing and adjusting an organization's structure to achieve its goals.

organizational life cycle The differing stages of an organization's life from birth to death.

organizational politics The use of power and influence in organizations.

organizational socialization The process by which newcomers are transformed from outsiders to participating, effective members of the organization.

organizational structure The linking of departments and jobs within an organization.

overdependence An unhealthy, insecure pattern of behavior that leads to preoccupied attempts to achieve security through relationships.

P

P-oriented behavior Leader behavior that encourages a fast work pace, emphasizes good quality and high accuracy, works toward high-quantity production, and demonstrates concern for rules and regulations.

participation problem A cost associated with absenteeism, tardiness, strikes and work stoppages, and turnover.

participative decision making Decision making in which individuals who are affected by decisions influence the making of those decisions.

people The human resources of the organization.

perceiving Preferring to explore many alternatives and flexibility.

performance appraisal The evaluation of a person's performance.

performance decrement A cost resulting from poor quality or low quantity of production, grievances, and unscheduled machine downtime and repair.

person–role conflict Conflict that occurs when an individual is expected to perform behaviors in a certain role that conflict with his or her personal values.

personal power Power used for personal gain.

personality A relatively stable set of characteristics that influence an individual's behavior.

personality hardiness A personality resistant to distress and characterized by challenge, commitment, and control.

planned change Change resulting from a deliberate decision to alter the organization.

political behavior Actions not officially sanctioned by an organization that are taken to influence others in order to meet one's personal goals.

position power The authority associated with the leader's formal position in the organization.

positive affect An individual's tendency to accentuate the positive aspects of himself or herself, other people, and the world in general.

positive consequences Results of a behavior that a person finds attractive or pleasurable.

power The ability to influence another person.

power distance The degree to which a culture accepts unequal distribution of power.

powerlessness A lack of power.

preventive stress management An organizational philosophy that holds that people and organizations should take joint responsibility for promoting health and preventing distress and strain.

primary prevention The stage in preventive stress management designed to reduce, modify, or eliminate the demand or stressor causing stress.

procedural justice The fairness of the process by which outcomes are allocated in an organization.

process consultation An OD method that helps managers and employees improve the processes that are used in organizations.

professional bureaucracy A decentralized form of organization that emphasizes the operating level and standardization of skills.

programmed decision A simple, routine matter for which a manager has an established decision rule.

projective test A personality test that elicits an individual's response to abstract stimuli.

psychoanalysis Sigmund Freud's method for delving into the unconscious mind to better understand a person's motives and needs.

psychodynamic theory The personality theory that emphasizes the unconscious determinants of behavior.

psychological intimacy Emotional and psychological closeness to other team or group members.

psychology The science of human behavior.

punishment The attempt to eliminate or weaken undesirable behavior by either bestowing negative consequences or withholding positive consequences.

Q

quality circle (QC) A small group of employees who work voluntarily on company time, typically one hour per week, to address work-related problems such as quality control, cost reduction, production planning and techniques, and even product design.

quality program A program that embeds product and service quality excellence in the organizational culture.

quality team A team that is part of an organization's structure and is empowered to act on its decisions regarding product and service quality.

R

rationality A logical, step-by-step approach to decision making, with a thorough analysis of alternatives and their consequences.

rationalization A compromise mechanism characterized by trying to justify one's behavior by constructing bogus reasons for it.

referent power An elusive power that is based on interpersonal attraction.

refreezing The final step in Lewin's change model, in which new attitudes, values, and behaviors are established as the new status quo.

reinforcement The attempt to develop or strengthen desirable behavior by either bestowing positive consequences or withholding negative consequences.

reinvention The creative application of new technology.

reward power Power based on an agent's ability to control rewards that a target wants.

risk aversion The tendency to choose options that entail fewer risks and less uncertainty.

robotics The use of robots in organizations.

role negotiation A technique whereby individuals meet and clarify their psychological contract.

rule-based theory An ethical theory that emphasizes the character of the act itself rather than its effects.

S

satisfice To select the first alternative that is "good enough," because the costs in time and effort are too great to optimize.

scientific management See work simplification.

secondary prevention The stage in preventive stress management designed to alter or modify the individual's or the organization's response to a demand or stressor.

secrecy Attempting to hide a conflict or an issue that has the potential to create conflict.

selective perception The process of selecting information that supports our individual viewpoints while discounting information that threatens our viewpoints.

self-efficacy An individual's beliefs and expectancies about his or her ability to accomplish a specific task effectively.

self-esteem An individual's general feeling of self-worth.

self-fulfilling prophecy The situation in which our expectations about people affect our interaction with them in such a way that our expectations are fulfilled.

self-image How a person sees himself or herself, both positively and negatively.

self-interest What is in the best interest and benefit to an individual.

self-managed team A team that makes decisions that were once reserved for managers.

self-monitoring The extent to which people base their behavior on cues from other people and situations.

self-reliance A healthy, secure, interdependent pattern of behavior related to how people form and maintain supportive attachments with others.

self-report questionnaire A common personality assessment that involves an individual's responses to a series of questions.

self-serving bias The tendency to attribute one's own successes to internal causes and one's failures to external causes.

sensing Gathering information through the five senses.

sensitivity training An intervention designed to help individuals understand how their behavior affects others.

simple structure A centralized form of organization that emphasizes the upper echelon and direct supervision.

skill development The mastery of abilities essential to successful functioning in organizations.

skills training Increasing the job knowledge, skills, and abilities that are necessary to do a job effectively.

social decision schemes Simple rules used to determine final group decisions.

social information-processing (SIP) model A model that suggests that the important job factors depend in part on what others tell a person about the job.

social learning The process of deriving attitudes from family, peer groups, religious organizations, and culture.

social loafing The failure of a group member to contribute personal time, effort, thoughts, or other resources to the group.

social perception The process of interpreting information about another person.

social power Power used to create motivation or to accomplish group goals.

social responsibility The obligation of an organization to behave in ethical ways.

sociology The science of society.

sociotechnical systems (STS) Giving equal attention to technical and social considerations in job design.

specialization The degree to which jobs are narrowly defined and depend on unique expertise.

standardization The degree to which work activities are accomplished in a routine fashion.

status structure The set of authority and task relations among a group's members.

stereotype A generalization about a group of people.

strain Distress.

strategic change Change of a larger scale, such as organizational restructuring.

strategic contingencies Activities that other groups depend on in order to complete their tasks.

stress The unconscious preparation to fight or flee that a person experiences when faced with any demand.

stressor The person or event that triggers the stress response.

strong culture An organizational culture with a consensus on the values that drive the company and with an intensity that is recognizable even to outsiders.

strong situation A situation that overwhelms the effects of individual personalities by providing strong cues for appropriate behavior.

structure The manner in which an organization's work is designed at the micro level, as well as how departments, divisions, and the overall organization are designed at the macro level.

superordinate goal An organizational goal that is more important to both parties in a conflict than their individual or group goals.

survey feedback A widely used method of intervention whereby employee attitudes are solicited using a questionnaire.

synergy A positive force that occurs in groups when group members stimulate new solutions to problems through the process of mutual influence and encouragement within the group.

T

task An organization's mission, purpose, or goal for existing.

task environment The elements of an organization's environment that are related to its goal attainment.

task function An activity directly related to the effective completion of a team's work.

task revision The modification of incorrectly specified roles or jobs.

task structure The degree of clarity, or ambiguity, in the work activity assigned to the group.

team A small number of people with complementary skills who are committed to a common mission, performance goals, and approach for which they hold themselves mutually accountable.

team building An intervention designed to improve the effectiveness of a work group.

team manager (9,9) A manager who builds a highly productive team of committed people.

technocentric Placing technology and engineering at the center of job design decisions.

technological interdependence The degree of interrelatedness of the organization's various technological elements.

technology The intellectual and mechanical processes used by an organization to transform inputs into products or services that meet organizational goals.

technostress The stress caused by new and advancing technologies in the workplace.

telecommuting Transmitting work from a home computer to the office using a modem.

terminal values Values that represent the goals to be achieved or the end states of existence.

tertiary prevention The stage in preventive stress management designed to heal individual or organizational symptoms of distress and strain.

Theory X A set of assumptions of how to manage individuals who are motivated by lower order needs.

Theory Y A set of assumptions of how to manage individuals who are motivated by higher order needs.

thinking Making decisions in a logical, objective fashion.

time orientation Whether a culture's values are oriented toward the future (long-term orientation) or toward the past and present (short-term orientation).

total quality management The total dedication to continuous improvement and to customers so that the customers' needs are met and their expectations exceeded.

trait theory The personality theory that states that in order to understand individuals, we must break down behavior patterns into a series of observable traits.

transformational change Change in which the organization moves to a radically different, and sometimes unknown, future state.

transformational coping A way of managing stressful events by changing them into subjectively less stressful events.

transnational organization An organization in which the global viewpoint supersedes national issues.

triangulation The use of multiple methods to measure organizational culture.

Type A behavior pattern A complex of personality and behavioral characteristics, including competitiveness, time urgency, social status insecurity, aggression, hostility, and a quest for achievements.

U

uncertainty avoidance The degree to which a culture tolerates ambiguity and uncertainty.

unfreezing The first step in Lewin's change model, in which individuals are encouraged to discard old behaviors by shaking up the equilibrium state that maintains the status quo.

unplanned change Change that is imposed on the organization and is often unforeseen.

upper echelon A top-level executive team in an organization.

V

valence The value or importance one places on a particular reward.

values Enduring beliefs that a specific mode of conduct or end state of existence is personally or socially preferable to an opposite or converse mode of conduct or end state of existence.

virtual office A mobile platform of computer, telecommunication, and information technology and services.

W

whistle-blower An employee who informs authorities of the wrongdoings of his or her company or coworkers.

work Mental or physical activity that has productive results.

work simplification Standardization and the narrow, explicit specification of task activities for workers.

Z

zone of indifference The range in which attempts to influence a person will be perceived as legitimate and will be acted on without a great deal of thought.

Company Index

A

Adobe [http://www.adobe.com], 297
Advantica, Inc. [http://www.advantica.com], 479
Aerobics Center, 211
Albany Ladder [http://www.albanyladder.com], 111
Alliance for Environmental Innovation [http://www.environmentaldefense.org/Alliance/], 127
America Online [http://www.aol.com], 14
American Airlines [http://www.aa.com], 151, 176, 225, 226, 430, 459, 477
    organizational behavior, 2, 3
American Heart Association [http://www.americanheart.org], 213, 292
American Red Cross [http://www.redcross.org], 30, 442
    committed involvement and, 155
    introduction to, 14–15,
    motivation without compensation at, 132, 133
    organizational design and structure of, 416, 417
    transformation of, 476, 477
    use of technology, 505
Anheuser Busch [http://www.anheuser-busch.com], 48
Apple Computer [http://www.apple.com], 297, 434, 435, 452
Arkhangelskgeologia [http://www.archangeldiamond.com], 478
Armstrong World Industries [http://www.armstrong.com], 83
AT&T [http://www.att.com], 49, 83, 213, 248, 297, 393, 406, 467, 468, 502
Atlantic Richfield (ARCO) [http://www.bp.com], 57
Auto-xchange [http://www.auto-xchange.com], 63

B

Bank of America [http://www.bankofamerica.com], 258
Bank of Montreal [http://www.bankofmontreal.com], 42
Baxter Export Corporation
    telecommuting and job sharing at, 405

Baxter International Inc. [http://www.baxter.com], 405
Beech-Nut [http://www.beechnut.com], 277
Bell Atlantic [http://www.verizon.com], 406
Bell Canada [http://www.bee.com], 51
BellSouth [http://www.bellsouth.com], 198
Binney and Smith [http://www.binney-smith.com], 433
Black & Decker [http://www.blackanddecker.com], 6, 171
The Body Shop, [http://www.bodyshop.com] 55, 321
Boeing [http://www.boeing.com], 275, 472
Boise Cascade [http://www.bc.com], 420
Boy Scouts of America [http://www.bsa.scouting.org], 453

C

Cable News Network (CNN) [http://www.cnn.com], 321
Campbell Soup Company [http://www.campbellsoup.com], 274
Capital City Corporation, 181
Cargill [http://www.cargill.com], 119
Carnegie-Mellon University [http://www.cmu.edu], 51
Carpoint [http://carpoint.msn.com], 63
Caterpillar, Inc. [http://www.cat.com], 469, 502
Chaparral Steel Company [http://www.chaparralsteel.com], 6, 177, 224, 306, 399, 454
The Charles Machine Works [http://ema.bentley.com/products/modeler/slides/sld029.htm], 452
Chrysler Corporation [http://www2.chryslercorp.com], 238, 314, 315, 378, 458
Cisco Systems, Inc. [http://www.cisco.com], 63
    employees' self-esteem, 75, 76
    teamwork at, 75, 76
Citicorp [http://www.citicorp.com], 239, 502
City of Phoenix [http://www.ci.phoenix.az.us], 259
Clif Bar, Inc. [http://www.clifbar.com], 453, 454
Coastal Corporation [http://www.coastalcorp.com], 389
Coca-Cola [http://www.cocacola.com], 31, 32, 33, 61, 120, 391, 420
Columbia-Health ONE [http://www.columbia.net], 358

Compaq [http://www.compaq.com], 13, 46, 116, 178, 468
Conoco, Inc. [http://www.conoco.com], 478
Continental Airlines [http://www.continental.com], 481, 482
Control Data Corporation [http://www.cdc.com], 15, 213
    STAY-WELL program, 7
Cooper Aerobics Center [http://www.cooperaerobics.com], 113
Coors Brewing Company [http://www.coors.com], 31, 45, 213
Cummins Engine Company [http://www.cummins.com], 469
Cushing & Company [http://www.cushingco.com], 480

D

DaimlerChrysler [http://www.daimlerchrysler.com], 238
Del Monte Foods [http://www.delmonte.com], 48
Dell [http://www.dell.com], 13
Deloitte and Touche [http://www.dttus.com/], 42
Delphi Automotive Systems [http://delphiauto.com], 378
Denny's [http://www.dennys.com/] 479
Digital Equipment Corporation [http://www.digital.com], 46, 178, 468
The Disney Company [http://www.disney.com], 45, 181, 284, 463
Dow Chemical Company [http://www.dow.com], 31

E

Eastern Airlines, 228
Eastman Kodak [http://www.kodak.com], 10, 18, 120, 148, 226, 231, 232, 398
Eaton Corporation [http://www.eaton.com]
    empowerment not for everybody at, 306
Electronic Data Systems [http://www.eds.com], 428
Eli Lilly & Company [http://www.elililly.com], 392
Ethics Resource Center [http://ethics.org], 121
Exxon Corporation [http://www.exxon.mobil.com], 372, 465, 481, 493
ExxonMobil [http://www.exxonmobil.com], 83, 466

F

FAA [http://www.faa.gov], 190, 386, 387, 464
FedEx [http://www.fedex.com], 31, 171–173, 234, 235, 500
FleetBoston Financial [http://www.fleet.com], 15
FMC Corporation [http://www.fmc.com], 59
Forbes [http://www.forbes.com], 14
Ford Motor Company [http://www.ford.com]
    conflict management at, 170
    employee involvement program, 151
    global strategy, 29, 30, 32
    introduction to, 9, 12
    leadership at, 316
    "Make Quality Job One," 12, 17
    medical costs due to cardiovascular diseases, 200
    quality, 241, 242
    relationship with UAW, 349, 350, 377, 378
    using technology at, 25
    using Theory Y assumptions at, 138
    work teams at, 220, 221, 232, 240, 422
Fortune [http://fortune.com], 41, 42, 53, 57, 262, 335, 479, 498
Frito-Lay [http://www.fritolay.com], 260
Fuji Xerox [http://www.fujixerox.co.jp], 340

G

Gallup [http://www.gallup.com], 195
Gateway [http://www.gateway.com], 13, 30, 497
    business strategy, 25
    introduction to, 11, 12
General Dynamics [http://www.generaldynamics.com], 120, 121
General Electric [http://www.ge.com], 171, 197, 315, 324, 478, 488, 494, 499
General Electric Medical Systems Group [http://www.gemedicalsystems.com/medical/], 38, 316
General Motors [http://www.gm.com], 6, 9, 165, 176, 220, 230, 234, 239, 264, 316–320, 349, 378, 428, 471
Gerber [http://www.gerber.com], 120
GNS Foods, Inc. [http://www.gnsfoods.com], 164
Graphics Control Corporation, 392
GTE Mobilnet [http://www.gte.com], 488

H

Hallmark Cards [http://hbe.hallmark.com], 230
Hampton Inn Hotels [http://www.hamptoninn.com], 263
Hanjin [http://www.hanjin.com], 461
Hardee's Food Systems [http://www.hardees.com], 207

Harley Davidson

Harley Davidson [http://www.harleydavidson.com], 502
Harpo Entertainment Group [http://www.oprah.com]
    introduction to, 12, 14, 30
    Oprah Winfrey and motivation, goals, and consequences of behavior, 160–161
Harpo Productions, Inc. [http://www.oprah.com]
    management style, 95–96
    mission statement, 95–96
    reflects Oprah's personality, 70–71
    Texas Cattle Ranchers, 284–285, 309
    The Oprah Winfrey Show, 185
Hartford Financial Services Group [http://www.thehartford.com], 479
Hawthorne Works, 9
Hewlett-Packard Company [http://www.hp.com], 83, 231, 232, 431, 452, 457, 483
Hitachi [http://www.hitachi.com], 262
Honda [http://www.honda.com], 31
Honeywell Corporation [http://www.honeywell.com], 83
Hospital Corporation of America, 224, 226
Humane Society [http://www.humanesociety.com], 285
Hyundai [http://www.hyundai.com], 220

I

ICN Pharmaceuticals [http://www.icnpharm.com], 57, 58
Industrial Light and Magic [http://www.ilm.com], 452
Internal Revenue Service [http://www.irs.gov], 423
International Business Machines Corporation (IBM) [http://ibm.com], 6, 15, 32, 34, 49, 60, 171, 197, 226, 392, 451, 455, 468, 502
International Harvester Company [http://www.navistar.com], 324
ITT [http://www.itt.com], 390

J

Jack in the Box [http://www.jackinthebox.com], 121
John Deere and Company [http://www.deere.com], 49
John Hancock Life Insurance Company [http://www.johnhancock.com], 389, 390
Johnson & Johnson [http://www.johnsonandjohnson.com], 6, 31, 53, 120, 213, 222, 335, 336, 406, 502
    credo, 61, 62
    "Live for Life Program," 7
Johnson & Johnson Health Management, Inc. [http://www.jjhcs.com], 213
Johnsonville Foods [http://www.johnsonville.com], 263

K

Kentucky Fried Chicken [http://www.kfc.com], 32, 46
Kim Dawson Agency, 123
Kimberly-Clark [http://www.kimberly-clark.com], 94, 502
Kinko's [http://www.kinkos.com], 480
KL Spring and Stamping Corporation, 232
Korean Airlines [http://www.koreanair.com], 461
Kraft General Foods [http://www.kraft.com], 207

L

Levi Strauss Company [http://www.levistrauss.com], 31, 54, 237, 308, 453
Lincoln Electric [http://www.lincolnelectric.com], 138
Lotus Development Corporation [http://www.lotus.com], 45
Lucent Technologies [http://www.lucent.com], 76
Lucky-Goldstar [http://www.lg.co.kr], 462

M

Malden Mills [http://www.polartec.com], 60
Marriott Corporation [http://www.marriott.com], 163
Marshall Industries [http://www.marshall.com], 178, 179
Matsushita [http://www.mew.co.jp/e-index.html], 262
Mazda [http://www.mazda.com], 31
McDonald's [http://www.mcdonalds.com], 32, 44, 45, 428, 429, 448, 458
McKinsey & Company [http://www.mckinsey.com.], 440
Medtronic [http://www.medtronic.com], 167, 168
Mercedes-Benz [http://www.mercedes-benz.com], 31
Mesa Petroleum, 449
Microsoft [http://www.microsoft.com], 76, 239
Mitsubishi [http://www.mitsubishi.com], 61
Mobil Corporation [http://www.exxonmobil.com], 465, 497
Monsanto Agricultural Company [http://www.monsanto.com], 493
    Valuing Diversity task force, 224
Motorola, Inc. [http://www.motorola.com], 42, 136

N

National Aeronautics and Space Administration [http://www.nasa.gov], 6, 267, 427
National Hispanic Leadership Agenda [http://www.nclr.org], 319
Neiman Marcus [http://www.neimanmarcus.com], 432
Netscape [http://www.netscape.com], 297
Nike [http://www.nike.com], 440, 452
Northern Telecom [http://www.nortelnetworks.com], 76, 272
Northwest Airlines [http://www.nwa.com], 15
Northwestern National Life [http://www.northwesternmutual.com], 15

O

Oak Imaging Group, 104
Oak Technologies [http://www.oaktech.com], 104
Office of Technology Assessments, 408
Ohio State University [http://www.osu.edu], 324, 325, 327, 328, 333
Onsite Engineering and Management, 9
Oracle [http://www.oracle.com], 63
Oregon Cutting Systems [http://www.oregonchain.com], 308

P

Pacific Bell [http://pacbell.com], 406
Pacific Gas and Electric [http://www.pgecorp.com/], 49
PacifiCare [http://www.pacificare.com], 358
Patagonia [http://www.patagonia.com], 43, 44, 60
PepsiCo [http://www.pepsico.com], 61, 260, 434
Perpetual Financial Corporation, 142
Pillsbury [http://www.pillsbury.com], 47
Pitney Bowes [http://www.pitneybowes.com], 120, 195
Pizza Hut [http://www.pizzahut.com], 44, 45
Planned Parenthood [http://www.plannedparenthood.org], 107
Polaroid [http://www.polaroid.com], 483
Precedent Health Center, 358
Prudential Insurance [http://www.prudential.com], 119
Purex [http://www.purex.com], 6, 171

Q

Quaker Oats [http://www.quakeroats.com], 454

R

Rand Corporation [http://www.rand.com], 270
Raytheon [http://www.raytheon.com], 238
Ritz-Carlton Hotel Company [http://www.ritzcarlton.com], 497, 498
Rotary International [http://www.rotary.org], 60
Royal Dutch Shell [http://www.shell.com], 375, 420

S

Sacramento Air Logistics [http://www.mcclellan.af.mil], 207
San Antonio, City of [http://www.ci.sat.tx.us], 319
Sanger-Harris, 168
SAS Institute [http://www.sas.com]
    family-friendly organizational design, 417
Scientech, Inc. [http://www.scientech.com], 15
Scott Paper [http://www.kimberly-clark.com], 94
Sears [http://www.sears.com], 420, 456, 483
Shell Oil Company [http://www.shell.com], 375, 420
Siemens [http://www.siemens.de/en], 76
Silicon Graphics [http://www.sgi.com], 197
Smith and Wesson [http://www.smith-wesson.com], 430
South Florida Water Management District [http://www.swfwmd.state.fl.us/], 432
Southwest Airlines [http://www.southwest.com], 30
    flexibility with job descriptions and work rules at, 387, 410, 411
    humor and handling stress at, 190, 214, 215
    introduction to, 13
    leadership at, 70, 315, 316, 459, 460
    organizational culture of, 447, 448, 452, 472, 473
Southwest Industries, 237
Southwestern Bell [http://www.southwesternbell.com], 450, 452
Square D Company [http://squared.com], 307
Starbucks Coffee Company [http://www.starbucks.com]
    environmental responsibility and, 127
    individual and group decision making at, 246, 247, 279
    introduction to, 13, 14, 30
    leadership and followership at, 314, 315, 341
    mission statement, 101–102
    value system, 101–102
Steelcase [http://www.steelcase.com], 502
Sun Microsystems [http://www.sun.com], 297
Sunbeam [http://www.sunbeam.com], 94
Sundstrand Corporation [http://www.hamiltonsundstrand.com], 480

T

Tandem Computers [http://www.himalaya.com], 116
Tavistock Institute [http://www.tavinstitute.org], 494
Tenneco [http://www.tenneco-automotive.com], 6, 152, 171, 172, 259, 497
Texaco [http://www.texaco.com], 61
Texas A&M [http://www.tamu.edu], 319
Texas Capital Bancshares, 234
Texas Industries [http://www.txi.com], 135, 138, 454
Texas Instruments Inc. [http://www.ti.com], 274
Texas Nameplate [http://www.nameplate.com], 471, 472
3M [http://www.mmm.com], 31, 120, 262, 502
Toyota Motor Manufacturing [http://www.toyota.com], 262, 271
The Travelers Company, 406
Travelers Insurance [http://www.travelers.com], 502

U

UCLA [http://www.ucla.edu], 406
United Auto Workers [http://www.uaw.org], 238, 349, 350, 377, 378
United Services Automobile Association, 406
United Technologies [http://www.utc.com], 480
Universal Studios [http://www.universalstudios.com], 284
University of Michigan [http://www.umich.edu], 201, 323, 324, 496
U.S. Air Force [http://www.af.mil], 228
U.S. Marines [http://www.usmc.mil], 250, 251
U.S. Navy [http://www.usn.mil], 228
U.S. Steel [http://www.ussteel.com], 9, 10, 194
USWeb/CKS [http://www.uswebcks.com], 195

V

Valero Energy Corporation [http://www.valero.com], 6, 399, 427
Virgin Atlantic [http://www.virginatlantic.com], 262
Virtual Office [http://www.virtualoffice.com], 4
Vitatron [http://www.vitatron.com], 168

W

Wallace Company [http://www.wallace.com], 225
Wal-Mart [http://www.wal-mart.com], 57, 319, 432, 449, 450, 451, 483
Wells Fargo [http://www.wellsfargo.com], 55
The Western Company of North America, 6, 169, 178

Westinghouse [http://www.westinghouse.com], 455

Weyerhaeuser [http://www.weyerhaeuser.com], 6, 499

The Workshoppe [http://www.theworkshoppe .com], 297

X

Xerox Corporation [http://www.xerox.com], 230, 233, 239, 340, 457, 597

Xionics Document Technologies, 104

Y

Yahoo! [http://www.yahoo.com], 63

Yugo, 220

Name Index

A

Adams, S., 148, 149, 158
Adkins, J., 207
Adler, A., 136
Agor, W., 259
Alderfer, C., 139, 146, 147
Allen, R. N., 248
Allport, G., 73

B

Baldrige, M., 18, 238, 471
Ball, L., 284
Bandura, A., 161, 165, 166, 450, 494
Barnard, C., 258
Barrett, C., 448
Barton, C., 15
Basadur, M., 262, 263
Beck, R., 258
Behar, H., 278, 341
Benson, H., 212
Bethune, G., 482
Blake, R. R., 325
Blanchard, K. H., 277, 331, 333
Blau, P., 146, 148
Blood, M. R., 135
Boisvert, H., 59
Bramson, R. M., 262, 365, 367
Brenneman, G., 482
Briggs, K., 80
Burke, J., 120, 335
Bush, B., 450
Bush, G., 18, 59

C

Campion, M., 398, 399
Cannon, W. B., 161, 191, 192, 198
Carson, J., 119
Carty, D., 430
Cattell, R., 73
"Chainsaw Al," see Dunlap, A.
Chambers, J., 75, 76
Cisneros, H., 319
Clinton, W. J., 58
Conger, J., 302, 317
Cooper, K., 113, 114, 211
Crandall, R., 459, 460
Currey, G., 452

D

Daft, D., 33
Dawson, K., 123
DeBree, D., 405
DeLorean, J., 317, 319
Deming, W. E., 232, 401
Demo, J., 405
Dewey, J., 136
Dole, E., 476, 477
Drucker, P., 171, 321
Dunlap, A. ("Chainsaw Al"), 93, 94

E

Edison, T., 430
Erickson, G., 454
Etzioni, A., 146, 148, 155, 291–293

F

Feuerstein, A., 60
Fiedler, F. E., 328, 330
Fielding, J., 406
Fisher, G., 18, 231, 398
Fleishman, E., 324
Fonda, J., 365
Forward, G. E., 135, 138
Fox, S., 297
Freud, S., 73, 135, 136

G

Gates, W., 70
Geneen, H., 390
George, B., 168
Gerstner, L., 197
Gilkes, R., 104
Gilligan, 125
Goodnight, J. H., 417, 418
Gothard, T., 307
Grant, J., 234
Green, O., 104
Greene, B., 161, 185
Gross, M., 453

H

Hackman, J. R., 394, 395
Hambrick, D., 238
Harris, P., 60
Hersey, P., 331, 333
Herzberg, F., 140, 141, 143–147, 154, 389, 392–393
Heskett, J. L., 455, 456, 457
Hill, A., 369
Hirschhorn, L., 231
Hitler, A., 321
Hofstede, G., 34, 36, 64, 273, 356
Howell, L., 358

I

Iacocca, L., 238, 314–315, 458
Isenberg, D., 258
Ivancevich, J. M., 167
Ivester, D., 33

J

Jago, A. G., 335–336
James, W., 5, 136
Janes, L., 297
Janis, I. L., 266, 267, 269
Jobs, S., 434, 435
Johnson, L., 252
Johnson, M., 287
Jordan, M., 94
Jung, C., 79, 80, 96, 97, 100, 161, 166

K

Kahn, R., 192
Kant, I., 53
Kanter, R. M., 293, 483
Kearns, D., 233, 340
Kelleher, H., 70, 190, 214, 215, 314, 316, 321, 447, 459, 460
Kelley, H., 181
King, R., 223
Kohlberg, L., 124, 125
Koop, C. E., 200
Korda, M., 293, 294
Koresh, D., 321
Kotter, J. P., 308, 315, 455–457
Kraemer, Jr., H. M., 405
Kroc, R., 458
Kvamme, M., 195

L

Landy, F., 403
Latham, G., 167
Lazarus, R., 192
Levinson, H., 192, 494
Lewin, K., 5, 70, 322, 325, 491, 493, 494
Likert, R., 494
Locke, E. A., 167
Lorenzo, F., 228
Lucas, G., 452
Lyman, H., 309

M

Machiavelli, N., 122, 124, 126, 128–130
Mao, Z., 94
Marriott, J. W., 163
Marshall, G. C., 317
Martin, J., 451
Martinez, A., 483
Maslow, A., 136–139, 143, 146, 147, 154, 463
Mastenbroek, W. F. G., 361
McCanse, A. A., 396
McClelland, D., 139, 140, 144–147, 154, 289, 290, 295
McGrath, J., 198
McGregor, D., 136–138
Merton, R., 6
Miller, D., 434
Mills, J. S., 53
Mintzberg, H., 258, 424
Montana, J., 450
Mouton, J., 325
Murray, H., 15, 139, 140, 145
Myers, I. B., 80, 254

N

Nasser, J., 12, 29, 30, 240

O

Oldham, G. R., 395
O'Loughlin, S., 454
Ornish, D., 212
Ostroff, F., 440

P

Panic, M., 58
Parton, D., 365
Pavlov, I., 161, 165
Peacock, K., 150
Peale, N. V., 277
Perot, H. R., 239, 428
Perrow, C., 429, 430
Peterson, D., 316
Pfeffer, J., 418
Pickens, B., 449
Pickford, M., 284
Platt, L., 231
Powell, B., 488, 489

R

Ramey, E., 202
Rhodes, R., 197
Roddick, A., 321
Rodin, R., 179
Rogers, C., 74,
Rokeach, M., 116, 129
Roosevelt, F. D., 321
Rudin, S., 355
Ryan, N., 450

S

Schein, E. H., 448, 453, 458, 499
Schultz, H., 14, 101, 246, 314, 315, 341
Scully, J., 434
Simmons, R., 114
Simon, H., 249
Sims, H., 397
Skinner, B. F., 494
Sloan, A. P., 316
Smith, A., 53, 135, 136, 153
Smith, D., 440
Smith, F. W., 172, 175
Smith, O., 341
Smith, R., 239
Springsteen, B., 94
Stayer, R., 263
Sullivan, L., 417
Szilagyi, A., 397

T

Taylor, F. W., 6, 136, 172, 390, 391, 401
Thayer, P., 398, 399
Thomas, C., 369
Thomas, L., 454
Thompson, J., 429, 430
Thurow, L., 15
Tjosvold, D., 376
Tomlin, L., 365
Trotman, A., 240
Turner, T., 321

V

Vroom, V., 154, 335, 336

W

Waitt, T., 13
Walton, S., 319, 321, 449
Watson, Sr., T., 451
Weber, M., 134, 135
Welch, J., 197, 315, 479
Winfrey, O., 14, 70–71, 95–96, 160–161, 185, 284–285, 309
Wofford, J. C., 319
Woodward, J., 429, 430
Wriston, W., 239
Wyatt, O., 389

Y

Yearwood, T., 450
Yerkes, R., 6
Yetton, P., 335

Z

Zaleznik, A., 320

Subject Index

ABC model of attitudes, 103–105
Ability diversity, 45–46
Accommodating style, conflict and, 372–373
Achievement, need for, 144
Adaptation perspective, in organizational culture, 456–457
Adaptive culture, 456–457
Adhocracy, 427
Administrative orbiting, conflict and, 369
Affect, of attitude, 103
Affective commitment, 112
Affiliation, need for, 145–146
Age diversity, 42–44
AIDS
    employee rights and, 54–55
    knowledge of, 56
Alderfer's ERG theory, 139
Ambiguity, questionnaire assessing tolerance for, 486–487
Americans with Disabilities Act, 409–410
Anthropocentric, 402
Anthropology, influence of, 6
Anticipatory socialization, 461
Artifacts
    ceremonies and rites, 450–451
    cultural, 449–453
    personal enactment, 449–500
    rituals, 452
    stories, 451–452
    symbols, 452–453
Assumptions of organizational culture, 453–454
Attitudes, 102–115
    ABC model, 103–105
    affect and, 103
    behavior and, 106–108
    changing of at Xionics, 104
    cognitive dissonance and, 105
    formation of, 105–106
    managerial implications, 126–127
    persuasion and change in, 116–117
    social learning and, 106
    social perception and, 86–87
    work and, 108–113
Attribution
    biases, 93–95
    internal and external, 92–93
    managerial implications, 95
    in organizations, 92–95
Attribution theory, 92, 181–183
    consensus, 181
    consistency, 182

distinctiveness, 181–182
informational cues and attributions, 182
model of, 183
Attributional biases
    in China, 93–94
    fundamental attribution error, 93
    self-serving bias, 93
Authority, 285
Authority-obedience manager, 327
Autocratic style of leadership, 322
Avoiding style, conflict and, 371–373

Balloons, 366–367
Bandura's social learning theory, 165–166
Barriers
    first-impression error, 89–90
    implicit personality theory, 89–90
    selective perception, 88–89
    self-fulfilling prophecy, 90–91
    to social perception, 88–91
    stereotype, 89
Behavior
    attitudes and, 106–108
    consideration, 324
    difficult, coping with, 365–367
    ethics and, 120–126
    group, 222–223
    initiating structure, 324
    of leaders, 458–459
    reactions to change, 489–491
    supervisor's leadership, assessing, 326
    at work, 17–18
Behavioral measures, of personality, 79
Belgium
    opening a foreign office, 38
    work definition, 388–389
Benevolents, 150
Bounded rationality model, 249–250
Brainstorming, 269–270
Bulldozers, 366–367

Career planning, 502–503
Centralization, 423
Ceremonies of organizational culture, 450–451
Challenge, 3
Challenge exercises
    ambiguity, tolerance for, 486–487
    brain hemisphere selection, 256
    change, perceptions of, 16
    company decentralization, 425
    conflict-handling style, 375

correcting poor performance, 180
effective followers, 339
employee empowerment, 235
employee value selection, 143
force field analysis, applying, 492
frazzle factor, 191
group cohesion, 229
healthy work environment, 404
job diagnosis, 396–397
job satisfaction, 109
knowledge of AIDS, 56
learning style inventory, 20
organizational culture and ethics, 470
Protestant ethic, 134
self-empowerment, 303–304
self-monitoring assessment, 77
self-reliance, 205
supervisor's leadership style, 326
work value inventory, 118
Challenger disaster, groupthink framework and, 267
Change, 3
    acquisition in socialization process and, 462
    analyzing perceptions of, 16
    applying force field analysis to, 492
    assessing tolerance for ambiguity, 486–487
    behavioral reactions to, 489–491
    challenge of, 15–18
    change agent's role, 483–484
    cultural assumptions and values and, 486–487
    disenchantment and, 490–491
    disengagement and, 489–490
    disidentification and, 490
    disorientation and, 491
    disruption of interpersonal relationships and, 485
    external forces of, 478–481
    fear of loss and, 485
    fear of failure and, 485
    fear of the unknown and, 485
    forces for organizational, 477–483
    in global marketplace, 32–33
    globalization and, 478–479
    incremental, 483
    internal forces of, 481–483
    interventions for organizational culture and, 467
    Lewin's model of, 491–494
    managing ethical behavior, 480–481

managing organizational behavior during, 18
managing resistance to, 487–489
in organizational culture, 465–472
personality conflicts and, 485
planned, 478
politics and, 485–486
process of, in organizations, 484–494
resistance to, 485–487
scope of, 483
strategic, 483
technological innovations and, 51–52, 480
transformational, 483
unplanned, 478
workforce diversity and, 479
Change agent, role of, 483–484
Character assassination, conflict and, 369
Charismatic leadership, 321–322
China
    attributional biases, 93–94
    business practices, 32
    Coca-Cola in, 33
    decision making, 273
    guanxi, 32
    team reward systems in, 178
Clams, 365–366
Classical conditioning, learning in organizations, 161–162
Coercive power, 286, 291–292
    guidelines for use, 288
Cognition, persuasion and, 114–115
Cognitive dissonance, 105
Cognitive moral development, 124–126
Cognitive structure, in social perception, 87
Cognitive style, in decision making, 253–254
Cohesion
    assessing, 229
    in groups, 222, 227–229
Collaborating style, conflict and, 372–376
Collectivism, 34
Commitment, in groups, 225–226
Communication
    conflict and, 356
    nonverbal, 87–88
    social perception and, 87–88
    socialization and, 463
    verbal, 87
Compensation, as defense mechanism, 363–364
Compensation award, 201–202
Competing style, conflict and, 372–374
Competition
    challenges for managers and, 30–31
    international business, 15–16
Competitive challenges, 30–31
Complainers, 365–366
Complexity, 420–421
Compromising, conflict style and, 372–374
Conflict, 350
    accommodating, 372–373

administrative orbiting, conflict and, 369
assessment of handling style, 375
authority relationships and, 353
avoiding, 371–373
causes of, in organizations, 352–356
changing personnel and, 370
changing structure and, 370
collaborating, 372–376
common resources and, 353
communication barriers and, 356
competing, 372–374
compromising, 372–374
confronting and negotiating, 370–371
consequences of, 351
coping with difficult behavior, 365–367
cultural differences and, 356
defense mechanisms, 363–365
distributive bargaining and, 371
effective techniques for dealing with, 369–371
emotions and, 356
ethics and, 354–355
expanding resources and, 370
forms of, in organizations, 357–361
functional vs. dysfunctional, 350–351
globalization and, 356–357
goal differences and, 353
importance of management skills, 350
ineffective techniques for dealing with, 369
integrative negotiation and, 371
interdependence and, 353
intergroup, 359
interorganizational, 357–358
interpersonal, 361–367
interrole, 359
intrapersonal, 359–361
intrarole, 360
jurisdictional ambiguities and, 354
management strategies and techniques, 367–371
management styles, 371–376
managerial implications, 376–377
nature of in organizations, 350–352
perceptions and, 354
personal factors in, 354–356
personalities and, 354
person-role, 360
power networks, 361–363
skills and abilities and, 354
specialization and, 352–353
status inconsistencies and, 353–354
structural factors in, 352–354
superordinate goals and, 369–370
values and, 354–355
win-lose vs. win-win strategies, 368
Consensus, attribution theory and, 181
Consequential theory, 53
Consistency, attribution theory and, 182

Contextual variables, of organizational design, 417
Continuance commitment, 112
Contributions, social exchange and equity, 147
Control, in groups, 226
Conversion, defense mechanism, 364
Counterdependence, 204
Counter-role behavior, 408–409
Country club manager, 327
Creativity
    in decision making, 259–263
    individual influences on, 259–260
    individual/organization fit and, 260–263
    in Japan, 262
    organizational influences on, 260
    in Poland, 262
    problem solving and, 261
Cross-cultural sensitivity, developing, 37–40
Cross-training, 392
Cultural differences
    conflict and, 356
    Hofstede's dimensions of, 34
    individualism vs. collectivism, 34–35
    masculinity vs. femininity, 36
    power distance and, 36
    time orientation and, 36
    uncertainty avoidance and, 36
    understanding, 34–37
    U.S. culture and, 36
    values and, 119–120
Cultural diversity, 40–41
Cultural theory, 54
Customer focus, 17

Decentralization, questionnaire assessing, 425
Decision making
    bounded rationality model, 249–250
    creativity and, 259–263
    decision support systems, 274–275
    effective, 248–249
    escalation of commitment, 252–253
    ethical issues in, 277
    expert systems, 273–274
    functions of left and right brain hemispheres in, 257
    garbage can model, 250
    in Germany, 264
    individual influences on, 255–263
    intuition, role of, 258–259
    Jung's cognitive styles and, 253–255
    managerial implications, 277–278
    Marines' "rule of three," 251
    models of, 248–250
    nonprogrammed decision, 247
    participation in, 263–265
    process of, 247–248
    programmed decision, 247
    rational model, 249
    risk and, 251–252

risk aversion, 252
technological aids to, 273–277
Z problem-solving model, 254–255
Decision making by groups
advantages and disadvantages of, 266
brainstorming, 269–270
cultural issues in, 273
Delphi technique, 270
devil's advocacy technique, 270–271
dialectical inquiry technique, 271
group decision support systems, 275–276
group polarization, 269
groupthink, 266–269
level of participation, 265
nominal group technique, 270
quality circles and quality teams, 271–272
self-managed teams, 272–273
social decision schemes, 265–266
synergy, 265
techniques for, 269–272
technological aids to, 273–277
virtual workplace and, 276
Defense mechanisms
compensation, 363–364
conversion, 364
displacement, 363–364
fantasy, 364–365
fixation, 363–364
flight/withdrawal, 364
identification, 363–364
negativism, 363–364
rationalization, 363–364
Delphi technique, 270
Demands, social exchange and equity, 146–147
Democratic style of leadership, 322
Desktop videoconferencing systems, 276
Devil's advocacy technique, 270–271
Dialectical inquiry technique, 271
Differentiation
between marketing and engineering, 419
in organizational design, 419–421
Discounting principle, situation's characteristics
and, 88
Discretion, having none and empowerment,
305–306
Disenchantment, change and, 490–491
Disengagement, change and, 489–490
Disidentification, change and, 490
Disorientation, change and, 491
Displacement, defense mechanism, 363–364
Distinctiveness, attribution theory and, 181–182
Distress, 190
Distributive bargaining, conflict and, 371
Distributive justice, 59
Diversity
ability, 45–46
age, 42–44
cultural, 40–41
gender, 41–42

Divisionalized form, 426–427
Due process nonaction, conflict and, 369
Dynamic follower, 338–340
Dysfunctional conflict, 351

Effective decision, 248–249
Ego-ideal, 192
Elaboration likelihood model of persuasion, 115
Emotions, conflict and, 356
Employee empowerment grid, 305–306
Employee rights, 54–55
Empowerment, 302
employee empowerment grid, 305–306
managing political behavior and, 302–308
mission defining and, 305–306
no discretion and, 305–306
organizational culture and, 471–472
and participation, foundations for in decision making, 264–265
participatory, 305–306
self-empowerment, 303–304
self-management and, 305–306
skills, 236
task setting and, 305–306
teams and, 234–238
Enacted values, 453
Encounter, socialization and, 461
Engineering, influence of, 6
Entitleds, 150
Environment, organizational design and,
431–434
Environmental uncertainty, 433
Equity sensitives, 149–150
Equity theory
Adam's theory of inequity, 148–149
demands and contributions, 146–147
new perspectives on, 149–151
resolution of inequity, 149
social exchange and, 146–151
ERG theory, 139
Escalation of commitment, in decision making,
252–253
Espoused values, 453
Ethics
behavior and, 120–126, 480–481
codes of, 60–61
cognitive moral development and,
124–126
conflict and, 354–355
consequential theory of, 53
considerations in organizational development, 503
cultural theory of, 54
employee rights, 54–55
four-way test, 61
issues in, 52–61, 122
locus of control, 123–124
Machiavellianism, 124
managerial implications, 126–127

model of ethical behavior, 123
organizational culture and, 469–470
organizational justice, 59
romantic involvements, 57–58
rule-based theory of, 53
sexual harassment, 55–57
social responsibility, 60
use of power, 288–289
value systems, 122–123
whistle-blowing, 59–60
Etzioni's power analysis, 292
Eustress, 198
Executives, tenure of and organizational performance, 239
Expatriate manager, 36
Expectancy model for motivation, 152
Expectancy theory
cultural differences in motivation, 154
expectancy, 151
instrumentality, 151
moral maturity, 153–154
motivation and, 151–154
motivational problems and, 153
valence of an outcome, 151
Experiential exercises
behavioral norms, identifying, 474–475
changes at work, 27
chaos and the manager's job, 412–414
Chinese, Indian, and American values,
129–130
correcting poor performance, 188
design and build a castle, 446
empowerment in classroom, 313
ethical behavior, 131
ethical dilemmas, 68
gender role stressors, 217
inequity, redressing, 158–159
international orientation, 65–68
job redesign, 414–415
layoff decision, making 280–282
leadership and influence, 346–348
MBTI types and management styles,
98–100
national culture and leadership, 343–345
organizational cultures, contrasting, 475
organizational diagnosis of a university,
507–508
reinforcement, positive and negative,
187–188
social power role playing, 311–312
stereotypes in employment interviews, 100
team building for effectiveness, 509
tower building group dynamics activity,
244–245
unethical behavior, conflicts over,
380–381
wilderness experience, 282–283
words and sentences company, 444–446
work needs, 157–158

workplace stress diagnosis, 217–218
world bank intergroup negotiation, 381–384
worst job, 28
Expert power, 287
  guidelines for use, 288
Expert system, 48
External attribution, 92–93
External incentives, motivation and, 135–136
Extinction, 165
Extroversion preference, 80–81

Familiarity, in social perception, 86
Fantasy, defense mechanism, 364–365
Feeling preference, 81–82
Femininity, 36
Fiedler's contingency theory
  leader-member relations, 329
  least preferred coworker, 329
  position power, 329
  situational favorableness, 329
  task structure, 329
First-impression error, social perception and, 89–90
Fit perspective, in organizational culture, 456
Fixation, 363
Flextime, 407
Flight/withdrawal, defense mechanism, 364
Followers
  dynamic, 338–340
  effective, 337–339
  types of, 337–338
Followership, 336–340
Force field analysis, 492
Formal leadership, 315
Formal organization, 9
  elements of, 10
Formalization, in organizational design, 423
Frazzle factor questionnaire, 191
Functional conflict, 351
Fundamental attribution error, 93

Garbage can model, 250
Gender diversity, 41–42
Gender
  leadership and, 321
  stress and, 202
  thinking/feeling preference, 81–82
Germany
  decision making in, 264
  work definition, 388–389
  work design in, 401–402
Glass ceiling, 41
Globalization
  changes in global marketplace, 32–33
  conflict and, 356–357
  developing cross-cultural sensitivity in, 37–40
  environment, managing in, 31–39

opening foreign offices, 38–39
organizational culture and, 468–469
organizational design and, 438
transnational organization, 31
understanding cultural differences, 34–37
Goal setting
  characteristics of effective goals, 168–169
  increasing work motivation and task performance, 169–170
  management by objectives, 171
  organizational design and, 434–436
  reducing role stress of conflicting expectations, 170–171
  stress prevention and, 209
  at work, 167–172
Great Britain, opening a foreign office, 38
Group behavior
  cohesion, 222
  formation of, 223–230
  loss of individuality, 223
  norms of, 222
  polarization of, 269
  social loafing, 223
Group development, stages of
  control and sanctions, 226
  decision making, 225
  motivation and commitment, 225–226
  mutual acceptance, 225
Groups
  behavior of, 222–223
  characteristics of effective, 221
  characteristics of mature, 226–230
  cohesion of, 222, 227–229
  formation and development of, 223–230
Groupthink, 266–269
  Challenger disaster and, 267
  guidelines for preventing, 268
  symptoms of, 268
Guanxi, 32

Hawthorne studies, 9
Health promotion programs, 502
Hersey-Blanchard situational leadership model, 335
Herzberg's two-factor theory
  critique of, 143–144
  hygiene factors, 142–143
  job reward factors questionnaire, 143
  motivation factors, 140–142
Heuristics, 249–250
Hierarchy of authority, 423
Hiring, in organizational culture, 459–460
Hofstede's dimensions of cultural differences, 34
Homeostasis, 192
Hostile-aggressives, 365–366
Human behavior
  in organizations, 3–7
  understanding, 4–5
Humanistic theory of personality, 74

Hungary, opening a foreign office, 38
Hygiene factor, 140

Identification, defense mechanism, 363–364
Implicit personality theory, social perceptions and, 90
Impoverished manager, 327
Impression management, social perception and, 91–92
Incremental change, 483
Indecisive stallers, 366–367
Individual differences, organizational behavior and, 71–72
Individual-organizational exchange relationship, 147
Individualism, 34
  loss of, 223
Inequity
  Adam's theory of, 148–149
  resolution of, 149
Influence, 285
  in political behavior, 295–299
  tactics for, 295–299
Informal leadership, 315
Informal organization, elements of, 9
Information-processing technologies, organizational design and, 438–439
Instrumental values, 116–117
Instrumentality, 151
Integrated involvement, in teams, 233
Integration, 421–422
Integrative approach to personality, 74
Integrative negotiation, conflict and, 369
Intentions, in social perception, 88
Interactional psychology, 71
Intergroup conflict, 359
Intergroup sources of power, 290–291
Internal attribution, 92–93
Internal needs, motivation and, 134–135
International competition, 15–16
Interorganizational conflict, 357–358
Interpersonal conflict, 361–367
  coping with difficult behavior, 365–367
  defense mechanisms, 363–365
  power networks, 361–363
Interpersonal demands, 462
Interpersonal power, 286–288
Interrole conflict, 359
Intrapersonal conflict, 359–361
Intrarole conflict, 360
Introversion preference, 80–81
Intuiting preference, 81
Intuition, role in decision making, 258–259
Israel, work definition, 388–389

Japan
  decision making, 273
  leadership styles in, 324–325
  lean production methods, 401

M-oriented behavior, 324–325
managing creativity in decision making, 262
opening a foreign office, 39
P-oriented behavior, 324–325
quality circles in, 271
social context and business in, 88
sociotechnical systems, 401
team reward systems in, 178
work attitudes and, 108, 112
work definition, 388–389
work design in, 401
Job characteristics inventory, 397–398
Job characteristics model, 394–395
Job characteristics theory, 393–398
Job descriptive index, 108, 110
Job design
alternative approaches to, 398–404
alternative work patterns, 406–407
cross-training, 392
flextime, 407
interdisciplinary approach to, 399–401
job characteristics inventory, 397–398
job characteristics model, 394–395
job characteristics theory, 393–398
job diagnostic survey, 394
job enlargement, 391–392
job enrichment, 392–393
job rating form, 396–397
job rotation, 391–392
job sharing, 405–406
managerial implications, 409–410
outcomes from various approaches, 400
skill development, 409
social information-processing model, 398–399
task revision, 408–409
telecommuting, 405–406
traditional approaches to, 390–398
virtual office, 407
Job diagnostic survey, 394
Job enlargement, 391–392
Job enrichment, 392–393
Job rating form, 396–397
Job redesign, 501–502
stress prevention and, 207–208
Job reward factors questionnaire, 143
Job rotation, 391–392
Job satisfaction, 108–111
assessing, 109–110
organizational citizenship behavior, 111–112
work attitudes and, 111–112
Job sharing, 405–406
Job strain model, 208
Jobs, 387
diagnosing, 396–397
in organizations, 389–390
Judging preference, 81–82

Jungian theory, 253–255, 258, 273
Jurisdictional ambiguities, 354

Kanter's symbols of powerlessness, 293–294
Kilmann-Saxton culture-gap survey, 464
Know-it-alls, 366–367
Knowledge
application of, 22–23
objective, 19
Korda's symbols of power, 294

Laissez-faire style of leadership, 322
Leader–member relations, 329
Leaders
allocate rewards, 459
behavior, 458–459
crises and, 458
as distinct personalities, 320
focus of, 458
hiring and firing by, 459–460
physical attributes, personality, and abilities of, 318–319
role in shaping and reinforcing organizational culture, 458–460
women, 321
Leadership
assessing supervisor's, 326
autocratic style, 322
behaviors, 324–325
charismatic, 321–322
consideration behavior, 324
cultural differences in, 340
democratic style, 322
effectiveness in the contingency theory, 330
formal, 315
guidelines for, 335–336
Hersey-Blanchard situational leadership model, 335
informal, 315
initiating structure, 324
laissez-faire style, 322
M-oriented behavior, 324–325
management and, 315–318
managerial implications for, 340–341
managerial grid, 325–327
P-oriented behavior, 324–325
path–goal theory of, 331–332
situational leadership model, 333–335
style and emotional climate at work and, 322–323
styles in Japan, 324–325
transformational, 319–320
Type I theories of, 318–322
Type II theories of, 322–328
Type III theories of, 328–330
Type IV theories of, 330–335
typology for theories of, 317

Vroom-Yetton-Jago normative decision model, 332–334
Lean production methods, in work design, 401
Learned optimism, stress prevention and, 209–210
Learning
Bandura's social learning theory, 165–166
classical conditioning, 161–162
operant conditioning, 162
about organizational behavior, 23
in organizations, 161–167
personality differences and, 166–167
strategies of reinforcement, punishment, and extinction, 162–165
from structured activity, 22
Learning style inventory, 20
Least preferred coworker, 328–329
Left brain hemisphere
functions of, 257
assessing, 256
Legitimate power, 286
guidelines for use, 288
Lewin's change model, 491–494
moving, 493
refreezing, 493
unfreezing, 491, 493
Locus of control, 123–124
characteristic in organizations, 75

M-oriented behavior, 324–325
Machiavellianism, 124
Machine bureaucracy, 426
Maintenance functions, in teams, 234
Management
development of, 501
ethical issues at work and, 52–61
in a global environment, 31–39
influence of, 6–7
leadership and, 315–318
of technological innovation, 48–52
of workforce diversity, 40–47
Management by objectives, 171
organizational development and, 496–497
Managerial grid, 325–327
Managerial implications
attitudes, values, and ethics at work, 126–127
changing nature of work, 409–410
creating a conflict-positive organization, 376–377
decision making, 277–278
facing challenges, 61–62
fitting people and structures together, 441
foundations for the future, 24–25
leaders and followers as partners, 340–341
managing change, 504
many ways to motivate people, 154–155
organizational culture challenge, 472
performance management is a key task, 184–185

personality, perception, and attribution at work, 95
productivity, quality, and teamwork, 240–241
stress without distress, 213–214
using power effectively, 308–309
Managers, 320
authority-obedience, 327
competitive challenges and, 30–31
conflict management for, 371–376
country club, 327
decision-making risk, 252
importance of conflict management skills, 350
impoverished, 327
organization man, 327
structural roles of, 439
team, 327
Managing political behavior in organizations, 299–300
Masculinity, 36
Mature groups, characteristics of
behavioral norms, 227
cohesion of, 227–229
purpose and mission, 226
status structure, 228–230
McClelland's personality and learned needs, 139–140
McGregor's X and Y theories, 137–138
Medicine, influence of, 7
Mentoring, performance and, 184
Message characteristics, persuasion and, 114
Michigan Organizational Assessment Questionnaire, 496
Miller's integrative framework of structural and strategic dimensions, 434
Minnesota Multiphasic Personality Inventory, 79
Minnesota Satisfaction Questionnaire, 108, 110
Mission
defining, empowerment and, 305–306
in groups, 226
Mood, in social perception, 87
Moral maturity, 153–154
Motivating potential score, 395, 397
Motivation
cultural differences in, 154
equity theory, 146–151
expectancy model for, 152
expectancy theory of, 151–154
external incentives and, 135–136
factors, 140–142
in groups, 225–226
Herzberg's two-factor theory, 140–146
internal needs and, 134–135
managerial implications, 154–155
Maslow's hierarchy of needs, 136–139
McClelland's needs theory, 139–140
McGregor's X and Y theories, 137–138

moral maturity and, 153–154
problems of, 153
and work behavior, 133–136
Multicultural teams, 239–240
Murray Thematic Apperception Test, 140
Mutual acceptance, in groups, 225
Myers-Briggs Type Indicator (MBTI) personality theory, 79–85
four basic preferences, 80–82
sixteen types, 82–85

Needs
for achievement, 144
for affiliation, 145–146
Alderfer's ERG theory, 139
internal, 134–135
job reward factors questionnaire, 143
Maslow's hierarchy of needs, 136–139
McClelland's personality and learned needs, 139–140
McGregor's X and Y theories, 137–138
for power, 144–145
Negative affect, 78
Negative consequences in reinforcement and punishment, 163
Negativism, defense mechanism, 363–364
Negativists, 366–367
Netherlands (The), work definition, 388–389
Nominal group technique, 270
Nonaction, conflict and, 369
Nonprogrammed decision, 247
Nonverbal communication, social perception and, 87–88
Normative commitment, 113
Normative power, 291–292

Objective knowledge, 19, 21
Operant conditioning, 162
Organization man manager, 327
Organizational behavior, 3
citizenship behavior, 111–112
individual differences and, 71–72
interactional psychology, 71
interdisciplinary influences on, 5–7
learning style inventory, 20
managing during change, 18
objective knowledge and, 19, 21
operant conditioning, 162
political, 295–300
skill development and, 21–22
Organizational commitment, 112
Organizational culture
adaptation perspective, 456–457
adaptive vs. nonadaptive, 457
artifacts of, 449–453
assessing, 463–464
assumptions of, 453–454
changing, 465–472

developing empowerment and quality in, 471–472
developing ethical, 469–470
developing global, 468–469
fit perspective, 456
functions and effects of, 455–457
hiring and firing and, 459–460
inventory of, 463–464
Kilmann-Saxton culture-gap survey, 464
leader's role in shaping and reinforcing of, 458–460
levels of, 448–449
managerial implications, 472
rewards and, 459
role of, 448–454
socialization, 460–463
strong culture perspective, 455–456
triangulation, 464
values of, 453
Organizational design
basic dimensions of, 423–424
centralization, 423
complexity, 420–421
contextual variables of, 427–436
demands on organizational processes and, 439
differentiation, 419–421
environment and, 431–434
formalization, 423
globalization and, 438
hierarchy of authority, 423
information processing technologies and, 438–439
integration, 421–422
key processes of, 417–422
life cycles in organizations, 436–440
managerial implications, 441
mechanistic and organic forms, 433
questionnaire assessing decentralization, 425
relationship among key elements of, 437
size and, 427–429
specialization, 419, 423
standardization, 423
strategy and goals, 434–436
technology and, 429–431
Organizational development
career planning, 502–503
cycle of, 495
diagnosis and needs analysis, 495–496
ethical considerations in, 503
evaluate effectiveness of, 504
health promotion programs, 502
individual-focused techniques, 500–503
interventions of, 494–503
job redesign, 501–502
large group interventions, 499
management by objectives, 496–497
management development, 501

managerial implications, 504
organization- and group-focused techniques, 496–500
process consultation, 499–500
product and service quality programs, 497–498
role negotiation, 501
sensitivity training, 500–501
skills training, 500
survey feedback, 496
team building, 498–499
Organizational distress
compensation award, 201–202
participation problems, 201
performance decrements, 201
Organizational justice, 59
Organizational life cycles, 436–440
Organizational politics, 295
Organizational socialization, 460–463
Organizational stress prevention
goal setting, 209
job redesign, 207–208
job strain model, 208
role negotiation, 209
social support systems, 209–210
Organizational structure, 9, 417
adhocracy, 427
cautionary notes about, 440–441
divisionalized form, 426–427
emerging, 440
machine bureaucracy, 426
managerial implications, 441
professional bureaucracy, 426
simple structure, 424–427
Organizations
attribution in, 92–95
formal and informal, 9–11
forms and sources of power in, 286–291
forms of conflict in, 357–361
human behavior in, 3–7
learning in, 161–167
power relationships in, 362
systems view of, 7–9
work in, 387–390
Overdependence, 204–205

P-oriented behavior, 324–325
Participation problem, 201
Participative decision making, 263–264
Participatory empowerment, 305–306
Path–goal theory of leadership, 331–332
People, as organizational resources, 8
Perceiver, characteristics of in social perception, 86–87
Perceiving preference, 81–82
Perceptions, conflict and, 354
Performance
actual and measured, 174
attribution theory, 181–183

coaching, counseling, and mentoring, 184
correcting poor, 180–184
defining, 172–173
feedback of, 175–176
managerial implications, 184–185
measuring, 173–175
rewarding, 177–180
Performance appraisal, 173
characteristics of effective, 177
developing people and enhancing careers, 176–177
Performance decrement, 201
Performance reward
individual incentive vs. profit sharing, 179
individual vs. team reward systems, 178
power of earning, 178–180
Personal enactment of organizational culture, 449–500
Personal power, 290
Personality, 72–79
behavioral measure of, 79
characteristics in organizations, 74–79
conflict and, 354
conflicts and change, 485
differences in learning, 166–167
hardiness of, 203–204
humanistic theory, 74
integrative approach, 74
and learned needs, McClelland's, 139–140
locus of control, 75
managerial implications and, 95
measuring of, 79
Myers-Briggs Type Indicator, 79–85
positive/negative affect, 78
projective test of, 79
psychodynamic theory, 73–74
self-esteem, 75–76
self-monitoring, 76–78
self-report questionnaire of, 79
theories, 73–74
trait theory of, 73
Person-role conflict, 360
Persuasion
attitude change and, 113–115
cognitive routes to, 113–115
elaboration likelihood model of, 115
message characteristics, 114
source characteristics, 113–114
target characteristics, 114
Physical appearance, in social perception, 87
Planned change, 478
Poland, creativity in decision making and new economy, 262
Political behavior
change and, 485–486
empowerment and, 302–308
influence tactics in, 295–299
managing relationship with boss, 300–302

in organizations, 295–300
in organizations, managing, 299–300
Position power, 329
Positive affect, 78
Positive consequences in reinforcement and punishment, 162–163
Power
analysis of, 291–293
coercive, 286, 291–292
coercive, guidelines for use, 288
concept of, 285–286
empowerment, 302–308
ethical use of, 288–289
Etzioni's power analysis, 292
expert, 287
expert, guidelines for use, 288
forms and sources in organizations, 286–291
guidelines for ethical use of, 288
intergroup sources of, 290–291
interpersonal forms of, 286–288
Kanter's symbols of powerlessness, 293–294
Korda's symbols of power, 294
legitimate, 286
legitimate, guidelines for use, 288
managerial implications, 308–309
managing relationship with boss, 300–302
need for, 144–145
normative, 291–292
in organizations, 286–291
personal, 290
powerlessness, 293
referent, 287
referent, guidelines for use, 288
relationships in organizations, 362
reward, 286
reward, guidelines for use, 288
social, 290
strategic contingencies, 291
symbols of, 293–294
utilitarian, 291–292
Power distance, 35
Power networks, 361–363
Powerlessness, Kanter's symbols of, 293–294
Preventive stress management, 205–213
comprehensive health promotion and, 213
framework for, 205
individual, 209–213
organizational, 207–209
primary prevention, 205, 207
secondary prevention, 205, 207
tertiary prevention, 205, 207
Primary stress prevention, 205, 207
Procedural justice, 59
Process consultation, 499–500
Professional bureaucracy, 426
Programmed decision, 247
Projective test, 79

Protestant work ethic, 134–135
    questionnaire for, 134
Psychoanalysis, 135
Psychodynamic theory of personality, 73–74
Psychological intimacy, in teams, 232
Psychology, influence of, 5–6
Punishment, 163–165
Purpose, in groups, 226
Pygmalion effect, 90–91, 304

Quality
    behavior at work and, 17–18
    customer focused for, 17
    developing in organizational culture,
        471–472
    managerial implications, 240–241
    total quality management, 17
    at work, 17–18
Quality circles
    in group decision making, 271–272
    teams and, 232
Quality program, organizational development
    and, 497–498
Quality teams, 232
    in group decision making, 271–272

Rationality, in decision making, 249
Rationalization, defense mechanism, 363–364
Referent power, 287
    guidelines for use, 288
Reinforcement, 162–164
    schedules of, 164
Reinvention, 52
Reward power, 286
    guidelines for use, 288
Rewards
    how leaders allocate, 459
    performance and, 177–180
Right brain hemisphere
    functions of, 257
    assessing, 256
Risk aversion, 252
Risk, decision making and, 251–253
Rites of organizational culture, 450–451
Rituals of organizational culture, 452
Robotics, 48
Role behavior, performance consequences of,
    408
Role demands, 462
Role negotiation, 501
    stress prevention and, 209
Romantic involvements, 57–58
Rule-based theory, 53
Russia, value differences and business in, 119

Sanctions, in groups, 226
Satisfice, 249
Scandinavia, work design in, 402–403
Secondary stress prevention, 205, 207

Secrecy, conflict and, 369
Selective perception, 88–89
Self-concept, in social perception, 87
Self-efficacy, in Bandura's social learning
    theory, 165–166
Self-esteem, 75–76
Self-fulfilling prophecy, social perceptions and,
    90–91
Self-image, 192
Self-interest, 135
Self-managed teams, 236–238
Self-management, empowerment and, 305–306
Self-monitoring, 76–78
    assessing, 77
Self-reliance, 204–205
    counterdependence and, 204
    overdependence and, 204–205
Self-report questionnaire
    Minnesota Multiphasic Personality Inven-
        tory, 79
    Myers-Briggs Type Indicator, 79
Self-serving bias, 93–94
Sensing preference, 81
Sensitivity training, 500–501
Sexual harassment, 55–57
Simple structure, 424–427
Situation
    characteristics of in social perception, 88
    discounting principle, 88
Situational favorableness
    leader–member relations, 329
    position power, 329
    task structure, 329
Situational leadership model, 334–336
Size, organizational design and, 427–429
Skill, application of, 22–23
Skill development, 19, 21–22
    in job design, 409
Skills training, 500
Social benefits of teams
    integrated involvement, 233
    psychological intimacy, 232
Social context, in social perception, 88
Social decision schemes, 265–266
Social exchange, equity theory and, 146–151
Social information-processing model, 398–399
Social learning
    attitudes and, 106
    Bandura's theory of, 165–166
Social loafing, 223
Social perception, 83–92
    attitudes and, 86–87
    barriers to, 88–91
    cognitive structure, 87
    familiarity, 86
    first impression error, 89–90
    implicit personality theory, 90
    impression management, 91–92
    managerial implications, 95

model for, 86
    mood and, 87
    nonverbal communication, 87–88
    perceiver's characteristics, 86–87
    physical appearance, 87
    self-concept, 87
    self-fulfilling prophecies, 90–91
    situation's characteristics, 88
    social context, 88
    target's characteristics, 86–88
    verbal communication, 87
Social power, 290
Social responsibility, 60
Socialization
    anticipatory, 461
    change and acquisition, 462
    as cultural communication, 463
    encounter, 461
    interpersonal demands, 462
    outcomes of, 462
    role demands, 462
    stages of, 460–462
Sociology, influence of, 6
Sociotechnical systems, in work design, 401
Source characteristics, persuasion and, 113–114
South Korea, opening a foreign office, 39
Specialization, 419, 423
    conflict and, 352–353
Standardization, 423
Status inconsistencies, conflict and, 353–354
Status structure, in groups, 228–230
Stereotype, social perceptions and, 89
Stories, of organizational culture, 451–452
Strain, 190
Strategic change, 483
Strategic contingencies, 291
Strategies in learning
    extinction, 165
    negative consequences, 163
    positive consequences, 162–163
    punishment, 164–165
    reinforcement, 162–164
Strategy, organizational design and, 434–436
Stress
    benefits of eustress, 198–199
    cognitive appraisal approach, 192
    consequences of, 198–202
    costs of distress, 199
    frazzle factor questionnaire, 191
    gender and, 202
    homeostatic/medical approach, 192
    individual distress, 199–201
    infotech stressor, 195
    interpersonal demands, 194, 196–197
    managerial implications, 213–214
    nonwork demands, 194, 197–198
    organizational distress, 201–202
    performance and health benefits of,
        198–199

personality hardiness, 203–204
person-environment fit approach, 192
physical demands, 194, 197
prevention of, 205–213
psychoanalytic approach, 192–193
role demands, 194, 196
self-reliance, 204–205
sources of, at work, 193–198
stress-strain relationship, individual differences in, 202–205
stress response, 193
task demands, 194–195
technostress, 407
Type A behavior pattern, 202–203
Yerkes-Dodson law, 198–199
Stressor, 190
Strong culture, 455–456
Strong situation, 78
Structural roles of managers, 439
Superagreeables, 365–367
Superordinate goals, conflict and, 369–370
Supervisor's leadership, assessing, 326
Survey feedback, 496
Survey of organizations, 496
Symbols of organizational culture, 452–453
Synergy, 265

Target
    characteristics of in social perception, 86–88
    characteristics, persuasion and, 114
Task demands, stress and, 194–195
Task environment, 8, 431–432
Task functions, in teams, 233–234
Task revision, in job design, 408–409
Task setting, empowerment and, 305–306
Task structure, 329
Tasks, performance and goal setting, 169
Team building, 498–499
Team manager, 327
Teams, 221
    comparison of new and old work environments, 231
    empowerment and, 234–238
    manager, 327
    managerial implications, 240–241
    multicultural, 239–240
    purpose of, 230–231
    quality circles and, 232
    self-managed, 236–238, 272–273
    social benefits of, 232–233
    task and maintenance functions, 233–234
    upper echelons and, 238–240
    at work, 230–234
Technocentric, 402
Technological innovation
    alternative work arrangements and, 49–50

changing nature of managerial work, 50–51
    helping employees adjust to change, 51–52
    managing, 48–52
    telecommuting, 49–50
Technological interdependence, 430
Technology, 48
    aids to decision making, 273–277
    change and, 480
    organizational design and, 429–431
Technostress, 407
Telecommuting, 49, 405–406
Terminal values, 116–117
Tertiary stress prevention, 205, 207
Thinking preference, 81–82
Time management, stress prevention and, 210–211
Time orientation, 36
Total quality management, 17
Trait theory of personality, "Big Five" personality traits, 73–74
Transformational change, 483
Transformational coping, 204
Transformational leadership, 319–320
Transnational organization, 31
Triangulation, in organizational culture, 464
Type A behavior pattern, 202–203
Type I universal trait theories
    charismatic leadership, 321–322
    leaders' physical attributes, personality, and abilities, 318–319
    transformational leadership, 319–320
Type II universal behavior theories, 322–328
Type III situational trait theories
    Fiedler's contingency theory, 328–329
    leadership effectiveness and, 329–330
Type IV situational behavior theories
    path-goal theory of, 331–332
    situational leadership model, 333–335
    Vroom-Yetton-Jago normative decision model, 332–334

Uncertainty avoidance, 35
United States culture
    decision making, 273
    individual reward system in, 178
    quality circles in, 271
    work definition, 388–389
Unplanned change, 478
Upper echelon teams, 238–240
    multicultural, 239–240
Utilitarian power, 291–292

Valence, of an outcome, 151
Value systems, 122–123
Values, 115–120
    change and cultural, 486–487

conflict and, 354–356
    cultural differences in, 119–120
    enacted, 453
    espoused, 453
    instrumental, 116–117
    managerial implications, 126–127
    in organizational culture, 453
    terminal, 116–117
    work, 117–119
Verbal communication, in social perception, 87
Virtual office, 4, 407
Vroom-Yetton-Jago normative decision model, 333–334

Whistle-blower, 59
Women
    glass ceiling and, 41–42
    as leaders, 321
    in workforce, 41–42
Work
    behavior and quality at, 17–18
    behavior motivation, 133–136
    creativity in decision making at, 259–263
    definition patterns by nation, 388
    goal setting, 167–172
    leadership style and emotional climate at, 322–323
    meaning of, 388–389
    in organizations, 387–390
    simplification of, 390
    technology at, 407–408
    values, 117–119
Work attitudes
    job satisfaction, 108–111
    organizational commitment, 112–113
Work design
    criteria for evaluating, 402
    emerging issues, 405–409
    in Germany, 401–402
    in Japan, 401
    in Scandinavia, 402–403
    well-being and, 403–404
Work environments, changing, 4
Work value scales, 389
Workforce diversity
    ability diversity, 45–46
    advantages of, 45–46
    age diversity, 42–44
    benefits and problems, 46–47
    changes in organization and, 479
    cultural diversity, 41–42
    gender diversity, 41–42
    managing, 40–47

Z problem-solving model, 254–255
Zone of indifference, 285